Window Room.

hest Brocad[d] Satten 75/. 1161.11.3

ocad[d] Borders ... 43/. 400:19:6

aded D[o] 30/. 453:7.6

D[o] 7/6. 40.10.–

k Room,

hest Brocaded

tern Silk .... } 115/6 2403.16.10

Border for D[o] ... 55/. 1005-2-6

1 3/4 Lustring

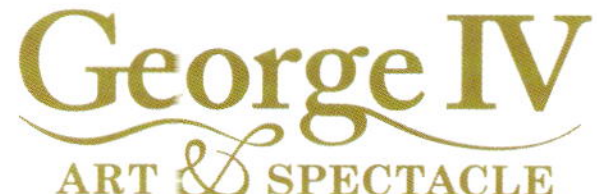
George IV
ART & SPECTACLE

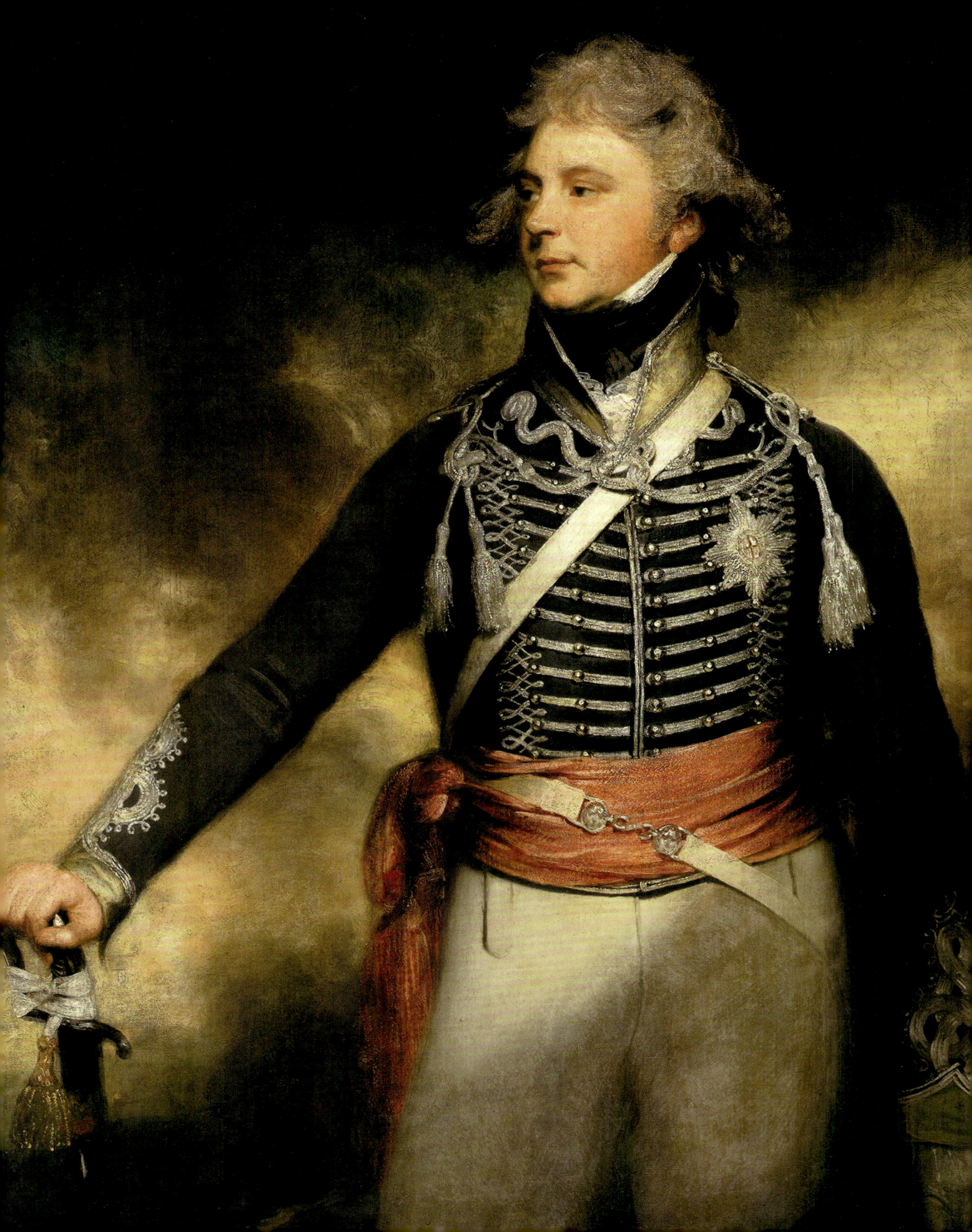

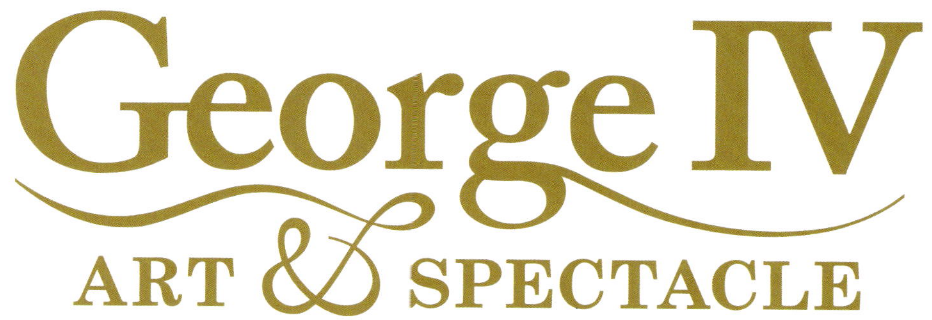

Edited by
KATE HEARD and KATHRYN JONES

ROYAL COLLECTION TRUST

Published 2019 by Royal Collection Trust
York House
St James's Palace
London SW1A 1BQ

Explore the Royal Collection at www.rct.uk

ISBN 978 1 909741 60 7

102113

British Library Cataloguing-in-Publication Data:
A catalogue record for this book is available from the British Library.

Designed by ADRIAN HUNT
Project Management by GEORGINA SEAGE & HANNAH BOWEN
Production Management by SARAH TUCKER
Colour reproduction by ALTA IMAGE
Typeset in Bulmer and printed on 150 gsm Arctic Matt
Printed and bound in the United Kingdom by GOMER PRESS

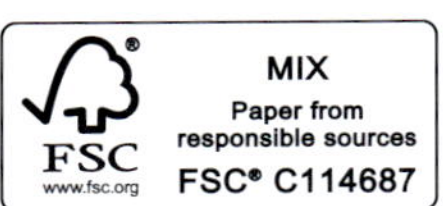

Published on the occasion of the exhibition *George IV: Art & Spectacle*, at The Queen's Gallery, Buckingham Palace, 15 November 2019–3 May 2020 and The Queen's Gallery, Palace of Holyroodhouse, 16 October 2020–5 April 2021

Frontispiece:
Sir William Beechey, *George IV when Prince of Wales*, 1803 (Fig. 2.17)

Facing page vi:
Charles Wild, *The Crimson Drawing Room, Carlton House*, 1816 (Fig. 5.20)

Endpapers:
Ibbetson, Barlow & Clarke, Mercers' bill for Carlton House, 1790 (RA GEO/MAIN/25094)

NOTE TO THE READER

George was Prince of Wales from 1763 until 1811, Prince Regent from 1811 until 1820 and King from 1820 until 1830. For clarity, he is here referred to as George IV throughout his life.

CONTENTS

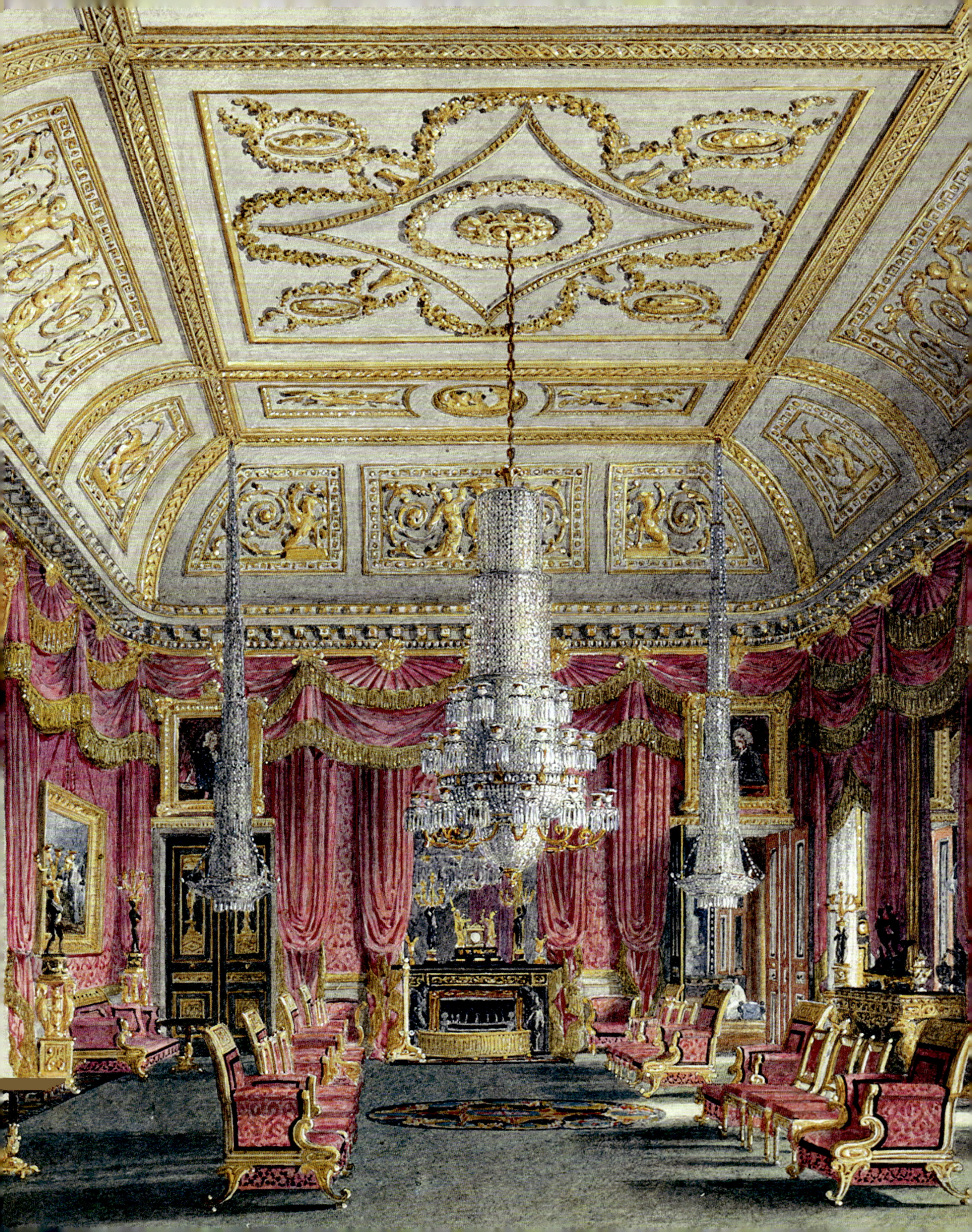

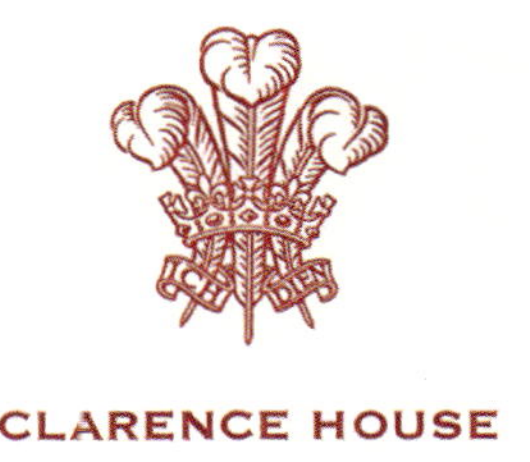

CLARENCE HOUSE

2020 marks the 200th anniversary of the accession of King George IV. The artistic legacy of this connoisseur monarch is witnessed by the thousands who visit Buckingham Palace and Windsor Castle every year to see the extraordinarily rich collections of paintings, decorative arts, books, prints and drawings that he amassed from across the globe. These palaces, too, bear George IV's mark: much of their appearance today is due to his creativity as an architectural patron, which can also be seen in the imaginative design of the Royal Pavilion that he built at Brighton.

King George IV is seen as one of the most colourful of sovereigns; his life was certainly not free from controversy and he was often the subject of satire. Yet as a collector he has always been admired. The Duke of Wellington called him 'the most accomplished man of his age' and praised his knowledge and talent. He might be celebrated alone as the most significant patron of the artist, Sir Thomas Lawrence, whose brilliant portraits of the leaders of Europe now hang in the Waterloo Chamber at Windsor Castle. He formed a magnificent collection of Dutch and Flemish paintings, and was also one of the greatest ever collectors of Sèvres porcelain and French furniture, English silver and arms and armour from around the world.

Nevertheless it is now almost thirty years since the last full-scale exhibition examining the work of this prodigious collector was held in The Queen's Gallery. This book is published to accompany the exhibition, *George IV: Art & Spectacle*, which will be mounted at The Queen's Galleries in London and Edinburgh to mark the anniversary of his accession. It presents some of the latest research into The King's collections, and seeks to place him on the contemporary European stage. Above all, it celebrates the magnificent works of art acquired by this 'first Gentleman of Europe', which remain at the heart of the Royal Collection today.

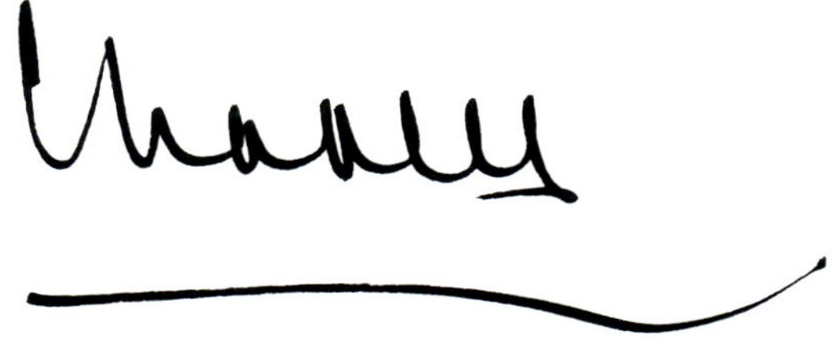

CARLTON HOUSE: ROOM NAMES AND FLOOR PLANS

The complicated history of Carlton House has led to a number of spaces being given different names at different times, as shown in the concordance table below. Spellings are those used in the source documents, including an inventory of 1819 and several inventories compiled in the late 1820s (see CH Inv. 1819, CH Inv. 1826 and Jutsham I, II and III, which are listed in Manuscript Sources on p. 285). Carlton House was built on a slope. Because of this, the principal apartments appear to be on the first floor when viewed from the garden and on the ground level when approached from Pall Mall. The names of rooms and spaces that were unfinished at the time when the source documents were compiled are shown in square brackets, while alternative or additional names are shown in round brackets.

The plans opposite show the rooms in the Lower (Basement) and Principal Floors as they were *c.*1825, but there is no plan of comparable date for the Attic Floor, so the one illustrated here dates from 1795. The names in the key to the plans are taken from the 1825 source. The sources for the plans lack a scale; the building was approximately 200 feet (61 metres) in length and 130 feet (40 metres) in depth.

	1784	1795	INTERVENING TITLES	1819	*c.*1825
ATTIC FLOOR	Prince's Bedchamber *or* Bow Bedroom	Library	Middle Room		Bow Room
	Dressing Room	Bedchamber			Bedchamber
	Breakfast Room	Armoury			(2nd, 3rd *and* Working Rooms *added to* Armoury)
PRINCIPAL (STATE) FLOOR	Hall and Pages Room	Tribune *or* Octagon *or* Octagon Hall		Vestibule	Vestibule
				Grand Staircase	Great Staircase
		Buffet			Plate Room
	[Courtyard]	[Courtyard]		West Anti Room	West Anti Room
	Dining parlour Dining parlour	*combined to become* Great Dining Room *or* Great Eating Room	(Scagliola Room)	Crimson Drawing Room	Crimson Drawing Room
	Waiting Room Presence Room Anti Room	*combined to become* Circular *or* Music Room		Circular Room	Circular (Dining) Room
	[Unfinished Ballroom]	Great Drawing Room	Gold Room *or* Ballroom	Throne Room	Throne Room
	State Room	State Room *or* Throne Room	Old Throne Room *or* Council Room	Anti Chamber (leading to the Throne Room)	Old Throne Room
	Anti Room	Second Anti Chamber (to the State Rooms) *or* Presence Chamber	(Crimson) Bow Room	Rose Satin Room	Bow Room *or* Rose Satin Drawing Room
	Drawing Room	First Anti Chamber		Anti Room	South Anti Room
	Bedchamber Closet	*combined to become* Princess's Private Drawing Room; *used as* Prince's Private Drawing Room	Admirals Room *or* Audience Room	Blue Velvet Room	(Large) Blue Velvet Room
	Dressing Room	(Princess's) Saloon; *used as* State Bedchamber	Military Tent Room	Blue Velvet Closet	Blue Velvet Salon *or* Closet *or* Small (Dark) Blue Velvet Room *or* Little Blue Room
		Anti Chamber			East Anti Room
		Library (and Closet)			Kitchen
LOWER FLOOR (BASEMENT)				Gothic Dining Room	Gothic Dining Room
		Bathing rooms	Roman Room	Golden Drawing Room	Corinthian Room *or* Colonnade Room
	Gallery	Gallery	(Gothic) Library	Library	Library
	Writing Room [Unnamed room]	*combined to become* First Anti Room		Lower Vestibule	Anti Room
	Anti Room	Second Anti Chamber		Bow Room	Bow Room
	Eating Room	Chinese Drawing Room		Anti Room to Dining Room	Anti Dining Room
	[Library, unfinished] [Music Room, unfinished]	*combined to become* Eating *or* Dining Room		Dining Room	Dining Room
				Conservatory	(Gothic) Conservatory

ATTIC (1795)

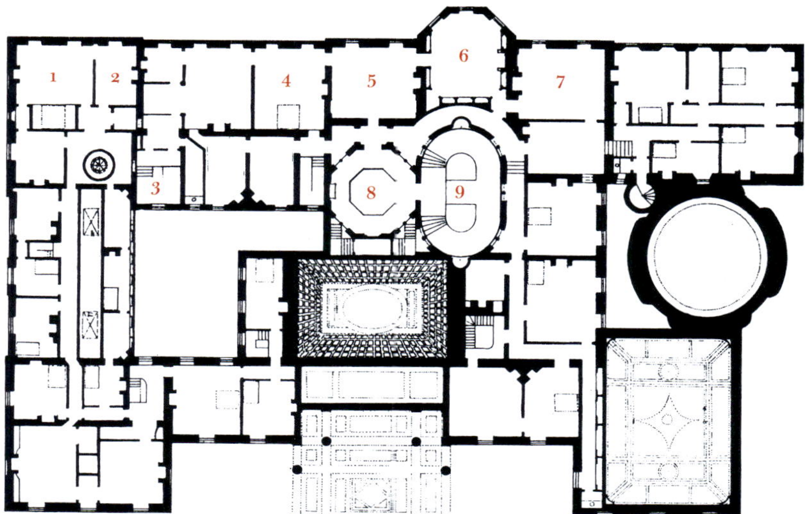

KEY

1. Bedchamber
2. Dressing Room
3. Private Stairs
4. Bedchamber
5. Anti Room
6. Bow Room
7. Armoury
8. Tribune
9. Grand Staircase
10. Vestibule
11. Grand Staircase
12. Plate Room
13. West Anti Room
14. Crimson Drawing Room
15. Circular Room
16. Throne Room
17. Old Throne Room
18. Rose Satin Drawing Room
19. South Anti Room
20. Blue Velvet Room
21. Blue Velvet Closet
22. East Anti Room
23. Kitchen
24. Gothic Dining Room
25. Colonnade Room
26. Library
27. Anti Room
28. Bow Room
29. Anti Dining Room
30. Dining Room
31. (Gothic) Conservatory

PRINCIPAL FLOOR (*c*.1825)

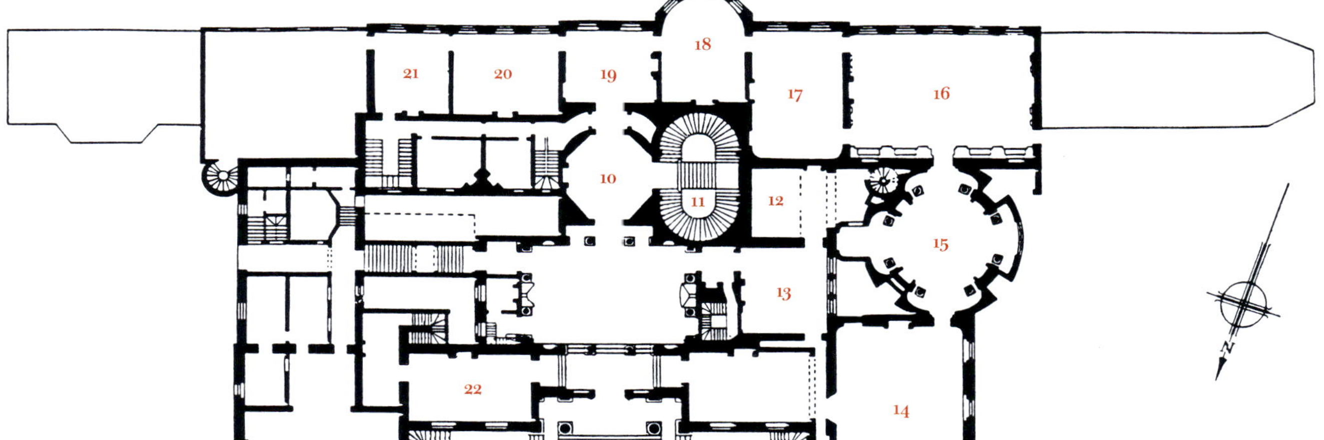

LOWER FLOOR (BASEMENT) (*c*.1825)

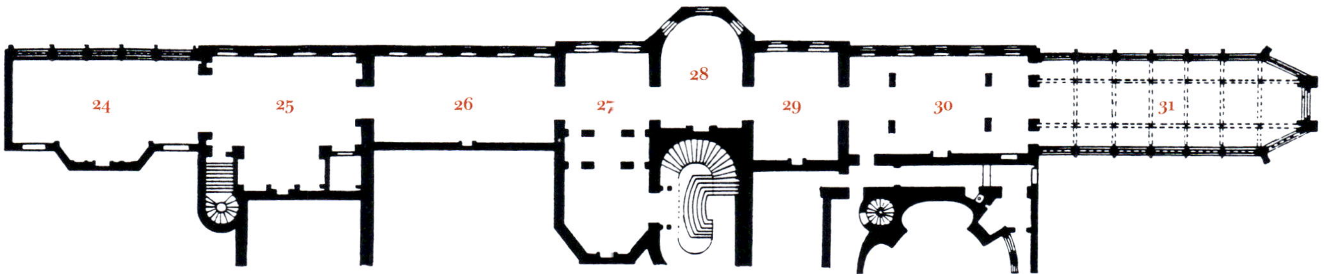

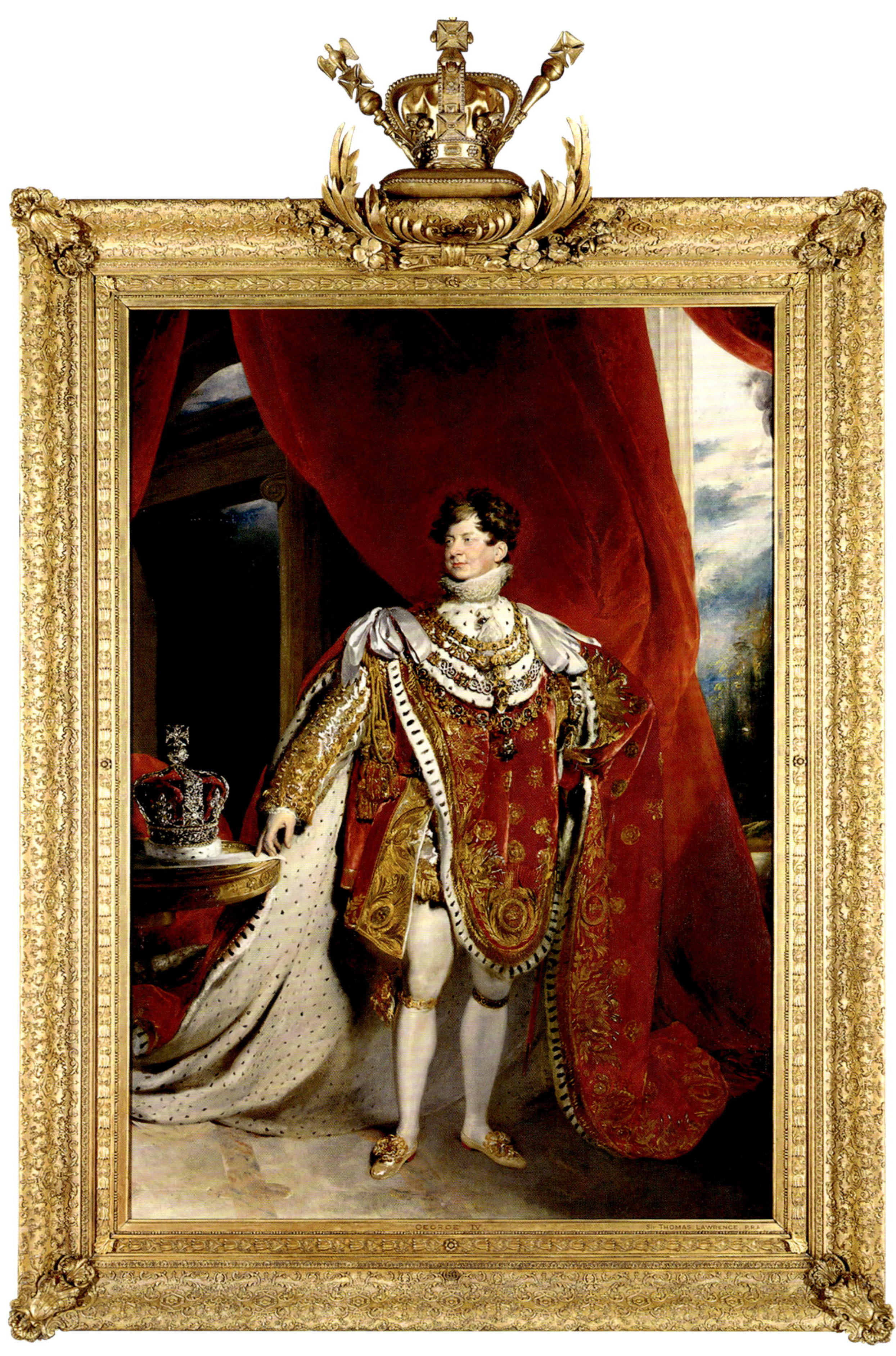
GEORGE IV.
Sir THOMAS LAWRENCE P.R.A.

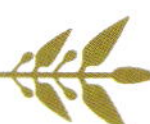

GEORGE IV: ART *and* SPECTACLE

KATHRYN JONES *and* KATE HEARD

One of the most revealing encounters of George IV's life must have been that which took place in Brighton on 15 April 1827. The elderly republican Albert Gallatin, born in Geneva but long resident in and acting as envoy for the United States, made a visit to pay his respects to the equally elderly king at Brighton Pavilion. The two men had first met more than ten years earlier, in 1815, when Gallatin's son had remarked on the difference between them: 'He [George] was superbly dressed … Father made such a contrast in his black shorts, white silk stockings, and black coat with his white choaker.'[1] At Brighton, the contrast between the infirm and dissolute monarch and the sprightly economist and politician was even stronger and the meeting even stranger:

> We only stopped one night at Brighton. Rooms had been prepared for us at a house close to the Pavilion, which the King keeps for his guests. We were received by his Majesty, who was lying on a divan – he could hardly hold himself up. Lady Conyngham was present at first, but at a nod from the King, retired. She looks as if she had something of a temper. The King spoke on several political subjects, and for a wonder with great lucidity. He said suddenly, 'Canning is a damned old woman'. We were bid to sup with the Royal circle. I could see that father could hardly dissemble his disgust. The conversation was boisterous and indecent. Cards after supper, and on a plea of being very fatigued father begged leave to retire. He and I went for a walk by the sea. The only remark he made was, 'And that is a King'.[2]

If Gallatin was disappointed by the reality of monarchy that he encountered at Brighton, so too, it seems, was George IV (Fig. 0.1). From the moment of his birth in 1762, George had been a focus of promise and hope: as Prince of Wales he had been heir to the throne; as Prince Regent (1811–20) he had headed the nation as it negotiated its monarch's illness and the threats of the Napoleonic Wars; as King from 1820, he had choreographed a vast and lavish

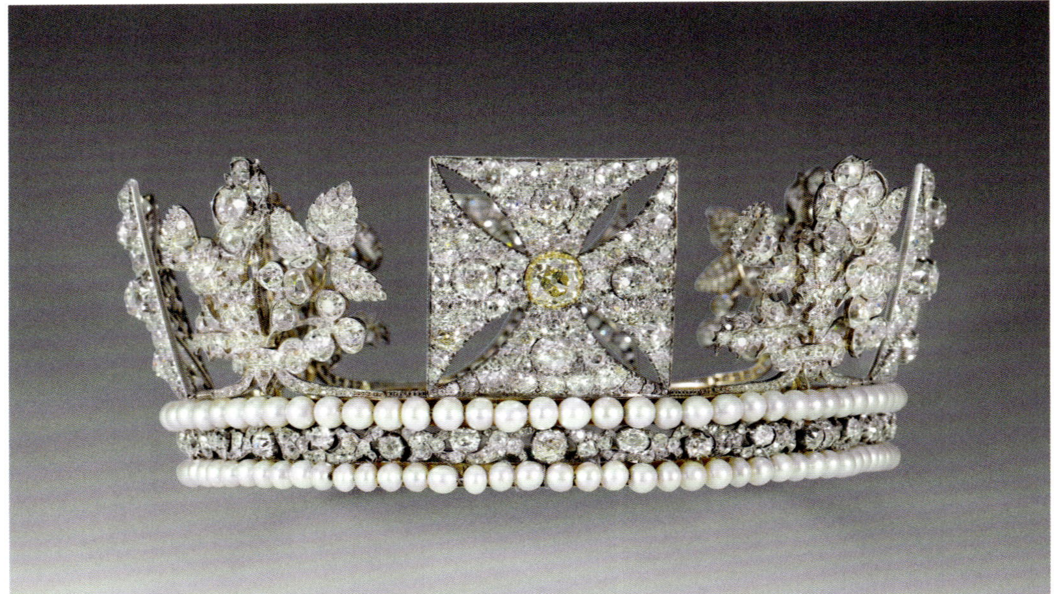

(p. x)
FIG. 0.1
SIR THOMAS LAWRENCE (1769–1830), *George IV*, 1821. Oil on canvas, 295.4 × 205.4 cm, RCIN 405918

FIG. 0.2
RUNDELL, BRIDGE & RUNDELL, *The Diamond Diadem*, 1820–1. Diamond, pearl, silver, gold, 19.0 × 19.0 × 7.5 cm, RCIN 31702

FIG. 0.3
Published by JOHN MARSHALL JUNIOR (active 1820), *The Kettle calling the Pot ugly names*, 1820. Etching with hand colouring, 27.9 × 38.4 cm (sheet), RCIN 751290

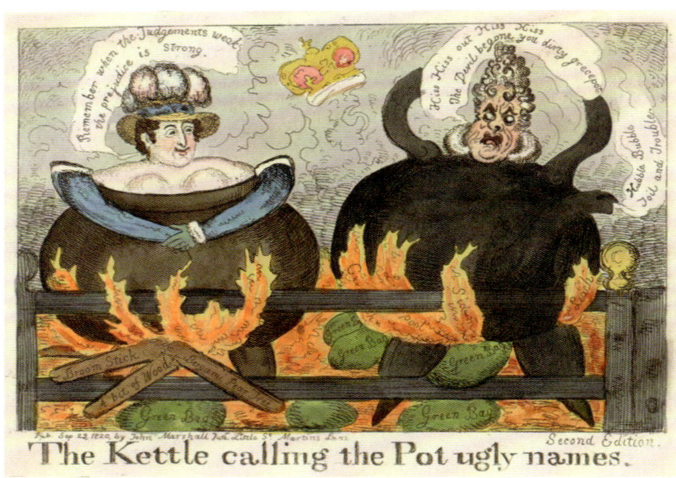

coronation, promising a glorious reign as George IV. His hugely successful visits to Dublin, Hanover and Edinburgh shortly after his accession revealed his great ability to charm and present himself to his people as one of their own, but this affection was shortlived. By the time he reached the throne, he was 57 years old, in poor health and disliked by a nation tired of his lavish lifestyle, extra-marital affairs and acrimonious marriage (Fig. 0.3). In 1819, in the aftermath of the Peterloo Massacre, he had been 'hissed by an immense mob'.[3] Instead of a decade of strong and brilliant leadership in the public eye, George's ten-year reign is characterised by the increasing reclusiveness of a monarch who largely retreated from public hostility to a residence hidden away in Windsor Great Park. By the time of his death, on 26 June 1830, he was so reviled that *The Times* could print a breathtakingly damning assessment of his reign: 'was there at any time a gorgeous pageant on the stage more completely forgotten than he has been, even from the day on which the heralds proclaimed his successor? … Nothing more remains to be said or done about George IV, but to pay – as pay we must – for his profusion.'[4]

George IV's life was indeed a 'gorgeous pageant' and one that has left a lasting legacy in architecture, in the magnificent works which he added to the Royal Collection and in the ceremony of monarchy. His Diamond Diadem (Fig. 0.2) and Imperial Mantle (Fig. 15.1) are still worn by the monarch, whose London residence remains the Buckingham Palace converted from a queen's lodging by George in the 1820s (Fig. 17.3). The splendid and familiar profile of Windsor Castle (Fig. 17.6), a medieval stronghold high above the Thames, is largely due to his architectural intervention. His seaside pleasure palace at Brighton (Fig. 10.10) continues to charm visitors with its inventive, fantastical design. His great London residence, Carlton House (Fig. 0.4), was demolished during his lifetime, but its ever-changing interiors can still be evoked through architectural plans and designs, the numerous bills for decoration and furnishing, and a series of interior views commissioned by the publisher William Henry Pyne to illustrate the relevant section of his *History of the Royal Residences* between 1816 and 1819 (Fig. 0.5).[5] To achieve these landmarks of building (each in its own way innovative), George employed a stable of adventurous architects, among them Henry Holland, John Nash and Sir Jeffry Wyatville (Fig. 17.7). In London, his architectural vision extended to the

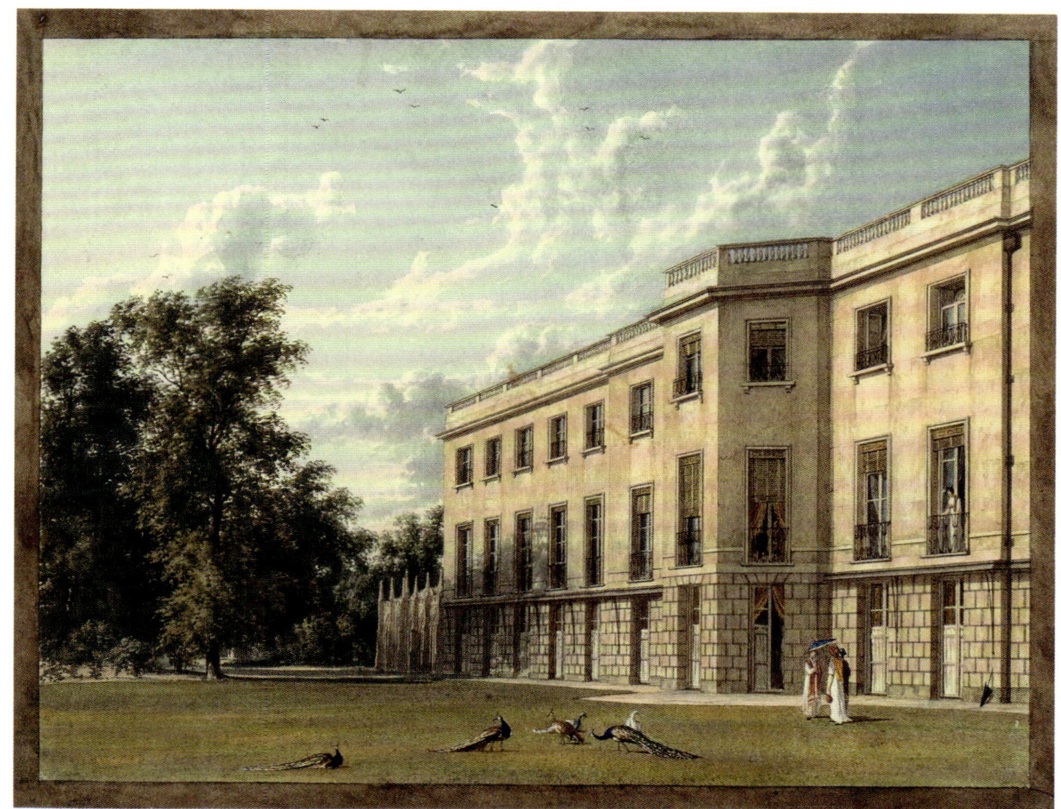

FIG. 0.4
WILLIAM WESTALL (1781–1850), *The South Front, Carlton House*, *c.*1819. Watercolour and bodycolour over pencil, 21.2 × 26.9 cm, RCIN 922169

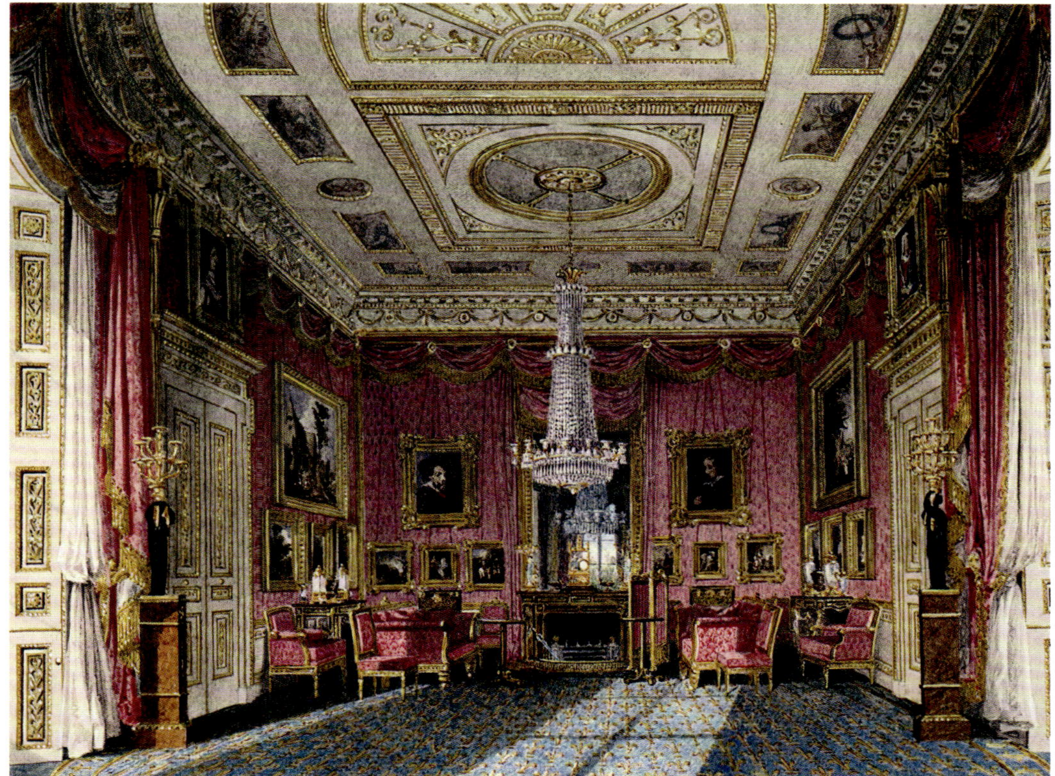

FIG. 0.5
CHARLES WILD (1781–1835), *The Rose Satin Drawing Room, Carlton House (looking North)*, *c.*1817. Watercolour and bodycolour with gum arabic over pencil, 20.6 × 27.0 cm, RCIN 922180

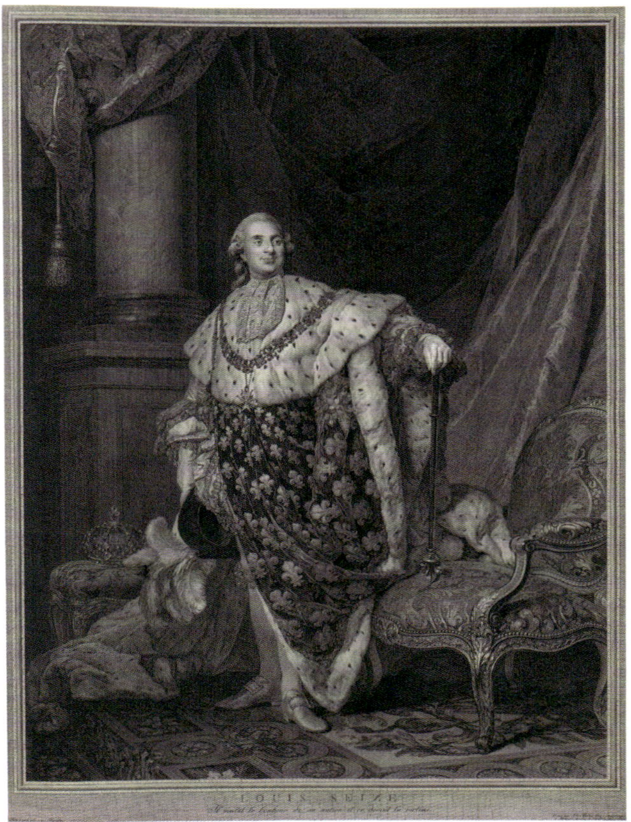

FIG. 0.6
JOHANN GOTTHARD MÜLLER (1747–1830), *Louis Seize*, 1792–3. Engraving, 68.6 × 50.8 cm (sheet), RCIN 617363

FIG. 0.7
FRANÇOIS GIRARDON (1628–1715), *Equestrian statue of Louis XIV (1638–1715)*, *c.*1696. Bronze, 105.5 × 92.0 × 50.0 cm, RCIN 31359. THOMIRE & CIE, *Pedestal*, 1826. Ebonised oak, bronze, gilt bronze, 102.2 × 129.5 × 82.5 cm, RCIN 31360

FIG. 0.8
ATTRIBUTED TO ADAM-FRANÇOIS VAN DER MEULEN (1632–90), *The Building of Versailles*, *c.*1680. Oil on canvas, 108.0 × 142.3 cm, RCIN 406554

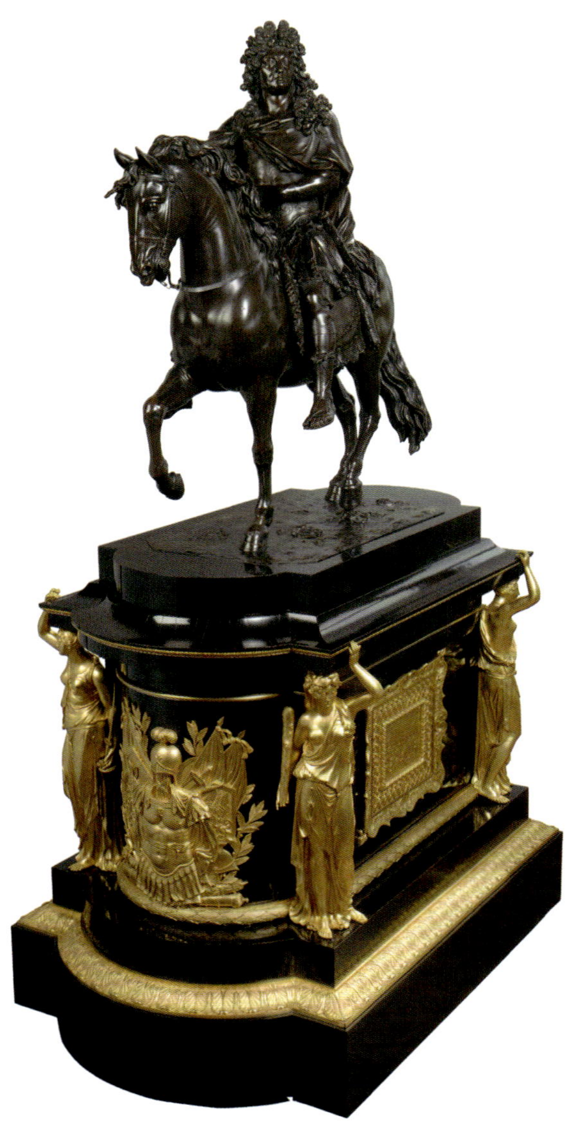

laying out of a grand new street, Regent Street, which runs between the site of Carlton House and Regent's Park, where George and Nash planned new residences around a large public garden.

The great architectural schemes which underpinned his life may be seen, to an extent, as George's attempt to create palaces for the British royal family of a suitable magnificence to rival those of the French monarchy, with which he was fascinated. A strongly Francophile flavour is apparent in many of the interiors in which he lived – David Oakey and David Beevers both argue in this volume that the earlier iterations of the architectural and decorative schemes at Carlton House and Brighton Pavilion, undertaken by Holland, were heavily based on the neo-classical *hôtels particuliers* of France (see chapters 5 and 10). His private apartments at Windsor Castle were, by his very personal choice, decorated with 'old French boiserie of the age of Louis XV',[6] and enhanced by the French furniture and gilt bronzes which were acquired by agents on George's behalf from the Parisian *marchands-merciers*, as well as their equivalents living in London, especially Dominique Daguerre (see chapter 6).

Within his residences, George formed a collection of paintings and decorative arts that was unrivalled in size or importance in the Britain of his day, and by few royal collectors

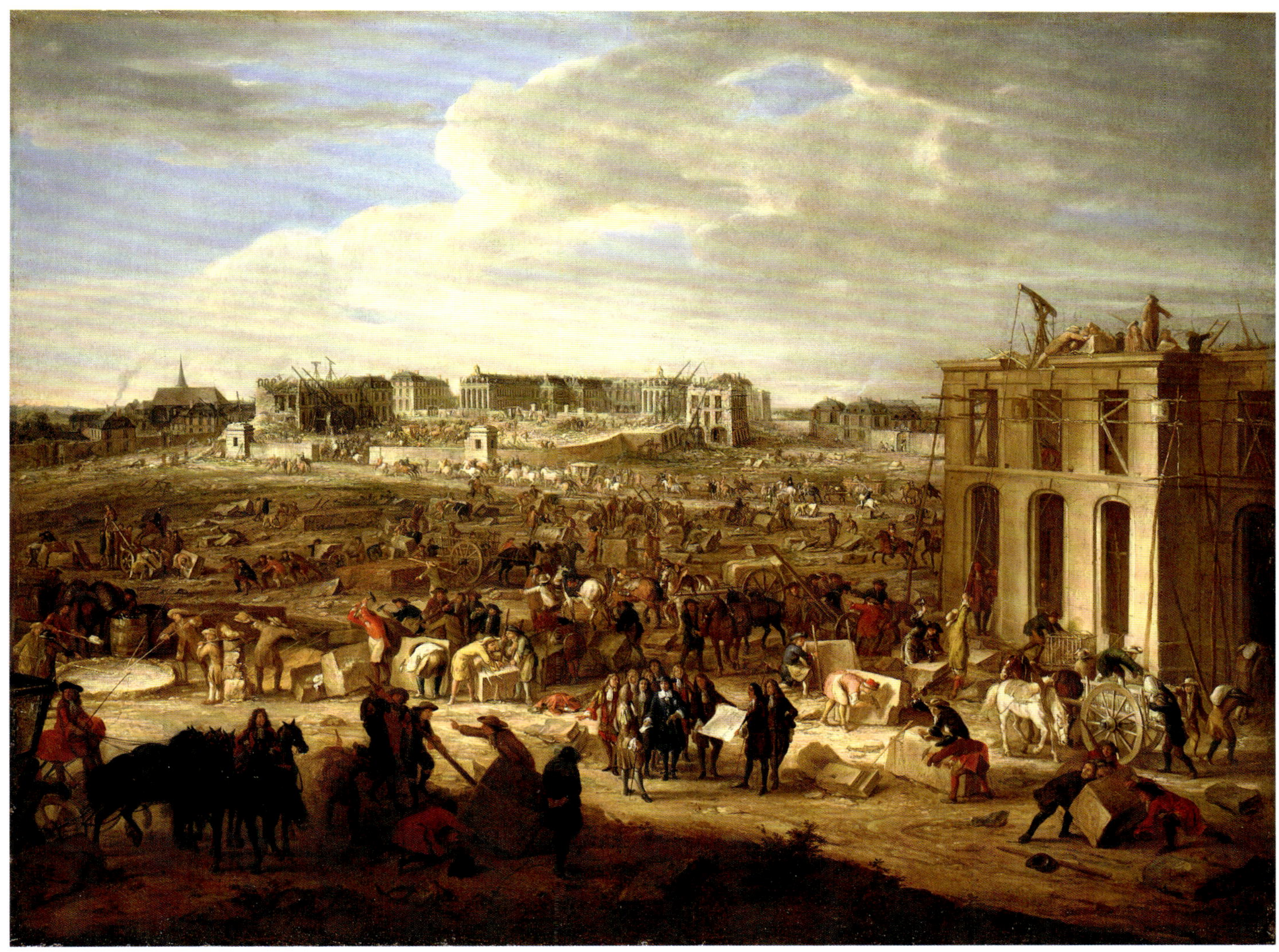

before or since. The extraordinary range of his acquisitions reveals a keen interest in Old Master and contemporary painting and sculpture, books, the print market and the decorative arts in all their forms. George's fascination with *ancien-régime* France manifested itself in the collecting of portraits of the French monarchs (Fig. 0.6) and associated courtiers from the fifteenth century onwards. Among the images of French monarchy he purchased was the large bronze of Louis XIV on horseback by François Girardon (Fig. 0.7), for which an ornate plinth was commissioned, complete with plaques depicting scenes from the seventeenth-century Franco-Dutch War, after the works of Adam-François van der Meulen. Indeed George amassed a large collection of Van der Meulen paintings, relating significant events from the reign of Louis XIV (1643–1715), including a record of building work under way at the Palace of Versailles in 1678 (Fig. 0.8). Undoubtedly George was attempting to emulate the splendours of Louis XIV's palace in his own residences. In later years, this taste for French furnishing was supplied by the London firm of Morel & Seddon. Nicholas Morel had originally been associated with such figures as Daguerre, but would later provide French-inspired decoration for Windsor Castle in partnership with George Seddon.[7]

George IV's collections were similarly inspired by the great connoisseurs of France. One of his early purchases, acquired before 1806, was Elisabeth-Louise Vigée-Lebrun's stylish portrait of Charles-Alexandre de Calonne (Fig. 0.9), the comptroller of finance to Louis XVI, who was himself a significant patron of furniture and paintings. George's beloved Dutch and Flemish pictures – which included luminous works by Aelbert Cuyp, intimate domestic scenes by Godfried Schalcken and Jan Steen, rowdy celebrations by David Teniers and Rembrandt's spirited *Shipbuilder and his Wife* (Fig. 0.10) – were undoubtedly in part

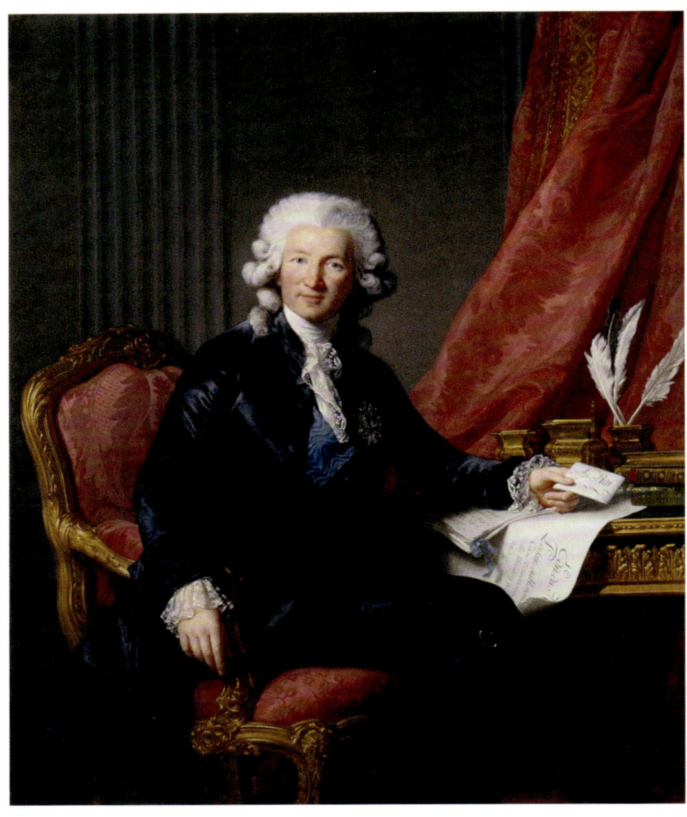

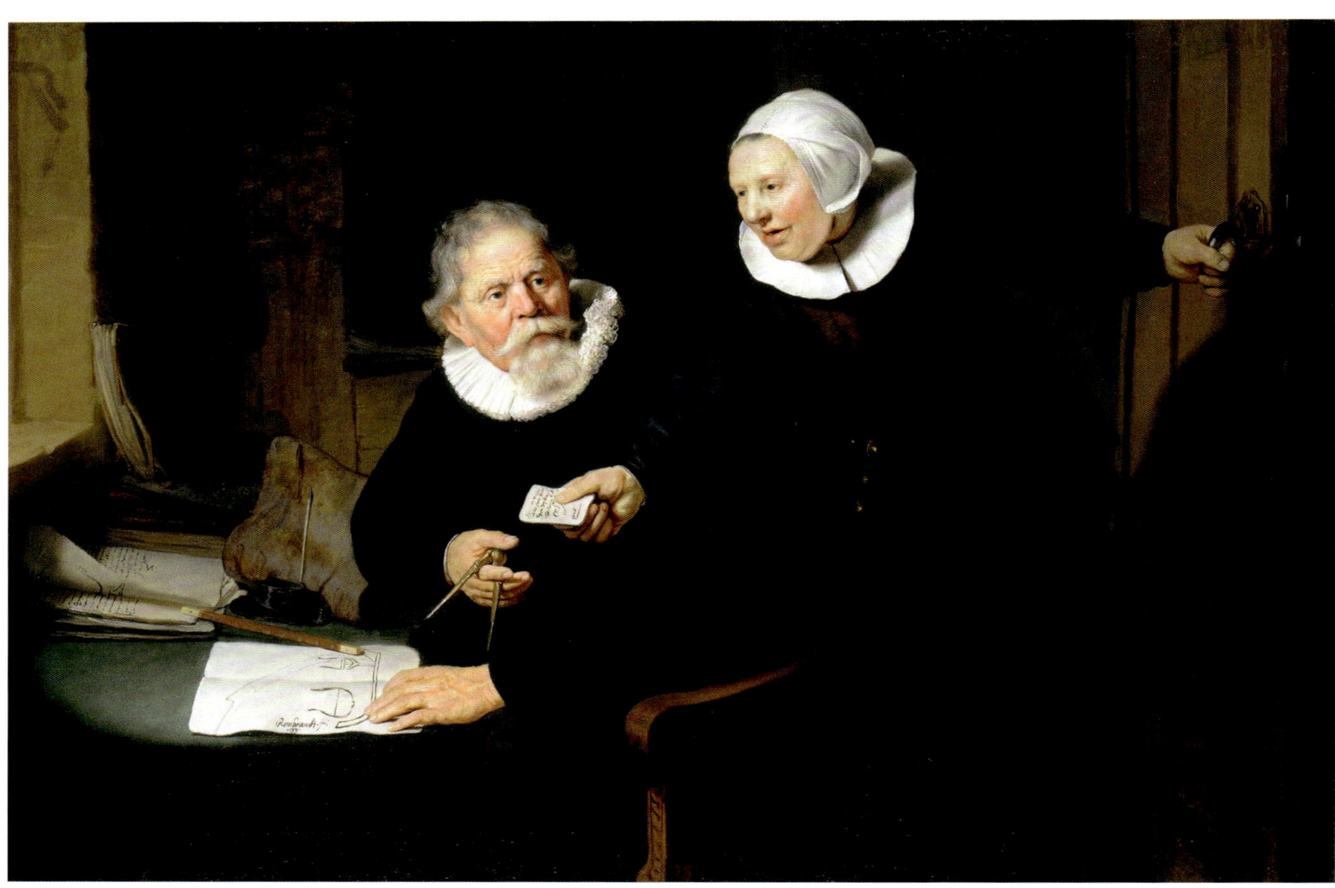

FIG. 0.9
ELISABETH-LOUISE VIGÉE-LEBRUN (1755–1842), *Charles-Alexandre de Calonne (1734–1802)*, 1784. Oil on canvas, 155.5 × 130.3 cm, RCIN 406988

FIG. 0.10
REMBRANDT VAN RIJN (1606–69), *Portrait of Jan Rijcksen (1560/2–1637) and his Wife, Griet Jans ('The Shipbuilder and his Wife')*, 1633. Oil on canvas, 113.8 × 169.8 cm, RCIN 405533

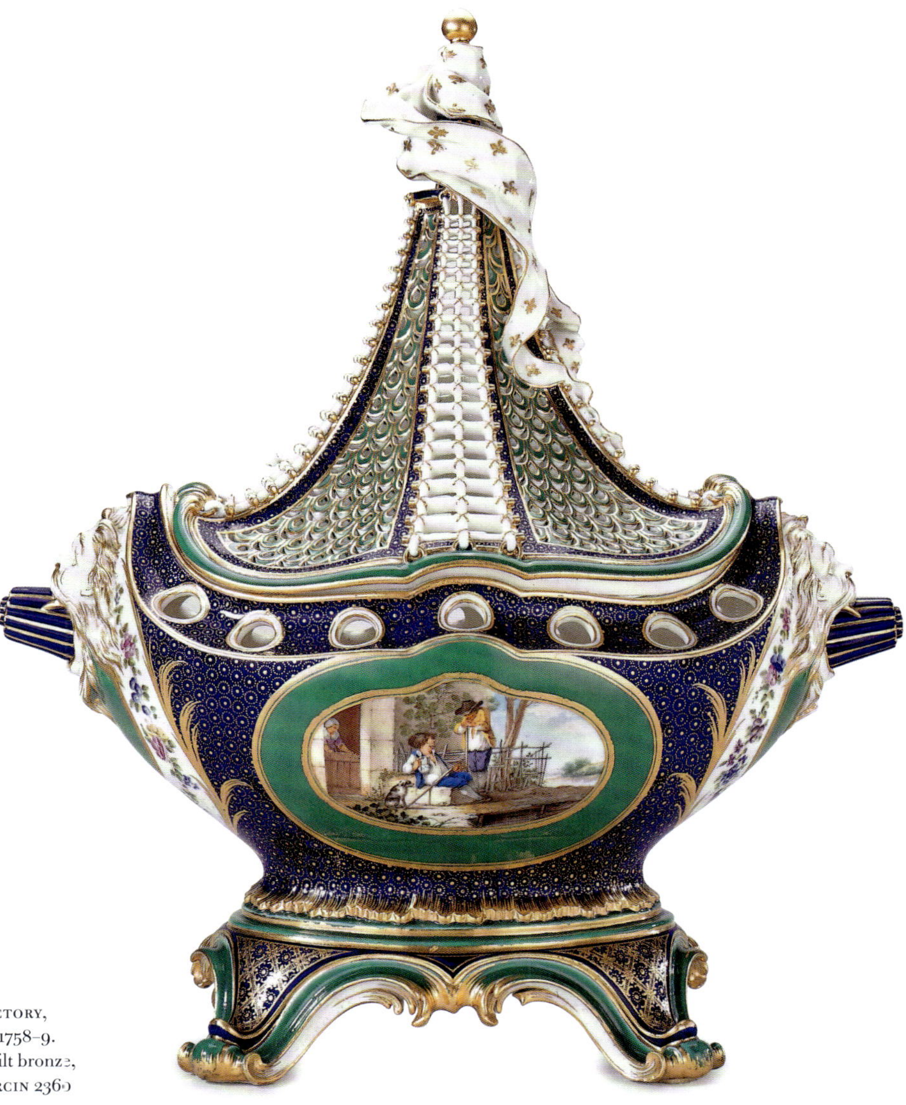

FIG. 0.11
SÈVRES PORCELAIN FACTORY,
Pot-pourri à vaisseau, 1758–9.
Soft-paste porcelain, gilt bronze,
55.1 × 37.8 × 19.3 cm, RCIN 2360

favoured by him as they were equally popular with the Bourbon dynasty.[8] The unparalleled quantity of Sèvres and Vincennes porcelain which he amassed at Carlton House, and later at Windsor, clearly reflected his own enthralment with the French royal collections. Perhaps the most celebrated example was the *vaisseau à mat* or potpourri vase in the form of a ship (Fig. 0.11), a great technical and artistic achievement produced at Sèvres and purchased in 1759 by Madame de Pompadour, and subsequently acquired by George.[9] Many of the vases George collected incorporated small painted genre scenes inspired by Dutch or Flemish artists, particularly the works of Teniers, and thus were an extension of his interest in this field. At the same time, the colourful palette and exquisitely executed gilding employed by the Sèvres manufactory were enormously appealing to George, whose love of highly finished surfaces was apparent in all his acquisitions.

In a similar vein, George bought pieces of furniture that were believed to have been owned by members of the extended Bourbon family – a superb marquetry rolltop desk attributed to Jean-Henri Riesener, thought to have been in the collection of Louis XVI;[10] a jewel cabinet with exquisite gilt-bronze mounts, from the collection of the comtesse de Provence (consort of Louis's younger brother); and a pair of marquetry pedestals supplied by Gilles Joubert that came from Louis's bedroom at Versailles.[11] George believed that the French Revolution represented a threat to all established government, yet as a collector the availability on the market of material associated with the French monarchy as a result of the Revolution was fortuitous and, in the first decade of the nineteenth century, he dispatched agents to France on his behalf to make extensive purchases from dealers and *marchands-merciers*.

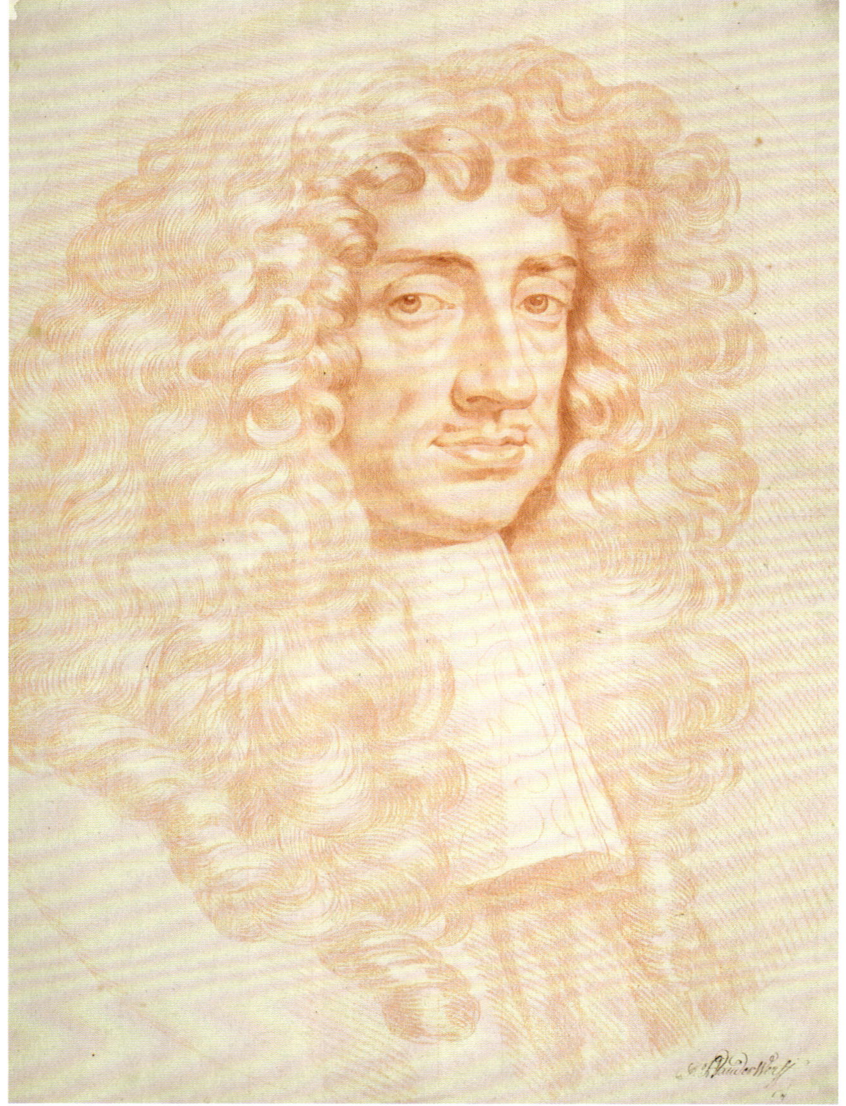

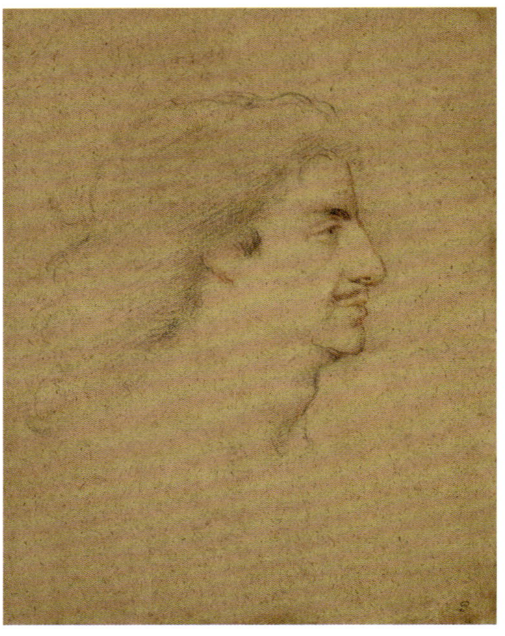

FIG. 0.12
ASSOCIATE OF SIR PETER LELY (1618–80), *Charles II (1630–85)*, *c.*1676. Red chalk (offset and worked up), 55.6 × 40.4 cm, RCIN 912839

FIG. 0.13
SAMUEL COOPER (1609–72), *Charles II*, 1660/62. Black and red chalks on faded brown paper, 17.8 × 14.0 cm, RCIN 914040

If George was inspired as a collector by French rulers past, he was also spurred on by a rivalry with the usurping (as he saw it) Napoleon Bonaparte, whose own extensive architectural and artistic schemes appear to have stimulated George's efforts as a patron. Where Napoleon was commissioning great dining services designed by Charles Percier and Pierre-François-Léonard Fontaine, George was doing the same from Rundell, Bridge & Rundell, to the extent that the emperor's *Grand Vermeil* of 1804 may well have lent its name to George's Grand Service of silver gilt, the first pieces of which were commissioned around 1806. The great sculptural schemes instituted in Paris from Antonio Canova were reflected in George's acquisition of three great marbles by the Italian master (see chapter 1) and Napoleon's coronation costume, designed by Jean-Baptiste Isabey, may have been the inspiration for George's own (see chapter 15). Indeed, George seems as likely to have collected 'relics' connected with Bonaparte as those relating to the Bourbons. Thus he acquired the sword commissioned by Napoleon as First Consul,[12] and the *Table des grands capitaines de l'antiquité* (Table of the Great Commanders of Antiquity). This was another great technical achievement by the Sèvres manufactory, intended for Malmaison, the home of the Empress Joséphine, which became one of George's most prized possessions (see Fig. 1.10).

If his Francophilia was evident in every facet of his collections, so too was George's own royal heritage. Much like his Hanoverian forebears, reaching back to the early eighteenth century, George showed an intense, if rather fanciful, interest in the Stuart dynasty. This was apparent in his collection of prints and drawings,

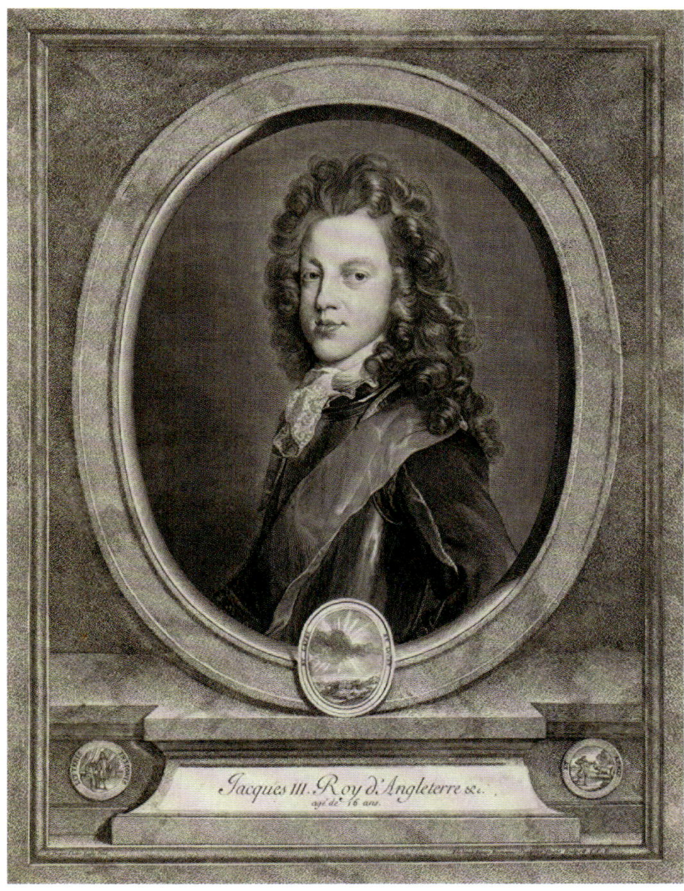

FIG. 0.15
GERARD EDELINCK (1640–1707), *Jacques III. Roy d'Angleterre &c*, *c.*1704–7. Engraving, 48.5 × 37.6 cm (sheet), RCIN 603505

which included numerous portraits of Charles I and Charles II, among them a beautiful chalk drawing by an associate of Sir Peter Lely (Fig. 0.12), as well as prints of the exiled Stuarts. He presented a drawing by Samuel Cooper of Charles II to his own father as a birthday gift (Fig. 0.13). The quasi-hagiographic exhumation of Charles I's coffin from the crypt of St George's Chapel, Windsor, on 1 April 1813, allowed George to encounter the most romantic of all the Stuarts in person. In the manner of a medieval touch relic, he had a small fragment of Charles's beard inserted into a seventeenth-century enamel and gold locket, apparently for presentation to his daughter, Princess Charlotte (Fig. 0.14). He retained a romantic interest, too, in the exiled Stuart family (Fig. 0.15), who argued a rival claim to the British throne, and acquired the important archive of Stuart papers after the death of Henry Benedict Stuart, Cardinal York in 1807.

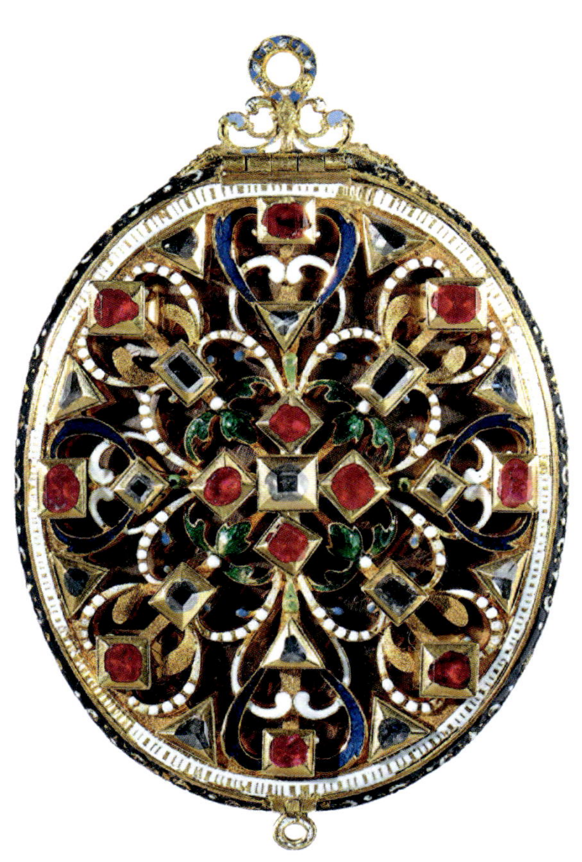

FIG. 0.14
ENGLISH (?), *Locket containing hair of Charles I (1600–49)*, *c.*1620 (with later additions 1813). Gold, enamel, Burmese ruby, diamond, 8.1 × 5.0 × 1.4 cm, RCIN 43778

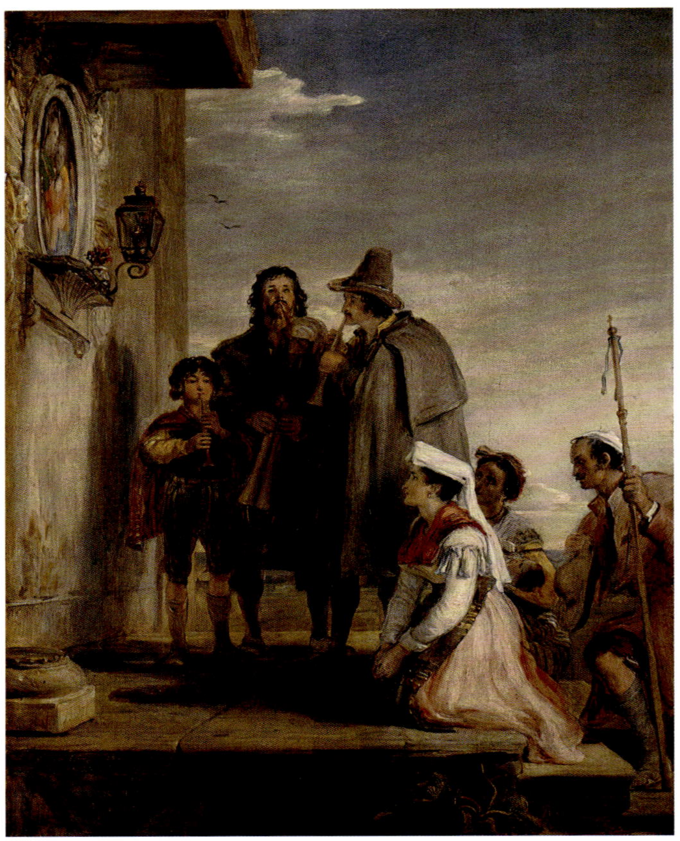

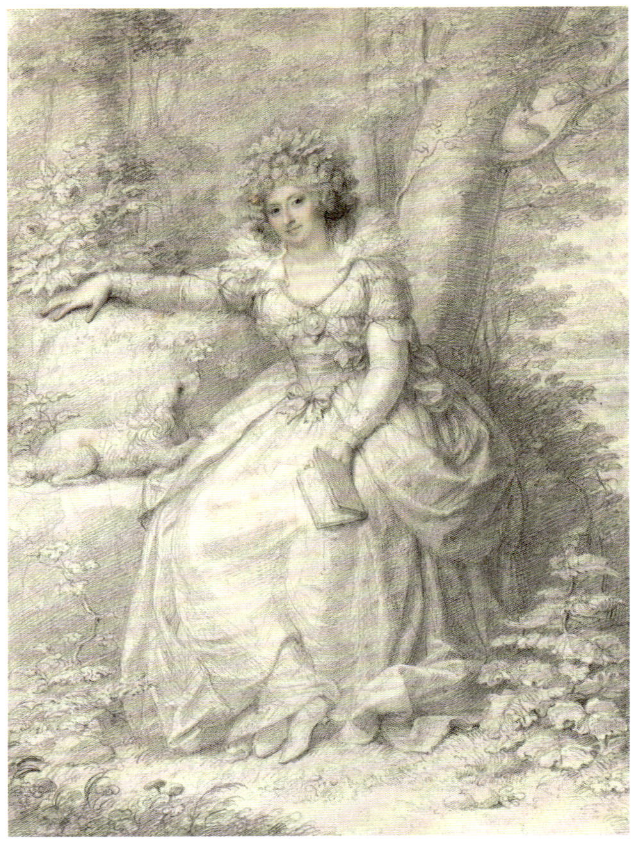

George was also a keen and significant supporter of British art, a strand of patronage that was especially apparent in his collection of portraits. He commissioned images of family and friends from William Beechey, who painted George's sisters, and John Hoppner, who depicted celebrities, among them Admiral Nelson and the composer Joseph Haydn. George was the most important patron of Sir Thomas Lawrence and David Wilkie (Fig. 0.16) in particular,[13] but also patronised Sir Joshua Reynolds, Thomas Gainsborough, George Romney, George Stubbs, James Ward and Richard Cosway (Fig. 0.17). Alongside these he commissioned two series of portrait busts in marble from Francis Chantrey and Joseph Nollekens. It should not be forgotten that in the area of contemporary art George was able to acquire works from artists he knew personally, as was the case with the Gainsborough painting of *Diana and Actaeon* (Fig. 0.18), which he purchased at the sale of works of art belonging to Gainsborough's nephew, the artist Gainsborough Dupont. This large mythological canvas sat as happily alongside George's Old Master paintings as it did his contemporary portraits and genre scenes.

George's collection can also provide a glimpse of the man behind the pageantry. A member of his household recorded how 'One great amusement of George IV was looking over his prints in the evening, when fatigued previous to his going to bed', and he formed a vast collection of works on paper. This was not a connoisseur's collection of fine prints and drawings, but the pursuit of a man who sought to understand his world, largely comprising portraits, topography, historical scenes and described as 'a most profitable and intelligent study, as it related to important events and distinguished characters'.[14] Surprisingly for one so often the target of satire, he collected more than 2,000 of the caricatures for which Britain was renowned in the late eighteenth century, although he was sensitive to scurrilous depictions of his own appearance and actions, which he sought to suppress. He formed a fine library of largely modern literature and many of those who met him discovered a well-read, witty man, who could talk intelligently on a wide variety of subjects, from politics and history to science and the natural world. He acquired an important collection of objects from beyond Europe through a network of contacts; displayed in his Armoury at Carlton House, these provided a taste of the wider world that he was unable to experience in person. He was a major patron of music both in London (where the chamber music concerts he held at Carlton House were serious affairs) and Brighton,

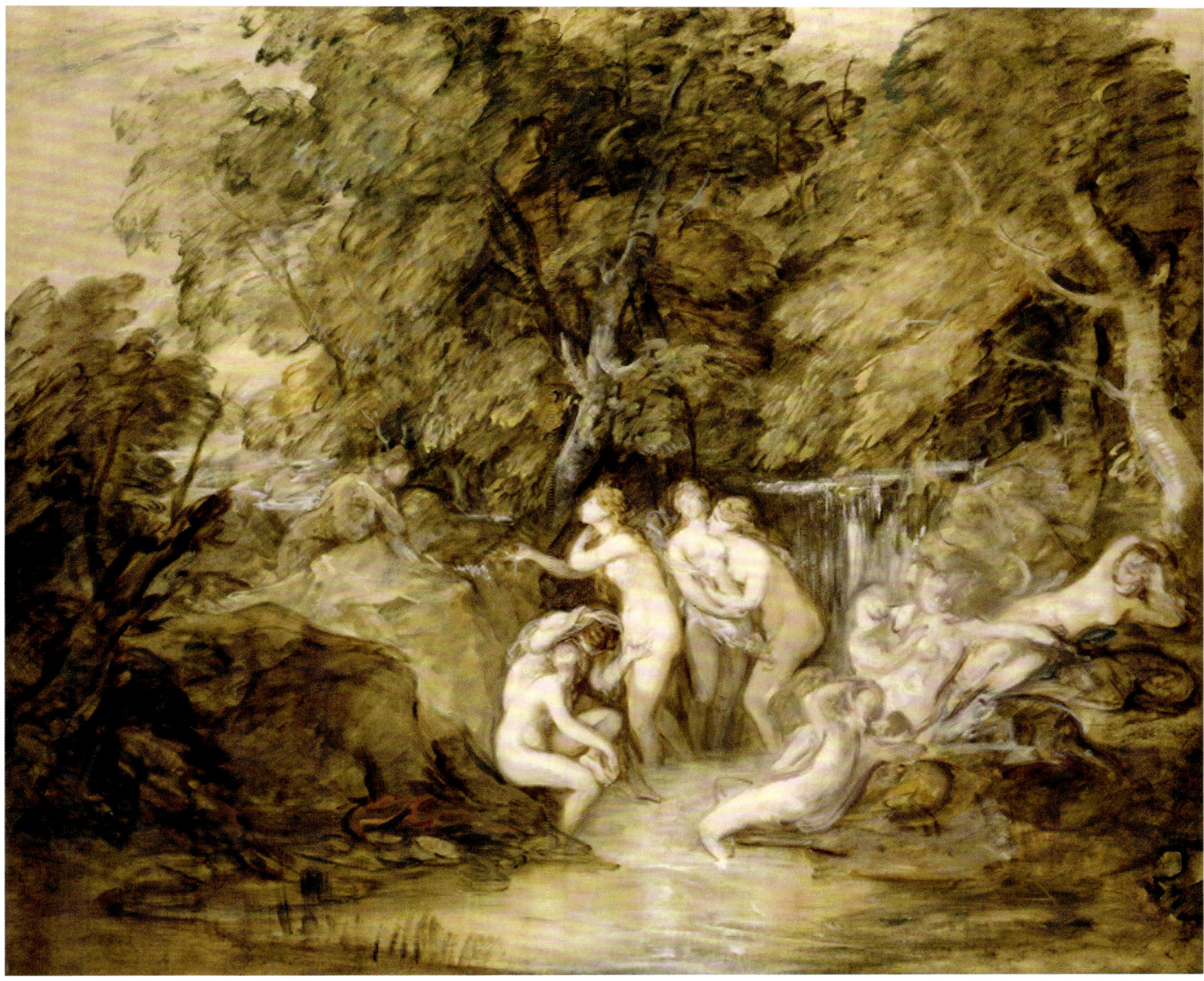

FIG. 0.16
SIR DAVID WILKIE (1785–1841), *I Pifferari*, 1827. Oil on canvas, 46.1 × 36.2 cm, RCIN 405861

FIG. 0.17
RICHARD COSWAY (1742–1821), *Maria Fitzherbert*, *c.*1789. Pencil and watercolour, 30.1 × 22.0 cm, RCIN 935221

FIG. 0.18
THOMAS GAINSBOROUGH (1727–88), *Diana and Actaeon*, *c.*1785–8. Oil on canvas, 158.1 × 188.0 cm, RCIN 405077

where Rossini was delighted to hear the wind band perform. A particular strand of George's personal taste is apparent in his adoption of the fashion for antiquarian collecting that was emerging at the beginning of the nineteenth century.[15] This was made manifest in the 1820s in particular, when the royal goldsmiths, Rundell, Bridge & Rundell, supplied him with an extraordinary group of wrought silver-gilt cups, dishes and mounted objects (Fig. 0.19), many of German sixteenth- and seventeenth-century origin. This collection drew parallels with a princely *Wunderkammer* of the Renaissance, and extended to natural curiosities such as mineral ores and specimens of hardstones, lodestones and pieces of petrified wood, musical instruments, quantities of snuffboxes and items of dress, jewellery (Fig. 0.20) and insignia.

Amassing such a stupendous collection was an expensive exercise, particularly so as George paid numerous figures to facilitate its formation: agents for the purchase of works, administrators of the collections that were acquired, and a group of fashionable architects and interior designers to provide the appropriate settings for them. Payment for art, buildings and staff came largely from the amount settled on George by Parliament from 1783, when he was awarded £50,000 per annum

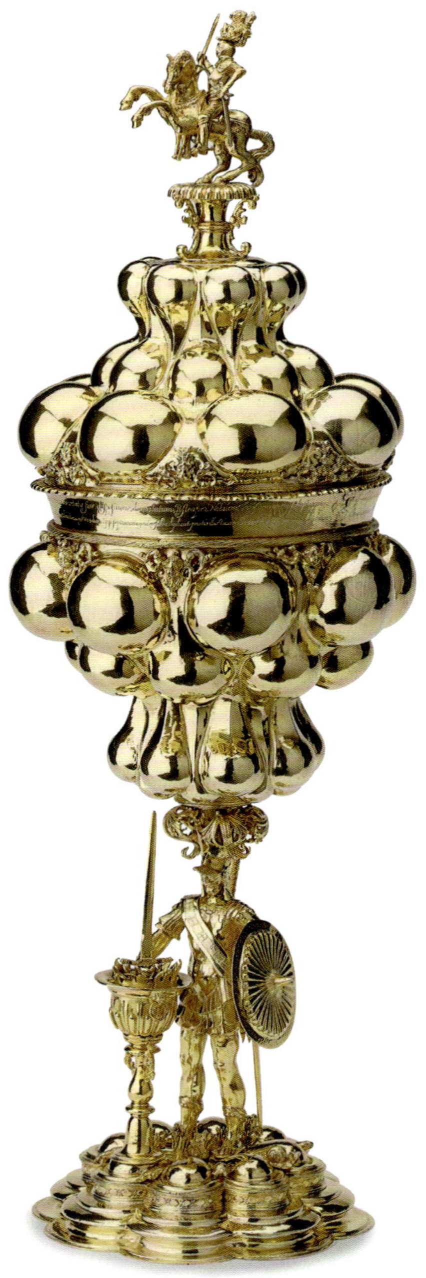

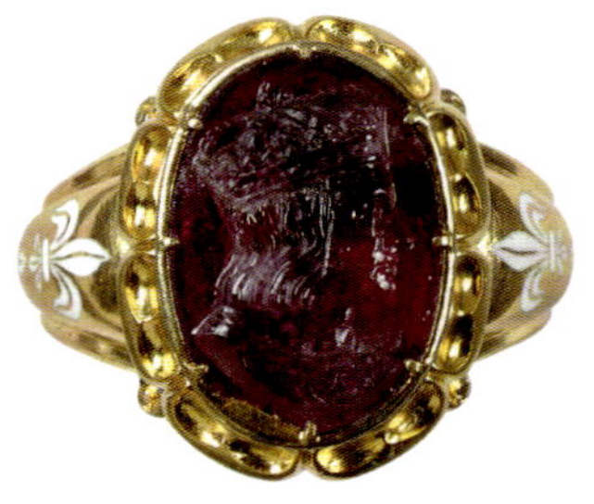

FIG. 0.19
FRIEDRICH HILLEBRANDT (b. 1555), *Standing cup and cover* (*Bukelpokal*), *c.*1596. Silver gilt, 59.0 × 17.0 × 17.0 cm, RCIN 51282

FIG. 0.20
FRENCH, *Ring with a bas-relief of Louis XII of France*, early 19th century. Rubelite tourmaline, gold, enamel, 2.0 × 1.6 cm, RCIN 65381

FIG. 0.21
RICHARD COSWAY (1742–1821), *Caroline, Princess of Wales (1768–1821), and Princess Charlotte (1796–1817)*, *c.*1797. Pencil and watercolour, 29.0 × 20.6 cm (sight), RCIN 452410

(in addition to the income from the Duchy of Cornwall, which was around £12,000 a year in 1783).[16] This sum was intended to cover all George's living expenses as a young man heading his own household, but he fell woefully short of Parliamentary expectation, becoming notorious among contemporaries as well as subsequent historians for living well beyond his means: by 1786, he was over £269,000 in debt.[17] Two years earlier, his treasurer George Hotham had admonished him for being 'totally in the Hands, & at the Mercy of your Builder, your Upholsterer, your Jeweller and your Taylor'.[18] By 1790, unable to raise funds at home, George and the dukes of York and Clarence borrowed a significant sum from Dutch moneylenders, a loan which would never be repaid. George's debts were the subject of much discussion, in newspapers and magazines, at coffee-house debating societies and in Parliament, which in 1795 appointed commissioners in an attempt to deal with his enormous arrears. George's disastrous marriage to Caroline of Brunswick (Fig. 0.21) in the same year has been viewed, with much justification, as largely driven by a wish to secure the larger annuity which would be due to a married man (and perhaps, too, access to the annuity settled upon his new wife). The couple were soon estranged, but the match produced one daughter, the spirited Princess Charlotte (Fig. 0.22), whose death in childbirth in 1817 devastated her father.

The chief cause of George's debts, as Hotham recognised, was his lack of restraint in all areas of his life, from drinking and gambling, to the keeping of a lavish stable, to the construction (and endless reconstruction) of his series of residences, to his penchant for fine tailoring, to the expensive works of art that he coveted. He provided annual sums to support a number of mistresses, among them Mary 'Perdita' Robinson and Maria Fitzherbert, and was prey to unscrupulous hangers-on (among them the appropriately named George Hanger, 4th Baron Coleraine, a failed army officer) who encouraged him to live an extravagant lifestyle from which they could benefit. George's financial affairs lurched from crisis to crisis and it was not until the 1820s that there was some success at retrenchment led by the formidable Sir William Knighton, who wielded much (and mistrusted) control over the elderly and ailing king. If George rarely settled

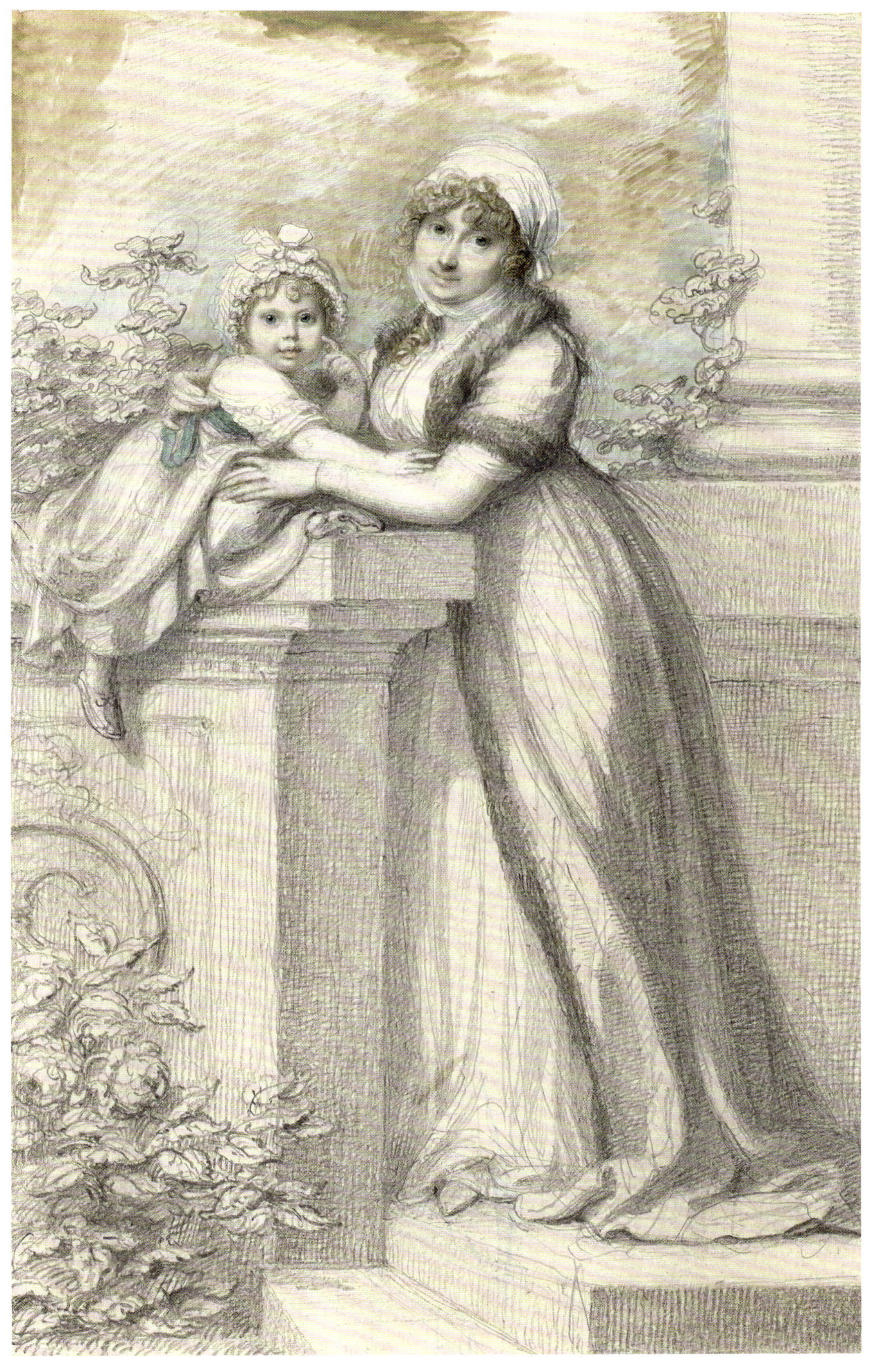

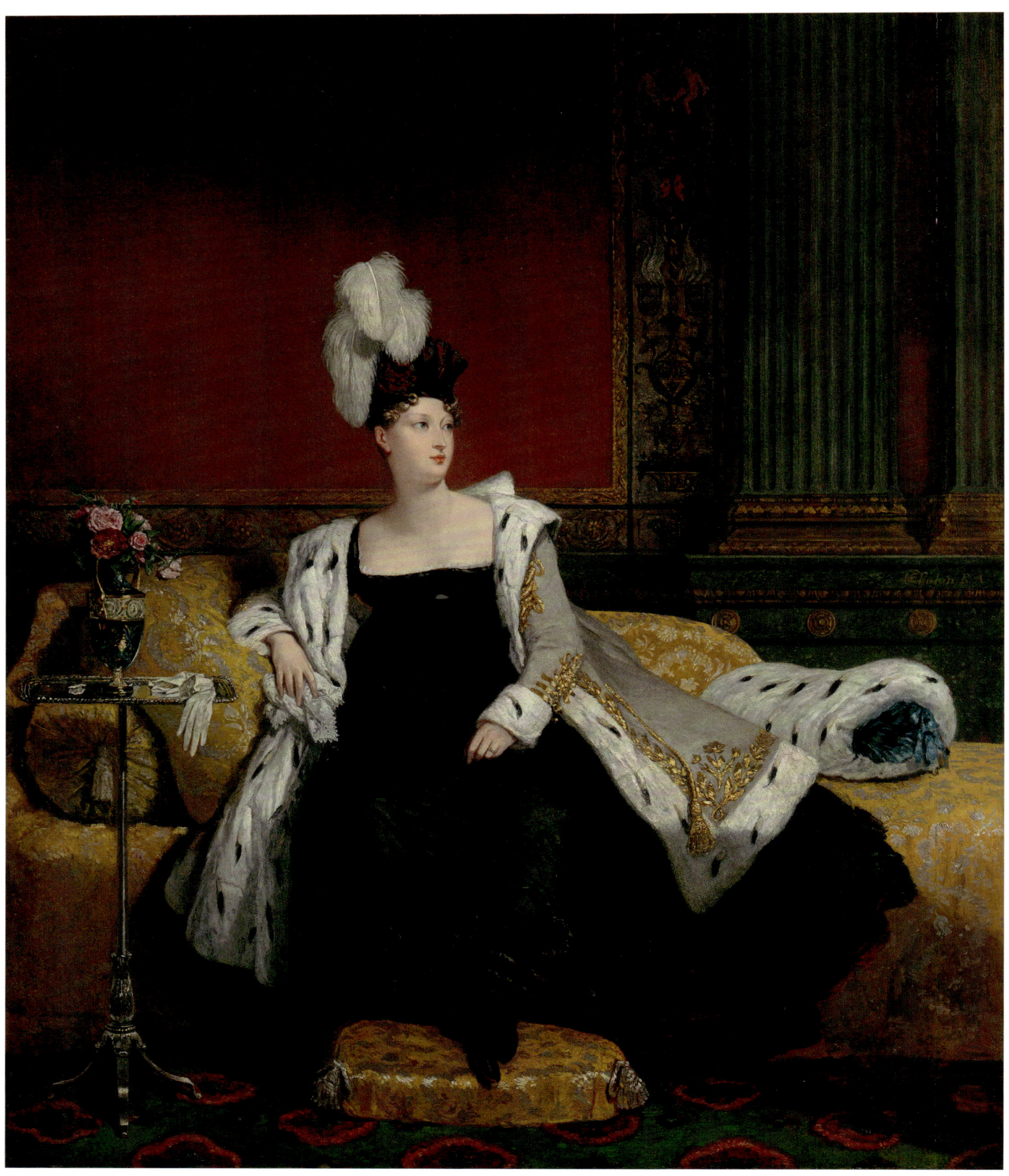

FIG. 0.22
ALFRED EDWARD CHALON (1780–1860), *Princess Charlotte of Wales (1796–1817), Princess of Saxe-Coburg-Saalfeld*, c.1817–19. Oil on panel, 76.3 × 63.9 cm, RCIN 405449

FIG. 0.23
JOHN RAPHAEL SMITH (1751–1812), *George IV when Prince of Wales*, c.1783. Mezzotint with pencil, 61.4 × 45.5 cm (sheet), RCIN 605110

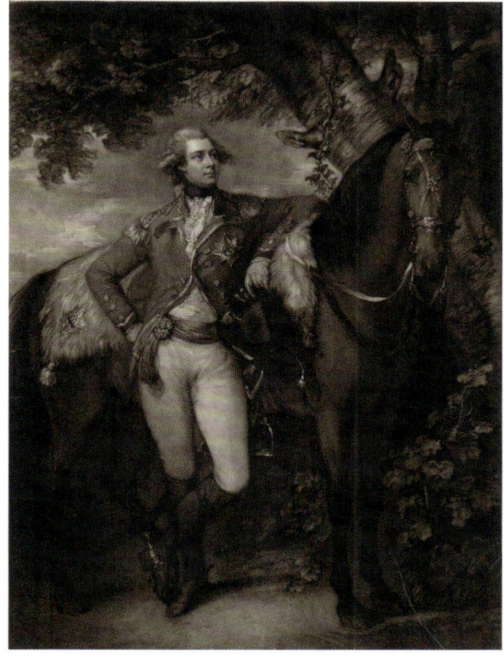

bills quickly, his reputation for late payment should be set against the record of his contemporaries, many of whom followed the same approach: George's position made him the subject of public appeals from tradesmen attempting to shame him into paying, but he was no different from other high-status collectors, many of whom delayed payment to their suppliers.[19]

George's financial extravagance was made all the more unpopular by the economic crisis which coincided with the beginning of his reign, when his country suffered under a large national debt incurred during the Napoleonic Wars, hardship and riots due to falling wheat prices, and a temporary but dramatic financial crash.[20] There was, wrote the MP William Huskisson, in March 1820, 'a soreness on every subject connected with expense, a feeling growing out of the present straitened circumstances of the yeomanry contrasted with the ease which they enjoyed during the war.'[21] Satirical prints of George's luxurious, vacuous lifestyle fed public perception of a monarch who failed to aid his country in its time of need: in *New Baubles for the Chinese Temple* (Fig. 10.11), Lord Liverpool, the prime minister, tells George that he cannot have a larger income, admonishing him to 'consider the poor starving manufacturers'.

In *New Baubles*, George's request to Liverpool is for half a million pounds extra income, a large sum in any age. It is very difficult to provide modern equivalents for the money George IV expended, particularly since he lived through a time of inflation, driven in large part by the Napoleonic Wars. The sums mentioned in this text, however, may set against the range of incomes with which Jane Austen provided her characters. Mr Darcy was extremely well-off on an income of £10,000 a year ('Tis as good as a lord!'), while Mr Bingley, a 'single man of large fortune', who also appears in *Pride and Prejudice* (1813), was considered extremely eligible with an income of £4,000–5,000 a year.[22] In this context, George's expenditure on the arts was lavish indeed.

George's endless indebtedness, if frustrating to contemporaries, provides rich evidence for the formation of his collection, since his multitudinous acquisitions were documented by a small team of financial staff who worked tirelessly to bring order to chaos. The invoices for George's purchases, letters to and from artists and suppliers, and the inventories compiled by his staff in an attempt to keep track of his gargantuan collection form the basis for many of the essays here.

The richness of both George's surviving collection and the documentary evidence for its formation has enabled a number of important studies on aspects of his collecting. Among these are a seminal exhibition held in 1991 on the lost palace of Carlton House and a comprehensive study of the furnishing of George's apartments at Windsor Castle.[23] Catalogues raisonnés of the Royal Collection have addressed his formation of important groups of Old Master paintings, arms and armour and Asian and Sèvres porcelain.[24] A recent biography has examined George's life as spectacle, while studies of figures such as Richard Cosway have focused on the men who surrounded and influenced him as he amassed his collection.[25] The present volume builds on this scholarship and is published on the occasion of an exhibition at The Queen's Galleries in London and Edinburgh. While a handlist at the back of the volume records the specific works on display in the exhibition, the accompanying essays are intended to range more widely, exploring George's life, from extravagant prince to magnificent king, through his art collecting and patronage. Assessing the documentary records for his art purchases, the surviving and lost buildings which he commissioned and his spectacular collections (which forms the basis of much of today's Royal Collection), the authors consider subjects as diverse as sport and fashion, paintings and furniture, formal ceremony and modern manufacture. George IV was a man of many parts and this is not intended to be a comprehensive biography of this most intriguing of kings, but rather a study of patronage which aims to shed new light on a life bounded by convention but enriched by art.

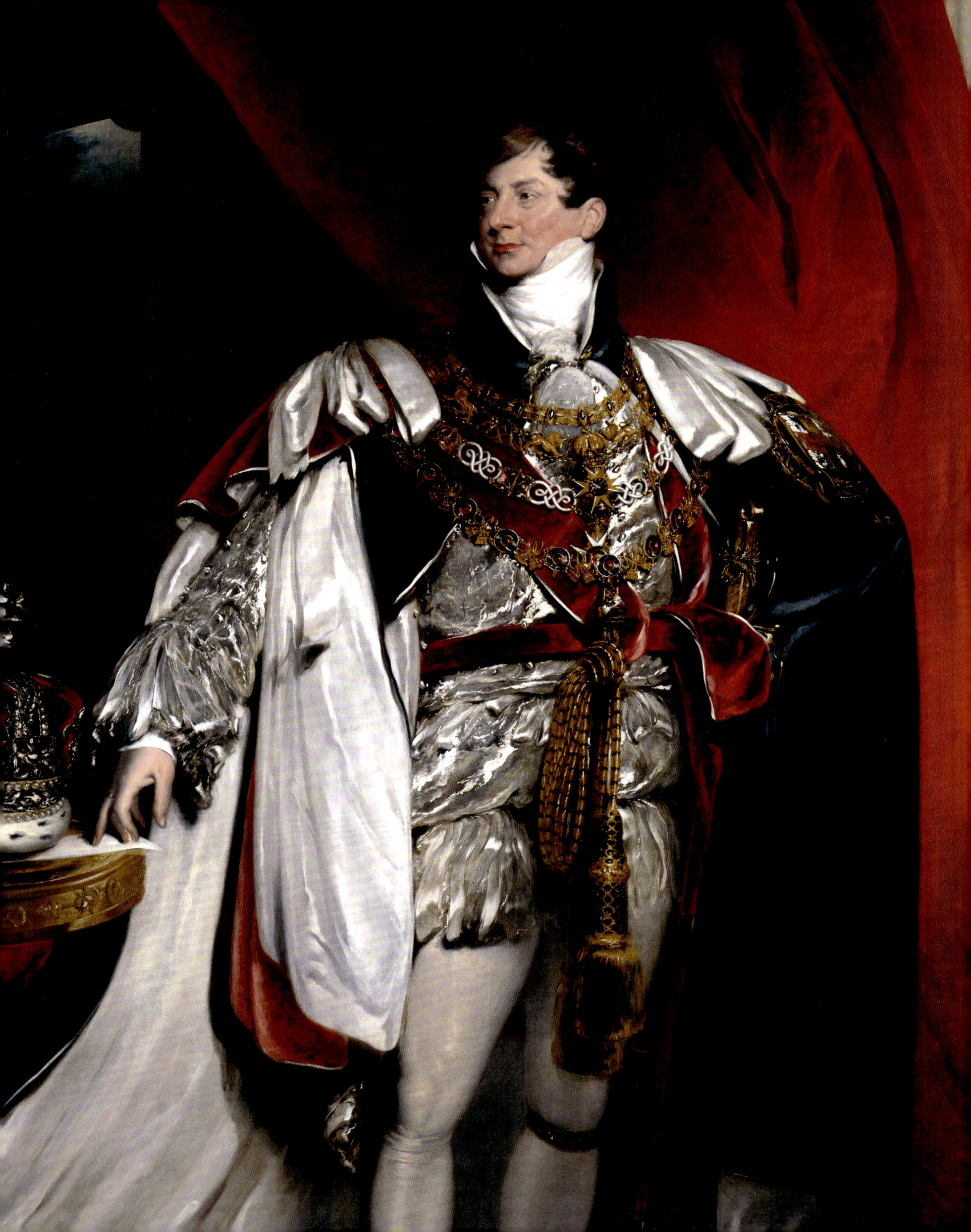

1

'FIRST GENTLEMAN *of* EUROPE'

JONATHAN MARSDEN

Those who admire every century but their own must surely find it difficult to justify their attitude when they reflect upon the conduct of a generation that conferred upon George Augustus Frederick, afterwards George IV, the title of 'The First Gentleman of Europe'.[1]

George IV was called many things in his lifetime, most of them far less flattering. But if we accept this Edwardian judgement on his credentials as a gentleman, it might yet be worth considering the terms 'First' and 'Europe'. How did this 'most munificent patron of the fine arts in Europe or the world'[2] compare with his contemporaries on the thrones of continental Europe as a patron, encourager and collector of art? How conscious was he of cultural and artistic movements beyond British shores? Did he regard himself in any sense as a European, and how did Britain's success in the Napoleonic Wars express itself through his patronage? To answer these questions, the circumstances of monarchs and monarchies in continental Europe during the first 15 years of the nineteenth century should quickly be reviewed. It will be clear that these circumstances were entirely different from those of George, as Prince of Wales, Prince Regent and King.

Prince Louis Stanislas Xavier, as heir to the abolished French monarchy, spent 23 years in exile, many of them in Britain, before assuming the throne as Louis XVIII, absenting himself from France during Napoleon's Hundred Days and then returning in 1815. Franz II was Holy Roman Emperor from 1792 to 1806 when, following the Battle of Austerlitz, his thousand-year-old empire was abolished. He reigned as Emperor Franz I of Austria until 1835. Emperor Alexander I, who came to the Russian throne in 1801 in circumstances that may have included complicity in the murder of his father, Paul I, was four times on different sides in the Napoleonic Wars, culminating in his leadership of the resistance to the French invasion of 1812, and the deployment of Platov's Cossacks in the decisive Battle of Waterloo. In Prussia, King Friedrich Wilhelm III retained his crown from 1797 until his death, but for much of his reign, Prussia was reduced to a vassal state at the mercy alternately of

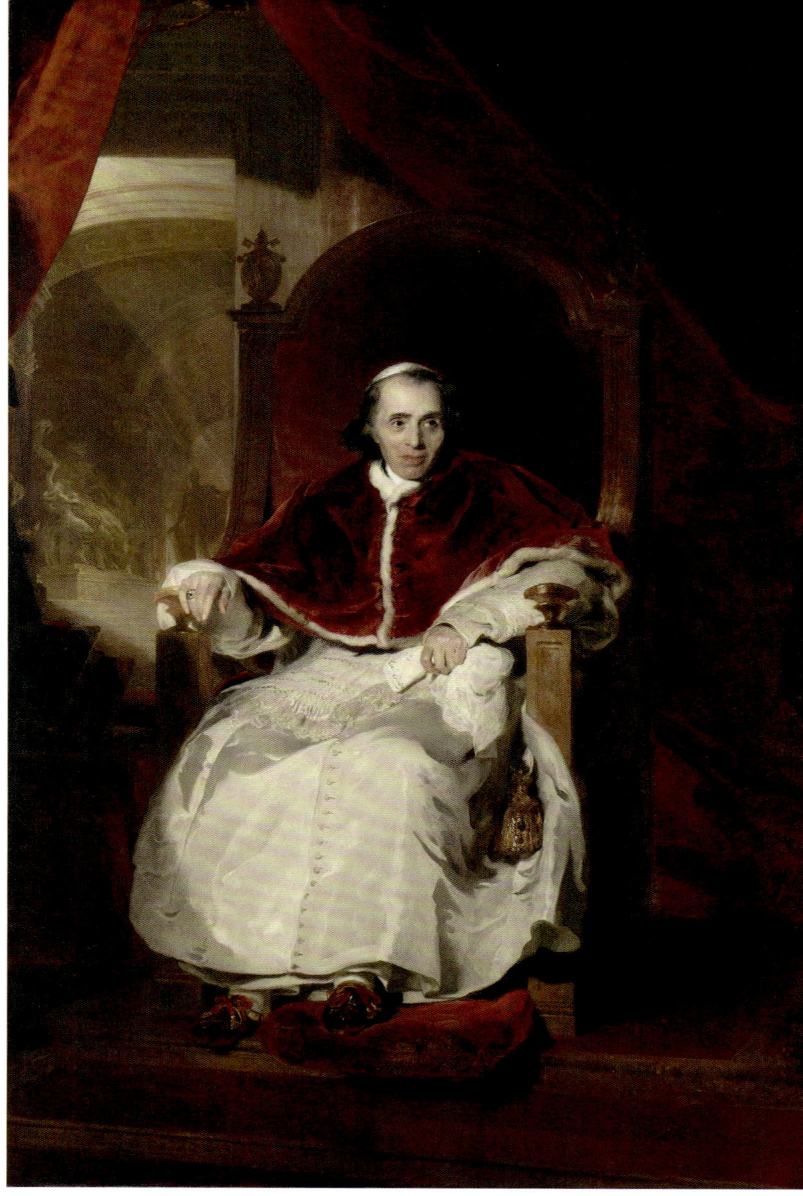

(p. 16)
Detail of Fig. 1.9, STUDIO OF SIR THOMAS LAWRENCE (1769–1830), *George IV*, 1821

FIG. 1.1
SIR THOMAS LAWRENCE (1769–1830), *Pope Pius VII (1742–1823)*, 1819. Oil on canvas, 269.4 × 178.3 cm, RCIN 404946

(opposite above left)
FIG. 1.2
BENJAMIN ROBERT HAYDON (1786–1846), *The Duke of Wellington describing the Field of Waterloo to His Majesty George IV*, 1840. Oil on canvas, 146.0 × 175.0 cm (Royal Hospital Chelsea, London: 579)

(opposite above right)
FIG. 1.3
CHARLES BRETHERTON (?1760–83), *Louis Weltje (1745–1810)*, 1781. Etching with hand colouring, 27.5 × 19.2 cm (sheet), RCIN 663659

(opposite below)
FIG. 1.4
JOHN HOPPNER (1758–1810), *Franz Joseph Haydn (1732–1809)*, 1791–2. Oil on canvas, 92.1 × 71.5cm, RCIN 406987

Napoleon or the Russian emperor, his territory and armed forces drastically reduced and his court for some years effectively exiled to the Duchy of Königsberg (now Kaliningrad). Maximilian I Joseph, the son of the Count Palatine of Zweibrücken, Friedrich Michael, served in the pre-Revolutionary French army, rising to the rank of major-general before succeeding his brother as Duke of Zweibrücken, a territory occupied by the French. In 1799 he became Prince-Elector of Bavaria and the Palatinate, and in 1806 the first king of the newly created monarchy of Bavaria. Max Joseph's successor, his son Ludwig I, did not share his father's Napoleonic sympathies, devoting himself instead to the nurture and preservation of the German nation. King Fernando VII of Spain was deposed by Napoleon in 1808 but regained his throne five years later. Finally, even the pope, Pius VII (Fig. 1.1), having been in attendance at the coronation of Napoleon as emperor in 1804, was held prisoner in France for five years from 1809.

Unlike his continental peers, George IV watched these existential struggles from the safety of the touchline, or perhaps, given his preferences, from a richly furnished box, fitted out 'in the best manner'. He followed the European wars with intense fascination, being careful to protect the interests (and possessions) of the Electorate of Hanover, took great pride in the acumen and the appearance of his armies and enjoyed discussing the details of particular actions with the Duke of Wellington.

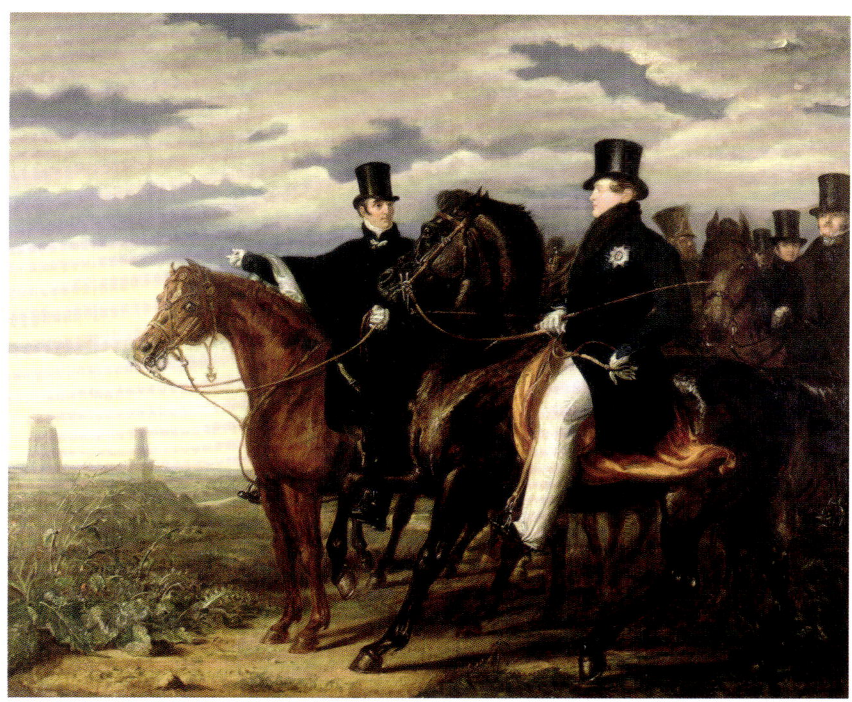

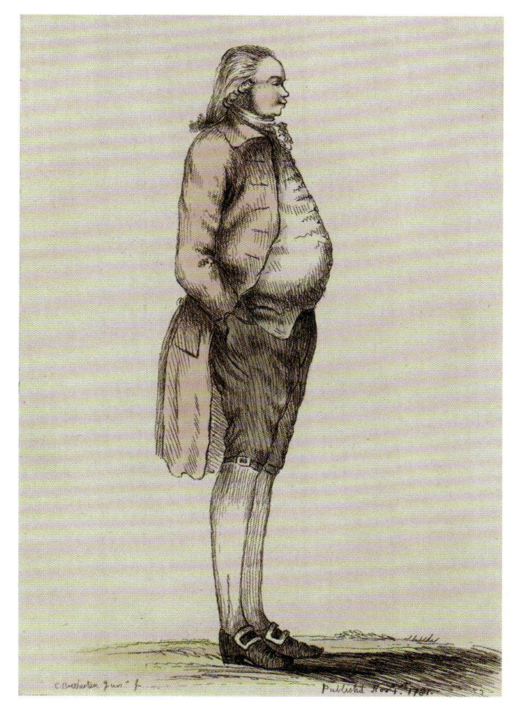

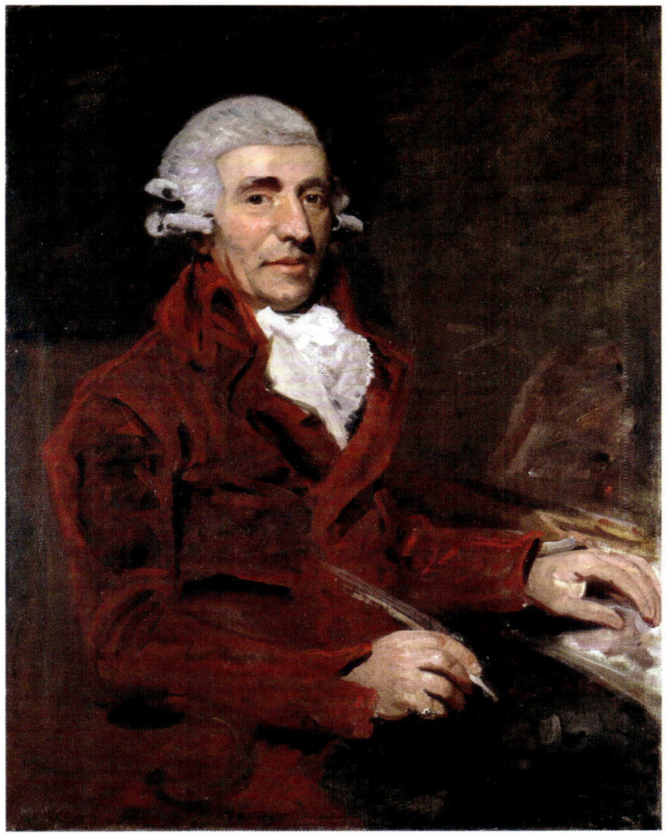

But the last King of Great Britain to lead troops into battle had been his great-grandfather, George II (at Dettingen in 1743), and by the time George IV visited the field of Waterloo with Wellington (Fig. 1.2) the guns had been silent for six years.

The education of the young Prince of Wales was designed to equip him with a good understanding of European culture. He read a great deal of French literature from his substantial library, and was fluent in the language. As a future Elector and King of Hanover he also mastered German. According to Joseph Haydn (Fig. 1.4), he had 'an extraordinary love of music and a lot of feeling'.[3] From the time of the establishment of his own household in 1783 his leanings towards the arts of France were cultivated and encouraged by a succession of French envoys to London,[4] and satisfied through direct purchases of new works of art from Paris and by the employment of the pre-eminent *marchand-mercier* Dominique Daguerre from 1787. Although he longed to visit the city himself, his acquisitions of outstanding furniture, bronzes and pictures from the dismantled collections of the French aristocracy were made at arm's length by the French-speaking members of his household – Jean-Baptiste Watier (*maître d'hôtel*), Louis Weltje (the German-born Clerk of the Kitchen; Fig. 1.3) and the confectioner, François Benois – or by friends and fellow connoisseurs such as Sir Harry Featherstonhaugh, Francis Seymour-Conway (later Lord Yarmouth and from 1822 3rd Marquess of Hertford) or Charles Long (from 1826 1st Baron Farnborough).[5]

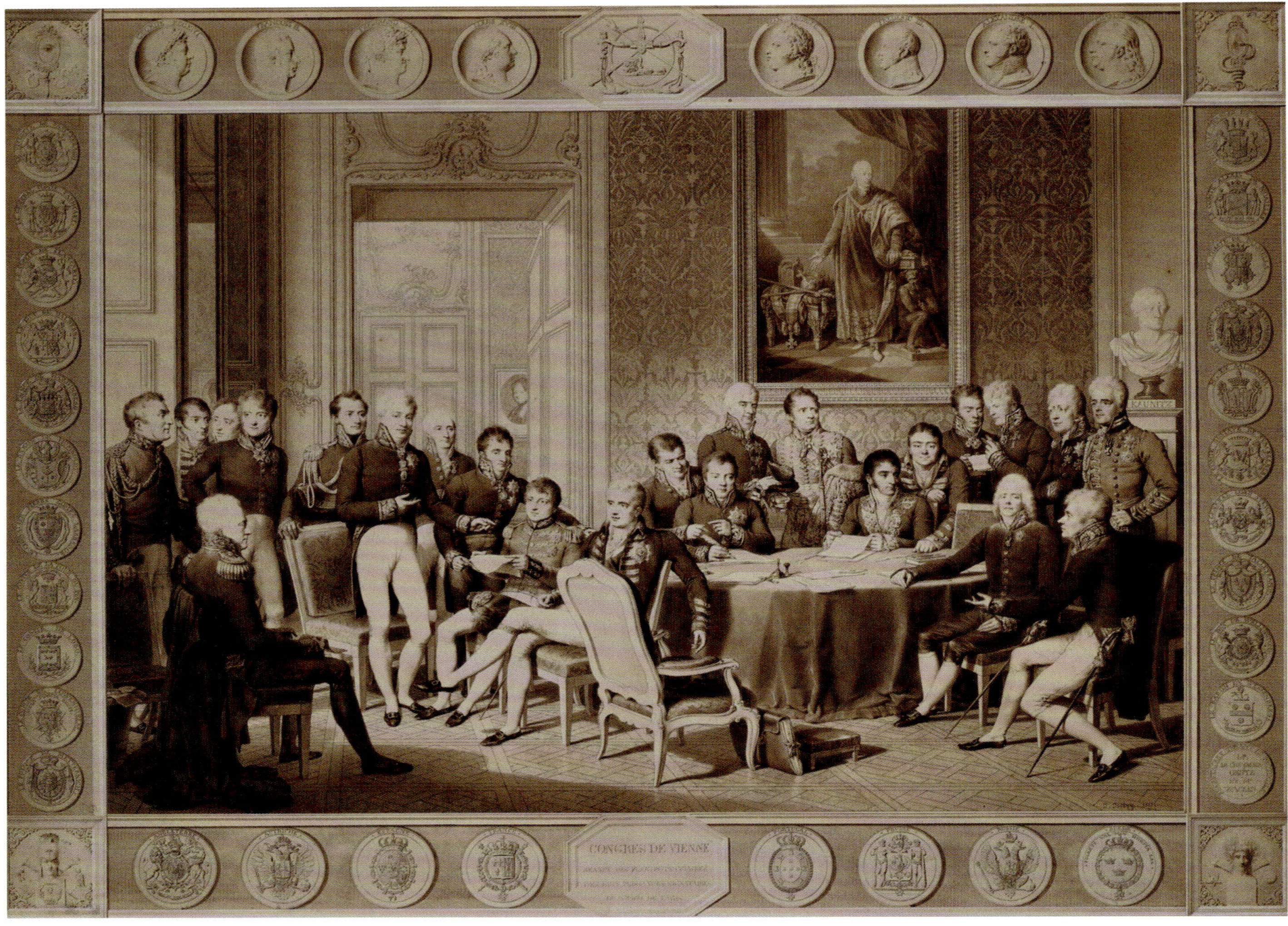

The notion that taste in architecture, fashion and the decorative arts emanated solely from Paris was of long duration. The court style of Louis XIV pervaded the German and other northern courts throughout the eighteenth century, but it had no such dominance in Britain. It was, however, perhaps the most consistent allegiance of George IV's life, despite the state of war that existed between Britain and France for almost all of the period between 1793 and 1815. In the prince's eyes this was not a war between nations, but between regimes; the enemy was not France but republicanism. In what seems a rare instance of responsiveness to the mood of the nation, the prince told Harriet Ponsonby, Lady Bessborough that he had decided to adopt the 'Chinese' style for the new phase of work at Brighton in 1802 'because at the time there was such a cry against French things, &c., that he was afraid of his furniture being accused of Jacobinism'.[6] If he meant this at all seriously, he presumably had in mind the dealings that he had with firms employed by Napoleon as First Consul, such as Thomire, Jacob and Lignereux. Otherwise there was no deviation from his life-long adherence to French style and manners. At the very end of the king's life we find the Duke of Wellington, who knew him better than anyone, who would become his executor and had tried over many years almost every means to secure his attention to serious matters, 'occupied for half an hour in endeavouring to fold a letter to his Majesty in a particular way, which he has prescribed, for he will have his envelopes made up in some French fashion'.[7]

As unstinting as his loyalty to the cultural world of the *ancien régime* was the prince's antipathy to Napoleon. Among the thousands of Britons who crossed the Channel after his first defeat were numerous artists, eager to see the unprecedented assembly of works of art brought by Napoleon to Paris from all over Europe and now on display in the Louvre. In the accounts of Thomas Lawrence and Benjamin Robert Haydon, who both admired the Prince Regent and enjoyed his patronage, we find

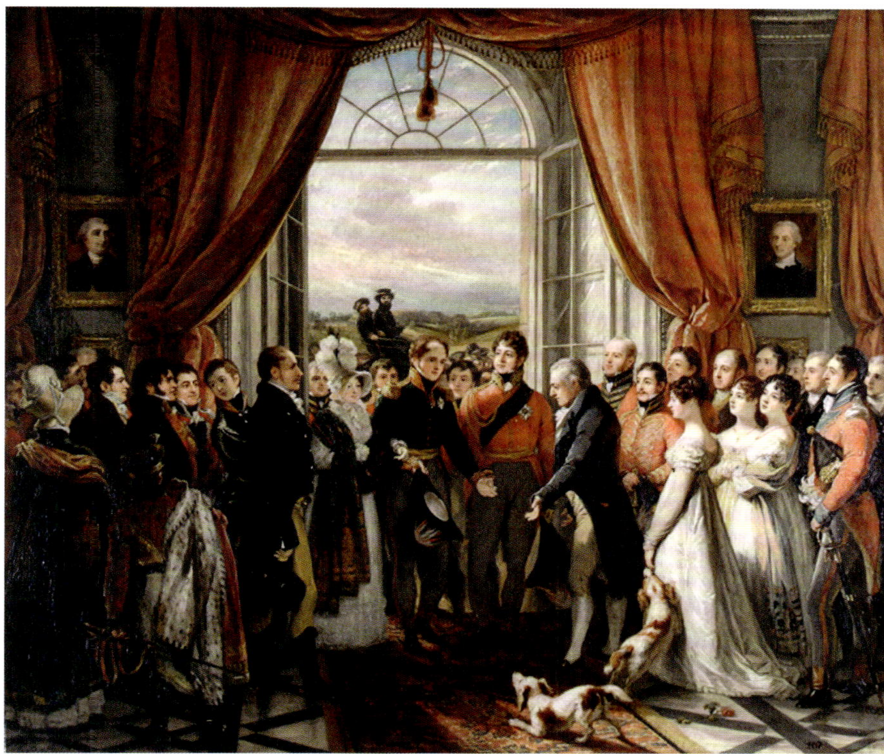

FIG. 1.5
JEAN-BAPTISTE ISABEY (1767–1855), *The Congress of Vienna*, 1815. Pen and ink with wash, 61.0 × 83.0 cm (sight), RCIN 451893.a

FIG. 1.6
THOMAS PHILLIPS, RA (1770–1845), *The Allied Sovereigns at Petworth, 24 June 1814*, 1817. Oil on canvas, 128.0 × 147.0 cm (National Trust, Petworth House: 486228)

more than a hint of admiration also for Napoleon. Lawrence, writing from Paris in May 1814, considered that 'No one can see France and Paris without bowing to the greatness of this man's conceptions … it is impossible that he can ever be separated from the past greatness of his country.' Yet, he added, 'That so much greatness of intellect, so vast a reach of thought (for the plans of improvement projected by Bonaparte are still superior to those effected), should have been mixed with such insensibility to virtue, is to my mind one of the most painful mysteries of Divine wisdom that can be contemplated.'[8] Haydon, who travelled to Paris with David Wilkie in the summer of 1814, was aghast at the 'hopeless confusion' of the city: 'All the nations on earth were there. The Louvre was in its glory. Such wonders can be only conceived. No human being hereafter can ever enter into the feelings of Europe when we heard Napoleon was in retreat; it cannot be comprehended.' No less than Lawrence he detested Napoleon's regime, but found himself 'affected with something like sympathy' as he walked through the deposed emperor's garden with the image of his eagle symbol in his mind: 'I sympathised with this romance of his nature, and I paced his favourite walk, drinking in sensations of ambition and glory, as if I was to be the next curse to the world.'[9]

While his generals waged war on the continent, George concentrated on enriching his collections, and on the decoration and redecoration of his palaces, Carlton House and Brighton Pavilion, but he also sought to promote architectural schemes for London that would, he said, 'eclipse' Napoleon's plans for Paris, such as the rue de Rivoli and Arc de Triomphe. This is how he is said to have reacted when Lord Glenbervie, First Commissioner of Woods, Forests and Land Revenues, presented to him the plans by John Nash for the creation of Marylebone (Regent's) Park in October 1811.[10] Yet the purchase that he and Nash could achieve against the 'barrage of frustration' presented by London's medieval street pattern, the ancient rights of markets, graziers and merchants, and the ruminations of the Commissioners of Woods and Forests, was never sufficient to deliver the scheme as he would have wanted. In truth there seems to have been no single grand plan, but rather a series of disconnected ones.[11]

The moment of greatest opportunity for the Prince Regent to occupy the spotlight as 'First Gentleman' arose in June 1814 when, as a preliminary to the planned Congress of Vienna (Fig. 1.5), he was able to take responsibility as head of the nation on behalf of his incapacitated father for the reception of Emperor Alexander I and the King of Prussia, together with members of their families, their ministers, generals and suites on a celebratory visit to England (Fig. 1.6). Over the previous decade, the relationship between the Russian emperor and the Prussian king had by turns been that of adversary and ally. They arrived together at

Dover on 6 June. As well as the tension between the emperor and the King of Prussia, it was already very clear that Alexander had taken great offence to the remarks made by the restored Louis XVIII on his taking leave of the prince in April to return to France, after six years' asylum in England, which had been printed in the press. Louis and George had invested each other with the orders of the Garter and Saint-Esprit, and the French king had declared that it was 'to your Royal Highness's Councils, to this great country, and to the constancy of its people that I shall always ascribe, under Providence, the restoration of our House to the Throne of our ancestors'.[12] Shortly after his return to Paris, Louis received the Russian emperor at Compiègne and such was Alexander's disgust at the manner of his reception that he declined to stay at the château, returning instead to Paris. His visit to Britain was marked by further snubs and perceived insults, which the earlier arrival of his sister Grand Duchess Ekaterina, widow of the Duke of Oldenburg, had fomented. In the course of a gruelling two-week programme of receptions and banquets, culminating at the Guildhall on 18 June with a banquet for 700 guests, the emperor and the Prince Regent spent only a short and awkward time together at Carlton House on the first evening of the visit.[13] The prince seems hardly to have managed to present himself in public as anything like the peer of his guests. According to Thomas Creevey, 'Prinny … lives only by protection of his visitors. If he is caught alone, nothing can equal the execrations of the people who recognise him.'[14]

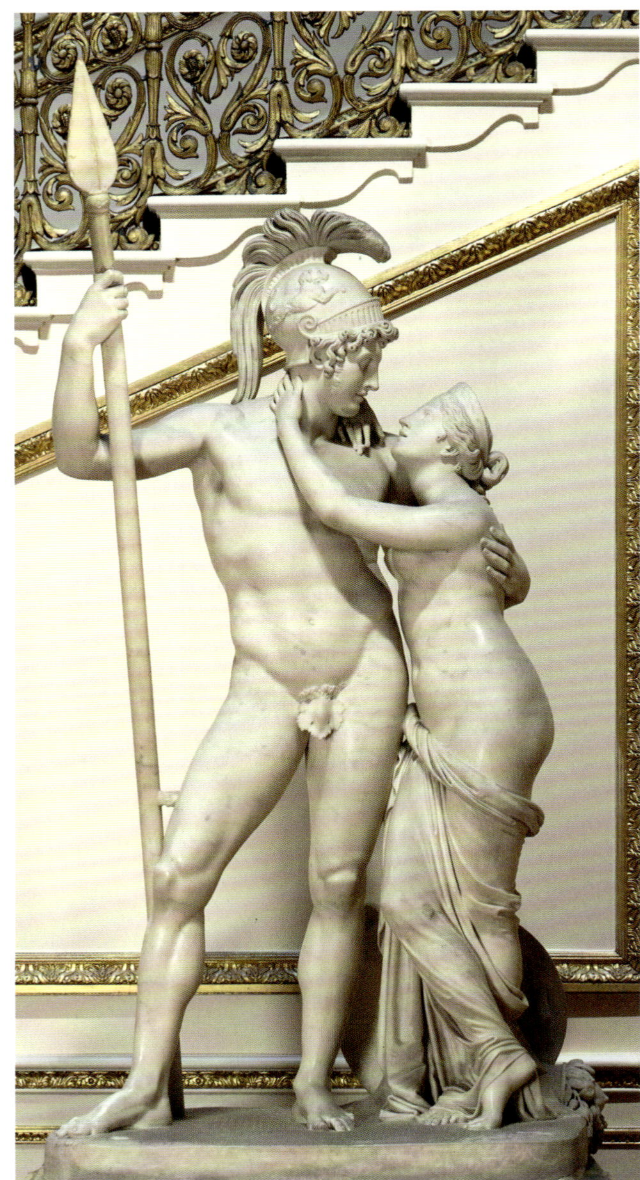

Some weeks later, on 21 July, after the sovereigns and their suites had long gone, the Regent gave a lavish fête at Carlton House in honour of the Duke of Wellington, and on 1 August he staged a celebration of peace which took place in St James's Park, Hyde Park and Green Park. Like the Carlton House occasion, it was remarkable for the extent and ingenuity of the temporary buildings and decorations, which included a Chinese bridge across the lake in St James's Park, and mock naval battles on the Serpentine (including a fireship which successfully destroyed the French fleet). A two-hour firework display in Green Park ended with the apparition of a Temple of Concord enriched with transparencies proclaiming Britannia's triumph, but the fireworks in St James's Park put paid to the superstructure of the Chinese bridge, which was engulfed by flames.[15] When Antonio Canova was asked what had struck him most about his visit to England in 1814, he is said to have replied: 'that the trumpery Chinese bridge in St James's Park should be the production of the government, whilst that of Waterloo was the work of a private company'.[16]

Something closer to the Russian emperor's idea of a victory celebration took place just over a year later, after the Battle of Waterloo, at the Plein de Vertus to the east of Paris on 11 September 1815. At its heart was a banquet which spread across 42 Gothic pavilions designed by the former imperial architect Pierre-François-Léonard Fontaine in collaboration with the celebrated chef Marie-Antoine Carême, attended by the emperors of Austria and Russia, the King of Prussia and the principal allied military commanders. Witnessing the march-past of 150,000 Russian troops the Duke of Wellington remarked to Lord Stewart: 'you and I never saw such a sight before and never shall again'.[17]

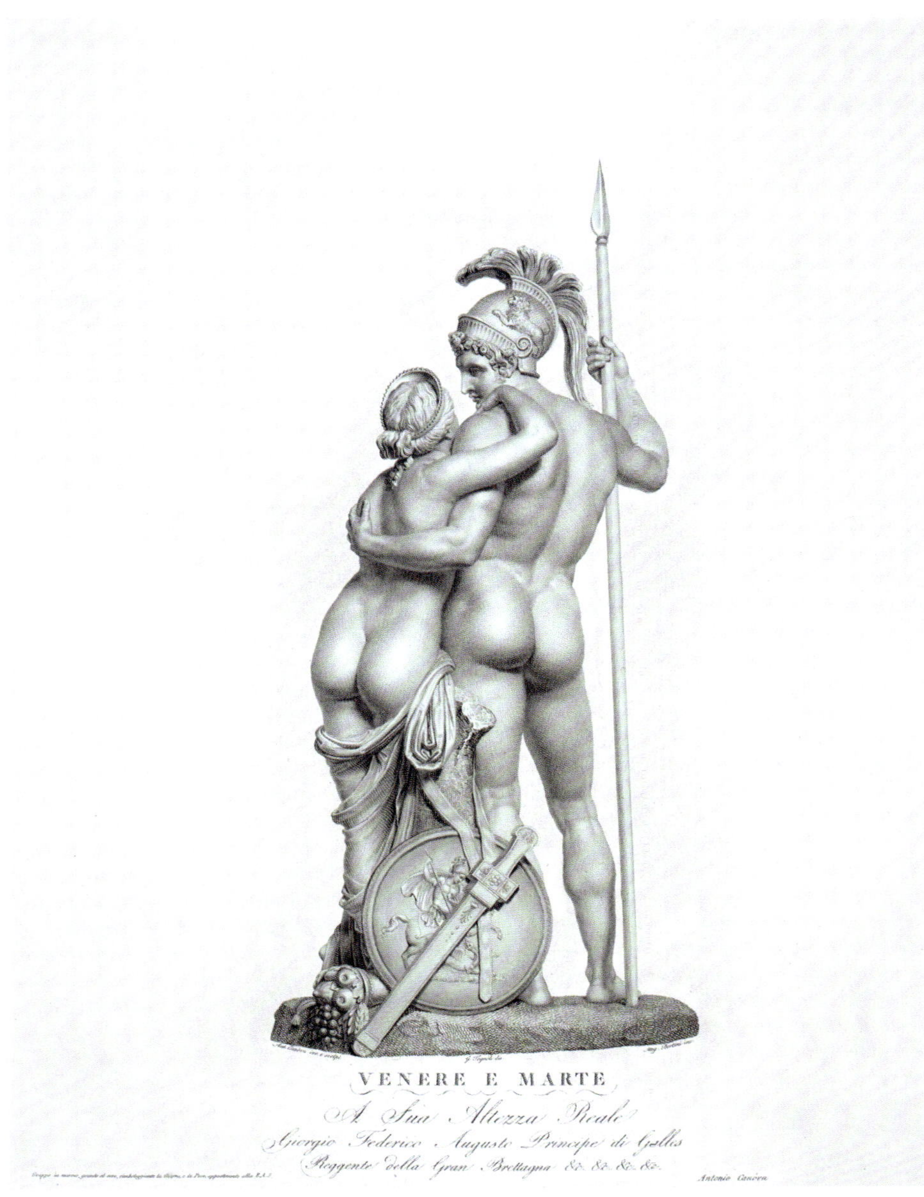

(opposite)
FIG. 1.7
ANTONIO CANOVA (1757–1822), *Mars and Venus*, 1815–19. Marble, 208.0 × 137.0 × 65.5 cm, RCIN 2038

FIG. 1.8
ANGELO BERTINI (1801–1900) AFTER GIOVANNI TOGNOLI (1786–1832) AND ANTONIO CANOVA (1757–1822), *Mars and Venus*, 1817–18. Engraving, 87.0 × 67.1 cm, RCIN 820841.at

One of the temporary buildings erected for the Duke of Wellington's fête at Carlton House, the 'polygon room', measuring 120 feet (37 metres) in diameter, was still in situ in 1818 when it served a surprising secondary purpose:

> There … were assembled, amidst the blaze of chandeliers and regal stars, at one period, the allied sovereigns, princes and chiefs from the Steppes of Tartary, warriors, statesmen, 'fair women and brave men', to celebrate the conclusion of that heroic period that had just terminated in the battle of Waterloo. And here was all that sublimity and beauty in ancient art, like the approving representatives of the gods of other times.[18]

The author was referring to the use of the polygon room as a depository for one of the several consignments of casts of ancient statues (and of the works of Canova) sent to the Prince Regent by the pope and intended for the students of the Royal Academy. This latest gift, which arrived early in 1818, proved too much for the Academy and following the intervention of the Irish peer Lord Listowel the casts were sent to the new academy in Cork.

The papal gift of casts was one of the consequences of the dealings between the Prince Regent and Antonio Canova.[19] The great sculptor, famous throughout Europe, was appointed by the Roman Senate on 12 August 1815 to treat with the King of France for the restitution of property from Roman and papal collections.[20] By this time Canova had undertaken commissions for several branches of the Bonaparte family, and had begun work on the *Three Graces* for the Empress Joséphine. He also had a number of aristocratic clients in Britain. With the support of the Duke of Wellington, the British foreign secretary, Lord Castlereagh (and especially his under-secretary, William Richard Hamilton), Canova was able to conclude an agreement to the restitution of works belonging to the Roman state by 30 September. He subsequently spent a month in London, attempting to raise funds to finance the removal operation. On his last day in London, 5 December, he was granted an audience with the Prince Regent and a meeting at the Foreign Office at which he received a promissory note for 250,000 *franchi*, of which 200,000 was for the costs of restitution and 50,000 was the prince's own contribution towards the completion of Canova's monument to the exiled Stuarts in St Peter's, Rome, progress on which had stalled.

Canova took leave of the Prince Regent with a snuffbox bearing the prince's cypher and containing £1,000, which must have been intended as a down-payment on the *gruppo ideale di Marte e Venere, simboleggiante la Pace e la Guerra*.[21] Canova's 'symbolic group' of Mars and Venus (Fig. 1.7), ordered in 1815, was among the first of George's major artistic commissions following the final defeat of Napoleon. In its final, marble state it is a sublime essay on an ancient theme, without any sense of triumphalism. But correspondence between Sir Charles Long and the sculptor during the period of its creation reveals that the prince had first suggested that Mars' shield should have at its centre his own portrait in profile – as if to imply that the god of war depended for his protection upon George himself. Long ensured in the end that the shield was decorated with stylised foliage.[22] An intermediate design, with a relief of St George and the dragon, is preserved in an engraving (Fig. 1.8).

This colossal marble group, which was only delivered in 1824, was intended as a focal point of the Circular Room at Carlton House, where the prince no doubt wished it to serve as a monument to his role in the allied victory. In September 1816, when work on the full-size model for *Mars and Venus* was well under way, Long wrote to Canova on the prince's behalf to ask whether he could have a version of the *Three Graces* instead, but received no reply.[23] In 1818 Sir Thomas Lawrence informed Canova that the Prince Regent 'spoke with the greatest delight of the prospect of possessing your works, and wished for nothing short of an entire monopoly of your genius'.[24] In the following year there arrived at Carlton House the 'Fountain Nymph', which had been commissioned by Canova's first British patron, John Campbell.[25] On his way back to Rome after his successful London visit, the sculptor had written to Campbell asking him to cede the commission to the prince, who had expressed a strong preference for *soggetti graziosi, e specialmente quegli di donna* ('charming themes, particularly of women').[26] But Canova's death in 1822 removed any prospect of 'an entire monopoly'. Not for the first time, the settling of the artist's final account fell rather short. W.R. Hamilton wrote thus to Long in August 1825 to confirm the somewhat reluctant acceptance of final payment by the sculptor's step-brother, Abbate Canova: 'I am persuaded he is highly flattered that these his brother's latest finished works, should be deposited in the palace of the King of Great Britain, to whom he considers himself, as his brother did during his lifetime, so mainly indebted for the halo of glory which shed fresh lustre over Canova's last days.'[27]

The frustration of George IV's ambitions in respect of Canova (of whom the king ordered a posthumous bust from Sir Francis Chantrey – a commission that was cancelled on George's death in 1830) may explain why the space at Buckingham Palace now known as the Marble Hall but originally designated 'Sculpture Gallery', lying directly beneath the Picture Gallery on the first floor, remained empty in the king's lifetime.

In his dealings with other foreign artists, George was inconsistent. When the painter Elisabeth-Louise Vigée-Lebrun, whose company he much enjoyed, found herself obliged to return from London to Paris under the measures introduced following the collapse of the Peace of Amiens in 1803, the prince assured her that he would intercede with his father, George III, to ensure that she had leave to remain.[28] (Vigée-Lebrun painted his portrait the following year.) Having sent the prince the manuscript of his composition *Wellington's Victory*, composed in 1813 after the Battle of Vittoria, and asking him to accept its dedication, Ludwig van Beethoven received no acknowledgement. He wrote from Vienna on 1 June 1815 to Johann Peter Salomon (addressing him as 'most renowned virtuoso in the service of His Royal Highness the Prince Regent') asking him to attempt to recover from the prince at least the copying costs for the score of his composition (which he had become aware was already being

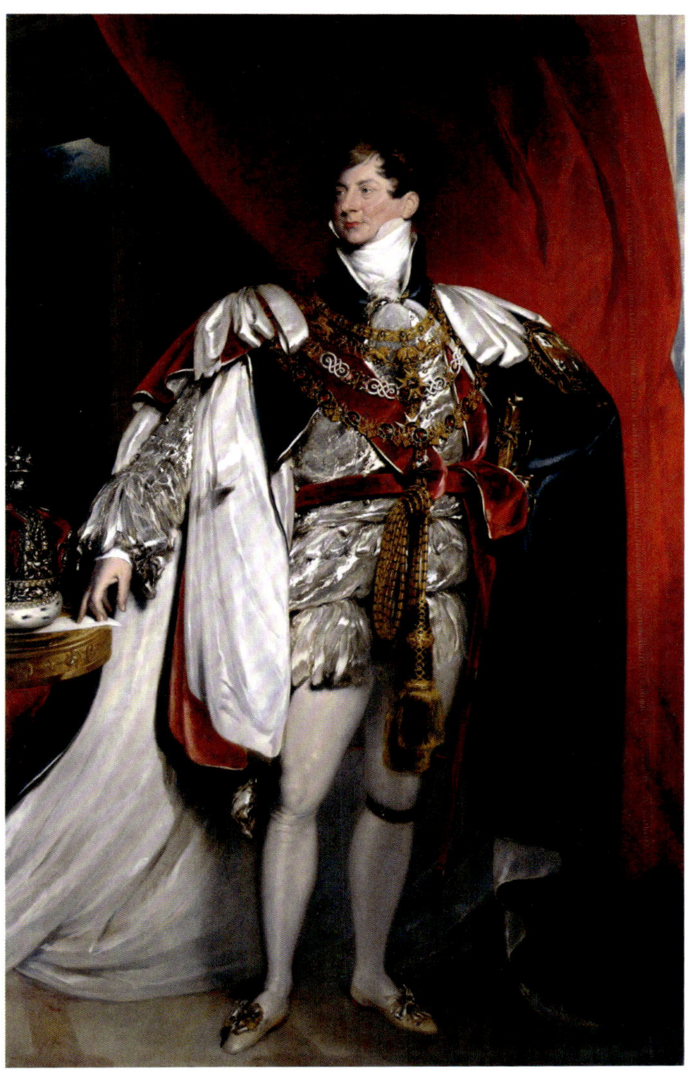

FIG. 1.9
STUDIO OF SIR THOMAS LAWRENCE (1769–1830) *George IV*, 1821. Oil on canvas, 271.5 × 190.4 cm, RCIN 404933

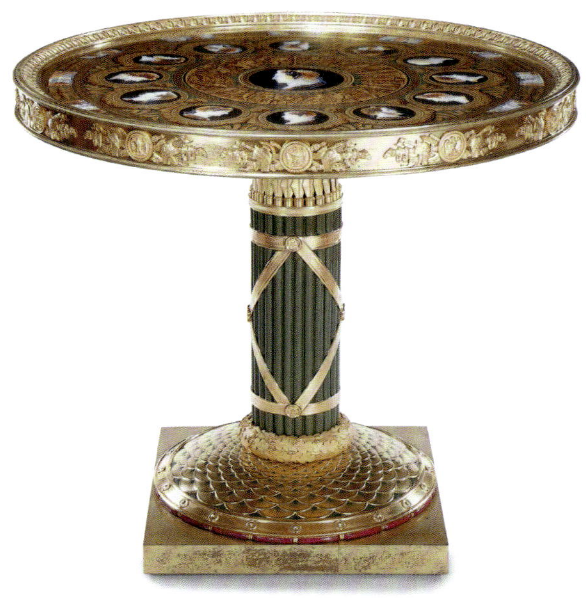

FIG. 1.10
SÈVRES PORCELAIN FACTORY, *Table des grands capitaines de l'antiquité*, 1806–12. Hard-paste porcelain, wood, gilt bronze, 92.4 × 104.0 cm, RCIN 2634

performed in a pirated piano version) but still to no avail.[29] The prince's employment of Carême – who of all chefs can be considered in the company of artists – was on the other hand brought to an end after eight months in February 1817, partly because George paid him too much in relation to the other members of his culinary establishment.[30]

In his famous full-length portrait by Sir Thomas Lawrence, painted in 1818 (for an example see Fig. 1.9), George IV stands in Garter robes and the historically inspired under-dress based on that of the early Bourbons, perhaps above all on that of his most-admired Henri IV. Without doubt it is an image of someone who seems to be in the ascendant, but not obviously of a military conqueror. In one version of the painting there are two identifiable objects. The first, in the foreground, is the extraordinary *guéridon* of Sèvres porcelain mounted in gilt bronze, the *Table des grands capitaines de l'antiquité* (Table of the Great Commanders of Antiquity), presented by King Louis XVIII of France in the previous year (Fig. 1.10). A masterpiece of Napoleonic propaganda and history-making that never reached the hands of the emperor himself, it serves eloquently in the portrait as a trophy of conquest. Victory here is signalled by the gentlest downward pressure of a fingertip. The gesture became less subtle in versions of the portrait painted after the accession of 1820 (see Fig. 0.1), when the feathered cap on the table was replaced by the rather heavier and more portentous Imperial State Crown of Great Britain. In the background of some versions of the picture is a partial view of a second object. It is the so-called 'font', a substantial ornamental tazza in gilt-bronze-mounted porphyry, presented to George by Pope Pius VII as a token of thanks for his help in the repatriation of the Vatican collections.[31]

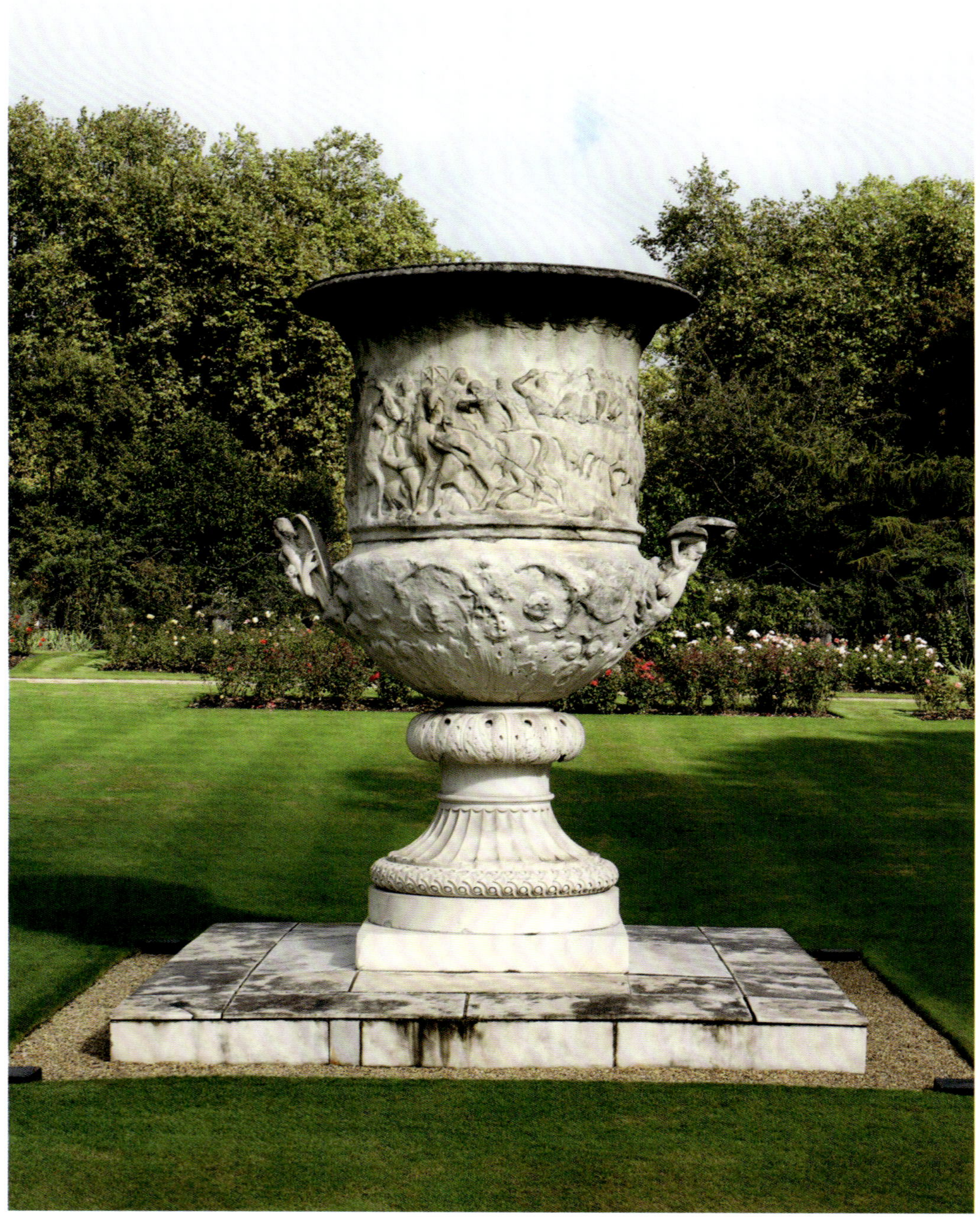

FIG. 1.11
SIR RICHARD WESTMACOTT (1775–1856), *The Waterloo Vase*, 1819–30. Marble, 550.0 × 267.0 × 267.0 cm, RCIN 68600

The two objects – to those who recognised them – represented both victory and the restoration of European cultural property.

On an early plan for Windsor Castle from the office of Jeffry Wyatville,[32] the large space in the upper part of an open court at the very centre of the state apartments is designated 'Sculpture Gallery'. This was instead to become the Waterloo Chamber, conceived as a hall of fame, not of Great Britons but of sovereigns, military commanders and statesmen of the nations of the victorious alliance against Napoleon.[33] The formats of the paintings were specified according to rank, with rulers and military commanders represented whole-length and politicians and diplomats in half- or three-quarter-length. The portraits may have originated in a plan for a single great picture by Lawrence featuring Emperor Alexander I, King Friedrich Wilhelm III and the Prince Regent, but during the years 1814–19, Lawrence was at work in London, Aix-la-Chapelle, Vienna and Rome on the principal paintings in a series that eventually comprised 29 canvases from his studio, to which were added eight by other artists (the last completed in 1848). At the centre of the chamber it was intended to place the Waterloo Vase (Fig. 1.11) by Richard Westmacott, 18 feet (5 metres) in height, with reliefs of Napoleon's defeat and an allegory of Europe under the protection of George IV, welcoming Peace. The vase, weighing 40 tons, was made from blocks of marble originally reserved at Carrara by Napoleon for a vase intended for the palace of the King of Rome.[34] No doubt advisedly, it was never placed in the chamber. William IV sent it in 1835 to the National Gallery (then under construction) whence, in due time, it came to reside in the garden of Buckingham Palace.

Symbols of military triumph were originally far more evident on the exterior of Buckingham Palace than they are today. Colossal stone trophies, resembling those composed by victorious Roman armies from the weaponry of their foes, formerly punctuated the skyline of the East Front. The Marble Arch, which stood between the ends of the two wings nearest to St James's Park, in the same relationship to them as the Arc de Triomphe du Carousel (on which it was directly based, although slightly larger) to those of the Louvre, was intended to support friezes of Napoleon's flight from Waterloo, and the death of Nelson, and at its apex a bronze equestrian statue of George IV by Chantrey (Fig. 1.12).[35] But inside the palace, symbols of victory were nowhere to be seen. What struck early visitors instead was 'the impress of nationality which [the interior] exhibits. All the ornaments have been formed to gratify national predilections'.[36] The writer must have had in mind the little Tudor roses that take the place of conventional fleurons in the capitals of the Grand Hall (just as the sunburst does at Versailles), and the national flowers cast in plaster in the ceilings or let into the borders of the wooden floors. In the Throne Room, what seems at first sight to be a copy of an ancient frieze (of the kind employed by Decimus Burton for his Athenaeum club house and the screen at Hyde Park Corner) was devised by the elderly Thomas Stothard with scenes from the Wars of the Roses (earlier designs seem to have been on the theme of Edward III's foundation of the Order of the Garter).[37] A telling comparison can be made with the contemporary frieze in Leo von Klenze's Walhalla on the Danube at Regensburg, completed in 1837 by Martin von Wagner, the sculptor who was Ludwig I's long-term agent for the formation of his collection of ancient art. The subject of the Buckingham Palace frieze was presumably chosen to highlight the union of the Houses of York and Lancaster as a foundation-stone of the British monarchy, but Ludwig's frieze, which also appears at first sight to be ancient, narrates nothing less than the progress of the German people.

Stothard's original design for the decoration of the tympana of the South Drawing Room (now known as the Blue Drawing Room) – a sculptural development of his painted ceiling in the library of the Faculty of Advocates in Edinburgh, which the king had admired on his visit in 1822 – was for a Parnassus in plaster relief. The early drawings represent poets of all times and nations in one single assembly, but as executed, after the king's death, there are three separate scenes celebrating only British poets.[38] How this change came about is unknown, but it may provide a telling contrast to the manner in which these matters were settled in Napoleonic France, where the choice of ornamental vocabulary was an affair of state and the new authorities took extreme pains to develop and design national emblems that would give a visible stamp to the eradication of the monarchy.

It has been argued that Napoleon's artistic imperialism and his concentration of works of art of the highest quality in a national museum accelerated the foundation of such institutions in other capitals.[39] In Berlin and Munich it was the monarchs – Friedrich Wilhelm III and Ludwig I – who brought into being respectively the Altes Museum, the Glyptothek and Alte Pinakothek. The contents of these museums were the property of these sovereigns but were intended to be generally accessible to the public, with the aim of developing the cultural life of the people.

After Napoleon's defeat in June 1815, George took a close interest in the proposed repatriation of the works of art from Italy, Germany and the Netherlands which had been appropriated for the musée Napoléon in Paris (renamed the musée Royale in 1814). This was a delicate question because the removal of works of art from the Vatican and most other Italian states had been given a form of legal sanction under the Treaty of Tolentino (1797–8), and British diplomats were anxious not to wound the pride of the restored French monarchy by denuding the new museum. A correspondence between the prime minister, Lord Liverpool, and the foreign secretary, Lord Castlereagh,

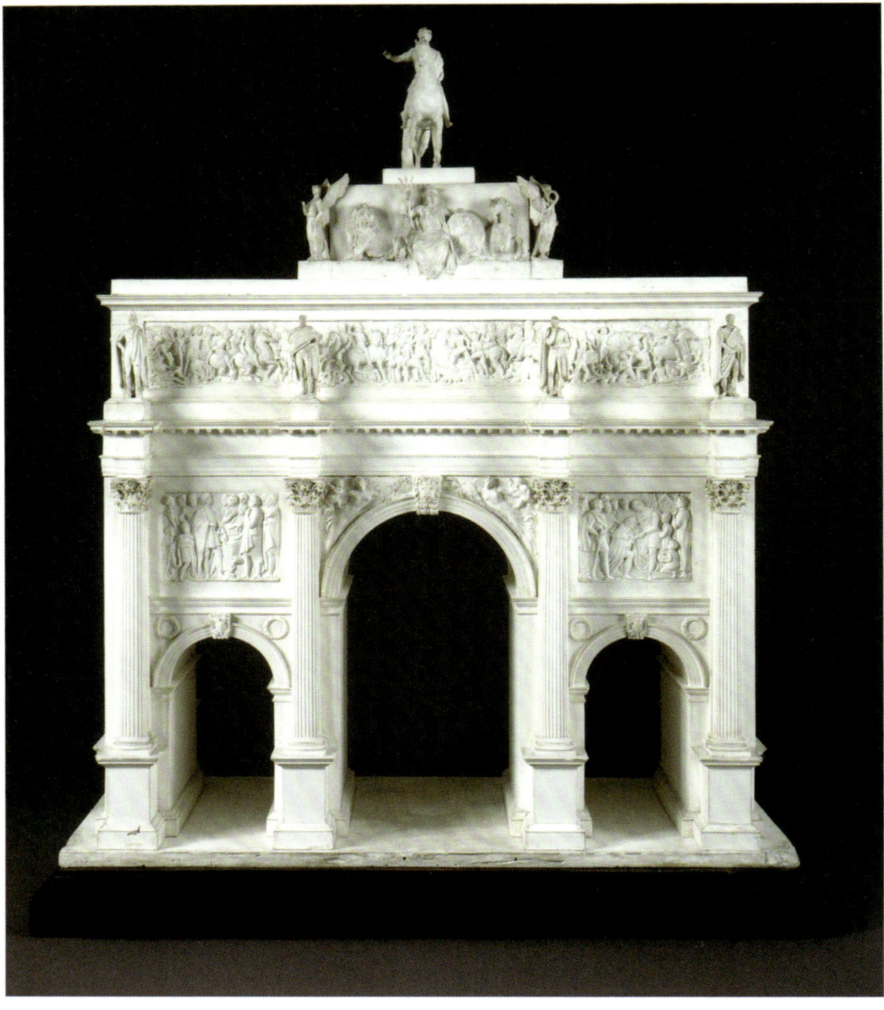

FIG. 1.12
OFFICE OF JOHN NASH, *Model for the Marble Arch*, c.1826. Cast plaster, 72.5 × 59.0 × 30.5 cm. (V&A, London: A.14-1939)

somewhat earlier that summer suggests that the prince had previously harboured different plans for the contents of the musée Napoléon. Liverpool wrote on 15 July 1815:

> I am particularly directed by the Prince Regent to call your attention to the collections of statues and pictures of which the French plundered Italy, Germany and the Low Countries. Whatever it may be fitting to do with them, whether to restore them to the countries from which they were taken, or to divide them amongst the allies, the Allied forces have the same title to them by conquest as that by which the French authorities acquired them.[40]

Liverpool stressed the prime importance of removing the treasures from Paris, where their continuing presence would 'have the effect of keeping up the remembrance of their former conquests'. Castlereagh was non-committal in his response, and the prime minister wrote again on 3 August:

> [Hamilton] will explain to you the strong sensation in this country on the subject of the spoliation of statues and pictures. The Prince Regent is desirous of getting some of them for a Museum or a gallery here. The men of taste and virtú encourage this idea. The reasonable part of the world are for general restoration to the original possessors; but they say with truth, that we have a better title to them than the French, if legitimate war gives title to objects; and they blame the policy of leaving the trophies of the French Victories at Paris, and making that capital in future the centre of the arts.[41]

If the prince did indeed have plans to create a national, public museum in Britain, this is the only time he ever mentioned them.

In the 25 years since the French Revolution, countless individual works of art and whole collections had changed hands in what might be termed irregular ways, and the prince's antennae clearly twitched at the opportunity of adding in some way to the artistic heritage of Britain.

One way of assessing George IV's achievements as a patron and collector between his accession as Regent in 1811 and his death in 1830 in relation to those of his European counterparts, is to do so in terms of means, motivation and opportunity. In strict monetary terms, the availability of funds was never a constraint in George IV's career as a collector, patron and builder. There remains, though, an important distinction between what was achieved in court cities such as Paris, Berlin and Munich (where such all-powerful figures as a Director of Buildings, or Museums, and a Court Architect or *Hofbaumeister* were royal appointments) and in London, which was emphatically not centred on the court,[42] and where major projects of urban planning were the responsibility of the Commissioners of Woods and Forests, civil, not royal, servants. The opportunity certainly existed to maximise the advantages presented by the relative continuity of Britain's government, the country's prosperity and its share in the eventual victory over Napoleon, to make London unquestionably the world's artistic capital (as Napoleon, by different means, had done momentarily in Paris). It may all come down to the question of motive. Without doubt, what Friedrich Wilhelm III was doing in Berlin, under the strong encouragement of his queen Luise of Mecklenburg and with his architect Karl Friedrich Schinkel, and likewise Ludwig I with Leo von Klenze in Munich, was novel. This new form of royal patronage had at its heart the idea of enriching the cultural life of the people, placing royal possessions at the disposal of the new middle classes in new public institutions. That George IV as a collector and patron enriched Britain's cultural possessions and architectural heritage is beyond question. Yet while the civic museums, the universities and institutes of Paris, Berlin and Munich were under construction, George IV was aggrandising and furnishing in the highest luxury the medieval fortress that had belonged to 30 of his predecessors, and erecting in London a British palace which – as much as it has served the country so well in subsequent reigns – he himself would never occupy. His ideal remained the luxurious, 'handsome', 'enriched' surroundings furnished 'in the best manner',[43] an evocation of the *gloire* of the *ancien régime*. As the machinery of commercial London ran hot in the new world of post-Napoleonic Europe, he remained to the end in a world of his own.

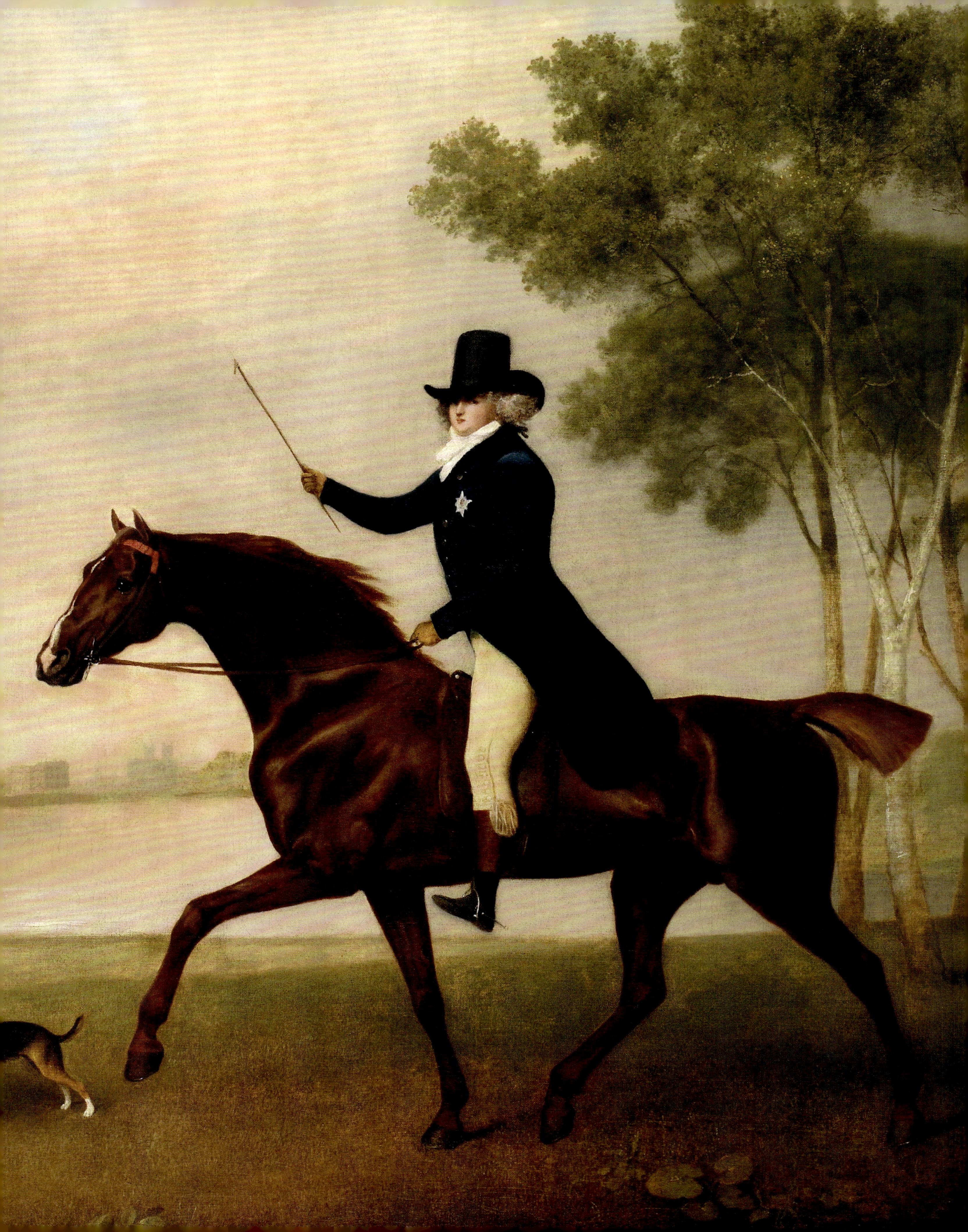

2

MAN *of* FASHION: GEORGE, PRINCE *of* WALES *and his* IMAGE

STEVEN PARISSIEN

Lecturing in America on the subject of the Hanoverian monarchs in the mid-1850s, the celebrated English novelist William Makepeace Thackeray – born in Calcutta in 1811, the year George, Prince of Wales had attained the Regency – regaled his audiences with a description of the prince having dressed

> in every kind of uniform and every possible court-dress – in long fair hair, with powder, with and without a pig-tail – in every conceivable cocked-hat – in dragoon uniform – in Windsor uniform – in a field-marshal's clothes – in a Scotch kilt and tartans, with dirk and claymore (a stupendous figure) – in a frogged frock-coat with a fur collar and tight breeches and silk stockings – in wigs of every colour, fair, brown and black.[1]

Thackeray's opinions were largely derived from the prints and pictures of 30 and 40 years before; his derision of George's Scottish costume of 1822, for example, was clearly inspired by David Wilkie's decidedly uncomfortable full-length portrait of 1829 (see Fig. 16.13). (Wilkie himself privately admitted that George merely looked 'like a great sausage stuffed into the covering'.[2]) However, as early as 1782, George's friend, Georgiana, Duchess of Devonshire observed that the prince was 'fond of dress even to a tawdry degree', and that 'his person, his dress and the admiration he has met … from women take up his thoughts chiefly'.[3] Certainly the prince's letters to his brother Frederick of the early 1780s are full of fashion gossip. Thus in March 1781 George wrote to Frederick informing him that

> By ye next messenger I will send you two uniforms at least, with ye dress and undress of my hunting uniform … If there are any other cloaths of any sort or kind besides these and yr Vandyke dress, wh. you wish to be sent over, I will take care of it. I shall also send you some new buckles together with ye sword you ordered … 'tis excessively pretty, a mixture of gold & steel beads.[4]

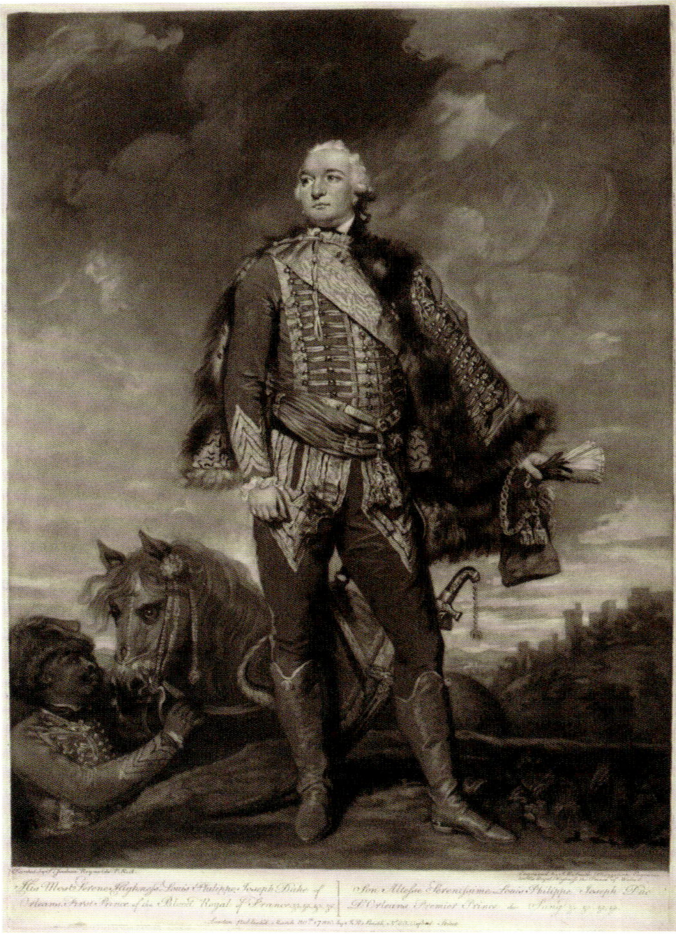

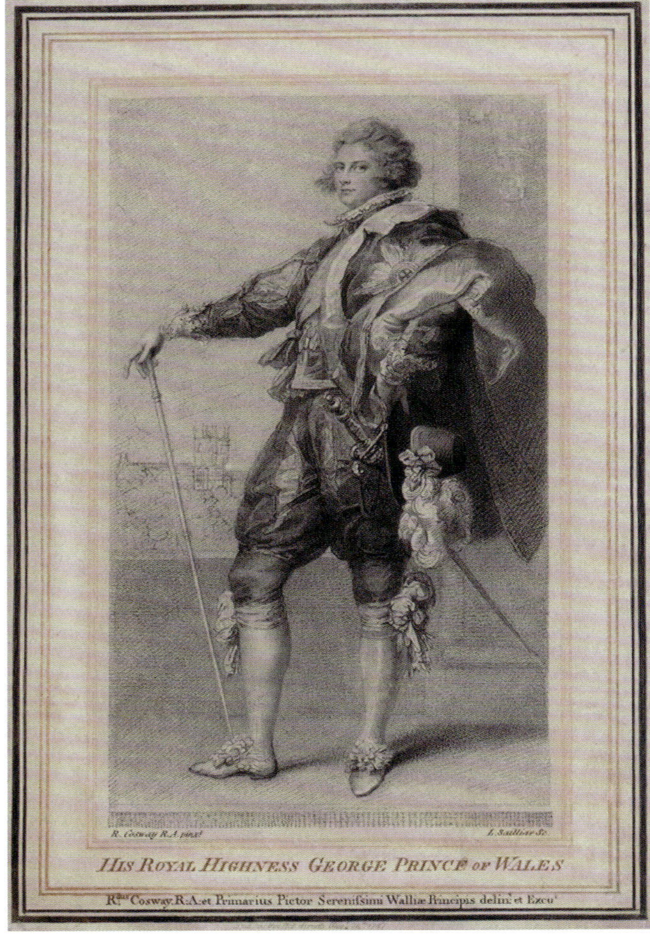

From his earliest years George's principal concern had been how he appeared, as communicated to his subjects by paint, by clothing and by association. In his recognition of the importance of image and iconography, he can perhaps be regarded as the first truly 'modern' monarch. His self-image was influenced by his friends and advisers, shaped by his awareness of the crucial role fashion could play in updating and elevating the reputation of the royal family, and bolstered by the heroic portraits of himself that he commissioned from artists and sculptors. Art, architecture and the decorative arts were all enlisted to create a picture of an heir to the throne who was virile, martial and – in contrast to his parents – at the cutting edge of fashion and taste. Unfortunately, as George grew older, his subjects increasingly recognised that this carefully crafted image was becoming ever more distanced from reality.

Even before his coming of age, George was taking his cue on both fashion and conduct not from his family but from the rakish set he collected around him at Carlton House: raffish Whigs or Whig sympathisers such as Charles James Fox, George Hanger, the Duchess of Devonshire and, on the occasions when he visited London, the anglophile Louis-Philippe, duc d'Orléans. In response, George III made it clear that he regarded Fox and his Whig coterie as largely responsible for his eldest son's massive debts, incorrigible womanising and incessant gambling.[5] For George, both fashion and portraiture were employed to make a statement: one that distanced him from his abstemious parents and which also at least notionally allied him with the political causes which his father abhorred. Thus, when George III rode down the Mall to open Parliament following the 1784 general election (which had, to his delight, seen the incumbent coalition between Fox and the veteran politician Lord North heavily defeated by his protégé William Pitt), his carriage had to pass a loud party for Fox being hosted at Carlton House by his eldest son, who donned the buff and blue of the Foxite Whigs for the occasion.

While the young prince paid lip service to Foxite Whiggism, however, rather closer to his heart was a love of dressing up and of militaria that he shared with the duc d'Orléans. The two also shared the same mistress on at least one occasion.[6] In 1785 the prince commissioned Sir Joshua Reynolds, already well established

(p. 30)
Detail of Fig. 2.3, GEORGE STUBBS (1724–1806), *George IV when Prince of Wales*, 1791

FIG. 2.1
JOHN RAPHAEL SMITH (1751–1812) AFTER SIR JOSHUA REYNOLDS (1723–92), *His Most Serene Highness Louis Philippe Joseph, Duke of Orleans (1747–93)*, 1786. Mezzotint, 67.3 × 47.7 cm (sheet), RCIN 640933

FIG. 2.2
LOUIS SAILLIAR (1748–95) AFTER RICHARD COSWAY (1742–1821), *His Royal Highness George, Prince of Wales*, 1787. Stipple, 30.8 × 20.7 cm, RCIN 605140

FIG. 2.3
GEORGE STUBBS (1724–1806), *George IV when Prince of Wales*, 1791. Oil on canvas, 102.6 × 127.7 cm, RCIN 400142

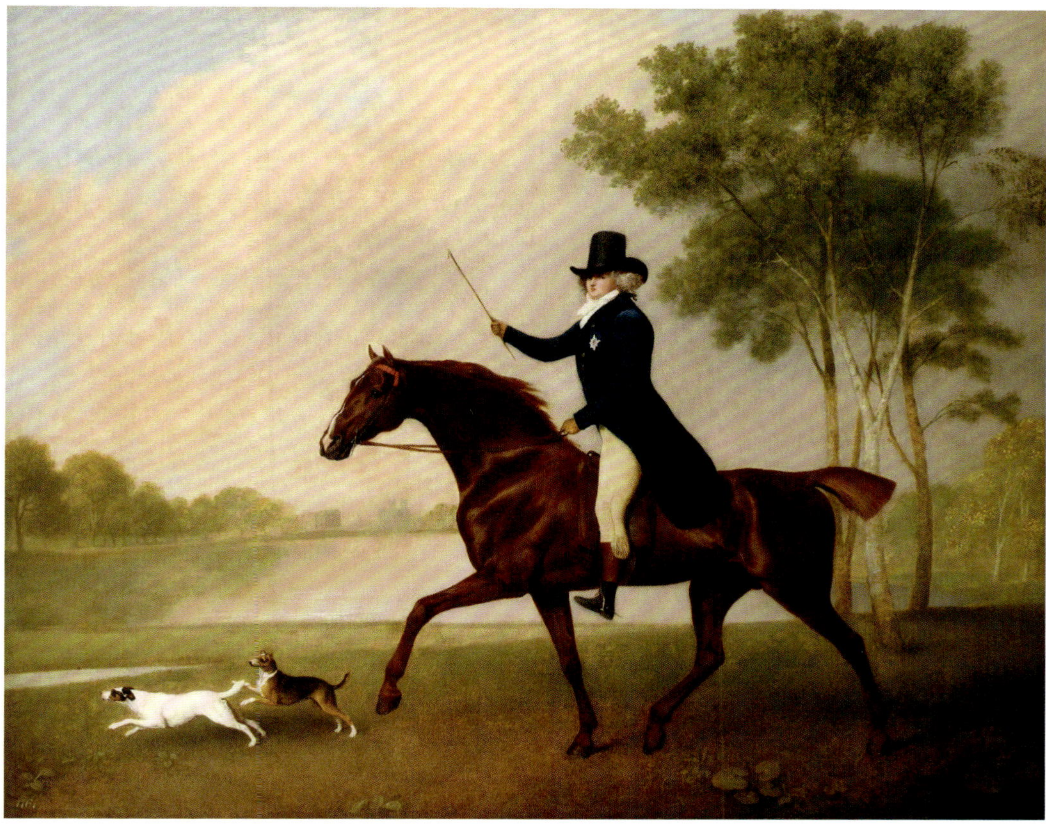

as the official painter of the Whig court – and, as such, shunned by George III, who reluctantly knighted the artist but never commissioned him to paint anything – to depict Orléans in a gaudy hussar uniform (Fig. 2.1). By 1789 George and the duke appeared inseparable, and in 1790 Orléans lent George the vast sum of £75,000.[7] This, however, still had not been repaid when the duke met his death at the guillotine in November 1793 – by which time Orléans's reinvention of himself as the revolutionary 'Philippe Egalité' and his vote for his cousin Louis XVI's death had convinced George that he was now absolved from the debt. Reynolds's canvas had, meanwhile, already been put into store.

Orléans was not the only arbiter of fashion to influence the young prince. In 1787 the man who had become one of George's closest confidants, the extrovert and eccentric miniaturist Richard Cosway (appointed Principal Painter to the prince and the first Surveyor of Pictures at Carlton House two years before), depicted his royal friend as the epitome of sartorial confidence: clad in 'Vandyke dress' and wielding a long cane, a costume which alluded to the fashionable trend to reference the court of Charles I, George wore an over-large star of his beloved Order of the Garter on his shoulder (Fig. 2.2). As has been observed, it was Cosway who helped instil in George an awareness of the power of the image.[8] In 1795 the artist was commissioned by George to paint a series of miniatures of the entire royal family – George's riposte to the series of half-length oils that his mother had commissioned from Thomas Gainsborough in 1782. Cosway subsequently lent his royal master what was, for him at least, a considerable amount of money: £1,500. Before it could be repaid, however, the miniaturist was abruptly dropped from the prince's circle in 1808. The ailing Cosway later pointedly refused invitations to the celebrations of George's Regency four years later.[9]

As his friends were chosen so as to appal his frugal father, George III, so George's excessive expenditure on fashion was an implied rebuke to a king whose creation (in 1777) of the staid, red-and-blue court 'Windsor uniform' represented the high point of his foray into the world of fashion.[10] George had already, as a young man, discovered the imposing and slimming effects that dark colours and subtle cuts could achieve, as seen in Stubbs's fine equestrian portrait of 1791 (Fig. 2.3), in which the prince is depicted wearing a long, dark blue coat with buff breeches – the colours of the Foxite Whig opposition (which were themselves borrowed from the uniforms of George Washington's American revolutionaries of a decade earlier). Indeed, George was still wearing the same figure-reducing combination a decade later (Fig. 2.4).

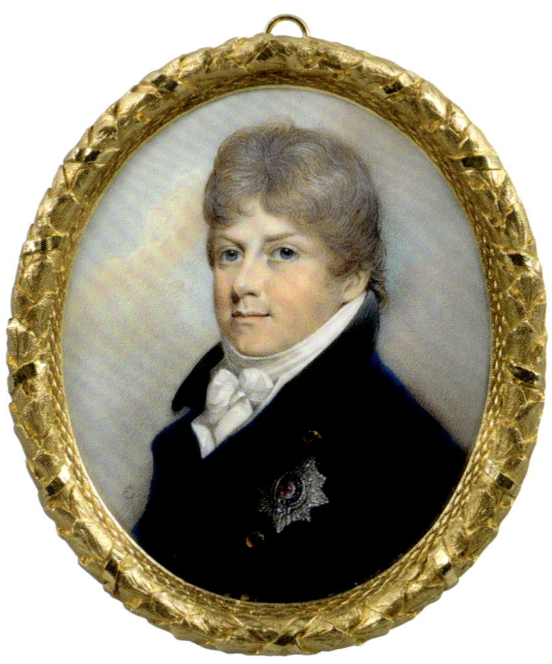

FIG. 2.4
GEORGE ENGLEHEART (1752–1829), *George IV when Prince of Wales*, 1801–2. Watercolour on ivory, 7.1 × 5.8 cm, RCIN 420207

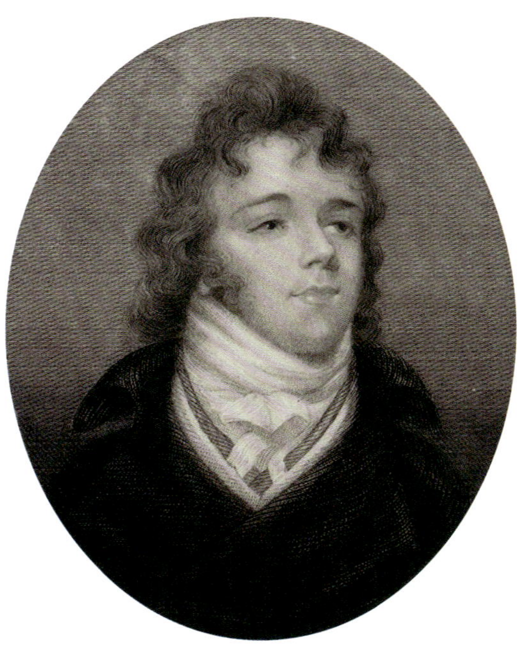

FIG. 2.5
JOHN COOK (active 1819–62), *George Brummell Esqr*, 1844. Stipple and engraving, 23.4 × 14.7 cm (sheet) (National Portrait Gallery, London: D1124)

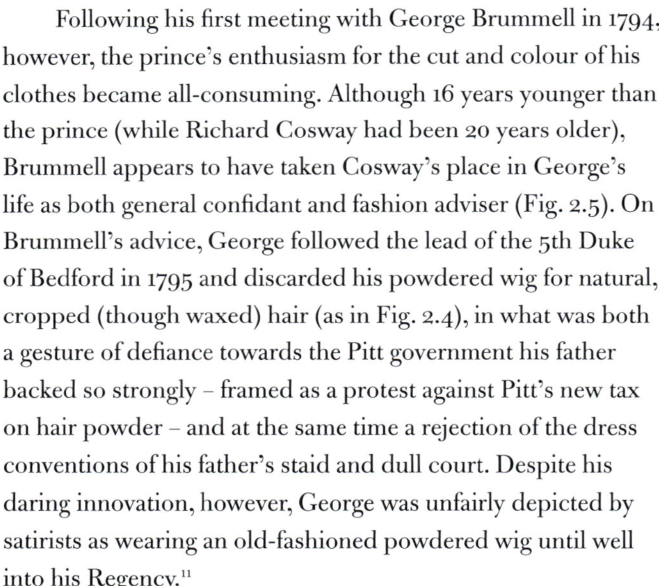

Following his first meeting with George Brummell in 1794, however, the prince's enthusiasm for the cut and colour of his clothes became all-consuming. Although 16 years younger than the prince (while Richard Cosway had been 20 years older), Brummell appears to have taken Cosway's place in George's life as both general confidant and fashion adviser (Fig. 2.5). On Brummell's advice, George followed the lead of the 5th Duke of Bedford in 1795 and discarded his powdered wig for natural, cropped (though waxed) hair (as in Fig. 2.4), in what was both a gesture of defiance towards the Pitt government his father backed so strongly – framed as a protest against Pitt's new tax on hair powder – and at the same time a rejection of the dress conventions of his father's staid and dull court. Despite his daring innovation, however, George was unfairly depicted by satirists as wearing an old-fashioned powdered wig until well into his Regency.[11]

Brummell and George became, as Orléans and the prince had once been, quite inseparable – particularly after Brummell quit George's hobby regiment, the 10th Light Dragoons, in 1798 in protest at its dispatch to Manchester (which Brummell derided as 'foreign service').[12] Brummell's first biographer, Captain William Jesse, related an incident when, on a visit to Belvoir Castle in 1799, Brummell's fur-clad figure was actually mistaken by the locals for that of the prince.[13]

It was Brummell, it has been argued, 'who turned the art of masculine attire into the supreme expression of being a gentleman: he helped create a look which relied on exquisite tailoring and the careful selection of accessories for its effect'.[14] The celebrity courtesan and subsequent memoirist Harriette Wilson noted that what Brummell dictated on dress was invariably adopted: fashionable men 'made it a rule to copy the cut of [his] coat, the shape of his hat, or the tie of his neckcloth', and observed that even the prince (one of the few not to be counted among her clients) watched Brummell dress.[15] The masculine image that Brummell sought to create – an image so enthusiastically adopted by his princely pupil – was not that of the dandy.[16] The Brummell 'look' was never exaggerated, nor relied on bright colours or dramatic cuts for its effect: '[Brummell's] morning dress was similar to that of every other gentleman – Hessians and pantaloons, or top-boots and buckskins, with a blue coat, and a light or buff-coloured waistcoat … His dress of an evening was a blue coat and white waistcoat [and] black pantaloons.'[17] Brummell took his inspiration from the figure-hugging, utilitarian casual sportswear and muted colours worn by the English country horseman: 'noble, muscular, self-evidently aspirational, utterly uneffeminate'.[18] A dark jacket, usually of what we would today call a navy blue,[19] was cut away at the back to form tails – notionally styled for ease on horseback. This feature not only implied that the owner of the jacket was a man of action, frequently in the habit of mounting a horse; more pragmatically, it also increased the apparent length of his legs.

With their deliberate austerity, understated cuts and sober, dark colours, Brummell's innovations – and George's patronage – had, by 1820, made London the global epicentre of men's fashion. Brummellesque clothes defined a quintessential Englishness; they did not advertise wealth and privilege, but instead subtly implied taste and discretion. Not everything was left to nature, however. George's coats were often padded at the front to suggest a full musculature and a slim waist. And the prince – among many others – soon mimicked Brummell's clever combination of a very high, starched collar which almost touched the ears with a soft neckcloth below, in George's case to hide his multiplying chins (Fig. 2.6). Below the waist, George adopted Brummell's novel abandonment of traditional knee breeches. The prince's legs were thereafter slimmed by a bewildering variety of pantaloons (some of which included feet, the ancestor of today's tights) and their looser-fitting cousins, trousers. Trousers could vary considerably in width – from thigh-hugging to capacious 'Cossack' trousers, named after the Russian specialist cavalry. Thus was the modern concept of trousers born, and the foundations laid for the ubiquitous modern suit.

Together, George and 'Beau' Brummell (the prefix appears to have been first used around 1800) changed the face of men's fashion irrevocably. The invoices for the prince's purchases of clothing show that George increasingly favoured sober, dark colours for his coats and greatcoats: dark blues, greens, browns and greys, which flattered the figure and were subtly cut to emphasise height over girth. Matt fabrics were preferred to gaudy, shiny cloths; vertical emphases to horizontal stripes or accessories. George's estranged wife, Caroline of Brunswick, later commented of her husband that 'he understands how a shoe should be made, or a coat cut … and would make an excellent tailor, or shoemaker, or hair-dresser, but nothing else'.[20]

As he reached his thirties, George's expanding girth made the need to flatter his figure even more pressing. James Gillray's savage print of 1792, *A Voluptuary under the horrors of Digestion* (Fig. 2.7), already shows a corpulent prince whose waistcoat barely restrains his burgeoning stomach and whose Carlton House room is full of references to excessive eating and drinking, with an overflowing chamber pot weighing down a collection of unpaid bills. As the years passed by, weight became an even more problematic issue. It has been noted how the officially sanctioned images of the prince were, by 1806, 'at least a tribute to the skills of his tailors, whose subterfuges to restrain the royal belly (clever interlining of coats, the use of "belts" or corsets) are

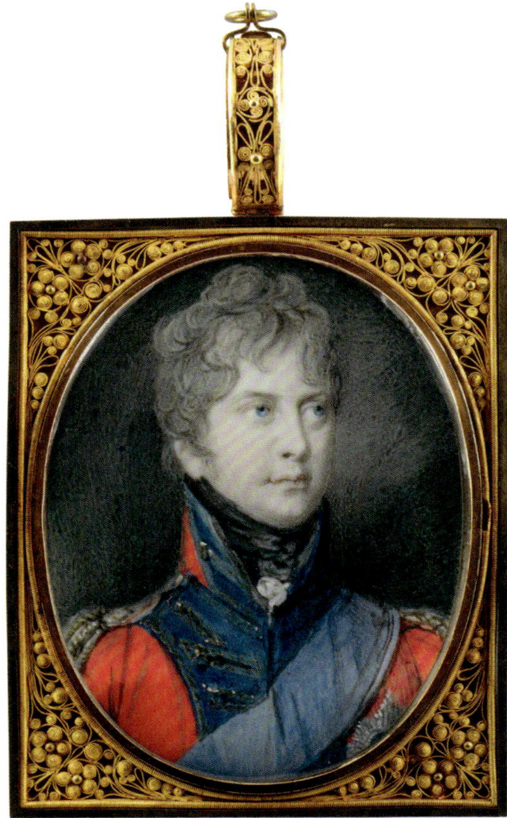

FIG. 2.6
RICHARD COSWAY (1742–1821), *George IV when Prince of Wales*, 1799–1800. Watercolour on ivory, 9.9 × 6.7 cm, RCIN 421981

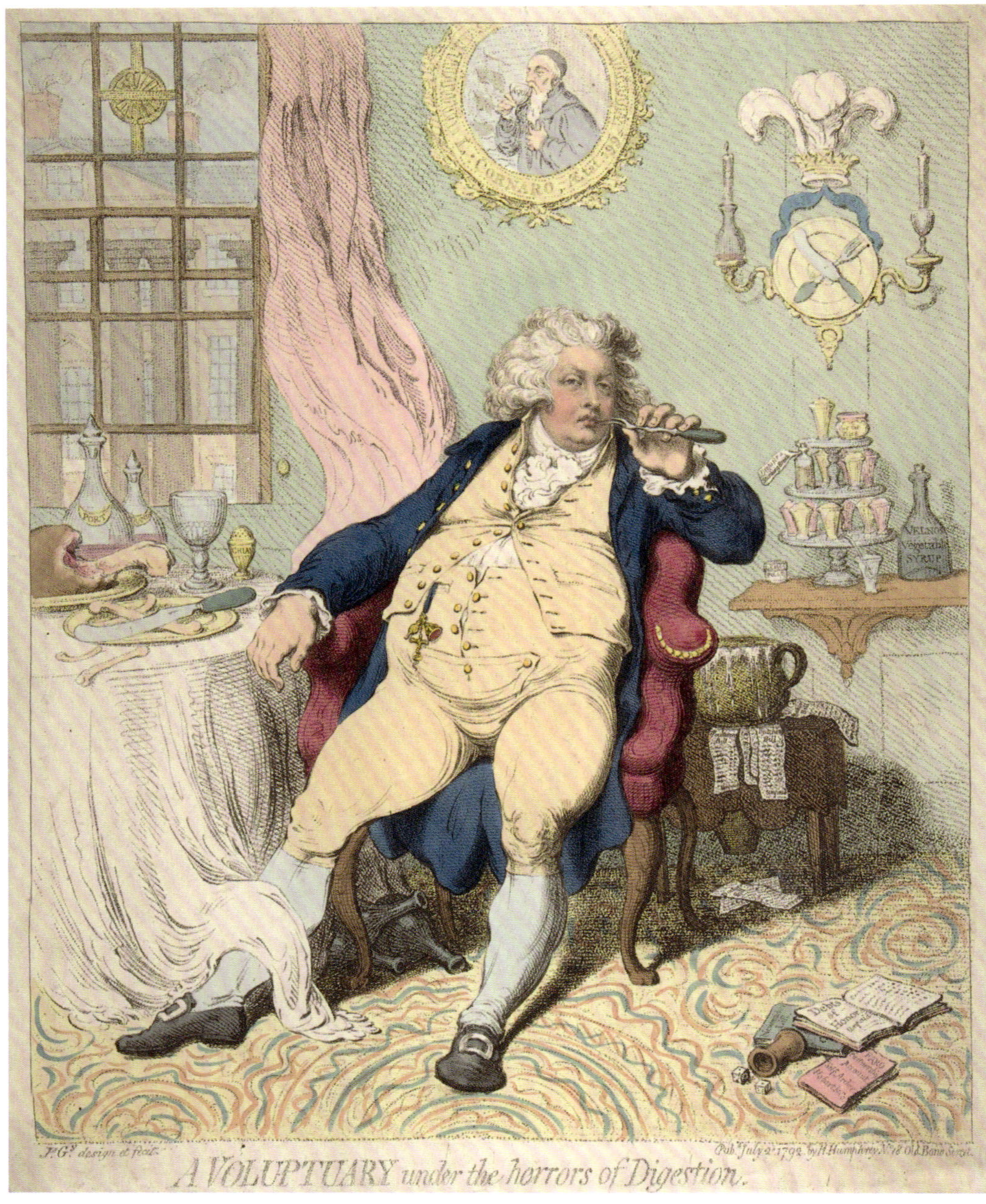

FIG. 2.7
JAMES GILLRAY (1756–1815),
A Voluptuary under the horrors of Digestion, 1792. Etching with hand colouring, 36.5 × 29.3 cm (sheet) (Metropolitan Museum of Art, New York, NY: 1976.602.22)

also revealed in the accounts'.[21] By that time, almost all George's clothing orders involved payments for 'letting out' clothes from his existing wardrobe (including his growing collection of field-marshal's uniforms) rather than for new purchases. Predictably, too, many of these orders were never paid for: the £350 George owed Greenwood, Cox & Co. for new pantaloons in 1815, for example, remained outstanding at the time of his death in 1830.[22]

As has been often rehearsed, Brummell's arrogance ultimately proved his undoing. His public pronouncements to the effect that he had 'made' the prince and could therefore just as easily unmake him, allied to his penchant for making disparaging comments about George's many mistresses, soon reached the ears of the prince's courtiers. The Carlton House fête of June 1811, held to celebrate George's assumption of the Regency, was the last royal event to which Brummell received an invitation. At a party held in February 1812 Brummell was ostentatiously cut by the Prince Regent; bereft of royal protection, he was easy prey to his many creditors and in 1816 fled to Calais to avoid them – foolishly rejecting George's generous offer of the British consulship there.[23] Nevertheless,

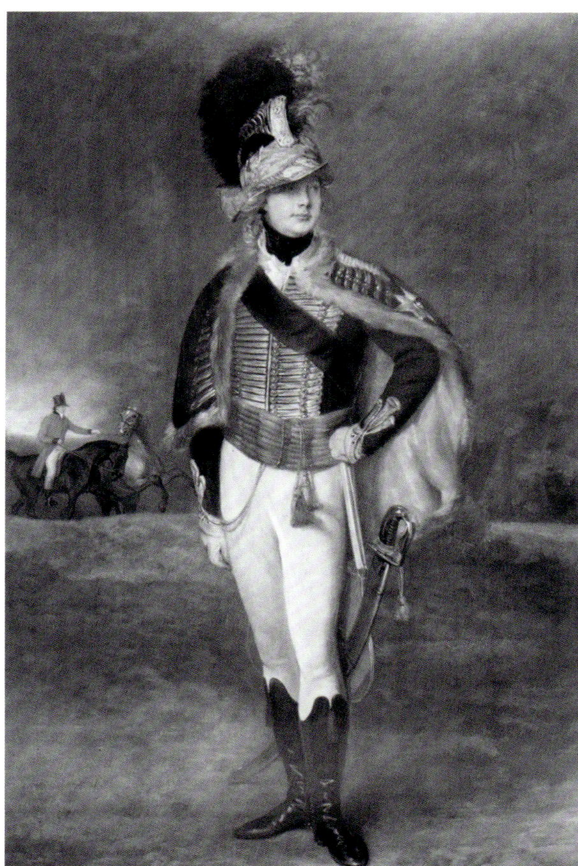

FIG. 2.8
THOMAS GAINSBOROUGH (1727–88),
George IV when Prince of Wales, 1784.
Oil on canvas, 247.0 × 156.5 cm
(private collection)

the prince was still being depicted by the satirists dressed as an imitation of Brummell as late as 1821, and for the rest of his life was constantly shown clad in Brummellesque buff and blue.

The cost of the prince's pursuit of pioneering fashion was substantial. On coming of age in 1783 he bought 23 pairs of boots, all from different makers. Three years later, in June 1786, he spent the vast sum of £2,041 1s 2d on lace from the venerable Catholic lacemaker Bryant Barrett and £38 10s on perfumes, while that September he ordered no fewer than 74 pairs of white-and-tan gloves from the glover Robert Bond – who was not paid for them for almost three years.[24] Bond was lucky: at least he eventually received his money. By 1787 the 25-year-old prince already owed his tailors nearly £17,000 – the equivalent of well over £1,000,000 today – and by 1793 his tailors' debt had risen to an astronomical £30,000. The artist and diarist Joseph Farington was not alone in denouncing the prince's lavish expenditure on fashionable clothes and accessories: in 1802 he noted that 'At one time silver buckles were taken from him which sold as old silver for £150 – [yet] they must have originally cost £900.'[25] But such criticisms had little effect on the prince's spending habits. In 1803 alone George spent £681 14s 9d on clothing – approximately £30,000 today. Three years later the London jeweller Nathanial Jeffrey, brought to bankruptcy by the prince's debts to him of £16,808, published a pamphlet bemoaning the many commissions from George and Mrs Fitzherbert for which he had never been reimbursed. But the pamphlet made no impression, and Jeffrey was never paid.

While, under Brummell's tutelage, George's everyday clothes grew snugger, darker and more subtle, he never abandoned his childhood enthusiasm for dressing up in uniform. George's unabashed love of militaria – doubtless fuelled by his father's understandable refusal to let him serve in the army abroad – persisted throughout his life. It can be seen in Gainsborough's full-length portrait of 1784 of the confident young prince in a uniform of his own invention for the 10th Dragoons while the storm clouds of war gather behind him (Fig. 2.8) – a concept also employed by Reynolds in the same year and adapted by Beechey 14 years later.[26] When his brother Frederick (who had been created Duke of York in 1784) visited Berlin in 1791, George gave him a vast shopping list of information he wanted about Prussian uniforms; while, when another soldier-brother, the Duke of Cambridge, was in Hanover in 1802, following the brief peace concluded at Amiens earlier that year, he was directed to send George sketches of the new pattern of Hanoverian army uniforms.[27] George's enthusiasms were shared by his brothers, too. In 1803 the Duke of Clarence eagerly sent his elder brother a detailed description of the uniform he had recently devised for the short-lived Royal Spelthorne Legion of Militia: 'The officers of the infantry will have a neat plain jacket with blue lappels with a gold epaulette[,] blue pantaloons and Hussar boots with a black tassel in front ... the serjeants and privates of the troop the same in red and blue and white and silver as your regiment in blue, yellow and white and silver.'[28] At the same time, George purchased 401 watercolours of military uniforms by brothers Robert and Denis Dighton and more than 500 watercolours and drawings of European military attire by the Dutch military artists Dirk and Jan Anthonie Langendijk.

George III was following long and sound historical precedent in refusing to let his eldest son serve in the army. The only post-medieval Prince of Wales to have seen active service had been the future Charles II, in the decidedly unusual circumstances of the English Civil War. In 1783 the new 10th Regiment of Light

Dragoons was at least honoured with the title of 'The Prince of Wales's Own', but the regiment's request (presumably at the prince's instigation) to have George appointed Colonel Commandant (the equivalent of the modern rank of Colonel-in-Chief) was refused by the king five years later. George III did relent when the French declared war on Britain in 1793, which produced a flurry of portraits in regimental attire (Figs 2.9–2.13), but made it clear that this was not to be regarded as a pathway to higher rank. This, however, merely encouraged the prince to enlist his brothers in a campaign to persuade his father to give him 'the rank of General, or Lt-General'. The king's withholding of such an honour was, George declared, a 'stigma … too heavy to be any longer endured', and one which he could 'no further suffer in silence'.[29] In 1795 he even disingenuously suggested to his father that his rakish behaviour was caused by the frustration of not being able to serve in the army. He then proceeded to compare himself somewhat ambitiously to the Black Prince, proposing that he and his father could command the army jointly, as Edward III and his eldest son had done at the Battle of Crécy.[30] George III did not reply to this appeal, which merely encouraged the prince to recruit the aged former army commander-in-chief, Lord Amherst,[31] in his crusade. This, though, proved equally futile: George III insensitively chose his eldest son's wedding day to write to him declaring that 'My younger sons can have no other situation in the State but what arise from the military lines they have been placed in … You are born to a more difficult one, and which I shall be most happy if I find you seriously turn your thoughts to.'[32]

Having failed to secure a genuine military role for himself, George resorted to dressing up both himself and his pet regiment (Fig. 2.14). The Royal Collection contains numerous items of militaria designed by the prince in an idle moment, from leopard-skin sabretaches (the long-strapped satchels that hung from cavalry officers' waistbands) to oversized gold epaulettes. In the splendidly comprehensive catalogue for the Royal Collection's 1991 exhibition on Carlton House, it was noted that George's passion for militaria was 'bordering on obsession'; much of his collection, it concluded, 'was probably used by the prince and his circle almost as a form of fancy or theatrical dress, in which they could imagine themselves in the roles of romantic, savage, warrior kings and princes'.[33]

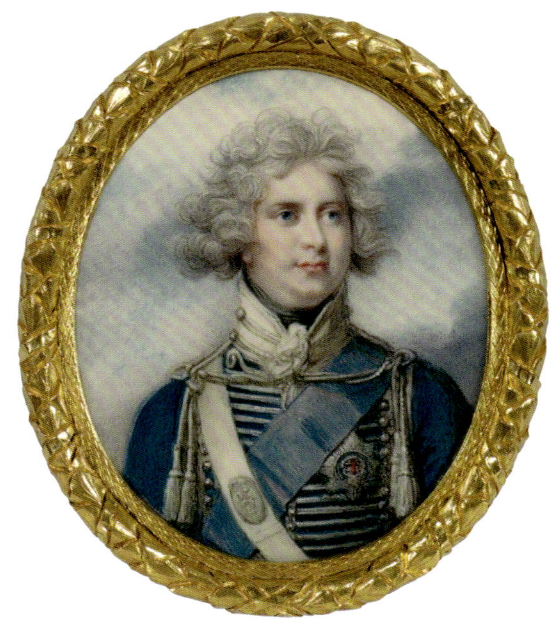

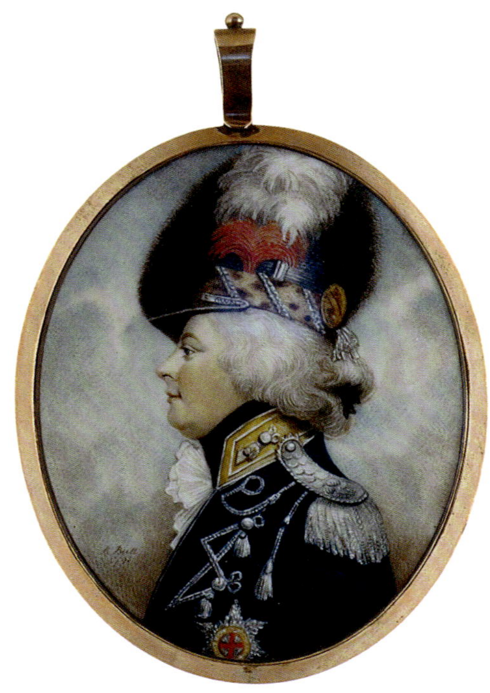

FIG. 2.9
RICHARD COSWAY (1742–1821), *George IV when Prince of Wales*, *c.*1793. Watercolour on ivory, 8.5 × 6.9 cm, RCIN 420004

FIG. 2.10
RICHARD BULL (1721–1805), *George IV when Prince of Wales*, 1793. Watercolour on ivory, 7.8 × 6.2 cm, RCIN 420984

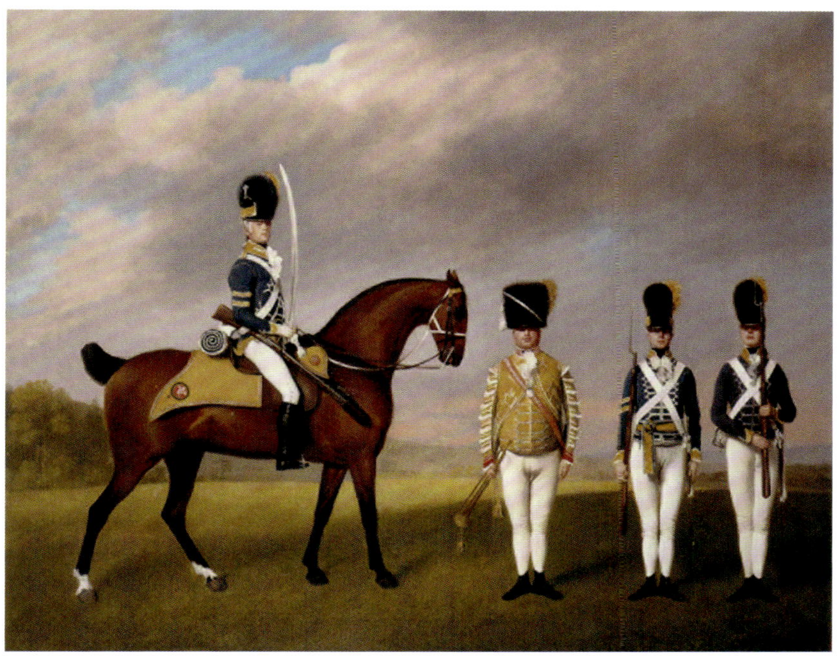

FIG. 2.11
GEORGE STUBBS (1724–1806), *Soldiers of the 10th Light Dragoons*, 1793. Oil on canvas, 102.2 × 128.1 cm, RCIN 400512

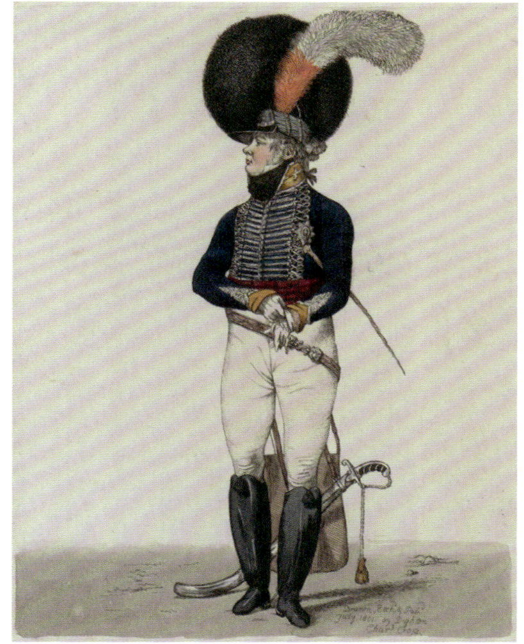

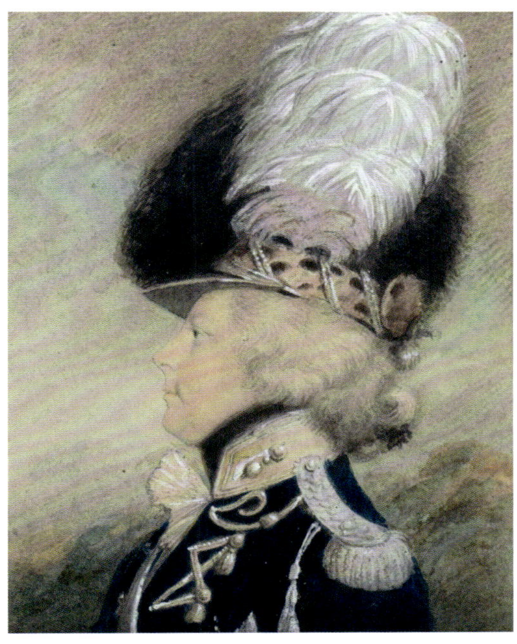

FIG. 2.12
ROBERT DIGHTON (1751–1814), *George IV when Prince of Wales*, 1801. Etching with hand colouring, 28.8 × 22.7 cm, RCIN 605186

FIG. 2.13
BRITISH SCHOOL, *George IV when Prince of Wales*, 1794. Watercolour and bodycolour over pencil, 11.1 × 9.0 cm, RCIN 421581

George dressed both himself and the 10th Light Dragoons in a bewildering variety of new uniforms, the results of which were frequently depicted by commissioned artists but also proved a gift to the satirical printmakers. The conversion of the 10th into a regiment of newly fashionable hussars in 1806 simply gave George, whose constant re-equipping of the regiment had made it an army joke, an excuse to design yet more new outfits, thereby instigating a short-lived 'hussar craze' in London's most fashionable circles.

Not all found George's enthusiasm for military posturing amusing. Gillray's celebrated 1796 print *Fashionable-Jockeyship* (Fig. 2.15) shows a massively overweight and ludicrously overdressed prince clad in one of his Ruritanian uniforms devised for the 10th Light Dragoons as he rides the cuckolded Lord Jersey to Lady Jersey's bed. Subsequent to Gillray's poisonous satire, George was frequently condemned as a dandy in popular prints until his very last years.[34]

Being unable to realise his military ambitions through an epistolary campaign, George turned not just to militaria and costume but also to painting to further his claims. The template – conceptualising the image of the heroic prince-patriot ready to dash to his nation's defence – was established in Reynolds's

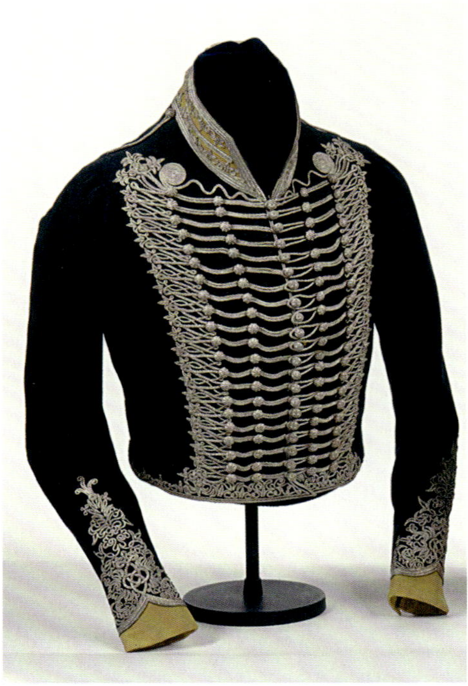

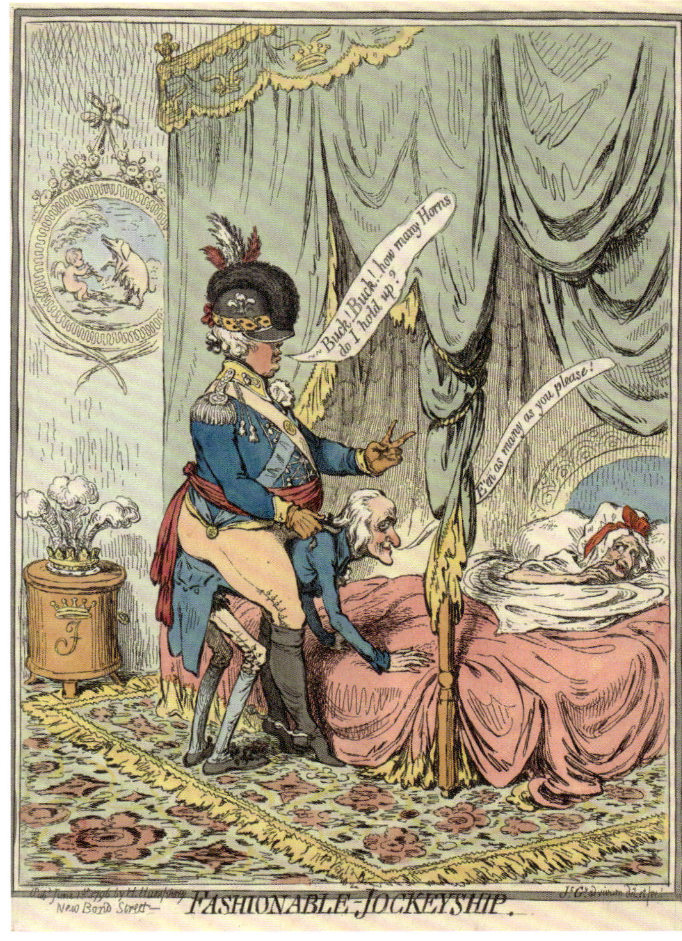

FIG. 2.14
J.C. FRANK, *Jacket*, 1800. Wool, silk, silver thread, 89.0 × 56.0 cm, RCIN 67195

FIG. 2.15
JAMES GILLRAY (1756–1815), *Fashionable-Jockeyship*, 1796. Etching with hand colouring, 33.3 × 24.6 cm (sheet) (Yale Center for British Art, New Haven, CT: B1981.25.1019)

dramatic canvas of 1784 (Fig. 2.16), in which George, sword in hand, was shown in the process of mounting a Titianesque white charger as ominous storms gathered in the background. A little later, George sat to Thomas Gainsborough for an equally dramatic equestrian portrait which was clearly based on Van Dyck's celebrated portrait of Charles I of *c.*1630, which itself recalled Titian's *Emperor Charles V* of 1548. Unfortunately, only a chalk sketch survives of this impressive concept, which presumably remained unfinished at Gainsborough's death in 1788. Around 1789 Mather Brown executed a more conventional portrait of George in military uniform, presumably about to join the battle proceeding in the background (Fig. 2.18), while George's image as a man of action was further enhanced by John Russell's attractive full-length painting of the prince in the green uniform of the Royal Society of Kentish Bowmen, the patronage of which he had eagerly accepted in 1788 (Fig. 13.13).

In 1798 – following yet another failed attempt by the prince to persuade the king to allow him to 'prove myself worthy of the confidence of my country … by staking my life in its defence' (to which George III had wearily replied that 'the approbation of the public should be your first object')[35] – the artist William Beechey was recruited to update Reynolds's imagery. Beechey's compelling martial three-quarter-length depiction (Fig. 2.17), presented to the Royal Academy in 1798 as his compulsory 'Diploma Work', showed George resting his hand assuredly on his sword, as if in the midst of battle. Beechey clad him in a new version of the uniform that the prince had recently devised for the 10th, with his fashionably high, Brummellesque collar and neckcloth lending him a firm, resolute jawline, and placed the Garter star prominently on his chest. Behind him swirled the smoke of war, very much as in Reynolds's full-scale portrait of the prince of 1784 and the same artist's three-quarter length of Lord Heathfield of 1787. George probably knew the latter picture: in 1810 he gave Gainsborough's 1782 portrait of himself as a languid country gentleman leaning against his horse (a far less appealing image to the aspirant military hero than Beechey's painting of 1798) to Heathfield's son, Lieutenant-General Francis Augustus Eliott, 2nd Baron Heathfield, who was himself featured as an

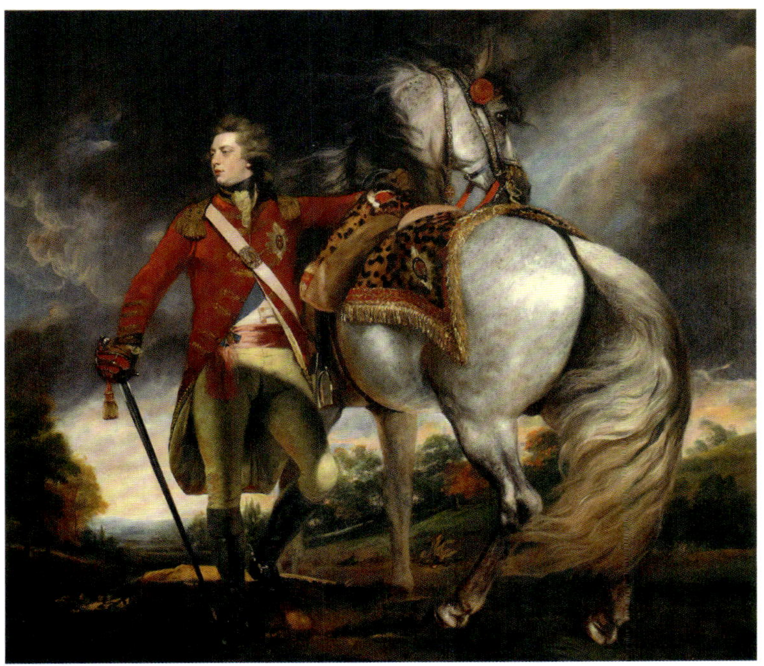

FIG. 2.16
SIR JOSHUA REYNOLDS (1723–92),
The Prince of Wales, later George IV,
1783–4. Oil on canvas, 238.8 × 266.7 cm
(private collection)

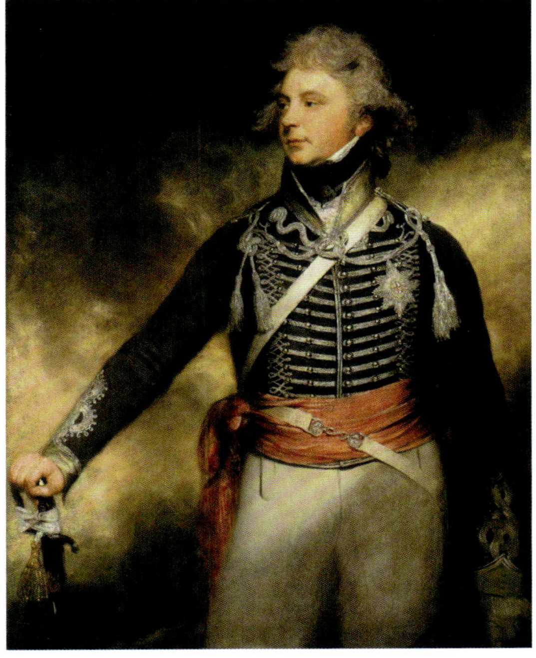

FIG. 2.17
SIR WILLIAM BEECHEY (1753–1839),
George IV when Prince of Wales, 1803.
Oil on canvas, 128.4 × 101.7 cm,
RCIN 400511

aide-de-camp in John Singleton Copley's speculative equestrian portrait of George at a review of the 10th Hussars of 1809.

Copley's ambitious but oddly lifeless composition clearly failed to enchant George in the way that the portraits by Reynolds and Beechey had. The prince refused to buy Copley's monumental painting, and it remained with the artist's son after Copley's death. Beechey's simpler and more effective image of 1798 was clearly of far greater appeal to George. In 1803 the artist was asked by the prince to paint a new version of the same subject for his brother Edward, Duke of Kent, the future father of Queen Victoria; it is this version that can be found in the Royal Collection today (Fig. 2.19). The timing of this commission was revealing: George had been bombarding the prime minister, Henry Addington, along with his father and his brothers, with yet more letters, using the excuse of the resumption of war to bid for a senior rank abroad. George informed Addington that 'I feel myself exposed to the obloquy of being regarded by the country as passing my time indifferent to the events which menace, and insensible to the call of patriotism', told the Duke of York that his 'idle, inactive rank' was of no help to anyone, and wrote to his father from Brighton that, given that 'Hanover is lost, England is menaced with invasion, Ireland is in rebellion, Europe is at the foot of France', his personal involvement in the war was crucial if Britain were to repel the Napoleonic tide. This time, however, not only was the king obdurate ('Should the implacable enemy so far succeed as to land,' he explained patiently, 'you will have an opportunity of shewing your zeal at the head of your Regiment'[36]) but even his brother Frederick found his pleas an unwelcome distraction from his duties as army commander-in-chief. (George responded by petulantly refusing him admission to Carlton House – almost the only sanction he could impose.) George reacted to their combined opposition by resorting to a very modern method of enforcing his argument: he brought the issue to the public's attention by publishing his purportedly confidential correspondence in December 1803. This deliberate flouting of royal and governmental protocol predictably enraged both the king and the queen, and made the likelihood of the appearance of the prince on the battlefield recede still further. It is significant that, on the recurrence of George III's illness in 1804, Queen Charlotte entrusted her husband's care not to the heir to the throne but to Henry Addington's government.

The same year as he presented his half-length of the prince to the Royal Academy, Beechey also exhibited a vast canvas at the same venue, commissioned not, this time, by the Prince of Wales but by the king himself. *King George III and the Prince of Wales Reviewing the 3rd (or The Prince Of Wales's) Regiment of*

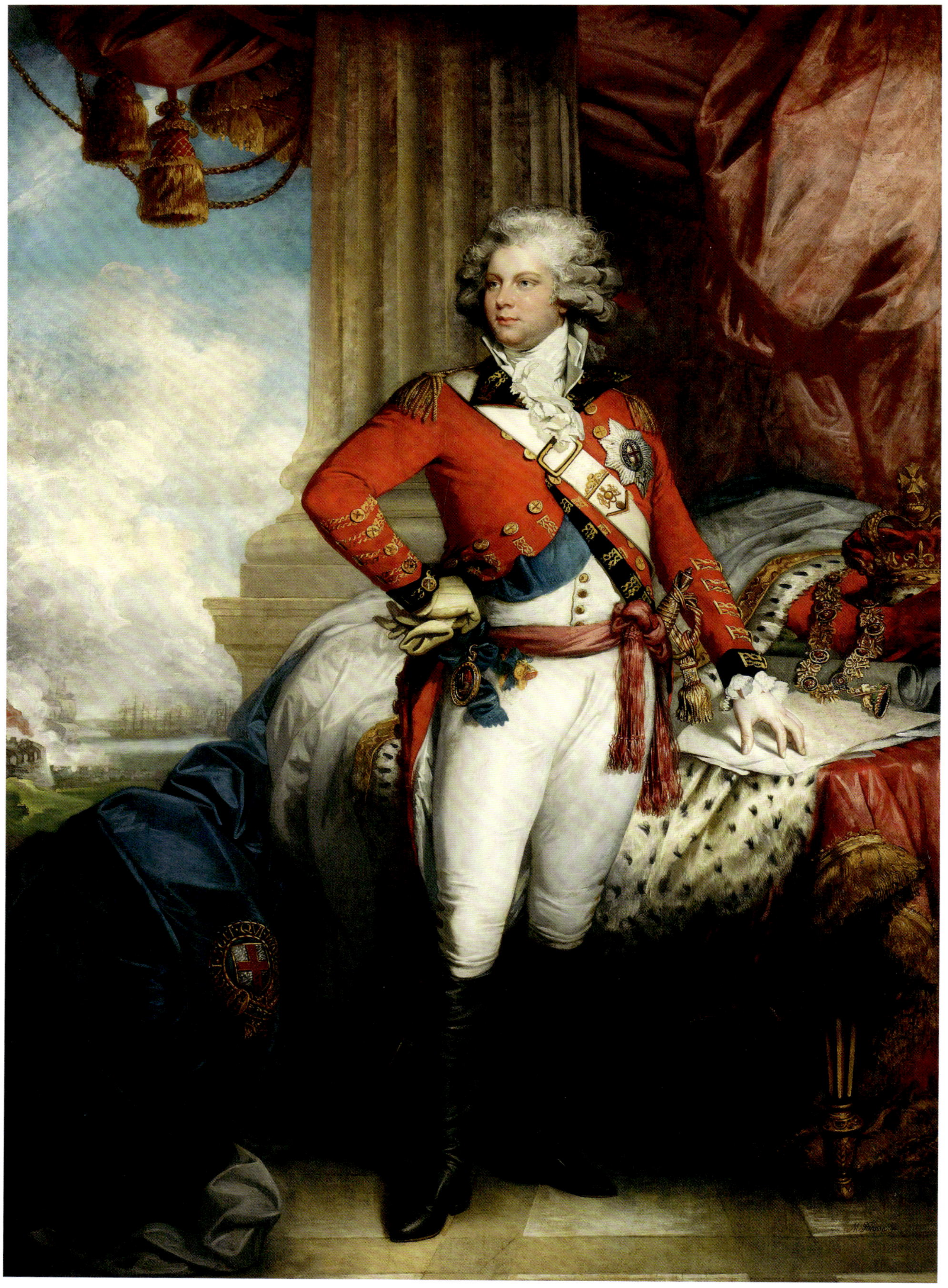

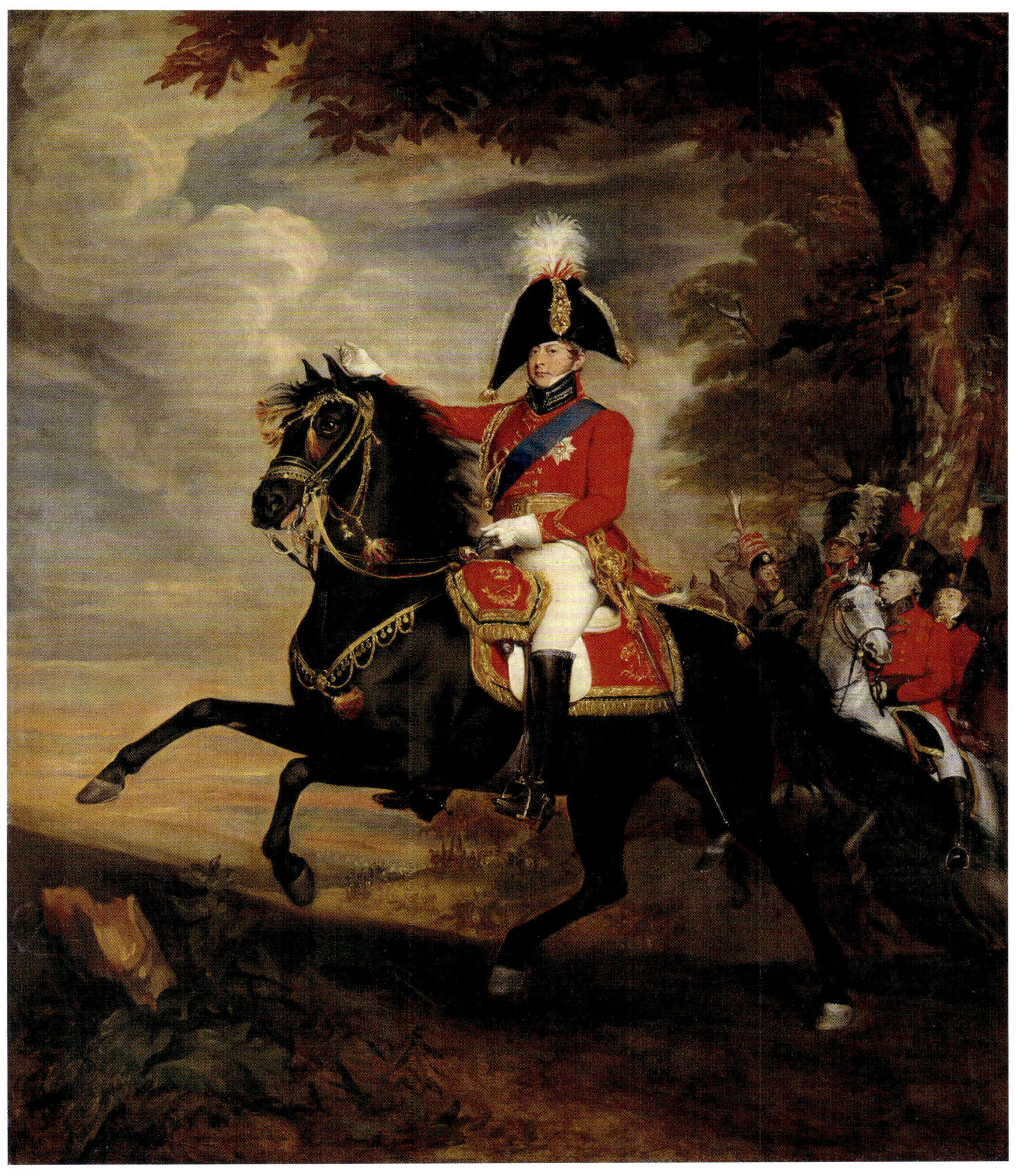

FIG. 2.18
MATHER BYLES BROWN (1761–1831), *George, Prince of Wales*, ?1789. Oil on canvas, 249.9 × 181.6 cm, RCIN 405135

FIG. 2.19
JOHN SINGLETON COPLEY (1738–1815), *George IV on horseback*, c.1813. Oil on canvas, 101.8 × 85.9 cm, RCIN 409290

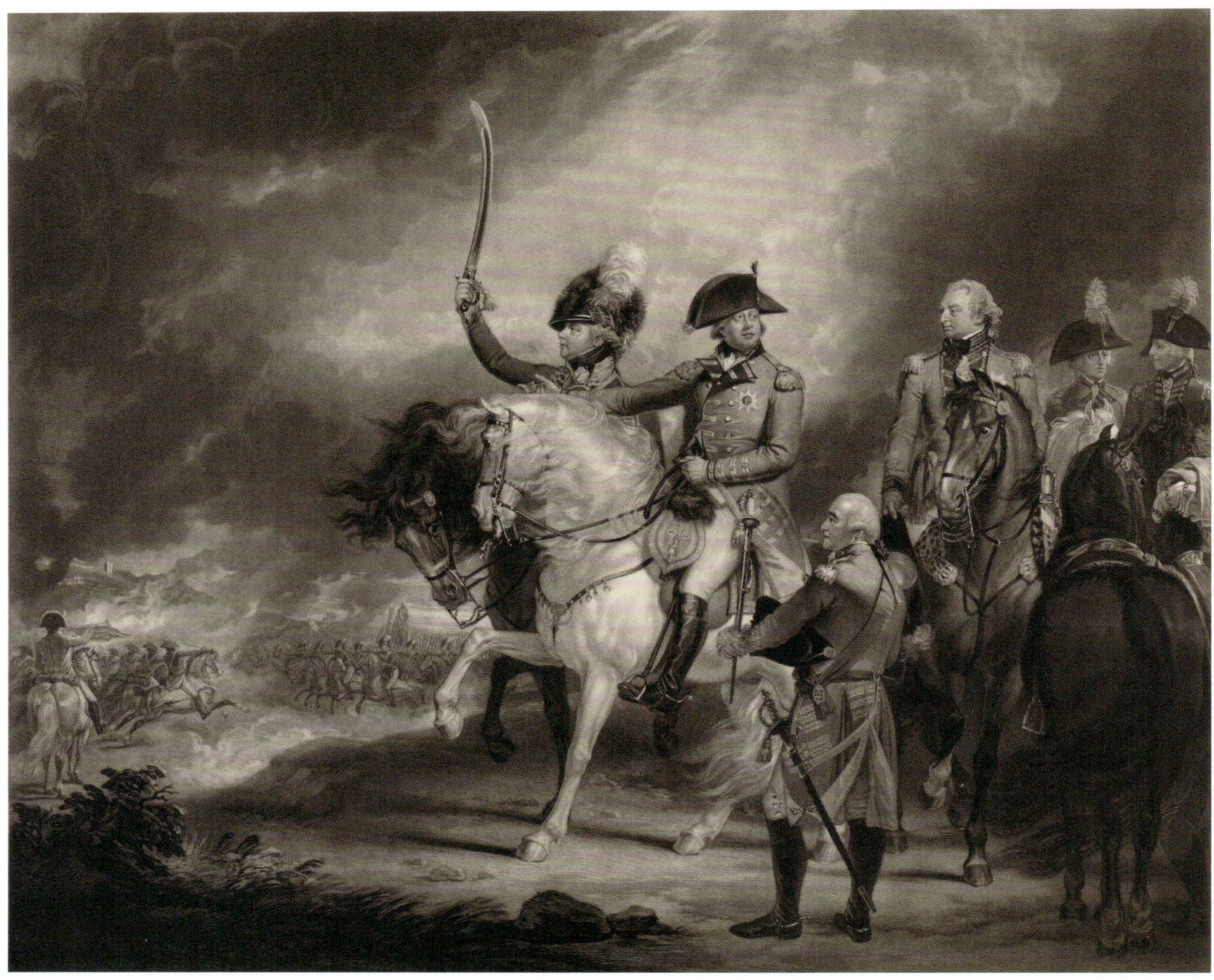

Dragoon Guards and the 10th (Or The Prince Of Wales's Own) Regiment of (Light) Dragoons, 1797 was Beechey's conjectural re-creation of an actual military review in Hyde Park. In this picture, however, George's martial ardour is exaggerated almost to the point of caricature (Fig. 2.20). While the king coolly gestures at the Dragoons as he addresses his attendants, the prince is pictured waving his sabre in the air somewhat histrionically and gazing into the middle distance. As a plea for George to be permitted to serve in the forces it is rather overplayed. Indeed, later versions of this composition somewhat revealingly omitted the figure of the prince entirely. (Although the original picture was lost in the Windsor Castle fire of 1992, William Beechey's composition can still be seen in the version of *c.*1830 by his son, George, in the National Army Museum.) And the painting failed yet again to persuade the king of the wisdom of posting the heir to the throne abroad. Possibly as a consequence of this disappointment, Beechey subsequently suffered the fate of Richard Cosway, John Hoppner and many of the other artists, architects and sculptors who had once worked for the prince, and was brusquely dropped. Although the prince was by now deeply in debt to Beechey – who had, like Cosway before him, lent George money, a sizeable £390 12s in 1801 – neither he nor his father ever again employed the artist, who died in 1839 at the age of 86.[37]

By the time he attained the full powers of Regency in 1812, George's public image needed revitalising. Typical of the popular prints of the time was George Cruikshank's savaging portrayal of *The Prince of Whales* (Fig. 2.21), after Charles Lamb's recent satire:

FIG. 2.20
JAMES WARD (1769–1859) AFTER SIR WILLIAM BEECHEY (1753–1839), *His Majesty Reviewing the Third or Prince of Wales's Regiment of Dragoon Guards*, 1799. Mezzotint, 58.6 × 66.7 cm (sheet), RCIN 630065

FIG. 2.21
GEORGE CRUIKSHANK (1792–1878), *The Prince of Whales or the Fisherman at Anchor*, 1812. Etching with hand colouring, 22.2 × 53.2 cm (sheet) (Metropolitan Museum of Art, New York: 17.3.888-128)

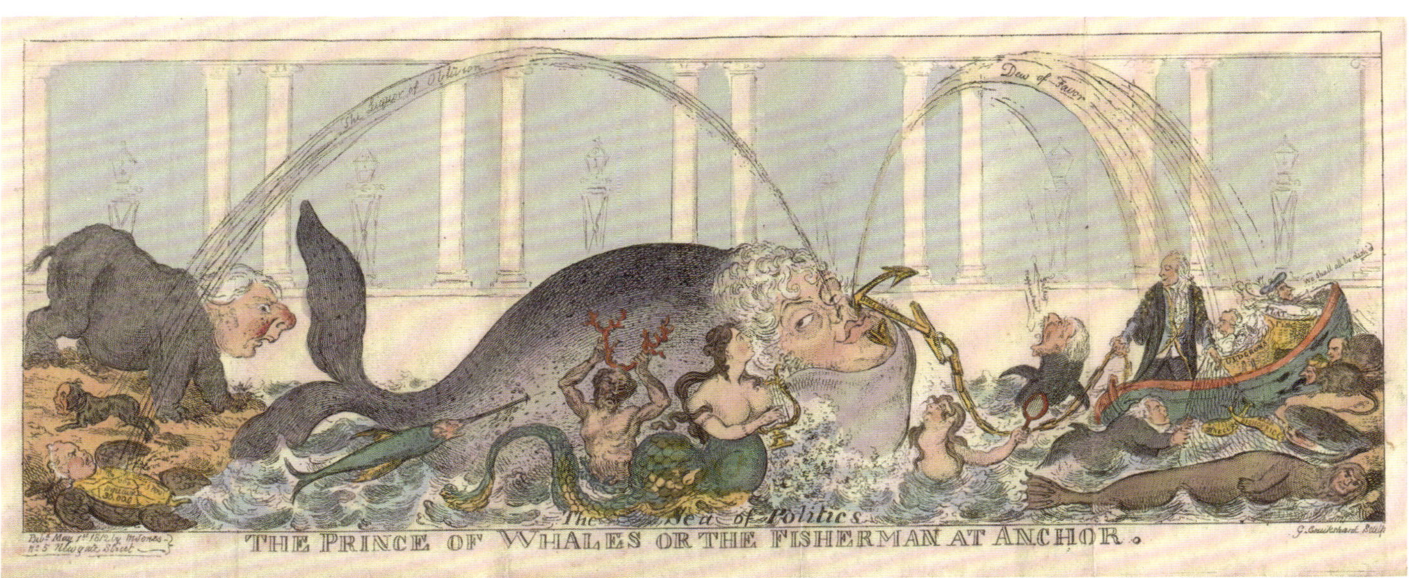

> … Not a fatter fish than he
> Flounders round the polar sea.
> See his blubber? – at his gills
> What a world of drink he swills![38]

As a consequence of his expanding waist, George had lost his enthusiasm for fashion, and was concentrating more on the acquisition of uniforms and military accessories than of modish everyday clothing. There were no longer any 10th Hussars to dress: after re-equipping the regiment one last time in 1811, George held a final review before the Hussars left, without their colonel commandant, to fight with the Duke of Wellington in Portugal and Spain. (An eyewitness of the review said of the prince that 'I fancy his whole soul is wrapped up in Hussar saddles, caps, cuirasses, and sword-belts,' adding that the soldiers of the 10th had themselves been 'amazingly disgusted' with their over-elaborate garb, which not only reinforced their unwelcome reputation as the prince's clothes-horses but too closely resembled the appearance of their French equivalents.[39])

And from 1815 popular prints were appearing which portrayed George as an obese figure in Chinese dress (see Fig. 12.6), a shorthand identity that referenced his Brighton Pavilion retreat to imply inordinate excess in food, fashion and sex, and the drug-fuelled stupor of a Regent who was increasingly distant from his subjects and was kept amused by a succession of mistresses and court cronies. The prince clearly needed a new image-maker. Fortunately, he was to find him in Thomas Lawrence.

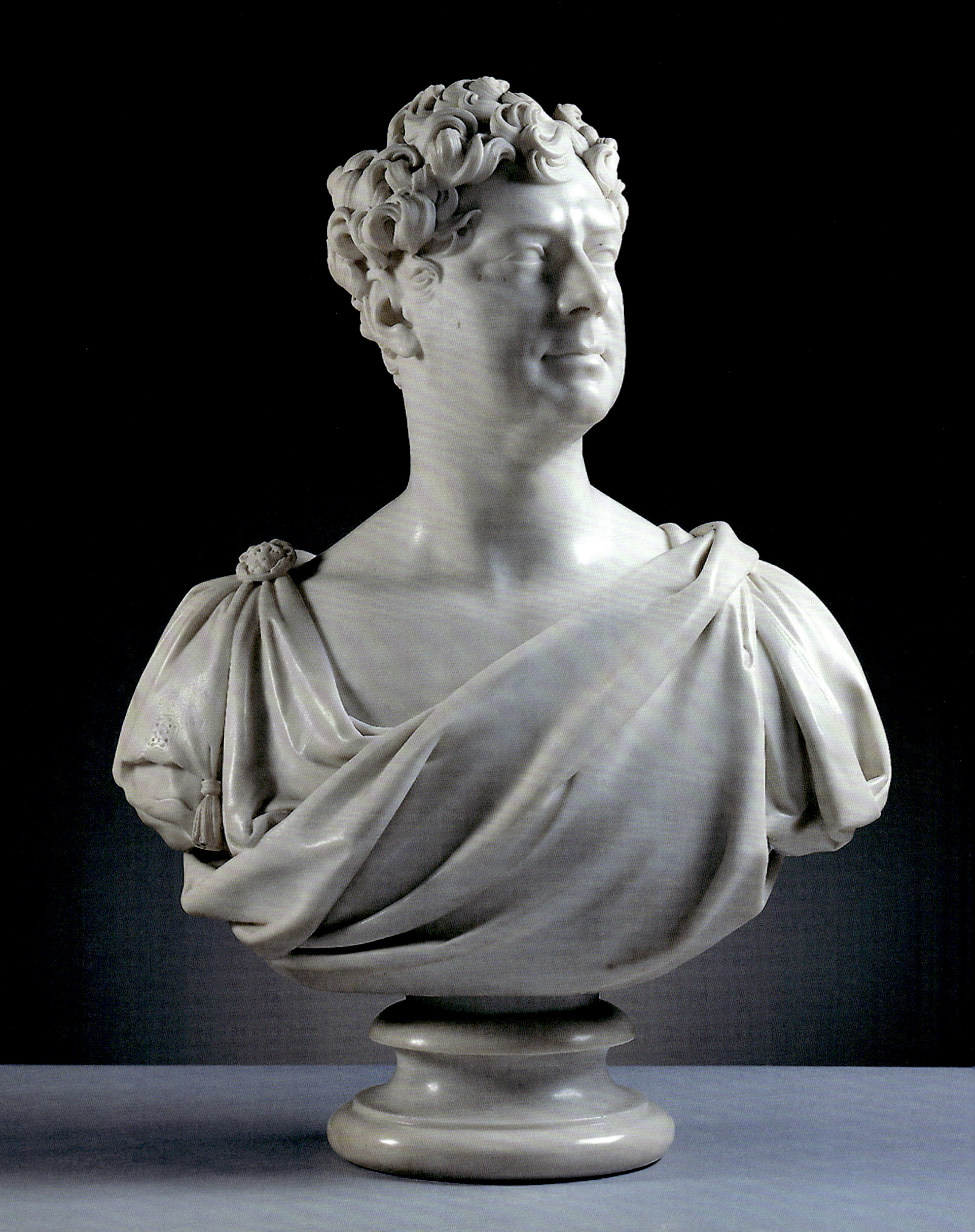

3

PRINCELY SPLENDOUR *and* POSTERITY: GEORGE IV'S PATRONAGE *and* DISPLAY *of* PORTRAITURE

REBECCA LYONS

PORTRAIT COMMISSIONS HAVE always formed the backbone of British royal collecting and the greatest court painters, such as Hans Holbein and Anthony van Dyck, have left to posterity some of the most compelling images of power and royalty ever produced. Full-length state portraits fulfilled multiple functions for monarchs – the most obvious being the display of wealth, status and splendour. They also provided visual evidence of the continuity of a royal line and its legitimacy, and performed as a proxy for the monarch in the physical absence of the royal person.

George IV was keenly aware of the nature and function of image-making, and was an avid collector and commissioner of portraits for private, public and political purposes throughout his life. These included portraits of himself, his family and his royal ancestors. Splendid images of George in paint and in sculpture would have greeted visitors to his royal residences. These asserted his status and magnificence through pose and regalia (see Fig. 0.1) or by alluding to Classical or historic precedent (Figs 3.1 and 1.12). George used larger-format works to maintain his presence in 'state' rooms, and in private and semi-private spaces in his own palaces. The tradition of portrait galleries within the aristocratic home harked back to the long galleries of country houses, wherein the lineage and dynastic ambition of their owners were arrayed in pictorial form. George IV's career as a collector of portraits spanned a transition period between such private displays and the formation of national, public institutions in the decades after his reign, and his later portrait hangs anticipated Victorian halls of fame and other public galleries where portraits celebrated bravery or outstanding achievement, or promoted national pride and individual virtue. His acquisition of portraits of his contemporary artistic, political and military peers can be seen in this context.

The commemorative function of portraits – giving pictorial form to the royal line of succession – was also important to George IV. Rather than attempting to demonstrate the importance of his own Hanoverian ancestors in particular, however, his later schemes for displays of royal portraiture at Windsor encompassed

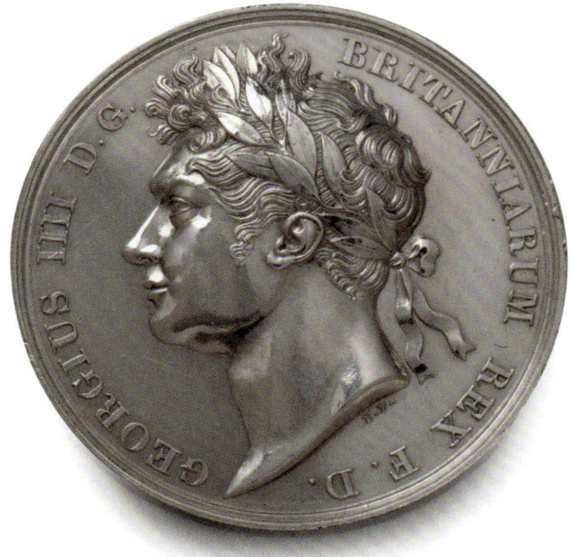

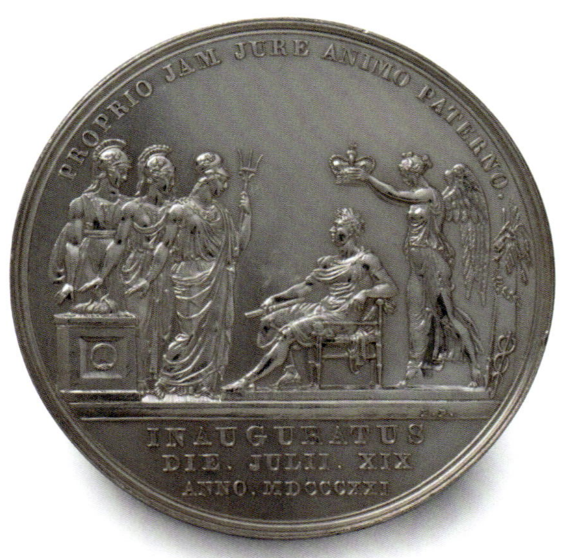

(p. 46)
FIG. 3.1
SIR FRANCIS CHANTREY (1781–1841), *George IV*, 1826. Marble, 80.0 × 58.0 × 27.0 cm, RCIN 2136

FIG. 3.2
BENEDETTO PISTRUCCI (1784–1855), *Medal commemorating the coronation of George IV*, 1821. Silver, 3.5 cm (diameter), RCIN 443328

the preceding Tudor and Stuart dynasties, revealing his broader aspirations for the institution of monarchy at a time when it was under threat elsewhere in Europe.[1]

As George travelled infrequently outside London and the southern counties, it was paramount that his image was present in other parts of his kingdoms, in representation, if not often in reality. Archival records, bills and receipts attest to the sometimes stultifying number of copies needed to fulfil the state business of image-distribution, which occupied the greatest portrait artists in Britain. Their works articulated the continued political and dynastic ambitions of the House of Hanover, and of George himself, and provide a visual record of allegiances and alliances across the late eighteenth and early nineteenth century. Portraits of George in other public spaces such as the Royal Academy provided a focus for public discourse, whether in light-hearted banter or political debates.[2] The production of commemorative medals at key points in George's Regency and monarchy, such as his coronation (Fig. 3.2), also kept the royal image in public circulation.[3]

Images of friends, mistresses and close family members formed part of George's more intimate visual environment and his firm attachment throughout his life to his brothers and sisters and dedication to friends and lovers is evident in his private portrait commissions.

Early portrait commissions and exchanges

The first record of a discussion about likenesses is documented in letters between George and his brother Frederick regarding an attempt to send to Hanover a sculpted wax portrait bust.[4] In December 1781 George wrote: 'I have sent you over a Wax Model of me wh. is reckoned by everybody yt. have seen it remarkably like except its being too fat, & especially about ye Chin.' He received some months later the news from Frederick that the bust in wax was 'all brok[e] into a thousand pieces'[5] – the precariousness of works of art in transit and the transience of commissions here succinctly summarised. Meanwhile, the 20-year-old George wrote again to Frederick in March 1782: 'I have had painted for you a Picture ye same as one I have given Gerrard; it is a half length painted by Gainsberough [*sic*] & reckoned remarkably like by every[one], I wish to know wh you think will be ye best way to send it over.'[6]

Some months later he referred again to the portrait, still taken with its likeness and still concerned for its safe passage to Frederick in Hanover.[7] His emphasis on the care to be taken suggests an appreciation for the work itself, but the commentary focuses on notions of vanity and verisimilitude rather than connoisseurship or the appreciation of stylistic or technical qualities. The work was valued by the brothers primarily in its functional capacity, providing an image of an absent loved one, and judged on whether the representation of reality compared well to the original. This may seem obvious – after all this is a

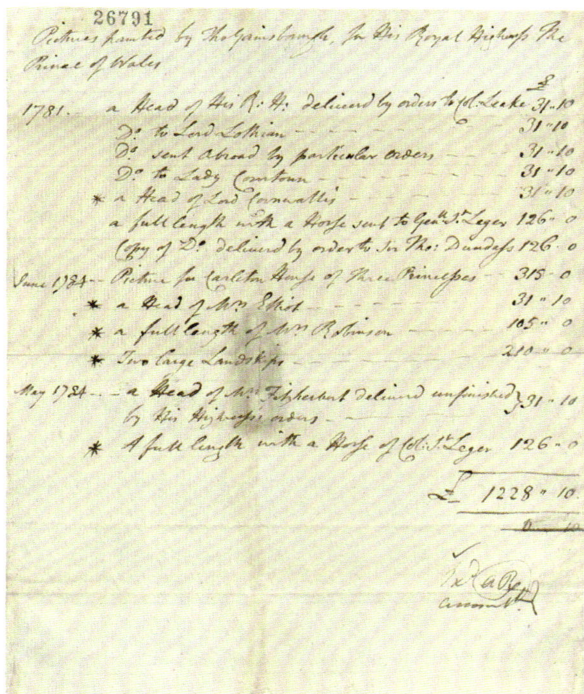
26791

Pictures painted by Tho. Gainsborough, for His Royal Highness The Prince of Wales

		£
1781.	a Head of His R: H: delivered by orders to Col. Leake	31 " 10
	D.o to Lord Lothian	31 " 10
	D.o sent Abroad by particular orders	31 " 10
	D.o to Lady Courtown	31 " 10
	* a Head of Lord Cornwallis	31 " 10
	a full length with a Horse sent to Gen.ll S.t Leger	126 " 0
	Copy of D.o delivered by order to Sir Tho: Dundass	126 · 0
June 1784	Picture for Carlton House of Three Princesses	315 · 0
	* a Head of Mrs Elliot	31 " 10
	* a full Length of Mrs Robinson	105 " 0
	* Two Large Landskips	210 " 0
May 1784	a Head of Mrs Fitzherbert delivered unfinished by His Highness's orders	31 " 10
	* A full length with a Horse of Col. S.t Leger	126 " 0
		£ 1228 " 10

FIG. 3.3
THOMAS GAINSBOROUGH (1727–88),
Bill for Pictures painted, 1784.
RA GEO/MAIN/26791

late eighteenth-century exchange between brothers, and not an aesthetic criticism – but it is important to note. It locates George's earliest interest in portraits squarely in the realms of mimetic and emotional concerns, and focused on private consumption. As George's tastes and connoisseurship developed, as his relationships with artists were forged and his knowledge of and exposure to art deepened and broadened respectively, his tastes and commissions would shift, to embrace portraits and image-making as a way of defining himself, his princely magnificence and the idea of authority and kingship in a wider world.

Letters of the early 1790s contain further observations of likenesses and references to the functional, familial use of portraits. Princess Augusta wrote to her brother, 'your *Dear Picture* has been so long promised to me … I … cannot bear to have a *Copy* or any other than the *very* one you *shew'd me*'.[8] Interestingly in this instance there is a higher esteem for the original work than for a copy, but again this may not be aesthetic preference. It is more likely that it had to do with an emotional connection, the original having been painted from life. The use of portrait miniatures was also significant in these familial exchanges and is discussed in this volume by Vanessa Remington (see chapter 4).

Many of George's early portrait commissions were given away as gifts and therefore no longer form part of the Royal Collection. The surviving bill from Gainsborough for paintings including the portrait mentioned above provides some vital evidence of this early patronage.[9] The list of recipients of the paintings (Fig. 3.3) demonstrates how George had begun to use larger-scale portraits of himself and others as tokens of appreciation and friendship as well as strategic and diplomatic gifts; they also reveal a more intimate circle of close friends and aides. 'Gen.ll St Leger', the John Hayes St Leger depicted by Gainsborough (Fig. 3.9), was sent a companion portrait of George which is now at Waddesdon Manor (Fig. 3.10). St Leger, who served in the 80th Regiment of Foot and had spent time at the court of Louis XVI, was a close friend of George, who admired him greatly. Both paintings show the friends in relaxed pose, at ease in their surroundings, with an effortless Van Dyckian elegance, confidence and sense of self-possession. The inclusion of their horses places them in the long Western European tradition of equestrian portraits, denoting authority and command, and their military dress lends a dashing glamour, yet the pastoral setting is rather more suggestive of the country gentleman than the battlefield-ready hero.

In the 1780s, while George was avidly patronising Gainsborough, he was also sitting to Sir Joshua Reynolds, President of the Royal Academy. Bills from Reynolds run from 22 April 1788 onwards[10] and the artist's own ledgers survive to corroborate various sittings.[11] Reynolds's rates were more expensive but the types of commission were broadly similar to those given to Gainsborough. Many of the resulting works also passed out of the Royal Collection to their intended recipients and, while there are several works by Reynolds in the Collection, some of these came in later by personal or diplomatic gift. The earliest Reynolds portrait commission, painted mainly in 1783, was given almost immediately to Peniston Lamb, 1st Viscount Melbourne in 1784. The work is grand and dramatic in style, a fusion of George's aspirations as military man and action hero and a reflection of Reynolds's desire to paint 'History' rather than simply copy nature (see Fig. 2.16). Unlike the pastoral portrait by Gainsborough, this shows a hero primed for action, sword at the ready, controlling an agitated horse, the storm clouds brewing behind – the painting had all the elements of robust baroque action, suggestive of one of Reynolds's own favourite painters, Rubens, and anticipating the military portraits that Thomas Lawrence would create for George and for the Waterloo Chamber (see below).

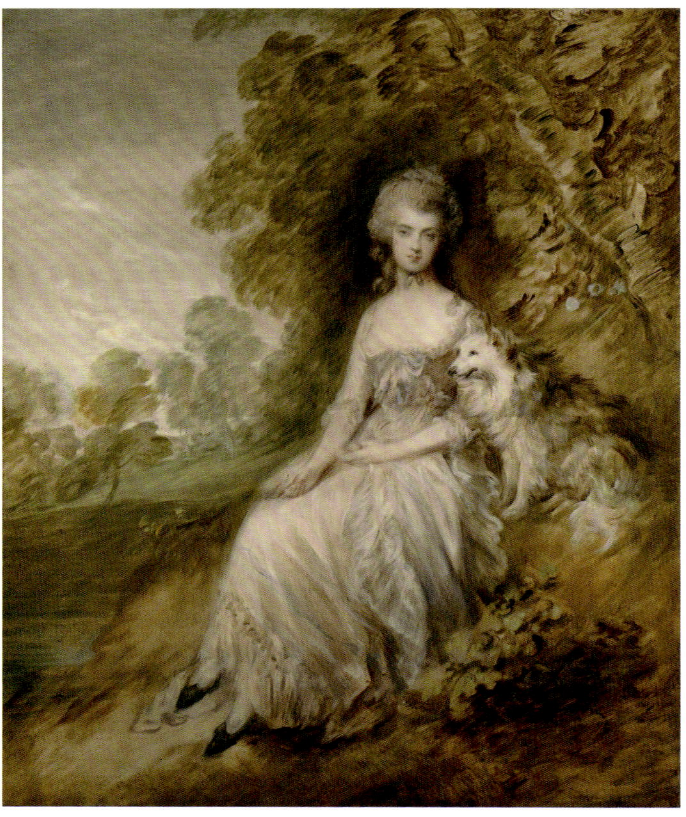

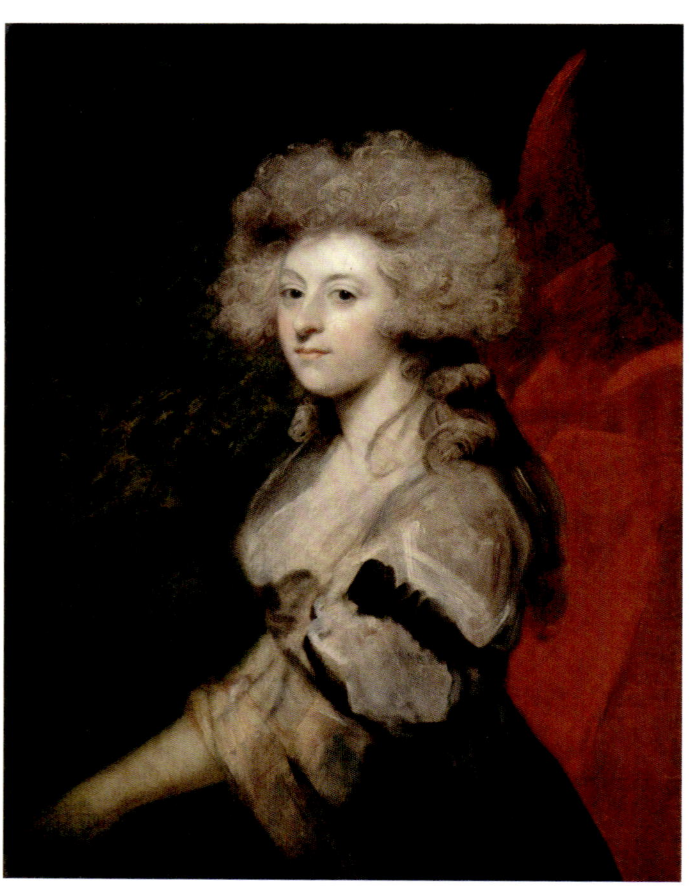

FIG. 3.4
THOMAS GAINSBOROUGH (1727–88), *Mrs Mary Robinson (1756/8–1800)*, *c.*1781. Oil on canvas, 76.0 × 63.2 cm, RCIN 400670

FIG. 3.5
SIR JOSHUA REYNOLDS (1723–92), *Maria Anne Fitzherbert* (1756–1837), *c.*1788. Oil on canvas, 91.4 × 71.1 cm (private collection; on loan to the National Portrait Gallery, London: L162)

FIG. 3.6
THOMAS GAINSBOROUGH (1727–88), *The Three Eldest Princesses: Charlotte, Princess Royal (1766–1828), Augusta (1768–1840) and Elizabeth (1770–1840)*, 1783–4. Oil on canvas, 129.7 × 179.8 cm, RCIN 400206

FIG. 3.7
SIR WILLIAM BEECHEY (1753–1839), *Princess Elizabeth*, 1797. Oil on canvas, 92.4 × 71.0 cm, RCIN 403412

Portraits of George's mistresses often graced his walls (Fig. 3.4), sometimes to be given away when the liaison became less desirable (Fig. 3.5). Sisters, though, remained. Gainsborough's painting of George's three eldest sisters, commissioned in 1783 (Fig. 3.6),[12] alludes to Van Dyck with its red curtain, architectural setting and landscape beyond, but marries these baroque elements with a fashionable aspect, a graceful rococo lightness of touch in the pastel-coloured dresses of the sisters and the delicacy of their rustling fabrics. Again, in 1800, George commissioned Sir William Beechey, who was Principal Painter to Queen Charlotte, for half-length portraits of his six sisters (Fig. 3.7).[13] These smaller, more domestic-scale works depict the women as attractive, accomplished and scholarly, and reflect their quiet and secluded life at Windsor and Kew – a far cry from the glamorous, full-length portraits of society women at the Royal Academy.

In 1807 George would commission portraits of his sisters again, this time from Peter Edward Stroehling (Figs 3.8A–D and 11.7), a German painter working in England and whose highly finished, jewel-like style probably appealed to George in the same way as works by Dutch painters such as Adriaen van der Werff or Godfried Schalcken. Portrait commissions to non-British painters were, on the whole, rare, although George's taste in interiors and furniture was markedly Francophile and his Old Master pictures predominantly Dutch and Flemish (see chapter 7). As Prince of Wales George was painted by Alexandre-Auguste Robineau, a French *émigré* artist and, sometime around 1803–4, by Elisabeth-Louise Vigée-Lebrun,[14] but generally his patronage of British portrait artists was notable.[15]

In 1811 Joseph Farington recorded George looking 'with attention' at pictures when he attended the Royal Academy dinner.[16] He went on to note that the prince spoke of his pride as an Englishman in seeing around him 'portraits which might vie with the pictures of Van Dyck'. As an Englishman 'he might with confidence expect that as this country had risen superior to all others in Arms, military and naval prowess so would it in Arts'.

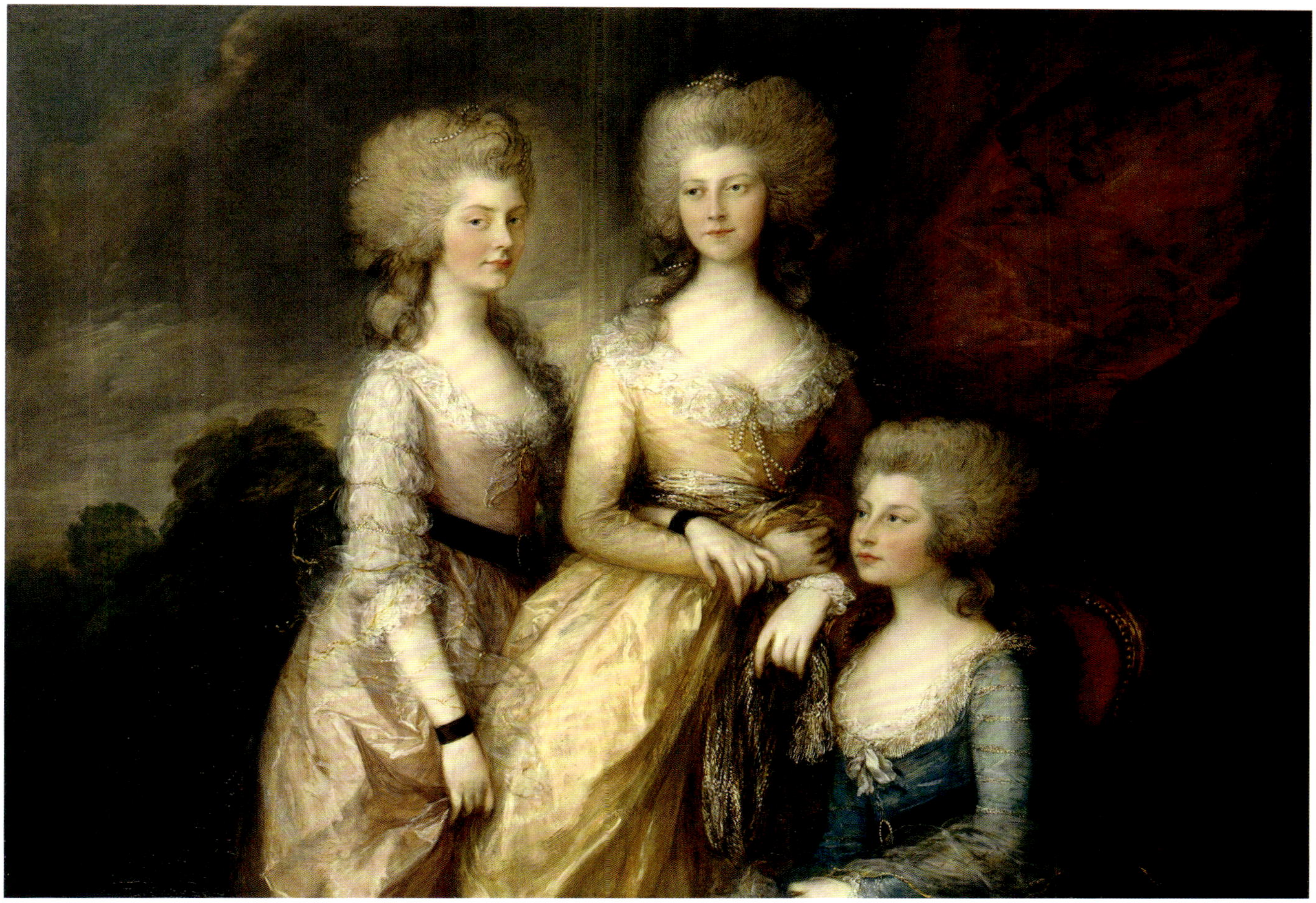

The expression of patriotic pride through the arts underpinned much of George's lifelong passion for collecting, but in his patronage of portraits it took a particularly British emphasis.

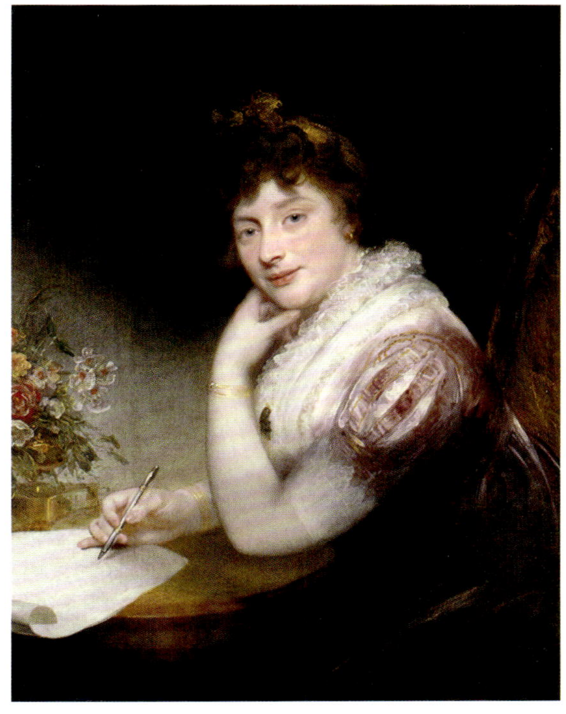

Public exhibition

Although many of George's portraits were privately exchanged, many were first publicly exhibited at the Royal Academy. Images of military figures in grand, full-length format had become an expected part of celebrity culture at the Academy, with the most famous artists of the day vying with one another in their depictions of these heroes, returned, triumphant or otherwise, from the battlefields of Europe and America.

The Gainsborough portraits of St Leger and George (see Figs 3.9 and 3.10) were exhibited together at the Royal Academy in 1782, as companions, with the same decorative saddle (a gift to St Leger from the prince) linking them. This attested to a friendship but also glamorised both sitters by association.

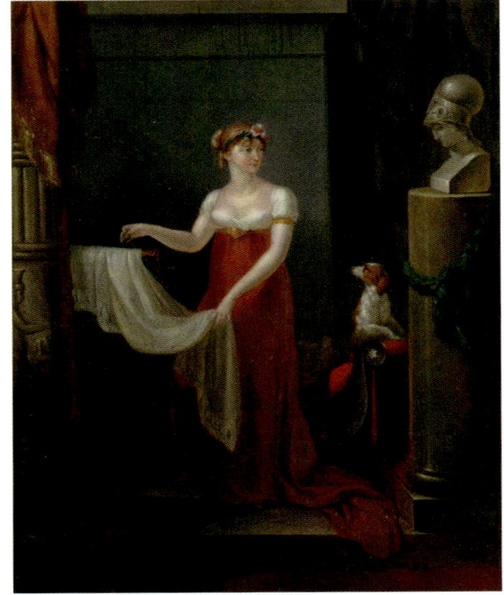

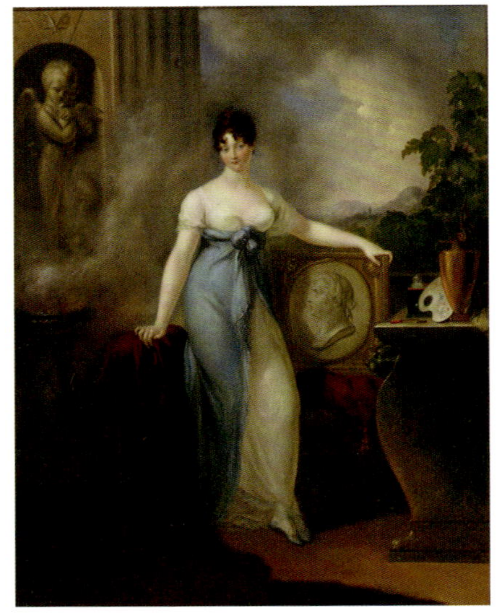

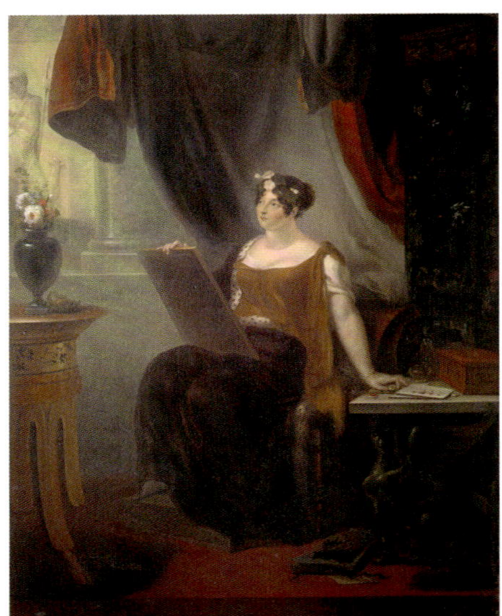

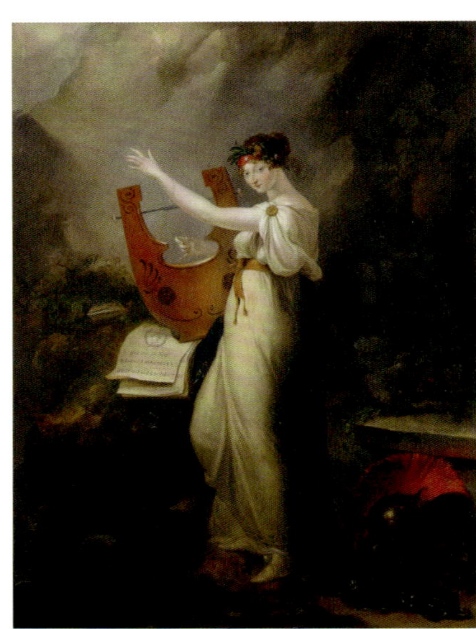

(above left)
FIG. 3.8A
PETER EDWARD STROEHLING (1768–*c.*1826), *Princess Sophia (1777–1848)*, 1807. Oil on copper, 60.8 × 48.3 cm, RCIN 404864

(above right)
FIG. 3.8B
PETER EDWARD STROEHLING (1768–*c.*1826), *Princess Mary (1776–1857)*, 1807. Oil on copper, 60.7 × 48.3 cm, RCIN 404866

(below left)
FIG. 3.8C
PETER EDWARD STROEHLING (1768–*c.*1826), *Princess Elizabeth (1770–1840)*, 1807. Oil on copper, 60.8 × 48.1 cm, RCIN 404870

(below right)
FIG. 3.8D
PETER EDWARD STROEHLING (1768–*c.*1826), *Princess Amelia (1783–1810)*, 1807. Oil on copper, 61.1 × 46.1 cm, RCIN 404871

One of the most notorious sitters in the same 1782 exhibition was Colonel Banastre Tarleton, painted by both Reynolds and Gainsborough in heroic, large-scale works. The Prince of Wales, in full uniform, took his place on the Academy walls that year among these veterans of bloody campaigns – it would not be the last time that he inserted himself into the pictorial records of military history, without ever having been permitted to take part in the action himself.

It is critical in considering George's portrait commissions to remember that their first exhibition was usually on the walls of the Royal Academy, whatever the subsequent or final royal destination might have been. Leading artists of the day competed for royal sitters, populating both the walls of Academy exhibitions and the royal residences with their latest commissions. Viewing portraits at the annual Royal Academy exhibition was part of the social calendar and the press eagerly reviewed the works and recounted the latest news of artists, sitters, celebrities and scandals. Viewers came to see, discuss, comment and criticise, and enjoyed making connections between society figures and the speculation that surrounded them, which was familiar to Academy visitors through print culture. Royal portraits, and in several years portraits of George himself, dominated the Academy displays.[17] His sovereignty in the exhibition space, particularly through the turbulent years of the French Revolution and the Napoleonic Wars, may have provided reassurance about the security of the monarchy itself. Though, of course, George himself did not determine the selection or hang of the paintings: it was a royal academy with royal patrons.

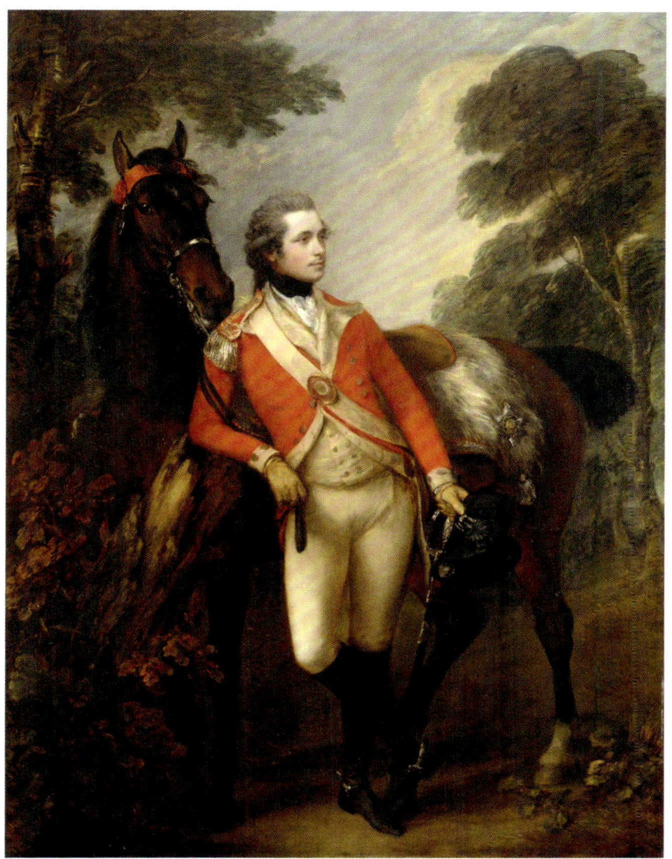

FIG. 3.9
THOMAS GAINSBOROUGH (1727–88), *John Hayes St Leger (1765–1800)*, 1782. Oil on canvas, 249.6 × 189.0 cm, RCIN 405726

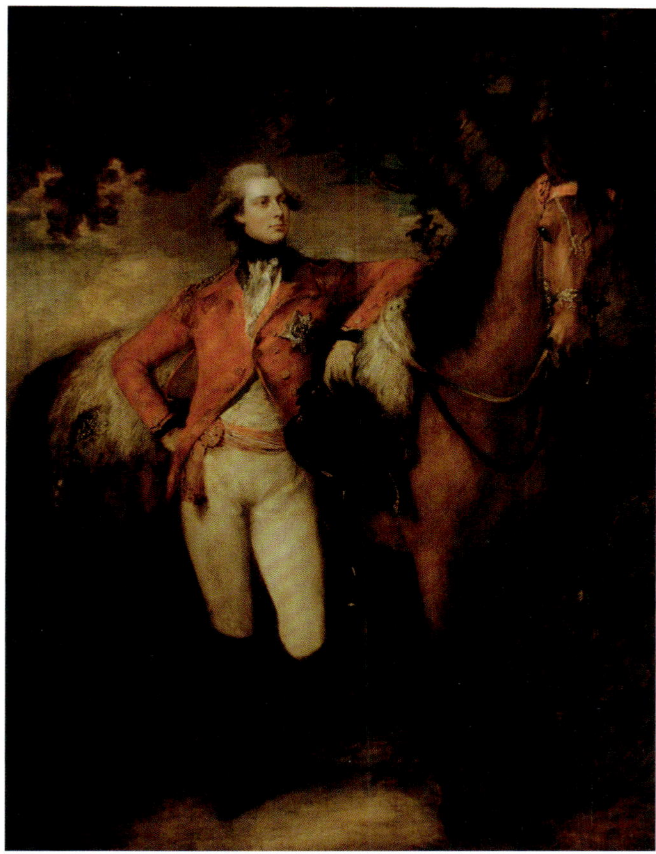

FIG. 3.10
THOMAS GAINSBOROUGH (1727–88), *George IV when Prince of Wales*, 1781. Oil on canvas, 250.1 × 186.0 cm (Waddesdon, The Rothschild Collection (The National Trust), Aylesbury: 2258)

George's patronage could bring difficulties as well as rewards for artists and sculptors. Royal Academician Joseph Farington's diaries are awash with tales of non-payment or late payment, as well as endless waiting times, as this one example attests:

> Smirke told me Rossi, the Sculptor, was with the Prince of Wales today modelling a small head of him in the Uniform of the 10th. regt. of Dragoons. Rossi waited 3 hours today before He was admitted, during which time the Prince was entirely engaged by a Shoemaker, and two Taylors who succeeded each other … Rossi, yesterday waited 5 hours in vain.[18]

Although such difficulties in arranging sittings or receiving payment, and the danger of falling out of royal favour, were some of the proven and seemingly well-known pitfalls of working for George, the benefits of producing a successful portrait and gaining royal preferment meant that several leading artists of the day decided it was a risk worth taking. In the competitive business that was portrait painting, a royal connection could provide a significant advantage in driving further commissions inside and outside royal circles.

The commission for *The Three Eldest Princesses* proved a controversial one for Gainsborough in the context of the Royal Academy. After an argument about the hanging of the work, Gainsborough withdrew it and never exhibited at the Academy again, but the combination of a long and successful career and royal patronage meant that this did not adversely affect his business. In 1786, *The Three Eldest Princesses* was exhibited at Gainsborough's premises at Schomberg House on Pall Mall, when it was noted in the press that the painting would remain with Gainsborough 'till the Picture Saloon at Carlton House is fitted for their reception'.[19] This episode illustrates the movement of works in George's picture collection, from private to public to semi-public to private space again, providing shifting contexts for their interpretation as a result.

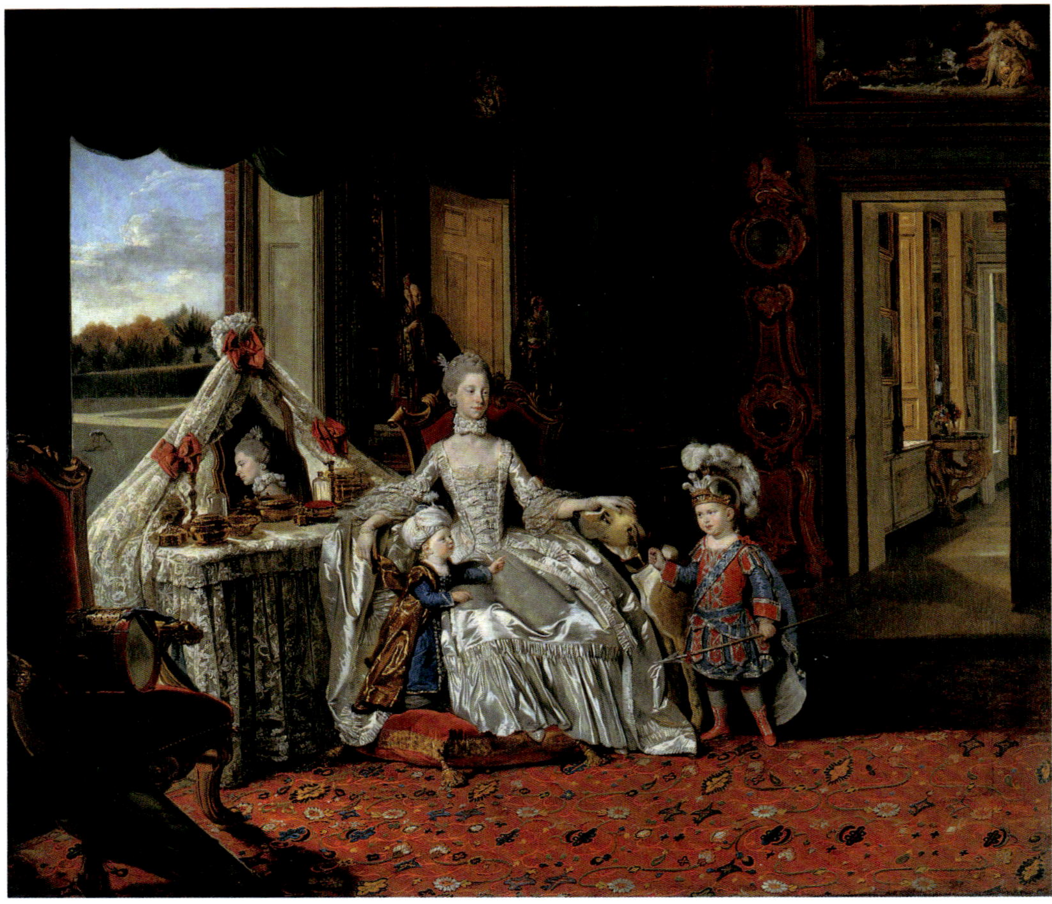

FIG. 3.11
JOHAN JOSEPH ZOFFANY (1733–1810), *Queen Charlotte (1744–1818) with her Two Eldest Sons*, *c.*1765. Oil on canvas, 112.2 × 128.3 cm, RCIN 400146

FIG. 3.12
JOHN HOPPNER (1758–1810), *Horatio, First Viscount Nelson (1758–1805)*, 1801–2. Oil on canvas, 239.0 × 148.0 cm, RCIN 405901

FIG. 3.13
SIR ANTHONY VAN DYCK (1599–1641), *Gaston de France, duc d'Orléans (1608–60)*, 1632 or 1634. Oil on canvas, 194.0 × 118.0 cm (musée Condé, Chantilly: PE125)

Portrait schemes and displays

The earliest plans for a family portrait hang at Carlton House survive only in press references, with two newspaper reports remarking not on the works commissioned by George but on those given to him by his father: 'The King has lately made the Prince of Wales a present of a most valuable collection of pictures, for the decoration of Carleton-house Palace; and among the rest the last paintings of their Majesties and the Royal children by Gainsborough, esteemed the greatest likenesses ever taken.'[20]

In discussing George's taste, the pictures he inherited should be considered alongside those he acquired or commissioned. It is clear that he received several of the Gainsborough portraits originally commissioned by his parents, along with other works from their collection. The concept of creating dedicated portrait rooms or galleries within his residences, combining works from previous royal collectors with his own acquisitions, runs more strongly throughout George's later plans, when he had full control of the whole collection, but is also evident to some degree in the early picture displays at Carlton House. These demonstrate from the outset the importance of portraits of family and friends. As early as 1784, George refers to the plan for hanging portraits of his brothers, Frederick, Duke of York and William, Duke of Clarence (later William IV) in a letter – 'I am keeping to [*sic*] places in my House, on purpose for Portraits of you & Billy'[21] – expressing a fond, fraternal wish, albeit for what may have been large-scale or grand paintings.[22]

In an extensive newspaper description of Carlton House in the *Morning Post and Daily Advertiser* in 1784, the State Room is noted as a work in progress. 'In this apartment the pictures of most of the Royal family are to be placed, but it contains at present only those of their Majesties.'[23] Almost a decade later, when the rooms had slightly changed in name, a 1793 Coutts inventory noted various portraits in this same, garden-facing, enfilade at the back of Carlton House. There the rooms are entitled 'State Apartments' and are separated into three distinct spaces. In the Anti Room 'Two portraits in Carved and Gilt Frames – Lord Rodney and Keppel'; in the Council Chamber 'Two large Portraits of the two late Dukes of Cumberland and Two Ditto of the Marquis of Rockingham and the Duke of Rutland';

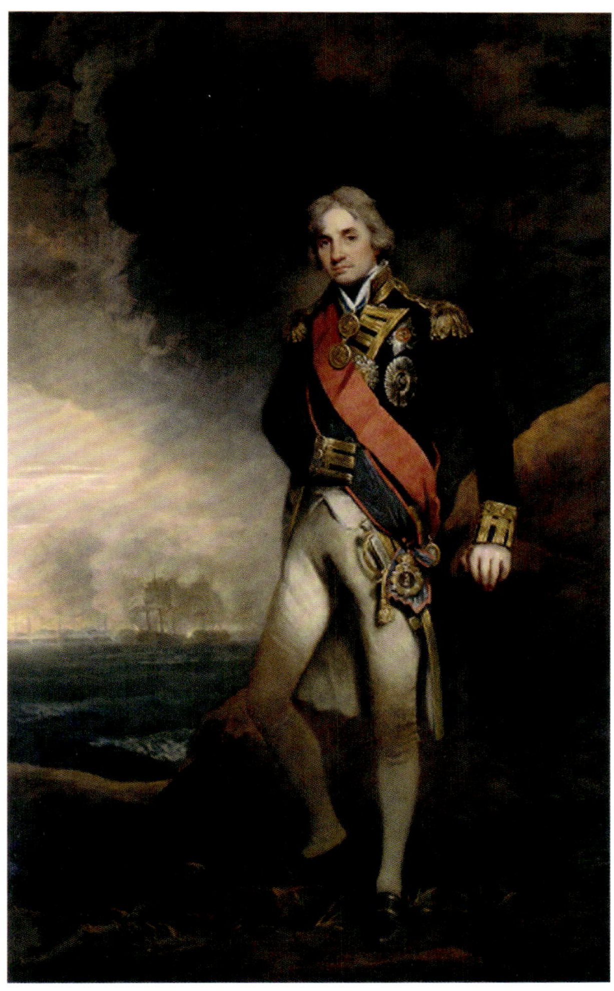

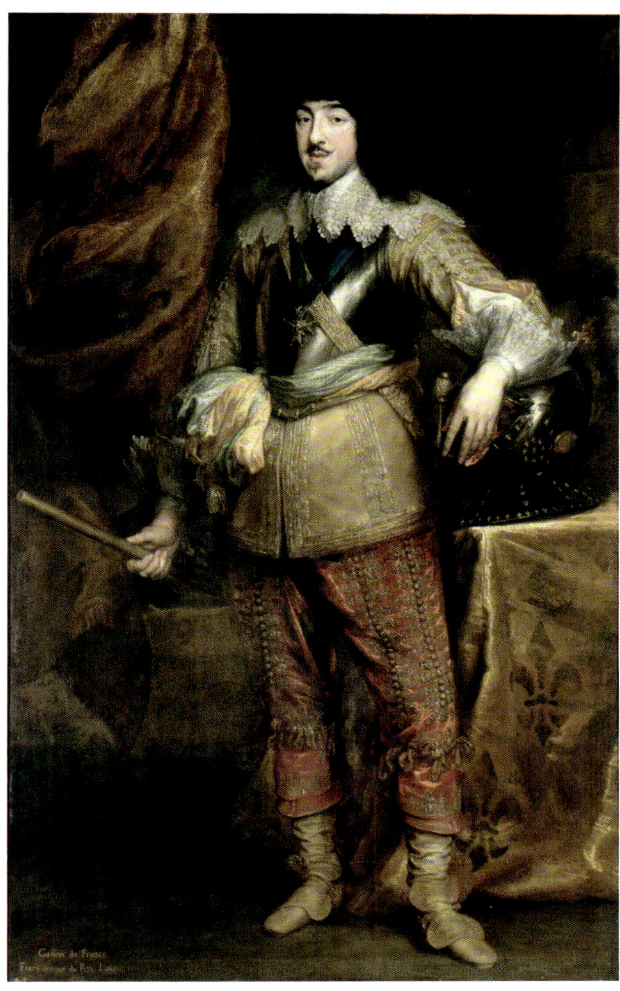

and in the Throne Room 'Five pictures, portraits of the Royal Family'.[24] These rooms functioned as the most formal receiving space in the house. Here George would have welcomed visiting nobility and other visitors of distinction as well as friends, and the display of military heroes, key political figures and royal family portraits reveals George's own vision of his place in the world, and as such can be seen as a forerunner of the great Waterloo Chamber scheme.[25]

In 1793 Johan Joseph Zoffany's painting of *Queen Charlotte with her Two Eldest Sons* (Fig. 3.11) was listed by the picture dealer George Simpson as one of the works being cleaned for the Prince of Wales, suggesting that it too had passed into George's own collection at Carlton House by that time.[26] It must have been a work that held some emotional and familial significance for him, but the childish dressing up of the young George as Telemachus, son of the great warrior and hero Odysseus, also referred to other portraits of child sovereigns and suggested the importance of military prowess even in boyhood.

Tracking exact picture movements around Carlton House on the basis of surviving inventories can be difficult due to the changing names of the rooms (see pp. viii–ix). What is clear from the comprehensive inventories of 1816 and 1819[27] (which vary only a little from each other) is that while sitters and artists changed, the martial or political character of several of the portrait displays remained. During the Regency, the East Anti Room held four full-length works by John Hoppner, who had been appointed as Principal Portrait Painter to the Prince of Wales in 1793. The four paintings had been commissioned at different points in previous decades and three of them had been exhibited at the Royal Academy. Hoppner's widow presented them to George in 1810. The portraits depicted military and naval heroes, including Lord Nelson (Fig. 3.12), and all were close and loyal allies to George.[28] Thus great heroes of British military and political power now came to take their place in the heart of Carlton House, recorded in these inventories at a time when national pride was at a post-1815 peak.

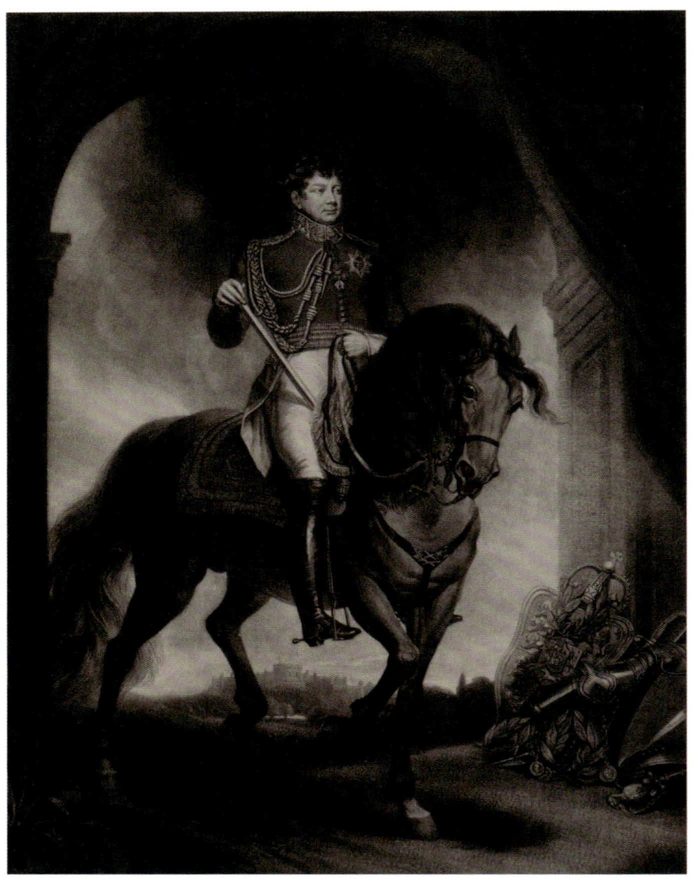

FIG. 3.14
SAMUEL WILLIAM REYNOLDS (1773–1835)
AFTER JAMES NORTHCOTE (1746–1831),
George IV, c.1828. Mezzotint,
73.5 × 53.8 cm (sheet), RCIN 605282

The West Anti Room, according to these same inventories, contained a mixture of English and French portraits, including a now destroyed portrait of Louis XV by Jean-Baptiste Greuze (presented by Louis XVIII) and a now much-damaged portrait of the duc d'Orléans by Reynolds.[29] This Anglo-French spirit was echoed in the South Anti Room where the Beechey portraits of George's sisters were joined by a portrait of Louis XV and another of his mistress Madame de Pompadour, and (noted in the 1819 inventory) the Van Dyck portrait of Gaston, duc d'Orléans, before it was given by George to Louis-Philippe, duc d'Orléans in 1829 (Fig. 3.13). These two rooms, with portraits of French royals alongside British nobility, demonstrated George's devotion to the *ancien régime* so much in evidence in other aspects of his art collecting.

The most interesting of these portrait displays during the Regency period was perhaps in evidence in the Crimson Drawing Room, where two Reynolds paintings depicting the heroes of the Seven Years' War, of the English Marquess of Granby and his German ally Wilhelm, Count of Schaumburg-Lippe,[30] took pride of place in the display alongside Rubens's *Landscape with Saint George and the Dragon*. The Rubens, painted for Charles I and reacquired by George in 1814, depicted the Stuart king as the saint (see Fig. 7.2). George was clearly making reference to his namesake, the Christian knight and patron saint of England, as well as incorporating Stuart ideals of chivalry and splendid artistic patronage into his own schemes. He would continue to refer to and collect Stuart-related paintings and portraits throughout his lifetime and some equestrian statues and paintings of him (Fig. 3.14) were also indebted to his Stuart predecessors.

Lawrence and the Waterloo Chamber

As has been noted, military halls of fame were a key feature of George's collecting and picture displays throughout his life. These martial narratives culminated in the portraits he commissioned from Sir Thomas Lawrence that he intended for display at Carlton House and which subsequently ended up at the heart of Windsor Castle, in the Waterloo Chamber.[31] Lawrence's connection to the royal family had begun long before this portrait commission. George III had supported his election as Academician, had commissioned a portrait of Queen Charlotte from him in 1789[32] and appointed him 'Painter-in-Ordinary' in 1792. This perhaps provides the opportunity to challenge a misconception about George III and his son in open animosity, apparently shown through opposing tastes in art. In fact, while they no doubt had major disagreements and differences, close examination of George's favoured portrait artists shows quite a lot in common with his parents, and much shared patronage of the great painters of the day such as Gainsborough, Beechey and Hoppner. Certainly George's early commissions relied on several 'inherited' artists rather than new ones. Despite his royal appointment and his prodigious talent, Lawrence did not work for George III very much, and it was only in the Regency that he began to gain royal commissions. This time it was in the Prince Regent's orbit, perhaps through the patronage of John McMahon, George's private secretary, although the young Lawrence had previously been part of the Francophile Whig circles at Devonshire House in the 1780s and shared many acquaintances with George.

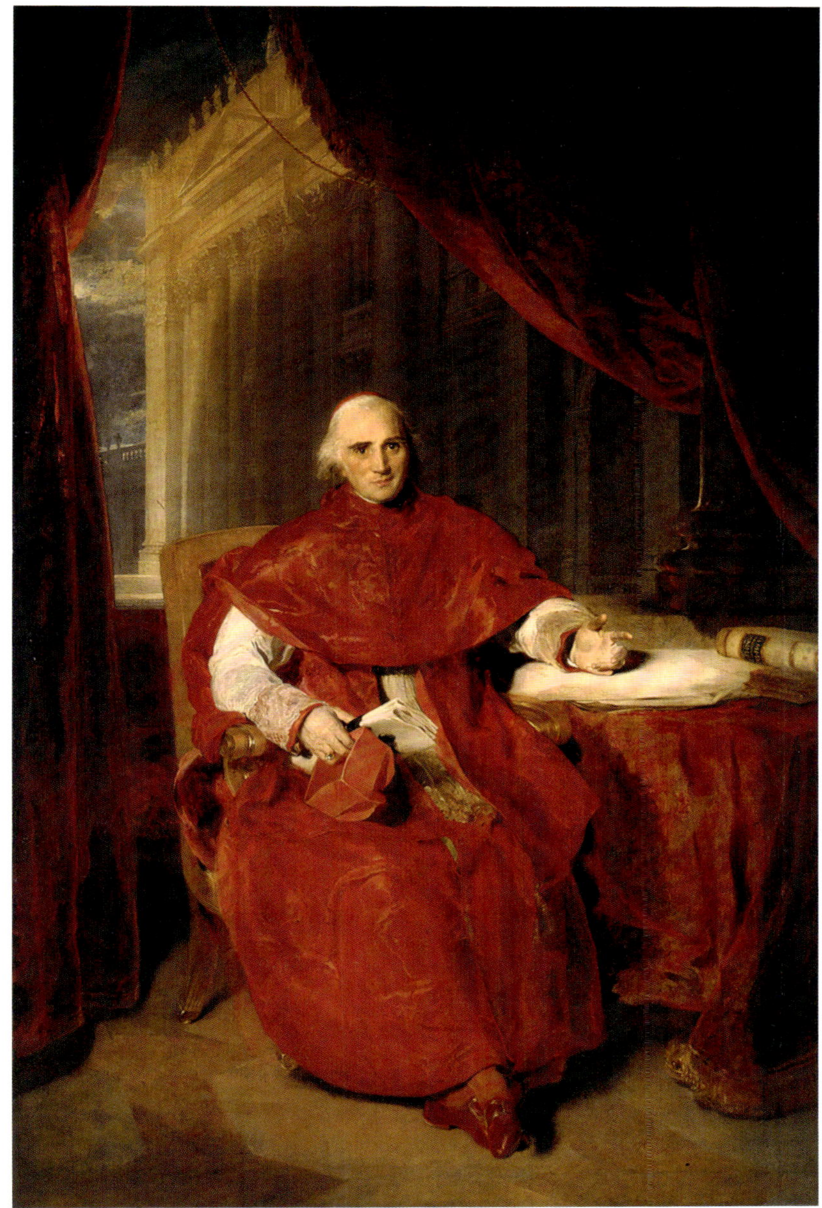

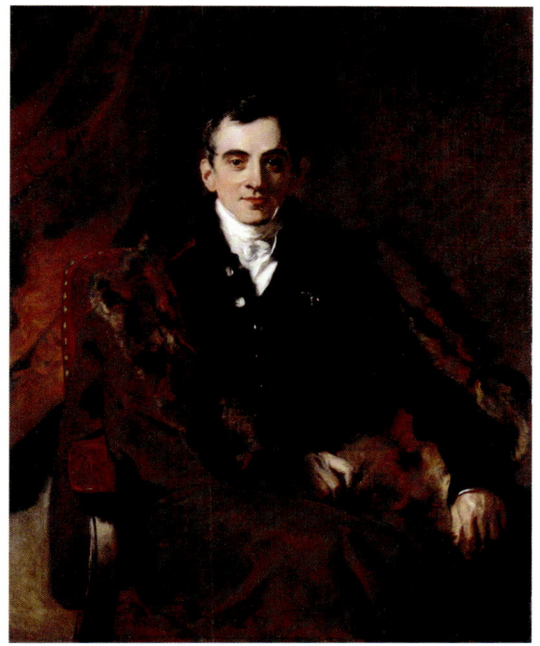

FIG. 3.15
SIR THOMAS LAWRENCE (1769–1830), *Ercole, Cardinal Consalvi (1757–1824)*, 1819. Oil on canvas, 269.2 × 175.8 cm, RCIN 404940

FIG. 3.16
SIR THOMAS LAWRENCE (1769–1830), *John, Count Capo d'Istria (1776–1831)*, 1818–19. Oil on canvas, 128.4 × 102.8 cm, RCIN 404947

By 1814 Lawrence could write to a friend:

> The Prince Regent was here on Saturday to see the Pictures – was pleased with them – desir'd to have the Duke of Yorks, another of Lord Castlereagh, with one of Lord Liverpool, and to crown this honor, engaged to sit to me at One today, and after a successful sitting of two hours has just left now, and comes again tomorrow, and the next Day.[33]

What followed was a whirlwind of commissions and royal business that had Lawrence occupied in painting the key Allied military and political figures of the day. An initial idea for two group portraits to commemorate the Allied victory over Napoleon fell away and Lawrence instead had individual sittings with military commanders and Allied heads of state and statesmen (Figs 3.15–3.17).[34] These sittings began in 1814 in London in Lawrence's studio, with the press eagerly seizing upon the arrival of celebrated 'foreign' military heroes Count Matvei Platov (Fig. 4.1) and Field Marshal Gebhard von Blücher.[35] Continuation of the scheme was delayed by Napoleon's escape from Elba, but resumed again after the victory of the Allies at the Battle of Waterloo. Other portraits were produced abroad, as Lawrence travelled to Aix-la-Chapelle, Vienna and Rome in order to paint the key figures in the campaigns against Napoleon.

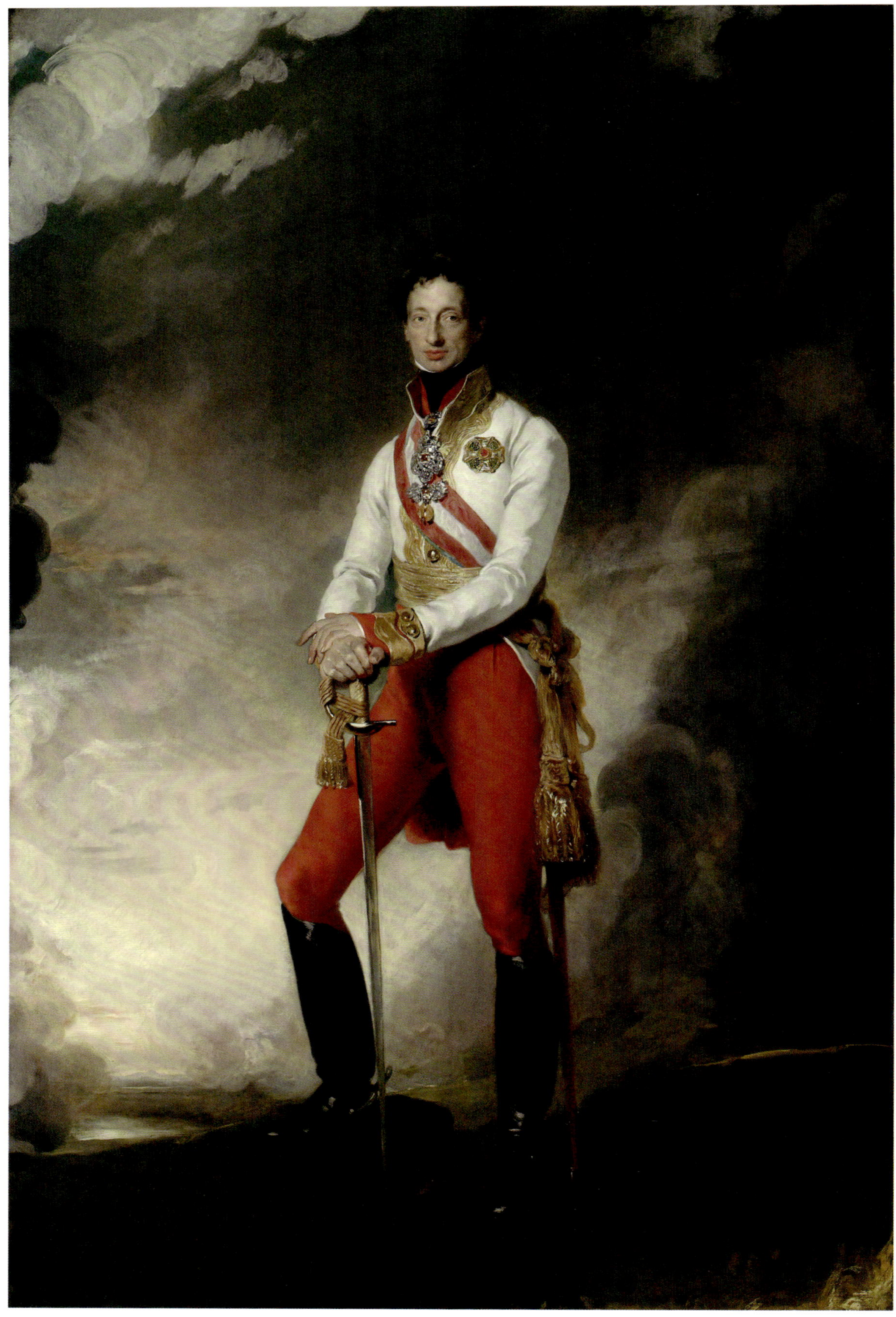

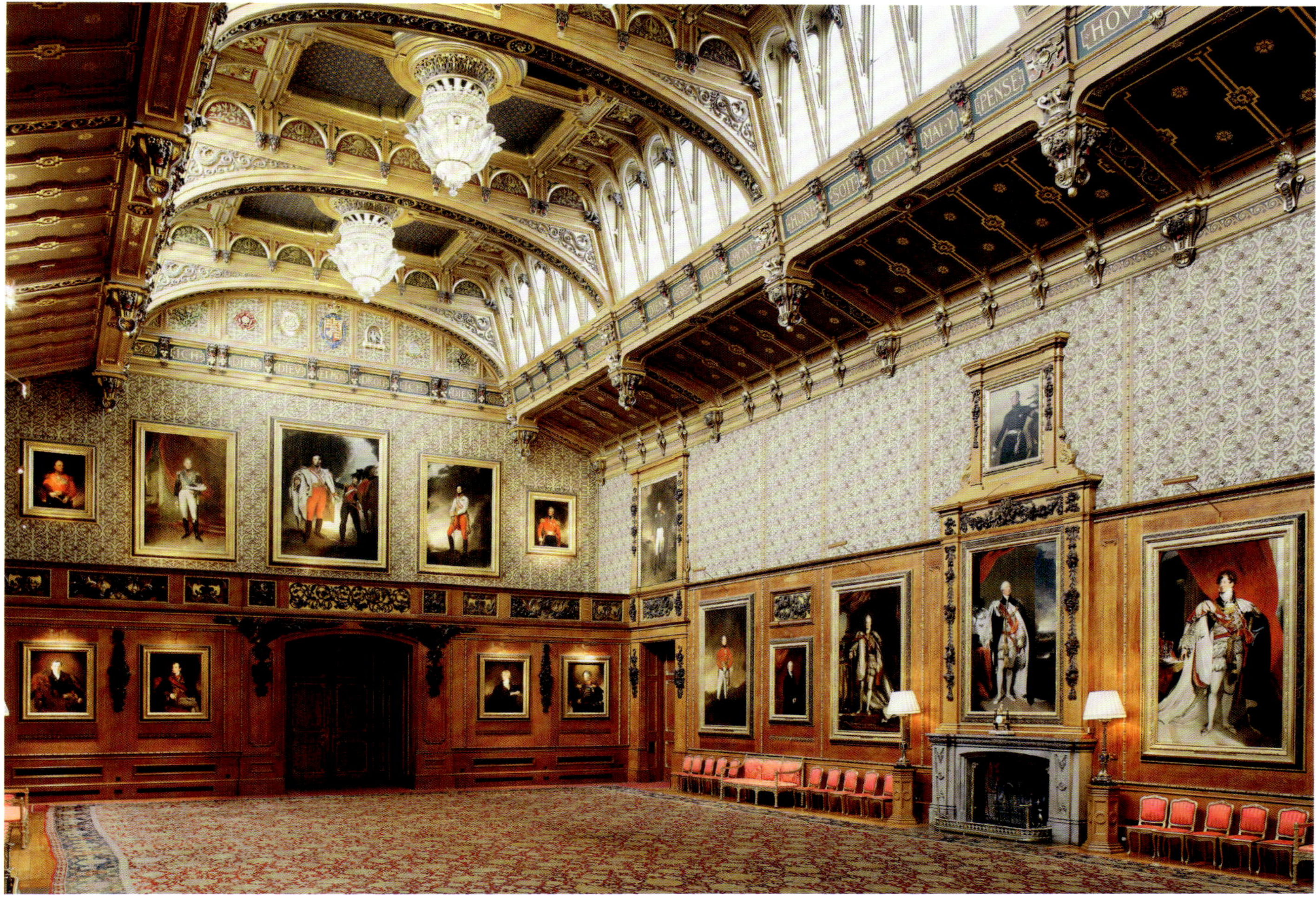

FIG. 3.17
SIR THOMAS LAWRENCE (1769–1830), *Charles, Archduke of Austria (1771–1847)*, 1819. Oil on canvas, 270.1 × 179.5 cm, RCIN 405140

FIG. 3.18
The Waterloo Chamber, Windsor Castle

Lawrence's letters of the period are fascinating, revealing studio conversations on politics and society and demonstrating how this brilliant, intelligent, charming artist became a key player in the recording of a moment in modern history.

As *de facto* head of state after 1811, George was able to play host to allied sovereigns in 1814, and to engage with those abroad in the years that followed. The planned portrait scheme for the Waterloo Chamber at Windsor gave this authority pictorial form. In addition to his role as statesman, George was also cast as a Maecenas, engaging with Antonio Canova to assist Pope Pius VII in recovering the Vatican marbles. Lawrence's papal portrait (see Fig. 1.1), made in Rome, was a *tour de force*, capturing the character and the spiritual authority of the pope in his sanctuary and setting this contemplative and more introspective figure against the hard splendour of those depicted fresh from the battlefield.

Even before he saw Lawrence's portraits painted abroad, the painter and president of the Royal Academy, Benjamin West, had remarked: 'Do not confound his pictures with mere portraits: painted as his are, they cease to be portraits in the ordinary sense; they rise to the dignity of history, and, like similar works of Titian and Vandyke, they may be said to be painted not alone to gratify friends and admirers in the present day, but rather for posterity.'[36]

George died before the portraits took their final place in the Waterloo Chamber and the display was finished under his brother William IV. He was nevertheless the driving force for this idea of a modern history installation as a celebration, a commemoration and also the formation of a historical narrative, with himself at the epicentre in portrait and as patron (Fig. 3.18).

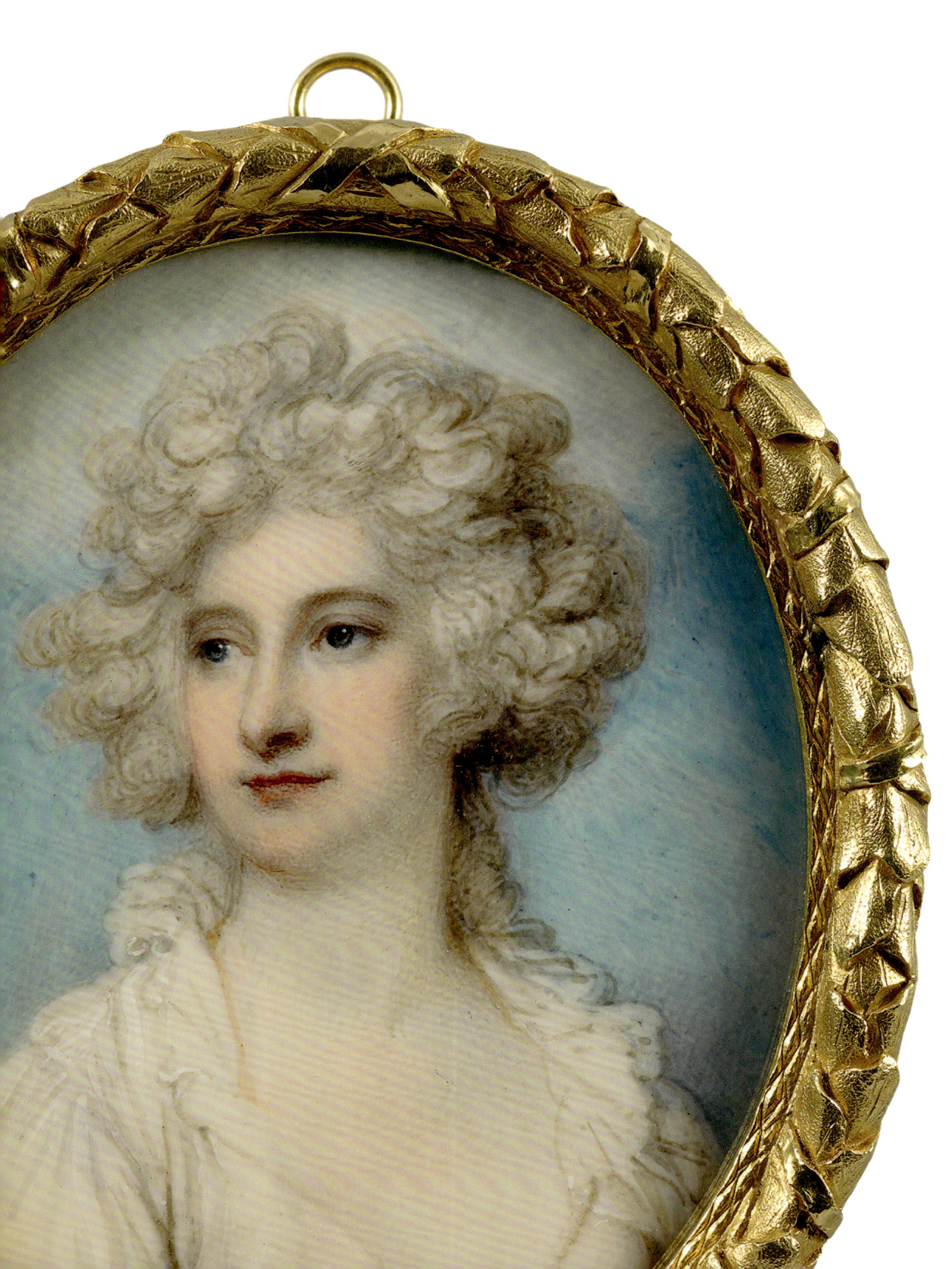

4

GEORGE IV *as a* COLLECTOR *of* PORTRAIT MINIATURES

VANESSA REMINGTON

George IV was an enthusiastic collector and commissioner of portrait miniatures, appreciating them for their traditional function as sentimental tokens for distribution and exchange, which suited his purposes perfectly. Queen Victoria recalled his gift of a miniature to her in early childhood:

> When we arrived at Royal Lodge the King took me by the hand, saying: 'Give me your little paw.' He was large and gouty with a wonderful dignity and charm of manner. He wore the wig which was so much worn in those days. Then he said he would give me something to wear, and that was his picture set in diamonds, which was worn by the Princesses as an order to a blue ribbon on the left shoulder. I was very proud of this, – and Lady Conyngham pinned it on my shoulder.[1]

Elizabeth, Marchioness Conyngham, George's mistress in his final years, had herself been the recipient of a similar miniature, dated 1817 and set in a frame of small diamonds (Fig. 4.2). Like the gift to Princess Victoria, this was an enamel miniature by the artist Henry Bone after Thomas Lawrence, one of many set into lockets, pendants and rings, and given to lovers, friends and associates of George IV.[2] For George, just as for monarchs dating back to Henry VIII, the miniature could serve as an intimate personal keepsake or a prestigious royal gift marking a diplomatic or political alliance. Count Platov, whose role in the defeat of Napoleon's army is commemorated by his portrait by Lawrence in the Waterloo Chamber, is shown there wearing a version of Bone's enamel set in diamonds (Fig. 4.1).

The potential of the art form must have become apparent to George early in life. As a child, he would have been familiar with the miniatures of his father, George III, which his mother, Queen Charlotte, wore prominently in jewellery and accessories in accordance with fashionable practice of the day (Fig. 4.3). And as a young man, he would have seen at the Queen's House (later Buckingham Palace) the 'six large frames, in one room, glazed on red Damask, holding a vast quantity of enamelled pictures,

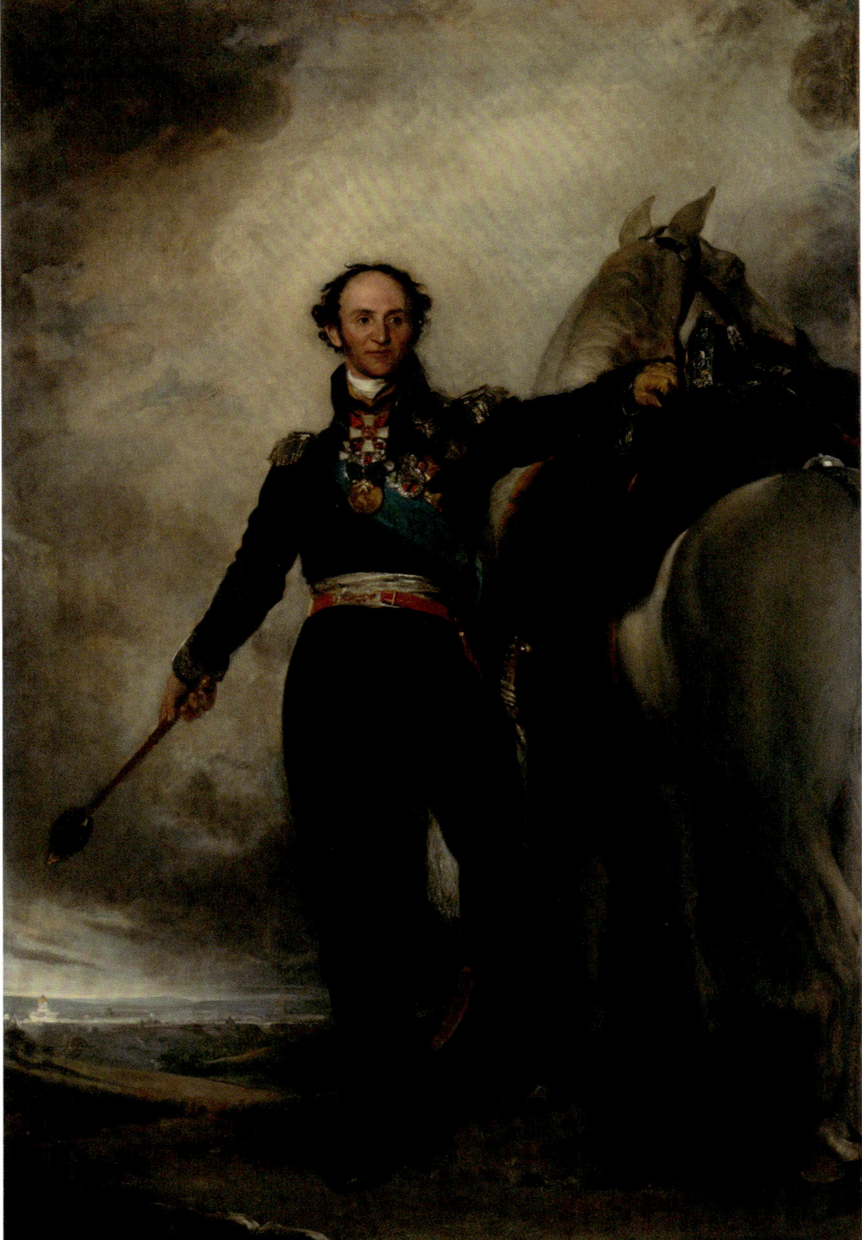

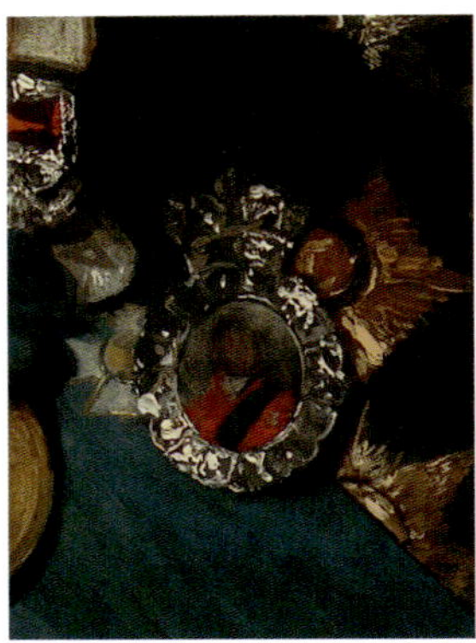

FIG. 4.1
SIR THOMAS LAWRENCE (1769–1830), *Matvei Ivanovitch, Count Platov (1753–1818)*, 1814. Oil on canvas, 270.5 × 179.6 cm, RCIN 405146 and detail

(p. 60)
Detail of Fig. A.24, RICHARD COSWAY (1742–1821), *Maria Fitzherbert (1756–1837)*, *c.*1789, RCIN 420928

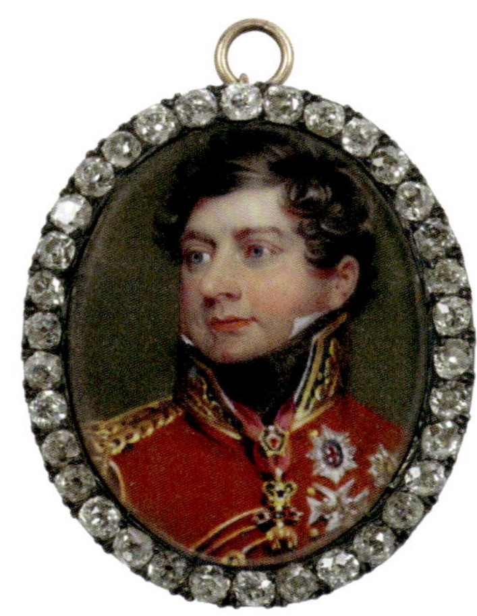

FIG. 4.2
HENRY BONE (1755–1834), *George IV when Prince Regent*, 1800. Enamel, gold, diamond, 3.3 × 2.6 cm, RCIN 421946

miniatures, & Cameos', also observed by Horace Walpole in the 1780s.[3] The display combined both contemporary portrait miniatures commissioned by George III and Queen Charlotte and miniatures from the historic collection formerly kept at Kensington Palace by Queen Caroline, George's great-grandmother. But as Prince of Wales and Prince Regent, George was to exploit the full potential of the portrait miniature in a way that his parents had not, seizing on the talents of one particular miniaturist whose works seemed to exemplify the spirit of George's circle and associates. In the hands of Richard Cosway (Fig. 4.4), the discreet and even muted nature of British portrait miniatures in the third quarter of the eighteenth century was transformed.

Painting miniatures of royal sitters and members of the court for George from 1780, Cosway adopted a new style that was as flamboyant and bold as his signature: *Pictor Primarius Serenissimi Walliae Principis* ('Principal Painter to His Royal Highness the Prince of Wales'). Cosway's portrait miniatures of George show this transition from the restrained depiction on

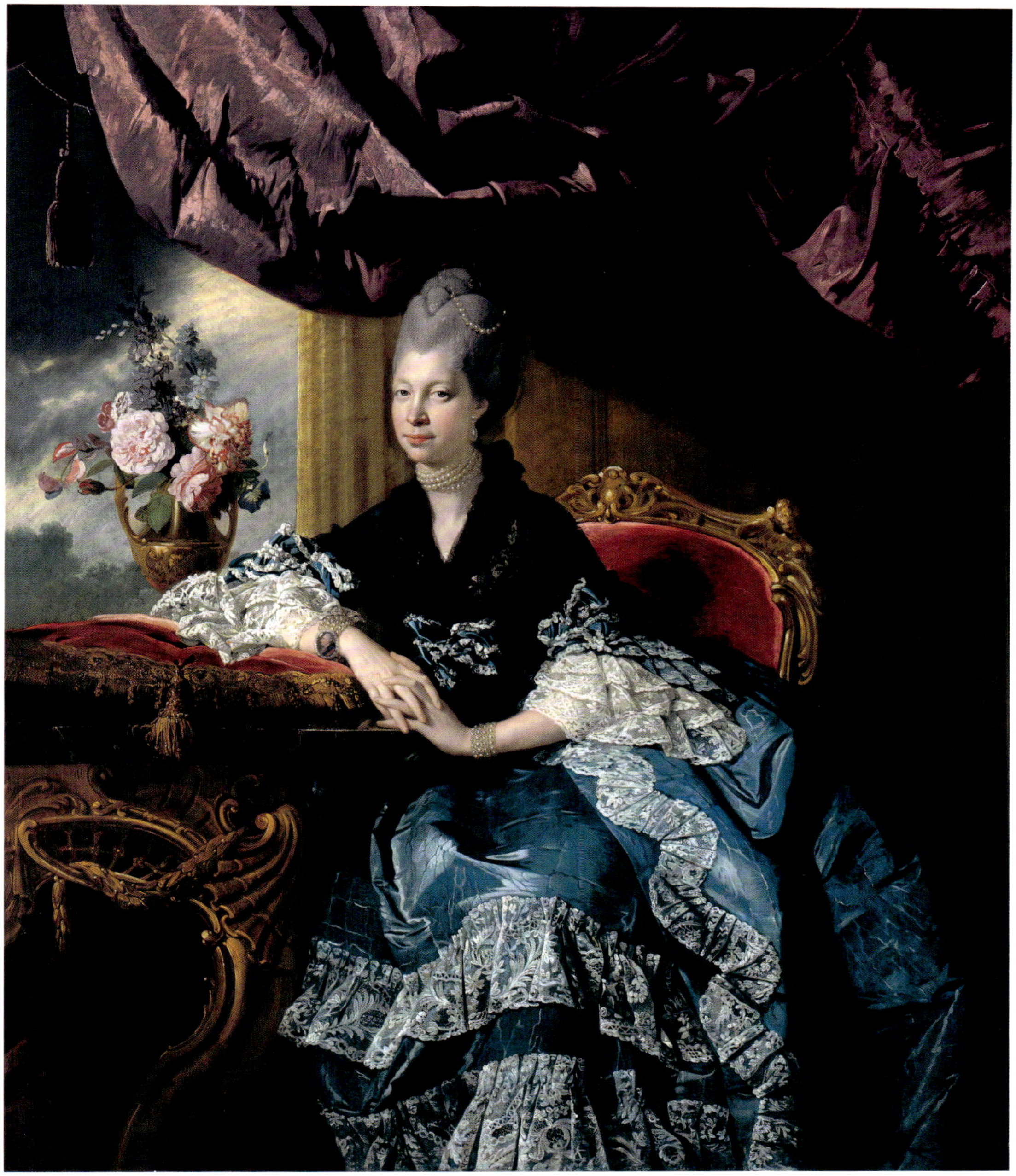

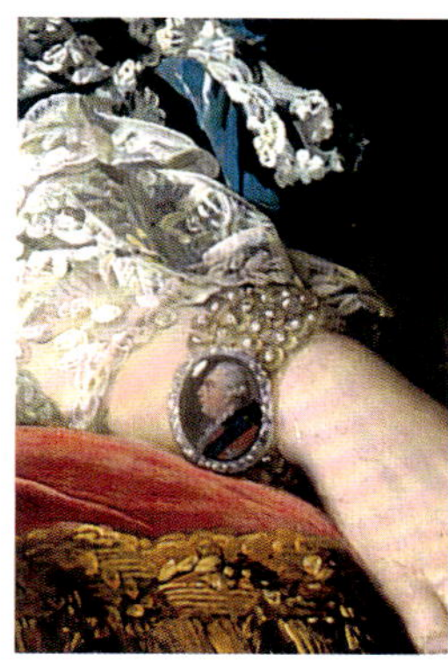

FIG. 4.3
JOHAN JOSEPH ZOFFANY (1733–1810), *Queen Charlotte (1744–1818)*, 1771. Oil on canvas, 162.9 × 137.2 cm, RCIN 405071 and detail

a small ivory roundel of *c.*1783–4 (Fig. 4.5) to the much more painterly style exemplified by his miniature of *c.*1795 (Fig. 4.6). Cosway brought drama and freedom to this most understated of art forms by using larger ivory bases, allowing the ivory to show through the pigment and lend translucency to the works, and by the sheer fluidity and movement of his brushwork. His flattering, fashion-conscious works found such favour at Carlton House that his accounts record no fewer than 73 miniatures produced between 1780 and 1808 for the Prince of Wales.[4] Some of these miniatures portrayed friends and family and were intended for the prince's private enjoyment, including miniatures of his sisters Princess Mary (Fig. 4.7) and Princess Sophia and 'A Picture of Prs Charlotte for a ring'.[5] However, more than 40 were miniatures of George himself, intended for distribution: 'with a hat', 'with Hat small', 'in uniform', 'in a ring' and even, in 1785, 'His eye' at a cost of £5 5s.[6] George sent this miniature of his eye to Maria Fitzherbert on 3 November 1785 with a letter in which he advocated their secret marriage: 'I send you at ye. same time

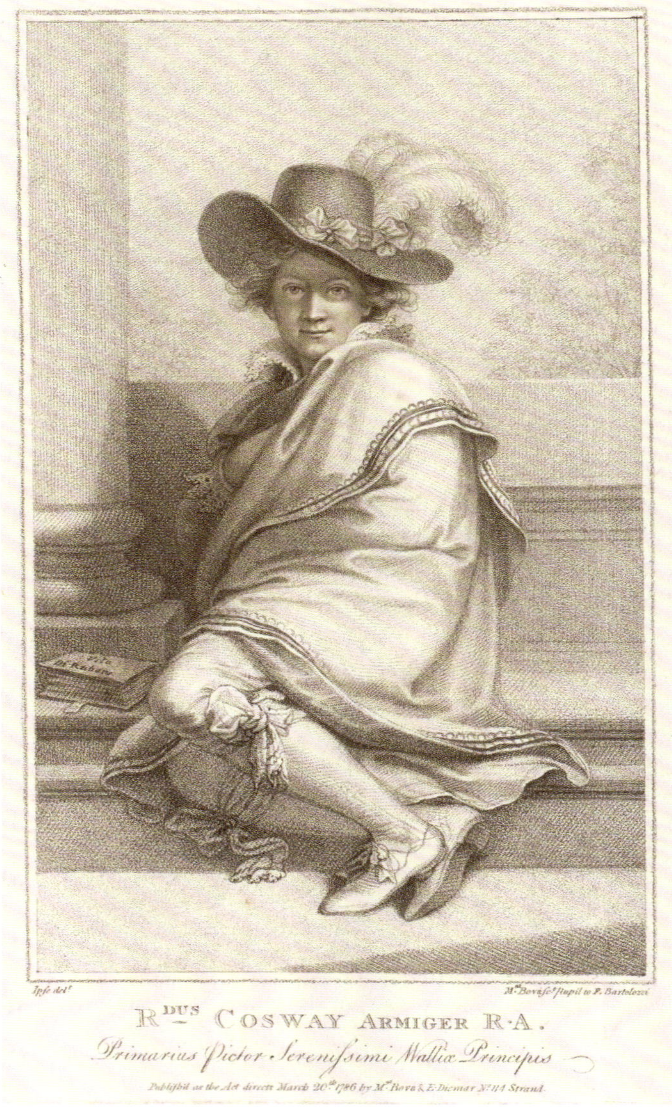

FIG. 4.4
MARIANO BOVI (1757–1813) AFTER RICHARD COSWAY (1742–1821), *Ricardus Cosway Armiger. R.A.*, 1786. Stipple printed in dark brown ink, 28.7 × 17.7 cm, RCIN 653006

an Eye, if you have not totally forgotten ye. whole countenance, I think ye. likeness will strike you.'[7] Miniatures played an important role throughout, and indeed long after the end of, George's clandestine relationship and marriage to Mrs Fitzherbert. The couple exchanged small gold lockets inset with miniatures of each other by Cosway: George's locket with her portrait was seen suspended on a ribbon at his neck as he lay on his death-bed, and the Duke of Wellington confirmed that it was buried with the king in line with the terms of his will; the miniature of George belonging to Mrs Fitzherbert, surrounded by diamonds, remained in her possession until her death and passed to her descendants (Fig. 4.8).[8]

As agent, dealer and artistic adviser to the Prince of Wales, Cosway's service to his patron was not limited merely to the supply of portrait miniatures, nor was George's patronage of miniature painters confined solely to Richard Cosway. Horace Hone was appointed Miniature Painter to the Prince of Wales in 1795 and George also acquired miniatures from William Grimaldi, Robert Bowyer and Anne Mee. Mrs Mee's early work had an affinity with Cosway's style and she was commissioned by the prince in 1812 to produce a 'Gallery of Beauties of George III' (Fig. 4.10), a series of 19 portraits of fashionable court ladies reminiscent of Sir Peter Lely's 'Windsor Beauties' painted for Anne Hyde, Duchess of York in 1662–5, or Sir Godfrey Kneller's 'Hampton Court Beauties' painted for Mary II *c.*1691. A contemporary account recorded that George was forming 'a superb boudoir for their reception'.[9] With their 'richly chased frames, antique scroll honey suckle, richly gilt … with chased Coronets &c.' they would have graced the opulent interiors of Carlton House, but no record of them survives in the inventories of 1816 or 1819.[10]

The Carlton House inventories, however, do record a unique and interesting hang of enamel miniatures commissioned from Henry Bone, a Cornish artist and miniature painter who was appointed Enamel Painter to the Prince of Wales in 1801. Bone produced enamels that conformed to the tradition of miniature painting in their technique but were unprecedented in size. He chose to copy mythological and biblical subjects by Italian sixteenth- and seventeenth-century masters, as well as works by contemporary British artists such as Sir Joshua Reynolds, including *The Death of Dido* (Fig. 4.9) and *Cymon and Iphigenia*. Twenty-one of these works in very rich carved and gilt frames hung in the Prince of Wales's Bedchamber at Carlton House (Fig. 4.11). This echoed the practice of Charles I, who had commissioned miniature copies of favoured Old Master paintings to be displayed in his private retreat at Whitehall Palace, the Cabinet Room.

Enamel miniature-painting reached its peak of technical accomplishment in the work of Henry Bone in the nineteenth century, but the first great exponent of the art was the seventeenth-century Swiss artist, Jean Petitot (Fig. 4.12). Petitot brought the

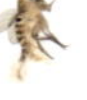

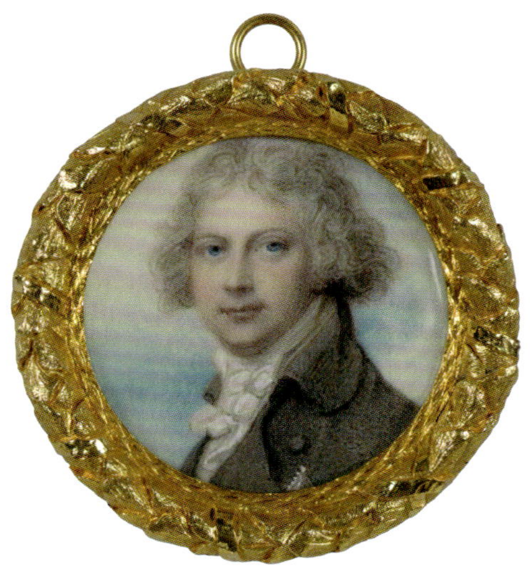

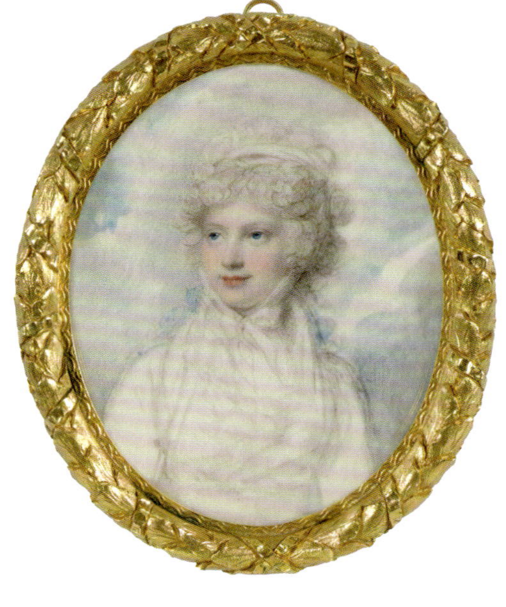

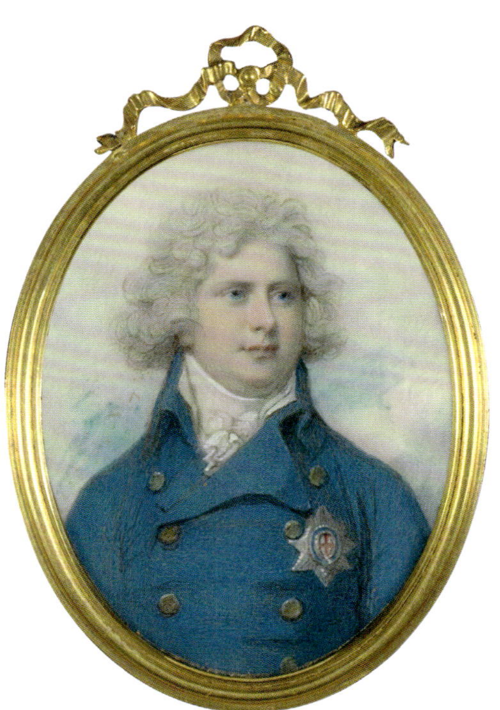

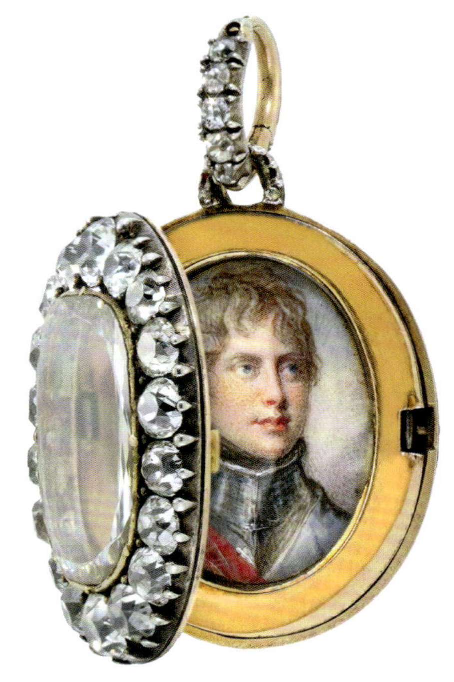

FIG. 4.5
RICHARD COSWAY (1742–1821), *George IV when Prince of Wales*, *c.*1783–4. Watercolour on ivory, 3.3 cm (diameter), RCIN 420005

FIG. 4.6
RICHARD COSWAY (1742–1821), *George IV when Prince of Wales*, *c.*1795. Watercolour on ivory, 7.5 × 5.6 cm, RCIN 421469

FIG. 4.7
RICHARD COSWAY (1742–1821), *Princess Mary, Duchess of Gloucester (1776–1857)*, *c.*1795. Watercolour on ivory, 7.9 × 6.4 cm, RCIN 420647

FIG. 4.8
RICHARD COSWAY (1742–1821), *George IV when Prince of Wales*, *c.*1800. Miniature on ivory in diamond-framed gold locket, 3.7 cm (height) (private collection)

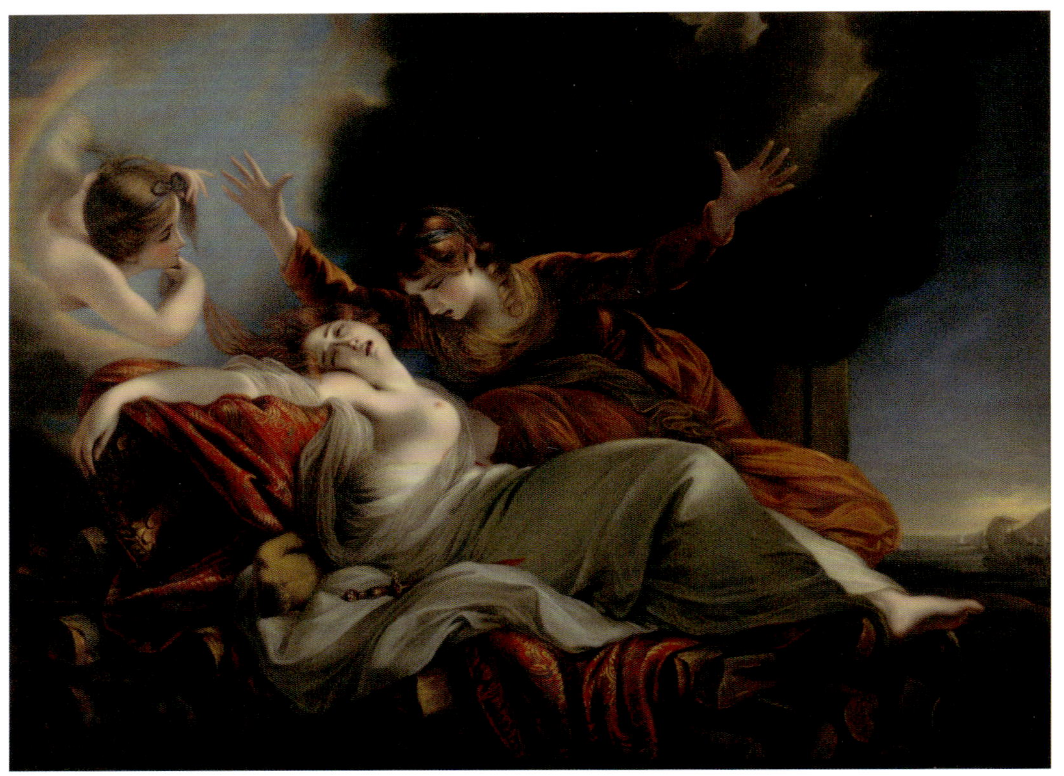

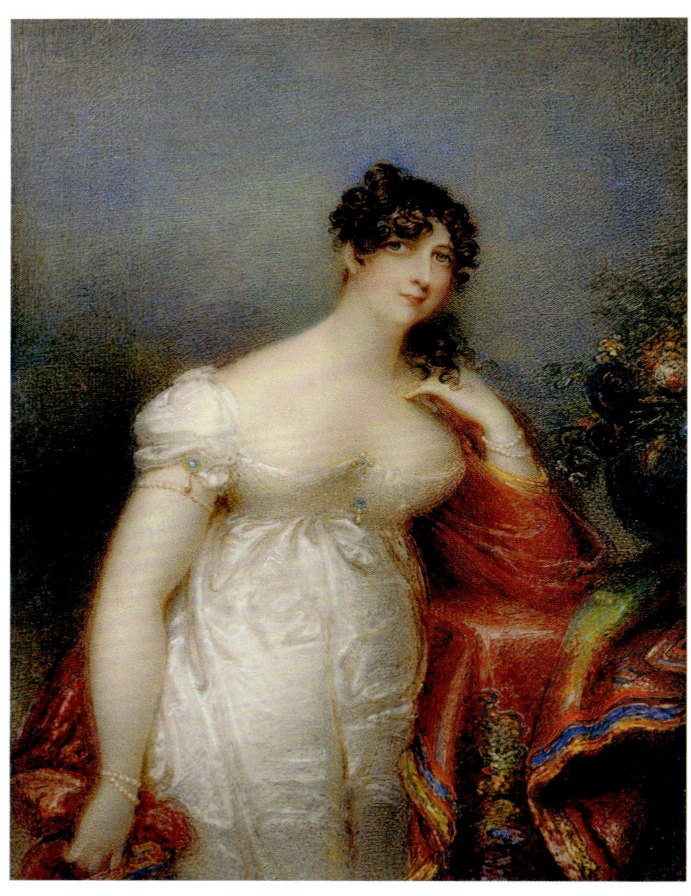

FIG. 4.9
HENRY BONE (1755–1834) AFTER SIR JOSHUA REYNOLDS (1723–92), *The Death of Dido*, 1804. Enamel on copper, 25.1 × 33.8 cm, RCIN 404284

FIG. 4.10
ANNE MEE (1770–1851), *Isabella, Marchioness of Hertford (1760–1834)*, 1812–14. Watercolour on ivory, 19.5 × 15.2 cm, RCIN 420869

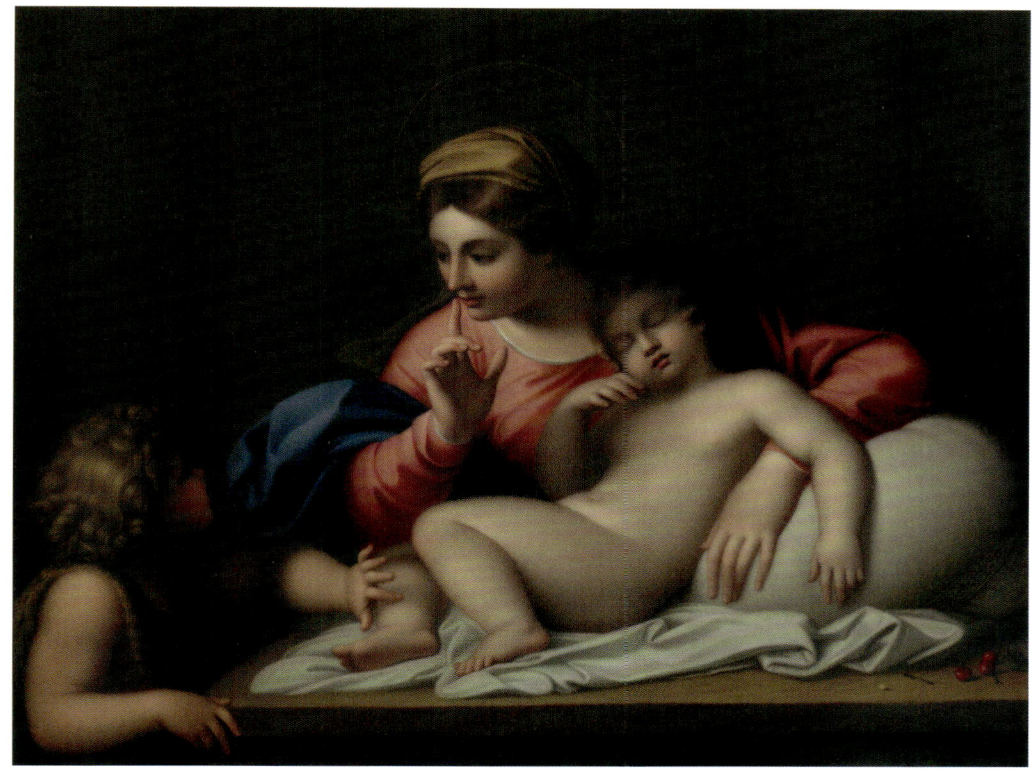

FIG. 4.11
HENRY BONE (1755–1834) AFTER ANNIBALE CARRACCI (1560–1609), *Holy Family ('The Silence')*, 1814, Enamel on copper, 24.6 × 32.0 cm, RCIN 404281

FIG. 4.12
JEAN PETITOT (1607–91), *Portrait of a Lady, called Marie, Marquise de Sévigné (1626–1696)*, *c.*1644–60. Enamel, 2.6 × 2.3 cm, RCIN 421373

FIG. 4.13
JEAN PETITOT (1607–91), *Snuffbox with inset miniature of Louis XIV*, *c.*1680. Tortoiseshell, gold, enamel, 3.9 × 7.6 × 5.4 cm, RCIN 3983

art of enamel painting to the court of Charles I in London and at the end of his long career he worked extensively for Louis XIV at the French court. George's accounts between 1799 and 1827 list the purchase of more than 50 enamels by Petitot. Of these, more than 27 represented, or claimed to represent, Louis XIV, and 14 of those were set into snuffboxes (Fig. 4.13). Many of these boxes were bought from Rundell, Bridge & Rundell, but as a large number were dispersed or re-set between 1830 and 1838, individual enamels remaining in the Royal Collection cannot now be associated with specific purchases. The records do, however, provide evidence of George IV's sustained and extensive interest in the acquisition of portraits of Louis XIV and members of his court. This sets the pattern of George's miniature collecting within the much broader framework of his fascination with French seventeenth- and eighteenth-century monarchy and patronage. George IV was not alone among British monarchs in this interest in enamels. Charles I's acquisition of enamel copies has already been noted and George II had commissioned an important series of enamel miniatures from Christian Frederick Zincke, but the scale of George IV's collecting in this area was unprecedented in British royal circles, and distinguishes his contribution to the royal collection of miniatures.

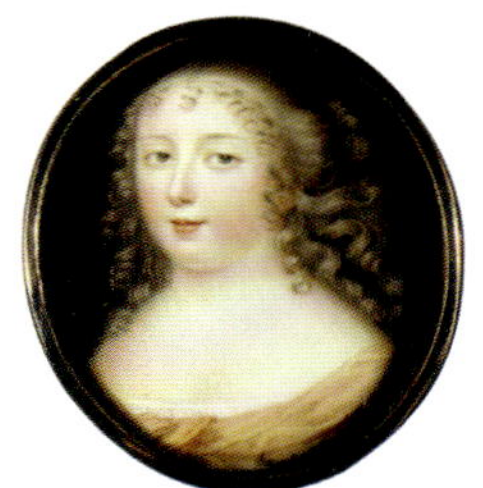

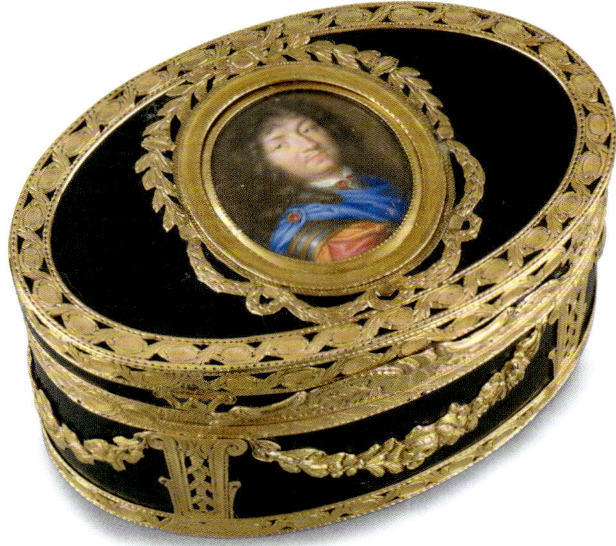

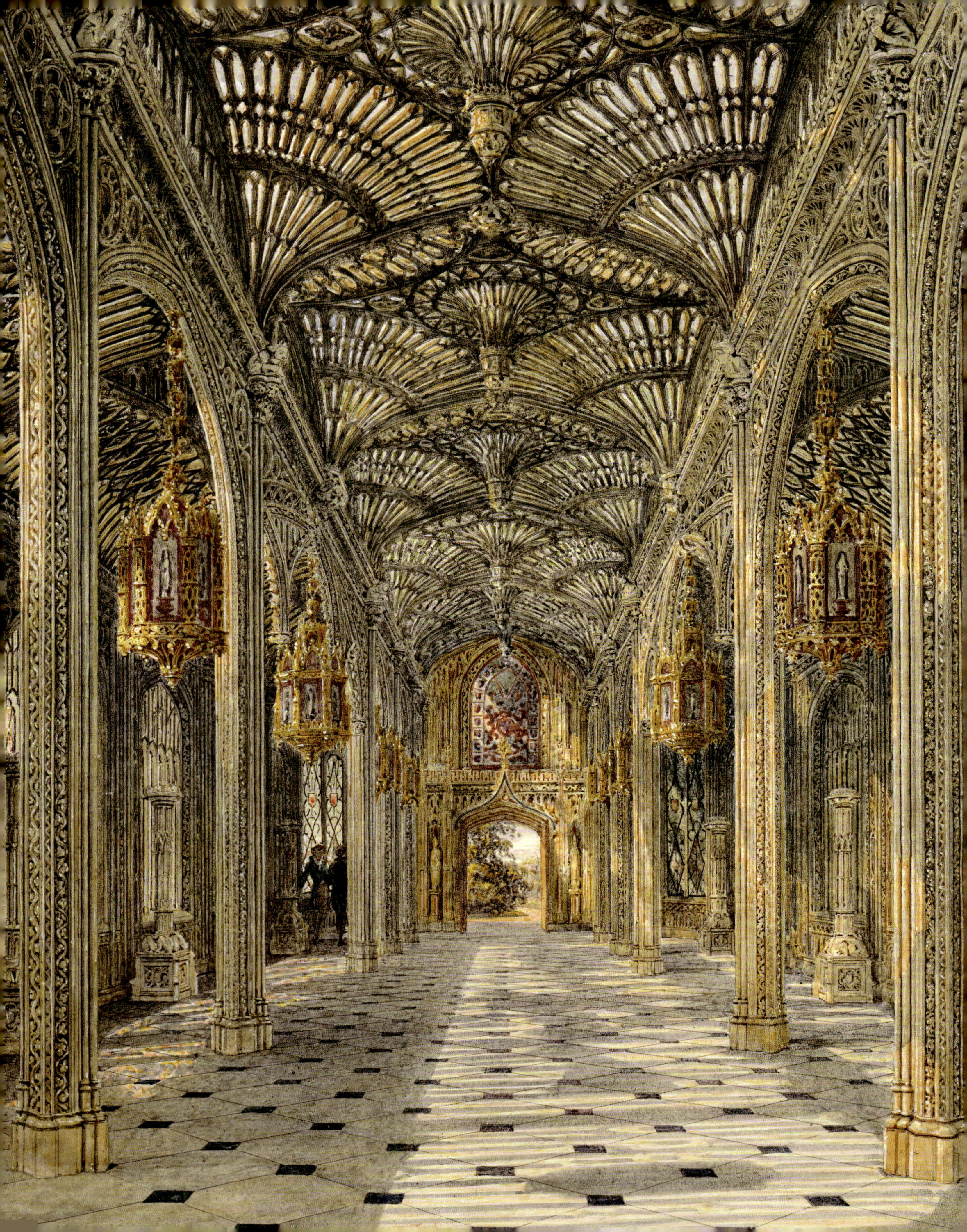

5

The CONSTRUCTION, DECORATION *and* DEMOLITION *of* GEORGE IV's CARLTON HOUSE

DAVID OAKEY

An illustration of Carlton House's reconstruction in the early 1780s confirms that when it was presented to George, Prince of Wales on his twenty-first birthday in 1783 the building was far from grand (Fig. 5.2).[1] Although facing on to London's fashionable Pall Mall,[2] with extensive grounds and direct access to St James's Park at its rear, its frontage was hemmed with private premises. Furthermore, it was on a sloping plot, meaning that in an odd arrangement for the era, the state rooms were on the ground floor (Principal Floor), with a suite of semi-state rooms below in a low-ceilinged basement (Lower Floor) opening on to the garden. It had been empty for 11 years since the death of its previous occupant, George's grandmother Princess Augusta; its interiors would have been both unfashionable and decrepit.

George III granted his son a modest £50,000 per annum from the Civil List for his establishment, to include the cost of renovating the house, to be combined with his annual revenues from the Duchy of Cornwall of £12,000. With this budget, the king envisaged 'painting it and putting handsome furniture where necessary'.[3] Yet by the end of the year the prince had dismissed his father's architect William Chambers, turning instead for inspiration to his Whig friends who gathered at Brooks's Club in St James's Street. Led by Charles James Fox, their radical politics and ardent Francophilia were informed by philosophical ideals as espoused by Voltaire and Rousseau. The 1780s was an exceptional era of peace with France that enabled French leaders of fashion such as the duc d'Orléans[4] (see chapter 2) to visit London regularly; he would become a member of this clique and friend of the young prince. It was this group's *de facto* official architect Henry Holland who was chosen to renovate Carlton House; he had trained with Lancelot 'Capability' Brown, and had recently applied the latest French-inspired neo-classical architecture, interior decoration and domestic comfort to several magnificent private residences,[5] as well as to Brooks's new building of 1776–8. We can assume the prince's French contacts were of crucial importance in organising for Holland to travel to France in 1785, almost certainly with the aim of gathering inspiration for Carlton House.[6] Although,

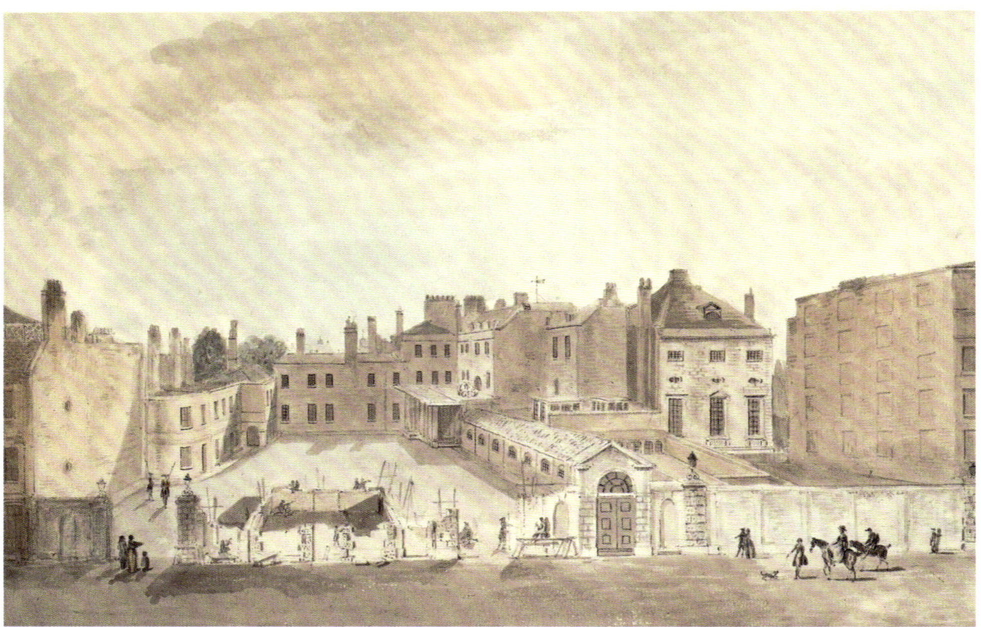

(p. 68)
FIG. 5.1
CHARLES WILD (1781–1835), *The Conservatory, looking towards the garden, Carlton House*, 1817. Watercolour and bodycolour over etched lines, 25.7 × 20.3 cm, RCIN 922191

FIG. 5.2
LOUIS BÉLANGER (1736–1816), *The Rebuilding of Carlton House*, *c.*1783. Pen and ink and watercolour over pencil, 31.8 × 44.3 cm, RCIN 913030

FIG. 5.3
HENRY HOLLAND (1745–1806), *Carlton Pallace with designs for the additions*, 1789. Pen and ink with wash and pencil annotations, 31.0 × 43.0 cm (British Library, London: Crace Port 12.9.(4))

FIG. 5.4
HENRY HOLLAND (1745–1806), *Carleton House, October 1794. Plan of the Principal Floor* (partially unrealised), 1794. Pen and ink with watercolour and wash, 34.0 × 48.6 cm, RCIN 918943

unlike many of his rivals, Holland did not have the opportunity to study Classical architecture first-hand, his work demonstrates a command of the manuals on the style that were available by this time, such as Stuart and Revett's *Antiquities of Athens* (1762) and Jean-François de Neufforge's *Recueil Elémentaire d'Architecture* (1757–80). In 1794–7, to add authenticity to his decorative choices, he sent his young employee, Charles Heathcote Tatham, to Italy to make drawings and retrieve Classical architectural fragments for replication at Carlton House.[7]

Holland's Carlton House

Despite its drastically altered appearance, an early 'working' plan (Fig. 5.3) reveals how much of the old house, shown in brown, was retained by Holland; here only the entrance areas and staircase have been erased and replaced. A new eastern wing built slightly later would balance the house (Fig. 5.4), containing kitchens and offices, accommodation for servants and storage of wine and coal in its basements. This 'staged' construction was probably executed both for financial reasons,[8] and because the prince remained in residence while works were carried out. The entire house, old and new, was united behind a uniform Portland stone rustication and centred with a striking hexastyle portico of colossal Corinthian columns (Fig. 5.5). According to the French concept of *convenance*, this order was reserved only for the most important public or royal buildings, here highlighted by the inclusion of a magnificent sculptural royal crest within the pediment. The portico was probably based on the Maison Carrée in Nîmes, lauded in the 1780s by the French neo-classicist Charles-Louis Clérisseau as being among the most complete surviving examples of a Roman temple (Fig. 5.6).[9] Its recently deciphered dedication to the sons of Emperor Augustus, 'the princes of youth', perhaps added to its appeal.[10] Holland spliced style and practicality in the portico, which for the first time in England acted as a *porte cochère* under which carriages could shelter on arrival at the entrance, as recommended by the French architectural theoretician Nicolas Le Camus de Mézières.[11] An architectural screen was devised to act as an effective cordon that could still afford ample views of the house beyond; here Holland may have been influenced by both Marie-Joseph Peyre's unexecuted plans for the Hôtel de Condé and Pierre Rousseau's Hôtel de Salm (which he must have seen during his visit to Paris) and the three screens, or 'peristyles', illustrated in Neufforge 'to enrich a court, such as those at palaces and grand houses'.[12] The doubling of Ionic columns on the screen was an elegant distribution used by Le Vau on the colonnade of the Grand Trianon at Versailles,[13] but a contemporary neo-classical flourish was intended in the sculptural decoration of vases (made from Eleanor Coade's artificial stone) based on 'drawings from William Hamilton's Collection in the Museum'.[14] The screen turned the house into a Parisian-style *hôtel entre cour et jardin*; an effect that would have been enhanced if plans for extra wings and lodges either side of the court (in a design that mirrored the

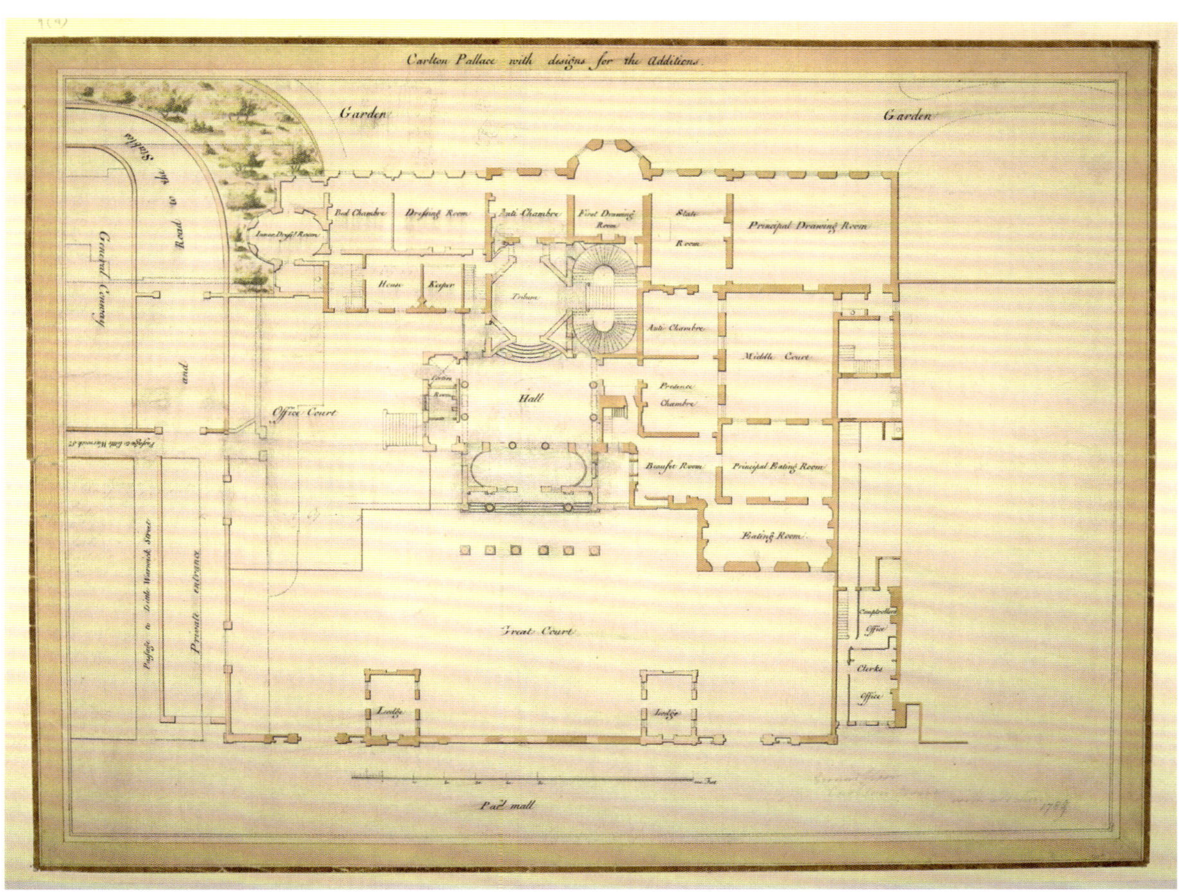
Carlton Pallace with designs for the Additions
Garden
Garden
Road to the Stables
and
Passage to Little Warwick Street
Private entrance
Bed Chamber
Dressing Room
Anti Chamber
First Drawing Room
State Room
Principal Drawing Room
House Keeper
Tribune
Anti Chambre
Middle Court
Hall
Office Court
Presence Chambre
Bouffet Room
Principal Eating Room
Eating Room
Great Court
Office
Clerks Office
Lodge
Lodge
Pall mall

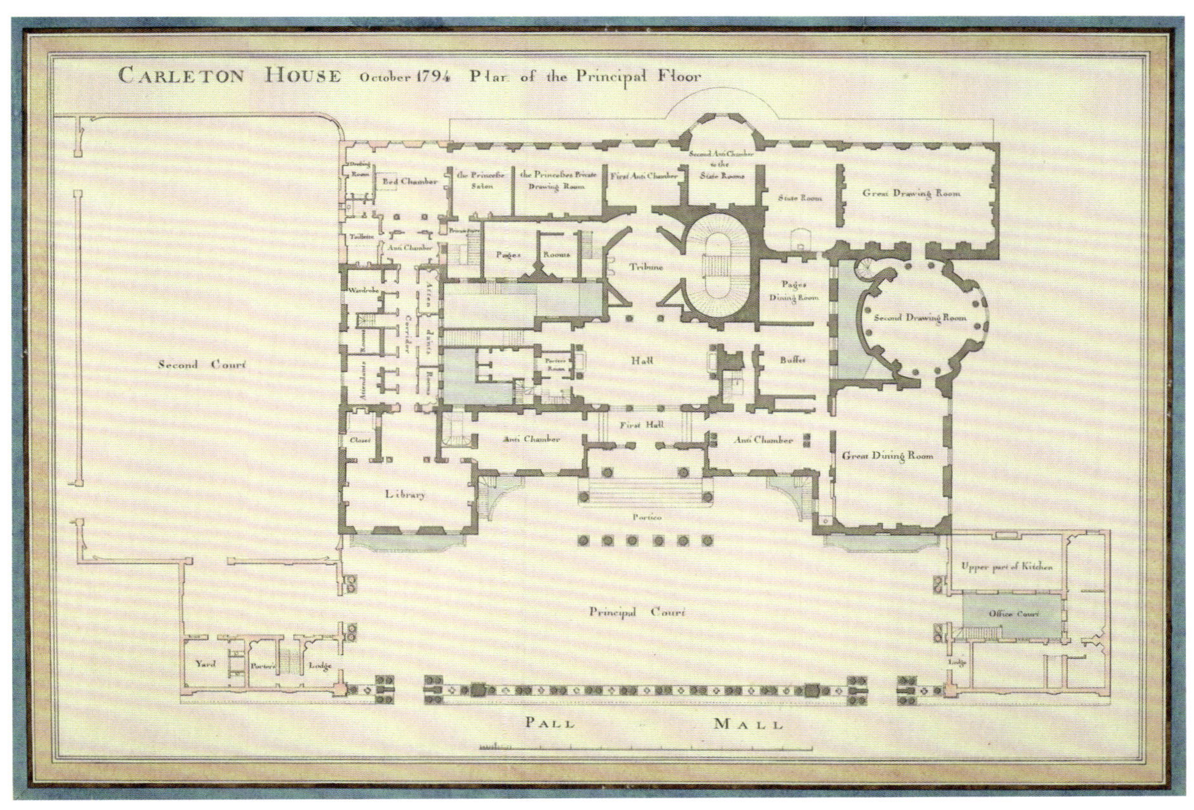
CARLETON HOUSE October 1794 Plan of the Principal Floor
Bed Chamber
the Princesses Private Drawing Room
First Anti Chamber
Second Anti Chamber to the State Rooms
State Room
Great Drawing Room
Toilette
Anti Chamber
Pages Rooms
Tribune
Pages Dining Room
Wardrobe
Second Drawing Room
Second Court
Hall
Buffet
First Hall
Anti Chamber
Anti Chamber
Great Dining Room
Closet
Library
Portico
Upper part of Kitchen
Principal Court
Office Court
Yard
Porters
Lodge
Lodge
PALL MALL

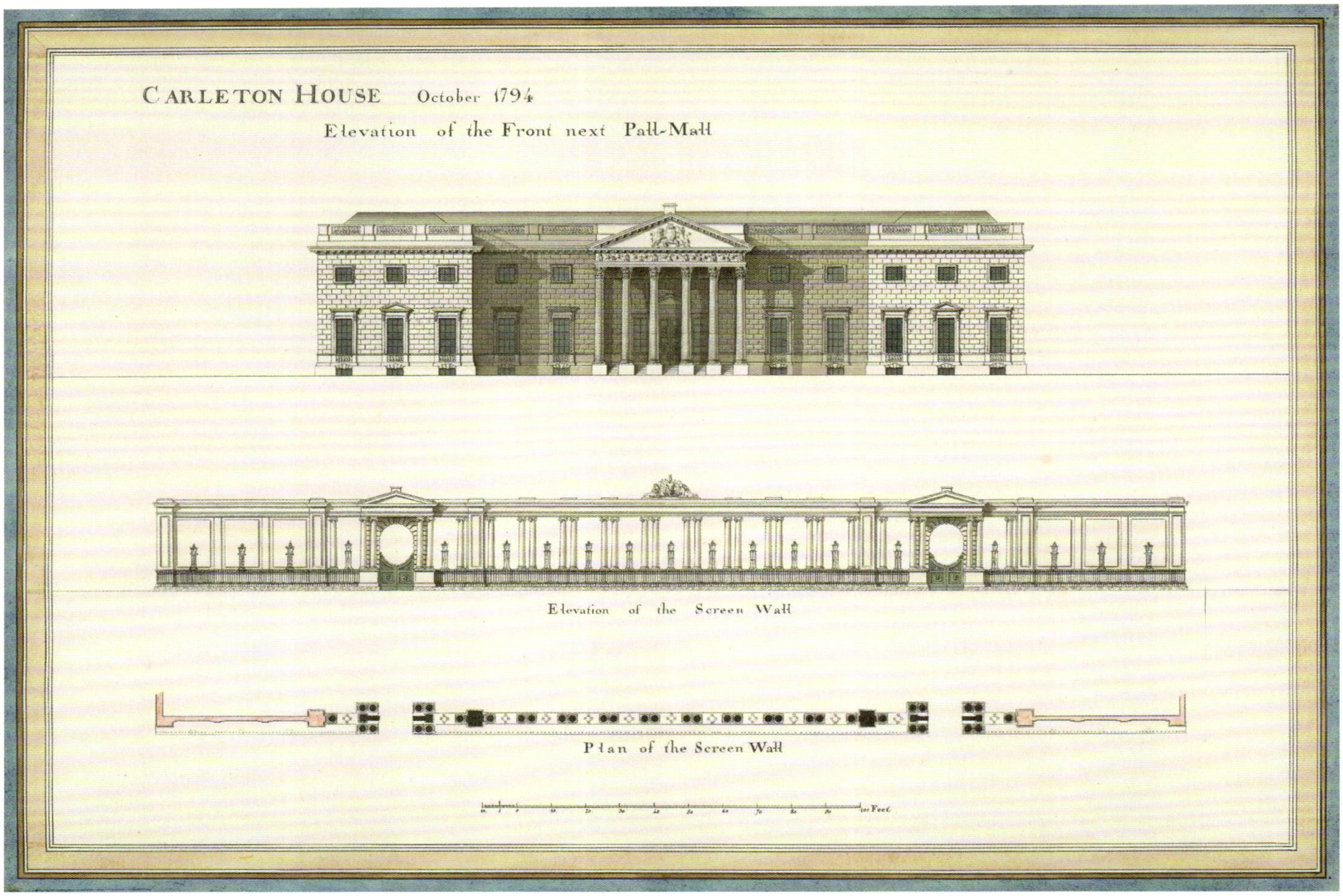

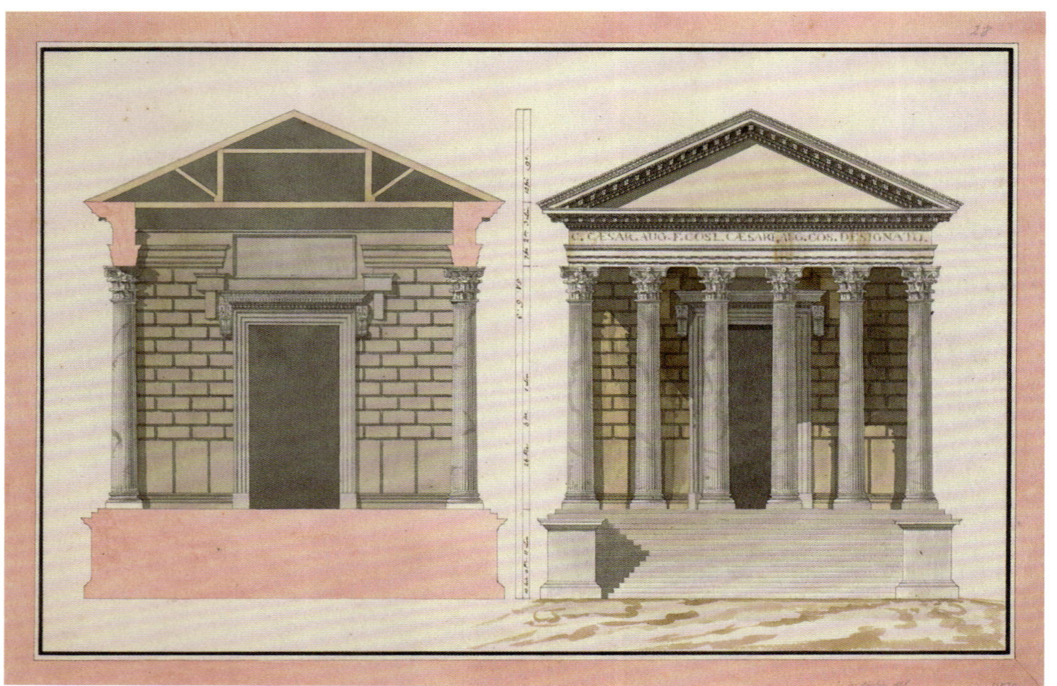

FIG. 5.5
HENRY HOLLAND (1745–1806), *Carleton House, October 1794. Elevation of the Front next Pall-Mall*, 1794. Pen and ink with pencil and wash, 33.5 × 49.3 cm, RCIN 918946

FIG. 5.6
WILLIAM KIRBY (active 1769), *Maison Carré, Nîmes*, *c.*1769. Pen and ink with watercolour over pencil, 35.1 × 52.8 cm, RCIN 911570

(opposite)
FIG. 5.7
HENRY HOLLAND (1745–1806), *Carleton House: section through the Portico, Hall and Tribune*, *c.*1787. Pen and ink with watercolour over pencil, 35.4 × 71.8 cm (Yale Center for British Art, New Haven, CT: B1975.2.640)

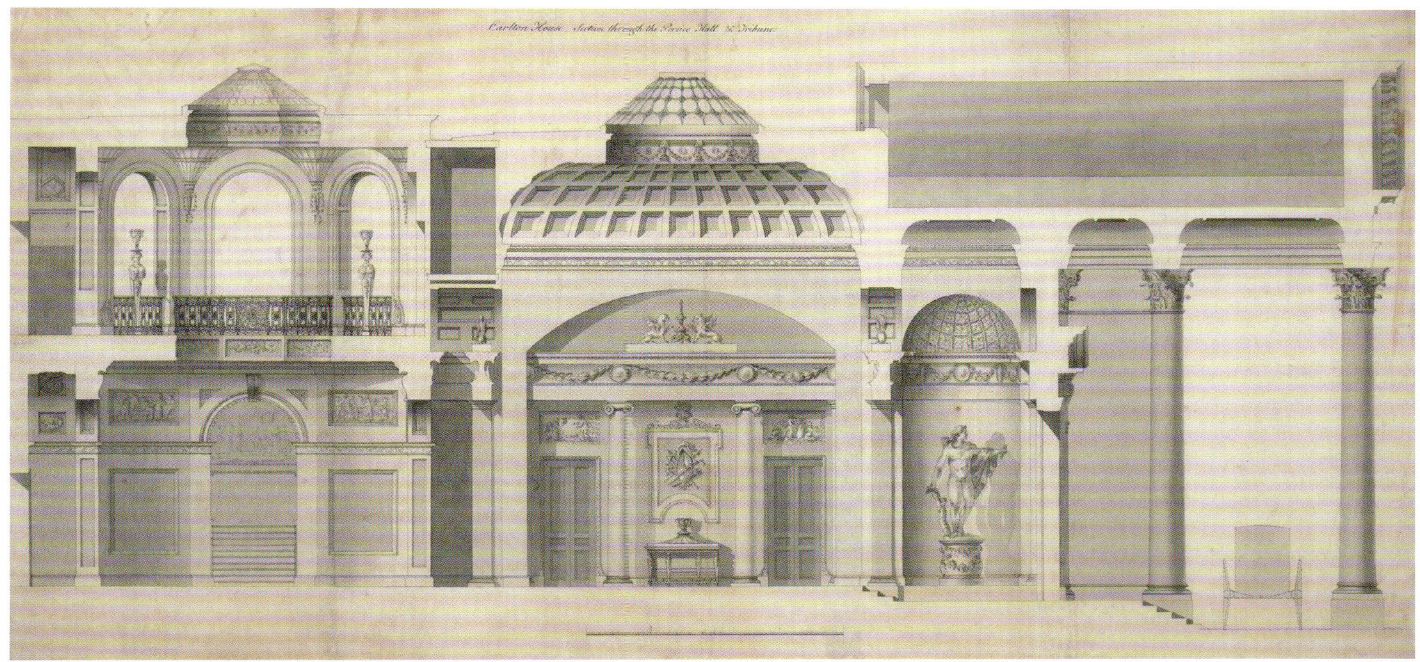

screen) had been executed. Architectural historians have referred to Peyre's designs for the Hôtel de Condé as 'a Roman version of a Parisian townhouse';[15] Carlton House was in much the same category. The new frontage was both an ingenious solution to the problems presented by the pre-existing situation, and a striking statement of modernity and sophistication.

Inside, new entrance areas were fitted out at considerable expense, estimated at £6,500 by Holland in 1784.[16] The Entrance Hall (Figs 5.7 and 5.8) was defined by scagliola columns and a geometrically tiled floor reflected by a simple coffered ceiling with an elaborately decorated skylight, shown to us fully in Holland's surviving sketchbooks (Fig. 5.9). Here he deployed Tatham's designs for sculptural schemes on the architraves.[17] the decorative painter Jirouard Le Girardy executed four imitation bas-reliefs of *trofés* [*trophées*] *De Guerre* painted against a gold ground,[18] while the four niches contained 12-foot- (3.5-metre) high sculptures of Antinous, Apollo, Prudence and Fortitude by John Baptist Giannelli.[19] With a chair passage leading directly to a side gate, it was a convenient arrival and departure point for sedan chairs. Beyond was the innovative, double-height, octagonal 'tribune', the shape perhaps inspired by the Tower of the Winds as featured in Stuart and Revett's *Antiquities*.[20] (Tribunes were a signature of Holland's, but at his previous projects they had always been circular.) The upper tribune area was a dramatic space, with a wide variation of light and dark, sweeping vaulting and archways that offered teasing glimpses of spaces beyond (Fig. 5.10). The adjoining new imperial staircase featured a balustrade of considerable complexity, designed by Holland and executed by Nathan Beetham,[21] with figures of Atlas bearing a map of the world with a wind dial, Time with a clock and several Coade stone eagles (Fig. 5.11). Most extraordinary of all was the installation of two enamel-painted glass-filled half-domes in the ceiling by John Theodore Perrache (Fig. 5.12).[22] A bricklayer's bill for 'making a furnace for Mr Parrache ... for enamelling glass'[23] confirms the glass for this installation was produced on site. Another new space was the circular, 40-foot- (12-metre) wide Music Room. Built in what had previously been a courtyard, it created communication between the two large entertaining spaces, the Great Drawing Room and the Dining Room. In his choice of a circular space here, Holland may have been evoking the Pavillon de Musique built for the comtesse de Provence in 1784 at Versailles by Jean-François Chalgrin.

Holland aligned all the doorways of the state rooms running along the garden front of the house on the Lower and Principal floors, and along the axis of the house, creating enfilades, an unmistakably French feature that prompted Horace Walpole on his visit in 1785 to exclaim the house was 'full of perspectives'.[24] Indeed, Carlton House's new plan contained no corridors, following the teachings of the French architectural theorist Jacques-François Blondel,[25] and was devised as a succession of different *appartements*, an idea that had been prevalent in

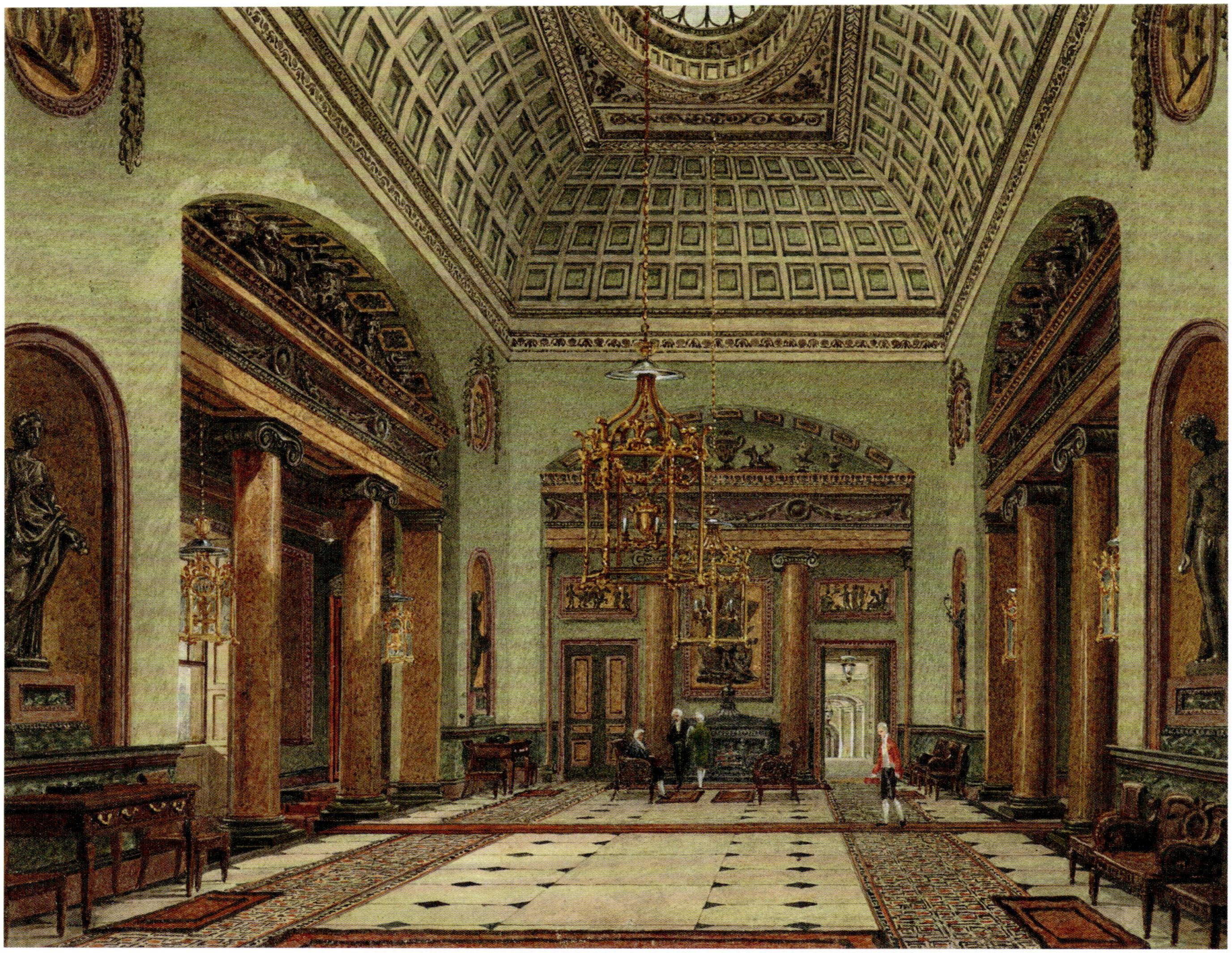

French house planning since the early eighteenth century. On passing through the entrance areas, the rooms towards the west, the Great Drawing Room, Music Room and Dining Room, were public state apartments for entertaining, what Blondel would have termed an *appartement de parade*. To the east were semi-private rooms for official business and meetings, the Council Chamber and ceremonial State Bedchamber, an *appartement de société*. (The inclusion of a State Bedchamber, for private audiences, was already old-fashioned for the 1780s, but was probably a further concession to the French tradition of house design.) The suite of rooms on the Lower Floor opening on to the garden was an *appartement de commodité* reserved for the prince's private relaxation and the entertainment of close friends, in the mode of the *petit appartement de la reine* at Versailles, which suited the otherwise problematic low ceilings. This suite

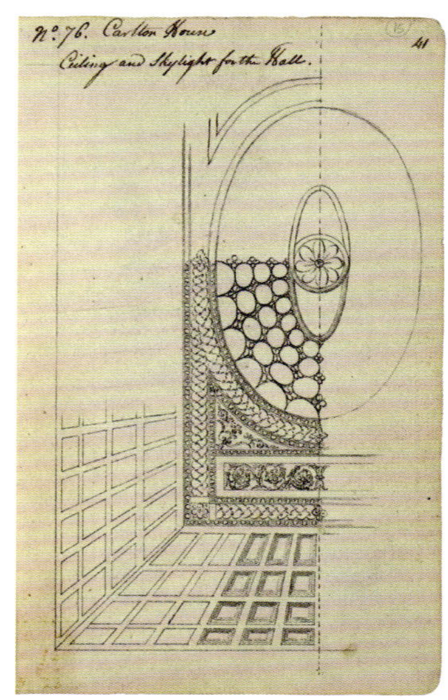

FIG. 5.8
CHARLES WILD (1781–1835), *The Hall of Entrance or Great Hall, Carlton House*, 1819. Watercolour and bodycolour, 20.2 × 25.6 cm, RCIN 922171

FIG. 5.9
HENRY HOLLAND (1745–1806), CHARLES HEATHCOTE TATHAM (1772–1842) and JEAN PIERRE THEODORE TRECOURT (d. *c*.1795), *Carlton House: design for ceiling and skylight of the entrance hall*, 1796. Pen and ink with pencil, 19.0 × 12.5 cm (RIBA Collections: SKB122/3, fol. 15r)

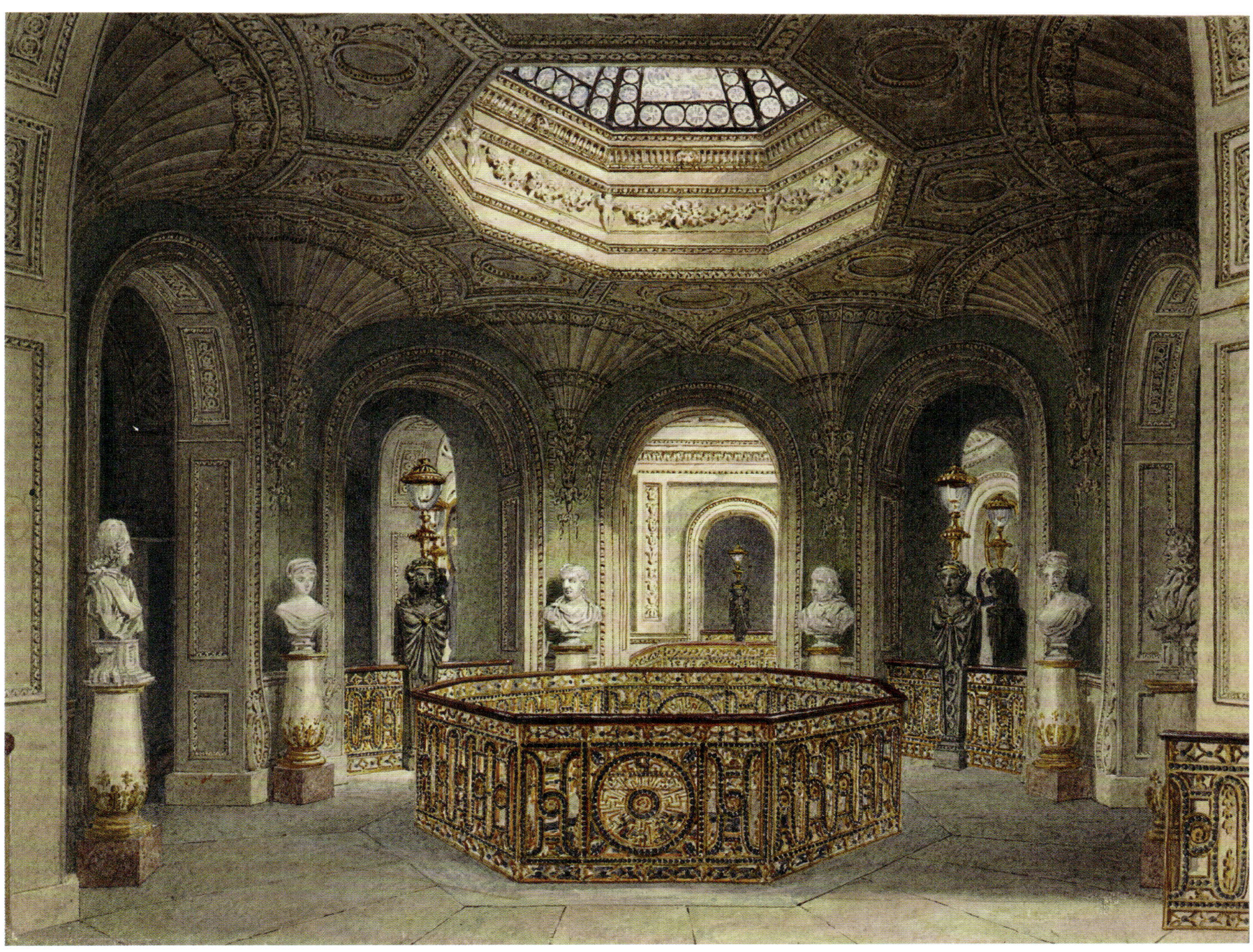

FIG. 5.10
CHARLES WILD (1781–1835), *The Gallery of the Staircase, Carlton House*, 1819. Watercolour and bodycolour, 19.5 × 25.4 cm, RCIN 922174

featured a private dining room, a gallery, a small library, the famous Chinese Drawing Room and bathrooms (Holland had placed bathrooms inside the living quarters at his other projects, including Claremont and Benham, following the most up-to-date French fashion). An elaborate entrance doorway was designed for this apartment to feature two female caryatids borrowed from the Erechtheion in Athens,[26] perhaps in emulation of the dining room of the Hôtel de Voyer in Paris, which had been adapted by Charles de Wailly in the early 1760s. The carver Thomas Alwood billed for 'a tablet emblem of familiarity' to surmount this doorway, further confirming the intended use of these rooms for the entertainment of friends, but ultimately the design was not executed.[27] Information about the upper 'attic' floor of the house is scant, except that it was the location of the prince's sleeping quarters for nearly all of the house's history, and the Armoury, which over the years would grow to occupy several rooms.

The house was equipped with an extensive new mews, essential to house the young prince's burgeoning collection of horses and elaborate carriages. It was connected to the front courtyard by a track, raised above the garden, and to the rear gate into the park. Most impressive was the two-storey riding house, where the riding school, accessed by ramps, was placed over the coach houses and forges, supported by a system of strong Purbeck stone pillars and bars.[28] There was space for at least 60 horses, with accommodation for the stable hands and

FIG. 5.11
UNKNOWN MAKER, *Eagle ornament from the staircase at Carlton House*, *c.*1784. Plaster (Sir John Soane's Museum, London: M431)

FIG. 5.12
AFTER JOHN THEODORE PERRACHE (b. 1744), *A View of the Dome of the Grand Staircase at Charlton House*, *c.*1798. Etching, 46.5 × 35.0 cm, RCIN 702857

FIG. 5.13
HENRY HOLLAND (1745–1806), *Carleton House. Elevation of the Entrance to Riding House*, *c.* 1786. Pen and ink and watercolour over pencil, 22.0 × 36.6 cm, RCIN 918953

FIG. 5.14
ATTRIBUTED TO FRANÇOIS RÉMOND (1747–1812), *Candelabrum*, *c.*1787. Gilt bronze, enamel, 149.8 × 58.4 × 35.6 cm, RCIN 2692

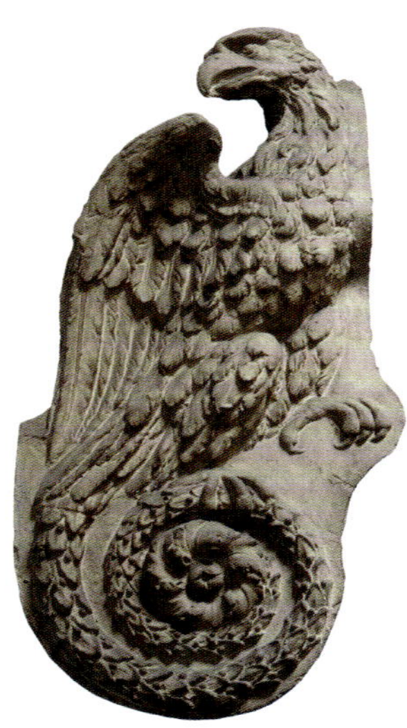

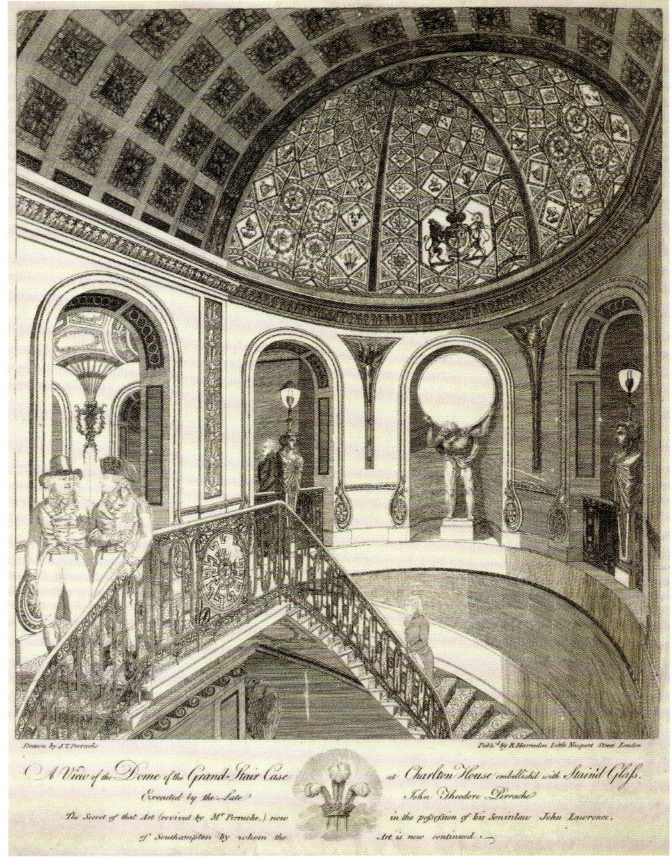

other staff located above the stables themselves.[29] Its garden front was ornamented by a magnificent doorcase with alcove costing around £9,000,[30] which seems related to the garden alcove and screen for Lansdowne House designed and built by Clérisseau for Lord Shelburne around 1772 (Fig. 5.13).[31]

The interior decoration

When Horace Walpole saw the house in 1785 he wrote to the Countess of Upper Ossory: 'We went to see the Prince's new palace in Pall Mall; and were charmed. It will be the most perfect in Europe. There is an august simplicity that astonished me. You cannot call it magnificent; it is the taste and propriety that strike. Every ornament is at a proper distance, and not one too large, but all delicate and new.'[32] By 1787 the architectural additions were largely complete,[33] but as the French writer Louis-Sébastien Mercier warned in 1782, 'when a house has been built, nothing has yet been done; one has not reached a fraction of the expense … the interior takes three times longer than the construction.'[34] The impetus for the decoration of the interiors would again be French; the château de Bagatelle, built by François-Joseph Bélanger and decorated by his brother-in-law Jean-Démosthène Dugourc for the prince's friend the comte d'Artois (later Charles X), seems to have been a key reference point, as it would also be at Brighton (see chapter 10). Bélanger was probably already a personal associate of Holland; like Clérisseau, he too had worked for the prince's friend Lord Shelburne, and further links are hinted at by his brother Louis's painting of Carlton House (see Fig. 5.2).[35] Although the prince could not directly employ the Bélanger–Dugourc team working at Bagatelle, he probably hoped to replicate it.

Thus, at Carlton House, Holland first collaborated with Frenchman Guillaume Gaubert, who had worked with a coterie of French craftsmen for George's friends the Duke and Duchess of Devonshire at Chatsworth in the 1770s. No doubt to George's delight, 1787 saw the arrival in London of the established Parisian *marchand-mercier*, Dominque Daguerre,[36] who had already enjoyed a notable career in France, where his clients had included Queen Marie Antoinette. Holland's journey to Paris in 1785 may have been undertaken at least in part to encourage the Frenchman to work for the prince; Daguerre would later claim *le prince ma envoyé chercher* ('the prince sent [him] to find me').[37] Unlike Gaubert, Daguerre was employed on an equal footing to Holland, collecting a commission of 5 per cent on all work he ordered.[38] His arrival ushered in a new phase of heightened sophistication which demonstrated the skills of decorative painters such as Biagio Rebecca, Jean-Jacques Boileau and Louis-André Delabrière, the last two recorded by John Woody Papworth in 1851 as being brought over by the wallpaper designer John Sheringham 'to do

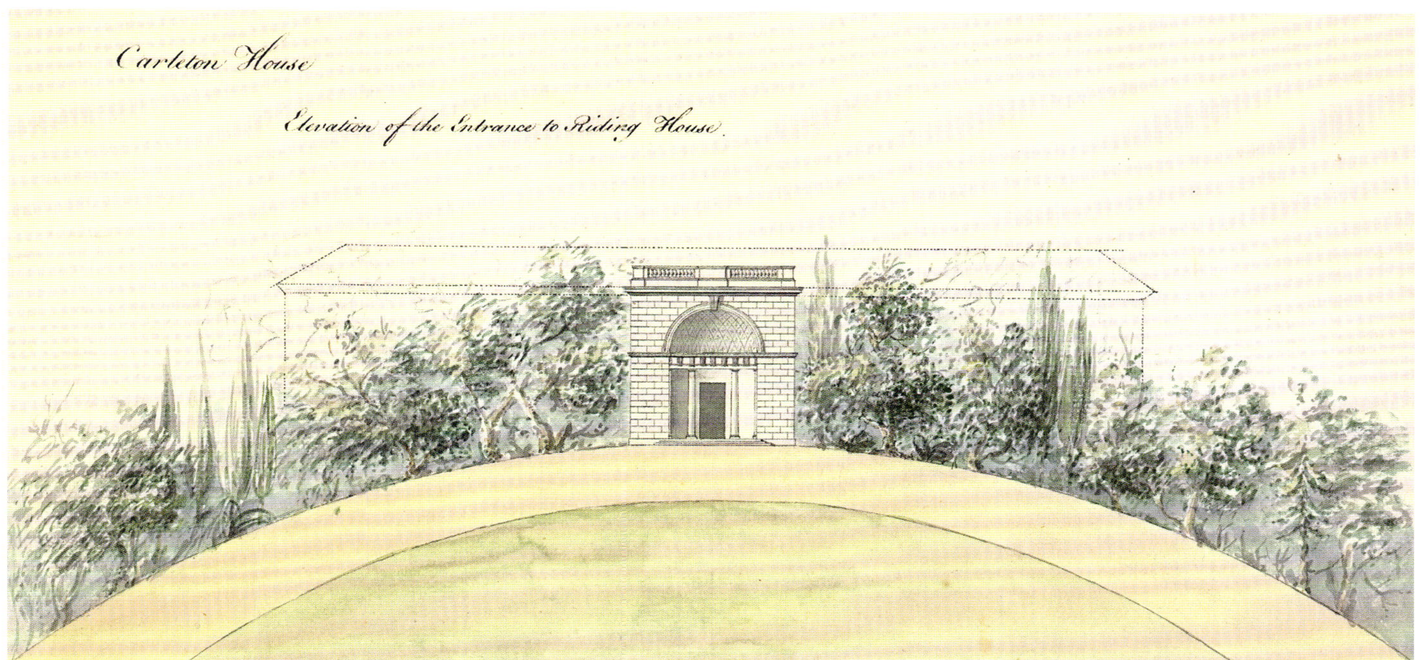

Carlton House under Henry Holland'.[39] Daguerre did not just act as an interior designer but also as a dealer in magnificent French furniture and could organise elaborate fixtures and fittings such as chimneypieces and candelabra by the Parisian *bronzier* François Rémond (Fig. 5.14).[40]

Some idea of the magnificent textiles used to decorate the house during this era is given by the silk brocade in the White Drawing Room at Houghton Hall in Norfolk which was a gift from the prince to his chamberlain, the 4th Earl of Cholmondeley, around 1797.[41] This material imitates the products of Lyons, demonstrating how the skill of English silk-weavers neared that of their French rivals. Edward Hasted recalled how 'in the year 1789 I saw in Mr. Calloway's looms the richest and most beautiful piece of silk furniture for the Prince of Wales's Palace of Carlton House'.[42] In 1790, 416 yards (380 metres) of the 'richest white brocade with an eagle pattern for the gallery at Carlton House' from Ibbetson, Barlow & Clarke cost an incredible £2,403.[43]

The Chinese Drawing Room on the Lower Floor (constructed *c.*1788–90) was conceived in the same vein as the so-called Turkish boudoirs created for members of the French aristocracy in the 1780s. Chinoiserie in the interior had declined in popularity with the rise of neo-classicism, and its idiosyncratic selection by the prince at this time was the earliest example of a taste that would become more pronounced at Brighton Pavilion. The prince's predilection for chinoiserie is sometimes traced to his mother Queen Charlotte but it was perhaps as much a result of interest

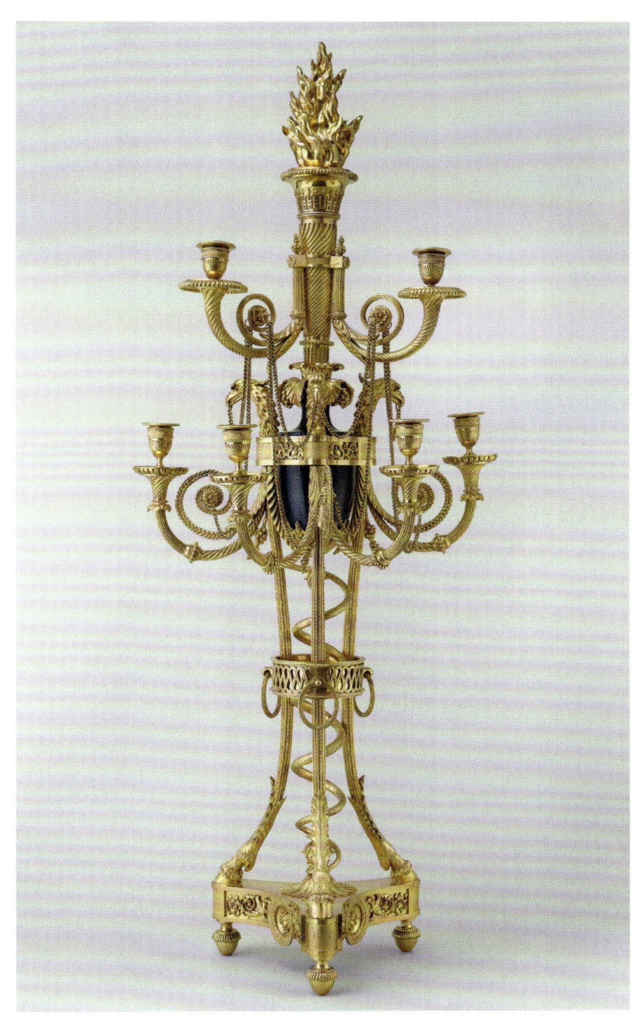

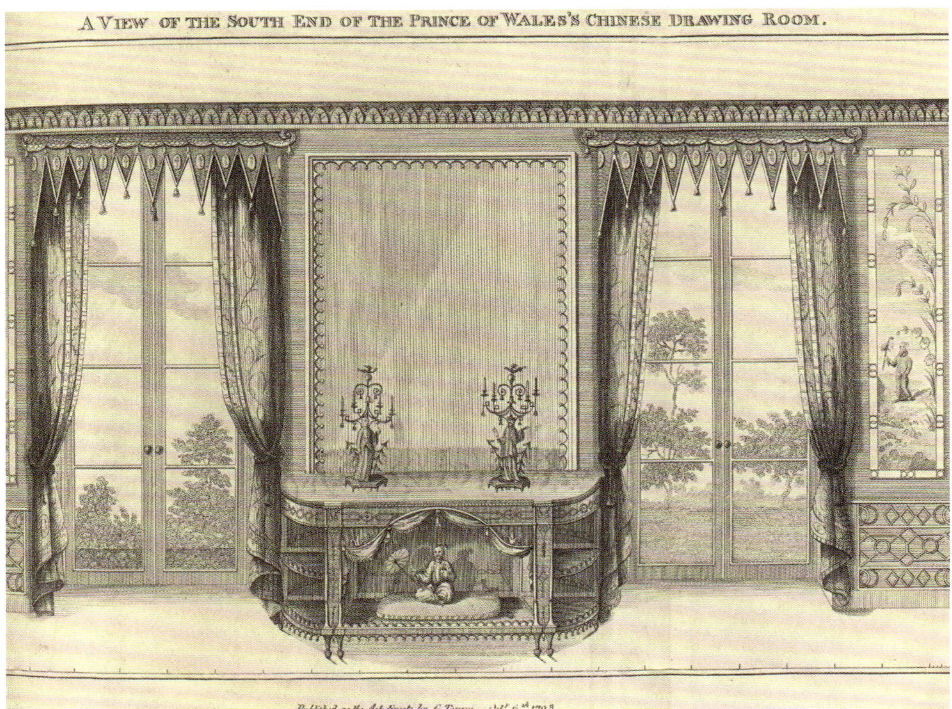

FIG. 5.15
THOMAS SHERATON (1751–1806), *A View of the South End of the Prince of Wales's Chinese Drawing Room*, 1793. Etching and engraving, 26.4 × 30.0 cm (sheet), RCIN 1115242

FIG. 5.16
ATTRIBUTED TO ADAM WEISWEILER (1744–1820), *One of a pair of console tables*, c.1787–90. Oak, ebony, gilt and painted bronze, marble, 96.0 × 162.0 × 52.0 cm, RCIN 181

FIG. 5.17
CHARLES WILD (1781–1835), *The Ante Chamber to the Throne Room, Carlton House*, 1816. Watercolour and bodycolour over etched lines, 20.3 × 25.4 cm, RCIN 922179

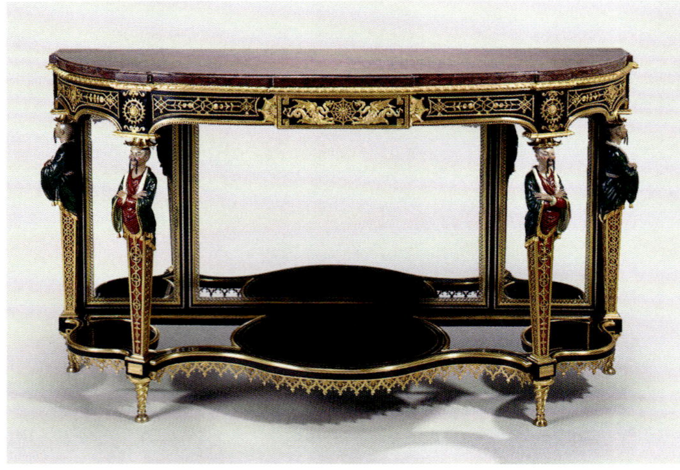

in the output of the designers working for the prince's French friends. Dugourc made drawings of a Chinese cabinet for installation at the Escorial outside Madrid in 1786 and Bélanger had used the style for the garden buildings at Bagatelle; another of his projects, the Folie Saint-James, completed around the same time, included a Chinese pavilion. Notably the prince planned to construct such a pavilion at Carlton House; in 1789 the builder John Groves charged for 'measured work in the brickwork to enclose ... the basement of the Chinese Temple',[44] although this was probably all that was built. The Chinese Drawing Room drew special attention, appearing in detail in Thomas Sheraton's *Cabinet Maker's and Upholsterer's Drawing Book* (Fig. 5.15).[45] It was here that Daguerre and Holland seem to have worked together most successfully, creating both an interior scheme and a set of furnishings of exquisite complexity, and much as in the French *turquerie* versions, with a range of bespoke decorative objects (Fig. 5.16).[46]

By comparing Holland's surviving drawings with the depictions of the house in Pyne's *Royal Residences*, it is clear that many aspects of his design survived any later architectural interventions. The original Throne Room retained Holland's ceiling scheme with sphinxes, symbolic of wisdom, exactly as in his sketchbooks (Fig. 5.17). Likewise, the original ceiling survived in the Great Dining Room, even after its reinvention as the Crimson Drawing Room (see below). The spectacular Great Drawing Room (later the Throne Room: Fig. 5.18) appeared to emulate examples such as the salon at the château de Brunoy designed by Dugourc for the comte de Provence. The earlier appearances of the circular Music Room and Great Dining Room are unknown, but both featured scagliola, fashionable at the time. In 1789 the renowned 'scagliolist' Domenico Bartoli installed 16 pilasters in *rosso sanguigno* and other elements in green *cipollino* in the Dining Room and columns of *porfido rosso* in the Music Room.[47] In the former room this had vanished behind crimson velvet swags by the time Pyne's views were painted, but in the

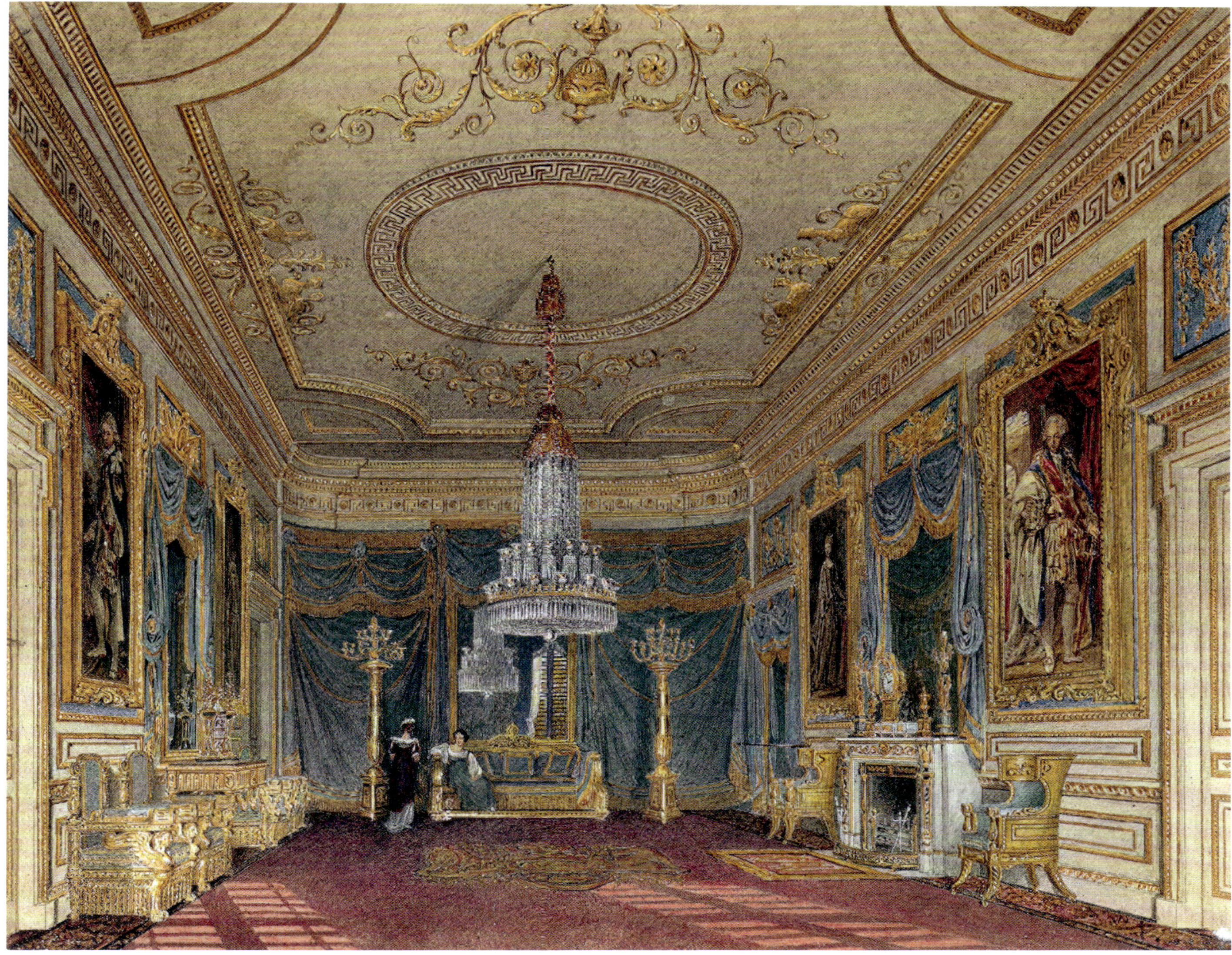

latter the scagliola still defined the scheme, and the intricate painted decoration visible in the watercolour probably also dated from the Holland era (Fig. 5.19).

Carlton House after Holland

Daguerre's sudden death in 1796, Holland's declining involvement[48] and external shifts in taste and fashion, coupled with alterations in the prince's personal circumstances and outlook, meant that the end of the century was a transitional period at Carlton House. The prince's increasing political importance as George III's health declined would see his youthful radicalism gradually replaced with an entrenched conservatism. War with France had returned in 1794, making the use of French products, designers and craftsmen problematic,[49] and the rise of Napoleon not only presented the nation with a new threat, but the prince with a rival in magnificence. The glamorous, Roman-inspired *Style Empire* devised by the French emperor's architects Charles Percier and Pierre-François-Léonard Fontaine set a new standard. George lost interest in the academic neo-classicism that underpinned the design of the house in the 1780s, instead displaying a growing predilection for the Gothic, which, along with obvious connotations of antiquarianism and historicity, was considered to be reassuringly British.

The prince turned to his friend Walsh Porter for inspiration in these renovations. Porter was an aesthete, socialite and antiquary, claiming descent from Endymion Porter, a seventeenth-century art collector and supporter of Charles I.[50] He had employed his architect Thomas Hopper to build a series of extraordinary

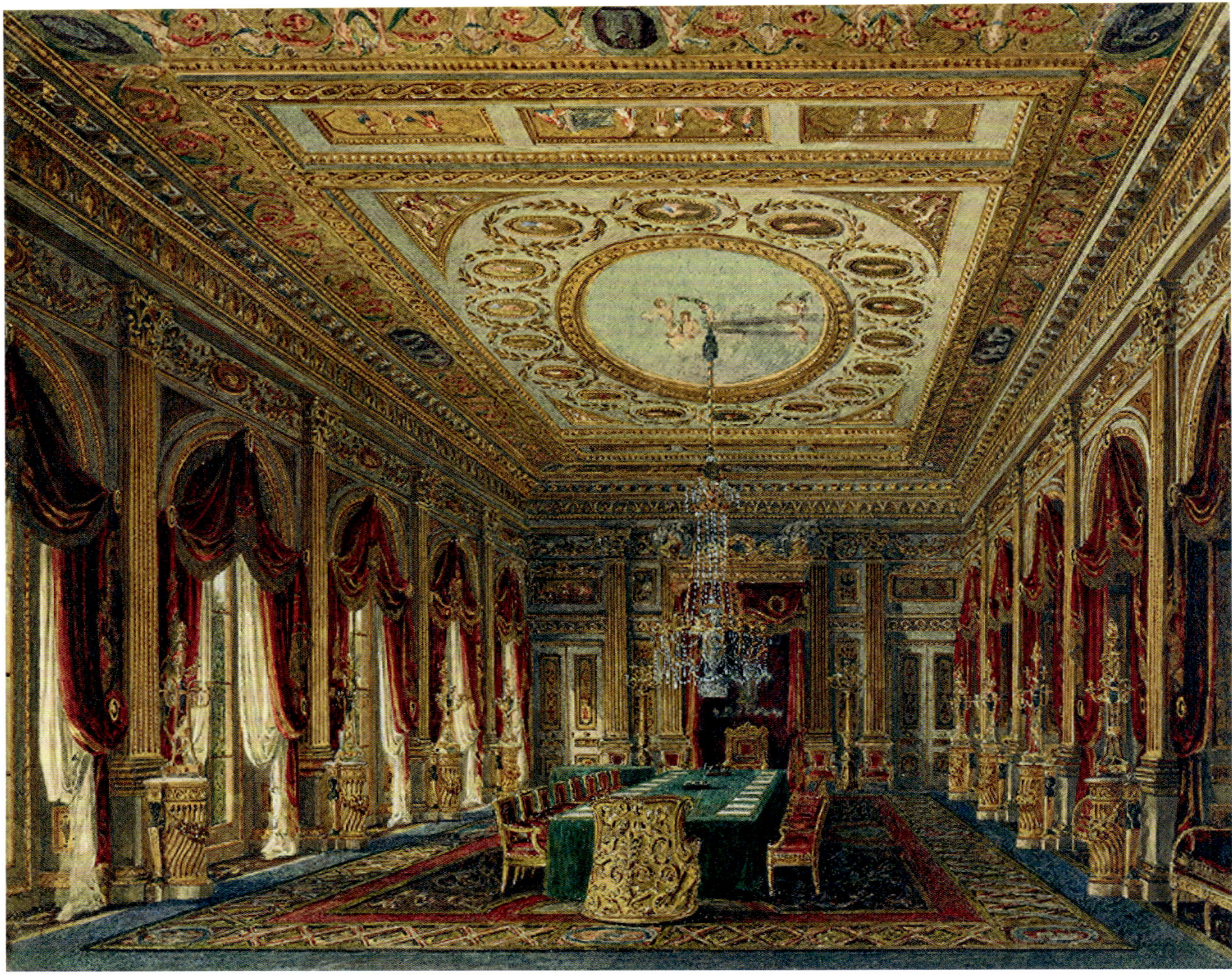

interiors at his home, Craven Cottage in Fulham, among them the Egyptian Hall in 'an exact copy of one of Denon's plates of Egypt'[51] and a 'Gothic chapel ... which purported to be an imitation of Henry VII's chapel at Westminster Abbey'.[52] He also owned a nearby banqueting house, Vine Cottage, which featured a 'robber's cave', 'lion's den' and a 'dining room, representing on a small scale, the ruins of Tintern Abbey', where he entertained the prince.[53] These conceits sound eccentric and frivolous, but Porter played an important role in increasing the theatricality, scale and eclecticism of George's taste at both Carlton House and in his subsequent projects. Porter was given considerable autonomy to execute his vision for Carlton House, writing to the prince, 'Sir I know full well, by observation, that the word "*no*" forms no part of y.[r] R[l]. H[ss]'s vocabulary'.[54]

A new scheme was devised for the public rooms on the Principal Floor, which Porter announced should be 'as refined & *classical* as possible'.[55] The Dining Room was converted into the Crimson Drawing Room and the Music Room became the new Dining Room.[56] Much of the redecoration was carried out by members of the Wyatt family, the sculptor Richard Westmacott and Italian plasterer Francis Bernasconi. In 1804 James Wyatt was commissioned to 'repair, paint and whitewash the whole of Carlton House; regild such parts as had been gilt before and to make some additions to the decorative part of the building'.[57] The new Crimson Drawing Room (Fig. 5.20) perhaps best demonstrates the increase in splendour during these redecorations. In February 1806, 91 yards (83 metres) of crimson Genoa velvet and 62 yards (57 metres) of crimson Italian 'Mantua' were purchased for £243 13s 1d from Joseph & William King,[58] augmented in 1807 by expensive gold embroidery, tassels, fringing and gimp braid from Barrett, Corney & Corney[59] with 'cut glass stars' on the pelmets,[60] and ten paintings were taken down from the ceiling 'to have gilt designs introduced instead'.[61] During this era the prince employed the Vulliamy family, previously

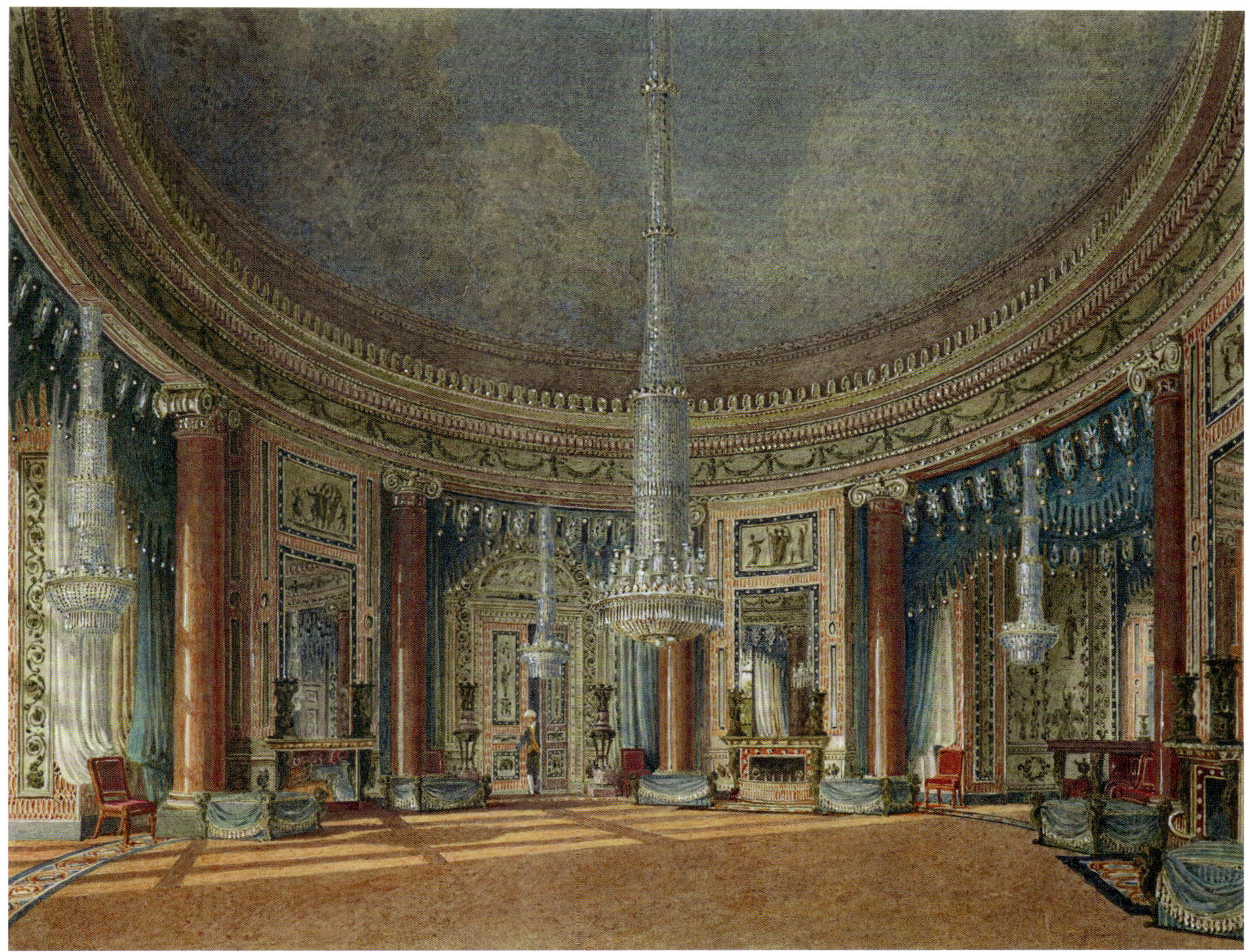

FIG. 5.18
CHARLES WILD (1781–1835), *The Throne Room, Carlton House*, 1818. Watercolour and bodycolour, 20.1 × 25.2 cm, RCIN 922178

FIG. 5.19
CHARLES WILD (1781–1835), *The Circular Room, Carlton House*, 1817. Watercolour and bodycolour over etched lines, 20.2 × 25.4 cm, RCIN 922177

clockmakers, to make forays into general bronzework, replacing many of Holland's classical marble chimneypieces with spectacular new examples of striking scale and complexity (Fig. 5.21). In February 1810 Richard Westmacott removed '3 dove colored marble chimneypieces' which 'did formerly belong to the Circular Dining Room and Crimson Silk Drawing Room' and placed them 'in rooms upstairs'.[62] The two new chimneypieces fashioned by the Vulliamys for the latter room cost £2,002 9d.[63] The other rooms were subjected to similar treatments: Edward Wyatt charged £300 for 'repairing the carving and regilding four very rich whole length frames with crowns' and 'richly carving and gilding in four pannels over doors … the orders of St George the Bath St Patrick and St Andrew in burnished gold' in the Throne Room.[64] Spectacular new chandeliers were ordered: in January 1807 Parker & Perry supplied for the new (Crimson) Drawing Room 'a magnificent 56 light lustre designed to represent a fountain falling into a large reservoir, the branches superbly chased and decorated with paste icicles, the whole finished in the most superior manner, the dimensions 6½ feet in diameter & the length 14 feet for the centre of the great drawing room at Carlton House',[65] costing the extraordinary sum of £1,050.

The Lower Floor suite was also subject to decorative changes. A new room was added at the eastern extreme, the Roman Room (later the Corinthian Room) which may have emulated the designs in Percier and Fontaine's *Recueil des décorations intérieures*. Judging by a surviving bookcase (supplied by Marsh & Tatham in 1806) it appears that the

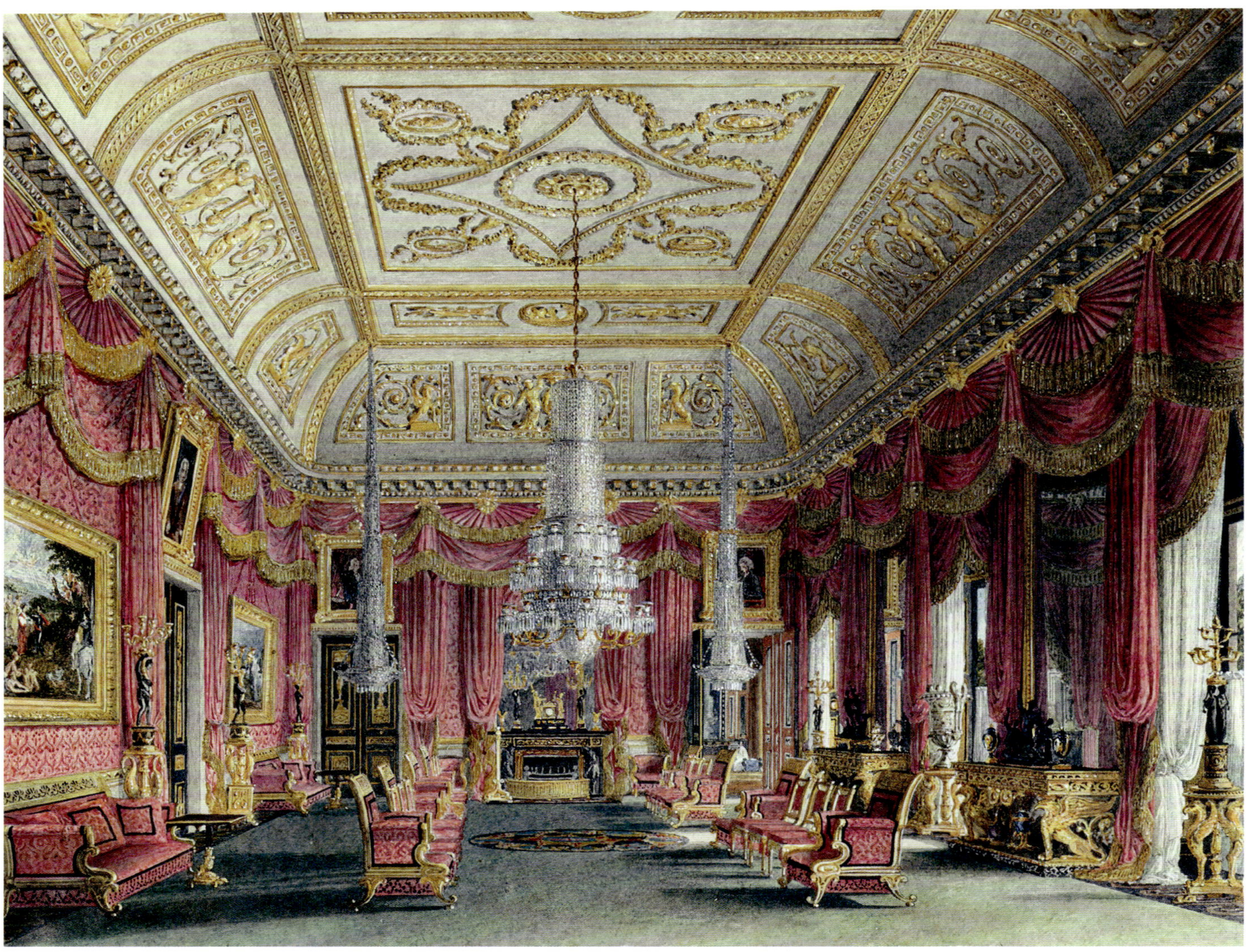

library was redecorated in an austere Empire style, perhaps in the vein of Napoleon's library at Malmaison.[66] This scheme must have been in place only briefly, as the library would see the prince's earliest experiments with Gothic style inside the house. In September 1808 Tatham billed for 'all the book cases from the west end of the room' and 'east end of the room', along with 'Two Large Gothic Oak Sofa's … Coverd with crimson Cloth ornamented with Black Velvet' for the 'Gothic library' and 'Two Large Indulgent Gothic Oak Chairs'.[67] This scheme may have been equally short-lived as it appears the prince was already disposing of elements of it by January 1810.[68] It seems Porter also reworked the Chinese Drawing Room, employing the Bond Street firm Fricker & Henderson, who from 1805 to 1807 submitted several bills for its renovation. Their work included 'six large panels of figures heightened in gold', 'eight rich Chinese pagodas … painted on a carmine background', 'two large Chinese canopies enriched with scales and paint highlighted with green and yellow gold' and 'painting the stiles of window shutters & window panes with gold scales & fillets'.[69] In July 1806 Parker and Perry supplied 'four large handsome flying dragons shaded & gilt, to hold lanthorns … by order of Walsh Porter'.[70] No visual record survives showing the room during this later incarnation, but the bills conjure an image closer to the theatrical chinoiserie later seen at Brighton Pavilion than Holland and Daguerre's version as published in Sheraton ten or so years previously, reinforcing the idea that Porter played an important role in developing the prince's taste in this area.

Porter also gave the Holland-era Council Chamber and State Bedchamber (the rooms intended for official business) a military theme, better suited for the prince of a nation at war. The former Council Chamber became the Admirals Room, prompted by the victory at Trafalgar in 1805. In February 1812,

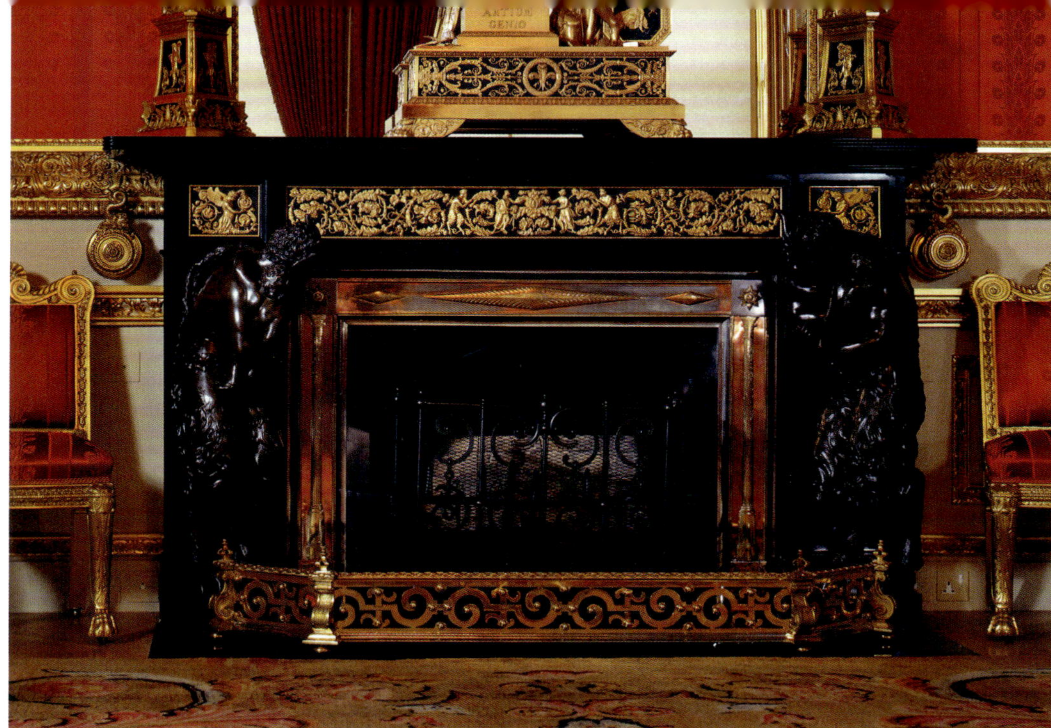

FIG. 5.20
CHARLES WILD (1781–1835), *The Crimson Drawing Room, Carlton House*, 1816. Watercolour and bodycolour over etched lines, 20.1 × 25.8 cm, RCIN 922176

FIG. 5.21
ATTRIBUTED TO BENJAMIN VULLIAMY (1747–1811), *Chimneypiece*, 1807–12. Marble, gilt and patinated bronze, 131.5 × 228.0 × 41.0 cm, RCIN 44193

three years after Porter's sudden death, Messrs Barrett & Corney delivered hundreds of 'Embroidered Articles in Gold' which 'were ordered by Mr Walsh Porter and was intended for the Pannels in the Admiral's Room or Old Council Room'.[71] The adjoining former State Bedchamber became the Military Tent Room in which in 1806 Tatham installed 'a temporary tent half circular and half square',[72] then 'hanging the roofs and sides of the tent with blue striped silk and making banners of ditto' all 'for Mr Porter's approbation'.[73] The doors placed between these two rooms during this era survive;[74] their elaborate painted decoration provides us with a small insight into these schemes, one side reflecting the military with a helmeted profile, the reverse celebrating the naval with a trident and shells. The two new military council rooms were probably conceived under the influence of Percier and Fontaine's installations for Napoleon, such as the tented council chamber at Malmaison. Yet in June 1811 more than 269 yards (246 metres) of 'Garter Blue Velvet' arrived 'for the Pannels in the Admiral's Room and the Room adjoining'[75] for their conversion into the Blue Velvet Drawing Room and Closet, recognisable in Pyne's views (Figs 5.22 and 5.23).

Perhaps Porter's greatest addition to Carlton House was the remarkable Gothic Conservatory, to the western end of the Lower Floor suite (Fig. 5.1). No doubt conceived under the influence of the Gothic rooms at Craven Cottage, its innovations were manifold: it was a conservatory, a novel concept in itself; it was Gothic, still a daring style choice; and it was made from the experimental materials of cast iron and 'Mr Parker's special concrete'.[76] Glasshouses and orangeries had been used in Britain since the seventeenth century, but the idea of building one adjoining the house, for use as an additional room, was a new idea. George's was likely conceived with the involvement of Humphry Repton, who in his *Observations on the Theory and Practice of Landscape Gardening* (1803) developed ideas for Gothic and Classical conservatories and examined ways of breaking down the barrier between the interior and exterior gardens of a house.[77] Designed and built by Thomas Hopper, who continued work on it after Porter's death in 1809,[78] the conservatory at Carlton House was a complex construction, fitted with remarkable and expensive Coade stone features. These included 'two statues of antient [*sic*] Kings and two ditto of bishops and one statue of a pilgrim for the niches', 'ten Gothic candelabra very richly ornamented seven feet high', several of which survive today (Fig. 5.24), and a large octagonal fountain whose decorative scheme included a 'bunch of leeks encircled by a coronet'.[79] The enamel-painted glass was probably the most spectacular feature: in 1807 Underwood, Doyle & Underwood supplied '17 mettle windows very richly ornamented to drawing (for the conservatory)'[80] and in June 1811 'A Handsome Painted Glass Window, with His Royal Highness's Arms painted on it' was placed at the west end.[81] In 1810, Richard Westall provided a drawing representing the Battle of Crécy, the greatest military triumph of the Black Prince, one of George's predecessors as Prince of Wales, intended as a design for a painted window for the conservatory,[82] suggesting the antiquarian aspect of the office was at play in the conception of the room. Despite its chronic structural issues and leakiness, the conservatory is remarked upon

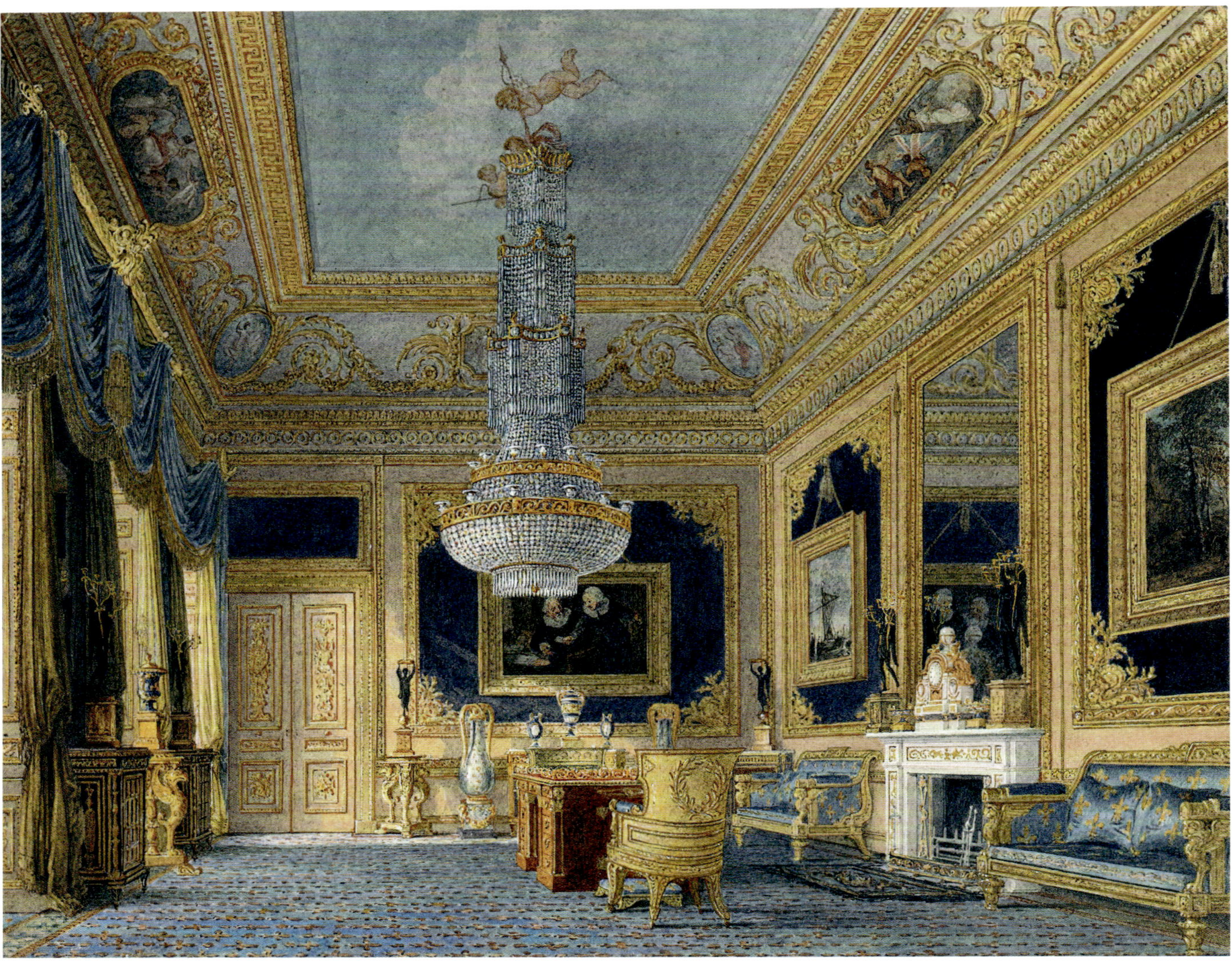

repeatedly in accounts of entertainments at the house. Sir George Jackson described it as 'really like what one would imagine a fairy hall to be ... a building of the lightest gothic, resembling the choir of a cathedral ... its beauties revealed by innumerable small coloured lamps placed all around the little cornices and in the niches of the gothic work.'[83]

Porter's activities at the house did not meet with universal approval; Joseph Farington wrote in May 1806 that 'although Carlton House as finished by *Holland* was in a complete & *new* state He [the Prince of Wales] has ordered the whole thing to be done again under the direction of *Walsh Porter*, who has destroyed all that Holland has done & is substituting a finishing in a most expensive & motley taste'.[84] A defensive letter of August 1805 from Porter to the prince's Treasurer Colonel McMahon suggests tension: 'I work like a Slave, & I exercise every possible œconomy that is not derogatory to the dignity of the Prince, nor have I done a single thing that was not originally proposed, or that has not met the entire & unqualified approbation of his Rl Highness.'[85] Some later critics have described Porter's redecorations of the house in disparaging terms. In reality, they often simply augmented or adapted the pre-existing schemes, and are of interest to us in the way that they reflect the evolving tastes and requirements of the prince and broader changes in fashion during the era.

The Regency and after

The unique conditions of the Regency, when George assumed the responsibilities of monarch, meant that in 1811 Carlton House became the leading royal residence of Great Britain. Because of the prince's increased importance, the old Throne

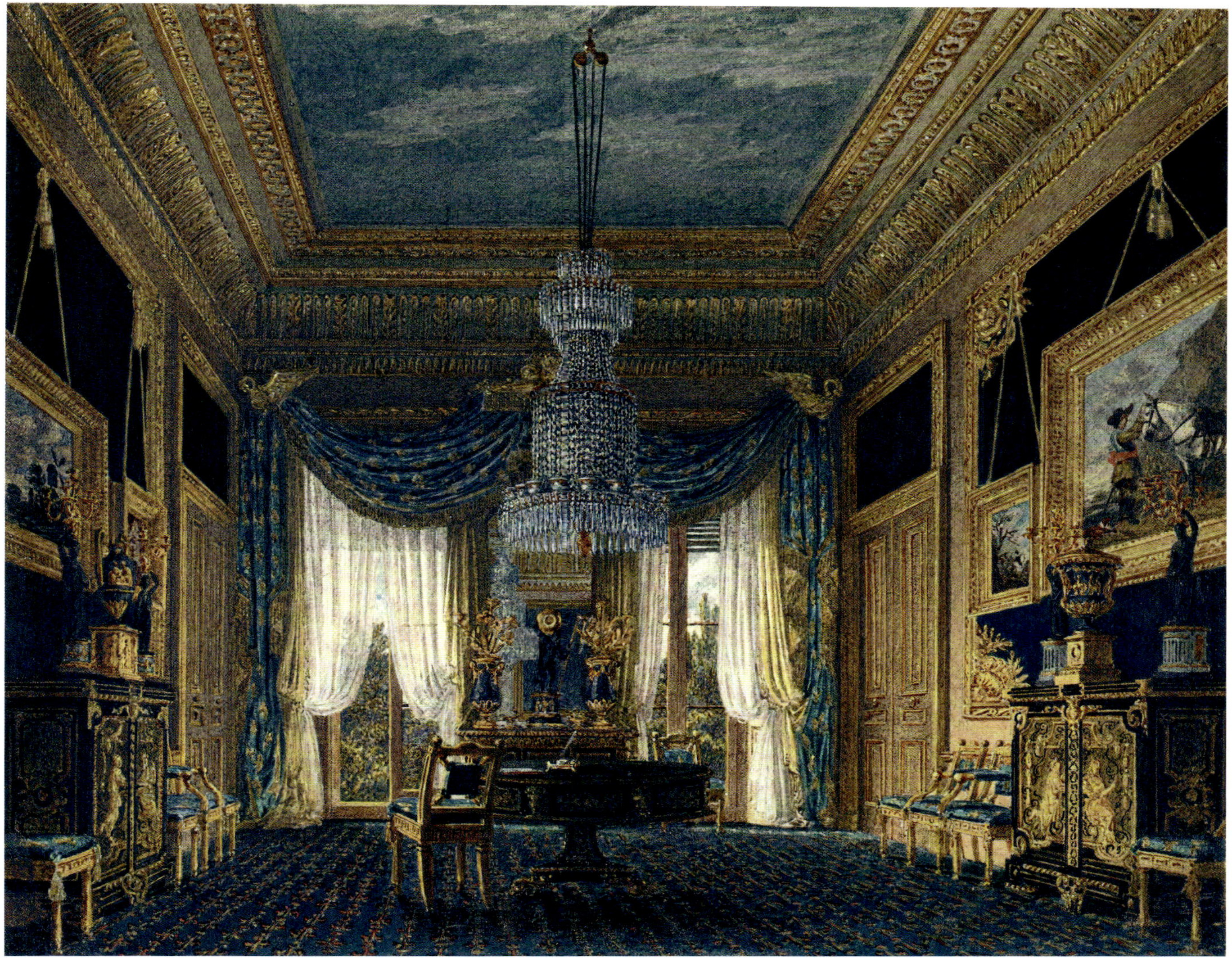

Room was deemed too small so the Great Drawing Room was converted to take on this role (see Fig. 5.18). Works and improvements continued in the house under James Wyatt. In September 1812 he was ordered 'to fit up a large room on the ground floor … adjoining the present library as an additional library, and in the same style; and to fit up the strong room'.[86] The magnificence was stepped up yet further; in 1811 Edward Wyatt billed for 'two pier Glass frames for the Blue Velvet room richly Carved laurel and berries and Oge [*sic*] roman strap leaves Gilt in Burnish'd Gold' and for 'richly Carving and Gilding in burnish'd Gold 24 emblematical Door Pannels [*sic*] for Throne Room';[87] these 'pannels' survive, reused to great effect in the semi-state apartments at Windsor Castle. During the Regency, which coincided with the culmination of the Napoleonic Wars, the house would become the setting for a succession of glittering celebrations (see chapter 15).

FIG. 5.22
CHARLES WILD (1781–1835), *The Blue Velvet Room, Carlton House, c.*1816. Watercolour and bodycolour with gum arabic over pencil, 20.1 × 25.2 cm, RCIN 922184

FIG. 5.23
CHARLES WILD (1781–1835), *The Blue Velvet Closet, Carlton House, c.*1818. Watercolour and bodycolour with gum arabic over pencil, 20.2 × 25.0 cm, RCIN 922185

Around 1814 Nash produced two designs for the complete rebuilding of Carlton House, one Gothic style and another Classical, perhaps hinting that the restrictions posed by the size of the house were becoming increasingly frustrating.[88] While the efficacy of these plans was questionable, Nash was able to improve the setting with the construction of Regent's Street as a processional approach, and a new, handsome square at its front, Waterloo Place.[89] Work began in 1813, and Waterloo Place was finished by the early 1820s. Nash designed and directed the construction of the new Gothic Dining Room in the Lower Floor

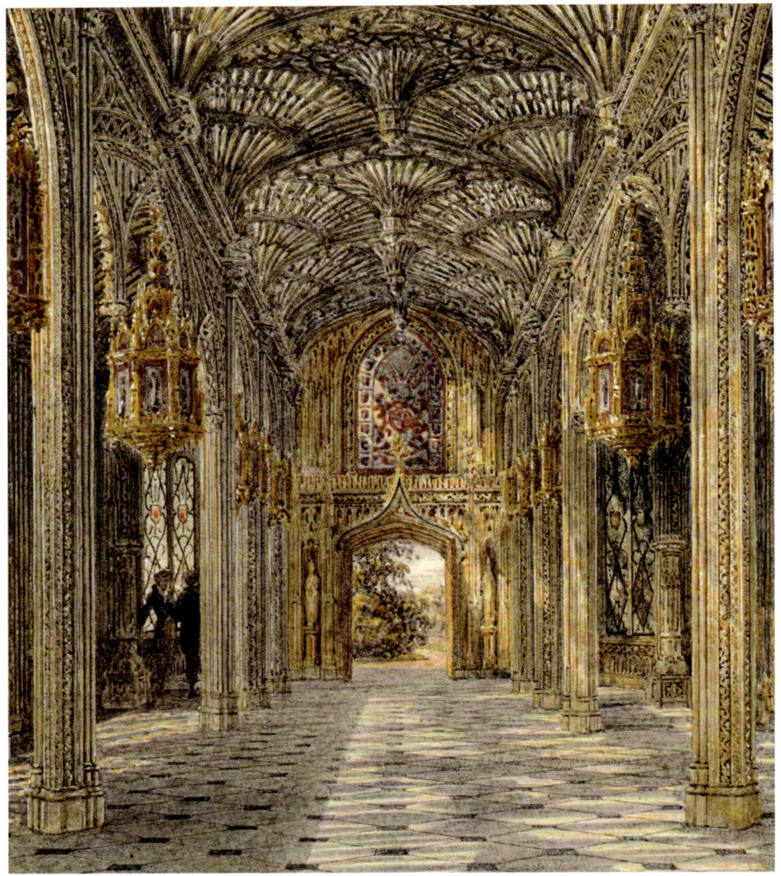

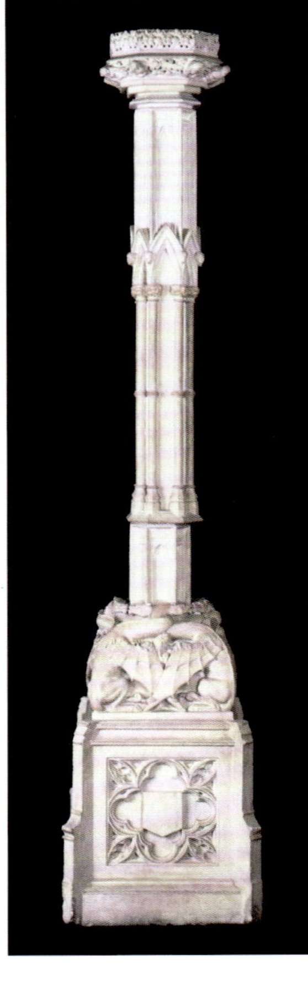

Detail of Fig. 5.1
CHARLES WILD (1781–1835), *The Gothic Conservatory, Carlton House*, 1817

FIG. 5.24
THOMAS HOPPER (1776–1856) and COADE AND SEALY, *Candelabrum*, 1810. Cast artificial stone (Coade stone), 205.9 × 43.2 cm (V&A, London: A.92–1980)

FIG. 5.25
CHARLES WILD (1781–1835), *The Gothic Dining Room, Carlton House*, 1817. Watercolour and bodycolour with gum arabic over etched outlines, 19.5 × 26.3 cm, RCIN 922189

suite at the opposite end of the range from the conservatory (Fig. 5.25).[90] Completed in 1816, it would be the last major architectural addition to the house.

It comes as a shock to think that – after playing such a leading role in national life, and the expense and effort of constructing a new street and square to improve its setting – Carlton House would be reduced to rubble just six years after the prince's accession to the throne as George IV in 1820. Despite its undoubted magnificence and fame, however, the house suffered from several fundamental drawbacks. It was never private enough, which developed into more of a problem as the aged king became increasingly reclusive, and the stark, temple-like façade was not in keeping with his mature tastes, nor could it easily be adapted or incorporated into something new. The house was smaller than Pyne's views would have us believe; the Entrance Hall, by far its largest space, had a floor area of 119 square metres; by way of comparison, the Throne Room at Buckingham Palace is 170 square metres. Lord Lonsdale summed up this problem to Joseph Farington in 1811 after a party at the house, noting that 'though there was much display & splendour, it fell far short of the magnificence of a Fete at Windsor given some years since by the king, where the large apartments of the Castle afforded more grandeur of effect'.[91] There were certainly no dedicated spaces to display the king's burgeoning art collection,[92] and Nash complained that the house was 'destitute of the necessary and usual accommodation for servants' and had 'but one entrance common to noblemen's carriages and wagons and carts'.[93] Most importantly, a shocking survey undertaken by Nash in March 1822 detailed a litany of cracks, sagging lintels, buckling and sinking floors, broken glass and leaking roofs.[94] We can assume many of these problems were owing to the degradation of the older parts of the house, along with the haste in which the new parts were constructed, and the use of untested experimental materials and technologies in areas such as the conservatory. The constant redecorations and architectural alterations, along with the heavy use of the Regency years, must have exacerbated the situation and a fire at the house in June 1824, which was severe enough to damage a number of works of art, may have sealed its fate. Perhaps if rebuilt from scratch, Carlton House would have survived; the Riding House,

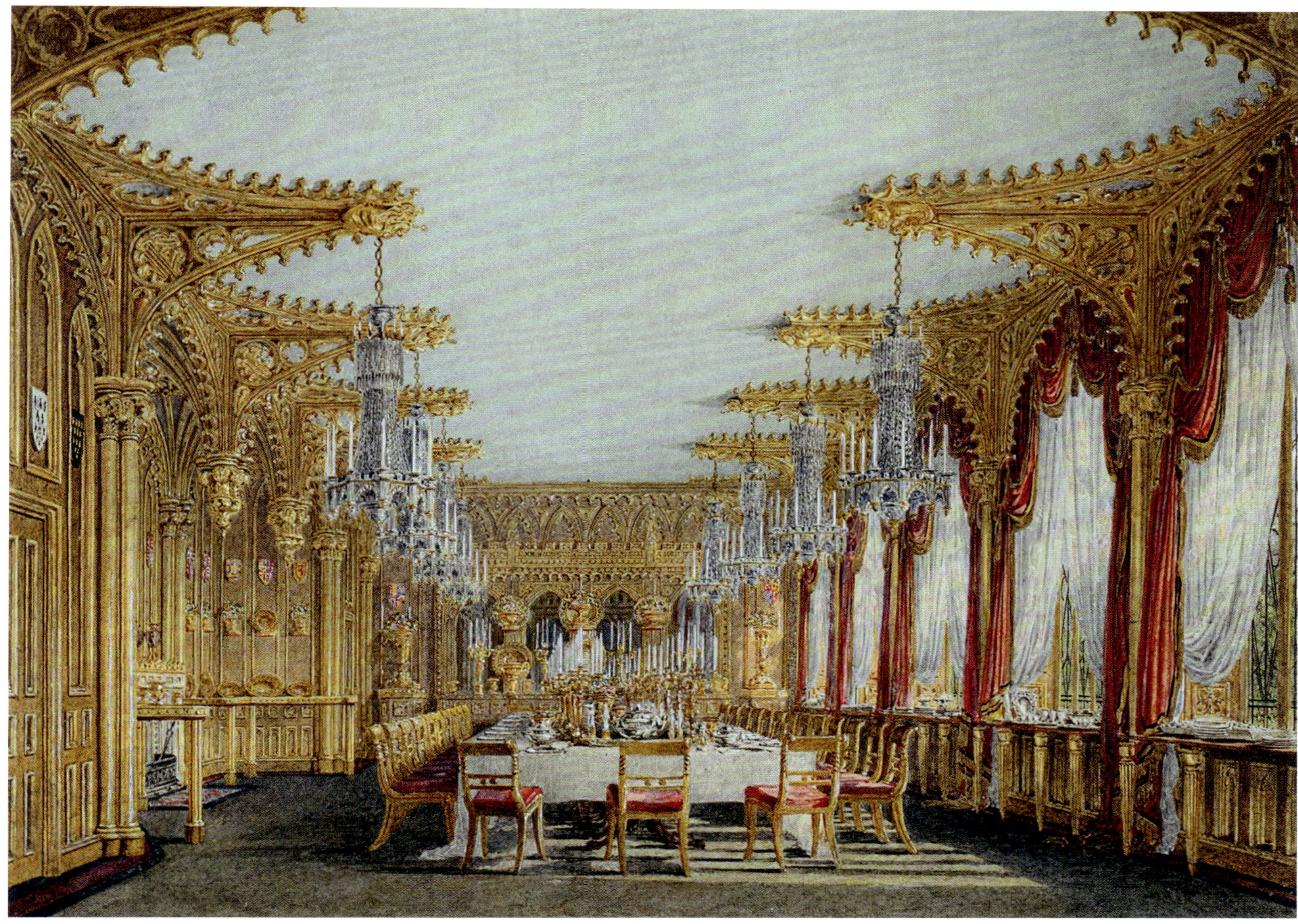

built completely anew, was retained until 1862 when it was demolished to make way for Carlton House Terrace Mews.[95]

By summer 1827 the demolition was well under way, and it was fully completed by 1829. Everything of value was carefully catalogued, first put into storage and then sent either to Windsor Castle or Buckingham Palace. Carlton House's existence was dazzling but brief, but its role as a testing ground for many of George IV's decorative and architectural tastes means that its spirit can be appreciated in his subsequent projects. One need not look much further than the semi-state apartments of Windsor Castle, where the Green and Crimson Velvet Rooms and grand Gothic Dining Room evoke the Blue Velvet Room, Corinthian Room and Gothic Dining Room at Carlton House. The influence of Carlton House is also discernible at Buckingham Palace, with its ubiquitous use of scagliola, magnificent ceilings and striking Grand Staircase with its complex glass roof. The relatively low-ceilinged rooms on the garden front of the ground floor, complete with a central bow, again seem to replicate the Lower Floor suite at Carlton House. The rooms at the castle and the palace were decorated by many of the same craftsmen and reused many actual decorative elements, including floors, fireplaces, giltwood carvings and chandeliers, not to mention furnishings.[96]

Perhaps George IV's destruction of his first house was not an act of capricious vandalism as it has sometimes been portrayed, but a way of liberating its essence from its crumbling and constricting shell, to be reapplied on the grander and more permanent scale which it so deserved. Nevertheless, the fact that Carlton House was constantly described in contemporary accounts in such terms as 'one of the grandest spectacles ever beheld',[97] 'eminently beautiful',[98] and 'the most perfect [palace] in Europe',[99] leave us in no doubt it was an enchanting and staggering sight that, lamentably, we can only imagine today.

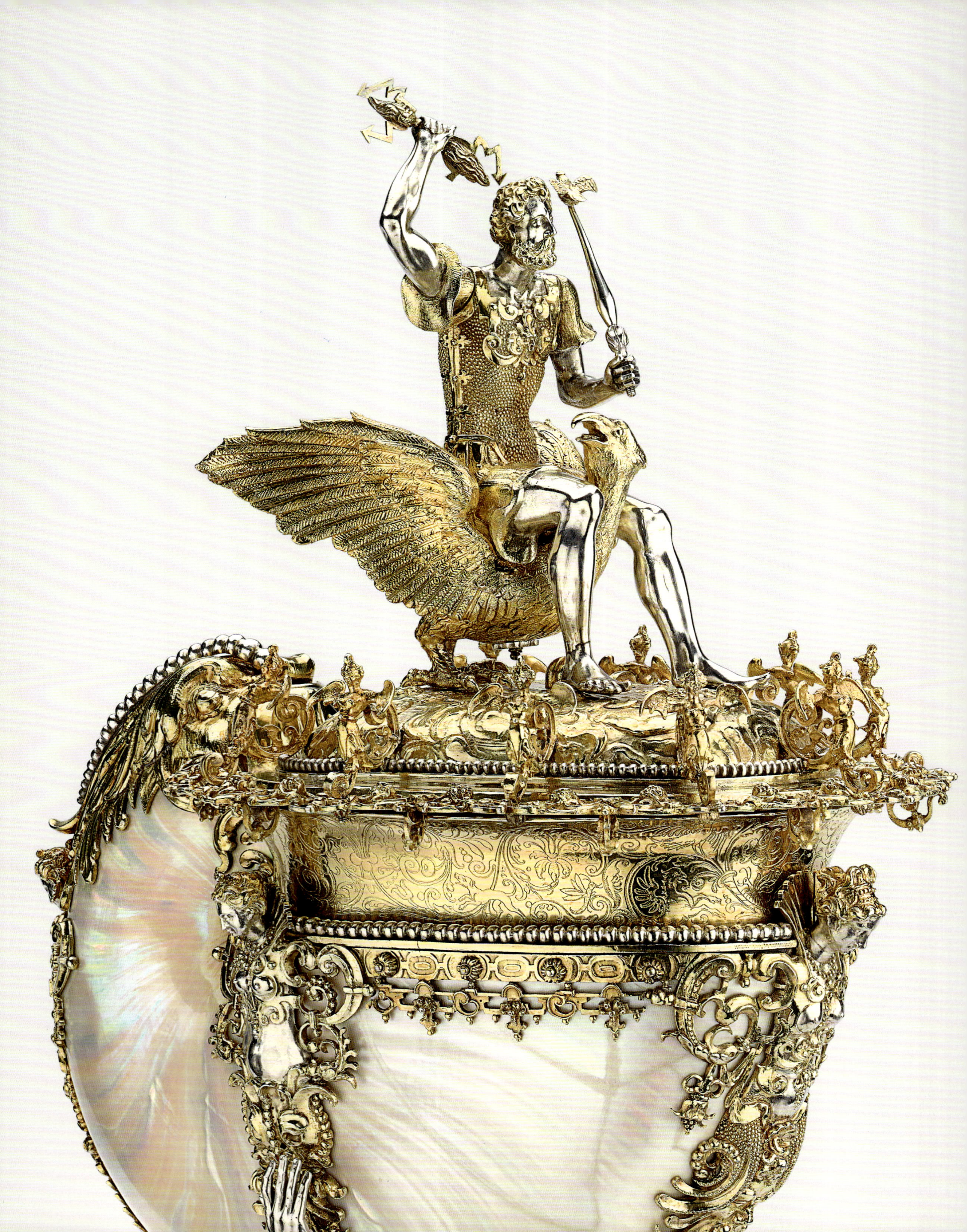

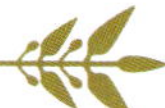 6

GEORGE IV
and the ART MARKET

RUFUS BIRD

As heir to the throne and as king, and as a collector of both great works of art and luxury trinkets, George IV's relationship with the art market was defined by the European geopolitical situation. The period from his coming of age in 1783 until his death in 1830 was one of remarkable opportunity for the collector: the auction sales in Paris which took place during and immediately after the French Revolution were a rich hunting ground for British and Parisian dealers who were able to buy at prices heavily reduced from the pre-Revolutionary years (although values later recovered). The sheer quantity of masterpieces which flooded on to the market in the wake of the Revolution generated great interest, particularly among Francophile British collectors. A number of French dealers targeted British buyers eager for the masterpieces of fine and decorative art which had formerly filled Parisian *hôtels particuliers*, and the collections formed by notable connoisseurs of the *ancien régime*. For example, during the short-lived Peace of Amiens (March 1802–May 1803) Sir Harry Featherstonehaugh, George's friend and fellow collector, purchased on his behalf a pair of ebony commodes in the newest Egyptian style, mounted with *pietre dure* plaques, from the Paris dealer Martin-Eloi Lignereux costing £671.[1] Miss Berry recorded in her journal the drop in cost of such luxury objects: 'These shops at present contain treasures of old Sèvres and rich ornaments of all sorts, which have been bought for nothing out of the great hotels and are now selling for a fourth of their original price.'[2] At the same time, the exodus – or the prospect of flight – of significant works of art from France caused some of its citizens to bid for pictures in the cause of patriotism.[3] The picture dealer William Buchanan summed up:

> The last thirty years have produced events in the history of Europe, which for a considerable length of time not only revolutionised her ancient politics, and impeded or diverted the natural current of her trade and commerce, but forced from their ancient sanctuaries those treasures of Science and of Art, that had long been the pride and glory of the states to which they belonged.[4]

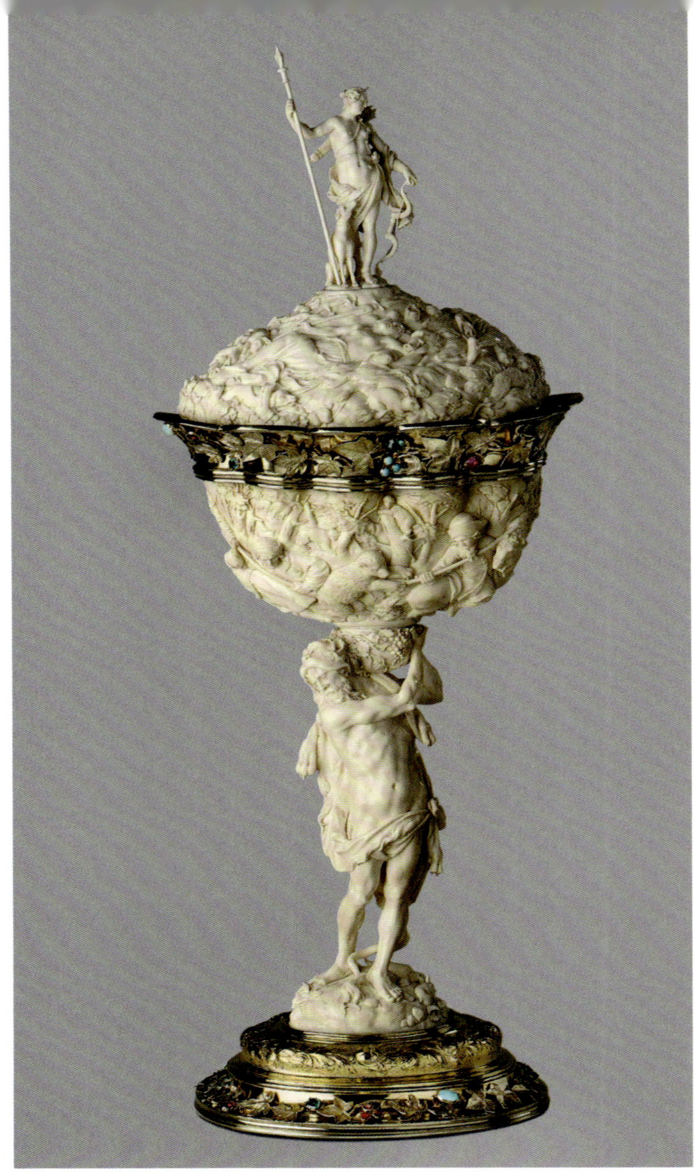

(p. 88)
Detail of Fig. 6.5, NIKOLAUS SCHMIDT (*c.*1550/5–1609), *Nautilus cup*, *c.*1600

FIG. 6.1
MARK OF D.G., SOUTH GERMANY OR AUSTRIA, ivory carving attributed to JOHANN GOTTFRIED FRISCH (active 1689–1716), *Cup and cover*, *c.*1700 (with later additions by Rundell, Bridge & Rundell, 1824/5). Ivory, silver gilt, ruby, emerald, turquoise, 49.8 × 16.6 × 20.2 cm, RCIN 50554

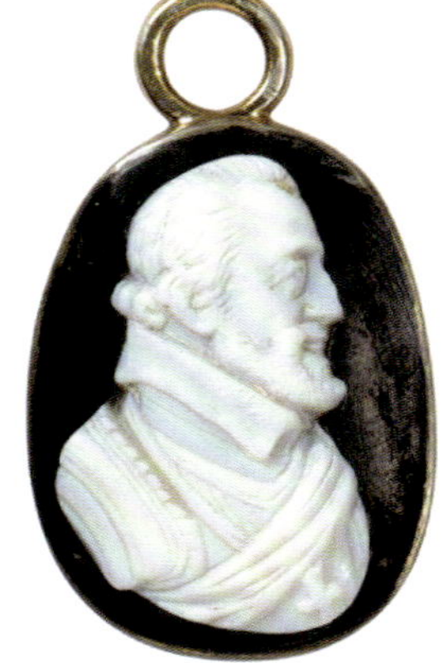

FIG. 6.2
FRENCH, *Henri IV (1553–1610)*, 1650–1700. Appliqué mother-of-pearl, cowrie shell, silver gilt, 3.0 × 2.1 cm, RCIN 65197

In spite of the opportunity caused by dramatic political events, as heir to the British and Hanoverian thrones George, like his father, was prevented from travelling to France – even before the Revolution. (For his post-accession visits to Dublin and Hanover in 1821, and to Edinburgh in 1822, see chapter 16.) So how did George make his acquisitions? The range of his collection was so enormous, its enlargement so continuous and the geographic spread of his purchases so wide that he did not and could not make every transaction in person. Over the course of almost 50 years George depended upon a network of agents, friends, household staff and dealers who provided advice and practical help in the creation of his magnificent collections and the splendid interiors in which they were displayed. George saw those interiors as an entity: paintings and furniture, porcelain and lighting were all acquired and presented in splendid surroundings often enriched by luxurious – and very expensive – textiles. This chapter will examine how he formed his collections of French furniture, silver, arms and armour, Chinese and Japanese porcelain, prints and sculpture. The collecting of Old Master paintings and the commissioning of modern furnishings and textiles for the remarkable project at Windsor Castle in the later 1820s are covered elsewhere in this volume (chapters 7 and 17 respectively). It is a matter of debate whether George perceived old and new furnishings differently: he must have been inspired by an antiquarian spirit in so many of his acquisitions, such as the German carved ivory cup which he purchased through Rundell, Bridge & Rundell (Fig. 6.1), or the numerous portraits in various media of Henri IV (Fig. 6.2). On the other hand, he was prepared to commission vast amounts of new silver from Rundells, and new furniture from Morel & Hughes and Tatham, Bailey & Sanders, alongside his purchases of historic French furniture which had been adapted or altered by London dealers such as Edward Holmes Baldock (see below).

Acquisitions made during George's early years at Carlton House were guided by the development of its interiors, overseen by the triumvirate of the French dealer Guillaume Gaubert, his fellow Frenchman Dominique Daguerre, and the English architect Henry Holland. For example, the cabinet-maker or 'Peintre-Ebéniste par Extraordinaire' George Brookshaw charged £50 for making a commode painted with flowers and repaired the gilding on a pair of candelabra to designs by Gaubert: his bill, dated 16 December 1783, was endorsed by Gaubert and Holland.[5] A few years later, Daguerre was responsible for directing decorations and sourcing

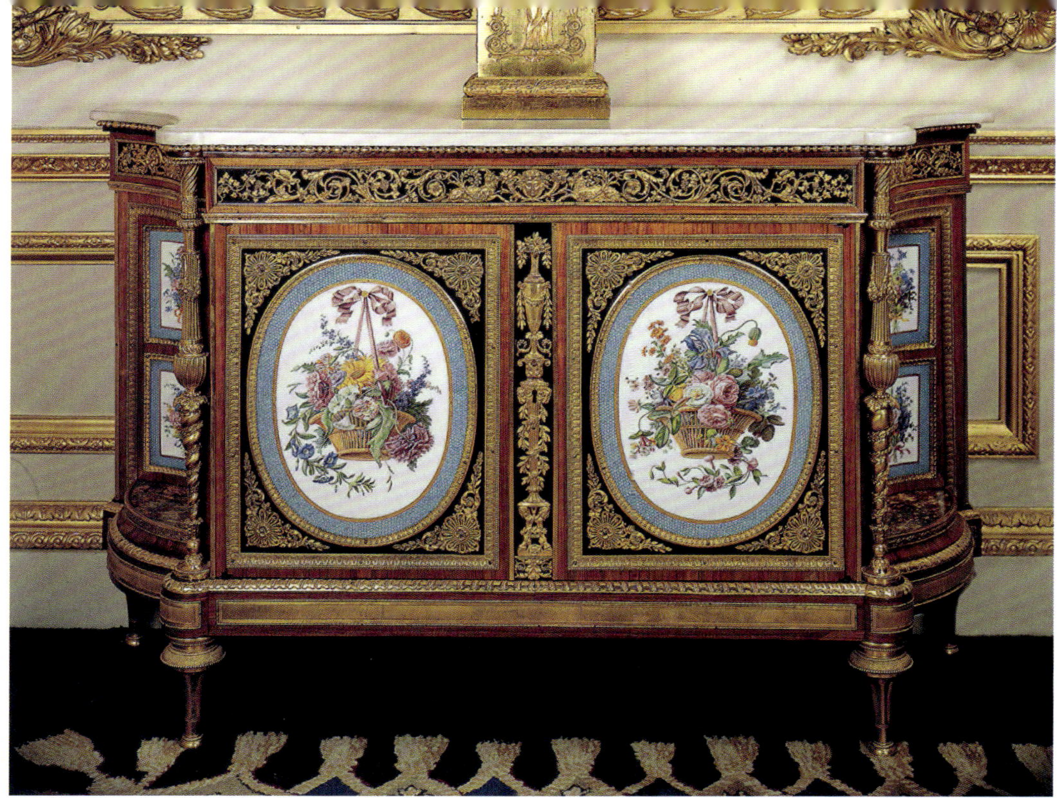

FIG. 6.3
MARTIN CARLIN (1730–85), *Cabinet*, *c.*1783. Oak veneered with tulipwood, purplewood, mahogany and boxwood, brocatello and white marble, gilt bronze, inset with soft-paste porcelain plaques, 95.9 × 152.4 × 50.8 cm, RCIN 21697

furniture and other works of art, among them a cabinet mounted with Sèvres plaques, which was placed in the Saloon at Carlton House (Fig. 6.3), and in the following year Gaubert withdrew entirely in the wake of financial irregularities, leaving Daguerre and Holland to oversee the early phase of decoration. Daguerre's involvement lasted until 1795. Unfortunately, relatively few invoices survive from this early phase, and documentation is scanty. After the turn of the century, the volume of surviving invoices for purchases of objects increases dramatically.

Besides Featherstonehaugh, the advisers who helped George acquire works in France included Walsh Porter, Lord Yarmouth and Sir Charles Long. George's closest adviser from 1803 until 1809 was Porter (see chapter 5), a remarkable man who encouraged George to introduce much bolder – and richer – antique Roman-inspired schemes throughout Carlton House which were overlaid onto the chaste neo-classical interiors he had preferred in the 1780s and 1790s.[6] Porter acted as intermediary in offering 12 pictures to George in 1806, writing that they were 'cull'd from the first Palaces & Collections in Europe, such as to set *criticism* at defiance … they have all been either imported by myself or I have directly purchased them … from those who *did* import them, & are (of course) all *undoubted* originals by the scarcest Masters.'[7] From 1809 to 1819 Lord Yarmouth acted as principal art adviser, often making purchases on behalf of George. For example, on 5 June 1813 Yarmouth purchased a bronze of Louis XV at Squibb's auction and in January 1818 he sent from Paris a quantity of bronzes and pieces of furniture purchased there.[8] The following year Lord Yarmouth bid successfully on George's behalf at Robins's auction sale of Lord Charles Townshend's pictures, buying Rembrandt's portrait of Agatha Bas (Fig. 7.13).[9]

In 1814, through Sir Charles Long, George made his most significant purchase of pictures *en bloc*: the Baring collection of 86 paintings by seventeenth-century Dutch and Flemish painters. Long told the artist and diarist Farington, 'Sir Thomas [Baring] has asked a moderate price'.[10] After this coup, Long took on an increasingly important role in George's acquisitions, including in 1822 the purchase of Van Dyck's *Charles I in Three Positions* (Fig. 6.4), which had been painted for Bernini as a guide for a portrait bust in marble. Long, like Yarmouth, also visited Paris to purchase works of art for George. He had a formative influence on the British art world of the first three decades of the nineteenth century, serving as a trustee of the British Museum from 1812 until his death and from 1824 as a founding trustee of the National Gallery.

Such was the breadth of his appetite for all forms of art, however, that George was never reliant on a single intermediary for all his purchases, which were made through a bewildering range of dealers and agents. Some were frequented more than others, reflecting George's passion for collecting the type of object in which that dealer specialised, and none more so than the firm of Rundell, Bridge & Rundell, goldsmiths based at 32 Ludgate Hill. Rundells, established by Philip Rundell in 1797,

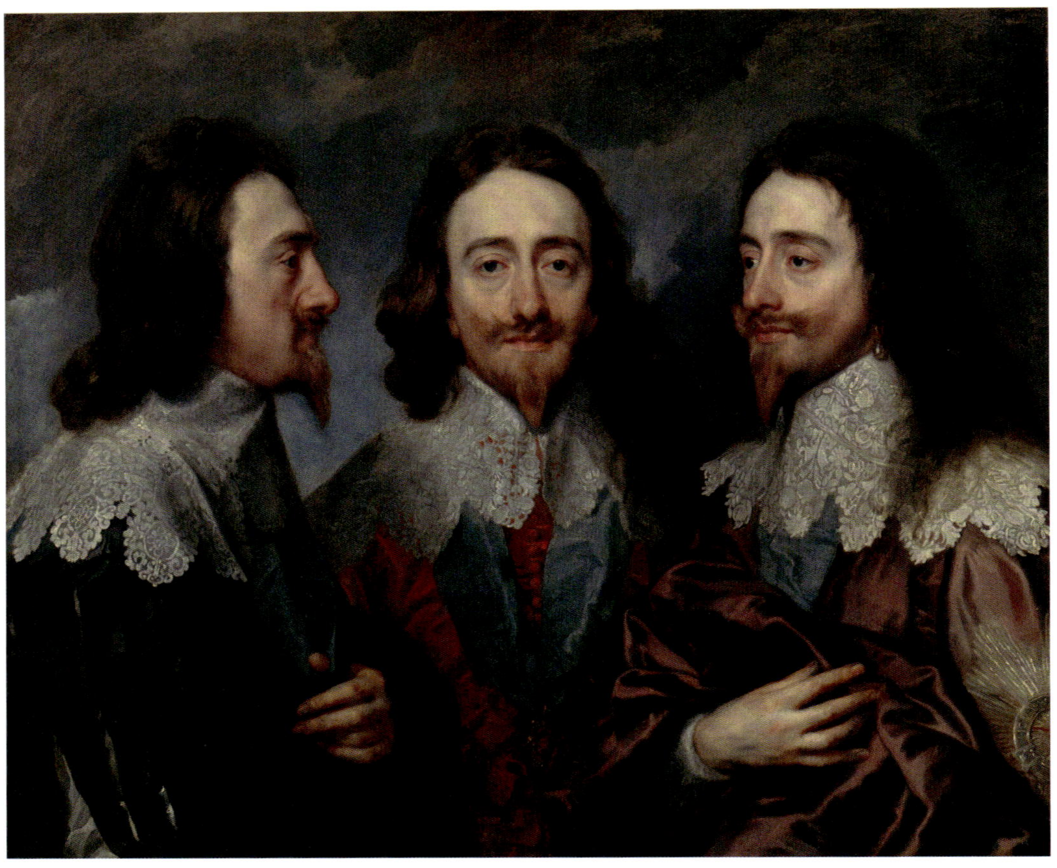

FIG. 6.4
SIR ANTHONY VAN DYCK (1599–1641), *Charles I (1600–49)*, 1635–6. Oil on canvas, 84.4 × 99.4 cm, RCIN 404420

FIG. 6.5
NIKOLAUS SCHMIDT (*c.*1550/5–1609), *Nautilus cup*, *c.*1600. Nautilus shell, parcel-gilt silver, 52.0 × 17.0 × 24.0 cm, RCIN 50603

FIG. 6.6
PROBABLY GERMAN, WITH ADDITIONS BY RUNDELL, BRIDGE & RUNDELL, *Sword and scabbard*, *c.*1750–1820. Steel, gold, diamond, ruby; wood, fishskin, diamond, gold (scabbard), 96.6 cm (length); 78.0 cm (blade length), RCIN 67134

was soon the leading London supplier of modern silver, much of it manufactured in the workshops of Paul Storr. The firm was adept at providing George with enormous quantities of dining and domestic plate. Rundells also retailed older pieces to service the antiquarian proclivities of early nineteenth-century British collectors. At the sale of Wanstead House in 1822, for example, Rundells bought a spectacular nautilus shell cup with parcel-gilt silver mounts, dating from *c.*1600, by the Nuremberg goldsmith Nikolaus Schmidt (Fig. 6.5).[11] The following year the cup was sold by the firm to George IV who paid 250 guineas for it, in the belief that it might be the work of the celebrated Renaissance goldsmith Benvenuto Cellini.

Though Rundells are perhaps best known for supplying plate to George, they originally supplied him with magnificent jewellery. Besides the usual accoutrements and jewelled insignia (including a Lesser George set with diamonds, acquired in 1829[12]), Rundells modified existing pieces, adding, for example, a diamond-studded hilt to an eighteenth-century dress sword which they sold to George in 1820 at a cost of £3,687 (Fig. 6.6), and an ivory hilt depicting Andromeda and Perseus to a seventeenth-century German steel blade.[13] The most spectacular of all their jewelled creations was the Diamond Diadem (see Fig. 0.2), an ornamental headdress to be worn by George in the procession to his coronation.[14] The circlet was set with 1,333 diamonds which were hired at a cost of £800. After the coronation George decided that he would retain the circlet intact and agreed a purchase price for the diamonds of £8,216.[15]

Demonstrating remarkable versatility, Rundells also sold George pictures and works of sculpture. A sale of miniatures was recorded in an invoice of 1807 which also included a painting of Henry VIII, described as 'a most capital and unique picture, undoubtedly original by Hans Holbein £150'. The same invoice notes pictures of Oliver Cromwell by Samuel Cooper (£63), Maria Theresa, Queen Consort of Louis XIV, by Petitot, in enamel (£130), and Anne Boleyn (£16 16s).[16] On 16 August 1824 Rundells invoiced for a large quantity of French bronzes, including Philippe Bertrand's *Prometheus* for £68 15s (one of two versions acquired by George), Bertrand's *Psyche and Mercury* (Fig. 6.7), a portrait bust of Henri IV, *Hercules and Antaeus*, *Pluto and Proserpina*, a bust of Marshal Turenne after Jérome Derbais and reductions of the Marly horses (Fig. 6.8), the Nile river god and Guillaume Boichot's *Hercules Seated*, the last by

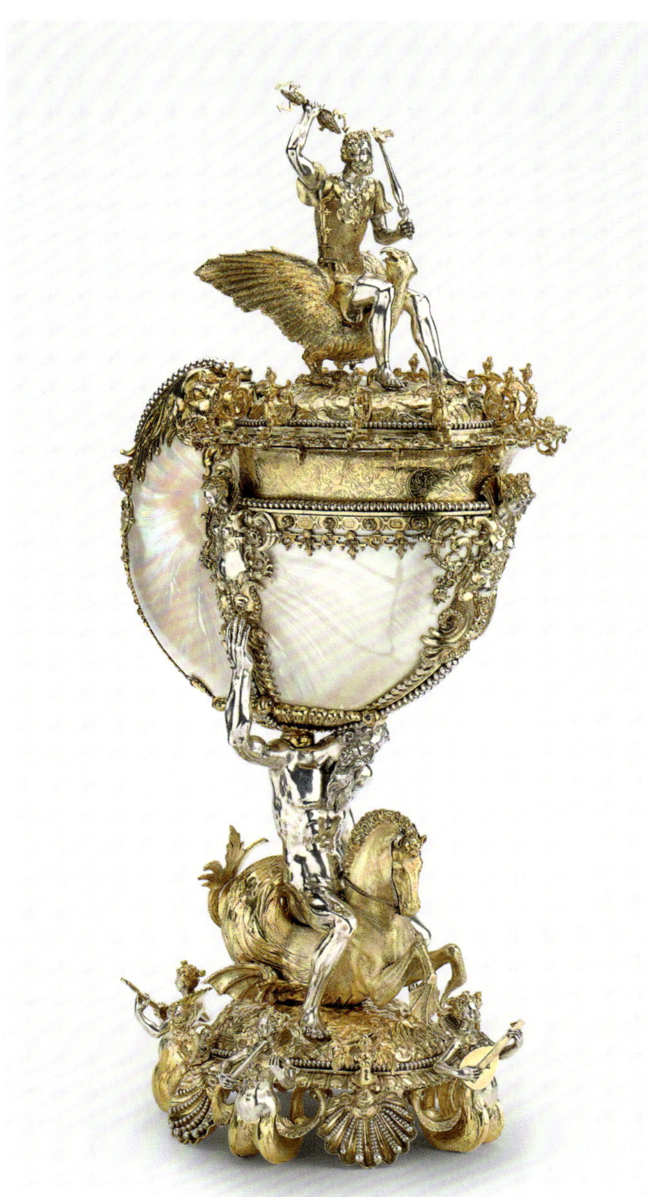

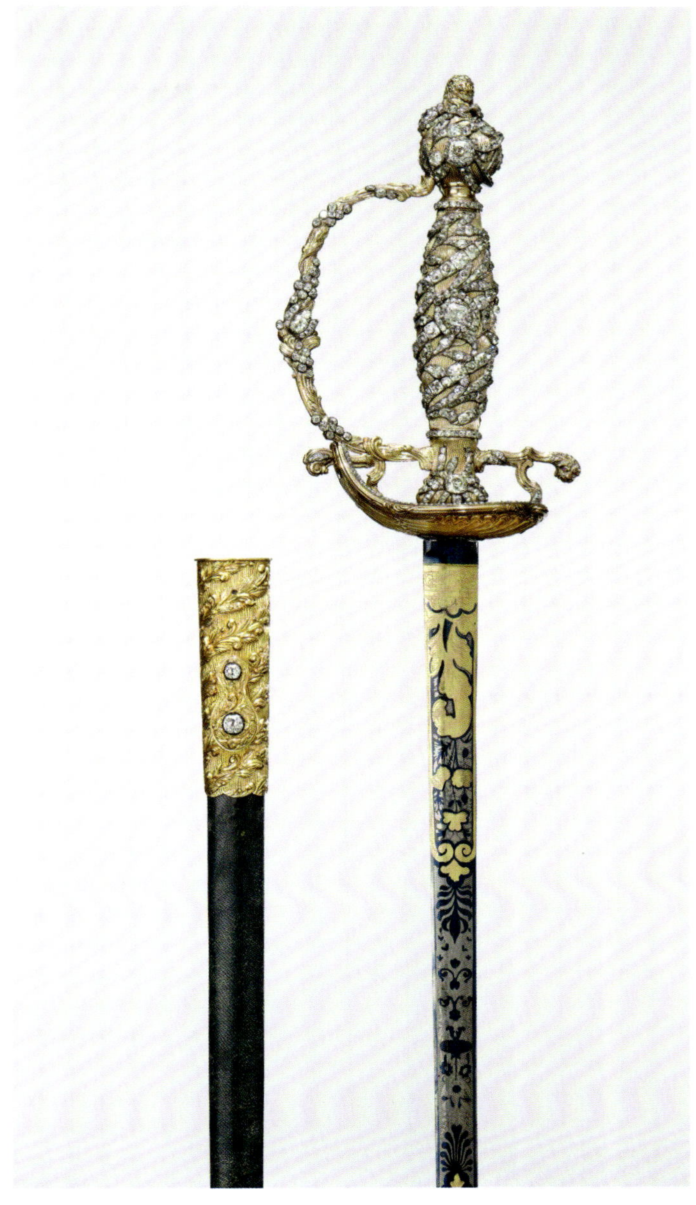

Charles Crozatier.[17] In 1828 George purchased from Rundells the large bronze relief of *Rudolf II introducing the Liberal Arts to Bohemia* by Adriaen de Vries for 100 guineas.[18]

At least ten French bronzes were bought for George by Lord Yarmouth, either from dealers in Paris or at sales in London. Among these were a bronze group of *Prometheus Bound*, by François Dumond, acquired by Yarmouth in Paris in 1818, and in the same year he acquired two bronze and parcel-gilt busts of the Roman emperors Vespasian and Augustus.[19] George sometimes acquired more than one bronze of the same subject: not only did he buy two versions of Bertrand's *Prometheus*, but he also acquired at least two examples of François Girardon's *Abduction of Proserpina*, the larger and finest of which had probably belonged to the artist himself.[20]

Some of the most significant of George's remarkable collection of bronzes were those bought at the sale of 88 selected pieces from George Watson-Taylor's collection, which had been quickly formed and equally rapidly dispersed. George IV did not just buy bronzes at this sale, which took place at Christie's on 28 May 1825, although he did acquire the three sixteenth-century busts by Leone Leoni (Fig. 6.9). The dealer Robert Fogg the Younger (see below) purchased 31 lots on George's behalf; all were intended for display and use at Windsor Castle, with the exception of a *bonheur-du-jour*, a small writing desk, by Martin Carlin which

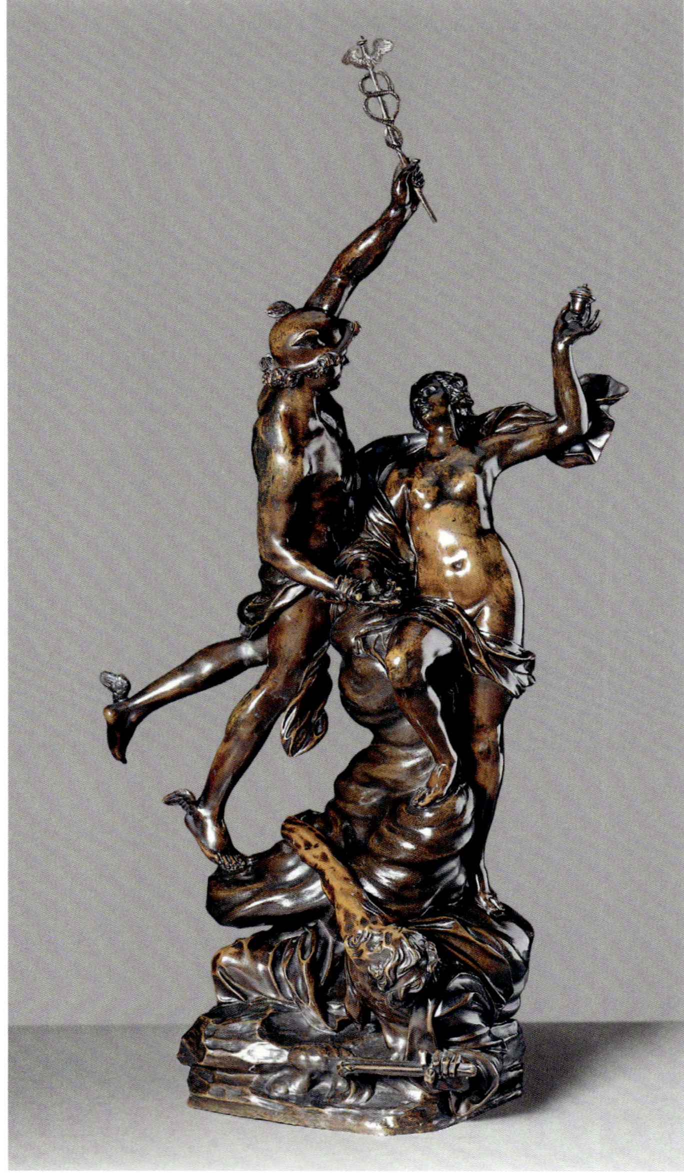

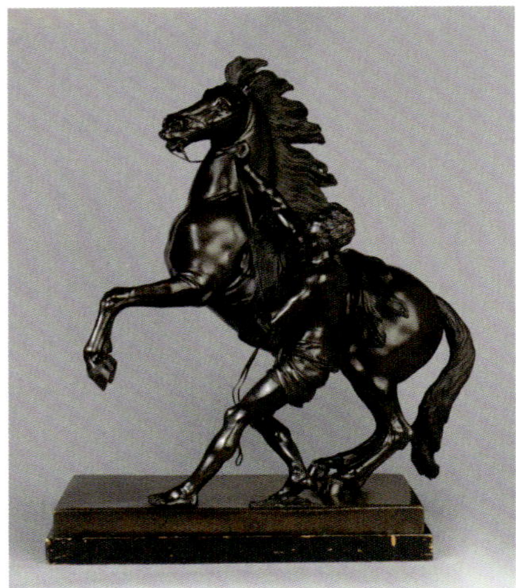

FIG. 6.7
PHILIPPE BERTRAND (1663–1724), *Psyche and Mercury*, *c.*1700. Bronze, 78.7 × 41.3 × 28.6 cm, RCIN 21641

FIG. 6.8
AFTER GUILLAUME COSTOU THE ELDER (1677–1746), One of *The Marly Horses*, *c.*1740. Bronze, 1746, 63.0 × 53.0 × 23.0 cm, RCIN 44189

was given to the king's mistress, Lady Conyngham (it is now in the Rothschild Collection, Waddesdon Manor).[21] This was the largest purchase George ever made at a single sale: two-thirds of the sale by value and a third by quantity were purchased by Fogg on his behalf for a total of £4,868 14s.

Fogg's was yet another firm of dealers to whom George turned for a range of acquisitions. The firm had been established by Robert Fogg the Elder in the 1750s 'At the China Jarr', 50 New Bond Street, and traded in tea, coffee and chocolate as well as European and Chinese porcelain. It was through his son, also Robert, and his nephew, Joseph, that large amounts of porcelain were sold to George. These included four very large porcelain pagodas; curiously the sale of the second pair took place more than ten years after the first.[22] These pagodas had been sourced by Fogg, perhaps by means of a direct commission to Chinese porcelain agents in Canton, and brought back by Dr Garrett (for whom, see chapter 18).[23] Fogg's most significant sale of porcelain to George was that of the dinner service commissioned by Louis XVI, the most expensive service made at Sèvres in the eighteenth century (Fig. 6.10). It had belonged to a Mr Würtz of Paris, and was bought by George in 1811 for £1,973 4s 8d. At that time, Britain was deep in conflict with France and yet Fogg, through his contacts in Paris, was able to continue trading. As has been noted by Geoffrey de Bellaigue, Fogg was not slow to take advantage of the relaxation of trade barriers in 1814; a memorandum of that year notes him importing 98 crates and packages (contents unspecified) from France.[24] Probably his most useful associate there was the *marchand-mercier* Philippe-Claude Maëlrondt, notorious for remodelling Sèvres through the addition of gilt-bronze mounts (Fig. 6.11).[25] Maëlrondt's probate inventory included 50 letters and accounts written by *M. Fogg marchand de curiosités demeurant à Londres* and a ledger of 255 pages entitled *les opérations que faisait le défunt avec Mr Fogg de Londres*.[26]

As well as using British agents such as Fogg, George established direct access to the French art market by dispatching francophone members of his household staff on buying trips. His confectioner, François Benois, was most frequently entrusted with these missions. Benois most likely came to royal attention through his role in establishing the embassy of Lord Whitworth in Paris in 1802. Benois and Lignereux were engaged to acquire works of art for

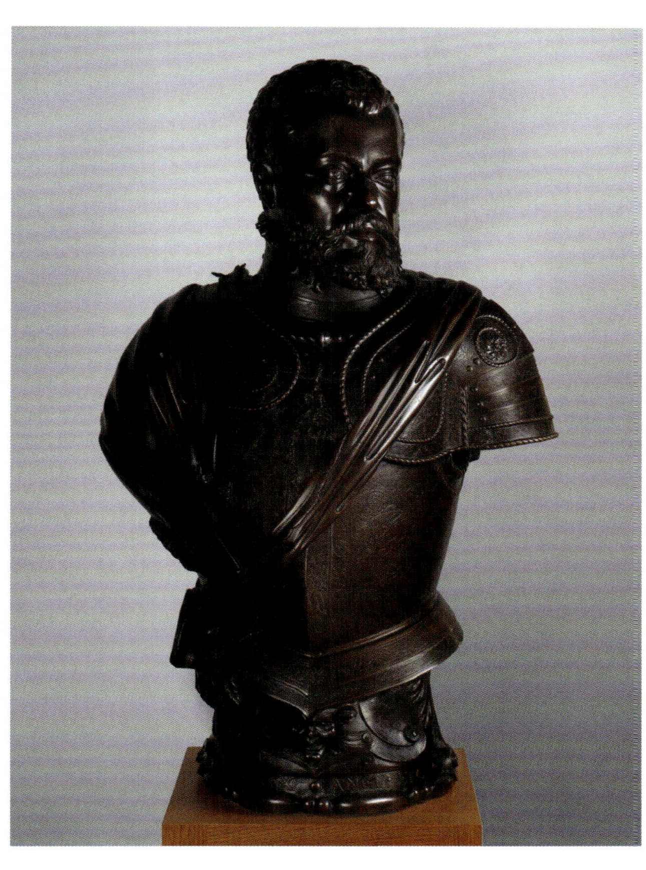

FIG. 6.9
LEONE LEONI (1509–90), *Philip II (1527–98)*, *c.*1555. Bronze, 88.9 × 57.5 × 30.5 cm, RCIN 35323

FIG. 6.10
SÈVRES PORCELAIN FACTORY, *Pieces from the Louis XVI Service*, 1783–92. Soft-paste porcelain, RCIN 5000017

the embassy as well as to pack them up and dispatch them to England when Whitworth's embassy came to an abrupt end in late spring 1803.[27] Benois was first recorded in the household of the Prince of Wales in 1804 when he was paid £62, just under half the monthly salary of the Keeper of the Privy Purse and three times as much as Joseph Ince, another confectioner in the prince's employ. He made an early buying trip for the Prince of Wales, not to his native France, but instead to Chester, where he was sent to buy two porcelain elephants and two porcelain dogs for a total cost of £8 8s.[28]

Benois's Parisian forays most often resulted in the purchase of quantities of porcelain, mostly Sèvres (Figs 6.12 and 6.13), but also Chinese and Japanese pieces, sometimes individually and sometimes in large quantity. In December 1815, he bought a service of *89 Pieces de Porcelaine ancien Sèvres fond bleu Claire à oiseaux* ('89 pieces of old Sèvres porcelain, light blue ground, with birds') from the dealer J.-F. Perregaux. It has been posited

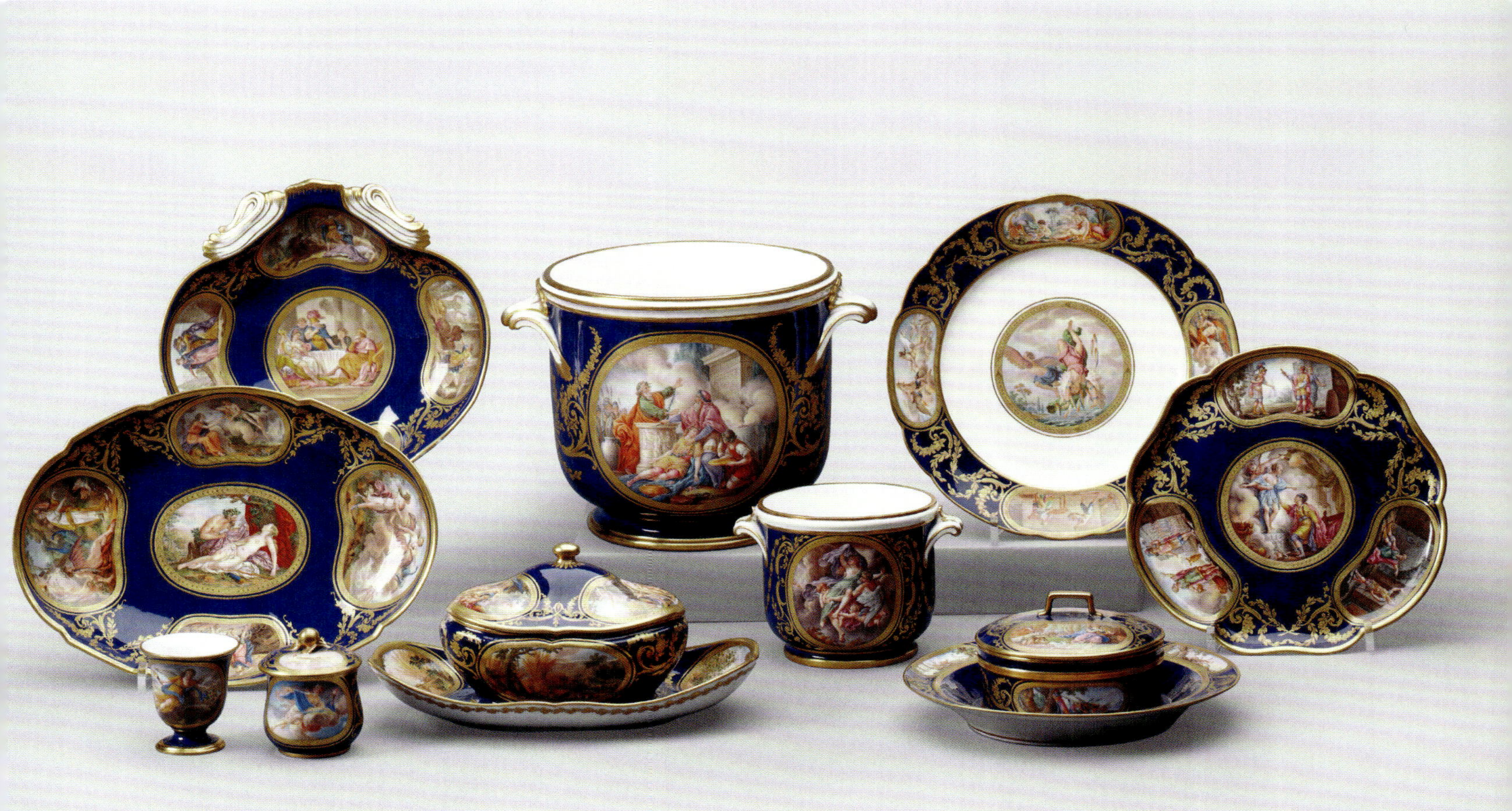

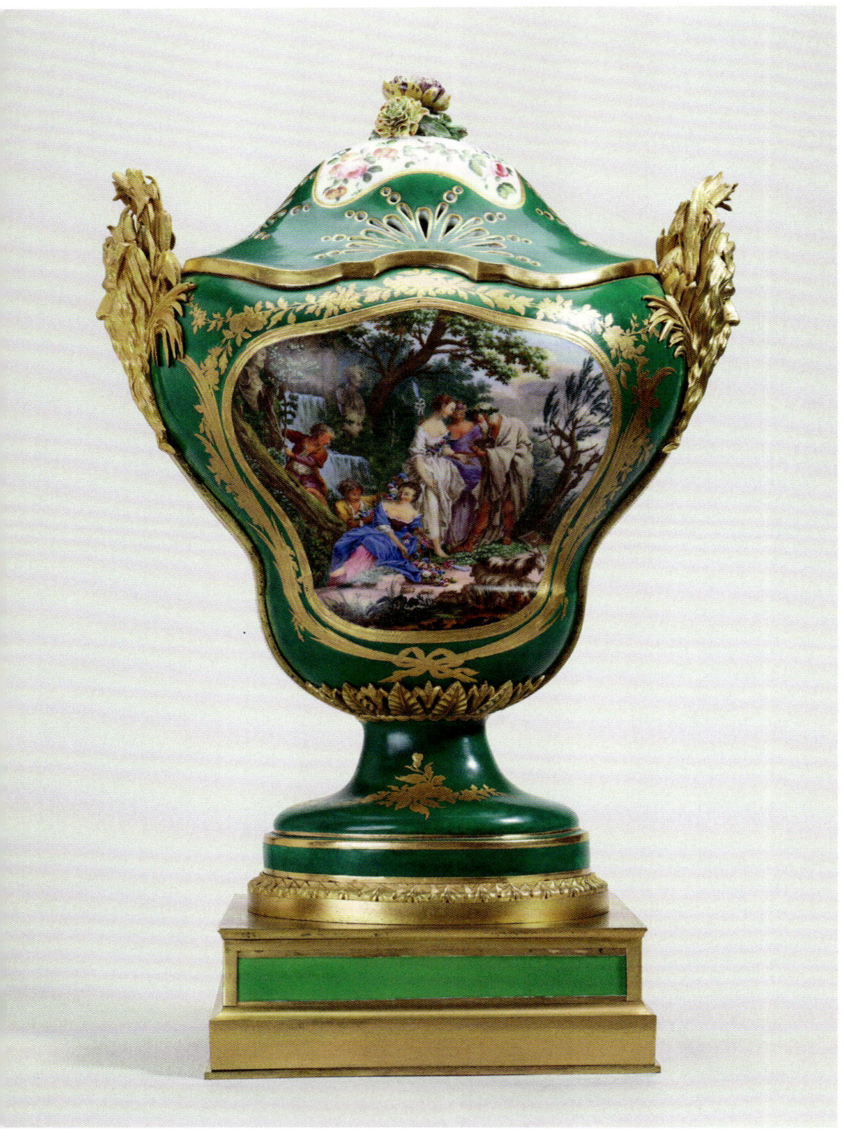

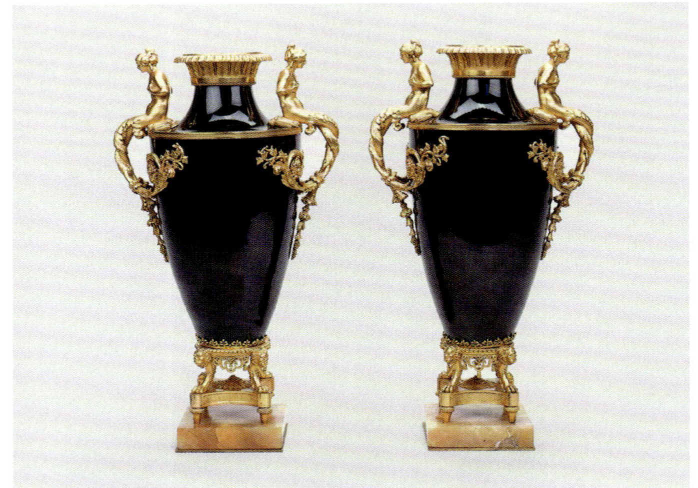

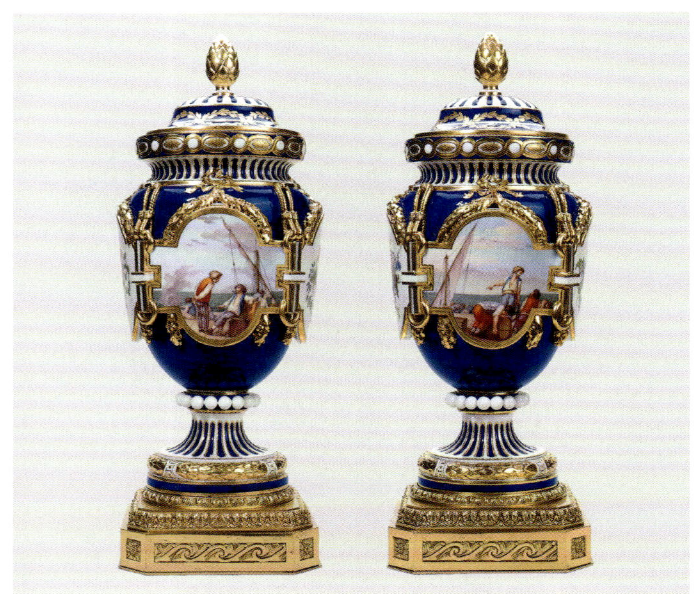

(above left)
FIG. 6.11
SÈVRES PORCELAIN FACTORY, *Pot-pourri Hébert*, 1763. Soft-paste porcelain, gilt bronze, 44.2 × 28.3 × 18.7 cm, RCIN 2361

(above right)
FIG. 6.12
SÈVRES PORCELAIN FACTORY with mounts by PIERRE-PHILIPPE THOMIRE (1751–1843), *Vases à monter*, c.1785. Hard-paste porcelain, gilt bronze, onyx, 35.0 × 19.2. × 12.8 cm, RCIN 253.1–2

(below right)
FIG. 6.13
SÈVRES PORCELAIN FACTORY, *Vases ferrés*, c.1780. Soft-paste porcelain, gilt bronze, 49.5 × 19.1 × 19.1 cm, RCIN 2286.1–2

that these pieces may at one time have been owned by Quintin Craufurd, the expatriate collector, adventurer, scholar, secret agent, servant of the East India Company and confidant of Louis XVI and Marie-Antoinette. If so, they were sold much earlier than most of Craufurd's collection, from which George acquired a number of pieces from Craufurd's widow in 1820.[29] Although presumably most familiar with porcelain, Benois's purchases for George ranged widely in media and value and were described in letters written to his masters in London. The large equestrian bronze of Louis XIV by Francois Girardon (Fig. 0.7) was the subject of a letter of 25 August 1817 from Benois to Sir Benjamin Bloomfield, George's Private Secretary, in which he suggested that there would be no space for this statue at Carlton House. Benois also described a *Grand Bureau et secretaire en marqueterie*, and

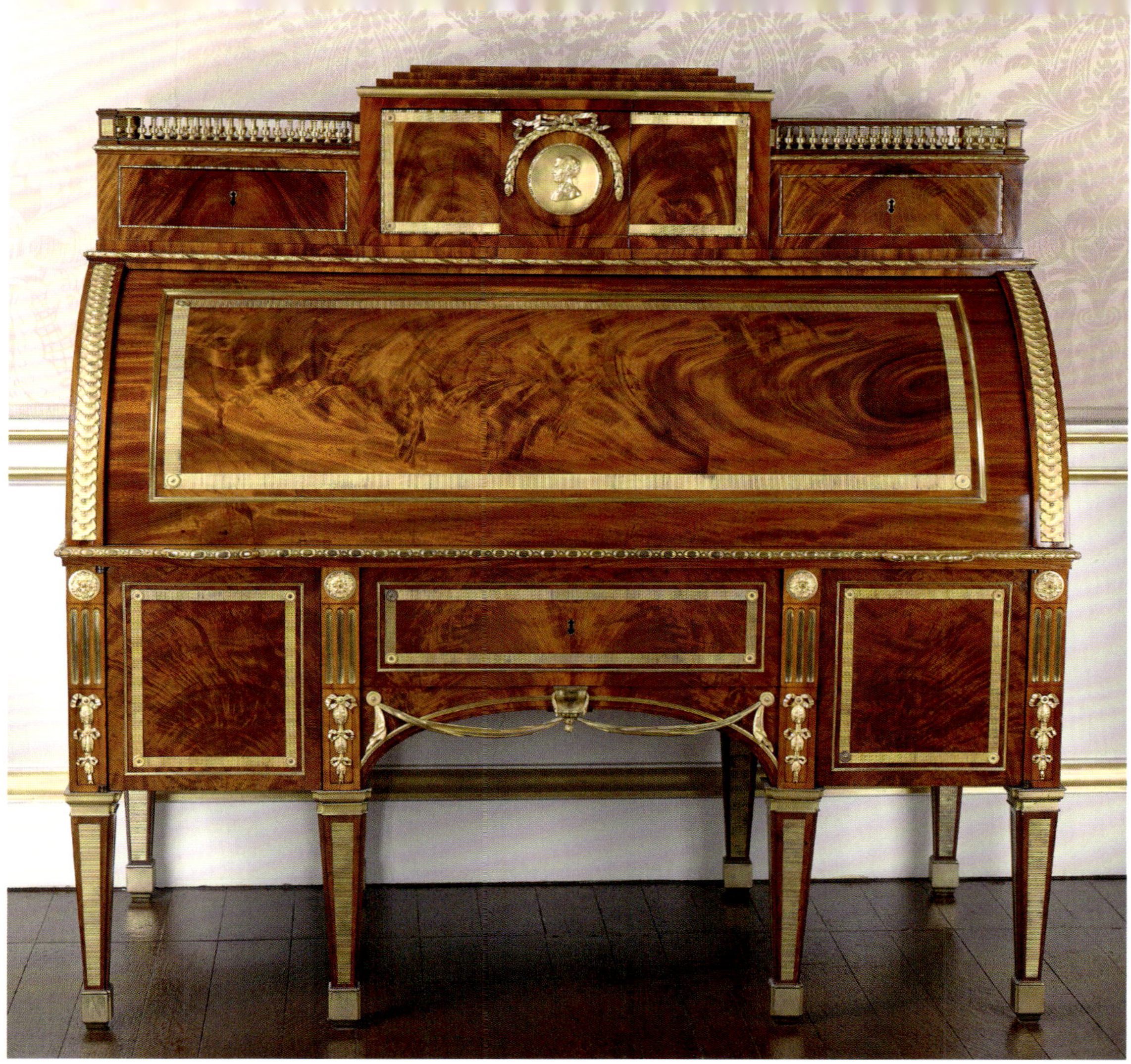

FIG. 6.14
ATTRIBUTED TO DAVID ROENTGEN (1743–1807), *Mechanical cylinder bureau*, *c.*1785. Oak and mahogany with gilt-bronze mounts, 148.0 × 142.0 × 83.0 cm, RCIN 293

recommended it should not be purchased.[30] In a subsequent letter, of 8 September, he expressed barely concealed glee at the news that George would not go ahead with recommendations made by another adviser-friend, Sir Jonathan Wathen Waller, who had recommended pieces judged by Benois to be *fort ordinaire* ('very ordinary'). This same letter mentions the Sèvres porcelain *Table des maréchaux* created for Napoleon as a tempting prospect for purchase.[31] The dealer Alexis Delahante wished to sell this, but only with some unspecified but apparently very beautiful paintings. The letter concludes with a word that the weather in France was of 'extreme warmth', giving hope that the wines of that year would be good, but not in abundance. Benois's next letter of three days later, 11 September, referred to a little drawing of a piece of furniture described as *très beau*. In the same letter he referred to a painting by Gerard ter Borch that had belonged to the politician Talleyrand and which had been offered for sale by Delahante, but now belonged to the dealer Bonnemaison, who would sell it at 27,000 francs (£1,225). The letter concluded by mentioning that Benois had not found anything else worth recommending, except a beautiful Meissen service.[32] Benois continued making significant purchases on regular forays to the French capital, among them the renowned mechanical cylinder bureau by David Roentgen (Fig. 6.14).[33] Like many of George's purchases, this probably appealed for its exalted French provenance. Three of this rare type of desk were made for Louis XVI and his brothers, the comte de Provence (later Louis XVIII) and the comte d'Artois (later Charles X). The one purchased in 1820 for George IV by Benois in Paris had cost £275, and was probably that which had been made for the comte de Provence.

Benois was responsible for numerous purchases of pieces of furniture of mainly low to middling value, spending on average about three months' sojourn in Paris, writing regularly and including little drawings of pieces seen at dealers (none are known to survive,

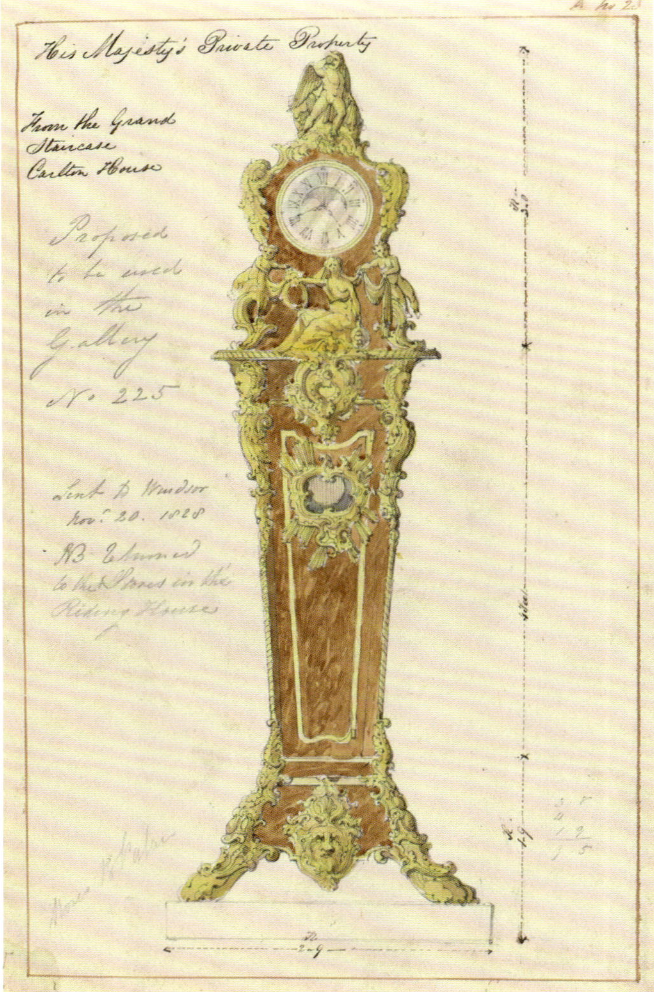

FIG. 6.15
OFFICE OF AUGUSTUS CHARLES PUGIN (*c.*1768–1832), *A floor-standing clock*, from the *Pictorial Inventory*, *c.*1827. Pencil and watercolour, 30.7 × 19.7 cm, RCIN 934764

but may be compared with those which make up the 'Pictorial Inventory'; Fig. 6.15).[34] In May 1814, Benois spent 31,289 francs (£1,501). Two years later, in the autumn of 1816, his purchases for George totalled 47,465 francs (£1,922) – the dealers or agents were named as Perregaux, Rocheux, Escudier, Coquille, Lefevre, Odiot, Dehaye, Paye, Jacob (the last not, in fact, for furniture, but for busts of emperors and Japanese and Chantilly porcelain).[35]

As Benois noted in another letter to Bloomfield of 22 September 1817, while he sourced objects of high value it was in fact left to Sir Charles Long to make the more costly purchases, no doubt based on intelligence provided by Benois in the form of letters and drawings.[36] In 1825 Long was in Paris and bought 19 objects at the posthumous sale of Philippe-Claude Maëlrondt, at which the Paris dealer Hasard seems to have been acting for Long, on behalf of the king.[37] On the same trip, Long purchased 37 pieces of Gobelins tapestry for the furnishing of Windsor Castle, including the *Story of Jason* series, which comprised eight panels.[38]

In furniture, George's taste was also competently serviced by the London dealer Edward Holmes Baldock. Baldock was able to source French furniture of the highest quality, and sold it to a band of English collectors, including George IV, all of whom shared an interest in collecting Boulle veneered furniture, exotic ebony and *pietre dure* cabinets and Sèvres porcelain, much of the latter recently mounted in gilt bronze, in much the same way that eighteenth-century Parisian dealers or *marchands-merciers* had mounted porcelain in gilt bronze or made furniture reusing seventeenth-century lacquer panels or hardstone plaques. Many of George's purchases from Baldock were made in the 1820s and included a large ebony writing-desk, almost certainly altered from its original form and with lettered gilt-bronze mounts reading 'DL' which had perhaps been taken from another piece of furniture altogether.[39] Such aggrandisement and alterations were typical of Baldock's trade, and supplied the market which readily accepted these creations, knowingly or otherwise.

Keeping furniture in its original form was evidently not a concern and, once acquired, it was often treated much like George's residences: subject to repeated cleaning, redecoration and modification. This quixotic approach to furniture was not unique to George IV. Many English collectors of the early years of the nineteenth century were just as flexible: George Byng of Wrotham Park, William Beckford, Lord Lowther and Walter Montagu-Douglas-Scott, 5th Duke of Buccleuch wanted a particular type of grand furniture – and that was what they were sold, albeit in an altered, adapted or aggrandised form. Dealers such as Baldock were only too ready to provide furniture which fitted the ideal of the early nineteenth-century English interior of the circle around George.[40] Not everything bought from Baldock by George had undergone surgery, however: a large Flemish secretaire-cabinet with a richly inlaid surface of pewter, turtle shell, hardstones and rosewood and mounted in gilt bronze was sold to George more or less intact following its sale from Clandon Park after the death of his friend the Earl of Onslow in 1827.[41] George bought the cabinet from Baldock in May 1828 for £350.

Equally, George was content to buy English reproductions, or interpretations, of early eighteenth-century Boulle furniture (Fig. 6.16). In 1815 he bought two tables (at £250 each) for the

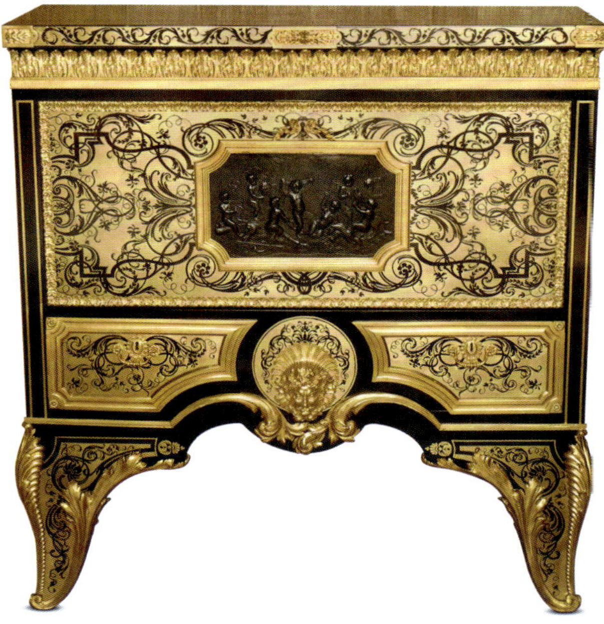

(above)
FIG. 6.16
ETIENNE LEVASSEUR (1721–98), *Secretaire*, *c.*1700 (with later adaptations, *c.*1770). Oak, ebony, tortoiseshell and brass, gilt-bronze mounts, 143.5 × 135.5 × 52.0 cm, RCIN 29945

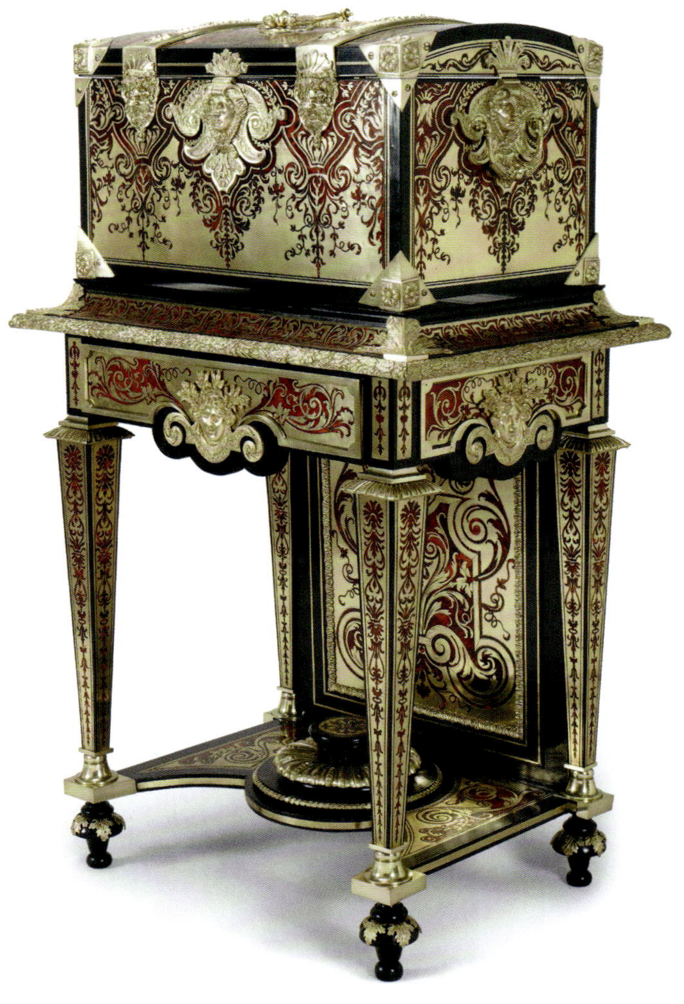

(right)
FIG. 6.17
THOMAS PARKER (active 1808–30), *Coffer-on-stand*, 1813. Brass-inlaid tortoiseshell, gilt bronze, ebony, 34.5 × 56.5 × 41.0 cm, RCIN 21624

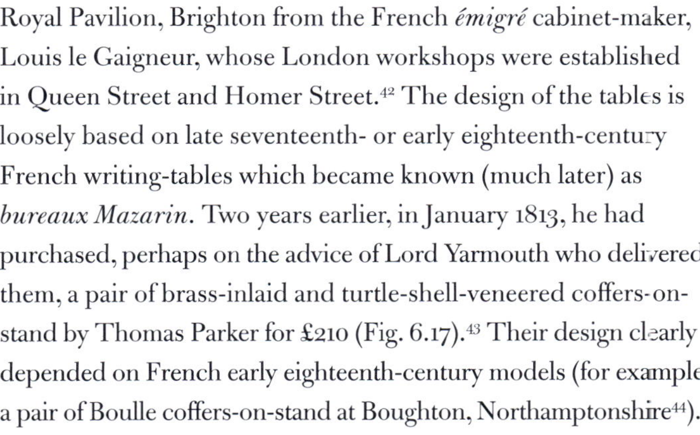

Royal Pavilion, Brighton from the French *émigré* cabinet-maker, Louis le Gaigneur, whose London workshops were established in Queen Street and Homer Street.[42] The design of the tables is loosely based on late seventeenth- or early eighteenth-century French writing-tables which became known (much later) as *bureaux Mazarin*. Two years earlier, in January 1813, he had purchased, perhaps on the advice of Lord Yarmouth who delivered them, a pair of brass-inlaid and turtle-shell-veneered coffers-on-stand by Thomas Parker for £210 (Fig. 6.17).[43] Their design clearly depended on French early eighteenth-century models (for example a pair of Boulle coffers-on-stand at Boughton, Northamptonshire[44]).

Other rich and exotic furniture was bought by George from Robert Owen, whose shop at 95 New Bond Street was known as the 'East India Warehouse'. Owen, rather like Baldock and other dealers, sold furniture which had been embellished, perhaps under his own direction. Among the porcelain, textiles and furniture sold to George was the commode stamped 'BVRB' which was made by the second-generation Flemish *émigré* cabinet-maker Bernard II van Risamburgh, one of the leading *ébénistes* in mid-eighteenth-century Paris.[45] The commode was made with expensive Japanese lacquer veneers, which had almost certainly been purchased by a Paris *marchand-mercier* such as Simon-Philippe Poirier or Thomas Joachim Hébert at great cost, and then sent to Van Risamburgh. It was bought by George in July 1829 for £110 5s.[46]

The firm of clockmakers Vulliamy & Co. played an important role in the sale, creation and maintenance of a wide range of works of art. The firm was established at 74 Pall Mall by the Swiss *émigré* François-Justin Vulliamy when he went into partnership with the royal clockmaker Benjamin Gray in 1743.[47] At first the business was solely concerned with clock and watch making (Fig. 6.18) and undertaking repairs but by the end of the eighteenth century

FIG. 6.18
PIERRE-PHILIPPE THOMIRE (1751–1843) with later movement by BENJAMIN LEWIS VULLIAMY (1780–1854), *Mantel clock*, *c.*1810 (movement 1834). Gilt bronze, blued steel, marble, glass, 75.0 × 78.0 × 26.0 cm, RCIN 2764

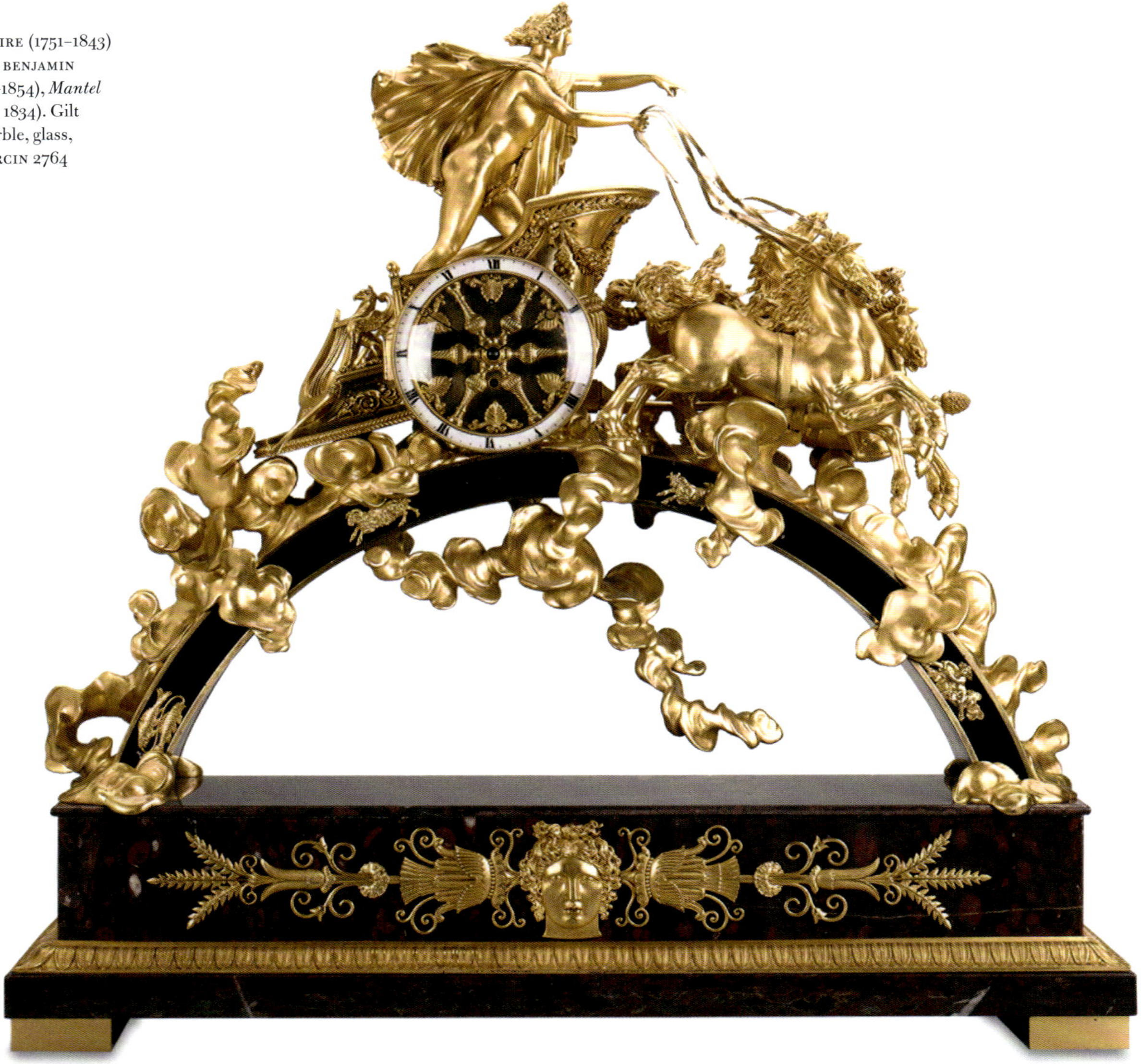

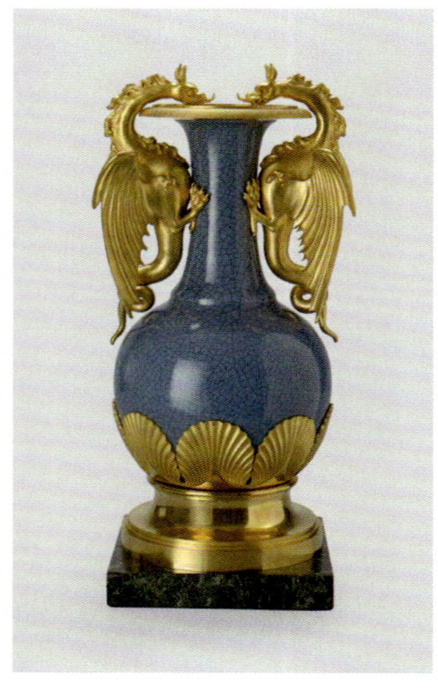

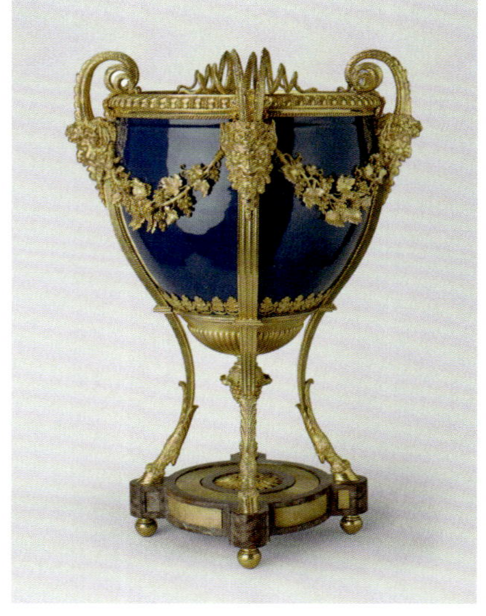

(left)
FIG. 6.19
JINGDEZHEN, CHINA, with mounts by BENJAMIN VULLIAMY (1747–1811), *Vase with mounts*, second half 18th century (mounts 1807). Porcelain, gilt bronze. 49.0 × 23.5 × 22.5 cm, RCIN 187

(right)
FIG. 6.20
JINGDEZHEN, CHINA, with mounts attributed to PIERRE-PHILIPPE THOMIRE (1751–1843), *Cistern with mounts*, mid-18th century (mounts last quarter 18th century). Porcelain, gilt bronze, 80.7 × 57.0 × 57.0 cm, RCIN 64062

FIG. 6.21
JOHANN GOTTFRIED HÄNISCH (1696–1778), *Crossbow*, *c.*1750–75. Steel, mahogany, ebony, horn, 65.3 × 55.0 cm, RCIN 61425

FIG. 6.22
DURS EGG (1748–1831), *Pistol*, 1787. Walnut, steel, gold, silver, 38.0 cm (length), RCIN 61166

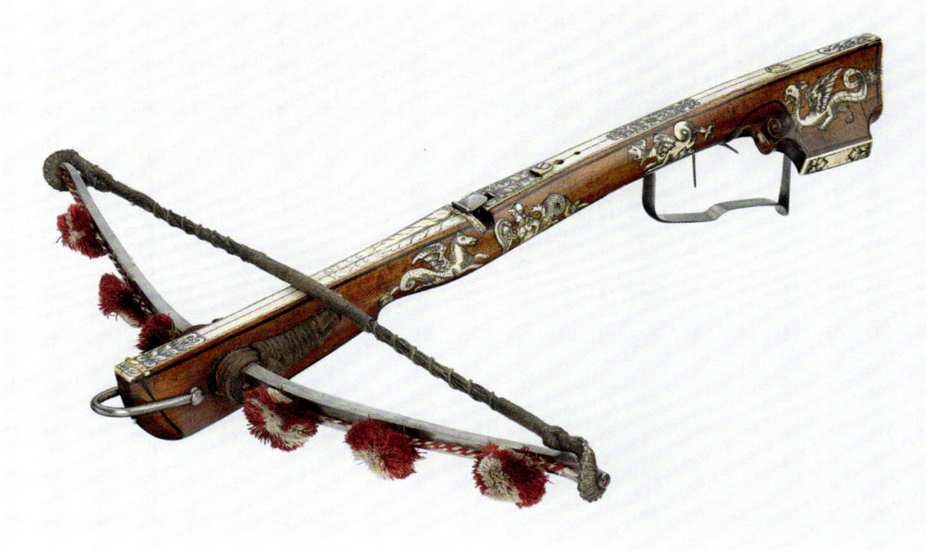

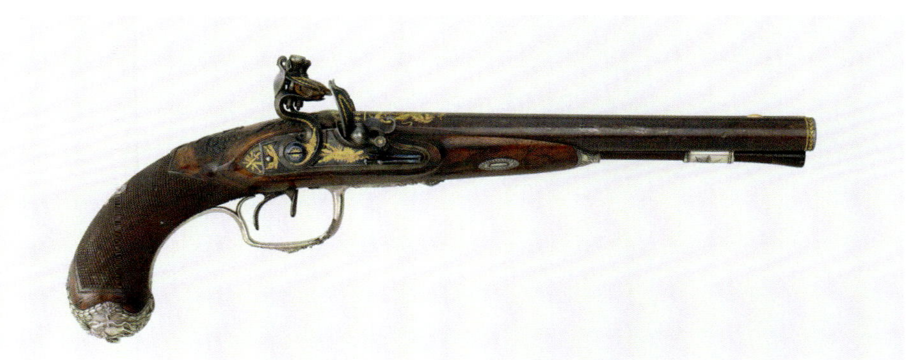

François-Justin's son Benjamin Vulliamy had assumed control and it was under his tenure that the firm expanded into making a wide range of mounts for Chinese porcelain (Fig. 6.19), adding fittings for lighting to vases and supplying candelabra, as well as repairing and replacing clock movements. Although dealing was not their primary concern, they did on occasion sell works of art to George, including the large Chinese blue porcelain cistern mounted in gilt bronze, perhaps by Thomire, purchased by the prince in March 1803 for £200 (Fig. 6.20).[48] After Benjamin Vuillamy's death in 1811 the firm continued to be closely associated with George, with Benjamin Lewis Vulliamy, grandson of the founder, at its head.

George's fascination with arms and armour was as long-lived as any of his other interests (Fig. 6.21). In the earliest period of his collecting, the 1780s, he bought swords from Thomas Bland, and firearms from London gunmakers Durs Egg, Henry Nock, Griffin & Tow and others.[49] Charles Brandt, a watchmaker, dealer and chapman, enjoyed particular favour, but mainly as a maintainer of weaponry and gilder of metalwork. In April 1821 George bought from him 'a Gun with Asiatic Barrel french mounted … £21'.[50] Egg, described by George in 1782 as 'ye best Workman we have here', seems to have encouraged George's antiquarian interest in arms and sold him a pair of Madrid pistols and a Turkish Damascus-barrelled gun, as well as modern arms such as the pair of double-barrelled flintlock pistols inlaid in silver with Prince of Wales feathers (Fig. 6.22).[51]

George's interest in all things military extended to his vast collection of prints and drawings, which included important material on army uniforms and battles (see chapter 9) and was formed mainly on the London market.[52] Pall Mall was at the centre of the London print trade and Carlton House was therefore situated close to the leading print shops, many of which supplied George. His main source of works on paper was the fashionable firm of Colnaghi & Co., who supplied him with tens of thousands of prints and drawings between at least 1792 and his death in 1830 (Figs 6.23 and 6.24). Unlike

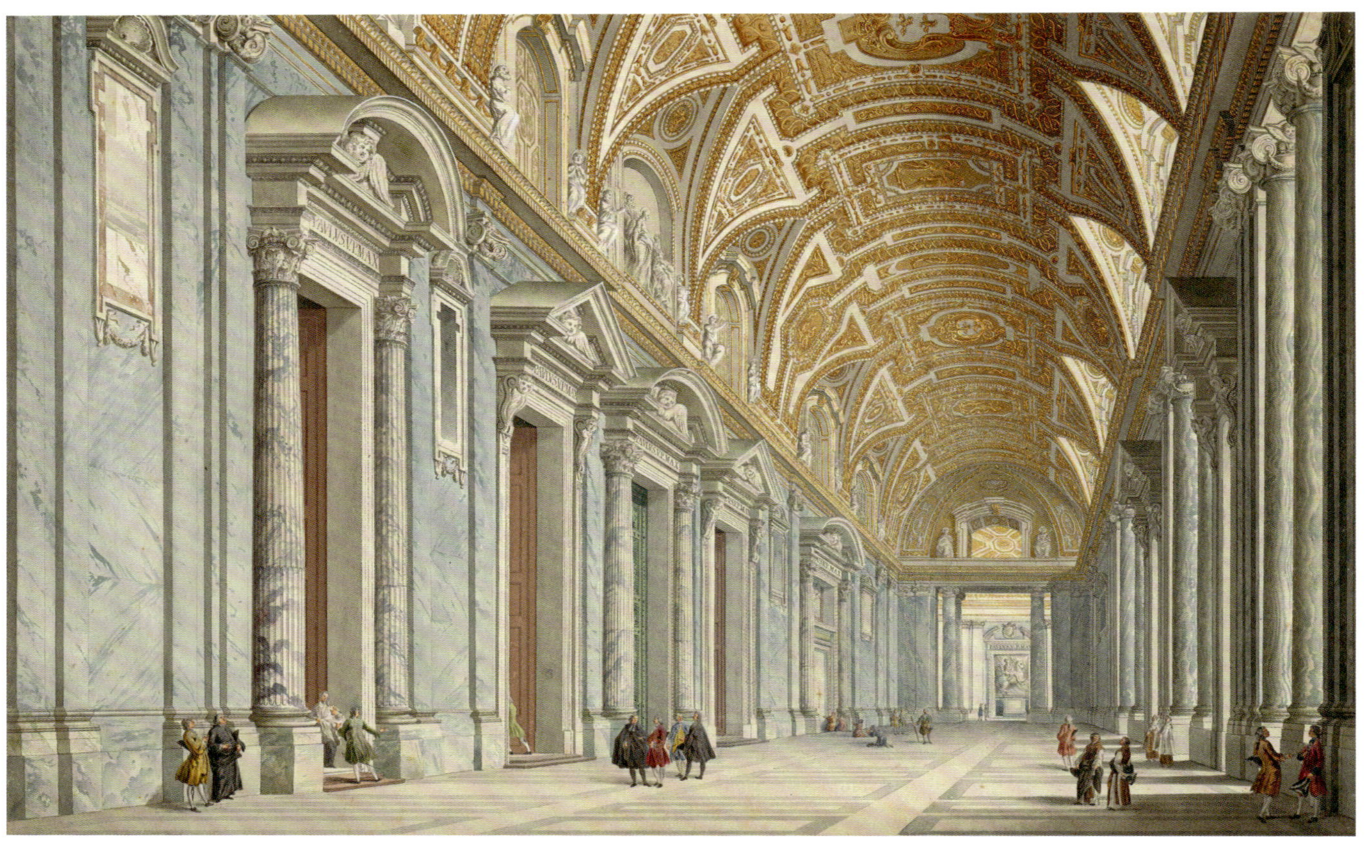

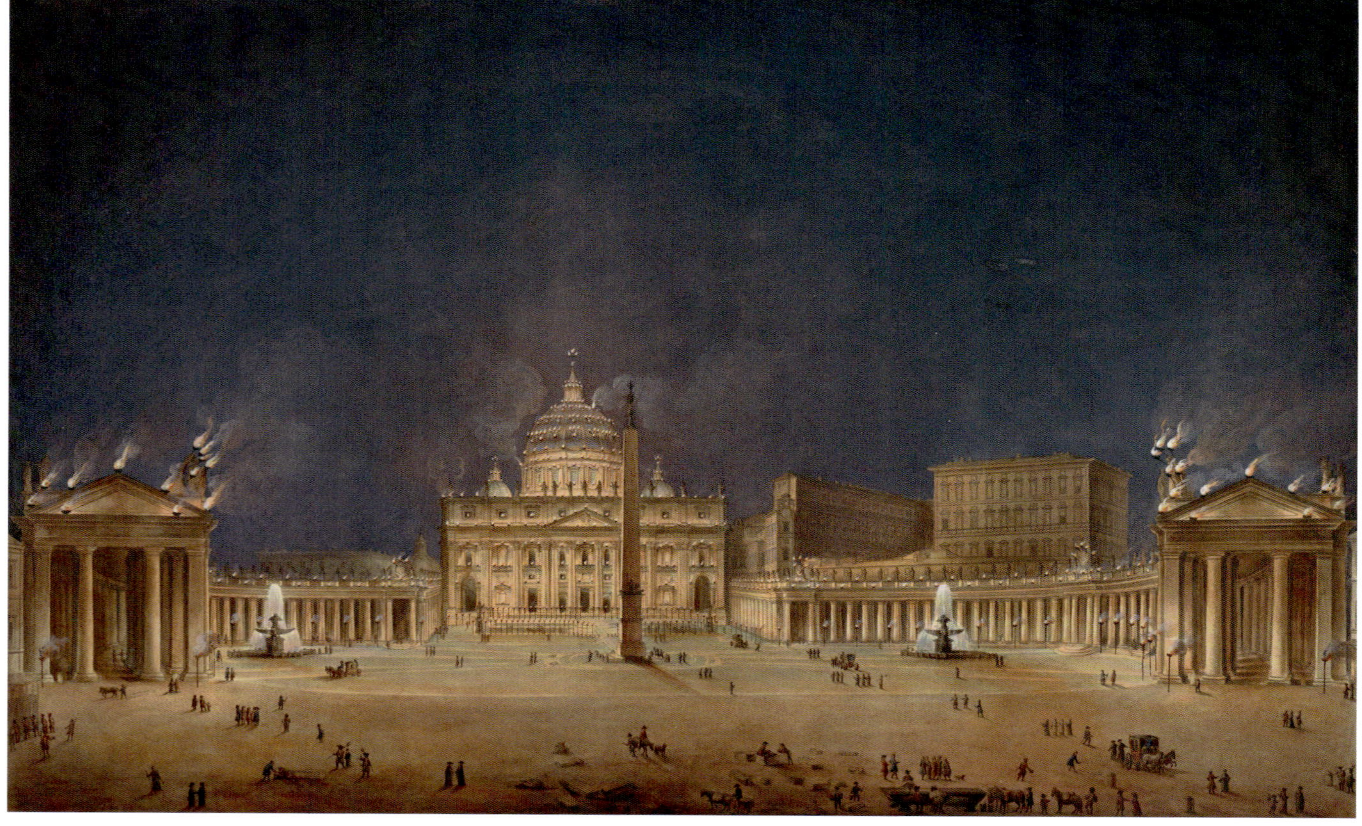

FIG. 6.23
FRANCESCO PANINI (1745–1812), *Prospetto Interno del' Portico della Basilica di San' Pietro nel Vaticano*, *c.*1770. Etching with watercolour and bodycolour and gold paint, 55.0 × 84.5 cm (sheet), RCIN 705163.c

FIG. 6.24
FRANCESCO PANINI (1745–1812), *Veduta della Piazza di S. Pietro illuminata dalle Fiacole*, *c.*1700. Etching worked in watercolour and bodycolour, 55.6 × 85.6 cm (sheet), RCIN 705163.f

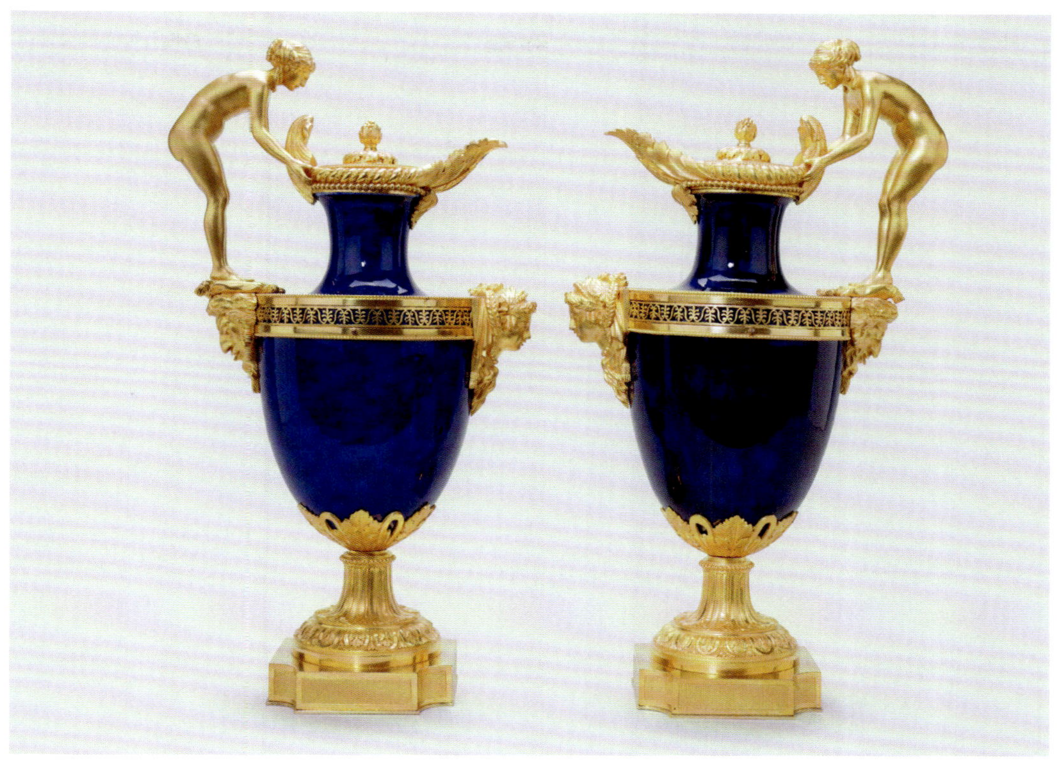

FIG. 6.25
SÈVRES PORCELAIN FACTORY with mounts by PIERRE-PHILIPPE THOMIRE (1751–1843), *Vases à monter*, *c.*1782–6. Hard-paste porcelain, gilt bronze, 41.0 × 23.0 × 13.5 cm, RCIN 35513.1–2

many print connoisseurs, George did not visit the Colnaghi shop (which moved between various addresses in Pall Mall and Cockspur Street), but rather chose prints from portfolios of material submitted for his consideration. Colnaghi & Co. also offered 'curatorial' services, with staff visiting the print collection on a number of occasions in 1813 'for the arrangt of His Royl Highness Collection of Drawings and Prints'.[53] Although Colnaghi & Co. were George's main suppliers, he patronised a number of the other leading firms, among them Edward Orme (who supplied topographical and sporting prints), John Boydell (to whose Shakespeare Gallery George was a typically late-paying subscriber) and Moon, Boys & Graves (who offered prints of society figures and notable paintings from 6 Pall Mall). The fashionable specialists in satirical prints William Holland and Hannah Humphrey were both important suppliers: Holland compiled albums of satirical material (containing well over 1,000 prints) around 1790 and from 1803 Humphrey sent regular deliveries of topical satires, which were apparently selected by George's Assistant Private Secretary, General Sir Tomkyns Hilgrove Turner, a knowledgeable connoisseur who acted as keeper of the prints and drawings. George's patronage was coveted by the London printsellers who won his custom. George's failure to purchase prints from the satirical printseller Samuel William Fores fuelled a feud which was conducted through hostile satires and threatened lawsuits (see chapter 12). For the printsellers of London, 'His Royal Highness the Prints of Wales' (as a hapless Colnaghi employee wrote in error on one invoice) was a valued and significant client.[54]

One of the greatest talents displayed by George was his ability to surround himself with like-minded advisers of enterprising spirit from whom he demanded a wide range of services. To take a single example, Dominique Daguerre was employed by the prince as interior decorator, but supported this role as both *marchand-mercier* and porcelain dealer (Fig. 6.25). George's friends, such as Charles Long or Lord Yarmouth, were similarly adaptable, often acting as intermediaries in the market as well as collaborating on the evolving interiors of the royal residences. Those external agents to whom George turned to supply his seemingly endless desire for new works of art were equally amenable to the varying demands from their royal patron – thus the royal goldsmiths produced works of sculpture or painting, his porcelain dealers supplied furniture, and one of the most successful nineteenth-century clockmaking firms took on the supply of a full range of mounts for porcelain. The lasting picture is of one in which George inspired those around him with great entrepreneurial drive to form a truly magnificent collection of masterpieces which he displayed in a series of interiors that were a harmonious whole, simultaneously comfortable and spectacular.

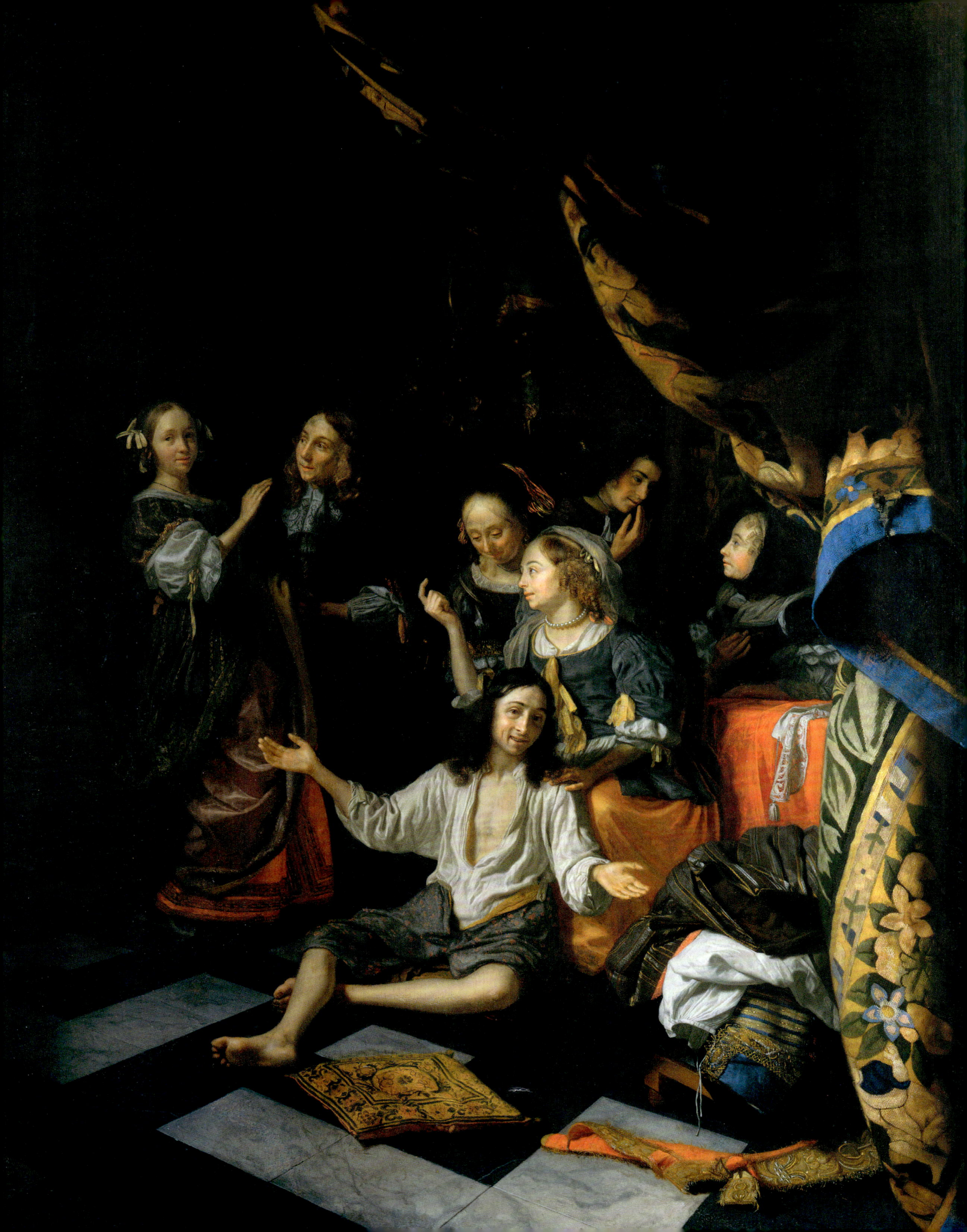

7

GEORGE IV *and the* LOW COUNTRY MASTERS

DESMOND SHAWE-TAYLOR

WITH SECOND-GENERATION COLLECTORS the first question that occurs to scholars is what did they grow up with and how did it affect their subsequent taste? George IV's childhood surroundings are recorded in Johan Zoffany's conversation piece of 1765, showing the three-year-old prince with his younger brother, Frederick, in the Warm Room at the 'Queen's House', as Buckingham Palace was called (see Fig. 3.11).[1] We can flesh out Zoffany's charming image with comprehensive documentation of the picture hang at the palace, from the 1780s until the accession of George IV in 1820.[2] A particular style of art earned its place in these surroundings, called the 'great style' by the first president of the Royal Academy, Sir Joshua Reynolds.[3] Based on the study of Classical Antiquity, the style was perfected by Raphael and practised during the sixteenth and seventeenth centuries by Italians and by Northerners, like Rubens (Fig. 7.2) and Van Dyck, who respected the same ideals. There was a landscape equivalent, of almost equal status and similarly imbued with Classical ideals, created in Rome by Claude Lorrain and Nicolas Poussin.[4] Such paintings filled the queen's apartments on the first floor of Buckingham House, the landscapes having a room of their own, all in carefully spaced and symmetrical arrangements.[5]

George IV did something different at Carlton House – employing the same careful arrangement but with a new type of painting. Many of the most important rooms at Carlton House, especially on the garden façade, were given over to rustic landscapes and genre paintings from the Low Countries, the very antithesis of the great style.[6] Illustrations of the interiors published by William Henry Pyne during the Regency show displays densely but carefully spaced and symmetrically arranged, featuring all manner of boors, braggarts and serving girls.

George IV was no pioneer in his taste for this 'Low Country Style'; the names in his inventories correspond to those sought out by collectors throughout the previous century.[7] Such a taste did not necessarily challenge academic teaching. Netherlandish art (usually called either 'Dutch' or 'Flemish' at the whim of the author) was generally accepted as something short of the highest art because it was particular and real rather than general

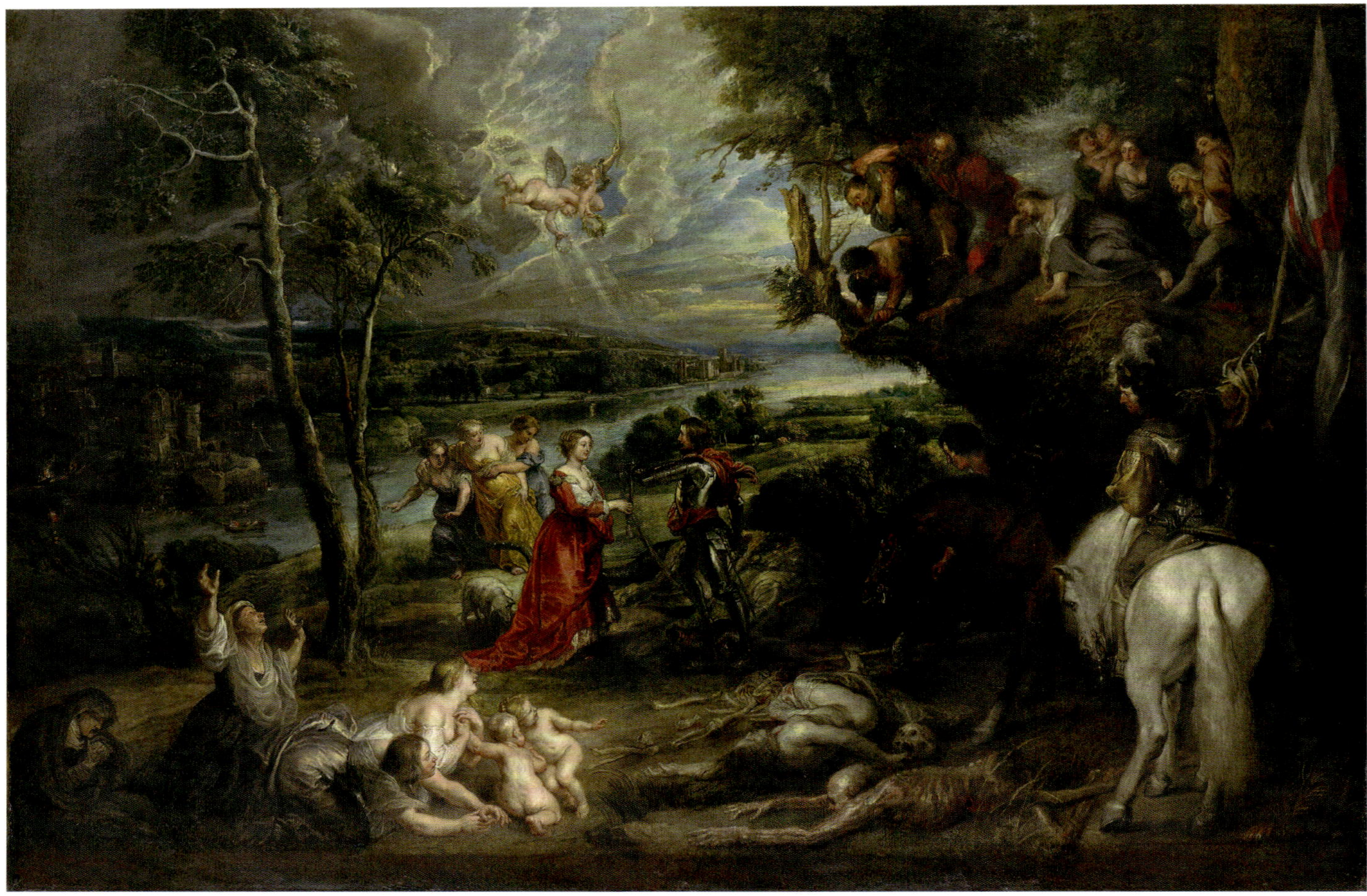

(p. 104)
FIG. 7.1
GODFRIED SCHALCKEN (1643–1706), *The Game of 'Lady, come into the Garden'*, late 1660s. Oil on panel, 63.5 × 49.5 cm, RCIN 405343

FIG. 7.2
SIR PETER PAUL RUBENS (1577–1640), *Landscape with St George and the Dragon*, 1630–5. Oil on canvas, 152.5 × 226.9 cm, RCIN 405356

and ideal; it was painted with brilliance rather than drawn with learning; and it was bourgeois or peasant comedy rather than princely tragedy.[8] The accommodation of peasant art into the royal cabinet took place most obviously in France and the easiest way to understand it is to consider the prestige of these painters' literary contemporary, Molière.[9] Court playwright to Louis XIV, Molière found inspiration in Classical precedents and occupied an assured place in the academic hierarchy; yet he wrote modern middle-class comedies rather than ancient heroic tragedies. Most European cultures could produce equivalents to Molière, even if, like William Wycherley, their fame was more parochial. Throughout the eighteenth century, a group of Dutch and Flemish painters commanded a comparable respect: finding their way into the most exalted collections, their fame disseminated through fine prints, often graced with French titles and the coat of arms of the collector. The most important was David Teniers the Younger; himself a landowner and court artist in Brussels to the Archduke Leopold William, his lively touch described an easily readable comedy of rustic clowns. His reputation carried two comparable Dutch purveyors of comic low-life, Isaac and Adriaen van Ostade. The second most popular artist was Philips Wouwerman, closely followed by Jan Wijnants; both depicted cavaliers, hunters or soldiers, in the picturesque setting of a camp, inn or fair. The Italian pastorals of Nicolaes Berchem, Karel du Jardin and Adriaen van de Velde were similarly picturesque with their prettily ragged shepherds and shepherdesses. The final category of artists embraced by aristocratic collectors were those who painted scenes of Dutch bourgeois prosperity, where the skill lay in depicting fine things in well-lit interiors and the comedy in amorous intrigues or sophisticated debauchery. The recommended artists of this type were Gerard ter Borch and the school of 'Leiden Fine Painters',

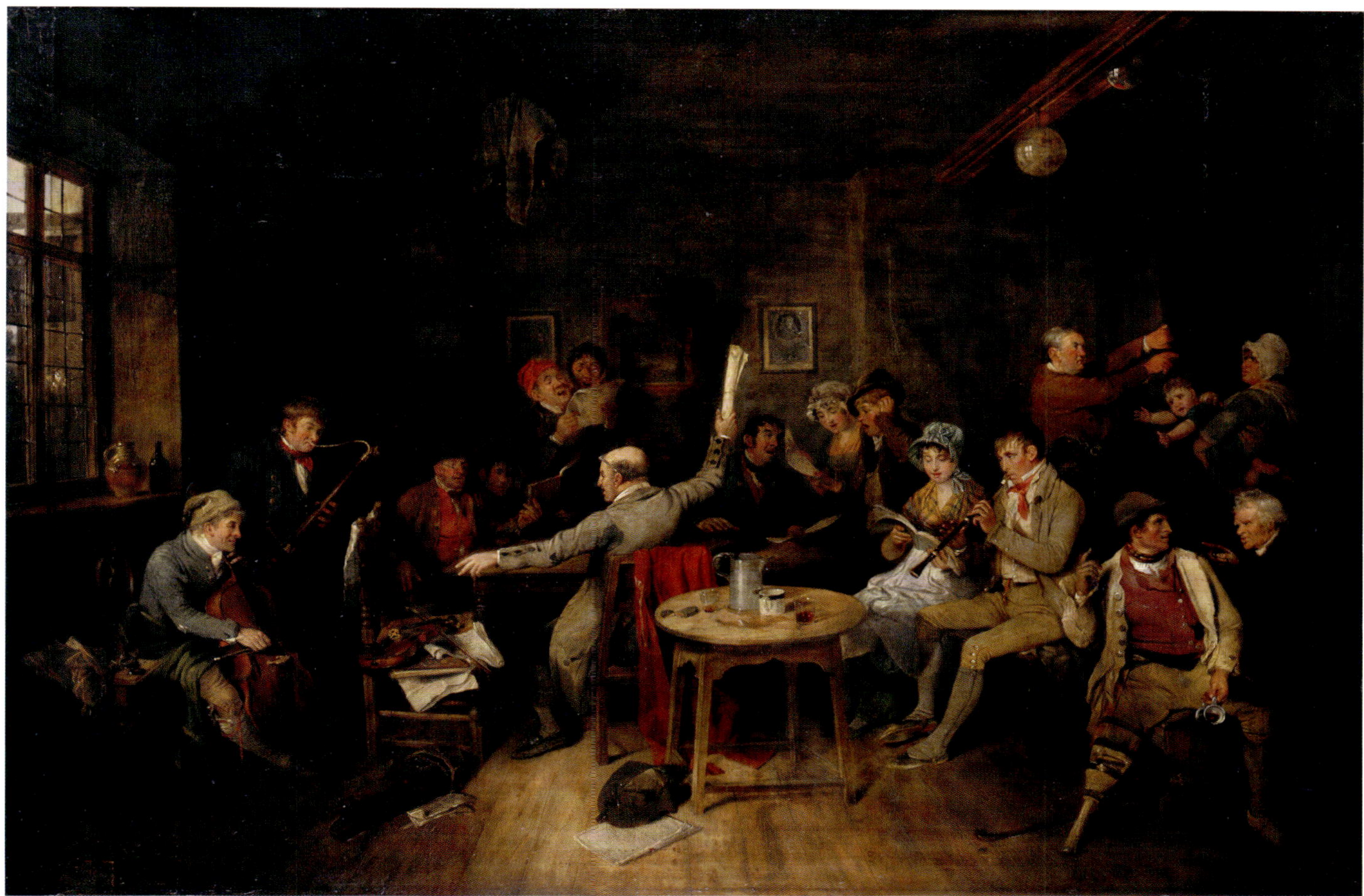

FIG. 7.3
EDWARD BIRD (1772–1819), *Village Choristers Rehearsing an Anthem for Sunday*, 1810. Oil on panel, 63.1 × 92.8 cm, RCIN 405540

Gerrit Dou, Gabriel Metsu, Godfried Schalcken, and Frans and Willem van Mieris.

There is no term of convenience to describe this restricted group of artists that made up *ancien régime* middle-brow taste, but their works appear reproduced or imitated on tapestries, porcelain and other decorative arts throughout Europe during the eighteenth century. They also made their way into the Royal Collection, through acquisitions by Frederick, Prince of Wales and George III of works by Teniers, Wouwerman, Wijnants, Berchem and Frans van Mieris.[10] Two of Frederick's Teniers paintings, both hanging at Carlton House, were reproduced by Thomas Major in 1749 and 1750 in fine engravings, complete with royal arms and in one case a comic-opera title – 'The Jealous Husband'.[11] Even Buckingham House displayed landscapes by Teniers and Wouwerman, if only in the miscellaneous hang of a lesser space, the queen's 'Wardrobe'.[12]

With George IV there was no change of heart, just a change of emphasis. He neglected the great style, or perhaps found that he could not afford examples to meet his high standards; at the same time, he brought these 'lesser masters' out of their wardrobes and closets.[13] We can trace the development of this taste through the impact of certain key sales. George IV was not a reclusive aesthete but a gregarious man of fashion, his taste influenced by advisers and fellow collectors, his bulk acquisitions often seeming as if he was winning a hand with the cards already arranged. George IV made a slow start as a painting collector: before the Regency in 1811, he had occupied Carlton House for 28 years and transformed it repeatedly (see chapter 5), while acquiring little of significance. This started to change during the first decade of the nineteenth century when Walsh Porter was advising George IV on its furnishings.[14] In a letter of 23 August 1806 Porter reveals that he has a 'rare assemblage of some of

FIG. 7.4
WILLIAM MULREADY (1786–1863), *The Wolf and the Lamb*, 1819–20. Oil on panel, 60.0 × 51.1 cm, RCIN 405539

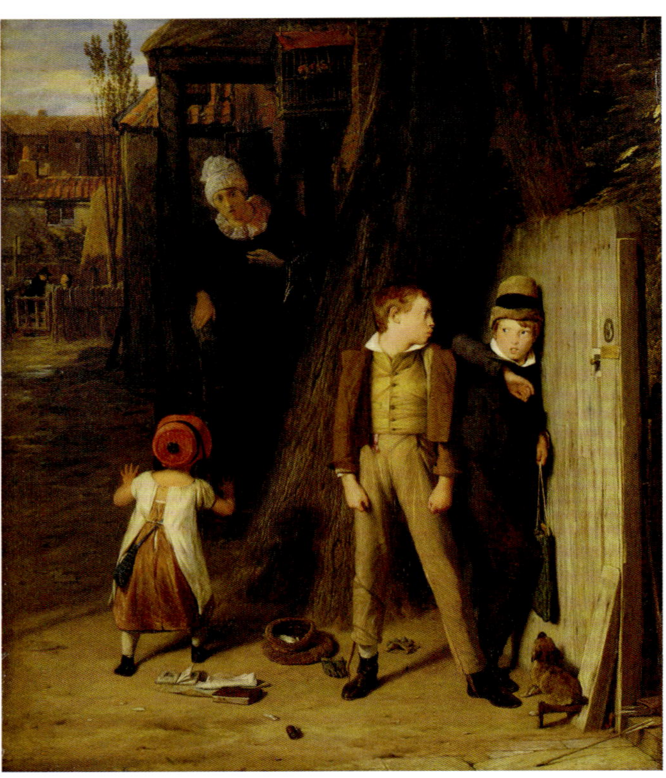

the finest things' that will make the apartments as 'refined & *classical* as possible'; he mentions 12 paintings, including fine examples by Rubens, Claude, Titian and Murillo.[15] George IV did not take up the offer and the paintings cannot be identified, but these four names and what we know of Walsh Porter's collection suggest that they were in the great style.[16] A few years earlier, in 1803, Porter had auctioned part of his collection and George IV spent £1,217 on four key works of the opposite type. He acquired a Teniers, a Le Nain (then attributed to Caravaggio), a Thomas de Keyser (attributed to Cuyp) and a Godfried Schalcken.[17] It is this final work, then called 'Le Roi Dépouillé' ('The King Despoiled'), now called *The Game of 'Lady, come into the Garden'* (Fig. 7.1), costing a considerable £409 10s, which epitomises George IV's taste at this date.[18] Created by a recognised master, and said in the sale catalogue to have been in the French royal collection, it comes with a French title and an arrangement of figures suggesting a risqué comedy.[19] Walsh Porter's death in 1809 provided George IV with a final opportunity to acquire works at his posthumous sale of 14 April 1810. This may give some insight into the works overlooked in 1806, as there are fine examples of the artists then mentioned by Porter – Rubens, Claude, Titian and Murillo.[20] In the event, the prince's only purchases were Dutch – a Wijnants *Hawking Scene* and a Jacob van Ruisdael *Landscape*.[21] In the same year George IV made some significant individual acquisitions, including an interior by Godfried Schalcken, already well known through a print of 1767 by Jean-Georges Wille, entitled 'Le Concert de Famille', as if it were another French bourgeois comedy.[22]

There is ample evidence of George IV's love of theatre and of the theatrical component of painting – its narrative and comedy. In the Middle Room Upper Floor at Carlton House he hung a 'scene from a French Comedy' attributed to Watteau, now identified as from Molière's *Monsieur de Pourceaugnac* and by Jean-Baptiste-Joseph Pater.[23] In the Upper Anti Room next door, George IV hung his first acquisition of English genre, Edward Bird's *Village Choristers* of 1810 (Fig. 7.3).[24] Though based upon and hanging in the company of Adriaen van Ostade, Bird's painting has a more sustained anecdotal narrative, inspired by the example of William Hogarth. At this date Charles Lamb was praising Hogarth as the second greatest *author* in the English language after Shakespeare and arguing that his reputation as an *artist* should be elevated. His remarks could be read as a defence of George IV's taste:

> It is the fashion with those that cry up the great Historical School in this country, at the head of which Sir Joshua Reynolds is placed, to exclude Hogarth from that school, as an artist of inferior and vulgar class. Those persons seem to me to confound the painting of subjects in common or vulgar life with the being a vulgar artist. The quantity of thought which Hogarth crowds into every picture, would alone *unvulgarize* every subject which he might choose.[25]

Lamb goes on to praise Hogarth for his cunning narrative devices and his generosity of spirit, which makes even his satire patriotic, as it shows characters 'cut out of the *good old rock*, substantial English honesty'.[26] In 1808, George IV acquired a very personal painting attributed to Hogarth (now without attribution), showing his grandfather Frederick, Prince of Wales, rubbing shoulders with these honest English folk in St James's Park, a few yards from Carlton House.[27] He retained his enthusiasm for this kind of modern narrative painting. He apparently spilt candle wax on the frame of Mulready's *The Wolf and the Lamb* (Fig. 7.4) of 1820 in his eagerness to explain its story to friends.[28]

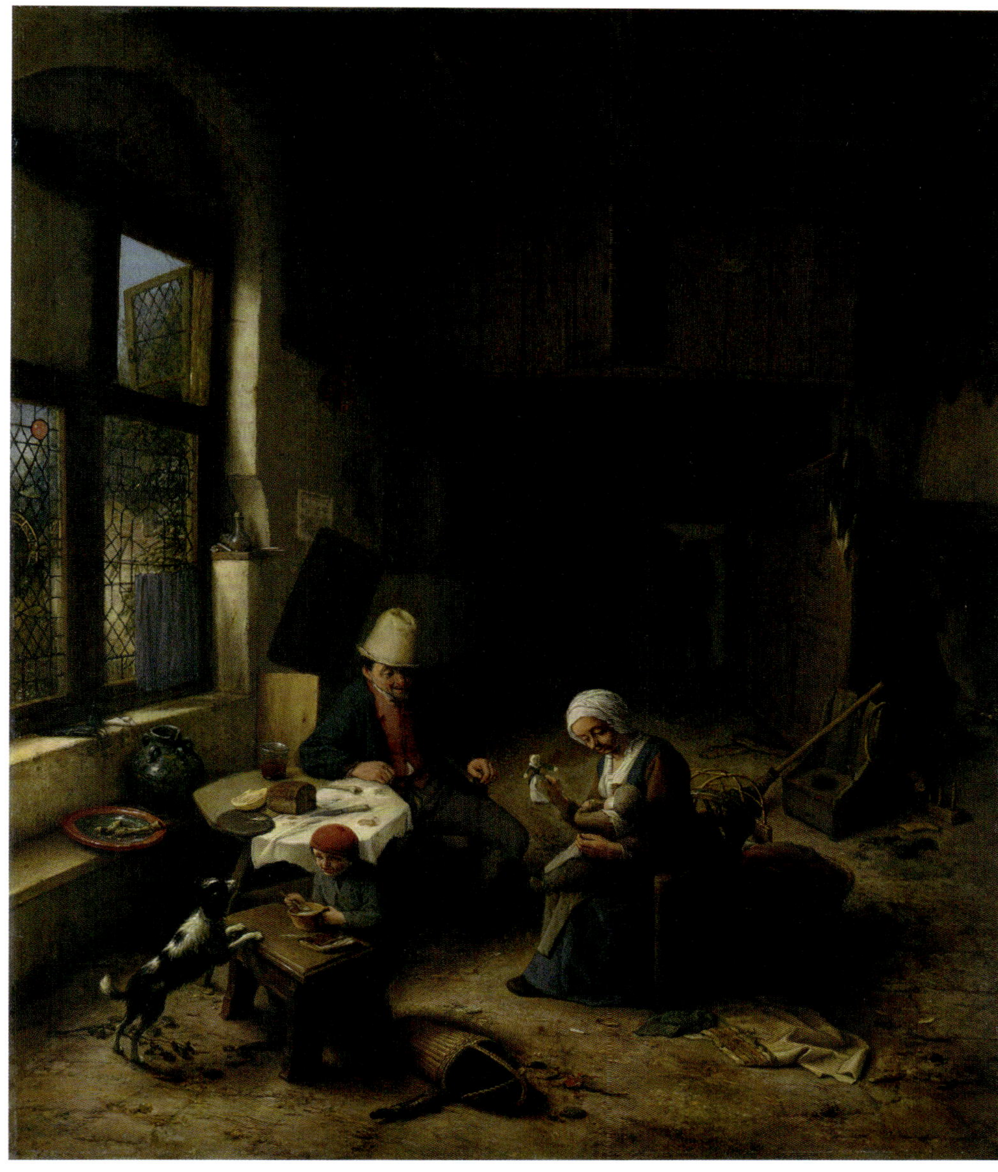

FIG. 7.5
ADRIAEN VAN OSTADE (1610–85), *The Interior of a Peasant's Cottage*, 1668. Oil on panel, 49.1 × 41.2 cm, RCIN 404814

George IV's final painting purchase was *The Duenna* by Gilbert Stuart Newton, illustrating his friend, Richard Brinsley Sheridan's famous opera of the same name.[29] The work, now known only through prints, appears to be a conscious imitation of the style of Gerard ter Borch.[30] Like so many of the contemporary theatrical paintings of Samuel de Wilde and George Clint, it reinforces the link between old Dutch paintings and modern British comedies.

On 5 February 1811, George became Prince Regent with access to considerably greater resources than hitherto. By this time Walsh Porter's role as chief artistic adviser had been taken over by George IV's friend and political associate Francis Charles Seymour-Conway, who became 1st Earl of Yarmouth in 1794 and 3rd Marquess of Hertford in 1822. His own acquisitions, now part of the Wallace Collection, closely resembled those of his patron, especially in fine examples of Dutch and Flemish Masters.[31] The Regent and his friend embarked on a four-year spending spree remarkable even by royal standards. The first important sale of the new era was at Christie's on 13 June 1811, featuring masterpieces from the collection of the Dutch aristocratic merchant, Peter de Smeth van Alphen.[32] George IV acquired four 'blue-chip' Dutch works: two landscapes by Wouwerman; a romantic pastoral by Adriaen van de Velde and a light-filled cottage interior by Adriaen van Ostade (Fig. 7.5), described by the dealer Christianus Johannes Nieuwenhuys as 'among his most renowned paintings'.[33] Two further purchases in this sale were more expensive and significant: Van Dyck's *Christ Healing*

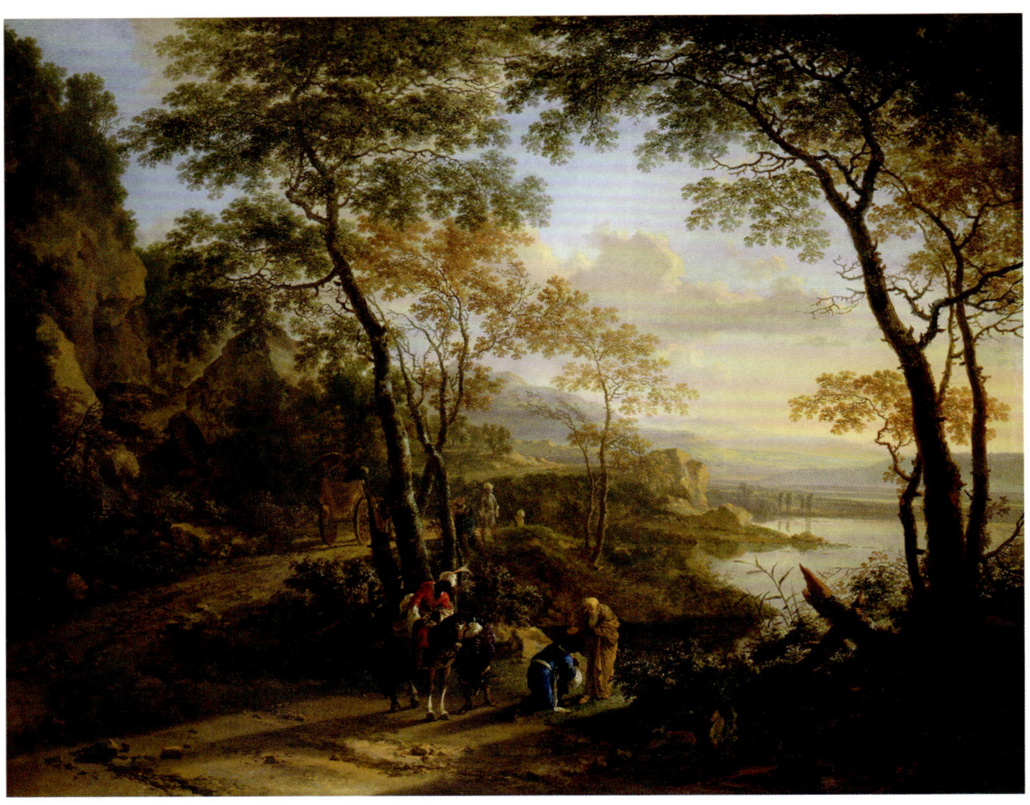

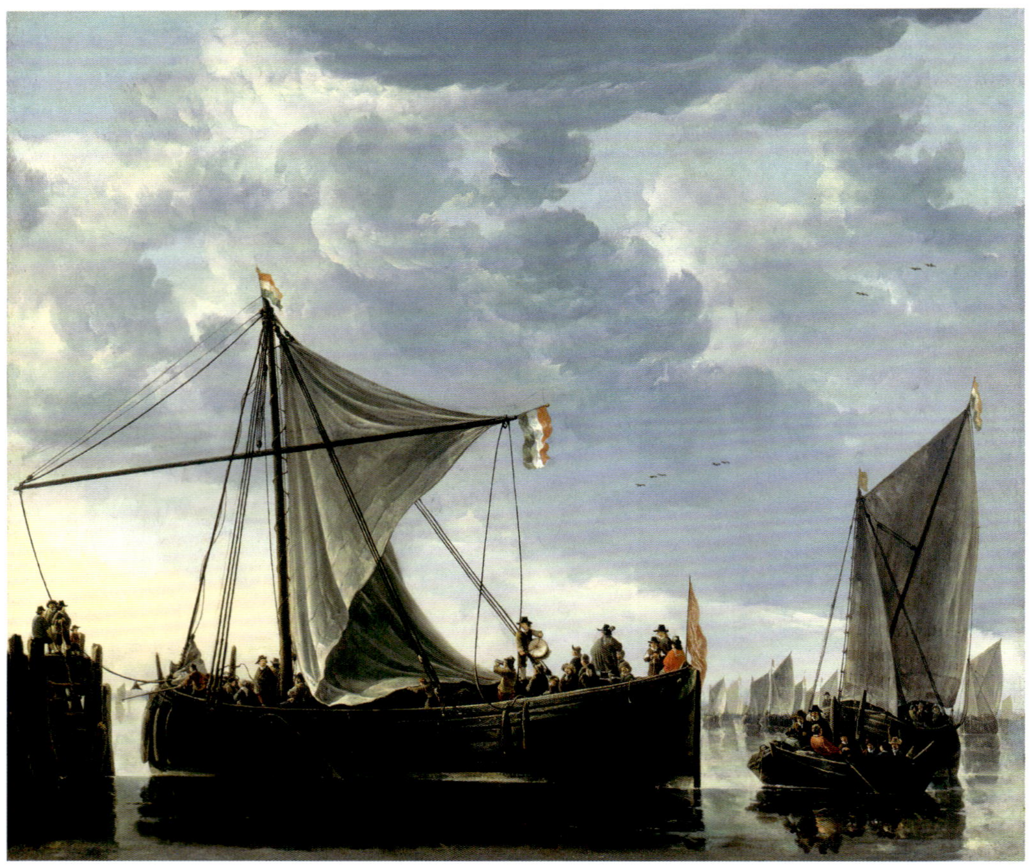

FIG. 7.6
JAN BOTH (*c.*1618–52), *Landscape with St Philip Baptising the Eunuch*, *c.*1640–9. Oil on canvas, 128.6 × 161.8 cm, RCIN 405544

FIG. 7.7
AELBERT CUYP (1620–91), *The Passage Boat*, *c.*1650. Oil on canvas, 124.0 × 144.4 cm, RCIN 405344

FIG. 7.8
DAVID TENIERS THE YOUNGER (1610–90), *Peasants Dancing Outside a Tavern*, *c.*1641. Oil on canvas, 135.7 × 205.4 cm, RCIN 406363

FIG. 7.9
AELBERT CUYP (1620–91), *An Evening Landscape with Figures and Sheep*, *c.*1655–9. Oil on canvas, 101.6 × 153.6 cm, RCIN 405827

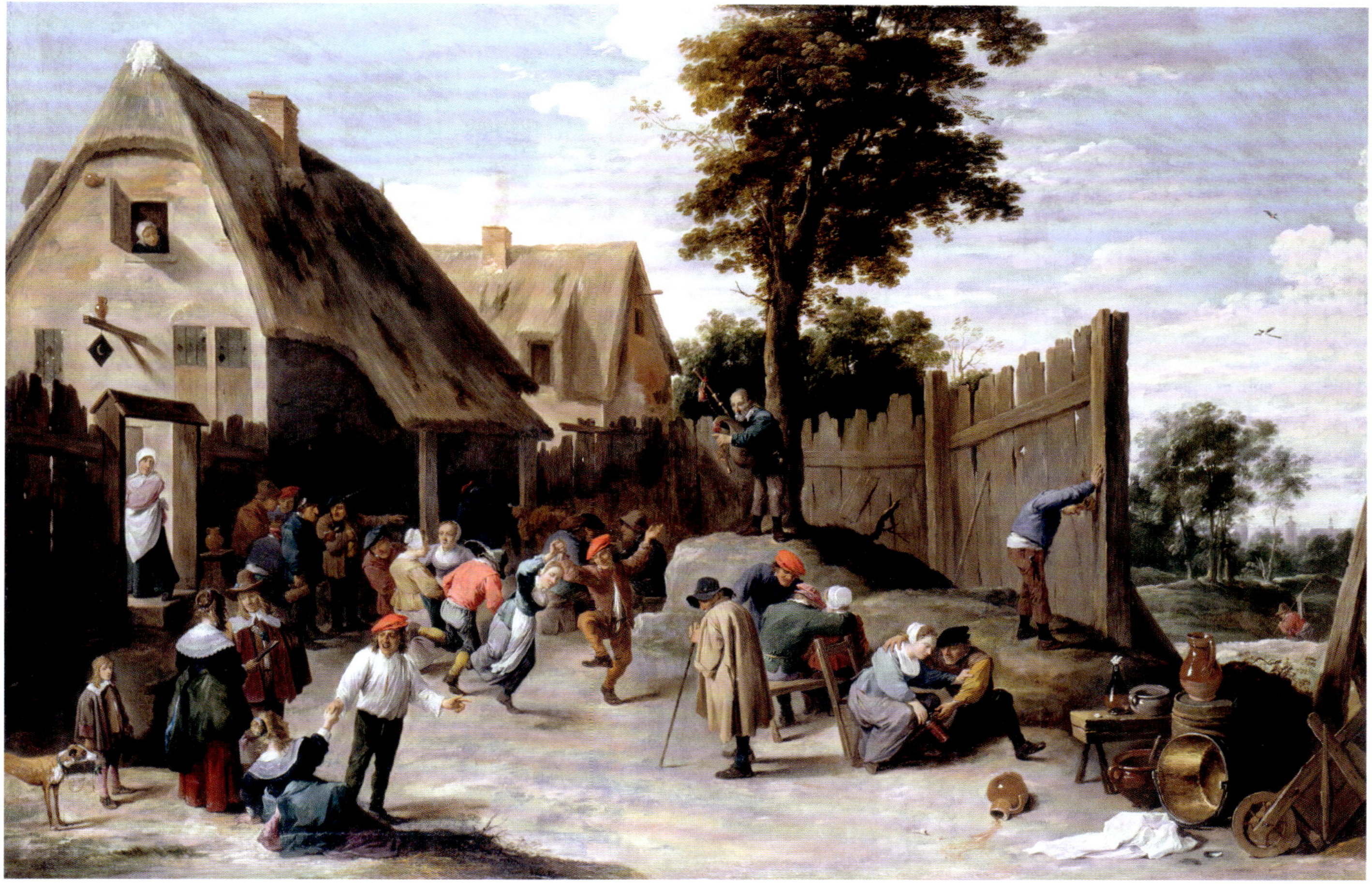

the *Paralytic* and Rembrandt's *Shipbuilder and his Wife* (see Fig. 0.10).[34] They immediately went as a pair to the Admirals Room (or Audience Room) on the Principal Floor of the garden front, a room decorated with patriotic ceiling paintings.[35] This was a first for Rembrandt. His work had been in the British royal collection since the reign of Charles I, but always in the form of character heads treated as colourful curiosities, within mixed cabinet hangs.[36] The Admirals Room paired Rembrandt's elderly couple – half-dignified, half-dithering – with a grand and imposing Van Dyck religious subject. This is in part a reflection of Rembrandt's rising reputation as an artist, but it tells us something about George IV that he could give prominence to so *unprincely* a couple. He must consciously have chosen to hang a merchant ship-builder in his Admirals Room, at a time when Britain was boasting of the wealth through trade that underpinned her military prowess.

George IV's next major painting acquisition occurred with the arrival on 8 May 1814 of the entire collection formed by two generations of the Baring family, Sir Francis and Sir Thomas Baring.[37] George IV's agent in this case was another political

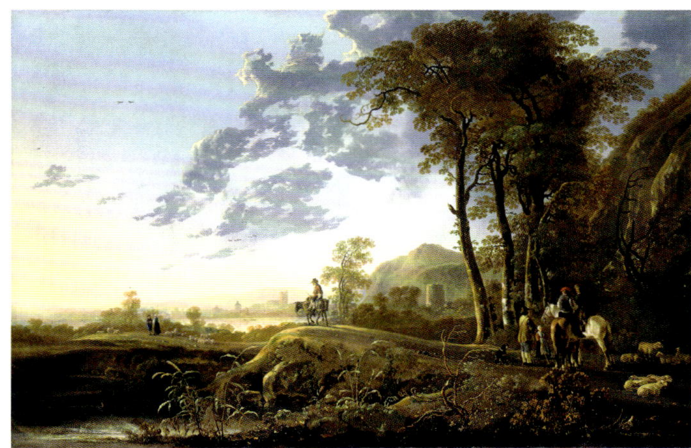

ally and friend, Sir Charles Long, created Baron Farnborough in 1826, a man described as the 'spectacles' through which the Prince Regent viewed art.[38] George IV's first reaction to this transformative purchase was to rationalise. On 26 May 1814, he offered 55 of his 'Old Collection' for sale at Christie's along with 15 unwanted works from his new Baring collection.[39] So

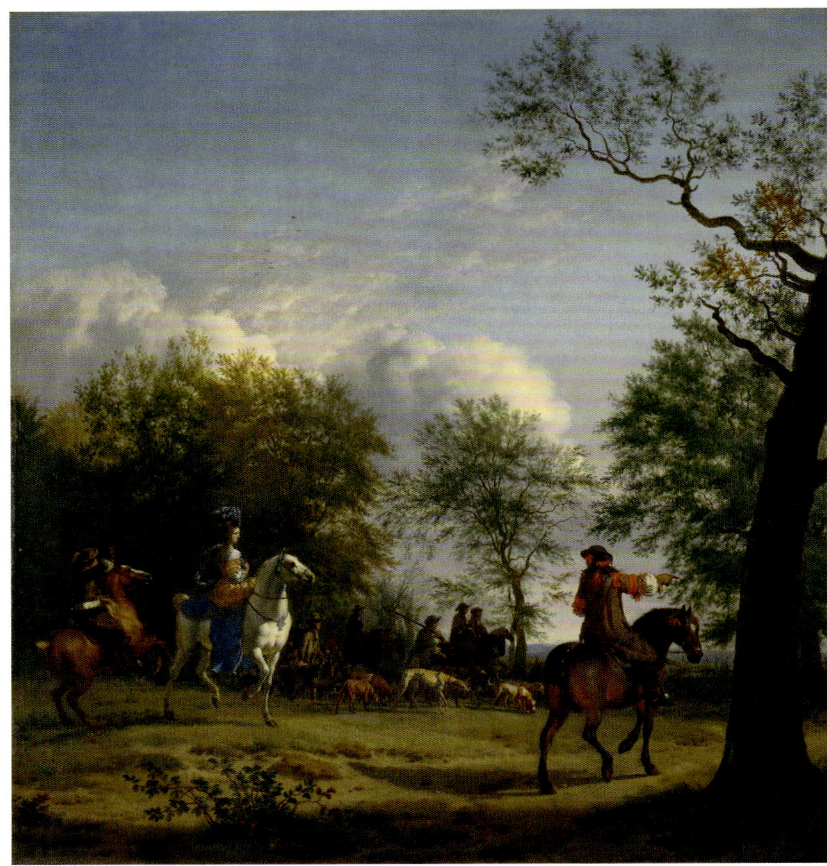

FIG. 7.10
ADRIAEN VAN DE VELDE (1636–72), *A Hawking Party Setting Out*, 1666. Oil on panel, 50.0 × 46.9 cm, RCIN 406966

FIG. 7.11
GERRIT DOU (1613–75), *The Grocer's Shop*, 1672. Oil on panel, 41.5 × 32.0 cm, RCIN 405542

FIG. 7.12
PAULUS POTTER (1625–54), *Two Sportsmen Outside an Inn*, 1651. Oil on panel, 53.3 × 43.7 cm, RCIN 400942

what was the rationale behind the rationalisation? The short answer is that George IV sought to improve his hand in the same suit. The Baring paintings he sold were by the same masters as the ones he kept, presumably just not as good.[40] As for the works from the 'Old Collection' sold on the same day, most of the named artists belong to the now familiar type, including Rubens, Teniers, Dou, Cuyp, Karel du Jardin and Van Mieris.[41] The final act in the great 'trade-up' of 1814 was the exchange with Mr Harris on 19 May of four paintings (two Van Huysum flower pieces and a Teniers from the Baring collection and an Ostade) for Rubens's *Landscape with St George and the Dragon* (Fig. 7.2).[42] Valued at 3,000 guineas in 1819, this was the most expensive of several acts of ancestral piety towards the greatest ever royal collector, Charles I.[43] It hung in the Crimson Drawing Room paired with Rembrandt's 'Burgomaster Pancras and his Wife', another demonstration of the latter's 'social arrival'.[44]

This purchasing campaign of only a few years resulted in the Old Master displays recorded in the Carlton House inventories of 1816 and 1819 and in Pyne's *Royal Residences*.[45] We can imagine George IV proudly arranging his recently arrived works. In the Admirals or Audience Room, Jan Both's *St Philip Baptising the Eunuch* (Fig. 7.6) from the Smeth van Alphen collection finds its pair in Cuyp's *Passage Boat* (Fig. 7.7), one of four paintings by this artist in the Baring collection.[46] Cuyp's depicting of daily life in Holland is dignified by its association with Jan Both's ideal religious landscape, just as Rembrandt was by association with Van Dyck. The remaining Old Masters at Carlton House hung in nine rooms along the garden front, two on the Principal Floor (Bow Room and Little Blue Room), five on the Lower Floor and two on the Attic Floor. These nine rooms contained 138 works, of which 99 were Dutch and 20 Flemish, most of them recent acquisitions, 59 from the Baring collection alone; the remaining works were by modern French, British and German painters.[47] The Old Masters reflected the old taste. The most represented artist, with 15 works, was David Teniers (Fig. 7.8), whose clumsy peasants cavorted happily above elegant French commodes and tables in seven out of the nine rooms. The most popular theme in his works that were owned by George IV was the village festival; two examples made a pair behind his informal throne in the Colonnade Room.[48] Presumably, the real-life 'Dutch Fête', which took place at Frogmore House in 1795 in the presence of the Prince of Wales

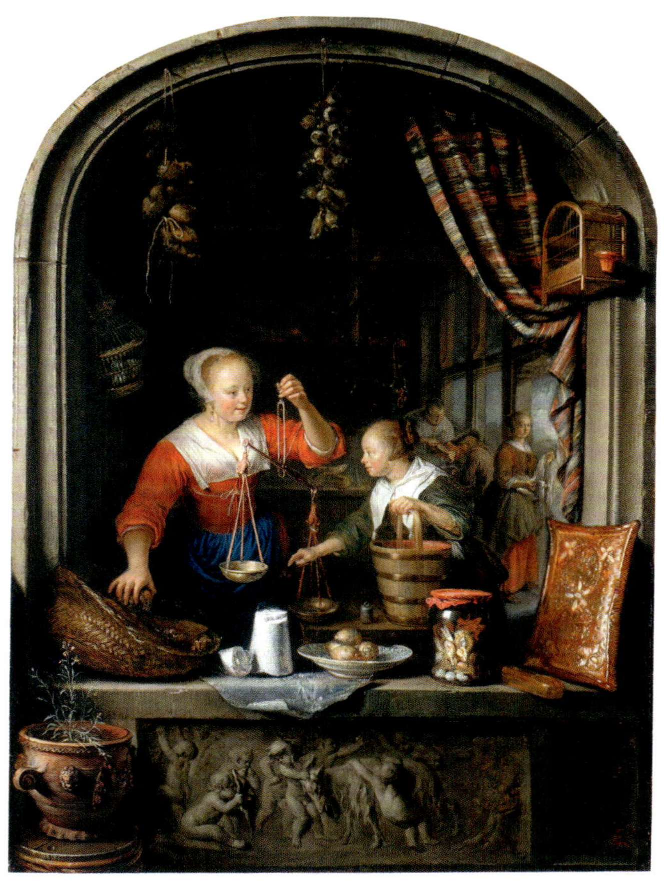

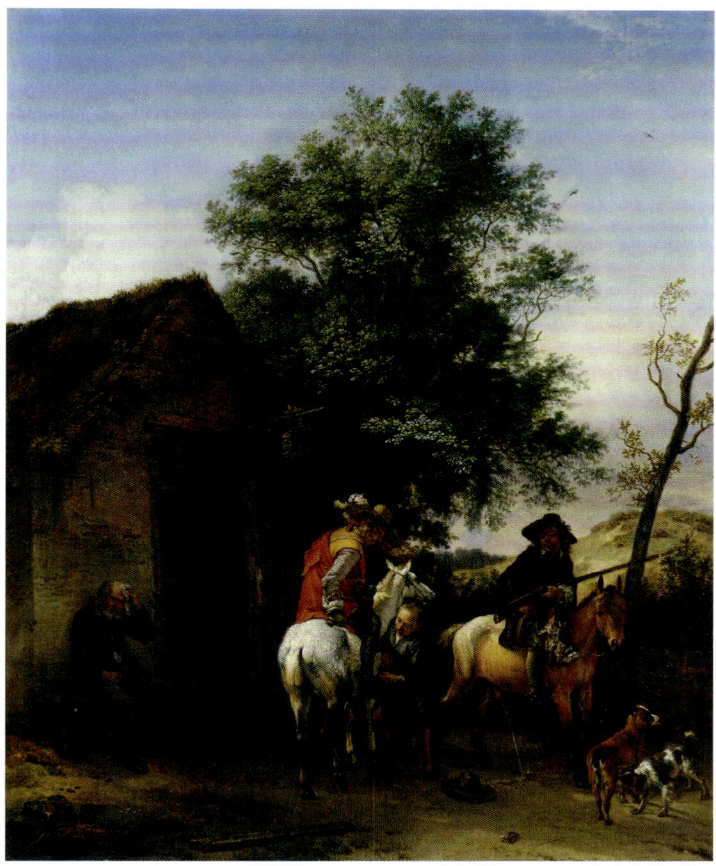

and the Prince of Orange, imitated just such a Teniers scene, suggesting that a political message was read into these depictions of rustic contentment.[49] The fairs and cottage interiors, usually with 'boors', by Adriaen and Isaac van Ostade accounted for 13 works, distributed among most of the rooms. Ten paintings by Wouwerman (one in collaboration with Wijnants) appeared, while the mostly Italianate pastorals of Adriaen van de Velde, Nicolaes Berchem and Karel du Jardin accounted for 20 works, almost all from the Baring collection. Bourgeois interiors by Ter Borch, Dou, Metsu, Schalcken, Frans and Willem van Mieris accounted for 20 works, generally with exceptionally high valuations. Carlton House displayed works by artists, like Willem van de Velde, Paulus Potter and Jan van der Heyden, who were appreciated throughout the eighteenth century, though never quite enjoying the popularity of the inner circle. There are some artists whose reputation was rising at this date: Jacob van Ruisdael and Meindert Hobbema were represented by three works between them, and Jan Steen by five, though none was given an especially high valuation. The only rising name strongly represented was Aelbert Cuyp (Fig. 7.9), with eight highly valued works, four of them from the Baring collection.

These Dutch and Flemish masterpieces were hung with system and flair. Two patterns appear in Pyne's illustrations: in the Bow Room a two-tier arrangement of one large over three small paintings and in the Little Blue Room a single-tier arrangement of one large flanked by two small.[50] It is clear from the inventories how carefully works of similar size or motif were paired off, often enjoying a compositional 'rhyme', as in the women descending staircases in interiors by Metsu and Nicolaes Maes, hanging opposite each other in the Little Blue Room.[51] Every group of three is something of a triptych. One such in the Bow Room has a central panel provided by Dou's *Grocer's Shop* (Fig. 7.11), with its frontal architectural niche, flanked by Adriaen van de Velde's modish hawking party (Fig. 7.10), riding in from the left, and Paulus Potter's mounted hunters (Fig. 7.12), arriving hungry at a squalid hut on the right.[52] These three paintings by different artists come from different collections; their only relationship lies in the symmetry of their compositions and the entertaining before-and-after narrative that can be read across them once you enter the spirit of Dutch painting.[53]

According to William Buchanan, the Prince Regent was offered the collection of one M. Aynard in 1819, but 'found

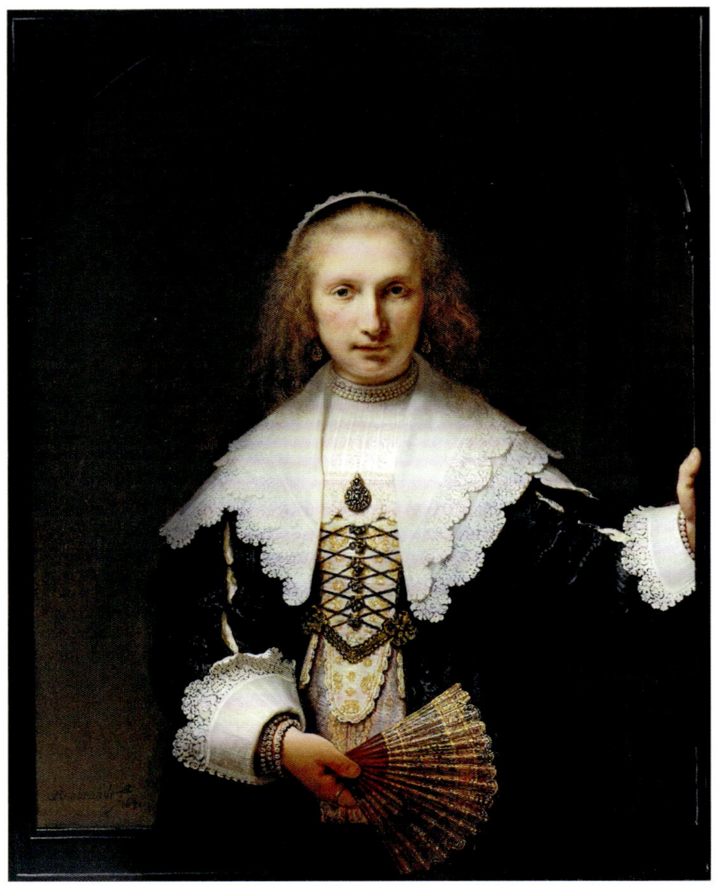

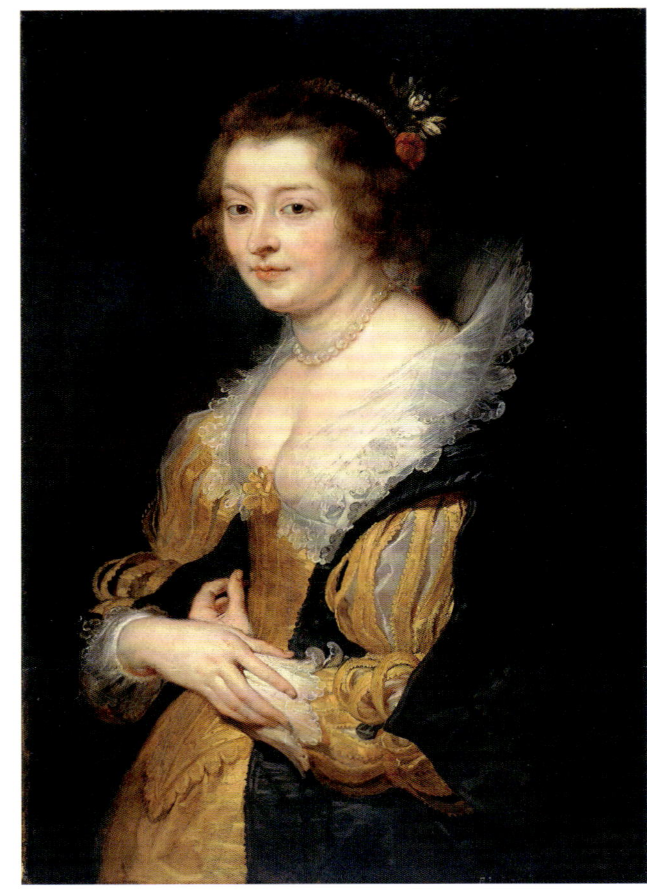

the list too general, and only desiring to possess certain works which the collection at Carlton House actually wanted, declined the offer of it in the aggregate'.[54] George IV made no more 'aggregate' purchases after 1814, but he did seek out individual works with, if anything, more discernment. Dou's *Grocer's Shop* was one such, formerly in the duc de Choiseul's collection, acquired on 21 June 1817 for 1,000 guineas.[55] However, the question remains, what did the collection at Carlton House 'actually want'? Sometimes the answer seems to be an even better example of the staple, sometimes a subtle extension of the range of the collection. In neither case do we know what place (if any) was intended for these later purchases, as the inventories record them as they arrived at Carlton House, not as they hung. For example, on 7 July 1819, George IV acquired two paintings from Lord Townshend: a Schalcken young woman called 'La Coquette' for 350 guineas and Rembrandt's *Agatha Bas* (Fig. 7.13) for 800 guineas.[56] The former is a fine single figure to join the groups by the same artist, the latter an extraordinary departure. It acts as an antidote to the 'Wife of Rubens' (Fig. 7.14), acquired from John Smith, the dealer and pioneer historian of Dutch art, for the same price in the previous year, and a visual jolt for a collection with so many queens and princesses by Van Dyck and Lely.[57] In the same month George IV did some more pruning, acquiring from M. Lafontaine a Wouwerman 'Horse Fair' and a Dou 'Interior of a Cottage', now attributed to Pieter Cornelisz. van Slingelandt, in exchange for eight works by various artists, including Teniers, Wouwerman, Willem van Mieris and Jan Steen.[58] Later that year he made a more venturesome exchange, also with M. Lafontaine – trading an 'Alchemist' by Teniers, a 'Herodias' by Leonardo da Vinci and two 'Calms' by Willem van de Velde for Rembrandt's incomparable *Christ and Mary Magdalen at the Tomb*.[59] We might ask where this would fit with the hunters and the coquettes. That would be to overlook the 'Wise Mens Offering' from the Baring collection then attributed to Rembrandt and valued at 1,800 guineas and Rubens's 'Assumption of the Virgin', acquired at the Hope sale on 1 July 1816, both paintings hanging in the Bow Room, Ground Floor.[60]

George IV acquired few Old Masters once he had become King, but the quality remained remarkable. On 7 July 1821, three paintings arrived at Carlton House from the French dealer M. Delahante: Teniers's 'Village Fête', Jan Steen's 'Interior of a bedroom with a Lady putting on her stockings' (Fig. 7.15) and Rubens's 'Chateau de Laeken'.[61] The first two are 'best in class';

FIG. 7.13
REMBRANDT VAN RIJN (1606–69), *Agatha Bas (1611–58)*, 1641. Oil on canvas, 105.4 × 83.9 cm, RCIN 405352

FIG. 7.14
SIR PETER PAUL RUBENS (1577–1640), *Portrait of a Woman*, c.1625–30. Oil on panel, 84.8 × 59.3 cm, RCIN 400118

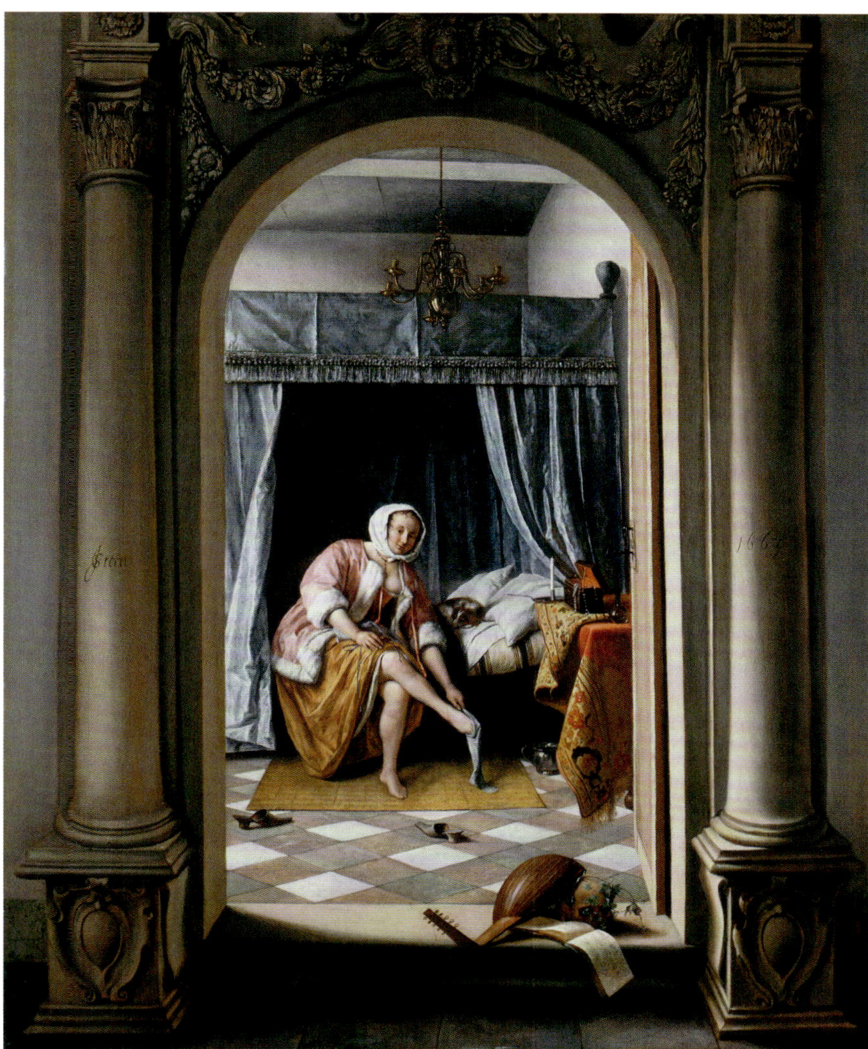

FIG. 7.15
JAN STEEN (1626–79), *A Woman at Her Toilet*, 1663. Oil on panel, 65.8 × 53.0 cm, RCIN 404804

the third is in a class of its own. At Mr Emmerson's sale at Phillips on 1 May 1829 George IV acquired for 400 guineas a 'View on a River in Holland', by Aert van der Neer.[62] A week later at Lord Gwydir's sale (Christie's, 9 May 1829), he acquired Claude's *Rape of Europa* for 2,000 guineas, a high price for the work of an artist he had avoided for so long.[63] Is it possible that he wished to create a new landscape room in which works by Rubens and Claude might 'unvulgarise' the recent acquisition of Aert van der Neer and the old stock of Jan Both and Aelbert Cuyp?

George IV's most exciting discovery in his later years was the painting of Pieter de Hooch. On 27 April 1825, John Smith submitted a receipt for £700 for De Hooch's *Card-Players*.[64] The other painting bought at the Emmerson sale of 1 May 1829, mentioned above, also for £400, was De Hooch's *Courtyard*.[65] According to Nieuwenhuys, it was at the exhibition for sale of the Smeth van Alphen collection on 2 August 1810 'that connoisseurs opened their eyes to the real value of this painter's merit'. One of the works in this sale was the same *Card-Players*, acquired by George IV 15 years later. Nieuwenhuys describes its apartment 'brilliantly lighted from a window in front' with open door and courtyard beyond; he concludes, the 'effect produced is perfectly illusive; and, for the management of its light and shadow, this is the most surprising picture I have ever seen of this painter.'[66] This description conveys the sense of wonder and novelty that Dutch realism could still evoke a century after it had become a normal addition to the European princely cabinet. It also suggests that there was a shift in taste for the art of the Low Countries, reflected in George IV's collecting career, beginning with Teniers and ending with Pieter de Hooch. Instead of enjoying an alternative set of conventions, collectors began to appreciate a type of painting that seemed, in its 'perfect illusiveness', not to depend upon conventions of any kind.

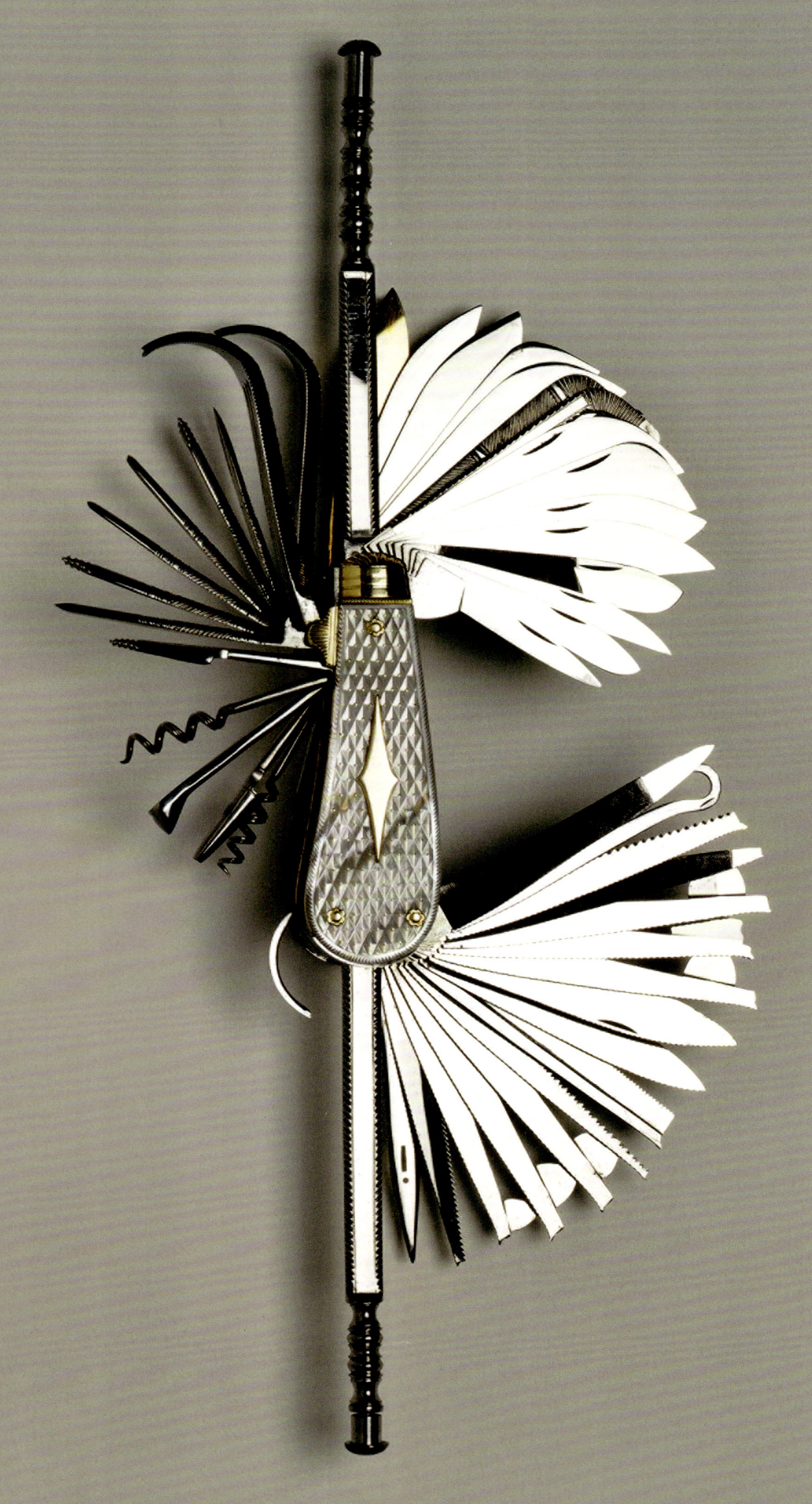

8

GEORGE IV *and* MODERN MANUFACTURING

KATHRYN JONES

PRESENTING A EULOGY TO GEORGE IV in the House of Lords, the Duke of Wellington spoke of the king as 'the most munificent patron of the fine arts … He possessed a larger collection of the eminent productions of the artists of his own country, than any individual'.[1] By artists Wellington was undoubtedly referring to painters and sculptors, rather than manufacturers. Yet his words might equally have been applied to those contemporary producers of decorative arts who supplied George in no small degree with individual works to furnish the magnificent interiors of his residences.

As a collector, George has been called 'both a modern and a conservative'.[2] Although he is perhaps better known for his interest in *ancien régime* France and his acquisition of historic and contemporary French decorative arts and furniture, there was a strong thread of support for British manufacture running through George's purchases. This may have been inculcated in him by his parents, who were staunch supporters of buying British and associated themselves in particular with the porcelain factories of Wedgwood and Worcester, the workshops of the goldsmith Thomas Heming and the cabinet-makers Vile & Cobb, and encouraged the silk trade in London. Such a concern for supporting domestic manufacturers was a perennial one among British sovereigns, and often underpinned by a political motivation, but George III and Queen Charlotte in particular had sought to patronise native craftsmen. As early as 1772, the young prince was following his father's example in buying a pair of 'wing-figured' bluejohn vases from Matthew Boulton.[3] And like his father, George sought out British manufacturers. Among the most successful partnerships between patron and supplier were those he formed with Morel & Hughes, and later Morel & Seddon, and with the royal goldsmiths Rundell, Bridge & Rundell. Their contributions are explored elsewhere in this volume (see chapters 6 and 17). At the same time, George's taste for works of art drawn from *ancien régime* France did not mean he was entirely wedded to the historic in his collecting – a good scattering of the objects he acquired reflect an interest in modern materials, techniques and technological advances.

To encourage George's patronage some English firms made him gifts, a number of which survive. A vase, for example, from the firm of Spode was presented by the Middletown Hill Mine in the early 1820s, to prompt his support for feldspar porcelain-

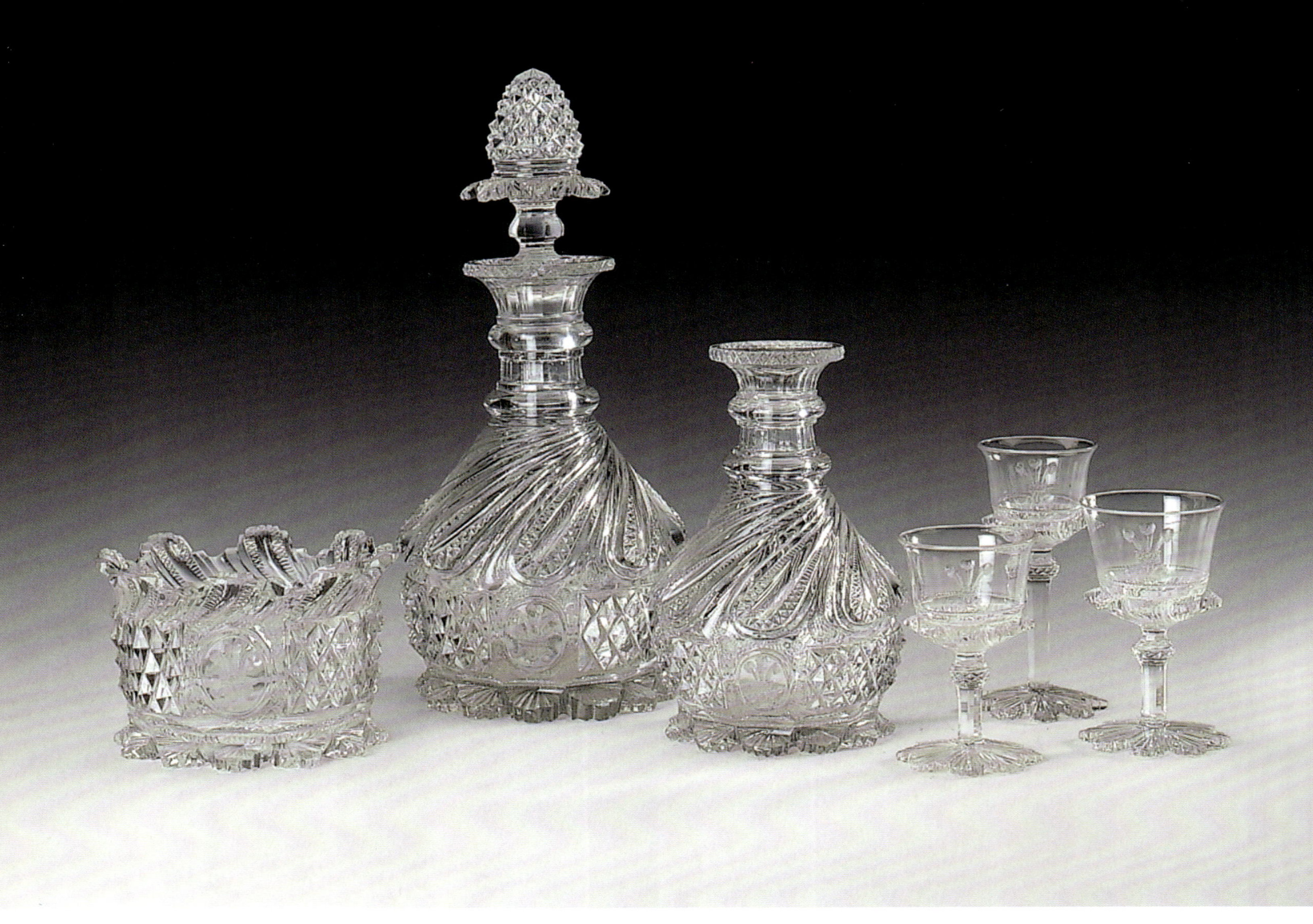

wares rather than the more traditional bone china associated with the Staffordshire region.[4] From Joseph Rodgers & Sons of Sheffield came the elaborate pocket knife, bristling with 46 individual blades and tools, which was presented to George in the hope that he would support the cutlers' arts of the city (Fig. 8.1). Most notably a gift was presented by the Corporation of Liverpool comprising a large service of lead glass, originally numbering well over 300 pieces, created by the Warrington firm of Perrin, Geddes & Co (Fig. 8.2). The service, designed so that the foot of each glass represents a star of the Order of the Garter, was based on a model seen by George at a dinner held in his honour in 1806, which prompted him to request a matching service for himself. As gifts these objects cannot perhaps claim to reflect any personal interest from the recipient, although the prince was certainly involved in selecting the design of the glass service.

George does appear to have kept up with some of the latest technological innovations, albeit straying on occasion into the field of novelty. Among his bills are listed objects such as an electrifying chair, a Merlin chair (a prototype of a wheelchair), an early version of a shower, and a vapour bath for use at Brighton, heated seating for Carlton House,[5] and a musical footstool which played four different tunes.[6] A small silver-gilt cup, known as the Galvanic Goblet (Fig. 8.3), is listed among the inventories of George's great dining service, the Grand Service, although no explanation for its name is provided in the bills or archives. The piece carries a hallmark for Paul Storr's

(p. 116)
FIG. 8.1
JOSEPH RODGERS & SONS, SHEFFIELD, *Pocket knife*, 1821. Steel, mother of pearl, 31.2 cm (length), RCIN 2451

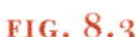

FIG. 8.2
PERRIN, GEDDES & CO., *Glass Service*, *c.*1807. Lead glass, RCINs 68275–68279 and 68281

FIG. 8.3
PAUL STORR (1771–1844), *The Galvanic Goblet*, 1814/15. Silver, silver gilt, 12.6 × 6.8 × 6.8 cm, RCIN 51444

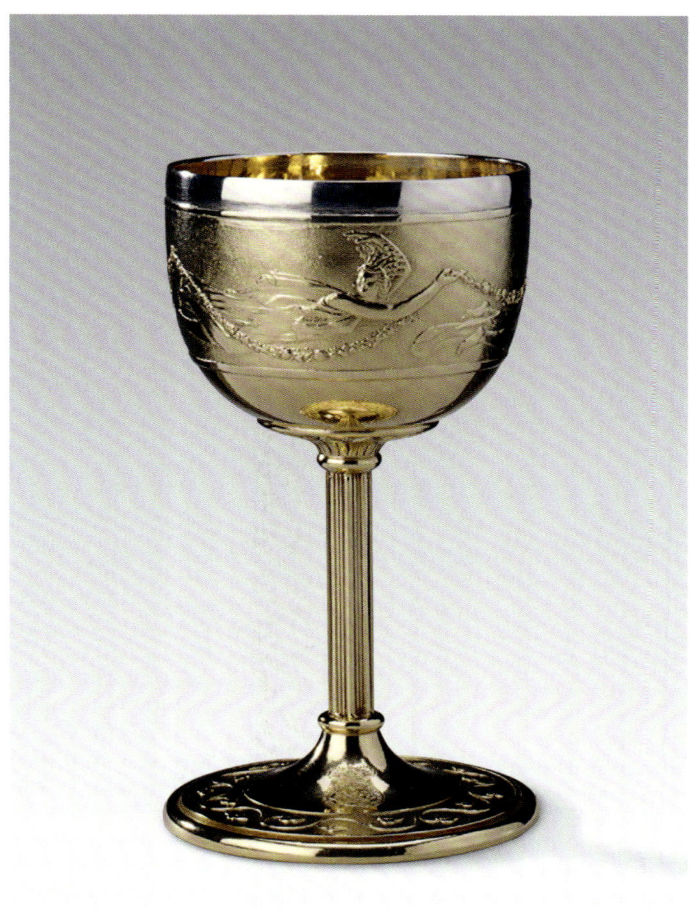

workshop in London for the year 1814/15, and it may have been an early attempt at electroforming or electrotyping (also known as galvanoplasty), a technique in use by medallists as early as 1810 although not pursued by goldsmiths until the 1830s. It is possible that the cup's name derives from another source, however: its ungilded rim, which has undergone metallurgical analysis, is formed from an unusual alloy of silver mixed with zinc rather than the traditional copper. It is possible that this alloy was thought to convey medicinal benefits, stimulating the muscles with electricity (galvanism), perhaps when combined with the drinking of mineral waters, and it may have given the goblet its name.[7]

While much of this interest in new technologies was more closely associated with George's health and concern for his own person than any scientific or patriotic sensibilities, it was, on occasion, a motivation for collecting works of art. This may be seen in his association with William Congreve, sometime equerry in George's household. George's interest in military life and, in particular, in the progress of the Napoleonic campaigns, led him to support the invention of Congreve rockets, which improved the black-powder rockets used by the British army at the end of the eighteenth century and increased their range fivefold. A Congreve rocket is depicted in the foreground of Pugin's watercolour of the Armoury at Carlton House (see Fig. 18.4). George also patronised Congreve's ventures into new forms of horological mechanism: his library at Carlton House contained, at various dates, both a long-case skeleton clock which housed Congreve's new extreme detached escapement (Fig. 8.4) and a table clock with a similar movement.[8]

In the same vein, George patronised the renowned French horologist Abraham-Louis Breguet, among whose innovative clocks was one which contained a double pendulum and housed within the case a brazier and chimney, which allowed for temperature regulation and thereby prevented the warping of the case and the subsequent problems of synchronising the clock (Fig. 8.5). George also owned a mantel chronometer by Breguet, which incorporated a metronome;[9] and one of Breguet's most unusual works, a so-called *Sympathique* clock and watch mechanism (Fig. 8.6), an invention which allowed the watch to synchronise with the clock when placed in the cradle fitted into the top of the clock case. The watch was regularly dispatched for repair during George's lifetime, which suggests that it was worn rather than simply being acquired as a novelty piece. Although many of George IV's clocks follow the pattern of his mother's collecting in their concern for the outward appearance of the case, in these instances we see the son following his father's interest in the inner workings.

As described elsewhere in this volume, George's architectural projects explored the potential of new materials such as cast iron or Coade stone, for example, in the conservatory at Carlton House and at Brighton Pavilion (see chapters 5 and 10). These innovations continued at Buckingham Palace under the supervision of John Nash, where all the principal joists and the Doric columns on the ground floor were of iron, cast in Staffordshire, and brought to London by the newly opened network of canals. Plate glass

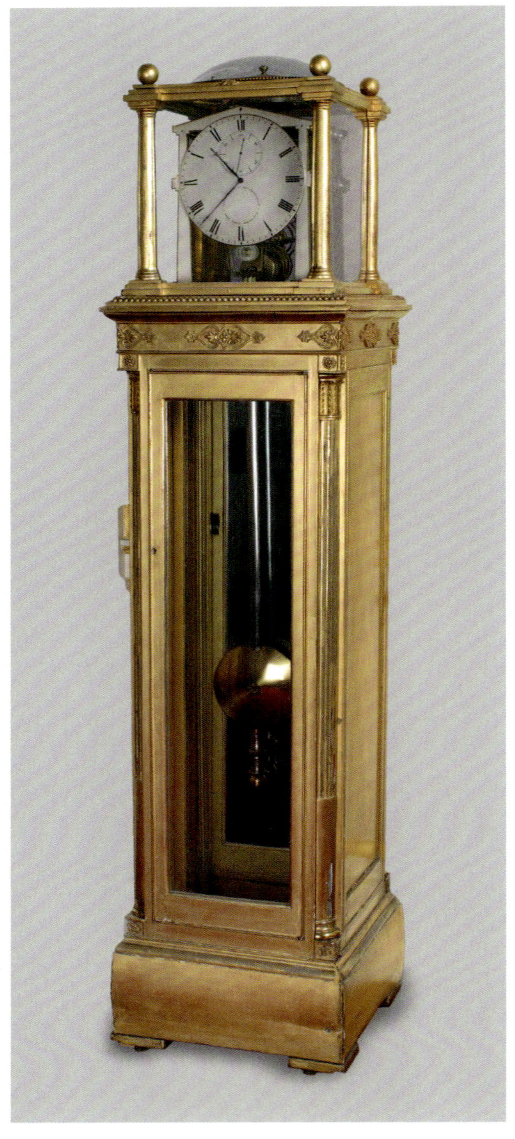

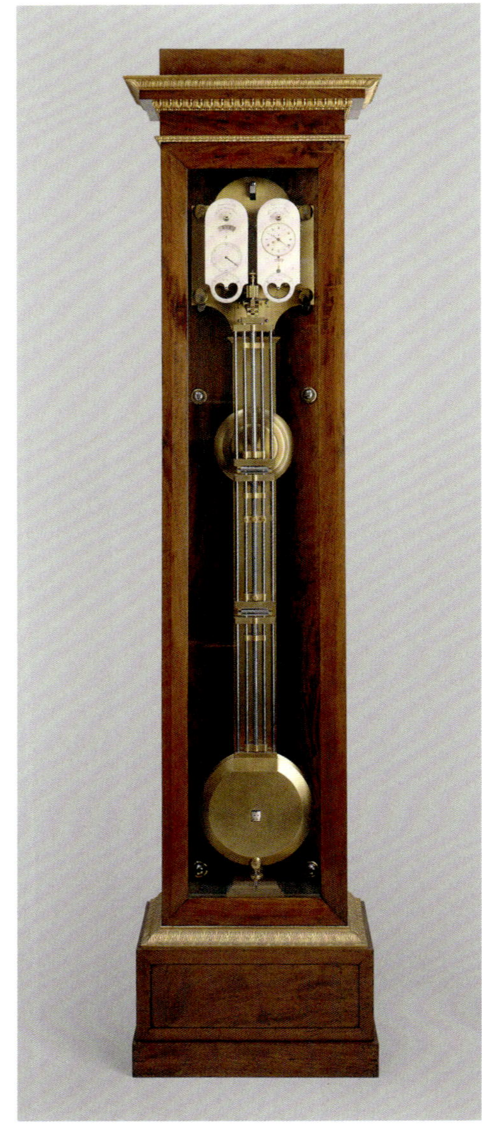

(left)
FIG. 8.4
SIR WILLIAM CONGREVE (1772–1828), *Floor-standing clock*, c.1800. Glazed giltwood case with brass, silvered metal and blued steel, 38.1 × 29.3 × 21.6 cm, RCIN 2869

(right)
FIG. 8.5
BREGUET ET FILS, *Regulator clock*, 1819–24. Glazed mahogany case with gilt-bronze mounts, silvered dial, zinc and steel, 203.8 × 49.5 × 29.5 cm, RCIN 2767

was employed at Carlton House for the doors of display cases in the Plate Closet. Although they were expensive, James Wyatt justified this measure as 'indispensably necessary, as it is intended that the Plate shall be seen and as the Plate is chiefly if not entirely ornamental; any glass but Plate [glass] therefore would cripple the forms and perhaps the most ornamental parts would be most injured'.[10] Plate glass was likewise used in Buckingham Palace for the new windows, and the mirrored and glazed doors were created in Vauxhall using increasingly industrialised techniques to produce ever larger sheets of glass.[11]

George seems to have been interested in new forms of lighting to an equal extent: Argand oil lamps, patented in the 1780s, were employed at Carlton House from at least 1806 and almost certainly before.[12] More significantly, at Brighton in 1821 George employed gas lighting on the exterior of the Pavilion. This was intended to act as back-lighting for the painted clerestory windows of the Music Room and Long Gallery. Much of the lighting at each of George's residences was supplied by William Parker, later of the firm of Parker & Perry, who became the manufacturer of lustres and chandeliers to George from as early as 1783. Parker & Perry were responsible for the numerous chandeliers utilising cascades of drops of lead glass, the designs of which were increasingly reliant on the latest cutting techniques to produce festoons or 'tents' that hid the metal framework of the lights entirely. Some sense of the intensive labour required in the cutting is apparent in the amount charged for these works. The example from the Saloon at Brighton, modelled to incorporate 28 lamps and branches, cost £950 alone; a further £150 was charged for the

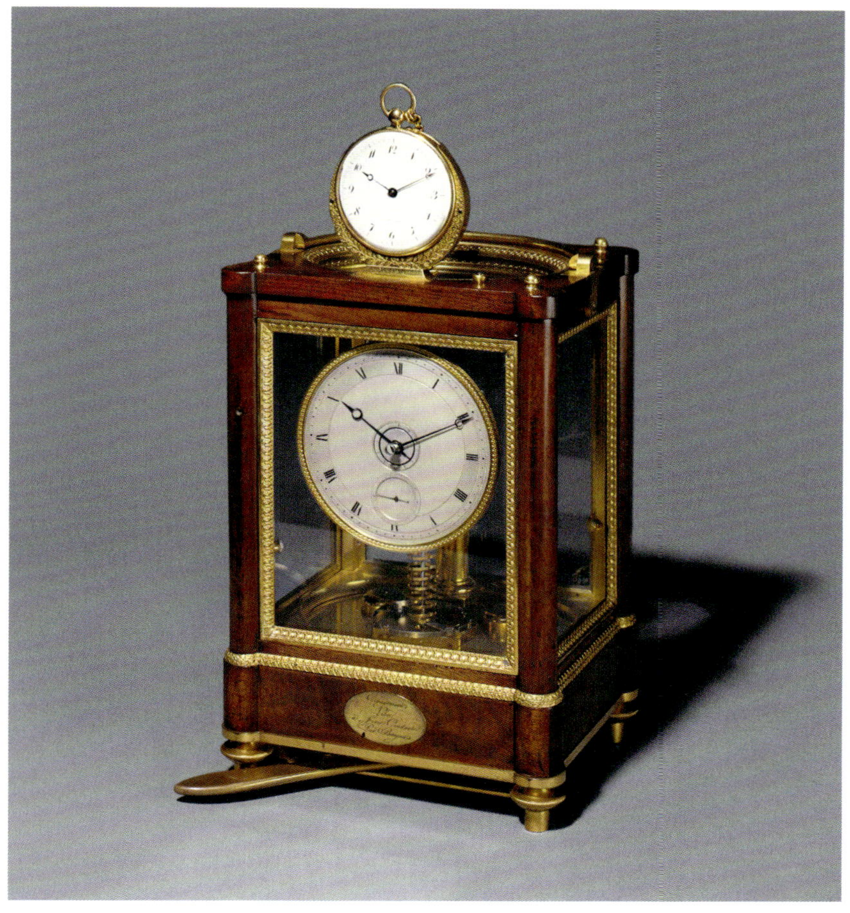

FIG. 8.6
BREGUET ET FILS, *The 'Sympathique' clock*, 1814. Glazed mahogany case with chased and gilt-bronze mounts, clock with silver dial, watch with enamel dial, 33.3 × 17.5 × 17.5 cm, RCIN 2861

cut-glass top section. The firm was also responsible for the enormous dragon, some 30 feet (9 metres) high, designed by Robert Jones, which formed the centrepiece of the Banqueting Room. Parker & Perry thereby demonstrated their versatility and at the same time their entrepreneurial drive. They were equally content to hire out chandeliers for the prince's events at Carlton House – for a party held in 1813, for example, 100 additional lamps were required for the conservatory alone – as Lady Elizabeth Fielding noted in a letter to Mary Frampton: 'I am afraid all my powers of description would fail to give you an idea of the oriental air of everything in that Mahomet's Paradise … the glitter of spangles and finery, of dress and furniture that burst upon you were quite eblouissant.'[13]

Indeed this entrepreneurial spirit infused all the architectural schemes under George's patronage, his own enthusiasms apparently encouraging his suppliers to new ventures. This is perhaps best exemplified by the versatile quality of the work supplied by Samuel Parker at Buckingham Palace. Parker created metalwork in all forms, from railings for the forecourt and gates for the Marble Arch, commissioned in 'mosaic gold',[14] to the magnificent gilt-bronze balustrade of the Grand Staircase, ornaments for the mahogany doors and marble capitals of the columns in the state apartments, and even gilt-bronze mounts for Chinese porcelain vases.

While Sèvres porcelain might have been George's choice for dining at his London residence, he was also aware of his parents' keen support of English porcelain makers and again here seems to have followed their lead. In 1806 the prince undertook a visit to Staffordshire with his brother William, Duke of Clarence to view the porcelain manufactories. This was followed by a commission for a 600-piece service from the Davenport factory, decorated with a pattern known as the Chinese Temple (Fig. 8.7). Over the following years he placed orders with firms in Derby, Worcester and Leeds as well as the Staffordshire-based Wedgwood, Spode and Minton. He seems to have felt that these manufacturers were more appropriate for the supply of smaller-scale services or for works for his out-of-town residences (although accompanying the Sèvres dining wares at Carlton House there were also services of Derby, Meissen, Berlin and Paris porcelain).[15] Thus he ordered a breakfast service from Chamberlain & Co., of Worcester, to commemorate the victory at Waterloo (Fig. 8.8). An extremely

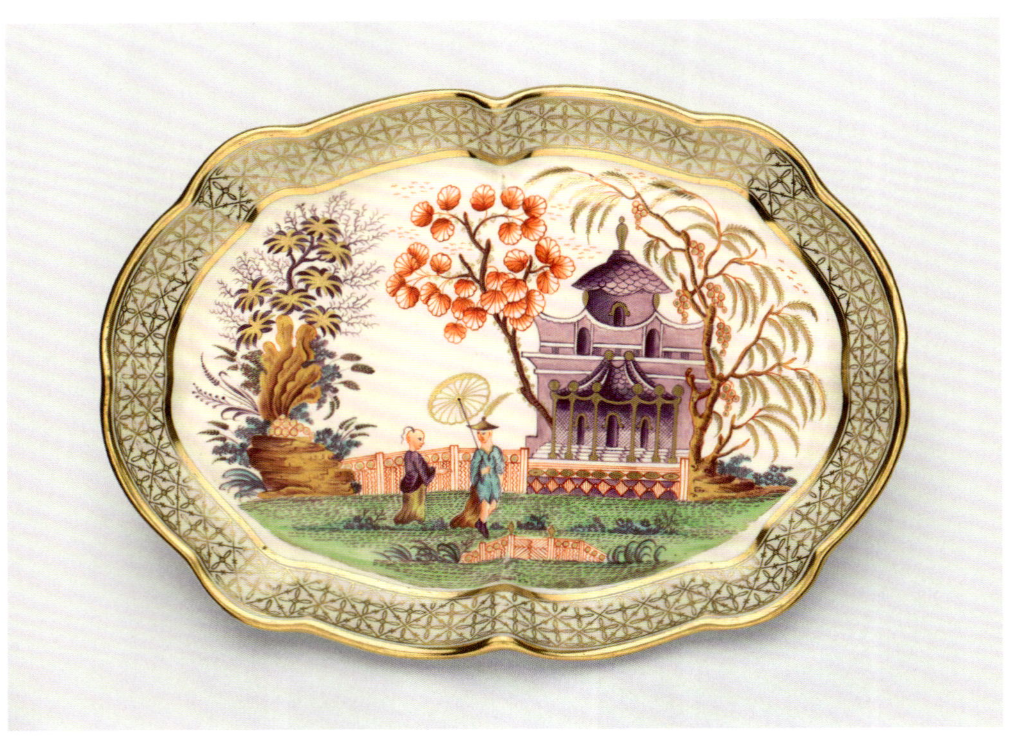

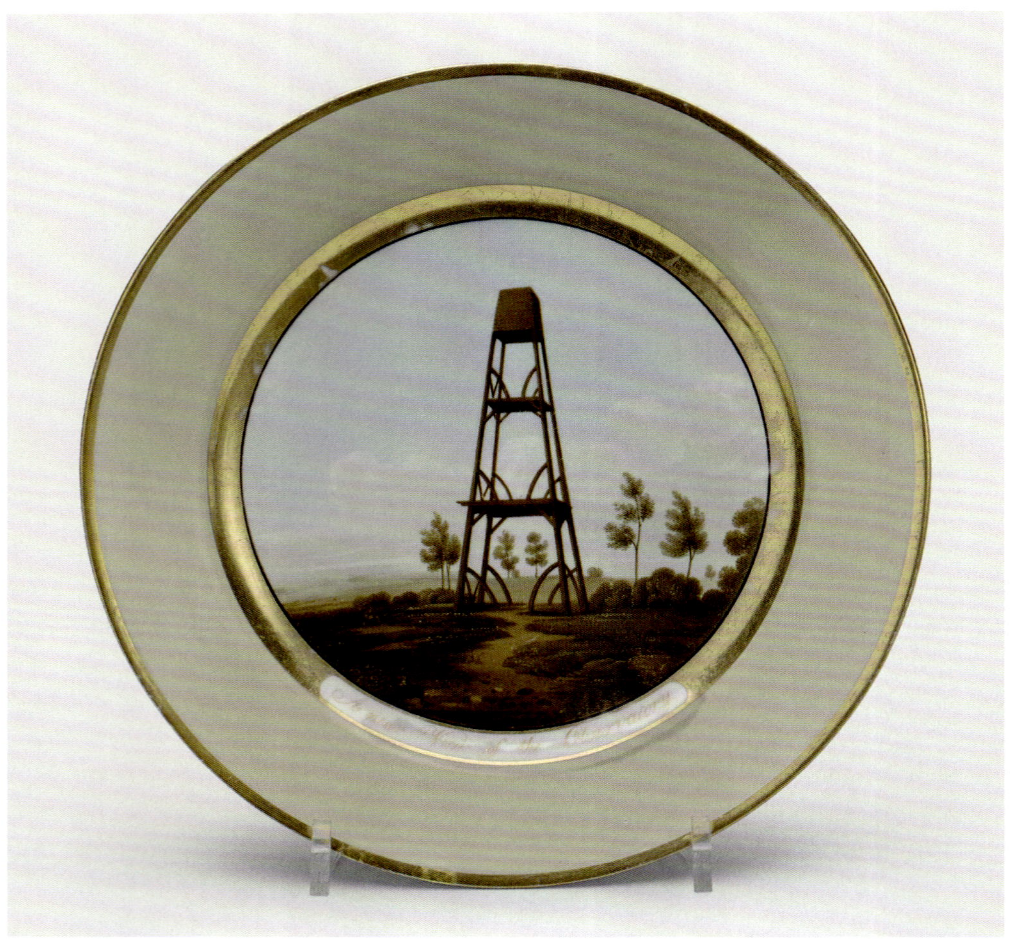

FIG. 8.7

DAVENPORT LONGPORT (*c.*1793–1887), *Lobed serving dish (part of the Chinese Temple dessert service)*, 1806–7. Bone china, 3.6 × 25.1 × 18.2 cm, RCIN 57210

FIG. 8.8

CHAMBERLAIN & CO., WORCESTER (*c.*1786–1852), *Plate commemorating the Battle of Waterloo*, 1816. Porcelain, 21.5 cm (diameter), RCIN 10884.5

FIG. 8.9

CHAMBERLAIN & CO., WORCESTER (*c.*1786–1852), *Pieces from the Harlequin Service*, 1807–16. Hybrid-paste porcelain (the 'Regent body'), RCIN 58403

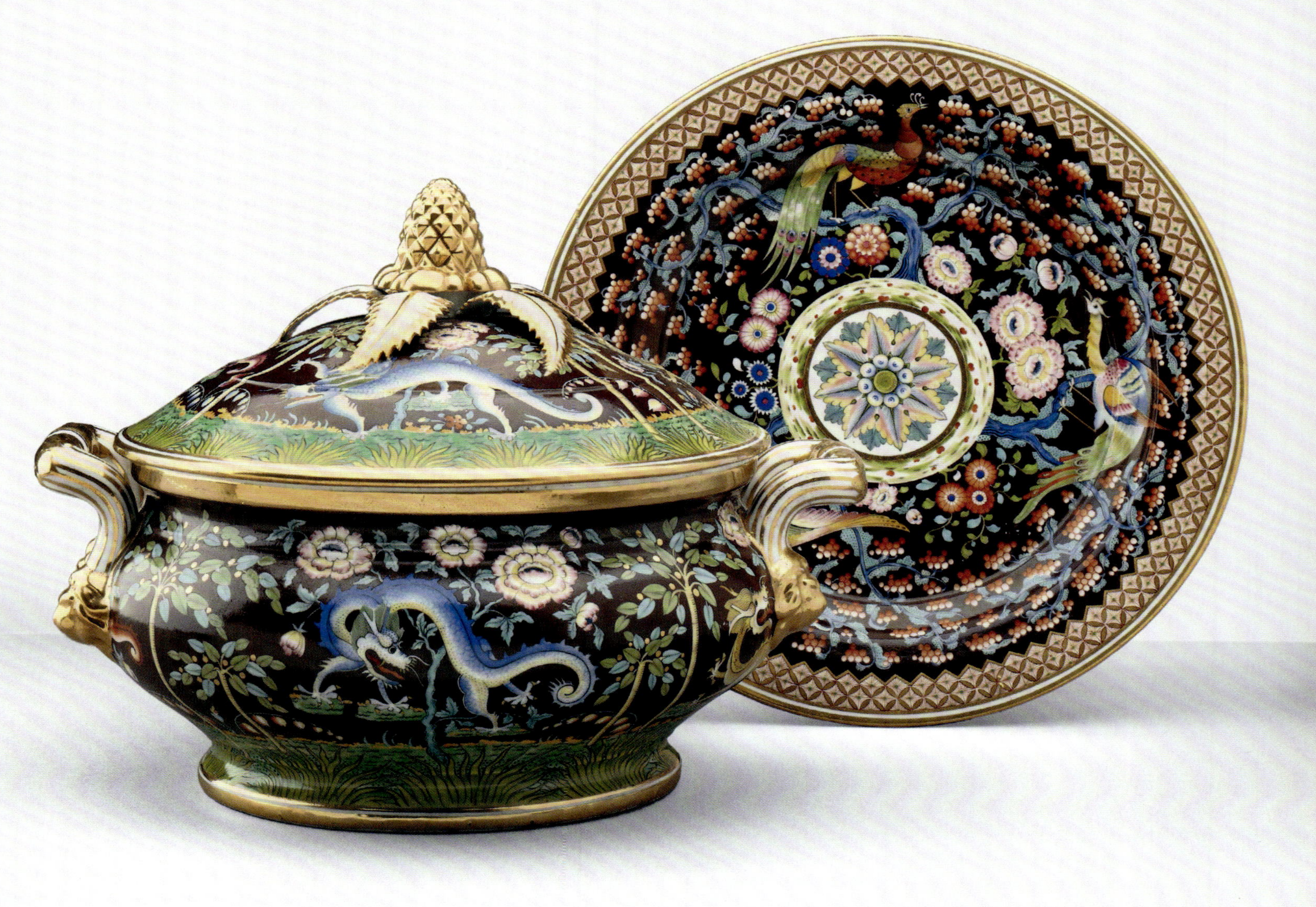

modest commission, for personal use, which included only 12 plates, the service was decorated after prints by S. Wharton, showing the battlefield and other significant locations connected with the Waterloo campaign.

By contrast, Chamberlain's also made one of the most extensive commissions from George, the large Harlequin Service (Fig. 8.9), and again it is possible to see the entrepreneurial spirit of the age in this commission. The service was ordered in 1807 and extended with an accompanying dessert service in 1811. The firm produced a large pattern book of designs all, by Robert Chamberlain's account, 'copied from old India and other China'.[16] According to the records at Worcester, the prince was unable to select a single pattern and therefore each piece of the service was decorated to a different design.[17] Moreover, Chamberlain took advantage of this important commission to develop the recipe for his porcelain body, creating a hybrid paste christened thereafter the 'Regent body'. As the ambassador Richard Rush noted, 'the English excel in cut glass … but I was not prepared to see their porcelain so good … the painting and gilding seemed not inferior to the French'.[18]

Much of George's patronage of modern technologies or English manufacturing has been overshadowed by his more overt fascination with history and indeed, many of the works of art he acquired are so overlaid with traditional detail and decorative motifs that it is often difficult to discern the novel materials and techniques hidden therein. Nevertheless, Wellington's assertion that George was to be seen as one of the greatest patrons in contemporary Britain still holds true – if only because as a catalyst whose own enthusiasms were constantly changing, he inspired the manufacturers of the day to explore and innovate.

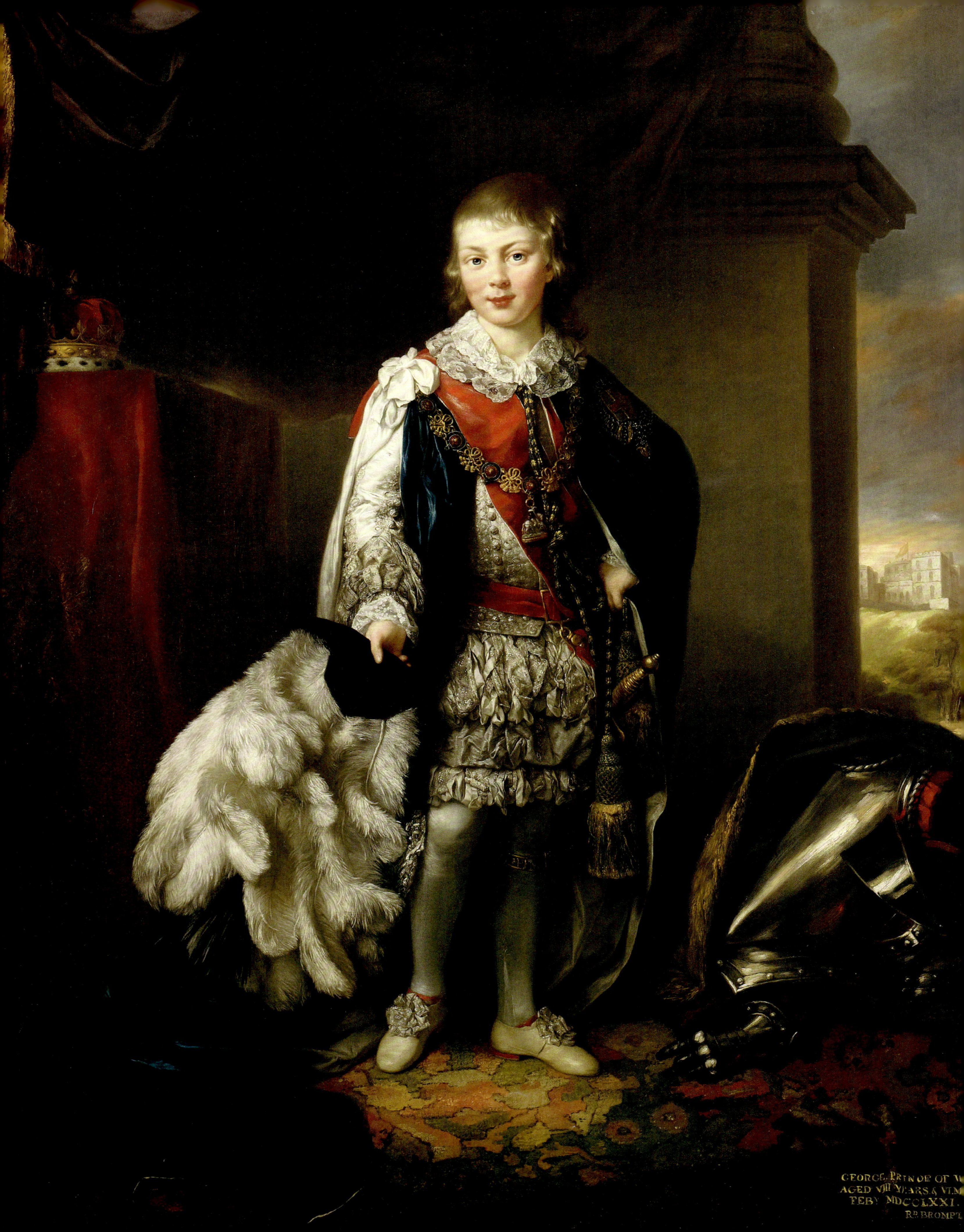
GEORGE PRINCE OF
AGED VIII YEARS & VI M
FEBY MDCCLXXI.
RD BROMPT

9

A NAIVE *and* SENTIMENTAL SOLDIER? GEORGE IV *and the* ART *of* WAR

KATE HEARD

On 25 June 1831, almost exactly a year after George IV's death, Thomas Creevey, Treasurer of the Ordnance, noted an unusual piece of business:

> I have been [given] a curious receipt upon a curious subject. The Duke of Wellington and Sir Wm. Knighton have this day paid me £3,170 as executors of his late Majesty. The money is for tents erected upon that part of Windsor Park called the Virginia Water. The canvas composing the tents is from Ordnance stores, and as His Majesty was pleased to imagine that whenever he *took the field*, his Ordnance Department must supply him with tents, he never meant to pay for these articles. Tennyson, finding the amount of this job in his books, has demanded payment from the executors.[1]

When we think of George and military affairs, we immediately think of him, as this anecdote suggests, 'playing soldiers': in encampment with the 10th Light Dragoons, or imagining himself leading the victorious charge at Waterloo. As Creevey's incredulous account shows, such aspirational play-acting continued to George's death. Yet considering his position and upbringing, it is unsurprising that George coveted thoughts of a military career. From a young age, he had been furnished with military toys and dress – '21 brass guns of 1lb calibre with travelling carriages' for his birthday in 1768, a set of guns made by John Hirst in 1773, and two small swords in 1772.[2] An early influence was Leonard Smelt, his sub-governor until 1776, who had previously had an army career and had fought at the battles of Dettingen and Fontenoy.[3] A portrait (Fig. 9.1), commissioned by his mother as a present for his governess, Lady Charlotte Finch, showed the nine-year-old prince in confident pose, standing next to pieces of shining plate armour, symbols of martial promise.

George showed a keen awareness, too, of the military exploits of his predecessors as Prince of Wales, notable among them Edward, the Black Prince, and the hot-headed 'Prince Hal', who would become the celebrated warrior Henry V. That both the Black Prince and Henry V had made their careers in combat with France (with which Britain was almost continuously at war between 1778 and 1783, and 1793 and 1815) was surely not lost on George. In 1771 he gave a tour of Windsor Castle to a group of visiting dignitaries, halting when he realised that a depiction of the Black Prince in St George's Hall would be offensive to the French ambassador.[4] As a love-struck teenager, he may have been attracted to the story of the Black Prince's love for and eventual marriage to Joan, the Fair Maid of Kent, despite his father's wish 'to match him to some foreign Princess'.[5] As King, he would commission full-length sculptures of the Black Prince and Edward III for the George IV Gate at Windsor Castle.[6] The comparison with these illustrious forebears went beyond George's own imagination: shortly after his death, an astoundingly flattering comparison was drawn between George IV and Henry V by Robert Huish, who asked 'where is the pretended similarity between the conqueror of Agincourt and the son of George III? ... Henry V was a hero, but not a gentleman, associating with the greatest blackguards of the day; – George, Prince of Wales, was a gentleman of the most finished stamp, and might have been a hero if the opportunity had been allowed him.'[7] Alas for George, comparison with his heroic ancestors was also used by those who sought to criticise him, notably James Gillray, who in his *Hint to Modern Sculptors* (Fig. 9.2) drew an unflattering comparison between the dashing Henry V and the overweight dandy prince.

As George reached his majority, he was only able to watch from the sidelines as his brothers embarked on their (admittedly largely unprepossessing) military careers.[8] Frederick, Duke of York, to whom George was closest, led the British army in the anti-Napoleonic push of 1793–5 and, despite a poor performance in that campaign, was promoted to field marshal in 1795 and commander-in-chief in 1798. William, Duke of Clarence (later William IV) pursued a naval career from an early age, rising to the rank of lieutenant before he returned home in 1788. Edward, Duke of Kent, Ernest, Duke of Cumberland and Adolphus, Duke of Cambridge all served with the Hanoverian army.

George's vast collections of military material benefited from the careers of his siblings – in 1794, for example, the Duke of Cumberland wrote to him from Arnhem to say that he was 'now getting you all the Cloathing of the new Corps here and shall send them over as soon as possible' – but he became increasingly frustrated at his own lack of military career.[9] Indeed, his envy of the Duke of York's army command led to friction between the two brothers, and it is possible to read George's formation of an important collection of arms and armour (discussed below) in the light of this rivalry. Pieces added to Frederick's own armoury at his Oatlands residence were eagerly reported in the papers, couched as the trophies of a conquering hero: 'Some military weapons for the *armoury* of the Duke of York arrived in town on Thursday,' reported the *Star* in 1791. 'His return from a campaign of *love* is thus preceded by the ensigns of war!'[10] Although it was praised in London guides such as Ackermann's *Microcosm of London*, such adulatory press coverage was never accorded to stay-at-home George's collection of arms and armour.

In response to George's demands that he be allowed to undertake military service, his father gave him nominal command of the 10th Light Dragoons in 1793, but was reportedly determined 'to resist every Idea that bore the Semblance of the Prince of Wales being in any other view or respect considered as a Military Man'.[11] In 1803, when war with France resumed after a brief peace, George's frustration became so great that his irritation made the press, through the publication of his letters to the prime minister, Henry Addington, requesting military service: '[t]he subject ... presses so heavily on my mind, and daily acquires such additional importance, that ... I find it impossible to withhold or delay an explicit statement of my feelings, to which I would direct your most serious consideration'. George argued that although 'I do not possess the experience of actual Warfare, at the same time, I cannot regard myself as totally unqualified or deficient in Military Science, since I have long made the Service, my particular study.'[12]

George's frustration is understandable: he was living at a time of heightened tension, when the British population felt threatened by both challenges to the country's overseas influence and the possibility of invasion. It has been estimated that between 1793 and 1815, around 250,000 British soldiers and sailors died in conflict.[13] Among them were Frederick Joseph Darby, rumoured (probably without foundation) to be George's illegitimate son, and George's acquaintances Major Frederick Howard and Major-General Sir William Ponsonby.[14] George, who remained at home while his brothers fought and his friends died, became Byron's 'Prince of Wales who *don't*', a sentiment expressed in a private letter, but undoubtedly typical of many opinions at the time.[15] Sir Gilbert Elliot noted George's frustration at being 'an idle spectator of the great events in Europe'.[16]

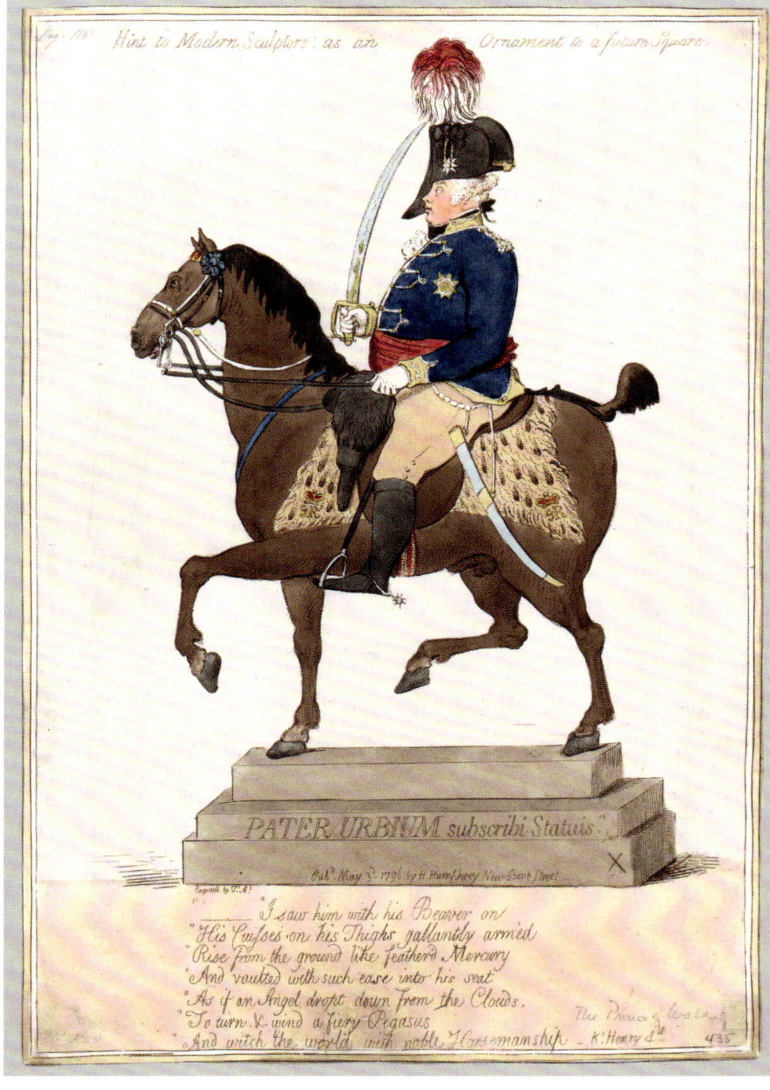

(p. 124)
FIG. 9.1
RICHARD BROMPTON (1734–88), *George IV when Prince of Wales*, 1777. Oil on canvas, 198.5 × 144.8 cm, RCIN 405067

FIG. 9.2
JAMES GILLRAY (1756–1815), *Hint to Modern Sculptors, as an Ornament to a Future Square*, 1796. Stipple and etching with hand colouring, 36.0 × 25.0 cm (sheet) (Lewis Walpole Library, Yale University, Farmington, CT: 796.05.03.01)

Denied military service, George's 'particular study' was partly carried out through his eager involvement with his Dragoon regiment (which became the 10th Light Hussars in 1806).[17] George joined the regiment for exercises in summer 1793, employing as his base a colourful marquee more suited to the masquerade than the battlefield.[18] He equipped the regiment with the newly developed Baker rifles, and splendid new uniforms.[19] As George would tell an acquaintance in 1805, his favourite print of himself was one after William Beechey's dashing portrait showing him in the uniform of the 10th.[20] As Steven Parissien shows in this volume (see chapter 2), dressing the part was ever important to the image-conscious George.

Besides interesting himself in army fashions, George took every opportunity to engage vicariously in the life of the military. His close circle of advisers was dominated by those who had seen service, among them Admiral John Willett Payne, who became his private secretary in 1786 after a respected naval career; Colonel Sir John McMahon, who had fought under the Duke of York in Flanders and served as George's Vice-Treasurer from 1800; Benjamin Bloomfield, who served with the Royal Artillery before joining George's household as Gentleman Attendant, Chief Equerry and Clerk Marshal from 1812; General Sir Tomkyns Hilgrove Turner, who had served in Europe and Egypt, and who was appointed to George's household in 1809; and Frederick, Baron Eben, author of a number of military texts (Fig. 9.3), who was described in the *Gentleman's Magazine* of 1817 as 'an aid-de-camp [*sic*] of the Prince Regent, of low extraction, but of considerable abilities, [who] has been elevated to his present rank from the humble station of a private soldier'.[21] These men were deeply involved in the formation of George's collection. Turner acted as the keeper of prints and drawings, and thereby oversaw the acquisition of works on

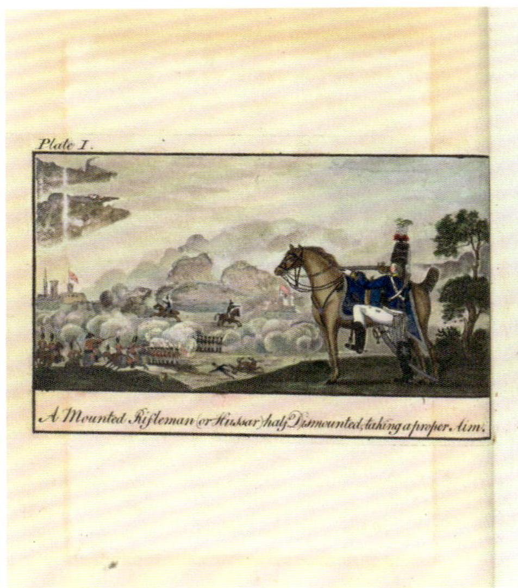

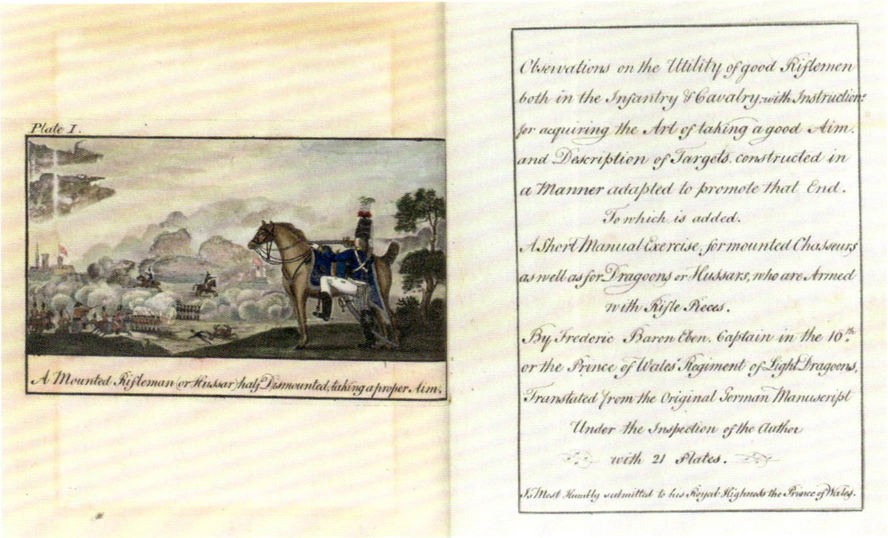

Plate I.

A Mounted Rifleman or Hussar half Dismounted, taking a proper Aim.

Observations on the Utility of good Riflemen both in the Infantry & Cavalry: with Instructions for acquiring the Art of taking a good Aim. and Description of Targets constructed in a Manner adapted to promote that End.

To which is added.

A Short Manual Exercise, for mounted Chasseurs as well as for Dragoons or Hussars, who are Armed with Rifle Pieces.

By Frederic Baron Eben. Captain in the 10th or the Prince of Wales's Regiment of Light Dragoons, Translated from the Original German Manuscript Under the Inspection of the Author with 21 Plates.

Is Most Humbly submitted to his Royal Highness the Prince of Wales.

FIG. 9.3
FREDERICK, BARON EBEN (1771–1832), *Observations on the utility of good riflemen both in the infantry & cavalry ... to which is added a short manual exercise for mounted chasseurs*, c.1804–6. Manuscript on paper, watercolour illustrations, 25.0 × 20.7 cm, RCIN 1047356

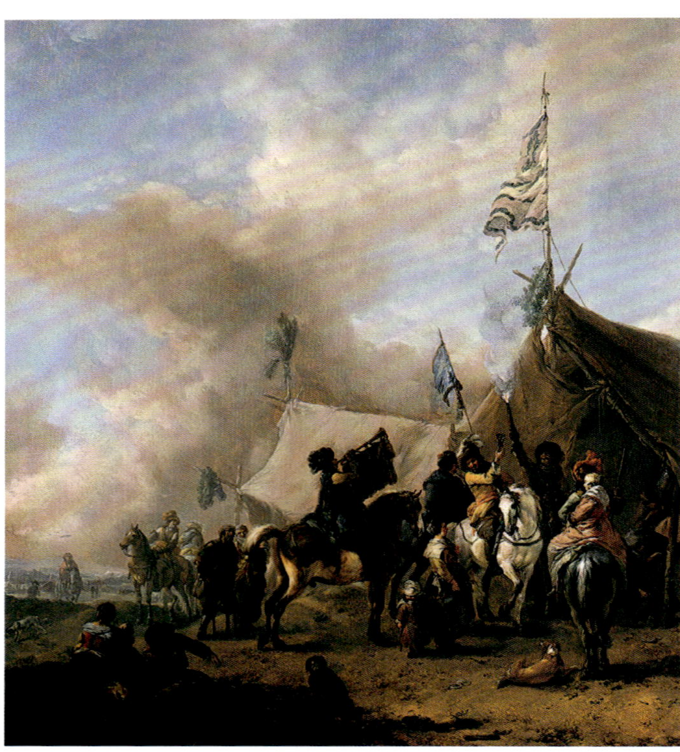

FIG. 9.4
PHILIPS WOUWERMAN (1619–68), *Cavalry at a Sutler's Booth*, c.1650–9. Oil on panel, 49.3 × 44.2 cm, RCIN 404615

paper of military subjects; McMahon, Payne, Bloomfield and Eben all presented items to the Carlton House Armoury. Eben, furthermore, dedicated his *Costumes of the Swedish Army* to George in 1808. It is surely no coincidence that Turner, Bloomfield and Eben appear with Lord Heathfield as attendants on George in a stubbornly martial equestrian portrait by John Singleton Copley (see Fig. 2.19), one which an unknowing observer would assume showed a great general, not a becalmed prince.[22]

Alongside military members of staff, George gathered vast collections of military art and memorabilia. Unlike the men with whom he could discuss the reality of life in the field, his art collection largely presented a romanticised view of warfare in which well-fed soldiers camped in verdant landscapes and engaged in thrilling hand-to-hand combat. Such paintings as Philips Wouwerman's *Skirmish of Cavalry* or Adam-François van der Meulen's battle scenes showed soldiers engaged in dramatic action in which the dead are visible, but not their terrible wounds, while the depictions of the battles of Vittoria and Waterloo which George commissioned from George Jones both concentrate on the figures of Wellington and his staff, with the fighting romantically depicted in a smoky haze. Similarly, Wouwerman's *Cavalry at a Sutler's Booth* (Fig. 9.4) and Aelbert Cuyp's *Two Cavalry Troopers Talking to a Peasant* depict the sort of easy camaraderie that appealed to George in all his social dealings.

Portraits of martial heroes, too, allowed George to celebrate a military ideal: at Carlton House around 1806 he planned an Admirals Room of naval heroes (perhaps pointedly, in the space previously allocated to his estranged wife for her suite of rooms).[23] The room was to be hung with paintings of Admirals Keppel, Rodney (Fig. 9.5), Nelson (see Fig. 3.12) and St Vincent by Sir Joshua Reynolds and John Hoppner.[24] George's other portrait purchases included Gainsborough's oval of Charles, 1st Marquess Cornwallis, veteran of the Seven Years' War and American War of Independence, and Thomas Phillips's picture of John Hely-Hutchinson, 2nd Earl of Donoughmore, who had been responsible for the defeat of the French in Egypt.[25] In 1820, he acquired Jean-Baptiste Isabey's group portrait of the attendees at the Congress of Vienna of 1814–15 (see Fig. 1.5). As Rebecca

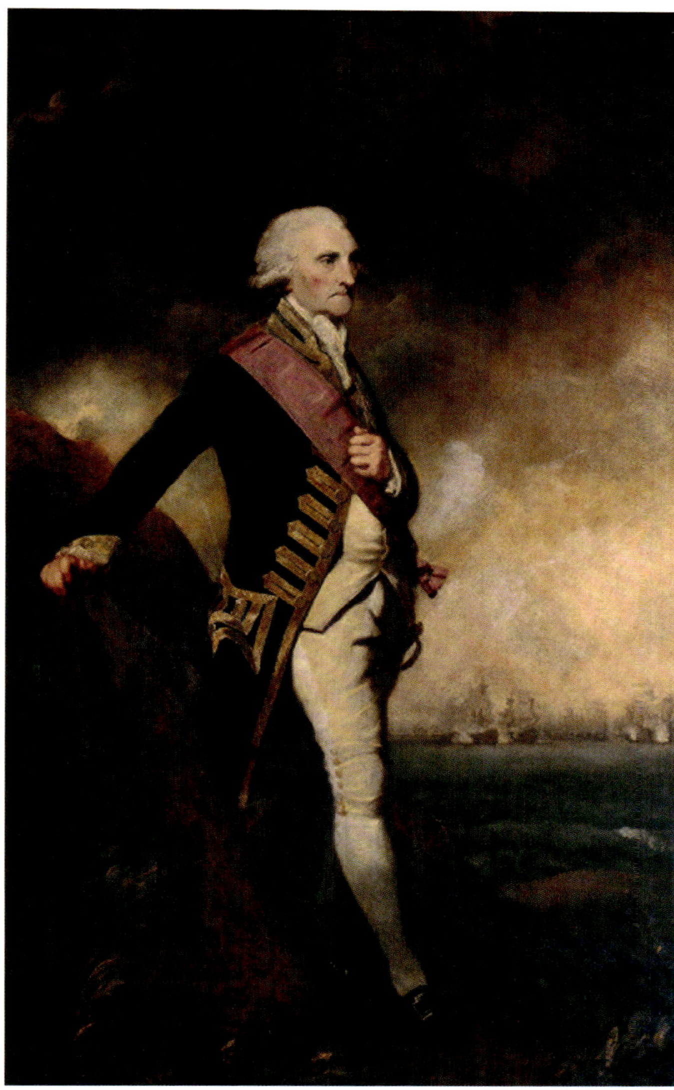

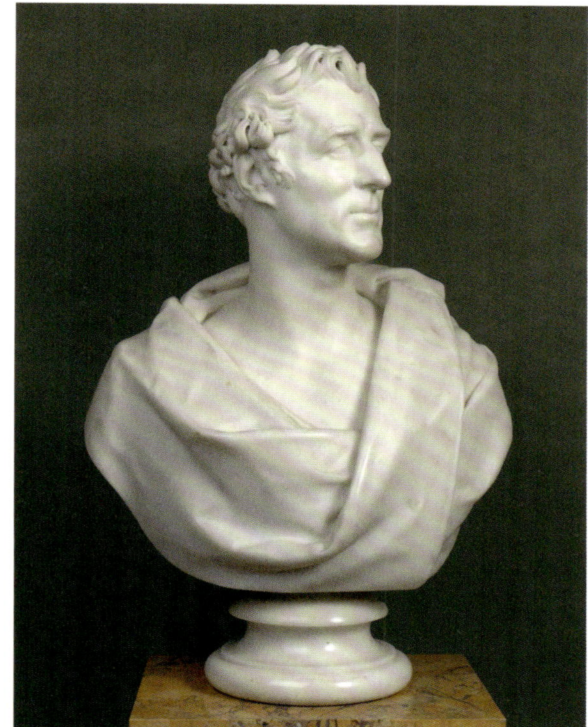

FIG. 9.5
SIR JOSHUA REYNOLDS (1723–92), *George Brydges, First Lord Rodney (?1719–92)*, 1788–9. Oil on canvas, 238.7 × 148.2 cm, RCIN 405899

FIG. 9.6
SIR FRANCIS CHANTREY (1781–1841), *Arthur Wellesley, 1st Duke of Wellington (1769–1852)*, 1828. Marble, 79.0 × 50.0 × 31.0 cm, RCIN 35422

Lyons discusses in this volume, George used portraiture to place himself among the military men he could not join in the field, and would later commission portraits of important military leaders, principal among them the Duke of Wellington, from Sir Thomas Lawrence to celebrate the end of the Napoleonic Wars. Such figures as Wellington (Fig. 9.6) and Nelson, of course, were national rather than personal heroes, but George's interest in them should be seen in terms of his fascination with military heroism rather than as jumping on a populist bandwagon.[26]

While the walls of his residences were hung with largely romanticised depictions of heroic warfare, George stocked his library with books, maps and prints of military subjects. This was not hankering after an idyllic military career, but a careful examination of military history, discipline and tactics. His books included discussions of strategy (Fig. 9.7), fortifications and army regulations (Fig. 9.8) for both the British and foreign forces and he purchased significant military volumes at the sales of Lord Heathfield in 1814, Major Charles James in 1819 and General Dowdeswell in 1820.[27] Alongside books, George studied military history and tactics through prints and drawings, buying illustrations of cavalry and infantry movements from Thomas Egerton's Military Library in Whitehall in 1799 and 48 drawings of sword exercises and 25 of lance exercises by Denis Dighton (each sheet showing a different drill position).[28] These were complemented by the numerous prints and drawings which he purchased of historic and contemporary battles, among them a series of prints of Marlborough's campaigns.[29] We know that he used maps and newspaper accounts to follow the progress of the British army on the continent: Thomas Creevey recounted how '[it] was a funny thing to hear the Prince, when the battle

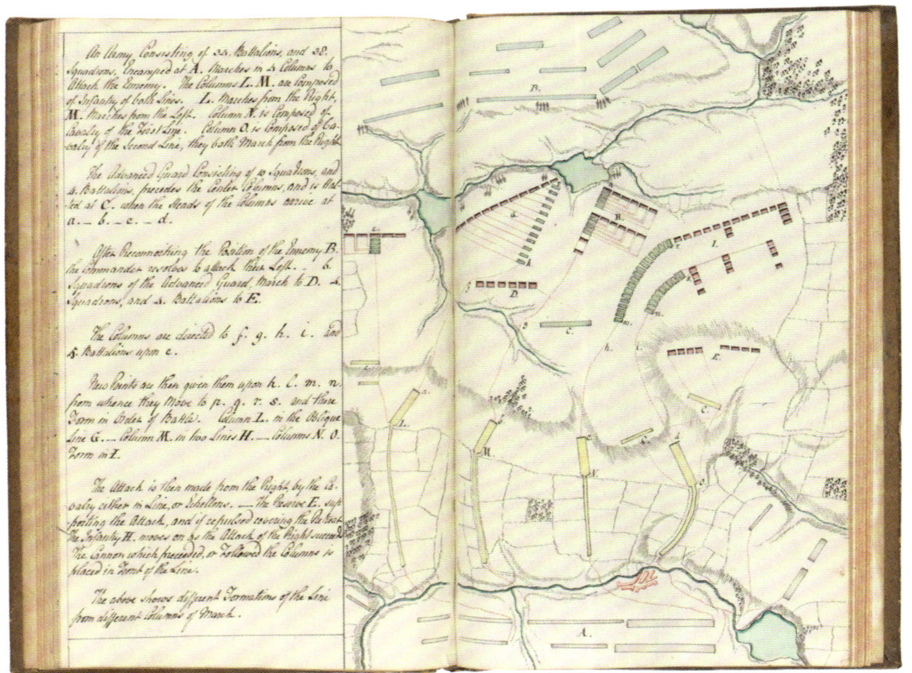
An Army Consisting of 34 Battalions and 38 Squadrons, Encamped at A. Marches in 4 Columns to Attack the Enemy. The Columns L. M. are Composed of Infantry of both Lines. L. Marches from the Right, M. Marches from the Left. Column N. is Composed of Cavalry of the First Line. Column O. is Composed of Cavalry of the Second Line, they both March from the Right.

The Advanced Guard Consisting of 10 Squadrons and 4 Battalions, precedes the Center Columns, and is Halted at C. when the Heads of the Columns arrive at a. _ b. _ c. _ d.

After Reconnoitring the Position of the Enemy B. the Commander resolves to attack their Left. _ 6. Squadrons of the Advanced Guard March to D. 4 Squadrons, and 4. Battalions to E.

The Columns are directed to f. g. h. i. and 5. Battalions upon e.

New Points are then given them upon k. l. m. n. from whence they Move to p. q. r. s. and there Form in Order of Battle. Column L. in the Oblique Line G. _ Column M. in two Lines H. _ Columns N. O. Form in I.

The Attack is then made from the Right, by the Cavalry either in Line, or Echellons. _ The Reserve E. supporting the Attack, and if repulsed covering the Retreat. The Infantry H. moves on as the Attack of the Right succeeds. The Cannon which preceded, or Followed the Columns is placed in Front of the Line.

The above shows different Formations of the Line from different Columns of March.

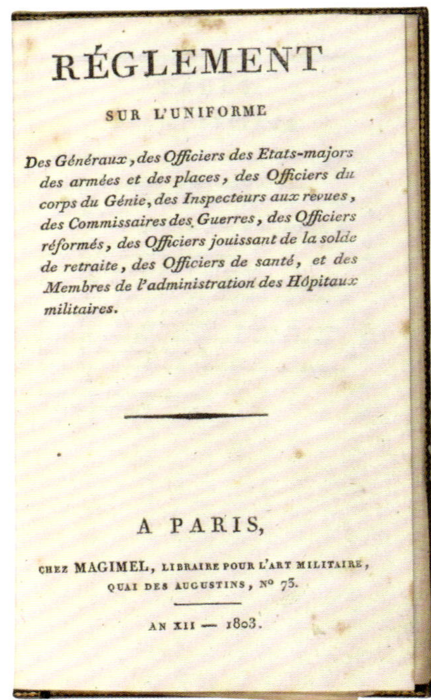
RÉGLEMENT

SUR L'UNIFORME

Des Généraux, des Officiers des Etats-majors des armées et des places, des Officiers du corps du Génie, des Inspecteurs aux revues, des Commissaires des Guerres, des Officiers réformés, des Officiers jouissant de la solde de retraite, des Officiers de santé, et des Membres de l'administration des Hôpitaux militaires.

A PARIS,

CHEZ MAGIMEL, LIBRAIRE POUR L'ART MILITAIRE, QUAI DES AUGUSTINS, N° 73.

AN XII — 1803.

FIG. 9.7
SIR DAVID DUNDAS (1735–1820), *Cavalry formations*, 1775. Manuscript on paper, watercolour illustrations, 32.0 × 20.5 cm, RCIN 1047113

FIG. 9.8
Published by MAGIMEL, PARIS, *Réglement sur l'uniforme des Généraux, des Officiers, des Etats-majors des armées et des places*, 1803. Printed book, 20.6 × 12.7 cm, RCIN 1082268

FIG. 9.9
Published by PIERRE JEAN (1754–1829), *Plan de la Bataille d'Austerlitz*, 1805. Engraving with hand colouring, 48.0 × 38.5 cm (sheet), RCIN 712608

had taken place, express the same opinion as was given in the London Government newspapers, that it was all over with the French – that they were all sent to the devil and the Lord knows what. Maps were got out to satisfy everybody as to the precise ground where the battle had been fought and the route by which the French had retreated.' The French had not in fact retreated at all – the battle in question was Austerlitz and soon news of the Austrian defeat began to arrive: 'when the truth began at last to make its appearance in the newspapers,' wrote Creevey, 'the Prince puts them all in his pockets, so that no paper was forthcoming at the Pavilion, instead of half-a-dozen, the usual number'.[30] If George could not influence the result of a battle through participation, he could at least control the flow of news about its outcome in his immediate circle. As well as general maps of the ground over which fighting took place, George purchased plans of specific battles, among them Austerlitz (of which he acquired at least seven depictions, including Fig. 9.9) and Marengo (the subject of at least six prints in his collection).

From the first years of the nineteenth century, George's understanding of the experience of battle could be fed by the flood of military memoirs published by those who had participated in the Napoleonic campaigns.[31] Among these many autobiographies, George was presented with a copy of Moyle Sherer's 1823 *Recollections of the Peninsula* in 1824.[32] If George read Sherer's enthusiastic account of his experiences on campaign he would undoubtedly have been struck by the contrast with his own restricted life. Among officers in the field, Sherer noted

> the conversation no longer ran in the same dull, unvarying strain, on scenes of expensive folly and fatiguing amusement … New prospects and eager hopes gave an animation and interest to the discourse, which, seasoned as it was by some excellent wine, made time fly swiftly, and it was midnight before I entered my tent … but I was far too happy to sleep.[33]

George's fascination with Napoleon, which permeated so many areas of his art collecting, was a catalyst for many of his military acquisitions. As well as books on all aspects of the Napoleonic campaigns and prints and drawings of the emperor

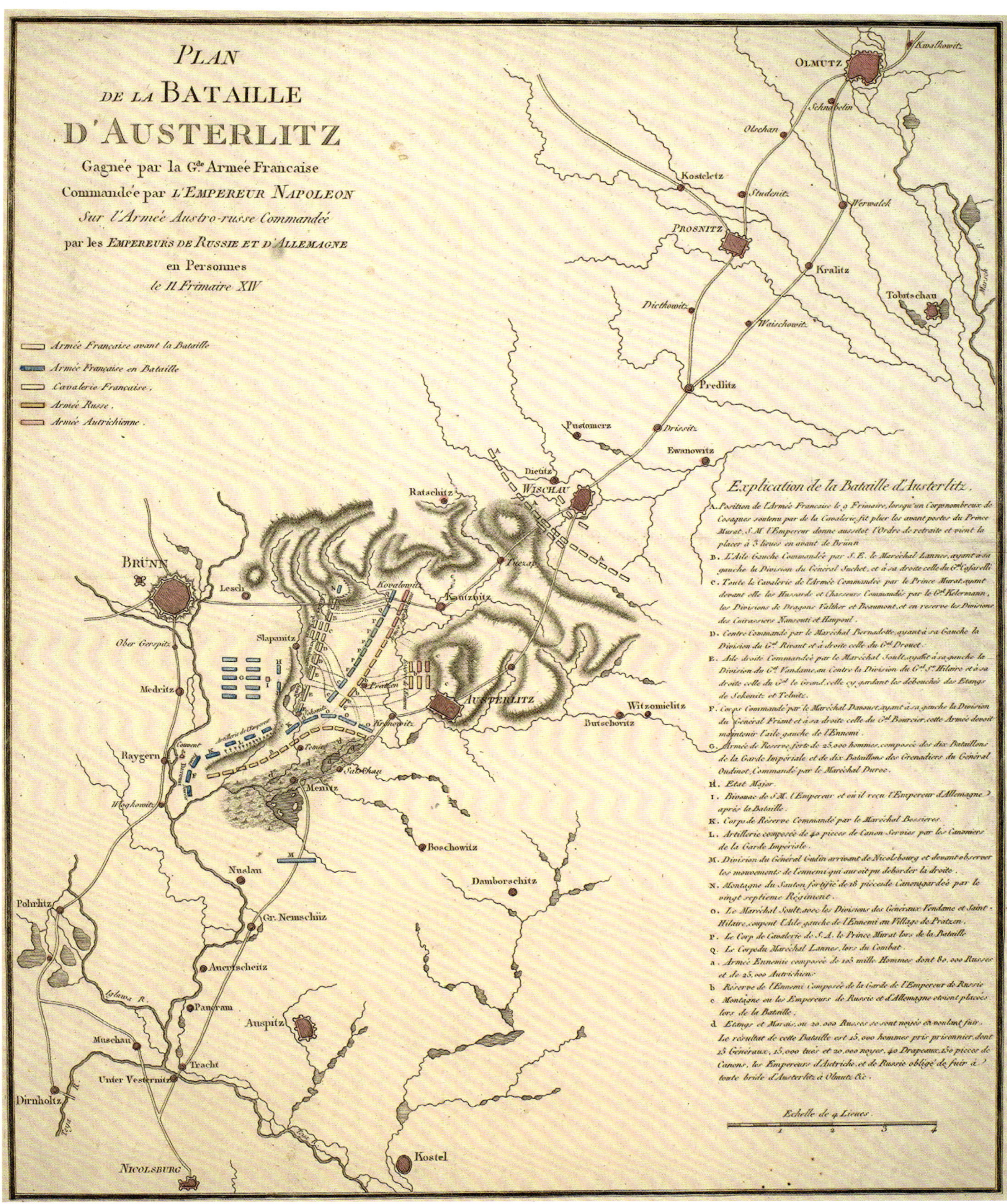
PLAN
DE LA BATAILLE
D'AUSTERLITZ
Gagnée par la Gde. Armée Francaise
Commandée par L'EMPEREUR NAPOLEON
Sur l'Armée Austro-russe Commandée
par les EMPEREURS DE RUSSIE ET D'ALLEMAGNE
en Personnes
le 11 Frimaire XIV
Armée Française avant la Bataille
Armée Française en Bataille
Cavalerie Francaise.
Armée Russe.
Armée Autrichienne.
OLMUTZ
Kwalkowitz
Schnabelin
Olschan
Kostelctz
Studenitz
Werwalck
PROSNITZ
Kralitz
Tobitschau
Dicthowitz
Waischowitz
Predlitz
Pustomerz
Drissitz
Ewanowitz
Dietitz
WISCHAU
Ratschitz
BRÜNN
Lesch
Kovalowitz
Kautzwitz
Tuczap
Ober Gerspitz
Slapanitz
Pratzen
AUSTERLITZ
Medritz
Witzomielitz
Butschowitz
Kritnowitz
Raygern
Telnitz
Satschau
Menitz
Wogkowitz
Boschowitz
Nuslau
Damborschitz
Pohrlitz
Gr. Nemschiz
Auerrscheitz
Panciam
Auspitz
Muschau
Tracht
Unter Vestemitz
Dirnholtz
Kostel
NICOLSBURG
Explication de la Bataille d'Austerlitz.
A. Position de l'Armée Francaise le 9 Frimaire, lorsqu'un Corps nombreux de Cosaques soutenu par de la Cavalerie, fit plier les avant postes du Prince Murat, S.M. l'Empereur donne aussitot l'Ordre de retraite et vient la placer à 3 lieues en avant de Brünn
B. L'Aile Gauche Commandée par S.E. le Maréchal Lannes, ayant à sa gauche la Division du Général Suchet, et à sa droite celle du Gal. Cafarelli
C. Toute la Cavalerie de l'Armée Commandée par le Prince Murat, ayant devant elle les Hussards et Chasseurs Commandés par le Gal. Kelermann, les Divisions de Dragons Valther et Beaumont, et en reserve les Divisions des Cuirassiers Nansouti et Haupoul.
D. Centre Commandé par le Maréchal Bernadotte, ayant à sa Gauche la Division du Gal. Rivaut et à droite celle du Gal. Drouet.
E. Aile droite Commandée par le Maréchal Soult, ayant à sa gauche la Division du Gal. Vandame, au Centre la Division du Gal. St. Hilaire et à sa droite celle du Gal. le Grand, celle cy gardant les débouchés des Etangs de Sokenitz et Telnitz.
F. Corps Commandé par le Maréchal Davoust, ayant à sa gauche la Division du Général Friant et à sa droite celle du Gal. Bourcier, cette Armée devoit maintenir l'aile gauche de l'Ennemi.
G. Armée de Reserve, forte de 25,000 hommes, composée des dix Bataillons de la Garde Impériale et de dix Bataillons des Grenadiers du Général Oudinot, Commandé par le Maréchal Duroc.
H. Etat Major.
I. Bivouac de S.M. l'Empereur et où il reçu l'Empereur d'Allemagne après la Bataille.
K. Corps de Réserve Commandé par le Maréchal Bessieres.
L. Artillerie composée de 40 pieces de Canon Servies par les Canoniers de la Garde Impériale.
M. Division du Général Gudin arrivant de Nicolsbourg et devant observer les mouvements de l'ennemi qui auroit pu déborder la droite.
N. Montagne du Santon fortifié de 18 pièces de Canons gardeé par le vingt septieme Régiment.
O. Le Maréchal Soult avec les Divisions des Généraux Vendame et Saint-Hilaire, coupent l'Aile gauche de l'Ennemi au Village de Pratzen.
P. Le Corp de Cavalerie de S.A. le Prince Murat lors de la Bataille
Q. Le Corps du Maréchal Lannes, lors du Combat.
a. Armée Ennemie composée de 105 mille Hommes dont 80,000 Russes et de 25,000 Autrichiens
b Réserve de l'Ennemi Composée de la Garde de l'Empereur de Russie
c Montagne ou les Empereurs de Russie et d'Allemagne etoient placés lors de la Bataille.
d Etangs et Marais, ou 20,000 Russes se sont noyés en voulant fuir.
Le résultat de cette Bataille est 15,000 hommes pris prisonnier, dont 15 Généraux, 15,000 tués et 20,000 noyes, 40 Drapeaux, 150 pieces de Canons, les Empereurs d'Autriche et de Russie obligé de fuir à toute bride d'Austerlitz à Olmutz &c.
Echelle de 4 Lieues.
1
2
3
4

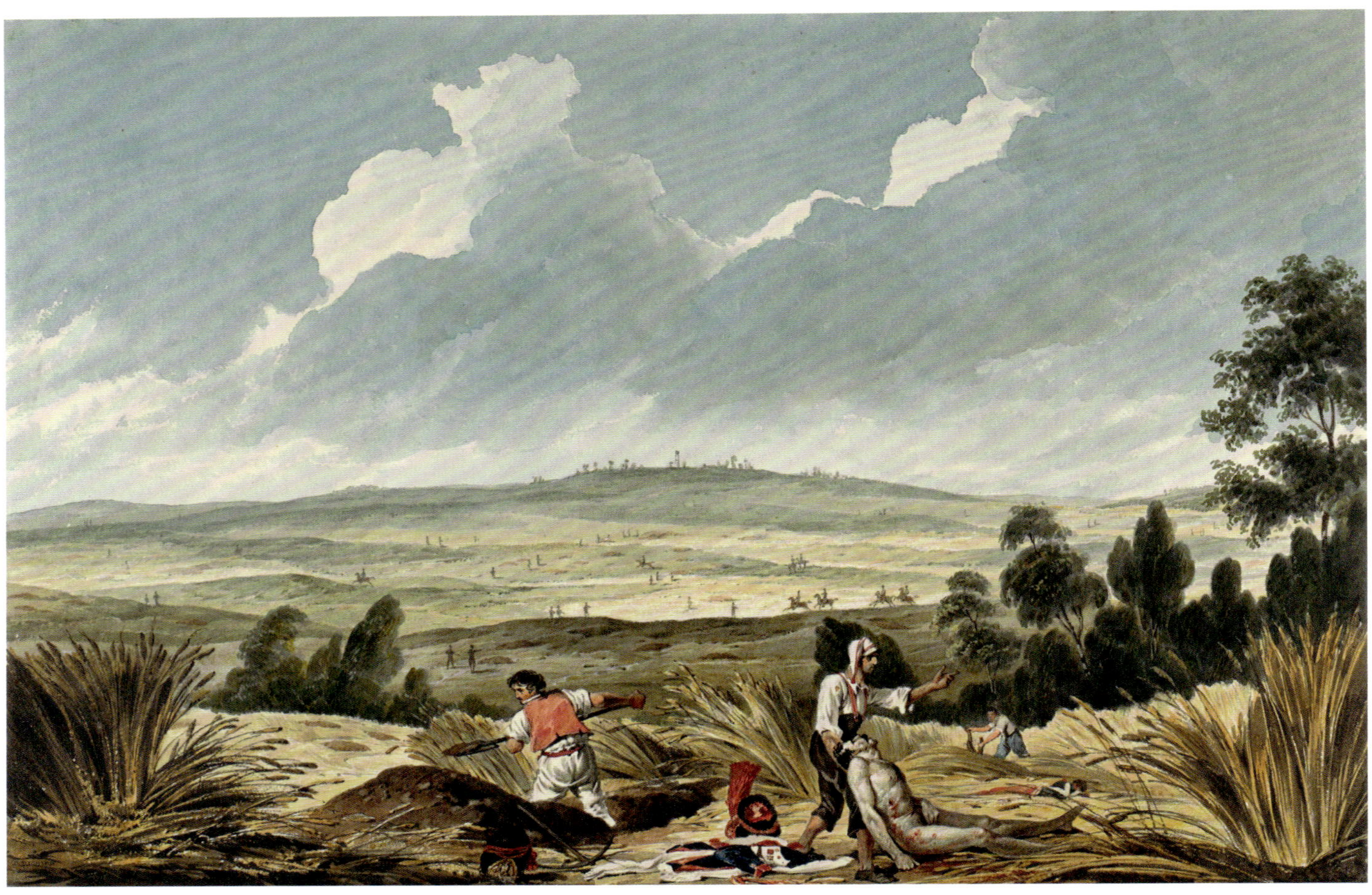

FIG. 9.10
DENIS DIGHTON (1792–1827), *View of the left centre of the French position with the Observatory, Field of Waterloo*, 1815. Watercolour and bodycolour with gum arabic over pencil, 29.0 × 44.5 cm, RCIN 915011

as a commander in battle, he acquired, by purchase and gift, many items of Napoleonic memorabilia which acted as contact relics of the great man (see Fig. 1.10). Among these were 'the Sword of the Legion of Honour, Sent by Bonaparte to the Prince of Peace', presented by Wellington in 1811, and 'a richly chased Sword – presented by the City of Paris to Bonaparte when First Consul', which he purchased in 1827.[34]

It is in the context of his collecting of battle accounts and fascination with Napoleon that George's acquisition of Denis Dighton's watercolours of the field of Waterloo should be seen. Dighton's brutal depictions of the aftermath of the battle are in stark contrast to the romantic paintings that hung on the walls of George's residences. George had long been a supporter of the military artist (see above), gaining him a commission in the 90th Regiment of Foot, and appointing him his personal 'Military Painter' in 1815. Thereafter, George purchased numerous watercolours from Dighton of military uniforms. Dighton's visit to Waterloo shortly after the battle, however, was not in response to a royal commission but taken on his own initiative (as Robert Gray in the Duchy of Cornwall Office noted in a memorandum: 'The Prince Regent was informed of Mr Dighton's intention to visit the field of Waterloo, but neither directed nor encouraged it').[35] Nonetheless, the graphic watercolours he produced as a result of the trip (Fig. 9.10), which show the dead and dying still lying on the battlefield, some being stripped of their clothes, others tipped with little dignity into hurriedly dug graves, were purchased almost immediately by George, who later acquired two equally unromanticised paintings by Dighton of the battle. Through Dighton's works, George could see the reality of the fierce fighting that had proved the final defeat of Napoleon and had led to his own triumph as the leader who had brought together the alliance which prevailed.

The greatest expression of George's military interests was the Armoury that he established at Carlton House.[36] It was here

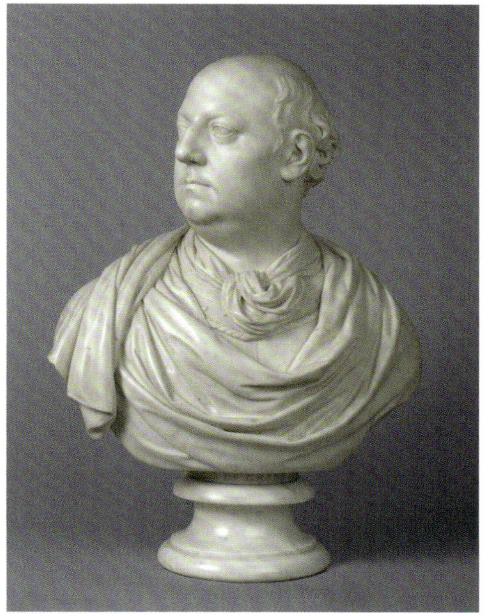

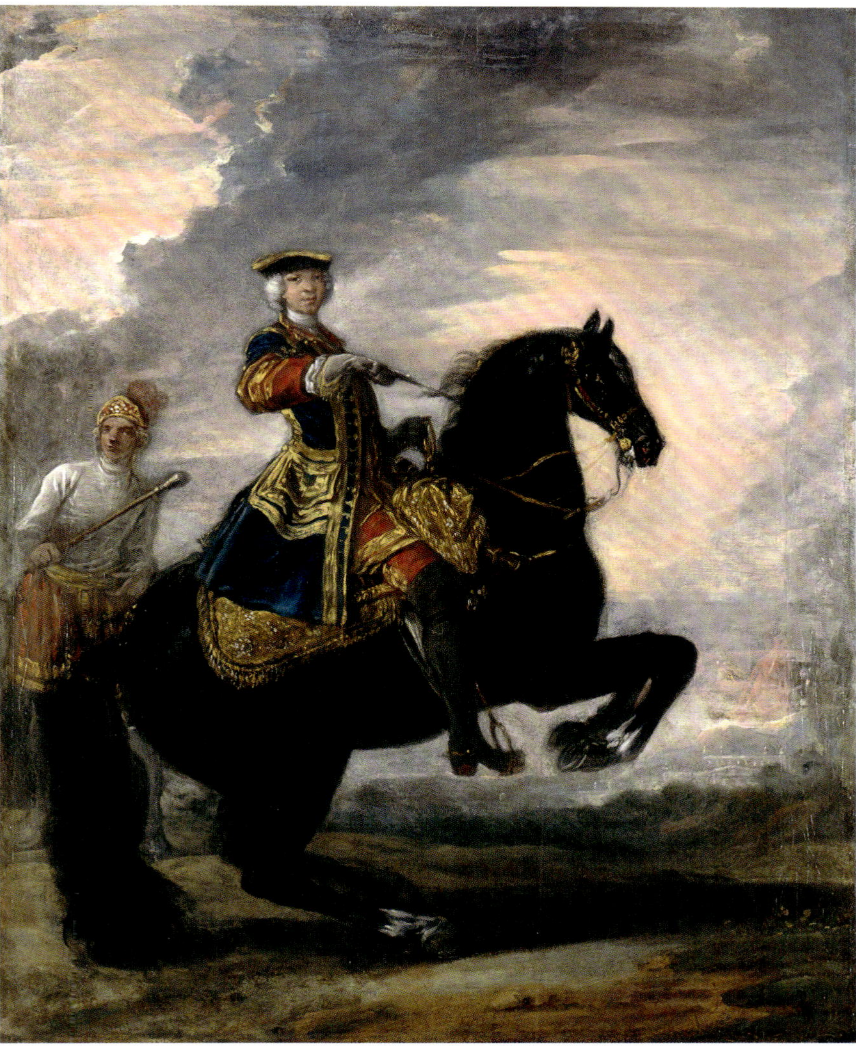

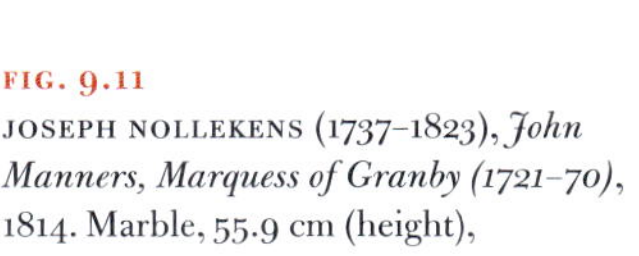

FIG. 9.11
JOSEPH NOLLEKENS (1737–1823), *John Manners, Marquess of Granby (1721–70)*, 1814. Marble, 55.9 cm (height), RCIN 45143

FIG. 9.12
CHARLES PARROCEL (1688–1752), *Charles, Prince de Nassau (1712–75)*, *c.*1725–50. Oil on canvas, 80.4 × 64.8 cm, RCIN 403390

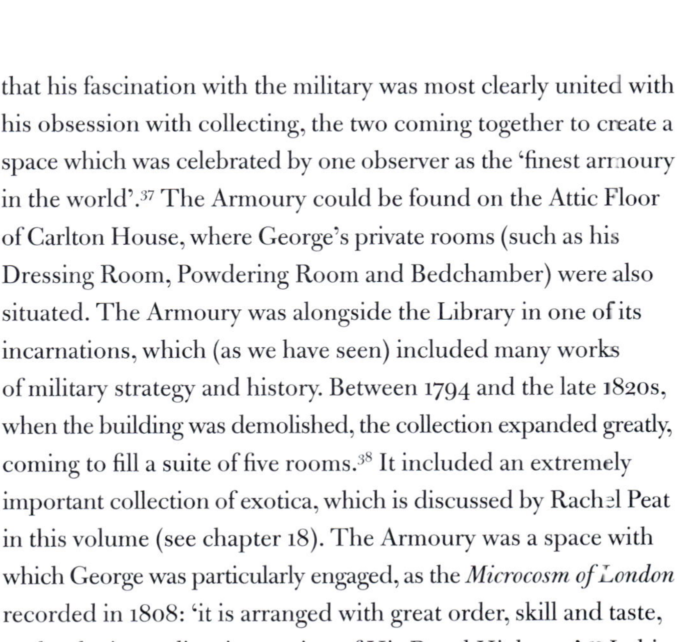

that his fascination with the military was most clearly united with his obsession with collecting, the two coming together to create a space which was celebrated by one observer as the 'finest armoury in the world'.[37] The Armoury could be found on the Attic Floor of Carlton House, where George's private rooms (such as his Dressing Room, Powdering Room and Bedchamber) were also situated. The Armoury was alongside the Library in one of its incarnations, which (as we have seen) included many works of military strategy and history. Between 1794 and the late 1820s, when the building was demolished, the collection expanded greatly, coming to fill a suite of five rooms.[38] It included an extremely important collection of exotica, which is discussed by Rachel Peat in this volume (see chapter 18). The Armoury was a space with which George was particularly engaged, as the *Microcosm of London* recorded in 1808: 'it is arranged with great order, skill and taste, under the immediate inspection of His Royal Highness'.[39] In his 1814 satirical poem *Chalcographimania*, William Henry Ireland described George's taste for old armour as 'a wond'rous passion'.[40]

Beyond the widespread interest in the collecting of armour seen in Britain from the late eighteenth century, George's models for his Armoury may have been the collections formed by his brother Frederick and by the artist Richard Cosway, who acted as an artistic mentor to the prince between 1780 and 1808.[41] Cosway's collection of arms and armour, which he displayed at his Stratford Street house, included 'a very rich and beautiful body suit of steel armour, with cuisses and helmet; the whole chased and engraved in a very masterly manner: of the period of *Benvenuto Cellini*'.[42] An early interest in such collecting is seen in George's purchase, in February 1787, of Francis Grose's *A Treatise on Ancient Armour and Weapons*, which had been published in 1786, and for which he paid the large sum of £2 2s.[43] George would undoubtedly have been aware, too, that Napoleon

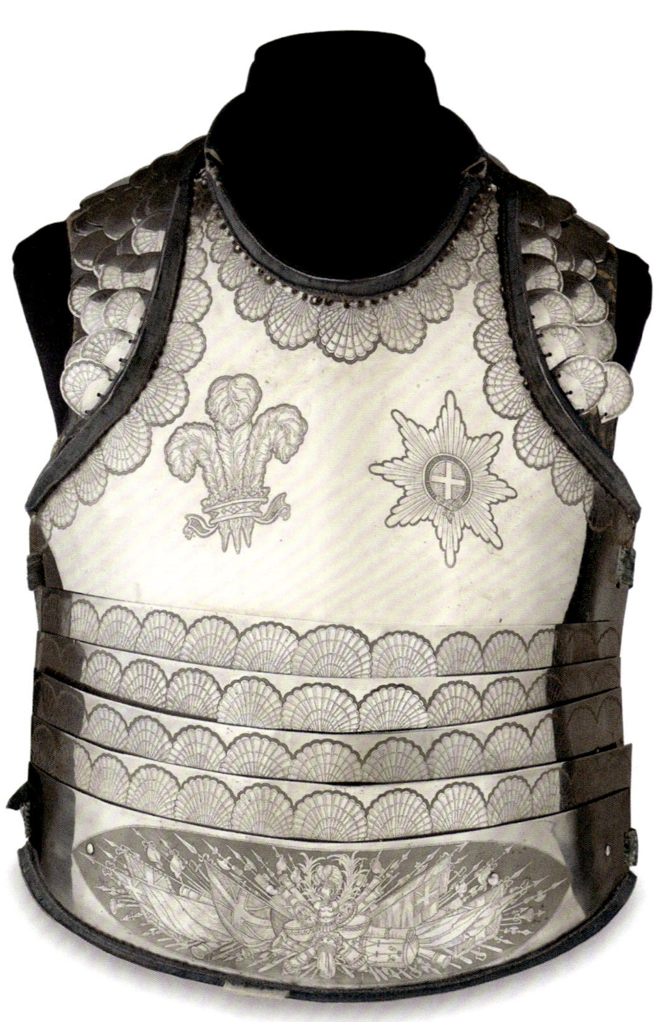

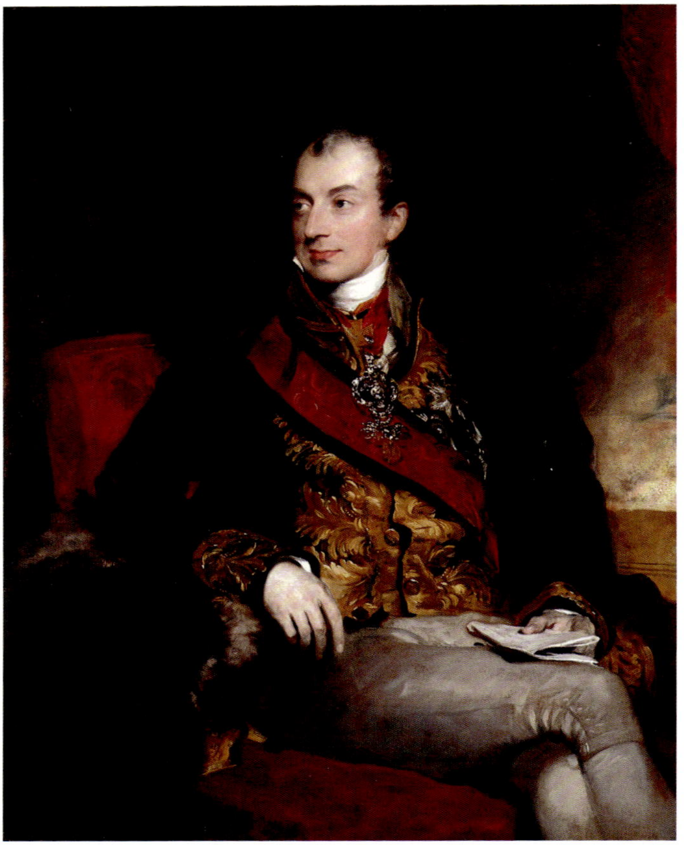

FIG. 9.13
ENGLISH (BIRMINGHAM), *Parade breastplate*, 1806. Steel, velvet, silk, 49.6 × 38.8 cm, RCIN 67162

FIG. 9.14
SIR THOMAS LAWRENCE (1769–1830), *Clemens Lothar Wenzel, Prince Metternich (1773–1859)*, *c.*1815. Oil on canvas, 131.2 × 105.0 cm, RCIN 404948

was forming a collection of such material, having appropriated the fine collection of arms and armour accumulated by the archdukes of Tyrol at Schloss Ambras.[44]

Something of the decoration of the Armoury can be seen in a watercolour by Augustus Charles Pugin (see Fig. 18.4), purchased by George in 1814. This shows cases of arms around the walls, with bows, crossbows and pikes suspended from the ceiling, and a central display of armour, with a group of visitors admiring the collections in the background. An inventory of the collection taken *c.*1826 recorded busts of the Marquess of Granby by Nollekens (Fig. 9.11) and the Duke of Wellington, General Blücher and Count Platov (by Turnerelli) in the second room.[45] The Armoury also included antique-style sculptures, supplied by Colnaghi & Co. in 1807, among them 'a Marble Figure of Venus Callipiga in the Palace Farnesi' and 'Two [Bronze figures] of Antique Psyche Lamps'.[46] Two equestrian paintings by the French artist Charles Parrocel were recorded hanging in the space in 1816 (Fig. 9.12).

Study of the contents of the Armoury benefits from a meticulous inventory compiled by Benjamin Jutsham, who acted as both Inspector of Household Deliveries and as Keeper of the Armoury.[47] As Jutsham's volumes show, George's Armoury fulfilled the roles of arsenal, wardrobe, museum, showpiece, study collection and Valhalla. It was here that George's own

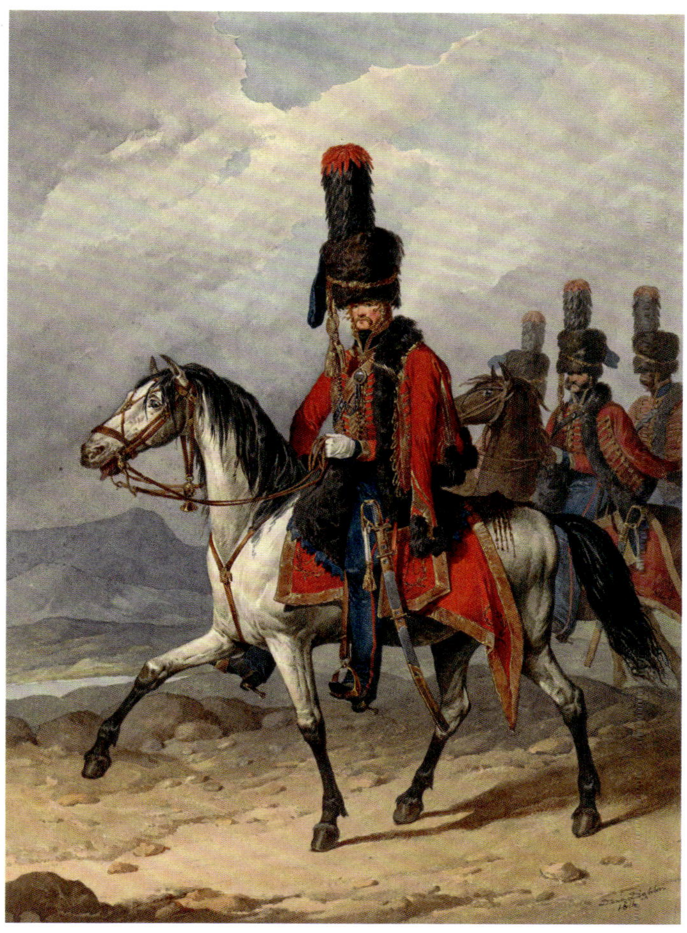

FIG. 9.15
DENIS DIGHTON (1792–1827), *Russian Army: Officer of the Imperial Guard*, 1814. Watercolour over pencil with gum arabic, 50.9 × 37.2 cm, RCIN 915144

uniforms and weapons were stored, as were the braces of pistols and swords purchased to arm his staff when they were travelling with him.[48] George's military-themed fancy dress was here, too, including 'A Chabraque. Green Velvet with Gold Embroidery in Flowers. Very Rich', which was described by Jutsham as 'For an Officer. Fancy Dress. Superbly Embroidered', and a breastplate with etched motifs used by George at a masquerade (Fig. 9.13).[49] Such costumes were certainly used by George: as late as 1821, the Austrian statesman Clemens Metternich (Fig. 9.14) described meeting him in Hanover. 'He was outstretched on a chaise longue,' wrote the amused Metternich, 'enveloped in an Austrian hussar's cloak of a tolerably fantastical cut.'[50] George was, as ever, sartorially prepared for any occasion.

As well as George's personal arms and dress, the Armoury furnished a reference collection of contemporary military uniform and arms, acquired for him across Europe by friends and family. These items were complemented by George's large collection of uniform drawings, purchased through agents on the continent and the London firm of Colnaghi & Co., which remains one of the greatest such collections in existence, and which is still used as a resource for the study of military costume. Benjamin West reported seeing these works in 1810, describing it to Joseph Farington as 'a large collection of drawings made abroad by Foreign Artists, representing the Military of various countries & their operations, with views of places'.[51] The collection included watercolours by specialist military artists such as Denis Dighton (Fig. 9.15), Jan Antonie Langendyk, Alexander Sauerweid, Carle Vernet and Noël-Dieudonné Finart. Like the group of personal arms, this was a working collection: material was lent to the painters David Wilkie and Sir Thomas Lawrence for use as models in paintings commissioned by George.[52] The formation of a reference collection of uniforms and uniform drawings was singled out for praise in the *Microcosm of London* in 1808, when it was noted that

> so extensive and multifarious are the objects of this museum, that to be justly appreciated it must be seen. His Royal Highness bestows considerable attention upon it, and it has in consequence, arrived in a few years to a pitch of unrivalled perfection. Among the dresses are sets of uniforms, from a general to a private, of all countries who have adopted uniforms, and military dresses of those who have not.[53]

Alongside this reference collection were examples of new military technology, among them the model of a cannon 'Made on a New Principal' and a new 'Marine Mortar' (intended to be effective in rough waters) designed and presented by William Congreve.

Most attention, however, was reserved for the 'museum' pieces which the Armoury boasted: items of arms and armour associated with particular historic figures or events.[54] The collection included weapons belonging to George's celebrated forebears (among them William the Conqueror, the Black Prince and Henry V) and that had been used at key battles (including two swords worn by the Marquess of Granby at the Battle of Minden, and a sword which 'bears the date of 1414, the Year preceeding [*sic*] the Battle of Agincourt, and might have been there'; Fig. 9.16).[55] George's interest in such evocative pieces was clearly well-known: for his forty-fifth birthday he was presented by Walsh Porter with a magnificent rapier (Fig. 9.17) – said to have been made by Benvenuto Cellini and owned by the parliamentarian John Hampden – and with General Moreau's favourite sword, a gift from the Duke of Sussex. As well as instilling knowledge of warfare in past ages, such pieces allowed romantic flights of imagination: William Henry Ireland described in 1805 how his own collection transformed his bedroom into 'a regular armoury; and on many occasions, when the moon has shone upon a full suit, I have sat upright in my bed, and pictured scenes from my lord Orford's Castle of Otranto'.[56] George, whose bedroom was situated not far from the Armoury and who had a fondness for Gothic literature, may well have recognised the sentiment.

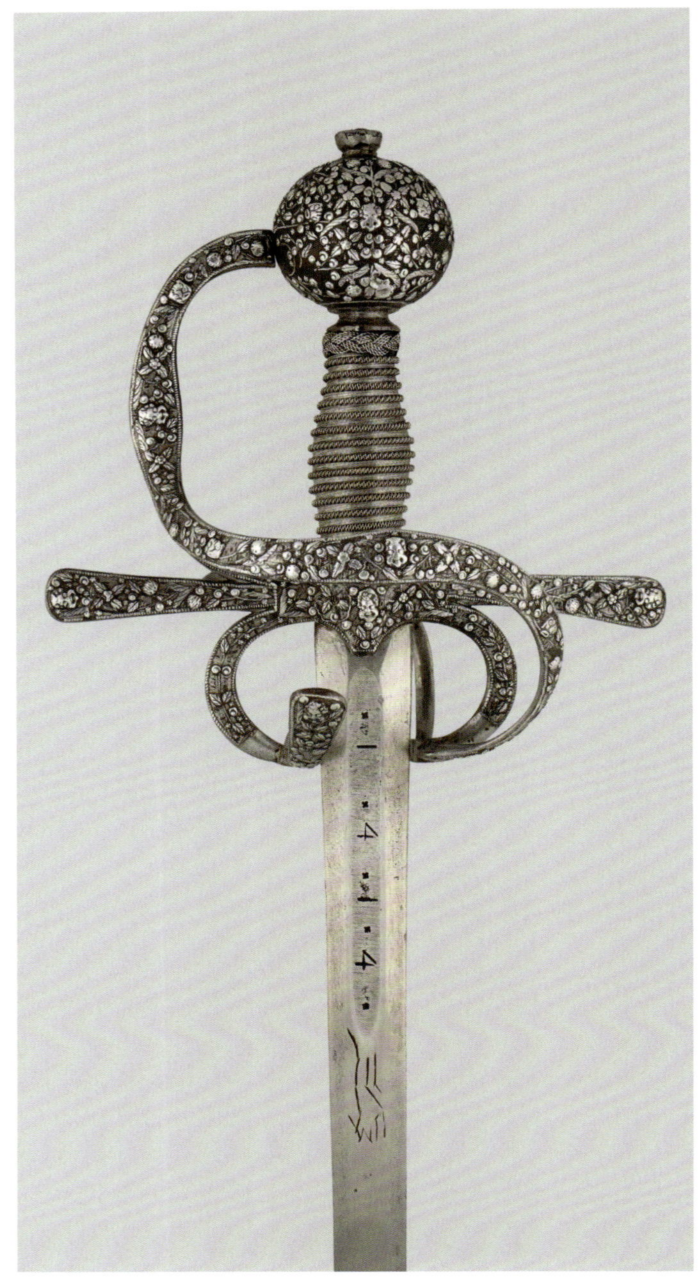

The Armoury was a repository of current as well as historic trophies. During the visit of the Allied Sovereigns in 1814, a number of George's guests presented him with items they had personally used during the Napoleonic campaigns. General Blücher made the gift of a sabre and General Platov gave a saddle, bridle and cloak: both of these are noted in the contemporary catalogue as having been used by their donors during the fighting. These gifts had a rich symbolism: their presentation was an acknowledgement by the donors of George as a military equal, and their 'laying up' in the Armoury at Carlton House suggested that they would no longer be required in battle, an indication of the faith of contemporaries in the peace agreed in the Treaty of Fontainebleau, ratified by Napoleon in April 1814.

The descriptions of these items in Jutsham's catalogue, along with those of a number of others presented by Wellington, are accompanied by breathless encomia to the heroic donors. 'Let the Trumpet Never Cease to Sound the British Hero's Praise' wrote Jutsham of Wellington in the entry for Marshal Jourdan's baton (see Fig. 15.6), which the duke presented in July 1813, and 'Immortal shall thy Name stand in the memory of ages to come' he assured Blücher in the entry for his sabre.[57] If the arms of deceased military heroes, and the presentation of the arms of contemporary warriors (placed amid the busts of celebrities such as Wellington and Granby), gave the Armoury the flavour of a Valhalla, this was a hall of heroes in which George himself was also placed. The Armoury included 'the First Sword His Royal Highness The Prince of Wales ever Wore' and the saddle cloth 'Used the Day His Royal Highness was thrown from His Horse at Canterbury in the Year 1798. The Month of October. Happy Escape. May God in his infinite Mercy long Preserve him'.[58] Jutsham's notes elevate these objects from items of everyday use to memorials of an illustrious career, one which is not distinguished from the military feats of those, such as the Black Prince, Wellington and Blücher, who saw action in the field.

Robert Huish's judgement that George 'might have been a hero if the opportunity had been allowed him' sounds as ridiculous to us as it probably did to contemporaries. George, with his sybaritic love of comfort and extravagance, his melodrama and hypochondria, and his tendency to rail against authority (in the form of his father), would probably have been a terrible soldier, although such faults may have been drummed out of him by an early military training. But if George never achieved the martial

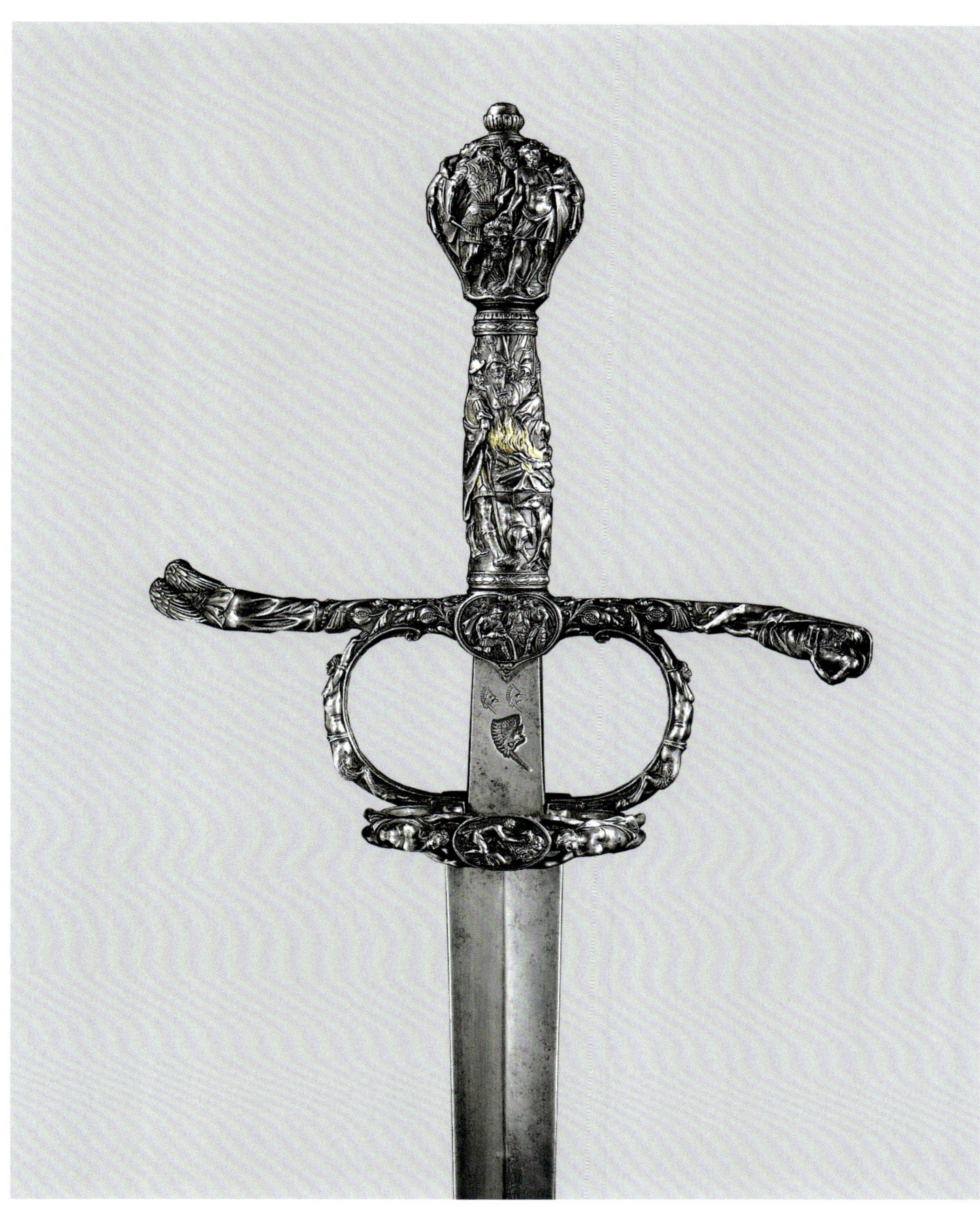

(opposite)
FIG. 9.16
ENGLISH OR FRENCH with blade from SOLINGEN, GERMANY, *Arming sword*, 1600–25. Steel, iron, wood, 102.3 cm (length), RCIN 62964

(left)
FIG. 9.17
NORTHERN EUROPEAN with blade from SOLINGEN, GERMANY, *Rapier*, c.1640. Iron, gold, 107.6 cm (length), RCIN 62994

career he so desired, his art collection speaks to a long and lasting fascination with the military, both as a focus of romantic heroism and as an object of serious study. This fascination led George to assemble a vast collection which in some areas (notably those of arms and armour, and uniform drawings) was unrivalled. As George abandoned Carlton House for Windsor Castle towards the end of his life, he took his Armoury with him, engaging Samuel Rush Meyrick, a collector and historian of militaria, to oversee the installation of his collection in the castle which Wyatville was turning into a Gothic fantasy. Parts of his collection were kept even closer: in 1827, certain swords were sent to Royal Lodge in Windsor Great Park, where George, by then unwell and immobile, lived in seclusion with a close and trusted circle of advisers. And George maintained the tents from the Ordnance Stores at nearby Virginia Water until the end of his life. The aged king, surrounded by paintings of heroic deeds and books of tactical theory, was ever ready to answer the call of battle, even if that call was never to come.

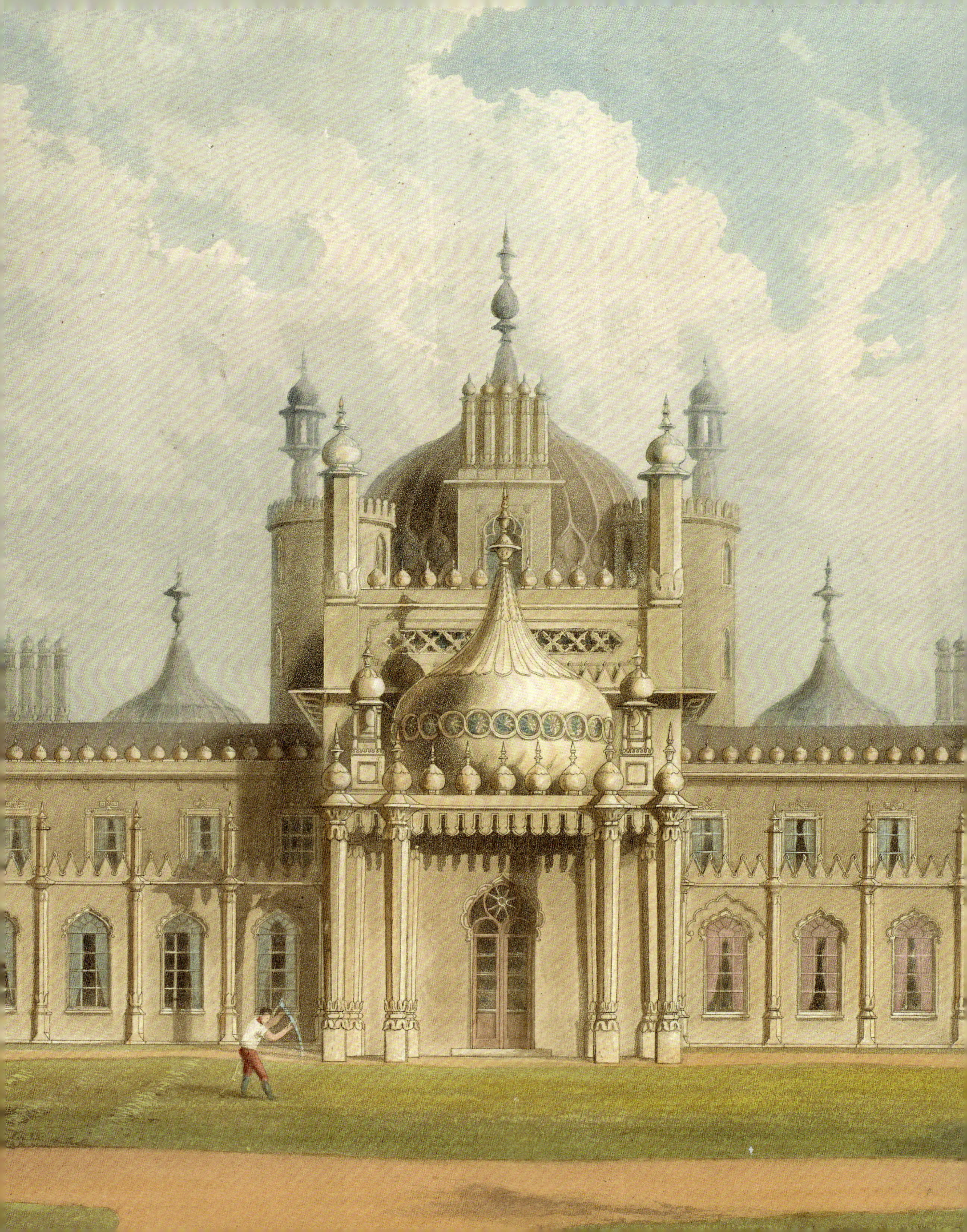

10

The ROYAL PAVILION *at* BRIGHTON

DAVID BEEVERS

George, Prince of Wales first visited Brighton in 1783, aged 21. He stayed for 11 days with his dissolute uncle Henry, Duke of Cumberland, a man whom George III regarded with particular aversion. Both his uncles, the Duke of Cumberland and William, Duke of Gloucester had discovered the town before George's first visit as Brighton offered all the leisure facilities pleasure-seeking aristocrats would expect; the first guide book, essential for a fashionable resort, appeared in 1769.

George came to Brighton to escape the restrictions imposed by his father and to see if bathing in and drinking seawater would ease his glandular swellings. He stayed with his uncle at Grove House (Fig. 10.1), built for Percy Wyndham, brother of the 3rd Earl of Egremont, *c.*1779–80. He enjoyed racing, gambling and fast living and returned to the town in 1784 and 1785. A year later, through his Clerk of the Kitchen and Brighton estate agent, Louis Weltje (see Fig. 1.3), he took a lease on a detached lodging house, with coach house and stables, known as Brighton House, situated south of Grove House and facing the area known as the Steine. In 1787 Weltje purchased the property for George. Here, together with Mrs Fitzherbert, whom he had married illegally in 1785, George lived a life of fashionable self-dramatising 'poverty', where, in view of fishermen drying their nets, he could indulge for a while in the illusion of a return to nature. The house was described by George Croly as 'a pretty and picturesque little fabric … where a few shrubs and roses shut out the road, and the eye looked unobstructed over the ocean'.[1] But, unsurprisingly, the simple life did not long appeal to George who, in 1786–7, employed Henry Holland, the architect patronised by the Whig aristocracy, to aggrandise his house (Fig. 10.2). The lodging house became the south wing of a greatly extended property with a suite of formal rooms, including the Drawing Room, later known as the Saloon, stretching to the north.

As extended and remodelled by Holland, the new residence was in an advanced French-influenced Graeco-Roman style somewhat resembling a neo-classical Parisian *hôtel particulier*. Together with Carlton House, it was one of the most advanced expressions of French neo-classicism ever to be built in Britain.

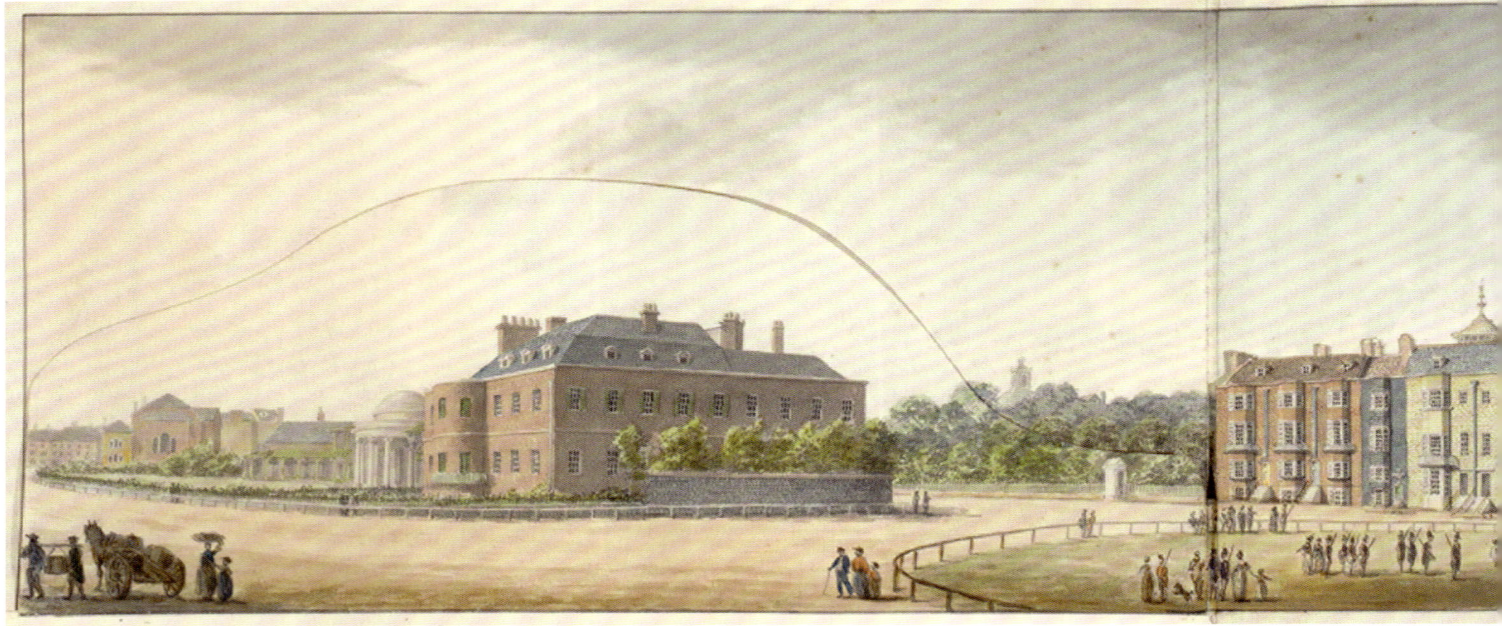

Holland had been in Paris in 1785, partly on a mission to recruit skilled craftsmen to work on Carlton House, and it is likely he saw Pierre Rousseau's Hôtel de Salm (1783) and F.-J. Bélanger's château de Bagatelle in the Bois de Boulogne (1777), where chinoiserie features in the grounds included a pagoda and Chinese bridge. Both have a marked resemblance to Holland's building at Brighton. Other French elements may derive from engravings in Jean-François de Neufforge's *Recueil élémentaire d'Architecture* (1757–68). Holland changed the angled bay windows of the original lodging house into bows and designed ground-floor windows which opened in the French manner directly on to the lawn. Immediate access to the garden was the essence of a *maison de plaisance* or pavilion, a word which accorded with the French-influenced architecture and interiors as well as suggesting a temporary structure or tent.

Little is known of the interiors of Holland's Pavilion as originally conceived. The ground floor consisted of a breakfast room and ante-room below the prince's apartment on the first floor. To the north of the Saloon were an Eating Room divided by a screen of columns and a Library. The only known depiction of a room in the first interior is a view of the Saloon published in Thomas Rowlandson and Henry Wigstead's *An excursion to Brighthelmstone made in the year 1789* (1790; Fig. 10.3). The letterpress by Wigstead remarks that 'the Grand Saloon is beautifully decorated with paintings by Rebecca executed in his best manner'. The involvement of the Italian-born Biagio Rebecca is confirmed by a payment to him of £150 in 1787.[2] Rebecca, who also worked at Carlton House, was a leading decorative artist of the late eighteenth century who specialised in *trompe-l'oeil* bas-reliefs painted in oil on paper. At Brighton he painted the ceiling and wall panels, the latter in a French-influenced neo-classical style marked by swags and cartouches. Two unexecuted designs for the Saloon in a Pompeian manner, dated 1787, may be by Jean-Jacques Boileau. They were delivered to Martin-Eloi Lignereux, a *marchand-mercier* and associate of Dominique Daguerre. The influence of France is again very marked.[3] Other rooms may have been decorated in a similar way; in 1787 payments were made to the decorator John Crace as well as to George Seddon and William Carrington for furniture, none of which is known to survive.[4] The furniture may well have been designed or influenced by Henry Holland.

In 1795 George married his cousin Caroline of Brunswick. Holland proposed additional wings to the Pavilion to accommodate Princess Caroline's household, but these were not executed. Holland was recalled in July 1801 and, clearly on George's instructions, proposed a Chinese exterior for the building (Fig. 10.4), the first hint of what was soon to happen inside. About a year later William Porden also prepared exterior elevations in the Chinese taste. Porden's drawings were exhibited at the Royal Academy in 1806 but neither his nor Holland's designs were carried out. Even George probably considered a Chinese elevation, generally associated with temporary garden structures, too frivolous for a royal building. Instead, two new wings projecting at a 60-degree angle were

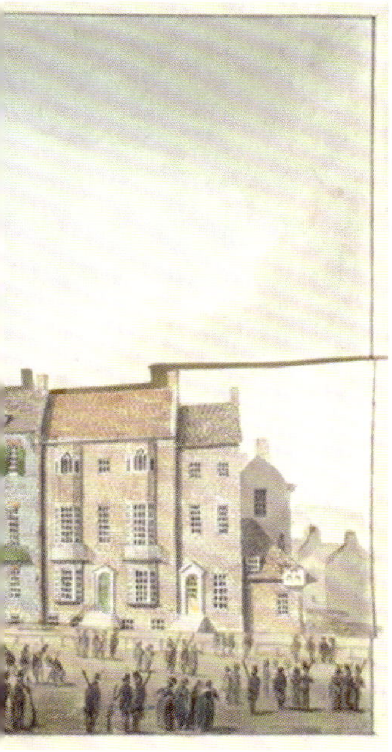

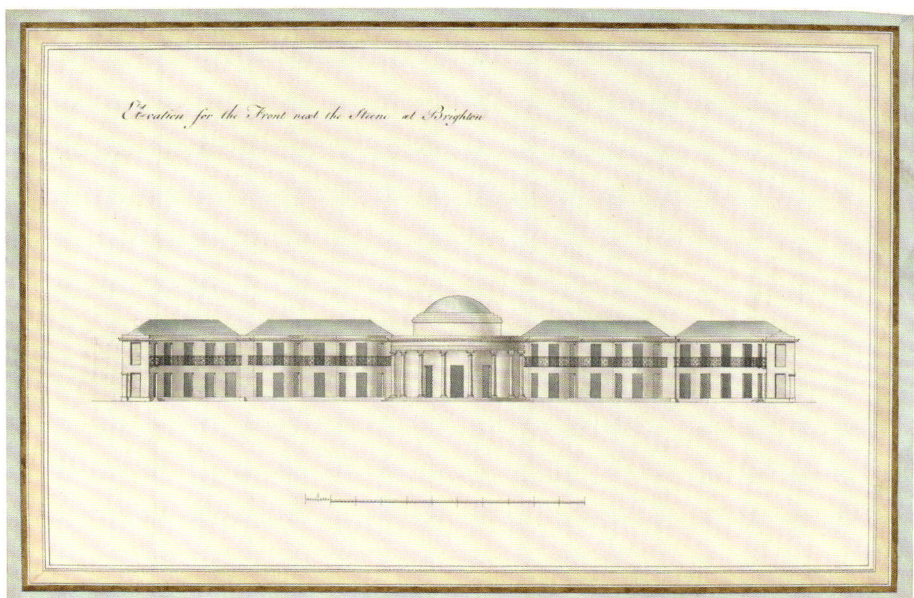

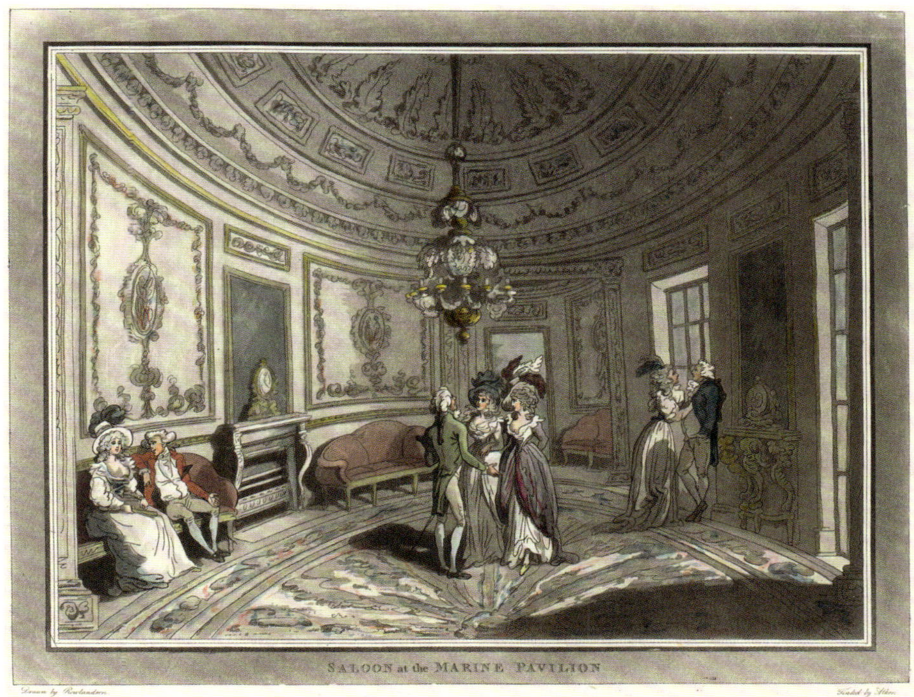

(p. 138)
Detail of Fig. 10.10, JOHN CLEGHORN (active 1827–80) AFTER AUGUSTUS CHARLES PUGIN (*c*.1768–1832), *Brighton Pavilion, Principal Entrance, West Front*, 1838

FIG. 10.1
HUMPHRY REPTON (1752–1818), *Designs for the Pavilion at Brighton: North Front towards the Parade*, 1806. Watercolour and wash over pencil, 25.2 × 77.6 cm, RCIN 918085. Image shown with flaps closed, with Grove House visible

FIG. 10.2
HENRY HOLLAND (1745–1806), *Elevation for the Front next the Steene at Brighton*, 1795. Pen and ink with watercolour and wash over pencil, 29.2 × 43.5 cm, RCIN 918956

FIG. 10.3
THOMAS ROWLANDSON (1757–1827), *Saloon at the Marine Pavilion*, from HENRY WIGSTEAD (*c*.1745–1800) and THOMAS ROWLANDSON, *An Excursion to Brighthelmstone made in the year 1789*, 1790. Etching and aquatint with hand colouring, 27.2 × 34.7 cm (plate), RCIN 1070419

added to accommodate a Conservatory and a Music Room to the south and a Dining Room to the north. It is unclear whether Holland or Peter Frederick Robinson, Holland's pupil, provided the designs. Robinson certainly supervised the work, since by 1803 Holland was no longer working in Brighton. The exterior of the Pavilion was stuccoed and lined in imitation of Bath stone and the surface was 'frescoed' in colour washes by the scene painter Louis Barzargo (variously spelt Buzarglo and Burzarglo among others), who had worked with Holland on the refurbishment of Drury Lane Theatre in the 1790s.[5] The exterior windows were provided with upcurved metal canopies painted green, a feature soon to appear on other Brighton buildings.

The first Chinese-inspired decorative interior schemes appeared in 1802–4. George had inherited from his mother a love of 'oriental' art (see chapter 11) and commissioned a Chinese Drawing Room at Carlton House in about 1788. Here at the

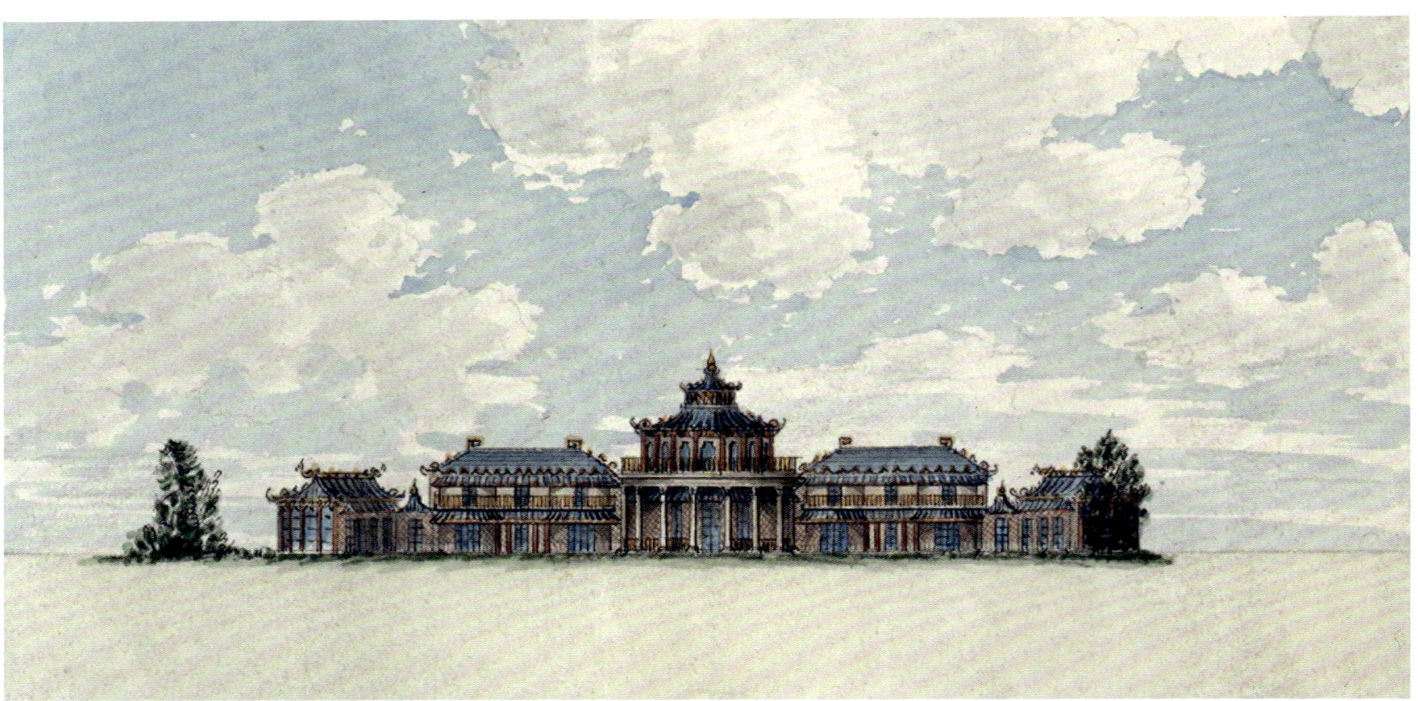

FIG. 10.4
HENRY HOLLAND (1745–1806), *Marine Pavilion, Brighton*, 1801. Pen and ink with watercolour over pencil, 17.2 × 21.4 cm (sight), RCIN 918957.d (detail)

Pavilion and uniquely in Britain, Chinese decorative schemes dominated the interior, intermingled with ideas and motifs from France and French chinoiserie. George's bedroom, for instance, was fitted up as a tent room (Fig. 10.5). Designed by Frederick Crace in about 1801, the room was influenced by French interiors of the 1790s inspired by military tents. The Eating Room had a painted sky ceiling by John or Frederick Crace, inspired by the French-influenced sky ceilings at Carlton House. The *London Chronicle* reported in 1802 that the Dining Room was to look like a Chinese tent.[6] The room was furnished by Nicholas Morel, 'who has been twice to Paris to procure patterns for the approbation of the prince'.[7] The *Advertiser* reported that Louis Barzargo, the 'frescoist' of the exterior, had repainted the dome of the Saloon having removed Rebecca's paintings. Corridors were painted 'French blue' and the Conservatory and Music Room had a roof of simulated teawood and rosewood supported on red columns with coiled dragons. Chinese export wallpaper completed the scheme. A glass passage, 12 feet (4 metres) long, linked the Conservatory and a Drawing Room. Designed probably by John Crace in about 1801–4, the corridor had painted glass walls lit from outside and looked like a Chinese lantern (Fig. 10.6).

These early interiors were a collaboration between the prince, Holland and Robinson and John and Frederick Crace, decorators who had already worked for George at Carlton House. John Crace, influenced by French decorators working at Carlton House, developed a range of illusionistic techniques which included marbling, graining and gilding along with the use of bold colour combinations. In addition, Crace had already worked with Holland on the Chinese Dairy at Woburn Abbey (1787) and quite possibly on the decorative schemes of the Chinese Drawing Room at Carlton House (1788–90). At this date the Craces also acted as agents acquiring Chinese porcelain, textiles and other works of art for the prince, the objects themselves often inspiring the interiors. Records of work by the Craces end in 1804 and do not resume until 1815 when many of the apartments became even richer after the appointment of John Nash as architect in 1814.[8] The use of Chinese motifs throughout this period may well be connected to George's fear that his Francophile tastes might be seen as unpatriotic at a time when Britain was at war with France. In 1805 Lady Bessborough recorded a conversation with the prince in which he remarked that Chinese-inspired furniture and decoration were used 'because … there was such a cry against French things … that he was afraid of his furniture being accused of Jacobinism'.[9]

Before considering Nash's extensive remodelling of the Pavilion from 1815, it is necessary to step back to 1803 when the extraordinary decision was made to provide new stables and a riding house in a style derived from Mughal India (Fig. 10.7). George chose William Porden as architect; his Chinese-inspired designs for the Pavilion date from about the same time. India and China were clearly confused in the prince's imagination, both

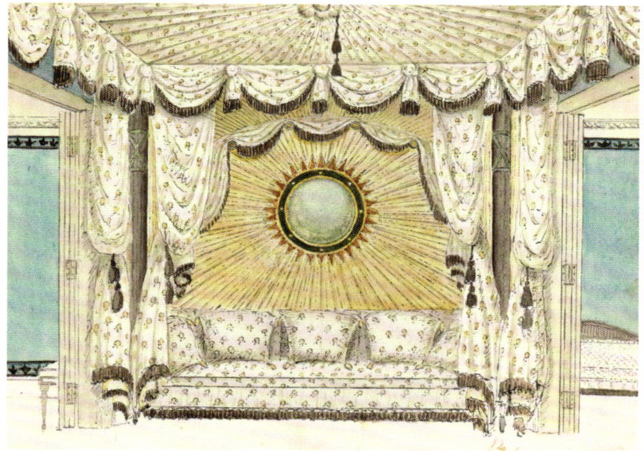

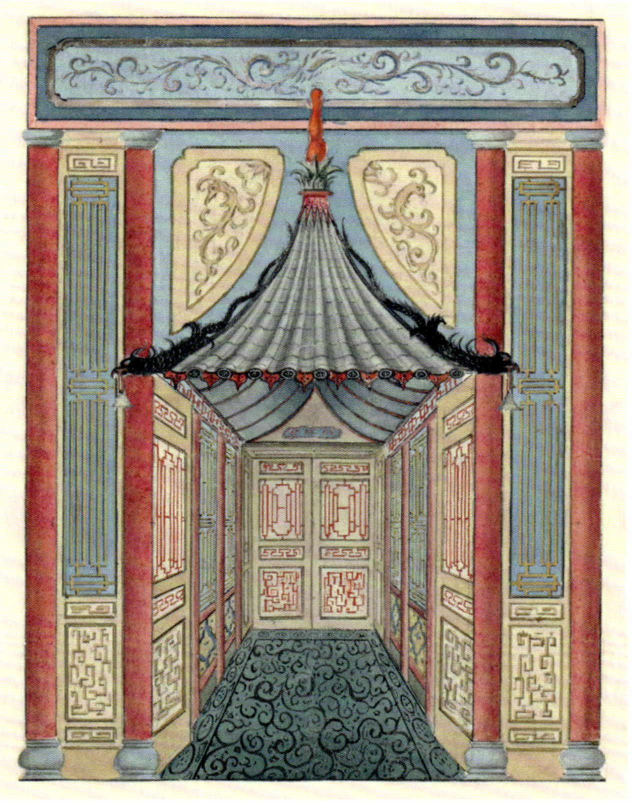

(above)
FIG. 10.5
FREDERICK CRACE (1779–1859), *Design for an alcove with a tented ceiling, probably for the Prince of Wales's Bedchamber, Royal Pavilion, Brighton*, *c.*1801–4. Pen and black ink, brush and watercolour, 20.3 × 27.9 cm (Cooper Hewitt, Smithsonian Design Museum, New York, NY: 1948-40-26)

(middle)
FIG. 10.6
JOHN CRACE (1754–1819), *Design probably for the Glass Passage, Royal Pavilion, Brighton*, *c.*1801–4. Pen and black and yellow-green ink, brush and watercolour, 23.3 × 17.0 cm (Cooper Hewitt, Smithsonian Design Museum, New York, NY: 1948-40-65)

(below)
FIG. 10.7
JOHN CLEGHORN (active 1827–80) AFTER AUGUSTUS CHARLES PUGIN (*c.*1768–1832), *Brighton Pavilion, Stables*, 1838. Etching with aquatint and hand colouring, 10.8 × 17.8 cm, RCIN 708000.bd

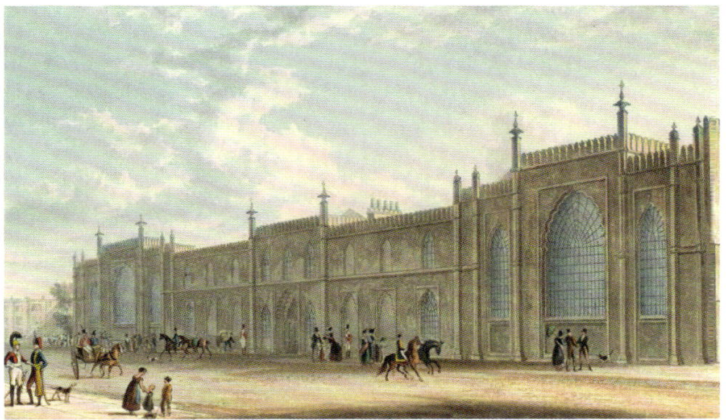

equally remote and exotic. Holland's Chinese Pavilion, as we have seen, was not carried out, but Porden's stables and riding house were built between 1803 and 1808, the first buildings of any size in Britain (and in Europe) to use Indian motifs with some consistency. Sezincote, in Gloucestershire, was built around 1805 in an Indian style to the designs of Samuel Pepys Cockerell, in whose office Porden had worked, but the stables at Brighton came first. Motifs were freely borrowed from Thomas and William Daniell's *Oriental Scenery* (1795–1808), and the Indian style was clearly the choice of the prince, whose desire for a smart originality may be connected with Britain's burgeoning imperial mission in India following the capture of Delhi by the British from the Mughal emperor in 1803.

The use of Indian, specifically Mughal, motifs on the stables and riding house was to dictate the future style of the Pavilion. From the start, the stables were regarded as one of the wonders of Europe: a palace for horses. They were to be flanked by a riding house built on a magnificent scale and an east wing intended as an indoor tennis court. The latter was not built. It was observed in 1809: 'Surely never were horses so splendidly lodged since the days of Caligula; indeed, the stables have eclipsed the glory of the Pavilion.'[10] The mass of the stables, towering rather threateningly above the Pavilion, was clearly intolerable. According to Sir John Summerson, it needed to be whipped into submission.[11] In 1805, before the stables were finished, the landscape gardener Humphry Repton was summoned to Brighton and was asked by George to provide, with the aid of his architect son John Adey Repton, an Indian elevation to the Pavilion which would trump the stables (Fig. 10.8). Repton had some experience of the style, having advised how Indian motifs might be used at Sezincote. In 1806 Repton delivered to the prince designs not only for the Pavilion but also for the grounds, which were to be turned into a Mughal-inspired paradise garden.

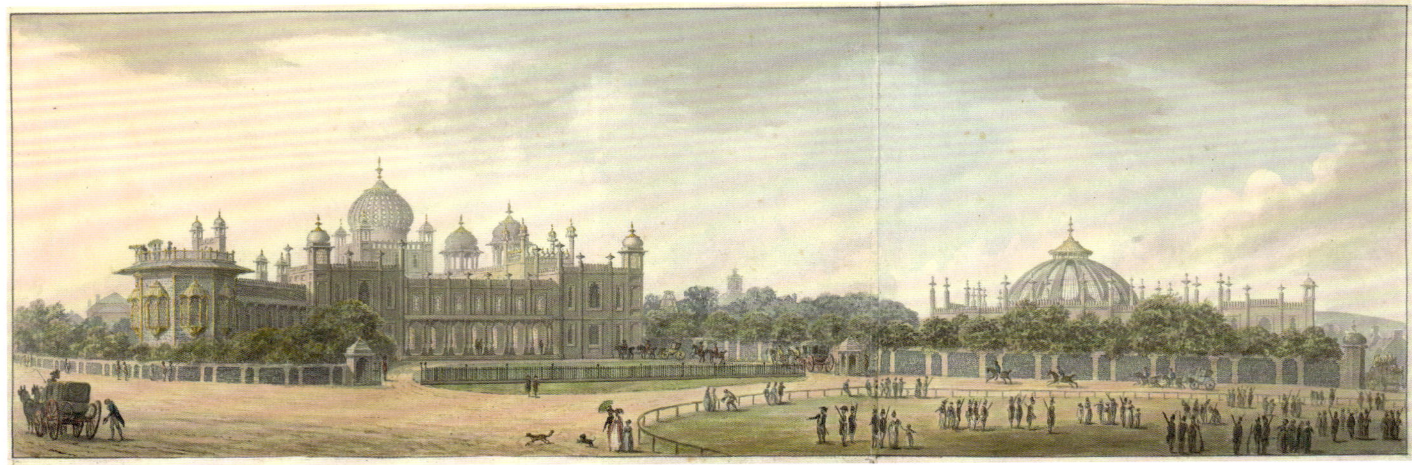

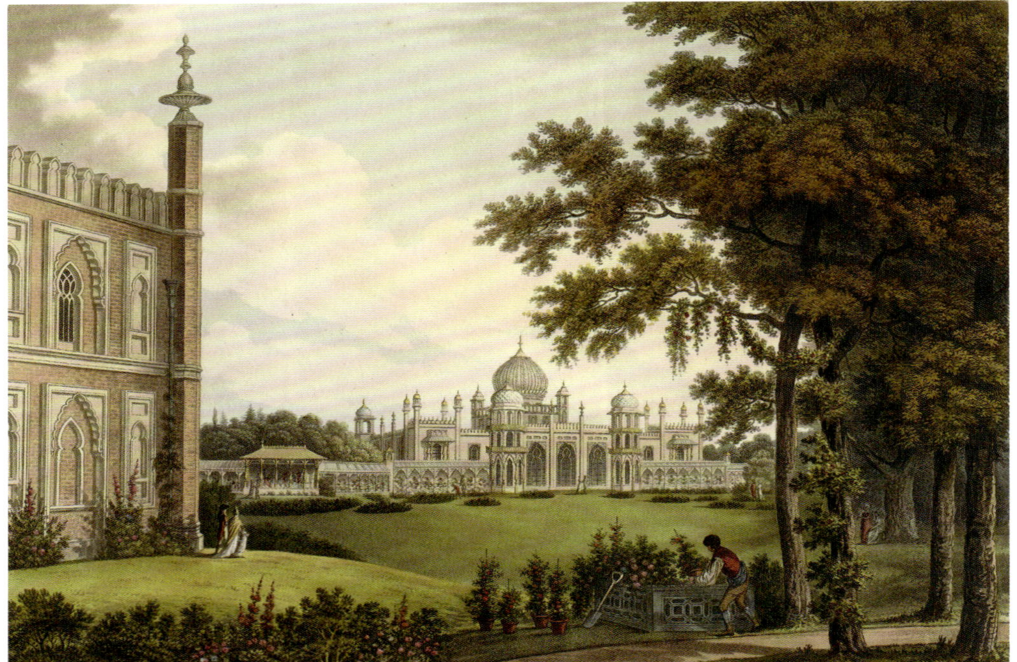

FIG. 10.8
HUMPHRY REPTON (1752–1818), *Designs for the Pavilion at Brighton: North Front towards the Parade*, 1806. Wash and watercolour over pencil, 25.2 × 77.6 cm, RCIN 918085. Image shown with flaps open

FIG. 10.9
HUMPHRY REPTON (1752–1818), *Designs for the Pavillon at Brighton*, 1808. Printed book, 54.0 × 37.4 cm, RCIN 1150259

FIG. 10.10
JOHN CLEGHORN (active 1827–80) AFTER AUGUSTUS CHARLES PUGIN (*c.*1768–1832), *Brighton Pavilion, Principal Entrance, West Front*, 1838. Etching with aquatint and hand colouring, 23.1 × 33.6 cm, RCIN 708000.n

Details for both were again taken from the Daniells' *Oriental Scenery*. Alas, this magnificent dream of India was not realised. The stables were absorbing too much money and Repton, in his autobiography, recorded that after showing his magnificent drawings to the prince, presented in the form of one of his famous Red Books, Mrs Fitzherbert's only response was 'And pray, what is this to cost?'[12] In 1808 Repton, immensely proud of being consulted by royalty, published the Red Book for Brighton as *Designs for the Pavillon at Brighton* (Fig. 10.9). It was the only Red Book to be published. But by then George's enthusiasm had waned, and to Repton's bitter disappointment, the whole project was abandoned.

Thus things stood until 1814 when John Nash, with whom Repton had been in partnership, was called in to advise on the Pavilion. As with Repton, Nash's brief was to remodel the building in such a way that the stables were no longer the dominant element of the estate. The prince was again determined on an Indian style, in conformity with the style of the stables and because Indian architecture evoked ideas of a pleasure palace. Work started in 1815 and was more or less complete by 1823. Classical in its main lines, the Pavilion took the form of an Indian palace conceived as a huge spreading tent (Fig. 10.10). Two large state rooms, the Music Room and Banqueting Room, replaced Holland's angled wings, the external forms characterised by

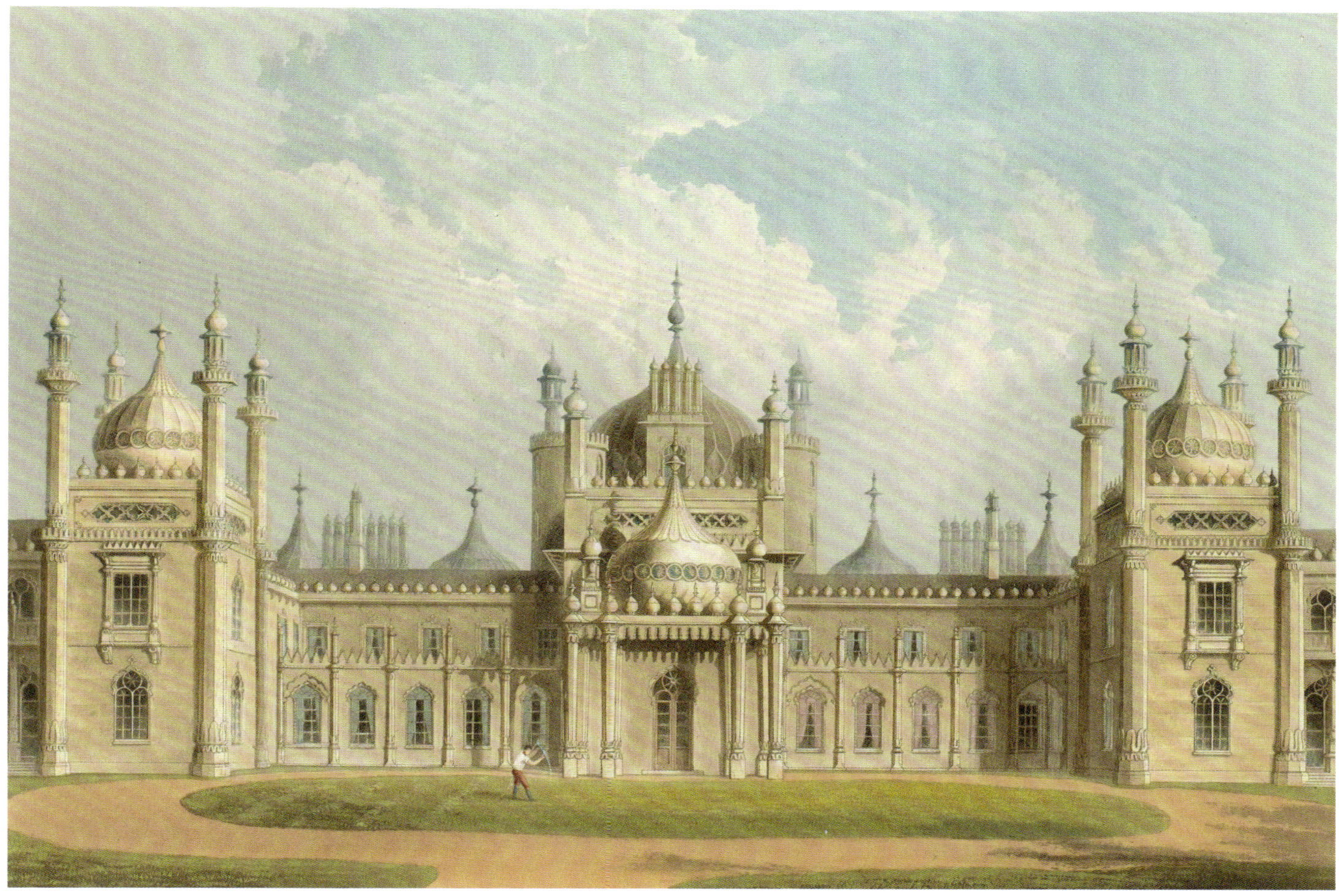

vast upswept Chinese-inspired roofs suggesting military tents. Nash's picturesque architecture is wildly eclectic: Indian motifs were culled not only from the Daniells' *Oriental Scenery* but also from Repton's *Designs for the Pavilion at Brighton*. Indian and Chinese designs are combined with purely decorative Gothic buttresses to form Nash's own fantastic version of the East, supported on a superstructure where cast iron is used on an unprecedented scale, both structurally and decoratively. Repton presciently considered that cast iron was 'peculiarly adapted to some light parts of the Indian style'.[13]

It is worth recalling that when the remodelling of the Pavilion started in 1815 Nash was 63 and George was 53. Neither was young, yet between them they created one of the greatest expressions of what in German is called a *lustschloss* and in French a *maison de plaisance*. The seaside location seemed to license a freedom from architectural restraint yet the Pavilion was also stately, suitable for the *de facto* monarch of a country that, following the defeat of Napoleon in 1815, was the richest and most powerful on Earth. The building is also an expression, like the stables, of Britain's burgeoning imperial project in India. Following the loss of the American colonies, Britain looked to Asia and with the Prince Regent often likened to the Emperor of India, an eastern-style palace by the sea of which Britons regarded themselves master was a striking expression of empire. Such symbolism was not lost on contemporaries, but in the European imagination India and the East also stood for luxury and pomp so that Nash's lush fantasy became, not least for the caricaturists, an expression of George's remoteness and extravagance (Fig. 10.11). What is clear is that the use of Indian architectural forms on the Pavilion estate over a period of 20 years suggests the close identification of the prince with India, not only symbolically but also as a source of new and unusual motifs that would astonish his friends.

In the interior, Nash created a sequence of rooms calculated to surprise and provide dramatic contrasts, becoming progressively more opulent and culminating in the extraordinary Music Room and Banqueting Room, where the land of Cathay is evoked in decorative schemes of imperial magnificence. Although the

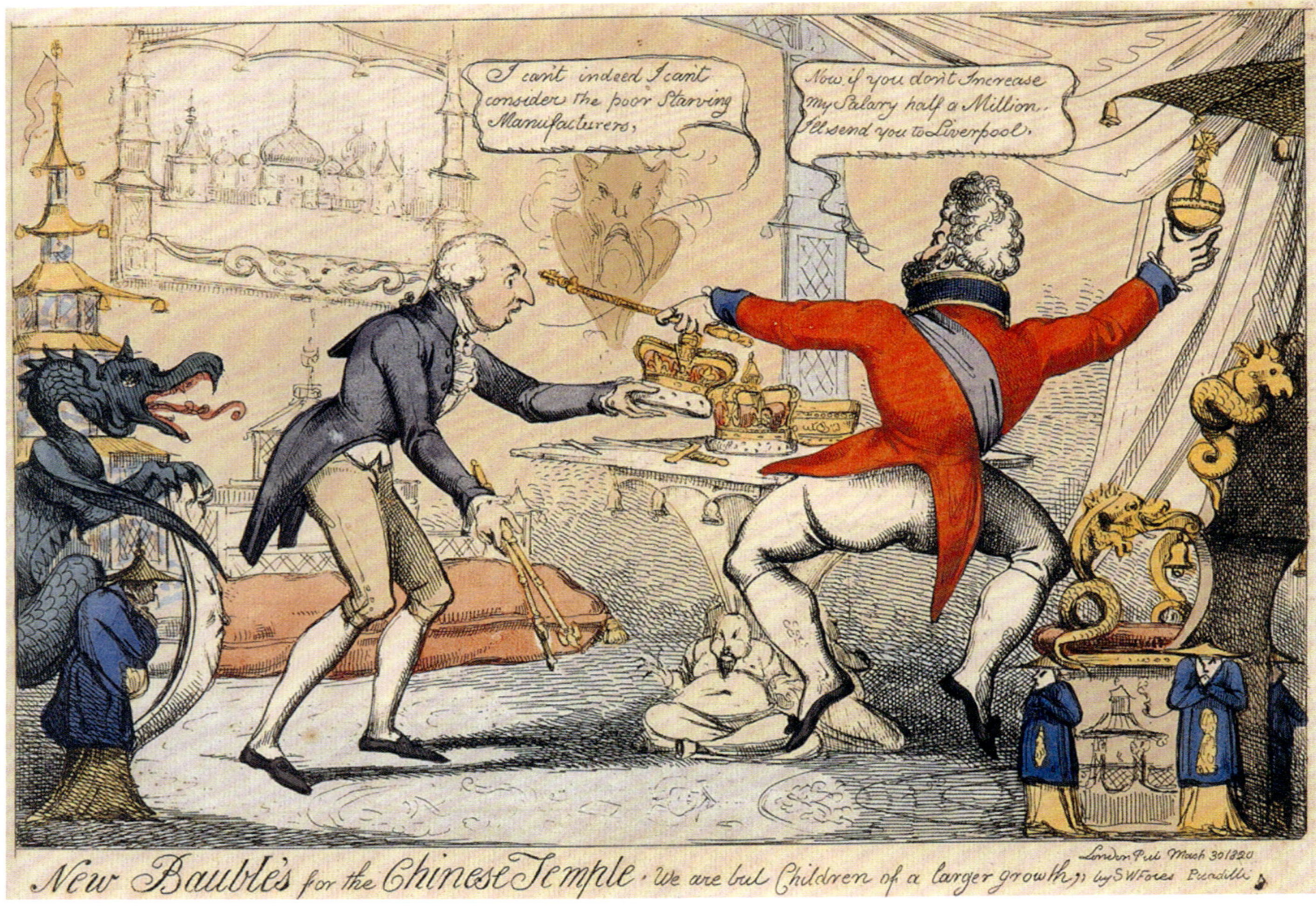

FIG. 10.11
PUBLISHED BY S.W. FORES (1761–1838), *New Baubles for the Chinese Temple*, 1820. Etching with hand colouring, 24.0 × 34.6 cm (sheet) (The Royal Pavilion and Museums, Brighton and Hove: FA 200652)

interiors are eclectic, Chinese themes continue to prevail. John and Frederick Crace, together with Robert Jones, subcontracted to the Craces but also working in several rooms on his own account, created for George a dream world of fantasy and imagination. Every detail of the decorative schemes created was supervised by the prince and changed, as often as necessary, until he was satisfied, for it is evident that George had an exceptionally fine sense of colour and design.

The connotations of China were contradictory: frivolity and a freedom from the rules of classicism on the one hand, but luxury and the trappings of rank on the other. Above all, the Pavilion represents a major departure in the history of chinoiserie, for the style was applied in various forms to the whole building, not just to a bedroom or drawing room. It was also very different from whimsical eighteenth-century rococo chinoiserie as the Craces used authentic Chinese sources such as costume, ceramics and Chinese export paintings as well as the drawings of William Alexander, an artist on Lord Macartney's embassy to China in 1793 and one of the few Englishmen to have been allowed beyond the confines of Canton (Guangzhou). The *ne plus ultra* of George's almost single-handed revival of chinoiserie was the Banqueting Room and Music Room. Although the architectural framework of the Banqueting Room was Nash's responsibility, the decorative scheme is by Robert Jones (Fig. 10.12). The room's shape is Classical – a domed square space with lateral extensions – but the overlay of decoration and the curved ceilings sweeping down from the cornice, resembling a sagging tent, create a room where classicism is far from the dominant impression. The room, particularly the ceiling, represents Nash's first exercise in the creation of the type of palatial interior that was to reappear at Buckingham Palace in the 1820s.

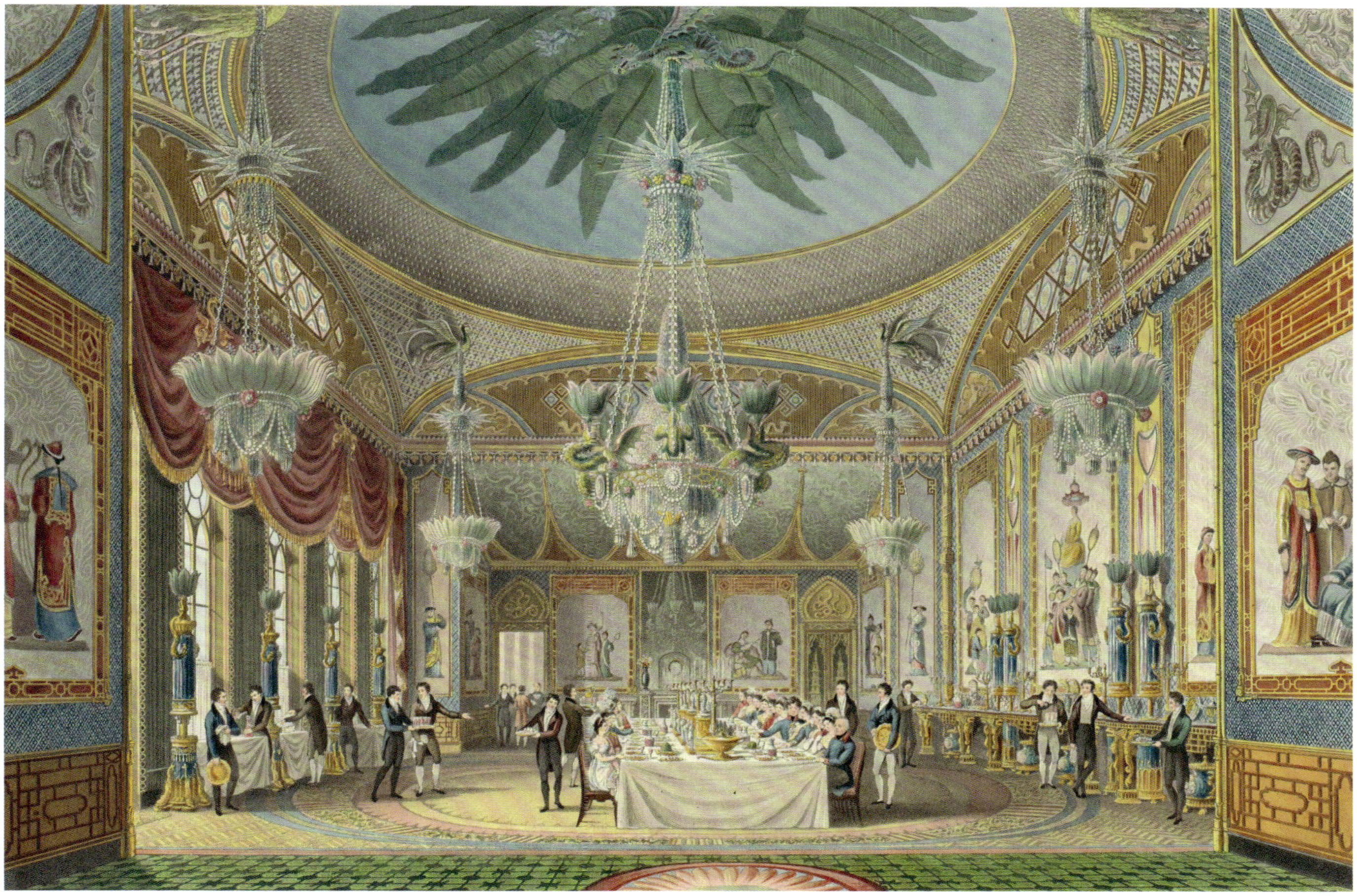

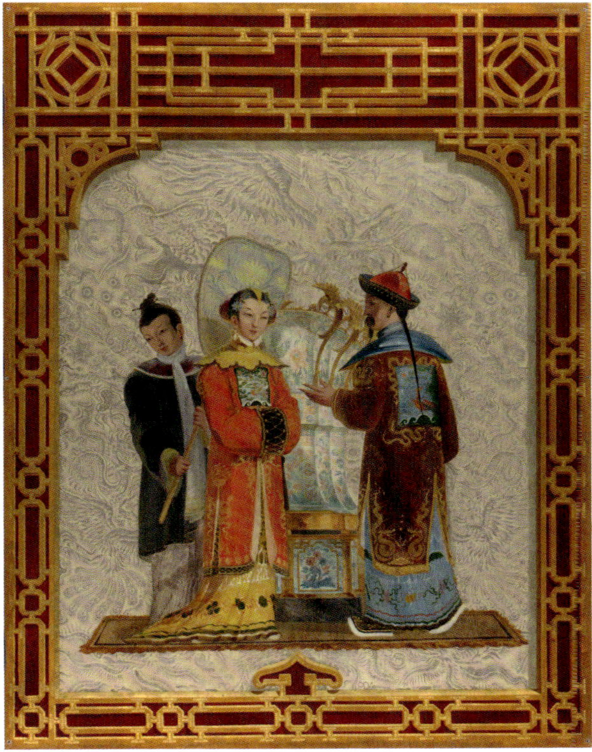

FIG. 10.12
JOHN LE KEUX (1783–1846) AFTER AUGUSTUS CHARLES PUGIN (*c*.1768–1832), *Brighton Pavilion, Banqueting Room*, 1838. Etching with aquatint and hand colouring, 26.2 × 38.7 cm, RCIN 708000.aq

FIG. 10.13
ROBERT JONES (active 1815–33), *Wall panel from the Banqueting Room, Brighton Pavilion*, *c*.1818–20. Oil on canvas, 297.0 × 228.0 cm, RCIN 11103

The basic structure of the Banqueting Room had taken shape by about 1817 but its decoration was not completed until January 1821. The *Sussex Weekly Advertiser* blamed Nash for the delays, referring in November 1820 to the 'unpardonable negligence of the head and chief of the works' and going on to say that 'scarcely an apartment throughout the whole is in a condition for even temporary accommodation'.[14] As late as December 1820 the same journal commented: 'Mr. Nash has taken especial care that there shall not be a room in the Palace fit for his Majesty's reception'.[15] What seems clear is that the famous dinner prepared by Marie-Antoine Carême on 15 January 1817 in honour of Grand Duke Nicholas of Russia, later Emperor Nicholas I, cannot have taken place in the Banqueting Room as the room still resembled a building site. It must instead have

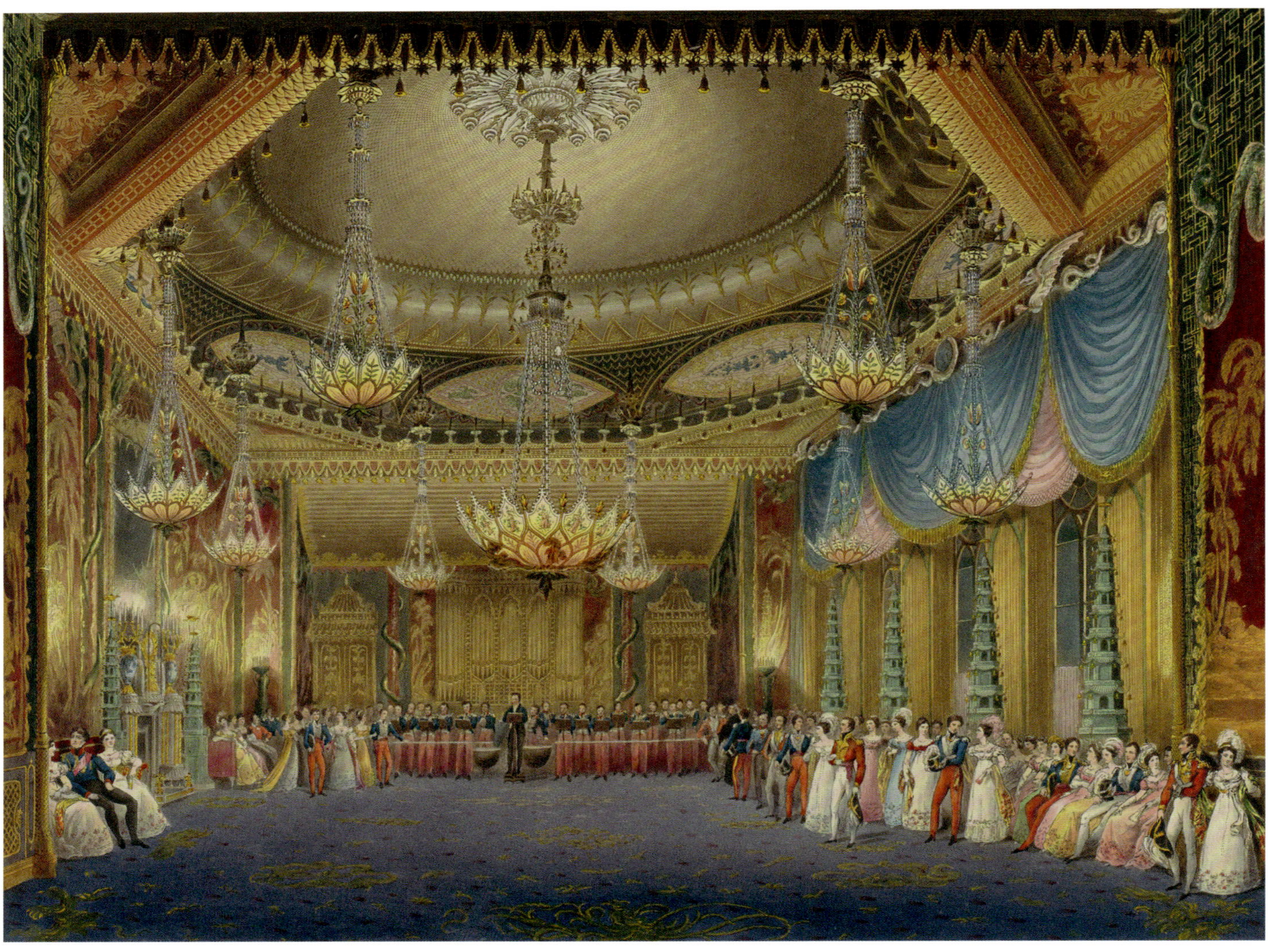

been served at Grove House (by this date known as Marlborough House), which was not finally demolished until March 1819. But after completion, the Banqueting Room was a source of wonder. Here Robert Jones excelled himself, designing the Axminster carpet, the magnificent chandelier made by William Perry & Co., the furnishings and the wall paintings of scenes from Chinese life (Fig. 10.13). The *Sussex Weekly Advertiser* commented in January 1821: 'the sensation of delight and astonishment is increased to one of inexpressible wonder and amazement … the whole appears as the work of enchantment'.[16]

No less magnificent was the Music Room, decorated by Frederick Crace (Fig. 10.14). Nash's architectural framework was in place by 1817 when the essayist John Wilson Croker reported that Nash had avoided an echo 'by some new theory of sound, which he endeavoured to explain, and which I did not understand nor I believe he neither'.[17] The decorative work, however, was completed only in 1820. The Music Room as designed by Crace sits easily within the tradition of Holland's French-inspired Chinese Drawing Room at Carlton House.[18] It is a reminder of the profound influence George's London residence had on the Pavilion; indeed, George moved many of the furnishings from Carlton House to the Pavilion both before and after the former building's demolition in 1827.

Prominent among the decorations in the Music Room are the wall paintings of Chinese landscapes painted by Henry Lambelet and assistants working under Frederick Crace. Here Crace used motifs from William Alexander's *The Costume of China* (Fig. 10.15) painted in gold on a crimson background, the whole resembling the inside of a vast 'oriental' lacquer box. From the ceiling hangs a magnificent chandelier by Perry & Co., probably designed by Frederick Crace, painted with scenes of Chinese figures, some derived from engravings after Alexander. The

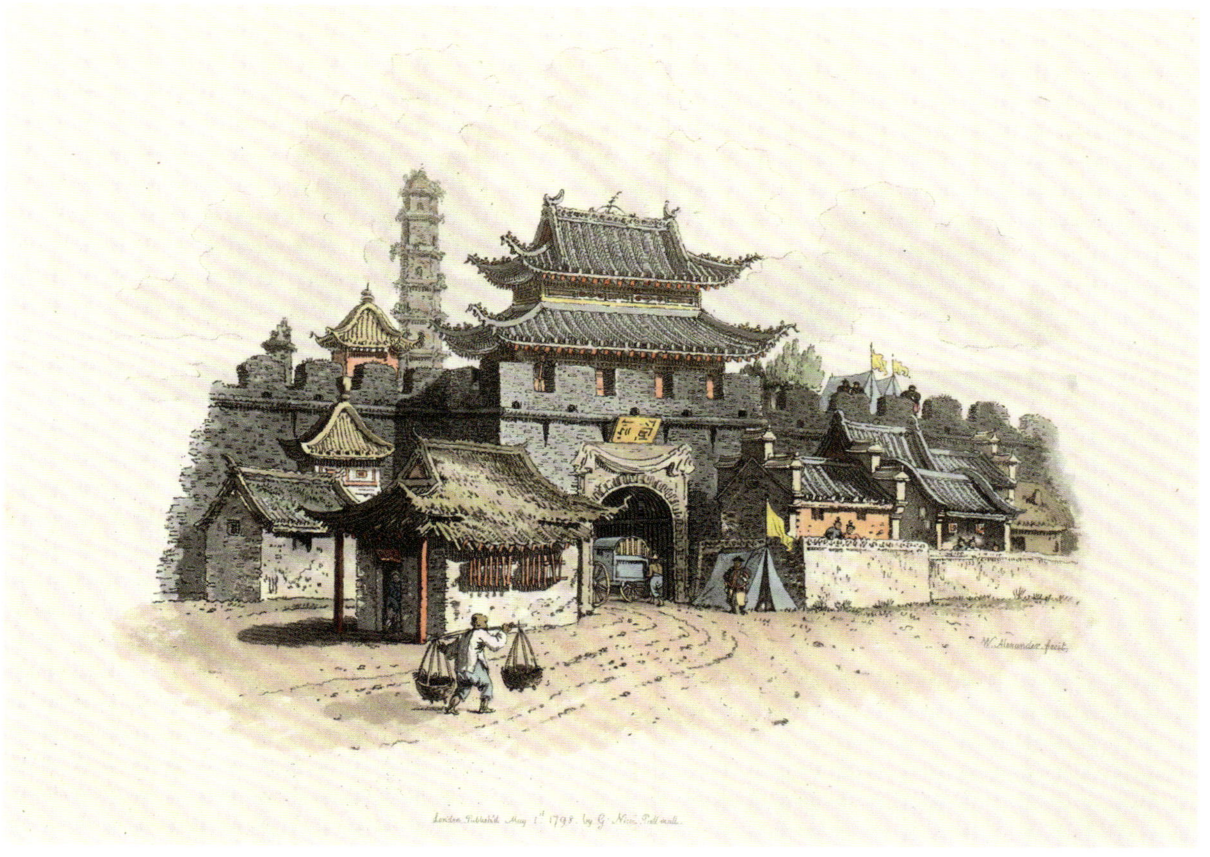

FIG. 10.14
JOHN SAMUEL AGAR (1773–1858) AFTER JAMES STEPHANOFF (1789–1874), *Brighton Pavilion, Music Room*, 1824. Etching with hand colouring, 26.6 × 34.8 cm, RCIN 708000.ai

FIG. 10.15
WILLIAM ALEXANDER (1767–1816). *The South Gate of the City of Ting-Hai*, from *The Costume of China*, 1805. Printed book, 34.0 × 27.0 cm, RCIN 1075234

chandelier, in the form of a water-lily, is flanked by smaller versions of similar shape. Chandeliers form a notable feature of interiors associated with George and must have had great importance for him. Those in the Music Room cost more than £4,000, a vast sum. A particular feature of the room is the interplay between three and two dimensions: dragons painted on the walls are matched by carved wooden dragons supplied by Tatham, Bailey & Sanders, as 'Ornament to Draperies & Curtains'.[19] Similarly, the set of Chinese export porcelain pagodas positioned in the window piers and either side of the chimneypiece are echoed by painted pagodas on the walls. This kind of visual trickery can be seen throughout the Pavilion.

The size and splendour of the organ (Fig. 10.16) on the north wall of the Music Room was frequently mentioned by visitors. It was one of the largest made for domestic use, with a delicacy of tone combined with great power.[20] Built in 1818 by Henry Cephas Lincoln, one of the leading makers of his day, who was paid more than £3,000,[21] it was described in the 1828 Royal Pavilion inventory as 'a very superb organ by Lincoln with 28 stops, 3 rows of keys, and row of pedals and lyre (shaped) desk'.[22] The organ case was designed by Frederick Crace and made by Tatham, Bailey & Sanders. It had doors with panels probably from a Coromandel lacquer screen: the Bailey & Sanders accounts record 'lining the front of the organ … with India screens and fixing carved and gilt ornaments'.[23] The organ was removed in 1847 and rebuilt in the 1850s at Buckingham Palace, where it remains.

Contemporary commentators saw the Pavilion in its final form, with its three great state rooms, as a palace worthy of Britain's status in the world. The *Sussex Weekly Advertiser* reported that the style of decoration in the Music and Banqueting Rooms 'will present to the eye a lasting exhibition

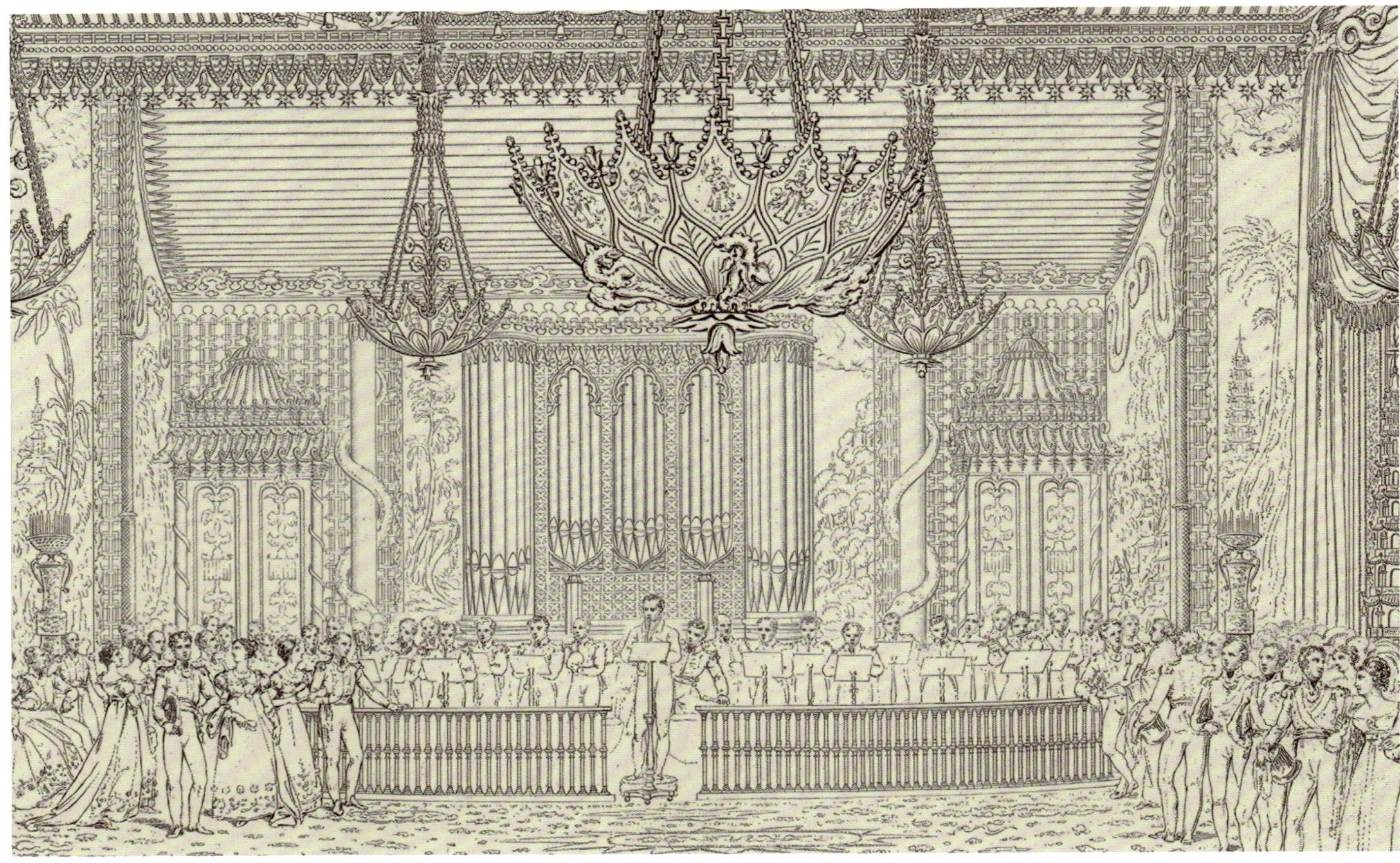

FIG. 10.16
JOHN SAMUEL AGAR (1773–1858) AFTER JAMES STEPHANOFF (1789–1874), *Brighton Pavilion, Music Room*, 1824. Etching, 33.4 × 38.7 cm (plate), RCIN 708000.ah (detail)

of the superiority of the arts and manufacturers of the day, and confirm His Royal Highness the Prince Regent as one of the first patrons for the encouragement of the arts, sciences and commerce of this nation'.[24]

It is appropriate that two of the most lavish rooms in the Pavilion were devoted to the delights of music and eating, pleasures that remained with George until the end. One of the earliest concerts in the Music Room was performed by the Prince Regent's private band of wind and percussion players in January 1818, when arrangements of works by Mozart, Handel and Beethoven were performed.[25] Formed by the prince in 1794, this group comprised musicians of many nationalities, including Germans and even French prisoners of war taken from prison camps and ships by the Hanover-born Christian Kramer, band leader from 1813. Numbers of musicians in the band, which was quite separate from the official state band, ranged from 32 to a maximum of 46; indeed, since George IV's death no monarch has maintained at his or her own expense a private band on such a scale.[26] Kramer arranged selections from Italian operas as well as works by Handel, Haydn, Mozart, Cherubini, Beethoven and Meyerbeer. As many as 300 parts would be given out for one evening's performance. The band performed, mainly at Brighton where it was largely based, every evening when George was in residence, its primary function being the provision of background music for dinner and social events.[27]

George himself was an accomplished musician. He took cello lessons from John Crosdill, the foremost British cellist of his day, and as a child he studied keyboard with Johann Christian Bach, son of Johann Sebastian, who was appointed music master to Queen Charlotte soon after 1762. The *Quarterly Musical Magazine* commented that the prince 'is really a judge of every description of Composition, from the comic opera to the grandest writing of Handel's inspired oratorios'.[28] George also enjoyed the company of musicians: he invited the great clarinettist Heinrich Baermann to play in Brighton in 1819, although his offer to Baermann of the position of joint leader of the band was rejected. In December 1823 Gioachino Rossini made a three-day visit to

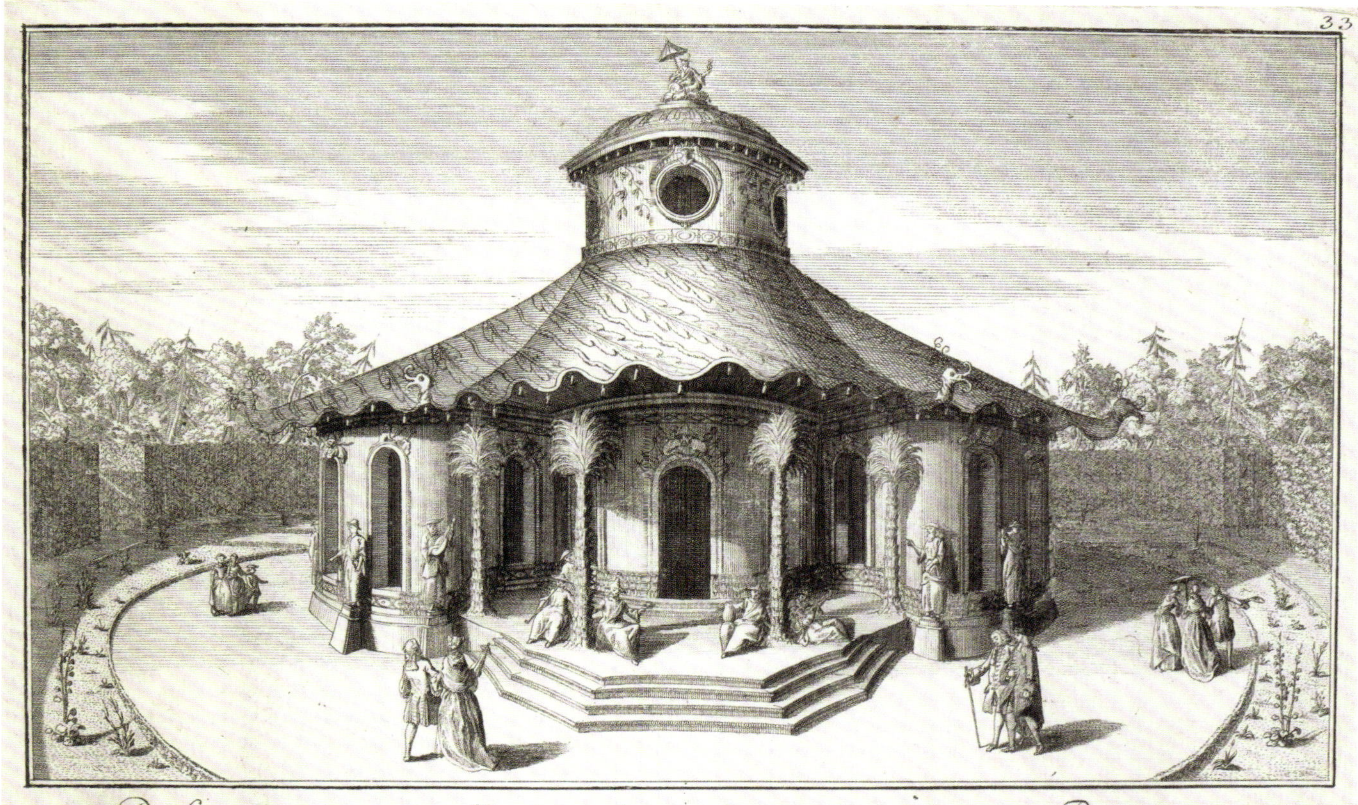

FIG. 10.17
JOHANN FRIEDRICH SCHLEUEN (1739–84), *Prospect des Japanischen Hauses im Königl. Garten sans Soucy bis Potsdam*, *c.*1756. Etching, 22.1 × 33.4 cm, RCIN 704633.c

Brighton. The *Morning Herald* reported a musical performance on 31 December: 'nothing can exceed the free and easy manner in which the notable composer demeans himself in the presence of royalty … (he) twirled his round hat on his finger before the King with all imaginable self-complacency.'[29] In his honour the band performed arrangements by Kramer of Rossini's music; the composer himself, sitting at the pianoforte, sang the 'Largo al factotum' from *The Barber of Seville* and the romance from *Otello*. Rossini was delighted by Kramer's arrangement of his music for wind band and the visit was a great success.[30]

The 37 years between the leasing of Brighton House and the completion of the Royal Pavilion show the development in George IV's taste from a brief flirtation with fashionable simplicity, through French-inspired neo-classicism, to its culmination in this picturesque building, with its Indian-style exterior and chinoiserie interior, that flouted conventional rules. Each phase of the building's development can be related to George's changing status as Prince of Wales, Prince Regent and King, his desire to establish himself as a major player on the world stage and to perform this role against an amazing background. But the Pavilion is not an architectural freak. It springs from two sources: the fashion for exotic buildings in gardens, of which the most famous is William Chambers's Pagoda at Kew, and the taste for 'oriental' pleasure palaces among European royalty.[31] The Pavilion can be seen as the last and most developed of those *maisons de plaisance* commissioned by the royal families of Europe. It is in the same tradition as Augustus the Strong's Chinese-style Wasserpalais on the banks of the Elbe at Pillnitz (*c.*1721); Frederick the Great's Chinese tea-house (1757) and Dragon House (1764) at Potsdam (Fig. 10.17); King Adolph Frederick of Sweden's Chinese House at Drottningholm (1769); Catherine the Great of Russia's Chinese village at Tsarskoe Selo (1770s); and La Palazzina Cinese in Palermo, Sicily, remodelled in a Chinese style for King Ferdinand IV and Queen Maria Carolina of Naples in 1798–1800. Seen within this tradition, George's Brighton Pavilion embodies his desire for a world of extravagant 'oriental' fantasy in an informal, seaside setting that allowed him to explore the possibilities of exoticism to the full.

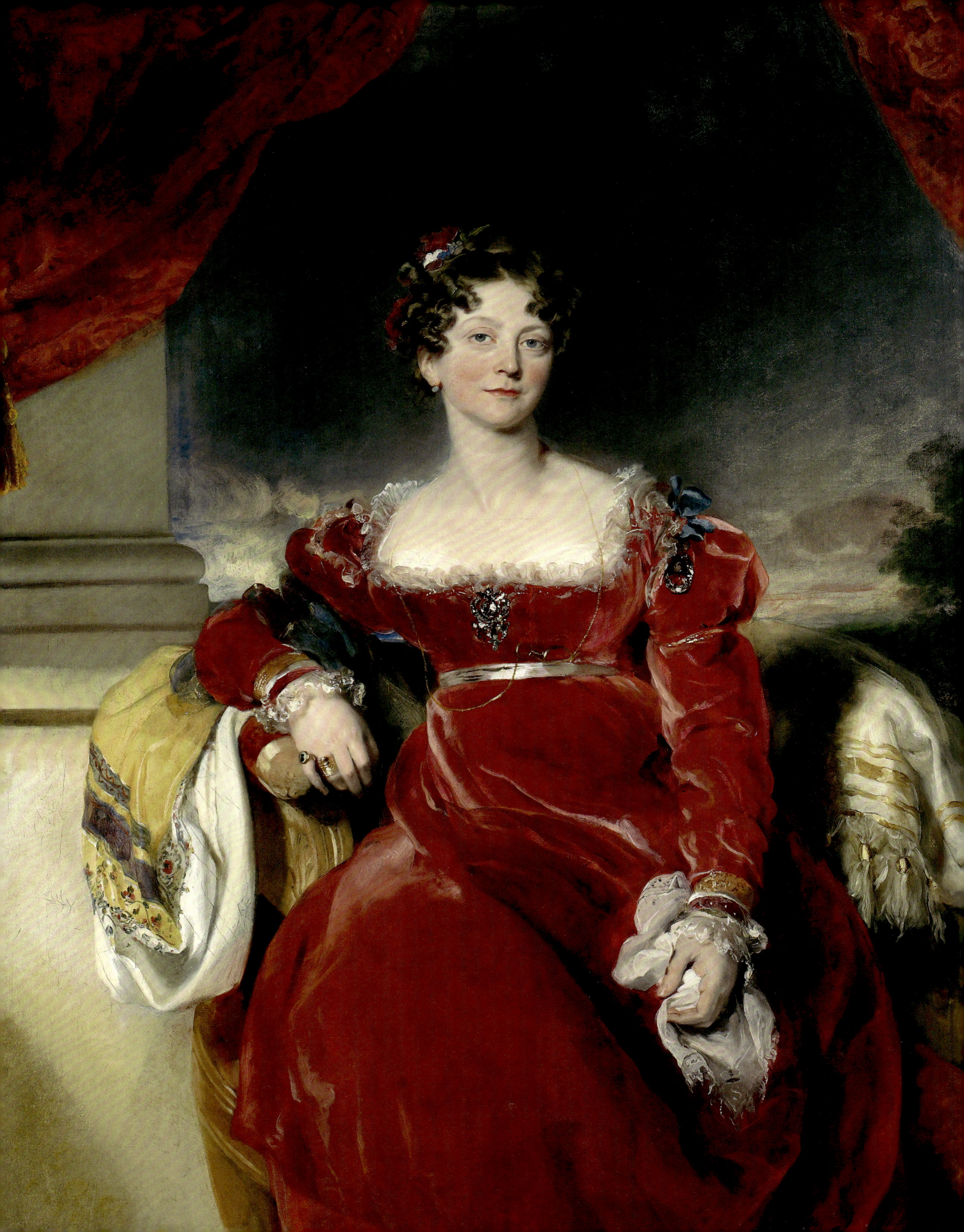

11

The FEMALE INFLUENCE *on* GEORGE IV'S TASTE *and* COLLECTING HABITS

ALEXANDRA LOSKE

As a collector and patron of the arts, George IV is often compared to his father (Fig. 11.3) and grandfather, or to his more distant forebear Charles I. While these male influences are important and indisputable, his mother (Fig. 11.2), grandmother and sisters also had a formative influence on the young prince's developing tastes. An exploration of the roles of Caroline of Ansbach (George's great-grandmother), Augusta of Saxe-Gotha and Charlotte of Mecklenburg-Strelitz at the British court has highlighted their significance as promoters of Enlightenment ideas in general and art patronage in particular, and suggested that their styles 'could be characterised respectively as philosophical, exotic, and whimsical'.[1] Both the latter characterisations can confidently be applied to George IV's architectural endeavours. In addition, all these women were important collectors in their own right and their interests can be seen to have encouraged George's own acquisitions in a number of areas. George's mother Queen Charlotte, for example, was a keen collector of Sèvres porcelain (of which George would form an important group) and Hogarth prints (which again, George collected comprehensively). Perhaps most importantly, mother and son shared an interest in the exotic, nowhere more evident than in George's embracing of the chinoiserie style in architecture and interior decoration. It has been noted that in this period 'chinoiserie and oriental artefacts were closely connected with notions of femininity and female patronage'.[2] It is therefore worth taking a closer look at how George's female relatives' interest in the style may have shaped his own explorations of the theme of exoticism.

Buildings that may have sparked George's interest in 'oriental' architecture include those in the so-called 'Wilderness' at Kew Gardens where, in 1757, George's grandmother Augusta commissioned the architect William Chambers to create several exotic structures (Fig. 11.4). Among other buildings, the infant prince would have seen an Alhambra, a mosque and the striking Great Pagoda, finished in 1762. Suspended from its roofs were 80 dragons, 'covered with a kind of thin coloured glass of various colours, which produced a most dazzling reflection'.[3] It is possible that these dragons were among the inspirations

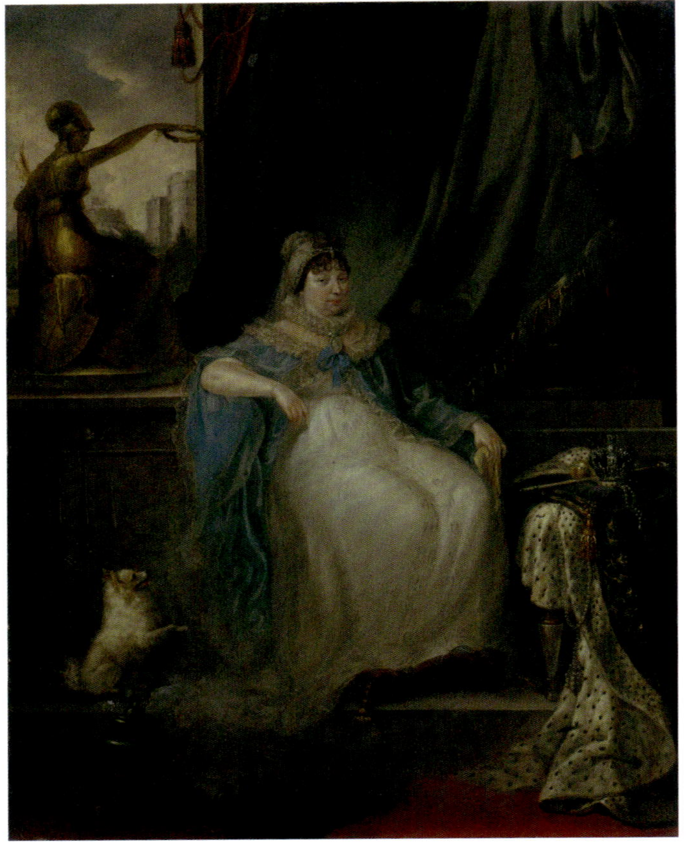

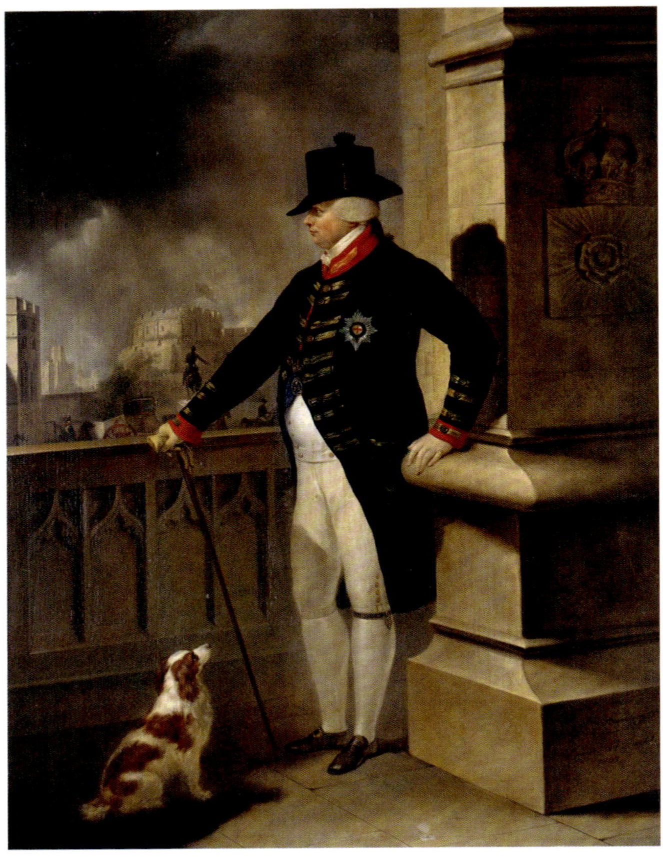

(p. 152)
FIG. 11.1
SIR THOMAS LAWRENCE (1769–1830), *Princess Sophia (1777–1848)*, *c.*1824. Oil on canvas, 141.2 × 111.9 cm, RCIN 403420

FIG. 11.2
PETER EDWARD STROEHLING (1768–*c.*1826), *Queen Charlotte (1744–1818)*, 1807. Oil on copper, 59.7 × 47.5 cm, RCIN 404863

FIG. 11.3
PETER EDWARD STROEHLING (1768–*c.*1826), *George III (1738–1820)*, 1807. Oil on copper, 60.7 × 48.2 cm, RCIN 404865

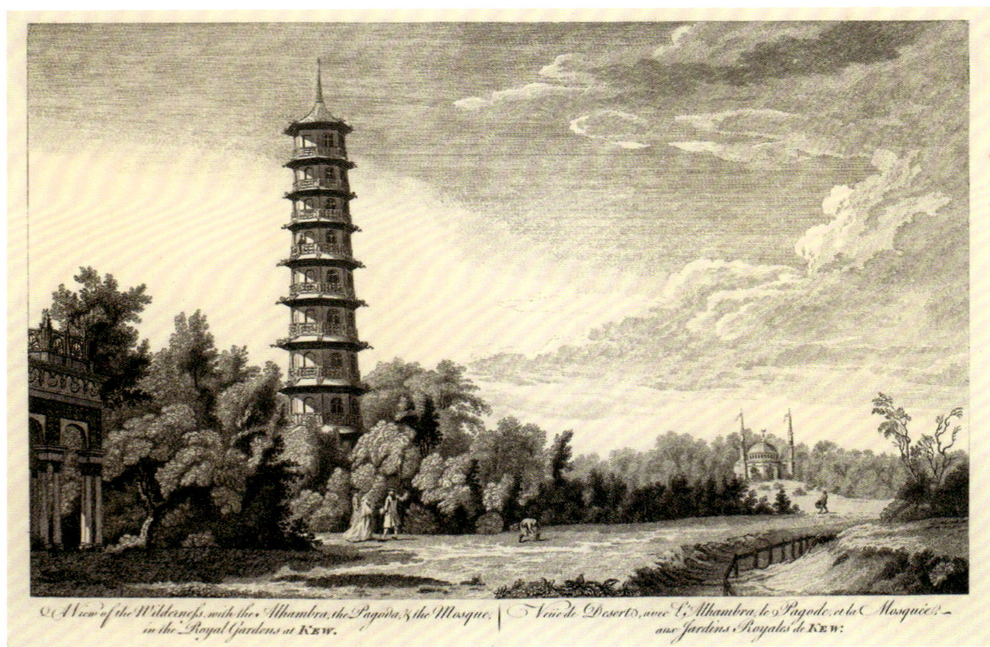

FIG. 11.4
EDWARD ROOKER (1711–74) AFTER WILLIAM MARLOW (1740–1813), *A View of the Wilderness, with the Alhambra, the Pagoda, & the Mosque, in the Royal Gardens at Kew*, *c.*1763. Etching and engraving, 35.5 × 51.2 cm (sheet), RCIN 702947.c

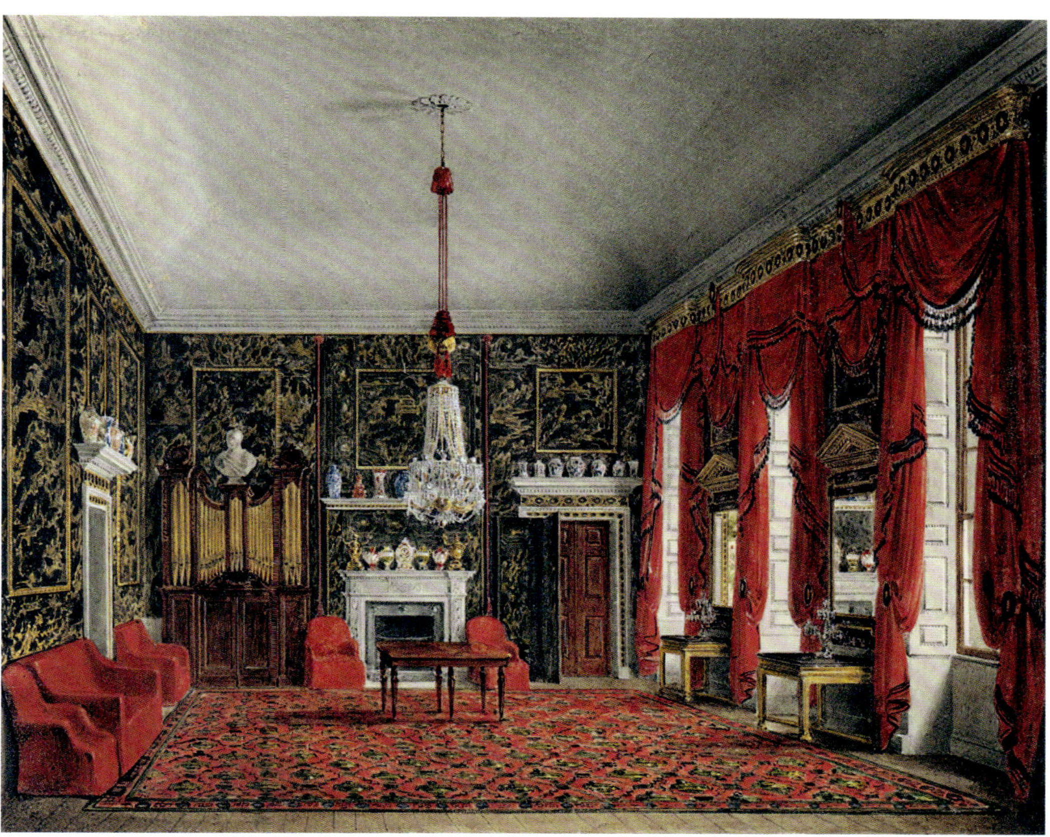

FIG. 11.5
JAMES STEPHANOFF (1789–1874), *The Queen's Breakfast Room, Buckingham House*, 1817. Watercolour and bodycolour, 20.2 × 25.3 cm, RCIN 922145

for the coloured glazes found on many silvered objects in the Royal Pavilion at Brighton: including, for example, the limewood dragons and snakes in the Music Room and the bells and the large dragon and phoenix birds that appear to be holding the Banqueting Room chandeliers (see chapter 10), as well as numerous cornices, capitals and smaller ornaments. The description of the central chandelier in the Banqueting Room in an 1828 inventory is reminiscent of that of the Great Pagoda's dragon ornaments: 'boldly carved, silvered and tinted: The body of this Lustre has a rich open work border of Metal, gilt with edges of silvered Bells – Six richly carved silvered and tinted dragons issuing therefrom'.[4]

While his grandmother Augusta's exotic buildings at Kew influenced George's taste generally, his mother and sisters played an important role in forming his ideas on interior design and collecting. A painting by Johan Zoffany (see Fig. 3.11) shows Queen Charlotte in a room in Buckingham House (later Buckingham Palace) *c.*1765, in the company of her young sons George and Frederick. The furnishings and decorative objects in the room reflect Charlotte's interest in Chinese export ware. On the table are two 'nodding' clay figures, similar to examples later purchased by George from 1803 for display in the Royal Pavilion. George would also have been familiar with his mother's collection of European porcelain, comprising historic pieces and commissions from British manufactories. In addition, there was the substantial collection of blue-and-white and Japanese porcelain (both export ware and European imitations) introduced to the English court by Mary II.[5] Its presence may well have triggered his interest in porcelain, especially Sèvres and Chinese export ware. As has been noted, Charlotte had also 'sought to create a "theatre of wisdom" or *Wunderkammer* at Buckingham House, encapsulating in microcosm elements of the whole world', a concept that may have fascinated the impressionable George and forged in him a passion for the dramatic display of art and decorative objects.[6] As Rachel Peat discusses (see chapter 18), George's own collections saw him gathering objects from across the world, particularly in the impressive Armoury that he established at Carlton House.

At Windsor Castle and Buckingham House Charlotte created several rooms decorated in a chinoiserie style or which incorporated export ware. Some of these schemes pre-date both the Pavilion and George's first chinoiserie interior, the Chinese Drawing Room at Carlton House, designed by Henry Holland *c.*1788 and furnished by Dominique Daguerre (discussed in chapter 5). Charlotte's Breakfast Room at Buckingham House (Fig. 11.5) was furnished with black-and-gold painted panelling that

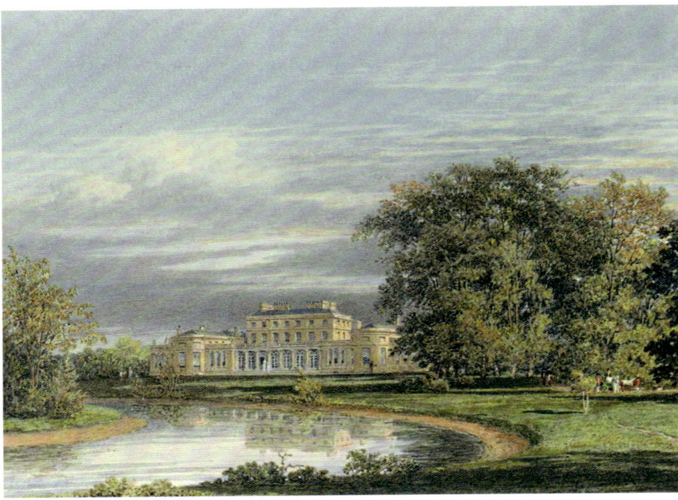

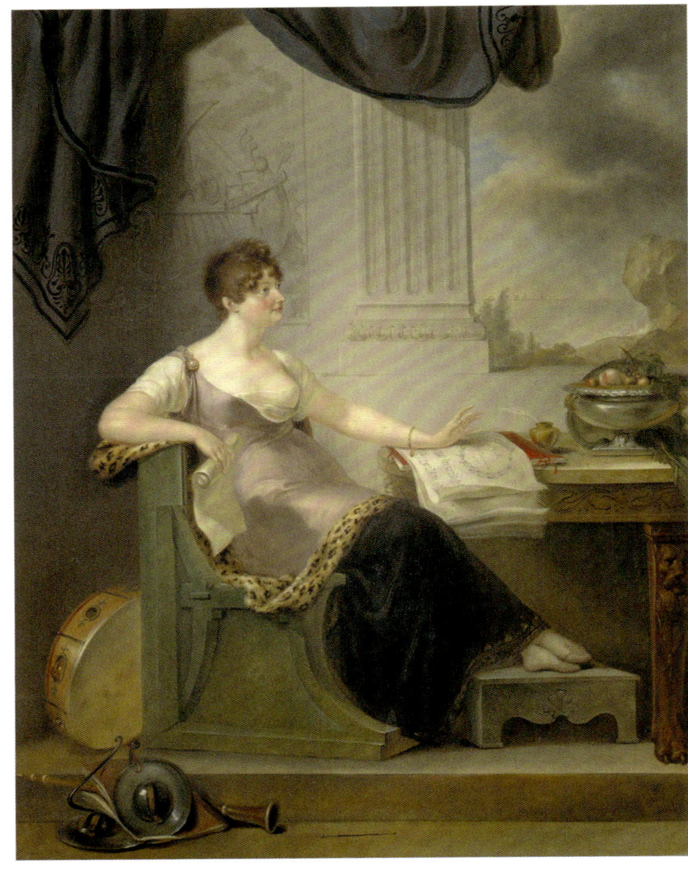

FIG. 11.6
CHARLES WILD (1781–1835), *The Garden Front, Frogmore House*, 1819. Watercolour and bodycolour, 18.4 × 24.9 cm, RCIN 922118

FIG. 11.7
PETER EDWARD STROEHLING (1768–*c.*1826), *Princess Augusta (1768–1840)*, 1807. Oil on copper, 61.0 × 47.9 cm, RCIN 404869

had been transferred from the Crimson Drawing Room in 1763.[7] Pyne described the panels as 'formed of beautiful japan, which has a pleasing effect'.[8] The room was further embellished with some of Charlotte's collection of East Asian and European china. The image in Pyne shows the arrangement of the room *c.*1817 but the porcelain was in situ from at least 1783, when it was described by Horace Walpole.[9] This room may have been among the inspirations for George's foray into the style at Carlton House, and eventually Brighton Pavilion.

The creativity of female members of the royal family saw the introduction of chinoiserie elements in the early nineteenth century at Frogmore House in Windsor Home Park (Fig. 11.6). In 1792 the lease of the original seventeenth-century house was acquired for Charlotte and the queen duly instructed the architect James Wyatt to convert it into a neo-classical villa. Following these improvements Frogmore was frequently used for fêtes, concerts and garden parties. It also became strongly associated with the queen's daughters, Charlotte, Princess Royal, Elizabeth and Augusta (see Fig. 3.6) and Sophia (Fig. 11.1).[10] Frogmore became a kind of 'Arcadian retreat',[11] where they pursued their interests in botany, literature, architecture and interior decoration.

While the Princess Royal and Princess Augusta had inherited their mother's interest in drawing, engraving and botanical illustration, Princess Elizabeth was particularly interested in interior decoration and is strongly associated with the three chinoiserie interiors at Frogmore, two of which she partly executed herself. In the Japan Room, according to Pyne, 'the walls … were painted, in imitation of rich japan, by her Royal Highness the Princess Elizabeth; the furniture was ornamented by the same tasteful hand'.[12] Displayed around the room were Chinese ceramics and European imitations. Elizabeth also appears to have created the walls of the Black Japan Room, a space in which 'an additional interest is excited, in knowing that the taste which the room displays, is all the work of female ingenuity', since the embroidery of the upholstery and soft furnishings was carried out by a school for orphans established under the patronage of Queen Charlotte.[13]

In Pyne two of the six illustrations of the house depict the Japan Room (Fig. 11.8) and the Green Closet (Fig. 11.9). These rooms are clearly represented as female spaces, occupied by seated women. Both the Royal Pavilion interiors and the Japan rooms at Frogmore were converted from Classically inspired settings to a bold chinoiserie style sometime before or in 1807. The Japan

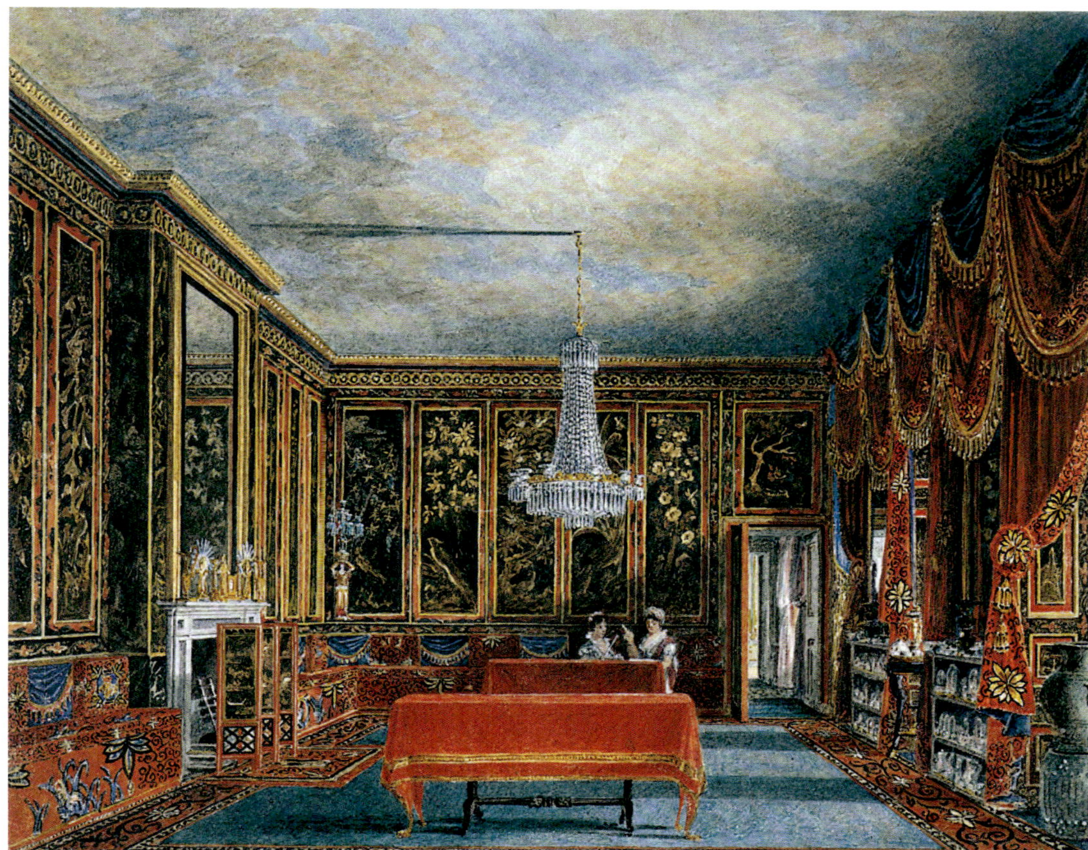

FIG. 11.8
CHARLES WILD (1781–1835), *The Japan Room, Frogmore House*, 1819. Watercolour and bodycolour, 20.3 × 25.2 cm, RCIN 922122

FIG. 11.9
CHARLES WILD (1781–1835), *The Green Closet, Frogmore House*, c.1819. Watercolour and bodycolour, 25.1 × 20.0 cm, RCIN 922123

Room was still decorated in the neo-classical style for a fête in 1797 but by late 1807 it had acquired its distinctive look: in a letter of 19 September that year, Princess Elizabeth told her friend Lady Cathcart, 'I am busy putting up my Japan room at Frogmore, which place is as dear to me as ever'.[14] This work thus coincides with the radical transformation of the Royal Pavilion interiors from neo-classical to exotic in the first years of the nineteenth century.

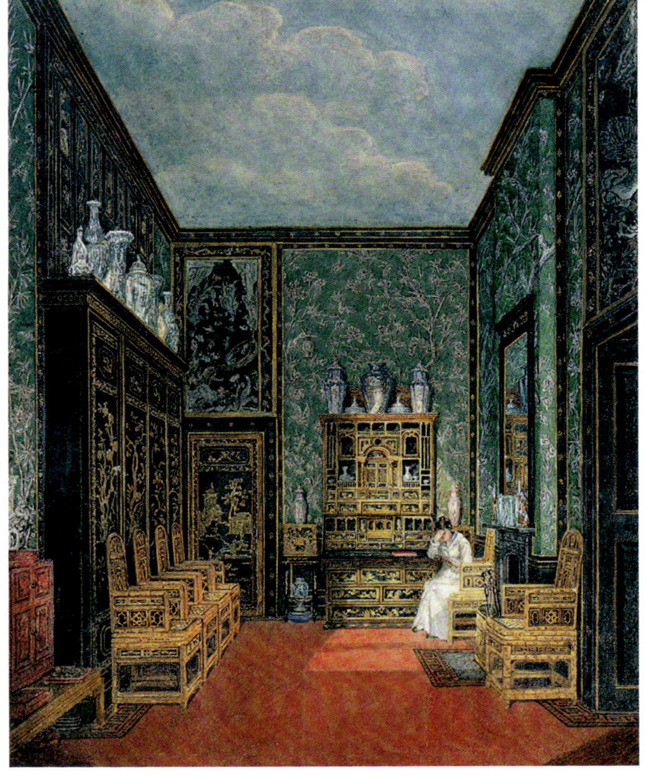

The Green Closet at Frogmore is described in Pyne's text as an 'apartment fitted up with original japan, of a beautiful fabric, on a pure green ground. The cabinets and chairs are of Indian cane'.[15] Some of the numerous 'oriental' objects seen in the illustration of the room for Pyne may have been presents given by the Emperor Qianlong to George III in 1793.[16] The Black Japan Room and an India Room are not illustrated in Pyne's publication. The India Room is described in only a few lines as featuring an elaborately carved ivory bed, white satin embroidered upholstery and red velvet cushions.[17] None of the 'oriental' interiors at Frogmore survive, but some of the lacquer panels were transferred to Elizabeth's married home, Schloss Homburg in Hesse, Germany, where they are installed in the 'English wing' of the palace.[18] Like the Pavilion's interiors, they

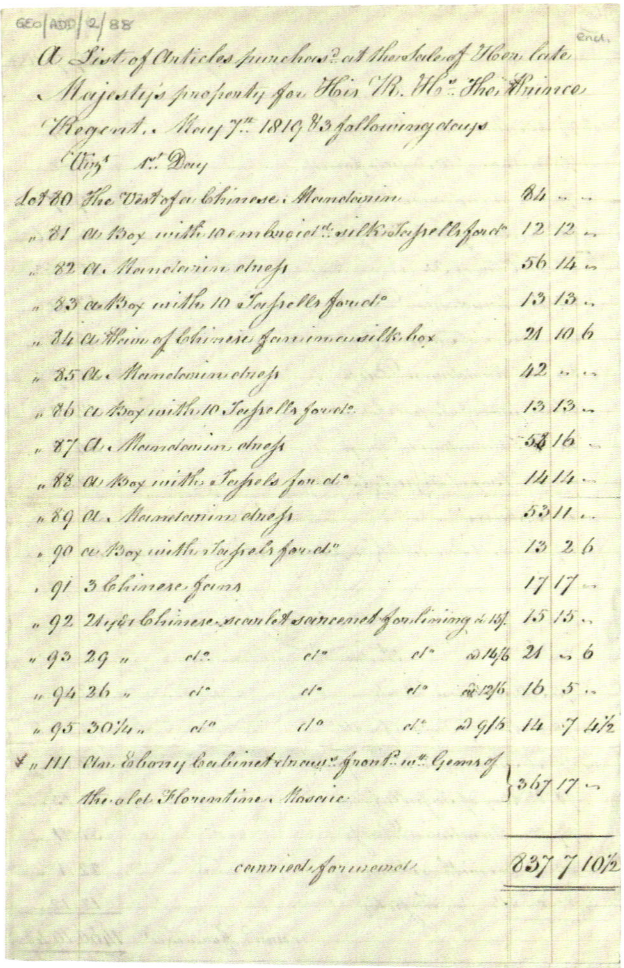

FIG. 11.10
A List of Articles purchased at the Sale of Her late Majesty's property for His R. H. The Prince Regent, *c.*1819–20. Royal Archives, GEO/ADD/2/88

FIG. 11.11
HENRY WINKLES (active 1819–32) AFTER AUGUSTUS CHARLES PUGIN (*c.*1768–1832), *Brighton Pavilion, The Gallery in its present state, looking towards the Music Room*, 1838. Etching with aquatint and hand colouring, 21.6 × 29.8 cm (sheet), RCIN 708000.ag

are a particularly vibrant and strongly coloured post-rococo manifestation of the chinoiserie fashion.

The 'oriental' interiors at Frogmore were stylistically close to the queen's japanned Breakfast Room at Buckingham House, and together these rooms may have inspired the wall decorations in the new Music Room at the Royal Pavilion, created to designs by Frederick Crace from *c.*1817 (see Fig. 10.14). The large red-ground paintings, which cover almost the entire wall space of the room, combine topographical and figurative motifs from William Alexander's images of his Chinese travels with painted effects imitating lacquered surfaces, as seen by George at Frogmore, Windsor and Buckingham House.[19] Mutual inspiration between George and his family members may explain this cluster of early nineteenth-century royal chinoiserie interiors in England.

Perhaps the most compelling and moving piece of evidence of Queen Charlotte's influence on her son's taste are the objects purchased by him at the posthumous sale of her goods in May 1819 (Fig. 11.10). George bought no fewer than 70 lots, at a total value of just over £2,735. Although these items included Sèvres vases, furniture, clocks, gold boxes and items of silver gilt, most of the items were of exotic style or origin, including Chinese fans, Indian furniture and boxes, items of 'Mandarin Dress', and 55 yards of Chinese scarlet silk.[20] The sale coincided with the busiest period of redecoration ever carried out in the Pavilion and many of the purchased items were incorporated there. A set of Indian sandalwood settees and chairs, veneered with ivory and originating in Vizagapatam (Vishākhapatnam), would become an important feature in the Royal Pavilion's Long Gallery (Fig. 11.11).[21]

If George looked to his mother and his sisters for some of his artistic inspiration, he may in turn have passed his own fascinations on to his only child, Princess Charlotte of Wales. Art was a means of expressing affection between father and daughter: the princess presented George with some elegant Chinese vases (Fig. 11.12), while he apparently presented his daughter with a seventeenth-century locket into which had been placed a lock of Charles I's hair, which had been taken from the tomb of the Stuart king when it had been opened in 1813 (see Fig. 0.14). Like her father, the princess commissioned equestrian paintings, favouring the artists Henry Bernard Chalon and Edmund Bristow.[22] The two were also both eager collectors of prints: Charlotte's 'large' collection was described by Sir Thomas Lawrence as 'all Sir Joshua, Vandyke's, &c'.[23] George's final artistic gesture for his daughter was her memorial by Matthew Cotes Wyatt, the model of which he approved in March 1820, which was placed in the medieval Urswick Chantry in St George's Chapel at Windsor Castle.[24]

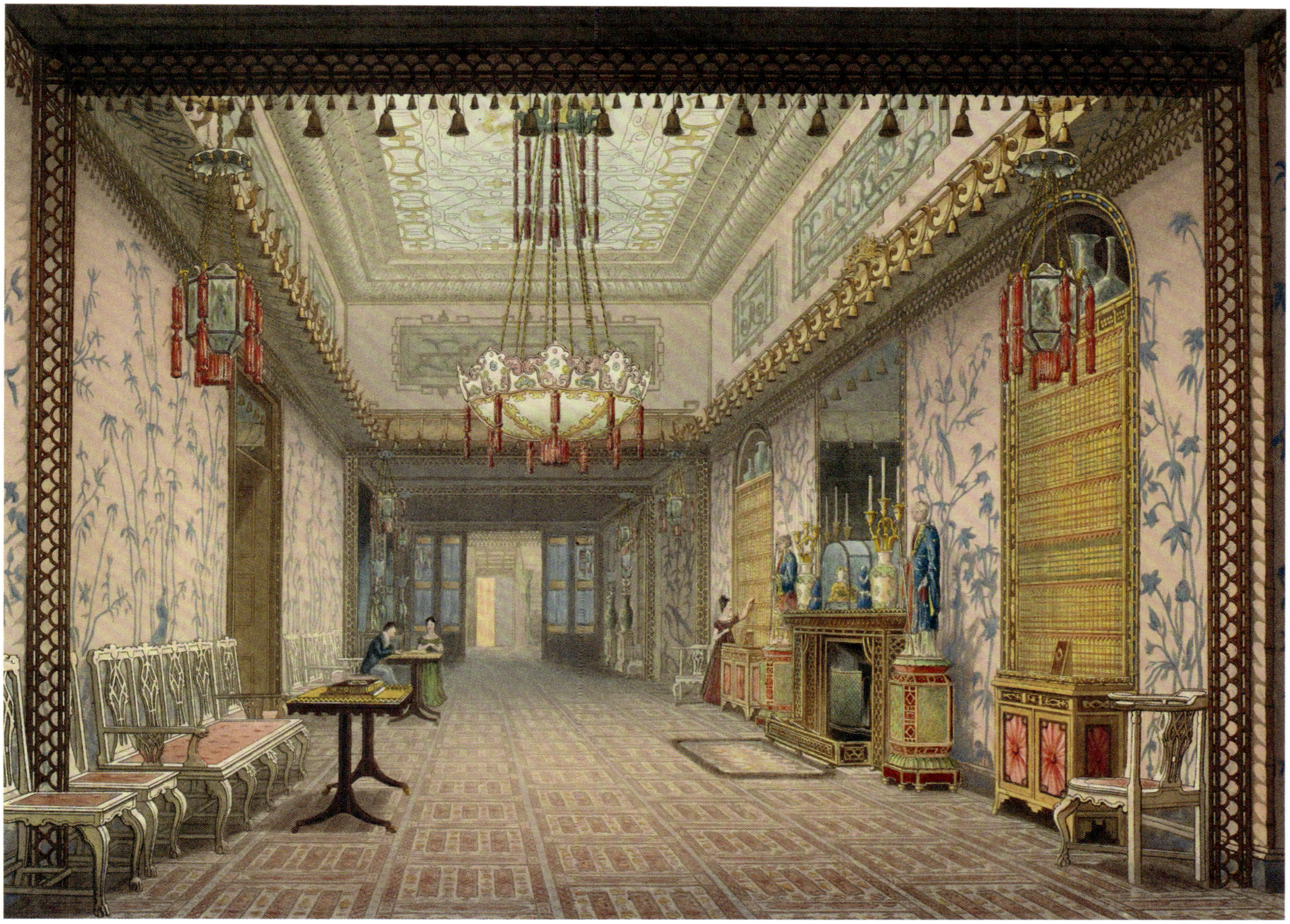

The many similarities between Queen Charlotte's collections and design decisions confirms she had as significant an influence on George's developing taste and collecting habits as his father. His sisters and grandmother, too, played a role in encouraging an interest in the exotic which would be expressed so successfully in the exuberant Royal Pavilion at Brighton.

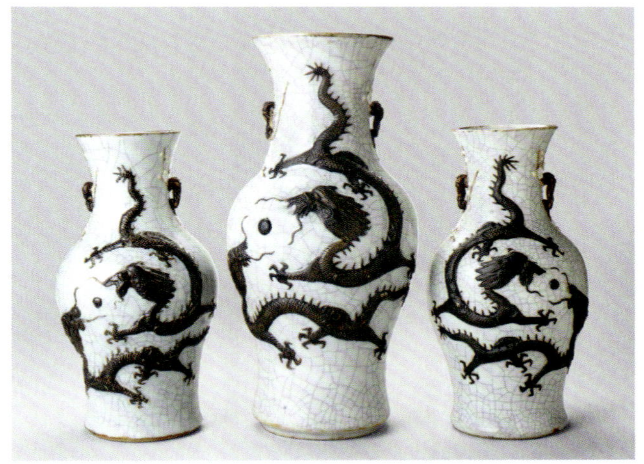

FIG. 11.12
SOUTH CHINA, *Garniture of three vases*, late 18th or early 19th century. Porcelain, craquelure glaze, slip, 45.9 cm (height), RCIN 11851; 35.4 cm (height), RCIN 692.1–2

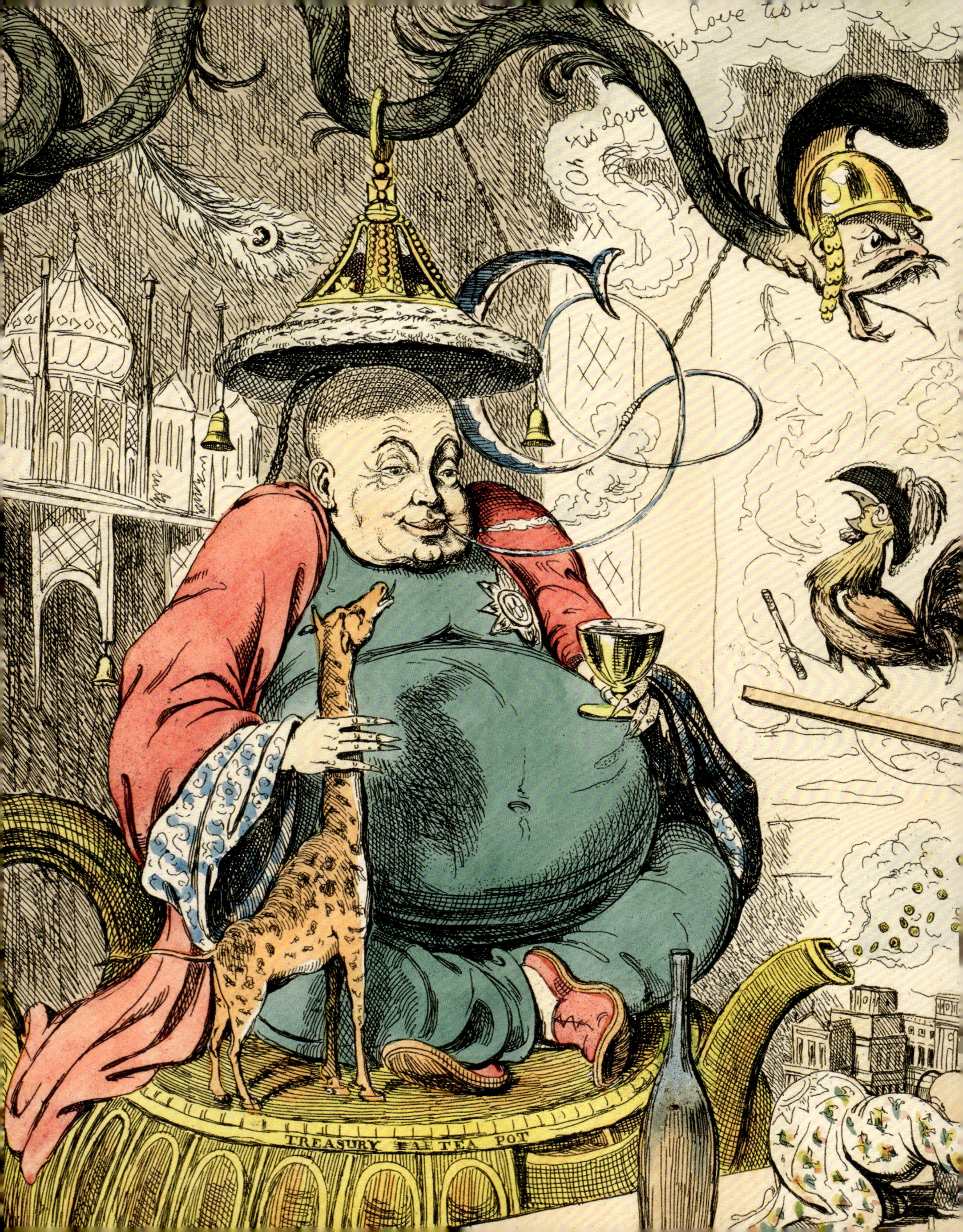
Oh 'tis Love
'tis Love
TREASURY TEA POT

The GREAT JOSS *and his* PLAYTHINGS: GEORGE IV *and* SATIRICAL PRINTS

KATE HEARD

George IV is largely known to modern audiences through satirical depictions by artists such as James Gillray, Thomas Rowlandson and George Cruikshank.[1] These humorously barbed images have fed his reputation as a drunken, womanising gambler, whose actions failed to live up to the position to which he had been born (Fig. 12.1). George was certainly sensitive to such depictions and spent much time and money attempting to suppress those prints that he felt were a particular challenge to his dignity, both by the threat of legal action and by using agents to pay off publishers who planned to issue derogatory material.[2] But he was also a purchaser of satirical prints who formed a fine group of such works as part of his vast print collection. This essay will examine George's reaction to contemporary satire through his print purchases, asking what appealed to him, and how far he was able to accept satirically critical depictions of himself.

On his death, George's collection included 2,750 satirical prints.[3] He had largely acquired these from three vendors: the satirical print specialists William Holland and the Humphrey family (see chapter 6), and the general London print dealers Colnaghi & Co. Other printsellers made occasional deliveries of satirical material: the artist Henry Wigstead, a close collaborator of Thomas Rowlandson, delivered satirical prints to Brighton in August 1788 and August 1789.[4] Among them were the anonymous *City Courtship* (1786) and the *Margate Hoy* (Fig. 12.2), both in uncoloured impressions. The delivery of these prints to Brighton, where George was in residence, provides a strong indication that the satirical prints he purchased were to be used and enjoyed.[5]

Henry Wigstead's bill shows a taste for contemporary social comedy, but William Holland's substantial sale of prints to George demonstrates much wider interest in the art of satire. Holland stocked a large selection of satirical prints at his fashionable shop on Oxford Street, and also compiled albums of such material for clients. In 1790, he put together sets of albums for both George and Frederick, Duke of York. Although neither set of albums survives intact, some of the contents of those compiled for George are known through a partially complete listing submitted by Holland to the commissioners appointed to settle George's debts in 1795.[6] Many of the prints in Holland's

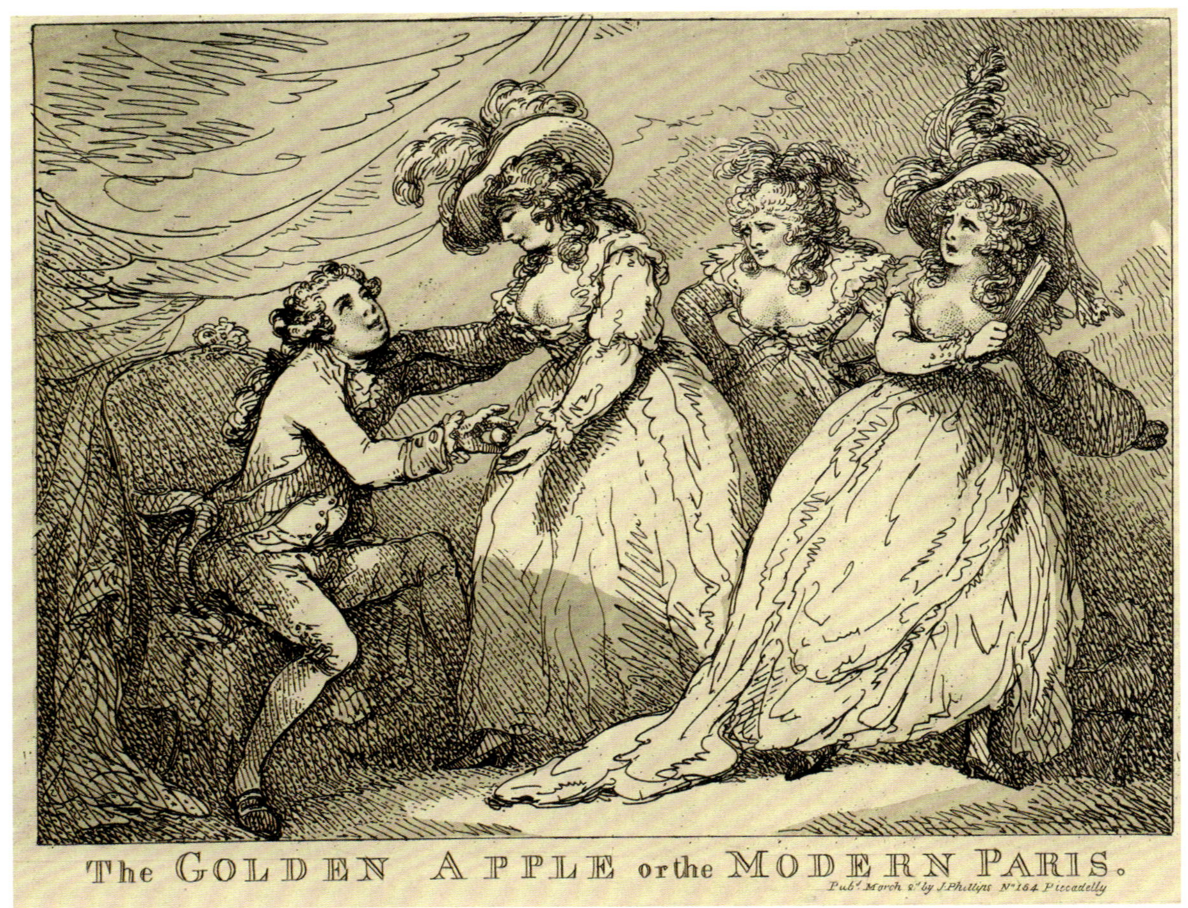
The GOLDEN APPLE or the MODERN PARIS.
Pub.d March 2d by J.Phillips No 164 Piccadilly

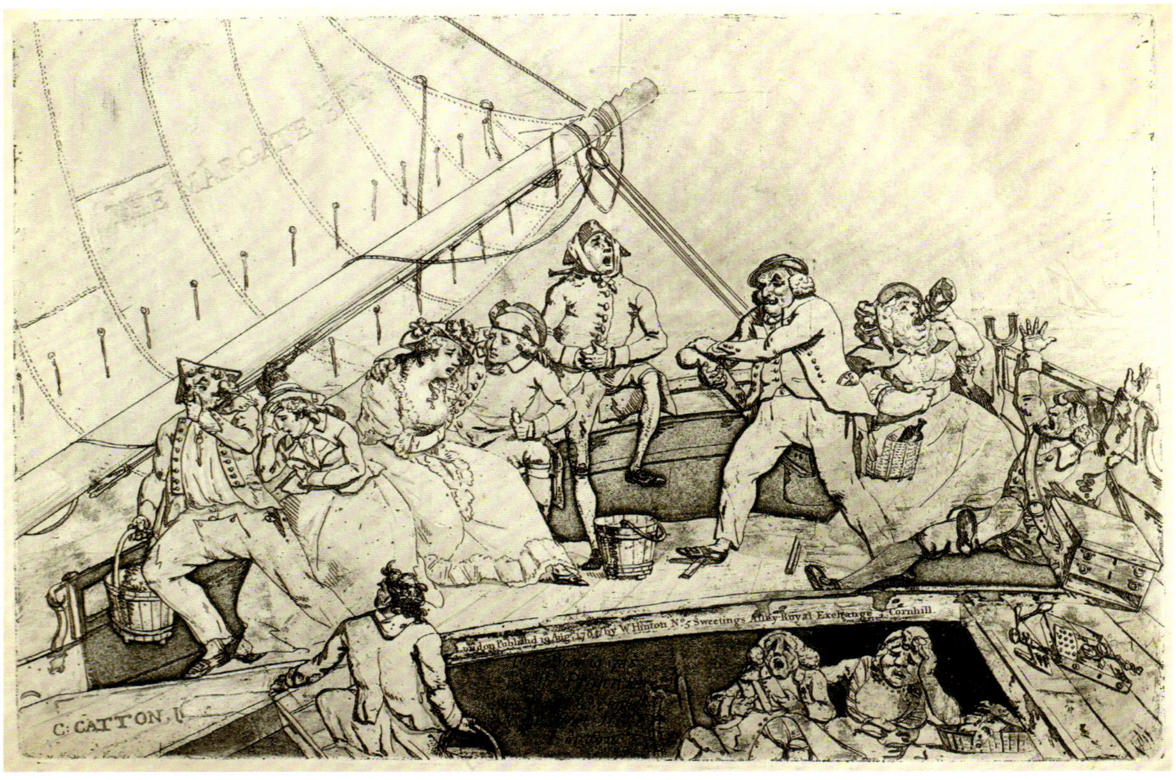
Publishd 19 Aug
by W Hinton No 5 Sweetings Alley Royal Exchange
Cornhill
C. CATTON,

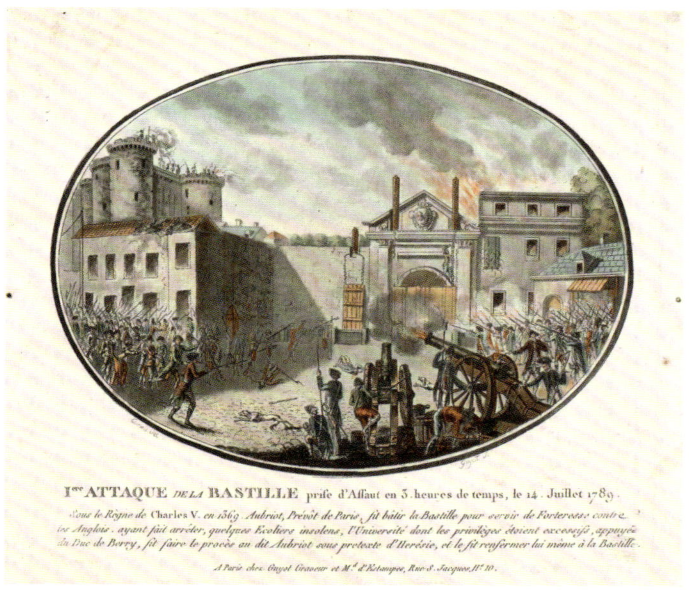

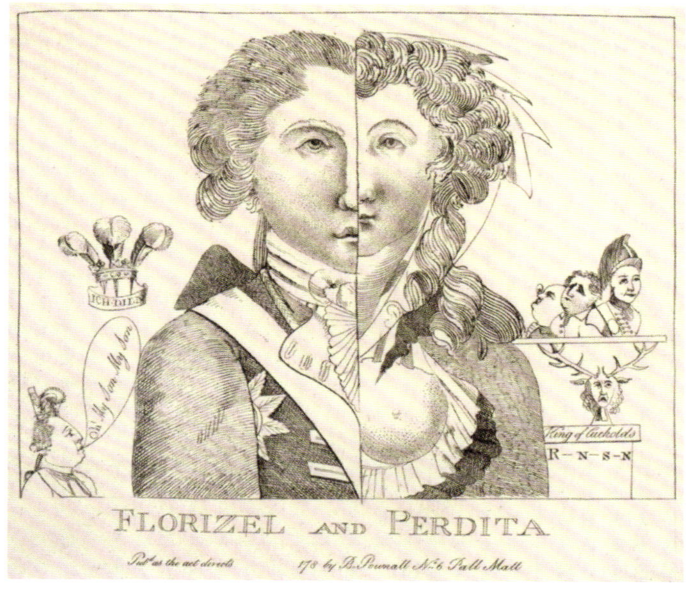

(p. 160)
Detail of Fig. 12.6, ROBERT SEYMOUR (1798–1836), *The Great Joss and his Playthings*, c.1829

FIG. 12.1
THOMAS ROWLANDSON (1757–1827), *The Golden Apple, or the Modern Paris*, 1785. Etching, 28.2 × 39.6 cm (sheet), RCIN 810123

FIG. 12.2
CHARLES CATTON JUNIOR (1756–1819), *The Margate Hoy*, 1785. Etching with aquatint, 32.5 × 48.0 cm, RCIN 810129

FIG. 12.3
LAURENT GUYOT (1756–1806) AFTER JEAN-ALEXIS CORNU (1755–1807), *Ière Attaque de la Bastille prise d'Assaut en 3. heures de temps, le 14. Juillet 1789*, c.1789–90. Etching with roulette work and printed colouring, 20.4 × 23.5 cm (plate), RCIN 755824

FIG. 12.4
PUBLISHED BY B. POWNALL (active 1783), *Florizel and Perdita*, 1783. Etching, 25.5 × 36.8 cm (sheet) (Library of Congress, Washington DC: PC 1-6266/ LC-DIG-ppmsca-38664)

invoice can be identified and show the impressive breadth of subject covered by the albums.[7] Holland provided George with historical as well as modern satires, among them an 'Old Print Pubd in the Reign of Henry 8th' (not yet identified) and some early eighteenth-century 'medley' prints, which purport to show a pile of prints and ephemera scattered on a surface. Alongside these were a fine collection of modern political and social satires, including a run of prints poking fun at the author Edmund Burke (portrayed as *The Knight of the Woeful Countenance*) and a group of satires on a 'Monster', who had terrorised London women with a series of knife attacks between 1788 and 1790. Although Holland described the contents of his albums as 'caricatures', a number of the prints included are not what we would class as satire. These include portraits of actors such as Henry Woodward and Charles Bannister, French genre prints such as a 'fi[ne] impression' of Philibert-Louis Debucourt's celebrated *Promenade de la Gallerie du Palais Royale* (1787), and an impressive series of prints documenting current events in France, among them Laurent Guyot's *Ière Attaque de la Bastille prise d'Assaut en 3. heures de temps, le 14. Juillet 1789* (Fig. 12.3).

Although the contents of the albums were undoubtedly selected from Holland's existing stock, these volumes were clearly put together with George in mind. Among the satires opening 'Vol. 12' (the first on the surviving invoice) were *The Prince's Bow* and *The Installation Supper*, two flatteringly humorous depictions of George as the object of admiration. The volumes included other satires of George, among them *Thing O'My in the Character of Macheath* (1786), which showed him surrounded by mistresses and prostitutes, and *Florizel and Perdita* (Fig. 12.4), which satirised his youthful affair with the actress Mary 'Perdita' Robinson. A few years earlier, in 1784, George had been happy to purchase *Money Lenders* from William Humphrey, which showed him, handsome and relaxed, discussing his debts with a pair of money lenders. All these prints, although critical of George's lifestyle, are flattering in their depiction of his person and George's purchase of them is indication that he was happy to be amused by gently humorous images of his misadventures, particularly those (such as the Robinson affair) which were firmly in the past. More surprisingly, the albums included the recently published *Who Kills Fi[r]st for a Crown*, which showed George and the duc d'Orléans as hunters pursuing crowned stags with packs of hounds bearing the faces of politicians: the French pack includes Orléans' mistress, the comtesse de Buffon (Fig. 12.5).

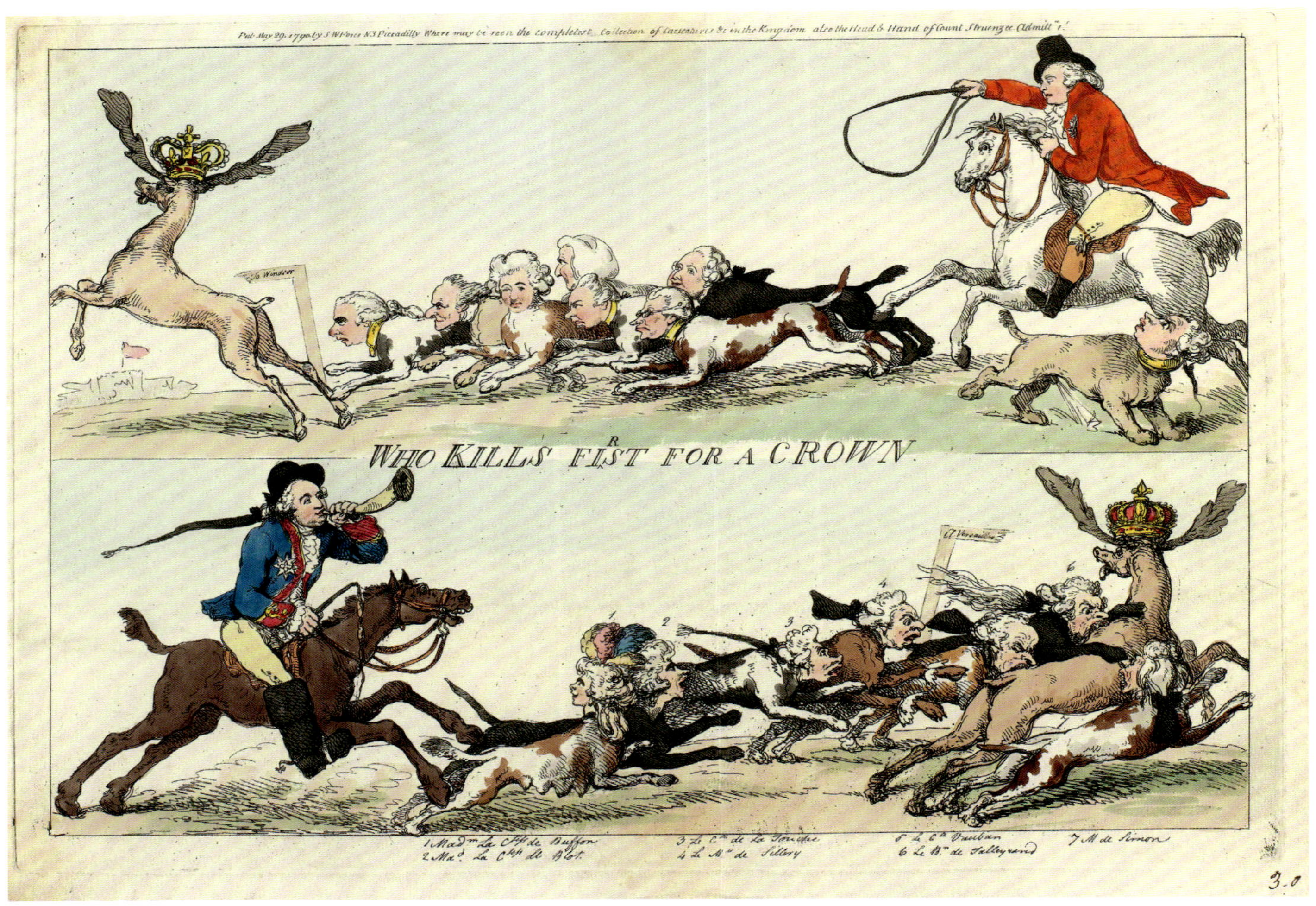

FIG. 12.5
THOMAS ROWLANDSON (1757–1827),
Who Kills Fi[r]st for a Crown, 1790.
Etching with hand colouring,
36.7 × 51.8 cm, RCIN 810385

Perhaps George regarded this print as denoting no more than his ambition to rule and favourably contrasting his well-ordered hounds with Orléans' bloodthirsty pursuit of power.

While William Holland compiled albums of satirical prints he thought George would enjoy, both the Humphreys and Colnaghi & Co. provided portfolios from which George could select those prints he wished to acquire. It is important to stress that such portfolios, like the Holland albums, would have contained only those prints thought likely to appeal to George: it is unlikely that he was ever offered such highly critical satires as Gillray's *A Voluptuary under the horrors of Digestion* (see Fig. 2.7), or Robert Seymour's *The Great Joss and his Playthings* (Fig. 12.6). The humorous prints supplied by Colnaghi's were usually sent as part of large consignments of printed material (often listed only as 'Various Humorous' at the end of invoices for portraits, topographical, military or theatrical subjects). But satirical prints were also sometimes listed separately among Colnaghi's itemised invoices – such works were often old material, perhaps valued by George as much for their historical as their comic appeal. These included *The Whigs Medley* and its *Answer* of 1711, *The Spy* of 1747 and *An Abridgment of Mr Pope's Essay on Man* of 1769, the latter a criticism of princely vanity which George does not seem to have taken to heart.

William Holland and Colnaghi & Co. provided George with historical as well as contemporary satires, but Hannah Humphrey, one of London's leading satirical print publishers and sellers, sold George almost entirely topical prints, most of which she had issued herself. George's patronage of Humphrey is particularly interesting as she published some of the most vicious satires on his conduct (some of which he sought to

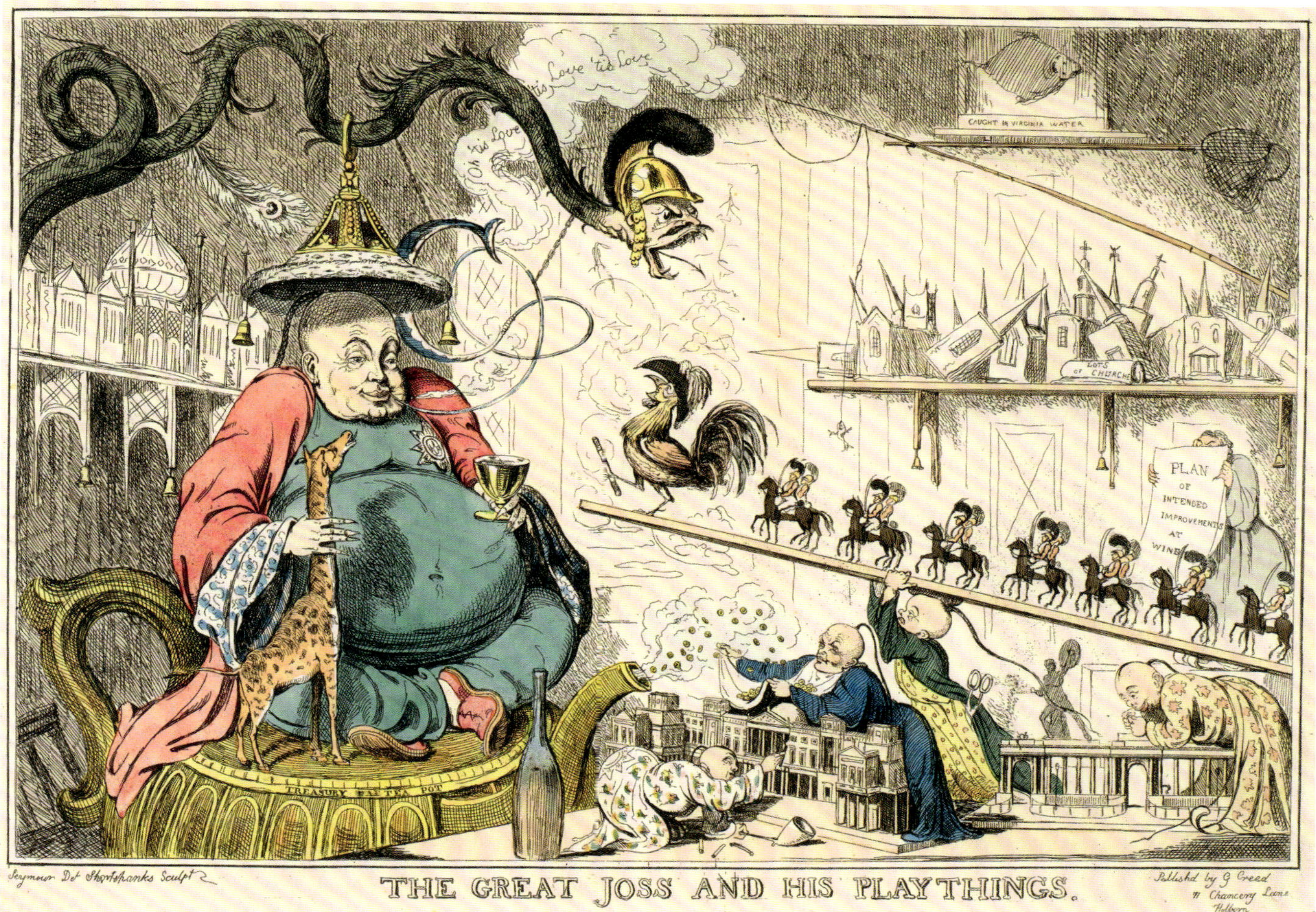

FIG. 12.6
ROBERT SEYMOUR (1798–1836),
The Great Joss and his Playthings,
*c.*1829. Etching with hand colouring,
25.2 × 35.3 cm, RCIN 751279

suppress). These attacks do not appear to have affected his purchases from her shop on St James's Street. Although he had made a major purchase from her brother William in 1784, George did not begin to patronise Hannah's shop until July 1803, when he paid a guinea to borrow a portfolio of prints.[8] The loan of portfolios, allowing the latest satires to be enjoyed by a host and his guests after dinner, was a service offered by a number of printsellers, but George's borrowing of prints from Humphrey may have been a means of sampling her publications prior to purchase. His interest may have been piqued by Humphrey's recent publication of a satire by James Gillray on the threat of a French invasion, a topic of particular fascination for him. Thereafter, George purchased numerous satires from Humphrey, for which he was invoiced quarterly (suggesting some form of standing arrangement). Prints may have been selected for George's consideration not by Humphrey herself, but by Sir Tomkyns Hilgrove Turner, who had the care of the print collection at Carlton House and who was himself a notable print collector.[9] Turner is likely to have selected prints on subjects that would particularly appeal to George, and to have avoided Gillray's cruel barbs. Although Humphrey overwhelmingly provided topical prints, she sometimes sent George works which had been published a few years earlier, among them Gillray's *Flannel Armour* (1793) and George Woodward's *Rogues in Grain* (1796).[10] A number of the prints that Humphrey sold had been issued by rival publishers, among them Rudolph Ackermann, demonstrating that her shop carried prints by other publishers as well as her own back catalogue.

George was happy to purchase prints from Humphrey, despite her publication of hostile satires, but the same patronage

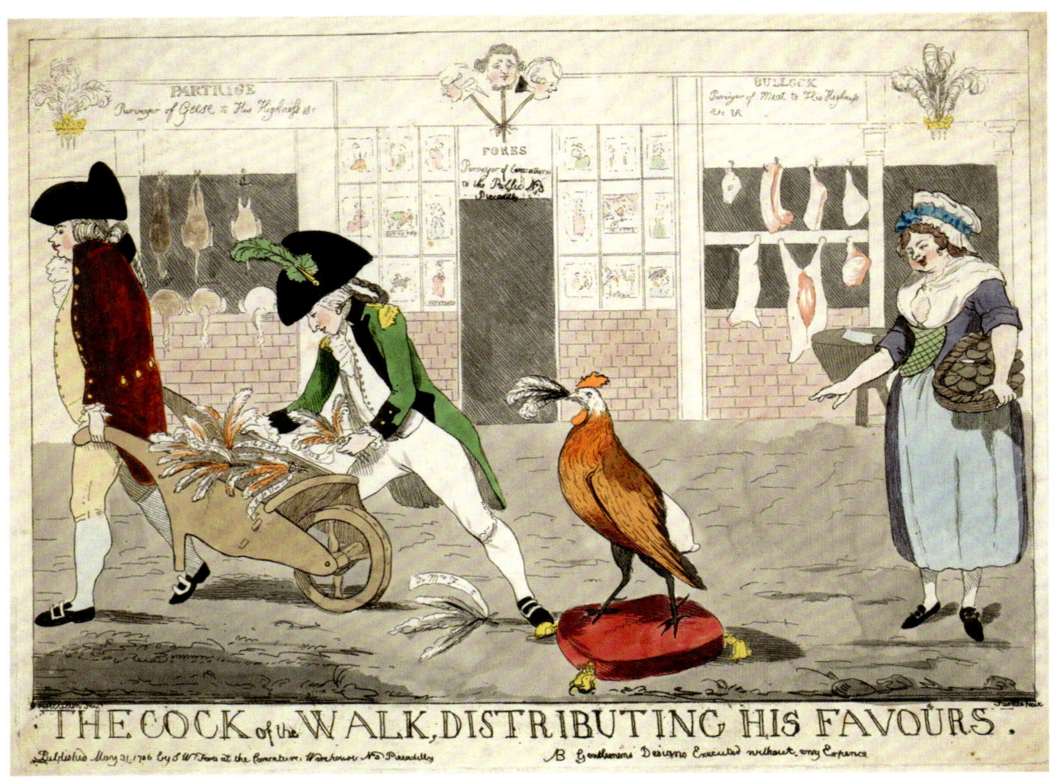

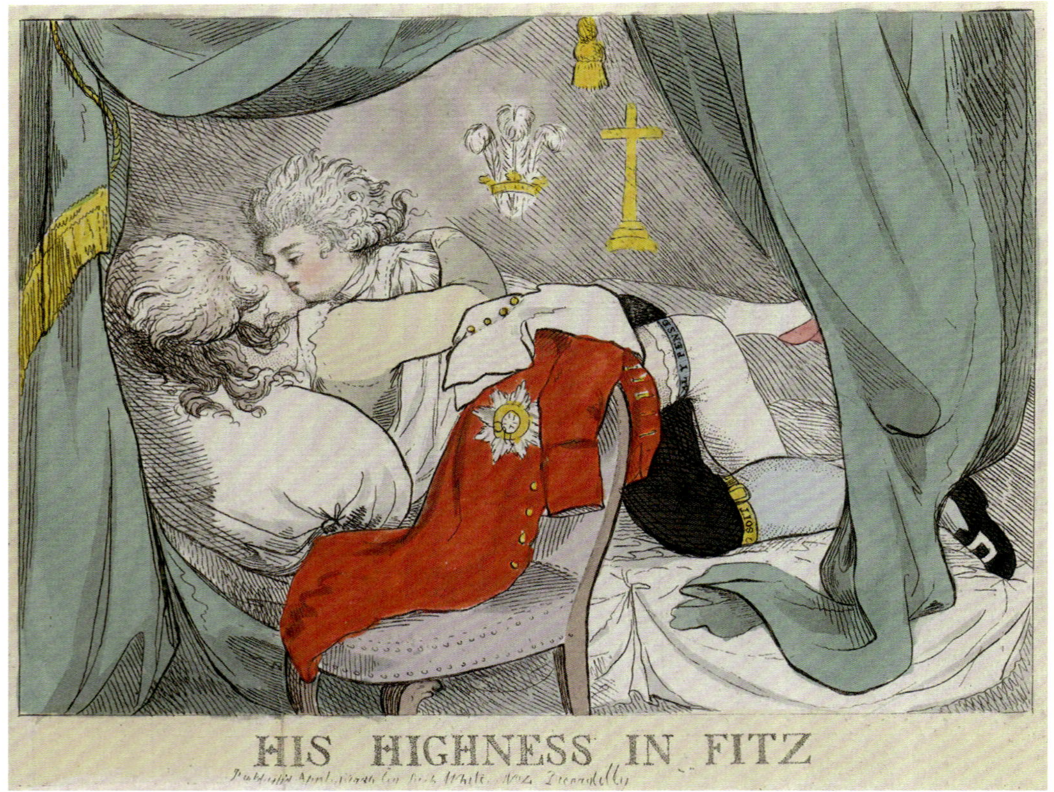

FIG. 12.7
PUBLISHED BY S.W. FORES (1761–1838), *The Cock of the Walk, Distributing his Favours*, 1786. Etching with hand colouring, 30.5 × 40.1 cm (sheet) (The Royal Pavilion and Museums, Brighton and Hove: FA 208002)

FIG. 12.8
ATTRIBUTED TO GEORGE TOWNLY STUBBS (1748–1815?), *His Highness in Fitz*, 1786. Etching with hand colouring, 17.6 × 25.3 cm (sheet) (British Museum, London: 1868,0808.5505)

FIG. 12.9
THOMAS ROWLANDSON (1757–1827), *Filial Piety!*, 1788. Etching with hand colouring, 25.6 × 37.5 cm (sheet), RCIN 810287

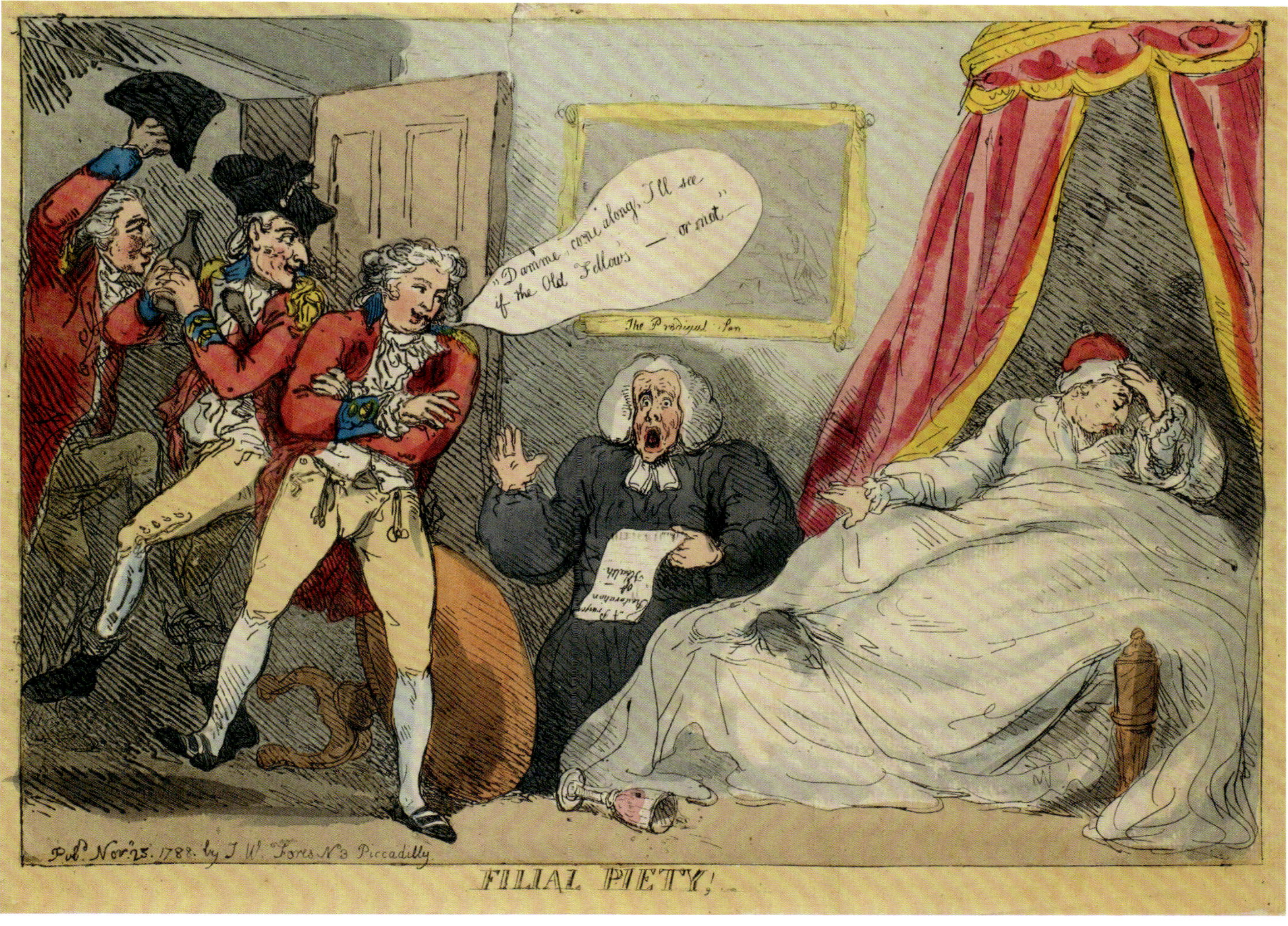

was not accorded to Samuel William Fores, the third (with Holland and Humphrey) of the triumvirate of major satirical print publishers in London. Fores was conscious of the withholding of royal patronage from his business: in 1786 he published *The Cock of the Walk, Distributing his Favours*, which shows his print shop passed by as the Prince of Wales (as a cockerel) hands out feathers to his favoured businesses (Fig. 12.7). George's unwillingness to patronise Fores's business appears to have been a reaction to Fores's publication of a viciously explicit satire on the prince's relationship with Mrs Fitzherbert, for which George had tried to take Fores to court in 1786 (Fig. 12.8), and on his bid for the Regency in 1788, which again led the prince to seek legal advice (Fig. 12.9).[11] Fores was to remain a thorn in the royal side, and was one of the printsellers who came under scrutiny in 1820, when George sought (unsuccessfully) to suppress satires on his treatment of his wife Caroline and his extra-marital affairs. By this time, Fores had been tormenting the prince for nearly 40 years.

George's decision not to purchase prints directly from Samuel Fores, but his willingness to purchase from Humphrey and Holland, gives us some indication of the limits of his humour. He was, as we have seen, able to accept satires which presented him in a flattering light: as a charmer of women or a handsome young buck. He could even stomach prints of affairs which had become 'old news', such as his fling with Mary Robinson (indeed, he would purchase Gainsborough's portrait of the actress in 1797). But George was, as Fores discovered, extremely sensitive to attacks on his current behaviour, on his present mistresses and on his recent political actions. He had a clear wish to preserve his immediate reputation, and an unwillingness to become the butt of public derision. His uneasy relationship with the satirical printsellers of London, which saw him acting as both collector and censor, tells us much about the line he, and they, trod between humour and offence.

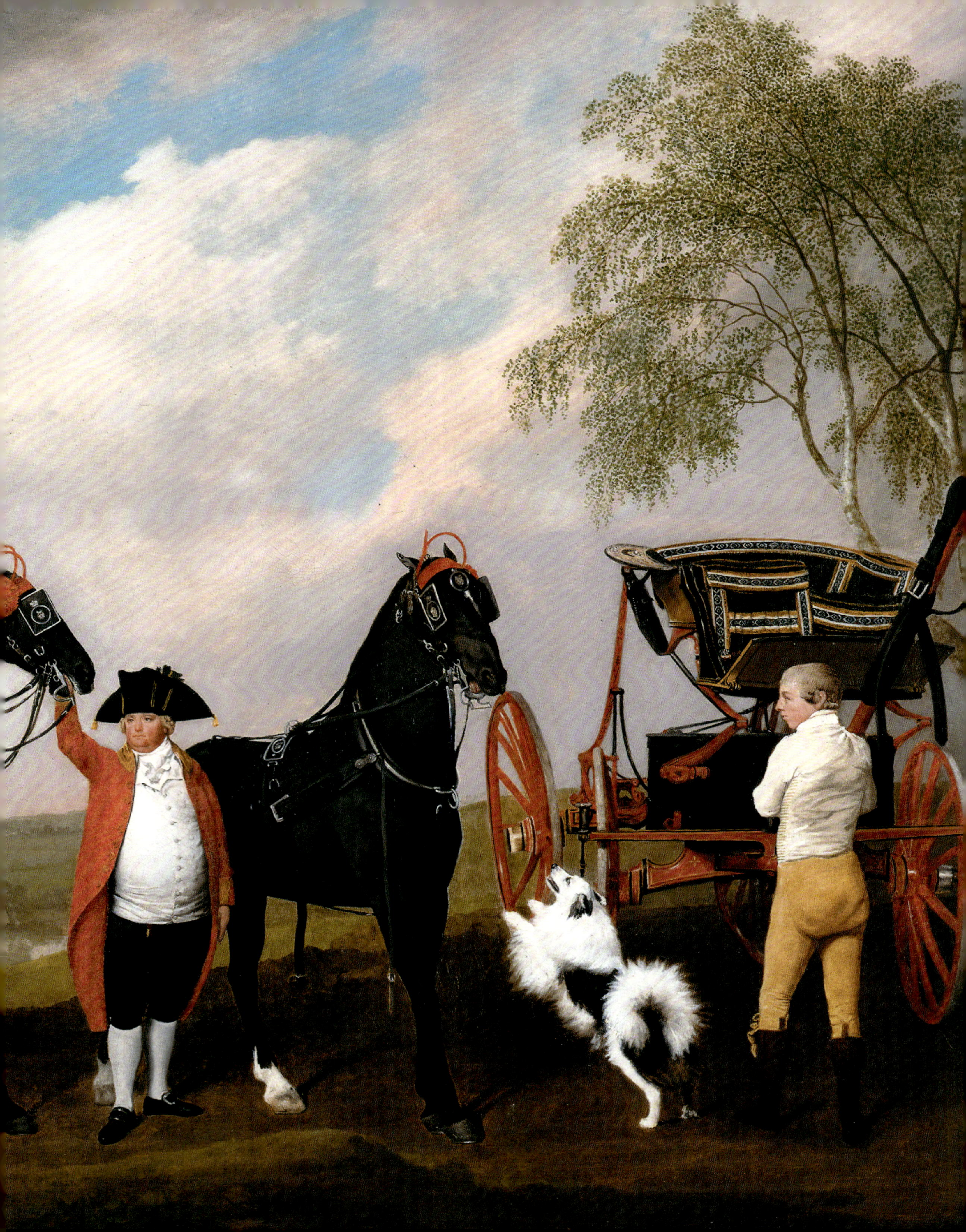

13

GEORGE IV *and* SPORTING ART

SALLY GOODSIR

> the one character in which he pre-eminently
> shone; that of an English sportsman[1]

THROUGHOUT HIS LIFE, George IV was an enthusiastic participant in and spectator of a wide range of sports. As with so many other of his fascinations, this interest was reflected in many areas of his art collecting and patronage. Of all sports, it was equestrian pursuits that he most consistently followed throughout his life. He may have been taught to ride by Sir Sidney Medows, an MP and equestrian who became Deputy Ranger of Richmond Park at the end of the reign of George II (1727–60). Medows's book, the *Art of Horsemanship*, was published posthumously in 1806 and dedicated to the prince, perhaps his most famous pupil.[2] In 1818, more than 20 years after his death, Medows was the subject of one of the prince's acquisitions, a portrait by George Stubbs showing him riding a muscular cream stallion, perhaps one of George III's Hanoverian Creams (Fig. 13.1).[3] The prince's adult riding style was captured in another Stubbs painting directly commissioned from the artist; unusually for a royal heir it shows him riding casually in a London park, rather than as a future head of state (see Fig. 2.3).

Hunting, racing and driving

Skill as a horseman led to a passion for hunting. At Windsor as a young man, the prince hunted on Tuesdays or Saturdays with his father. The presence of the royal family in the Great Park at Windsor was one of the few moments during George's childhood when he and his siblings might be seen outside their palaces; the young prince is reputed to have skated on the frozen Maastricht Garden to the north of the castle.[4] Aged 27 the prince leased his first hunting seat, Kempshott Park in Hampshire, in an area with established hunting and shooting. He maintained this lease between 1788 and 1795; plans dated 1795 for alterations to the house from the architect Henry Holland survive although it is unclear if any work was carried out (Fig. 13.2).[5] Holland was just completing initial works at Carlton House and at Brighton, and a pinch in the prince's finances curtailed work at Brighton in this year, which may explain the lack of obvious intervention by Holland at Kempshott. The plans show a house of relatively moderate proportions. At Kempshott, it was not only sport which was pursued. George and Caroline of Brunswick spent part of their honeymoon there, when the house party included several of George's drinking and hunting companions and his latest mistress, Frances Villiers, Lady Jersey, who had

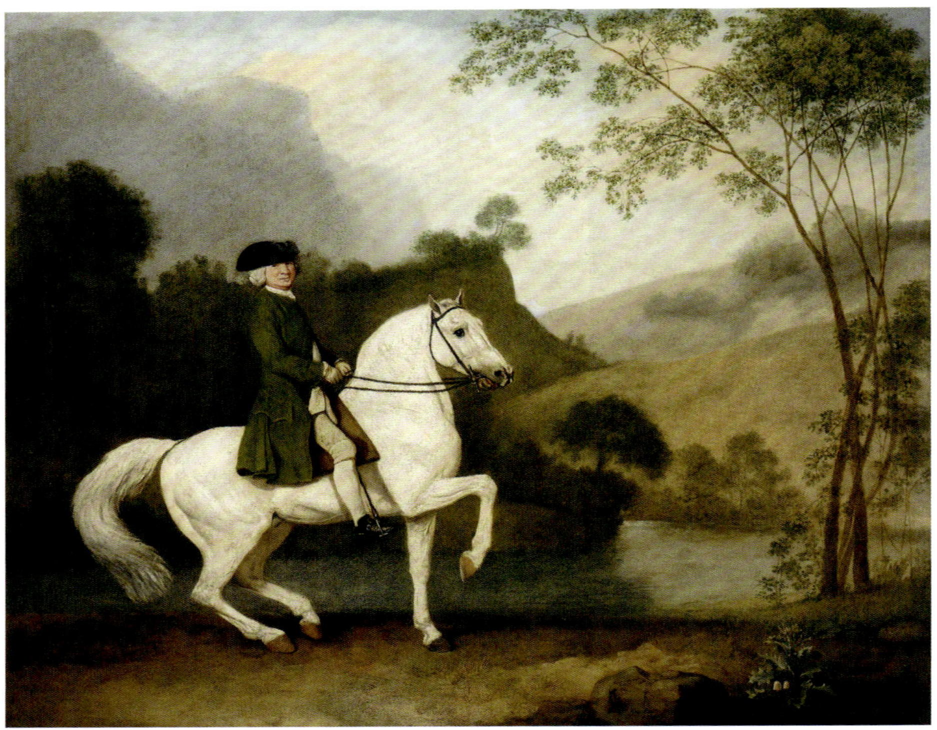

(p. 168)
Detail of Fig. 13.8, GEORGE STUBBS (1724–1806), *The Prince of Wales's Phaeton*, 1793

FIG. 13.1
GEORGE STUBBS (1724–1806), *Sir Sidney Medows (1701–92)*, 1778. Oil on panel, 82.6 × 101.6 cm, RCIN 400550

encouraged the match. Her husband held multiple positions in the prince's household through his wife's influence, but he was genuinely a keen huntsman, resulting in his appointment as the prince's Master of the Horse later the same year. The prince gave up Kempshott later in 1795; perhaps the associations with an unhappy honeymoon were too strong. The new 600-acre estate he leased at Northington Grange cost £900 p.a. in rent. The frequency of his hunting reduced and he gave up any regular presence in Hampshire in 1796.

The prince had acquired his first pack of staghounds for hunting deer in 1791 and named it the Kempshott Hunt. Hunts of four hours or more were recorded by the prince's hunt manager, William Poyntz, often running through several landowners' estates and farms.[6] One account of a hunt near Basingstoke in 1790 recorded that George only returned to Kempshott at 7pm, and that he 'expressed the highest satisfaction at the sport and the fineness of the country. He wore the uniform of the H.H. [Hampshire Hunt] and with his usual affability, conversed with every gentleman present.'[7] Loyal equestrian staff from this period remained with the prince for long periods; the hunting groom, John Gascoigne, rose through his household and ended as Clerk of the Stables. On his death in 1812 his colleague William Anderson succeeded him as Clerk. Both men were immortalised in canvases by George Stubbs commissioned by their employer during their time at Kempshott (Fig. 13.3).

Racing, like hunting, remained a lifetime's passion. No doubt the sport appealed to the young prince as a way of irritating his father, who disapproved of the expenditure and lifestyle which came with the pursuit of horseracing and racehorse breeding.[8] Racing was indeed an expensive sport: the Duke of York started to breed and race horses in the late 1780s, but had to sell them in the early 1790s due to financial constraints. The allure for George may have been increased by the success of the stud owned by his uncle, Henry, Duke of Cumberland, which during the prince's youth bred 26 winners of 94 races.[9] The prince registered the royal silks of crimson waistcoat, purple sleeves and black cap, which remain the royal racing colours today.

The prince's name first appears in the Stud Book in the mid-1780s, and between 1784 and 1792 his horses won 185 races, including 18 King's Plates and several Jockey Club Plates.[10] George's prominence in the equestrian world was celebrated by the equine auctioneers Tattersall's, located at Hyde Park Corner, who placed a bust of the prince in the middle of their sale ring (later transferred to their new yard at Newmarket). The prince also proved himself as a breeder; Annette became the first Classic winner bred by a member of the royal family, winning the Epsom Oaks in 1787, and George followed this with a Derby win with Sir Thomas the following year. Previous wins could also justify a purchase; Saltram was acquired in 1785, two years after winning

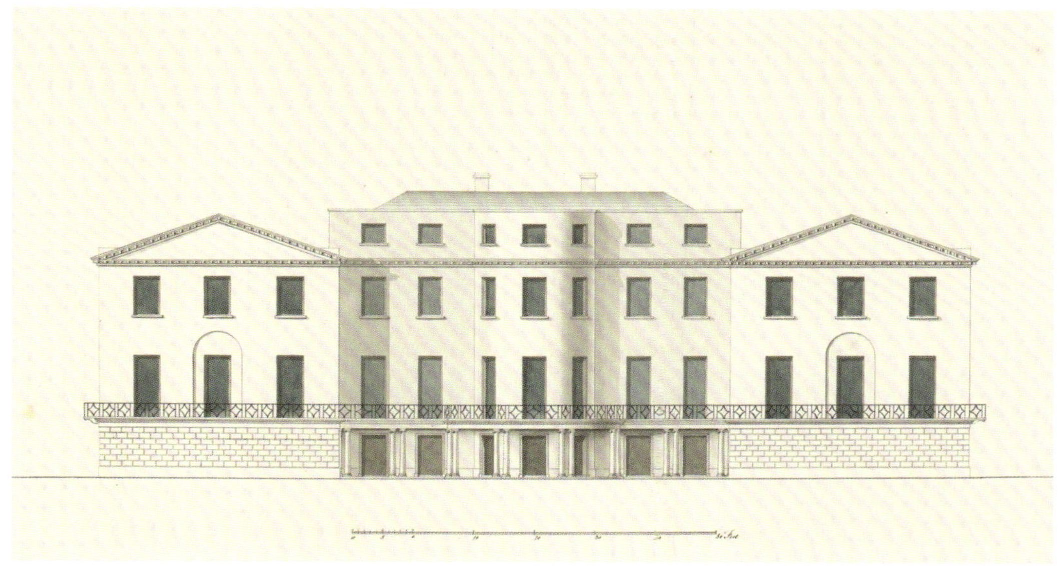

FIG. 13.2
HENRY HOLLAND (1745–1806), *Kempshott. April 1795. Elevation of the principal front*, 1795. Pen and ink with wash over pencil, 39.0 × 69.8 cm (sheet), RCIN 929634

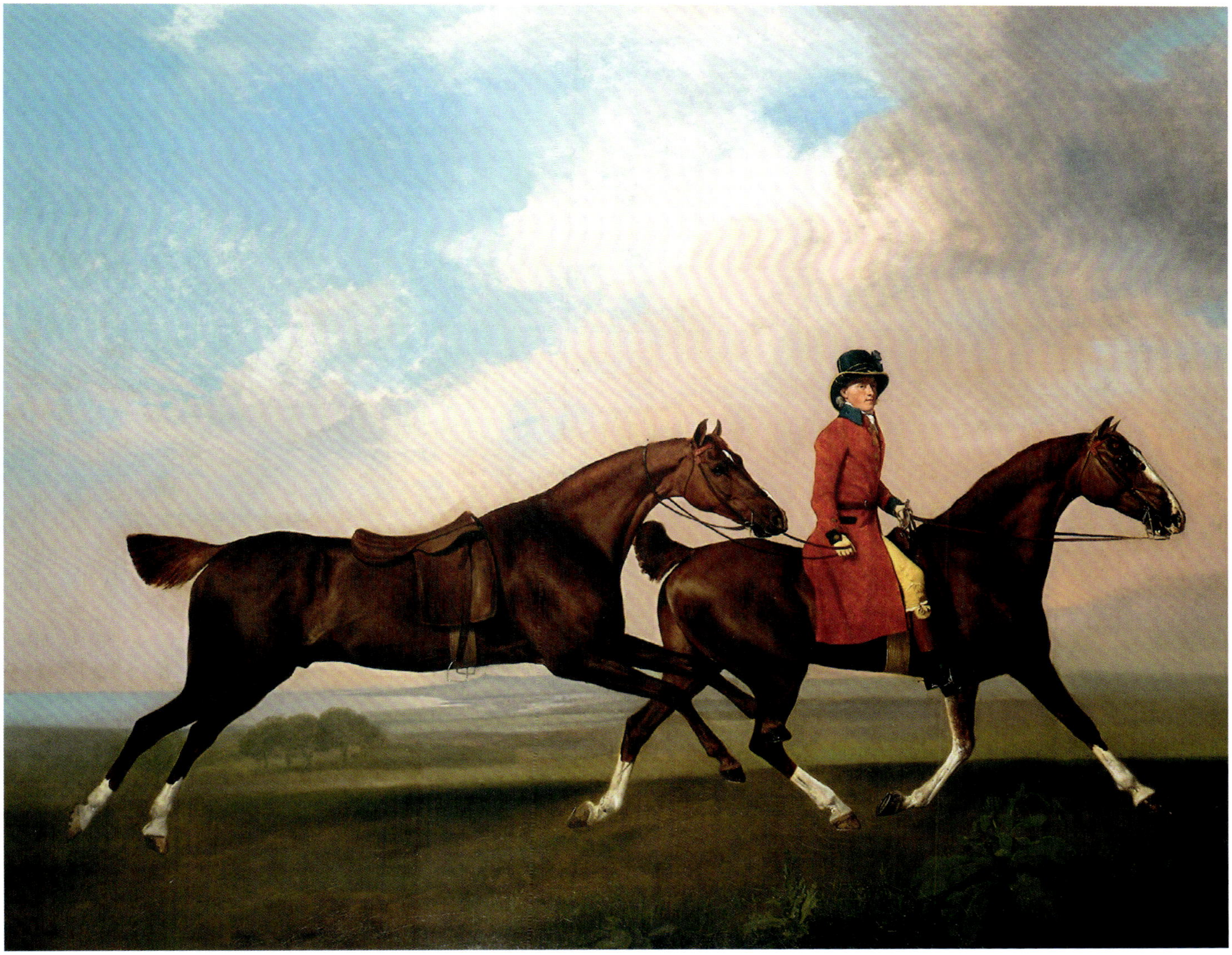

FIG. 13.3
GEORGE STUBBS (1724–1806), *William Anderson with Two Saddle-Horses*, 1793. Oil on canvas, 102.3 × 128.2 cm, RCIN 400106

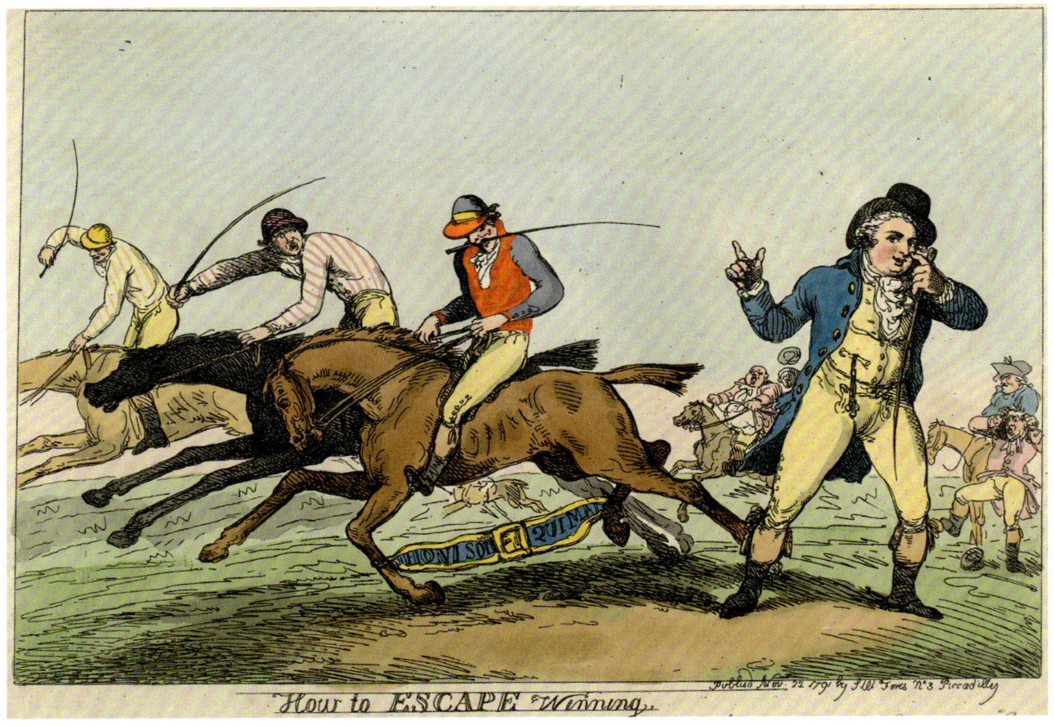

FIG. 13.4
THOMAS ROWLANDSON (1757–1827), *How to Escape Winning*, 1791. Etching with hand colouring, 27.2 × 39.7 cm, RCIN 810419

FIG. 13.5
MARK OF JOHN BRIDGE (1755–1834), *Lincoln Race Cup*, 1828/9. Silver gilt, 54.7 × 26.7 × 22.0 cm, RCIN 50269

the Derby for his previous owner. Occasionally the prince also sold horses; Mufti was sold to the Hon. Richard Vernon in the summer of 1786 and went on to win 14 races in the next six years. At the same time Rockingham sold for 800 guineas to the brewer Thomas Bullock, half the sum the horse was probably worth. The 1786 sales were part of the first complete dispersal of the prince's stud due to financial difficulties; one of the yearlings sold without yet having been named or raced was purchased by Mr Franco and developed a trick of opening his stable door. Named Escape by his new owner, he was later bought back by George and won four of his five starts.

After his reacquisition, Escape became part of an eponymous and notorious scandal, satirised by Thomas Rowlandson in a pair of prints, *How to Escape Winning* (Fig. 13.4) and *How to Escape Losing*. During the 1791 Newmarket meeting, Escape, ridden by the prince's favourite jockey Samuel Chifney, came fourth in his first race. The next day Escape won, and it was felt that the horse had been held back in the first race to skew the betting on the second. Chifney had won many races for the prince prior to this date, and had even been presented with a second version of George Stubbs's *Baronet with Samuel Chifney Up*; the original acquired by the prince remains in the Royal Collection.[11] The Escape scandal ended Chifney's career, but the prince presented him with an annual pension of £200. George never attended another Newmarket meeting although he continued to send his horses to race there. This was not his only involvement in shady practice: when his estate was tied up, his executors, the Duke of Wellington and Sir William Knighton, paid one 'Ruff' one hundred pounds, the outstanding amount 'in furnishing early racing intelligence, being in full of all demands'.[12]

In 1796 the prince made a second comeback with a re-established stud that he maintained for the rest of his life, increasing its breeding programme and purchasing young horses for further training. During this time his winnings became significant; the Brighton Pavilion Stakes of 1803 came with 1,900 guineas prize money, 200 guineas more than the Derby. The Brighton sum was no doubt boosted by the large crowds flocking to the seaside town to be in proximity to the prince and his circle.[13] As Prince Regent he owned the three best long-distance horses of his generation, Zinganee, The Colonel and Fleur de Lys, and in the first seven years of the nineteenth century his horses won over one hundred races and over 10,000 guineas of prize money. Fleur de Lys's win at Lincoln in 1829 was rewarded with a fine silver-gilt trophy presented by the Duke of St Albans (Fig. 13.5).[14] The duke was Hereditary Grand Falconer; thus the cup features a hooded falcon as its finial, and around the neck are naturalistically depicted horses chased in low relief, providing a marked contrast to the smooth gilded surface. The low relief echoes antique carved friezes of horses, such as those from the Parthenon which had arrived in London in the previous

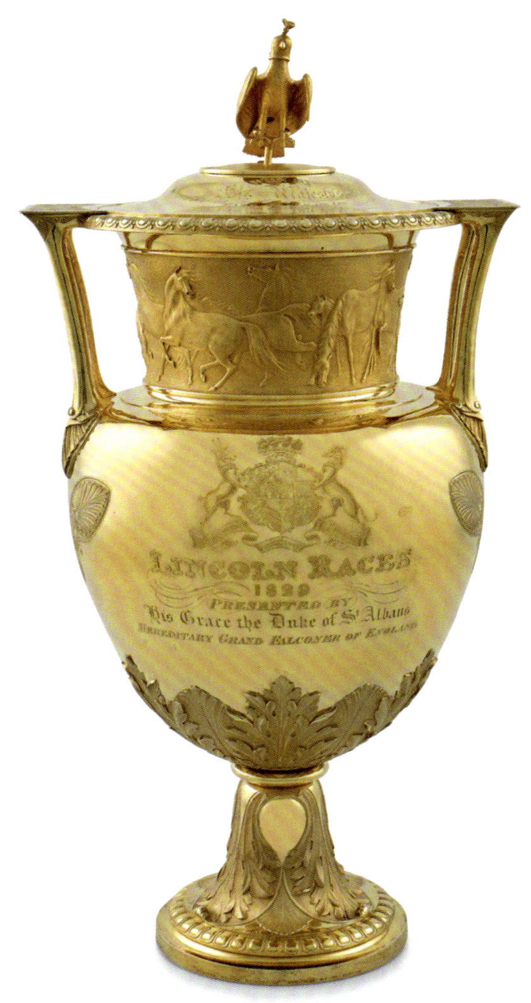

decade. Another win by Fleur de Lys the same year at Goodwood brought the prince an even larger silver-gilt trophy, the 1829 Goodwood Cup. Around its neck are depictions of a chariot race, probably inspired by ancient Roman prototypes.

George would frequently provide trophies for races, among them the 1805 Brighton Cup, which he purchased from Rundells. When his own horse Orville won the race, he presented the cup to Orville's previous owner, Christopher Wilson of Tadcaster. As with the prince's other sporting trophies, the Brighton Cup was a particular commission, 'An elegant rich chased cup and cover for Brighton races with device of the Pavillion [*sic*] chased out on one side and antique race the reverse, and His Royal Highness's crest on the top'.[15] In 1821 George visited Ireland as newly crowned King and attended racing at the Curragh. He was entertained in the new stand and presented a trophy as the prize for the Royal Whip Stakes.

> He addressed Mr. Prendergast in the Royal Room, and presented him with a whip (for a Jockey) to be run for and challenged every year, and to be hung up in the Club-room the week before the race — The whip is of the most elegant workmanship, and is ornamented in the most tasteful and costly manner; the Handle is of solid Gold, surmounted by a Gold Crown; all the other ornaments are likewise of pure Gold.[16]

Although George missed the end of the racing due to indigestion, he subscribed to the Irish Racing Calendar for the rest of his life.[17]

In 1814 Generals Blücher and Platov, the King of Prussia and the Emperor of Russia visited the races at Ascot. To please the crowds, Blücher, the Duke of York and Mr Warwick Lake, Clerk of the Stud, rode down the temporary booths to show themselves to the crowd. In 1825 George initiated the first royal carriage procession at Ascot:

> Contrary to his former practice, he drove up the Course to his stand, in the presence of everybody – himself in the first coach and four, the Duke of Wellington sitting by his side. There were three other carriages and four, and a phaeton after him, and I sh'd think 20 servants in scarlet on horseback, and as all his horses are of the greatest beauty, the whole thing looked very splendid; in short, quite as it should be.[18]

The royal box was directly opposite the finishing post; several redesigns of it were suggested during the prince's lifetime, including one by Thomas Sandby.[19] The final design was created by John Nash.

The prince regularly commissioned portraits of some of his favourite horses, and those of his friends and racing rivals, often to hang in groups. Notable among these are three paintings by James Ward from the early 1820s, depicting his riding horse Nonpareil and the stallions Soothsayer and Monitor (Figs 13.6 and 13.7). Ward recorded the circumstances of the commission in a letter to Sir William Knighton of *c.*1824: 'His Majesty directing my attention to some of the most beautiful Horses and some of which I was led to suppose it would be pleasing to His Majesty to see painted, and afterwards, upon Mr Wyatt accosting me the King observed "go into the stable and see what a beautiful

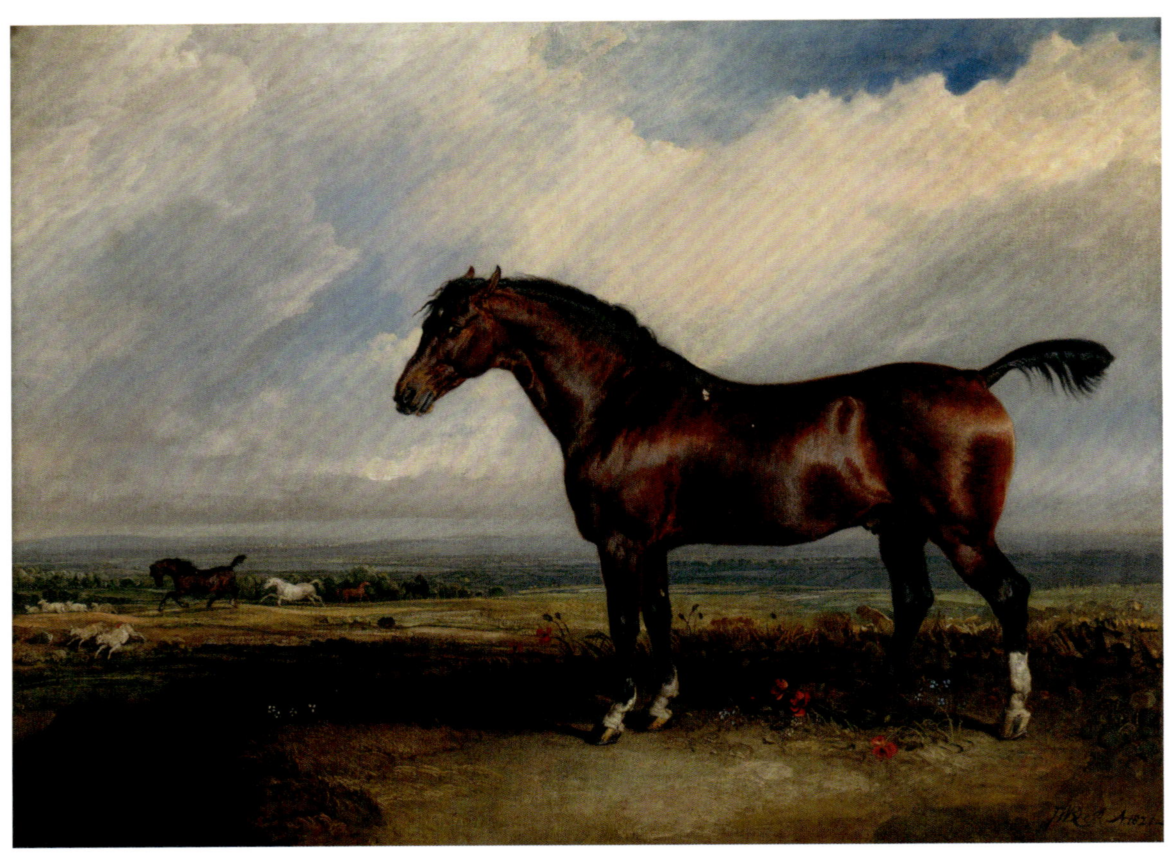

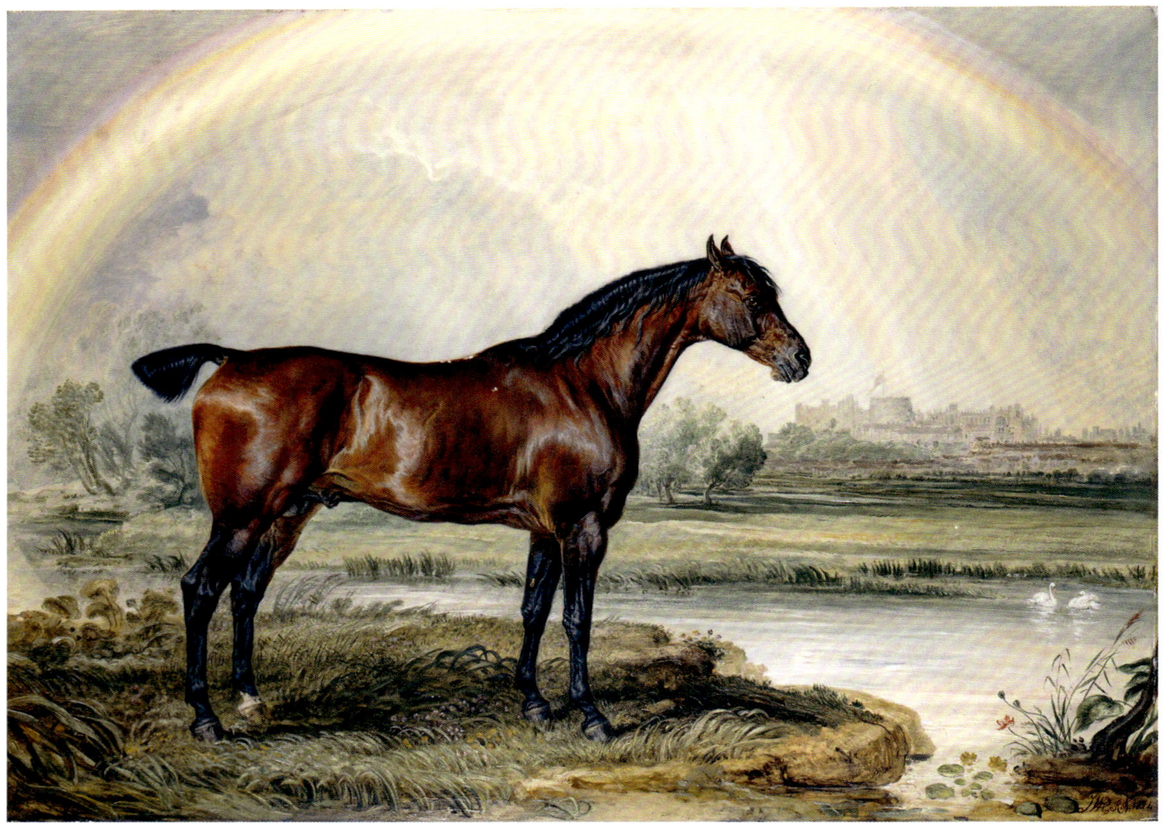

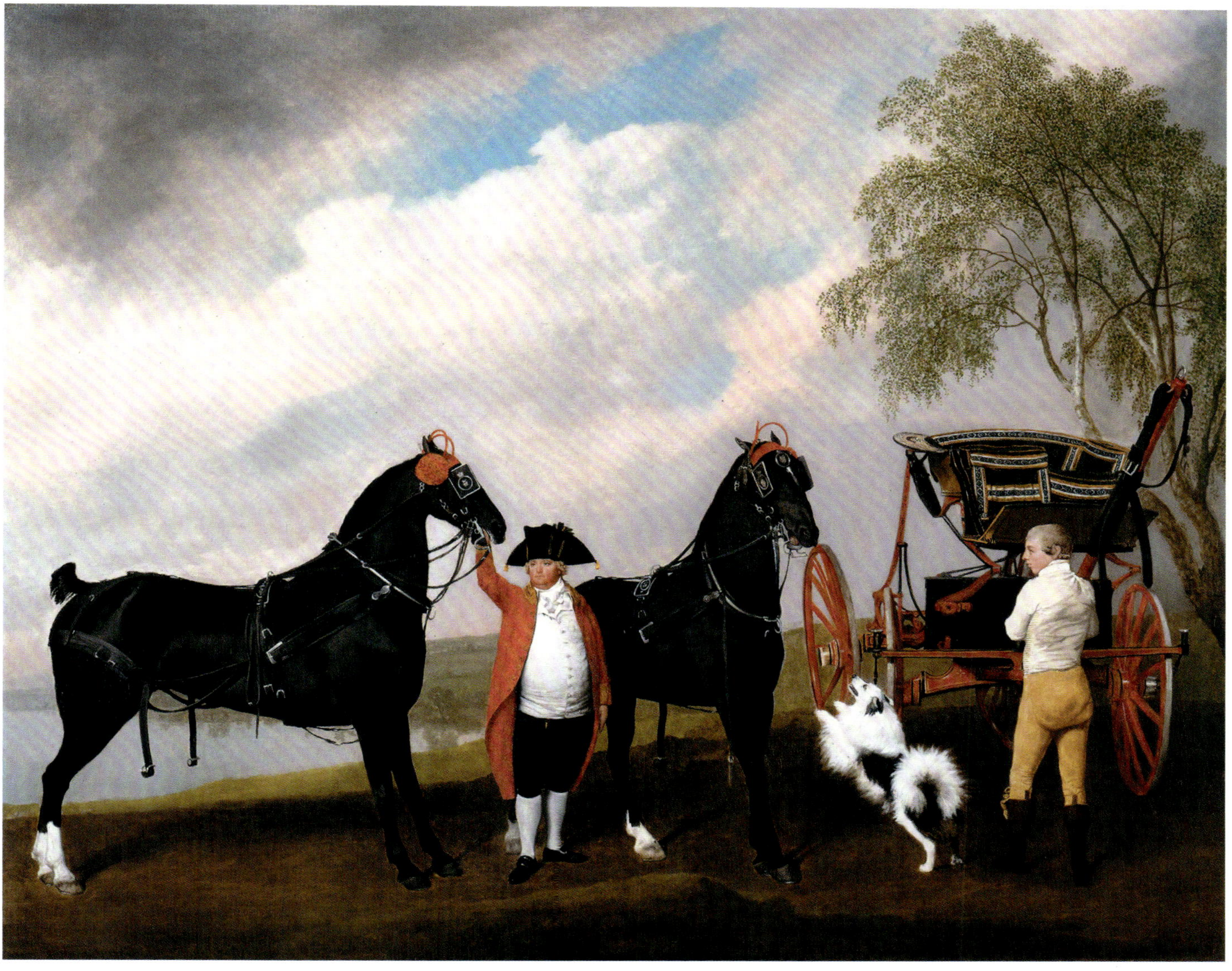

FIG. 13.6
JAMES WARD (1769–1859), *Monitor*, 1821. Oil on panel, 81.5 × 110.6 cm, RCIN 405017

FIG. 13.7
JAMES WARD (1769–1859), *Nonpareil*, 1824. Oil on canvas, 80.2 × 111.4 cm, RCIN 405018

FIG. 13.8
GEORGE STUBBS (1724–1806), *The Prince of Wales's Phaeton*, 1793. Oil on canvas, 102.0 × 128.1 cm, RCIN 400994

picture Mr Ward is painting for me".'[20] George clearly chose which subjects he wanted painted, his interest extending beyond his own stud: Ward later noted that George 'inquired after Soothsayer and Monitor' and described his work to complete the painting of Nonpareil: 'His Majesty's picture of his favourite Charger'.[21] By 1822, all but one of the canvases by George Stubbs either directly commissioned or acquired by the prince were hung at Royal Lodge in the Great Park at Windsor while the castle was undergoing significant alterations.[22] In 1825, John Wilson Croker described how, after a dinner at the lodge, George 'talked the rest of the evening chiefly in the character of a country gentleman about horses & hounds; & the pictures & books about the house are generally chosen with reference to those topics'.[23]

Beyond horses for racing and hunting, George also kept teams for driving. Towards the end of the eighteenth century smaller, lighter, often two-wheeled carriages which had previously been seen on the continent, including the curricle and the phaeton, appeared on British roads. The phaeton in particular was then overdeveloped into two types of taller, more suspended vehicle, the high-perch and crane-neck phaeton. Generally called highflyers, a term also used to identify the

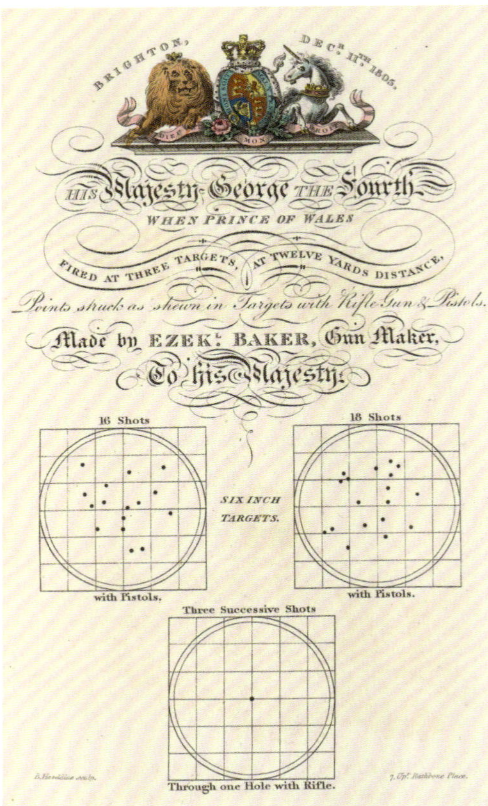

FIG. 13.9
EZEKIEL BAKER (1758–1836), *Remarks on Rifle Guns*, 1821. Printed book, 22.2 × 14.0 cm, RCIN 1080926

young, usually male drivers, they were difficult to drive and easy to overturn. The prince acquired a high-perch phaeton in 1792 through his friend, the skilled driver Sir John Lade, writing to him on its receipt, 'I am very impatient to have my Phaeton out'.[24] The prince's phaeton was driven usually with a team of blacks, such as those shown in a painting by Stubbs commissioned shortly after the carriage was acquired. This shows the carriage beautifully articulated to display its suspension, the best visual record of a high-perch in existence, and its unusual viewpoint must have been chosen deliberately (Fig. 13.8).

These new smaller carriages disposed of the requirement to have a coachman; a gentleman could drive himself, perhaps with a single passenger. Indeed, sometimes the prince's friends would act the part of servants; on one occasion 'the Prince's German waggon and six bay horses; the coachman on the box being replaced by Sir John Lade – issued out of the gates of the Pavilion'.[25] The prince once overturned his high-perch phaeton while Maria Fitzherbert was a passenger, an accident which occasioned a number of satires, one referring to the Fall of Phaeton of Classical Greek myth, and the others scurrilously suggestive. In his later years the prince reduced the high suspensions of the carriages of his youth and used a low pony phaeton to transport himself around the park at Windsor. Still known as a George IV Phaeton, such a vehicle was used by George to visit his menagerie at Sandpit Gate or travel between the castle, Royal Lodge and the Fishing Temple, where he could pursue the slower, more leisurely sporting activities of his later years.

Shooting

The prince often shot, generally at the same estates where he hunted. George was a skilled marksman with pistols or a rifle, as recorded in the frontispiece of the gunsmith Ezekiel Baker's *Remarks on Rifle Guns*, published in 1821 (Fig. 13.9). Baker assisted the prince throughout his life with gun sighting and designed a special carbine for the prince's regiment, the 10th Light Dragoons.[26] As with most aspects of his collecting George acquired a wide range of guns, irrespective of their potential use and some clearly only for decorative purposes. The leading London gunmaker and dealer Durs Egg was the major supplier; in one 1790 transaction the prince acquired a German rifle, a Turkish gun, a pair of Madrid pistols, a pair of Italian seventeenth-century pistols and a pair of pistols by Lewis Barbar decorated in gold and silver.[27] Many of these acquisitions were first displayed in his Armoury at Carlton House (see Fig. 18.4) and later at Windsor Castle, the latter arranged with the assistance of Baker. The prince also maintained an interest in new sporting literature, subscribing to W.B. Daniel's *Rural Sports*, the first volumes in 1801 and 1802 covering hunting, shooting and stalking, and the third in 1813 covering fishing.[28] Subscriptions to the 1807 publication by Thomas Williamson and Samuel Howitt, *Oriental Field Sports*, reflect both his interest in the wider world, and the sports enjoyed in those countries which he would never be able to visit but about which his friends and acquaintances could speak, including tiger, buffalo, leopard and peacock hunting. Many of these publications were supplied directly by publisher Edward Orme, who also sold the prince Samuel Howitt's *British Sportsman* and subscriptions to *British Field Sports* and *Foreign Field Sports*.[29]

As with racing, George presented trophies to shooting clubs where he was a member. The Red House Pigeon Club at Battersea was established in 1805, and is shown in Samuel

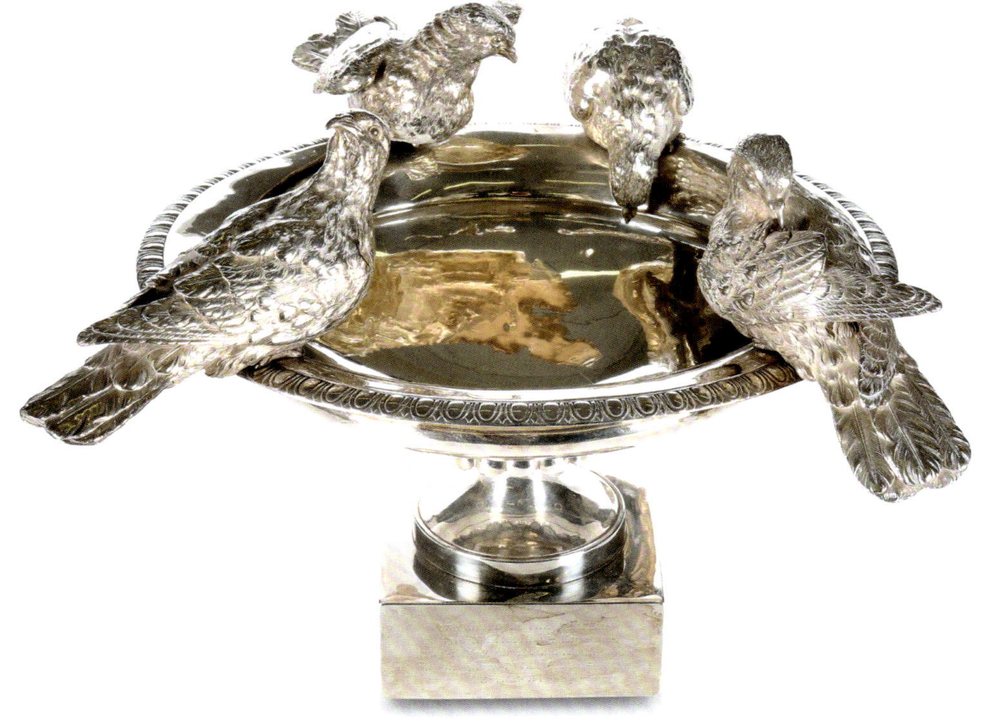

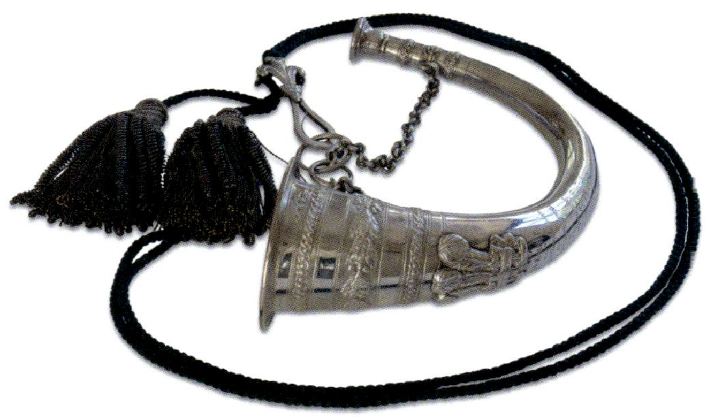

FIG. 13.10
PAUL STORR (1771–1844), *The Red House Pigeon Club Trophy*, 1828. Silver, 20.0 × 30.0 cm (diameter) (The Light Dragoons)

FIG. 13.11
WILLIAM FRISBEE (active 1782–1820), *The Crunden Bugle*, 1796. Silver, 21.9 × 12.7 cm (private collection)

Leigh's 1829 *Panorama of the Thames* and in an engraving by Henry Alken published in 1828. In that year George, now King, presented the club with a large silver bowl with pigeons perching on its edge (Fig. 13.10). The bowl, which was probably intended for use at dinners, was hallmarked by Paul Storr and therefore no doubt supplied through the royal goldsmiths Rundell, Bridge & Rundell, although it appears the bill for it does not survive. Storr was clearly looking to Classical precedents for the design, which brings to three-dimensional life the mosaic uncovered in Hadrian's Villa in Rome in 1737 of doves drinking from a fountain.

Archery

From the late 1780s the increased threat from France led to the re-formation of local militia, raised by the gentry, initially without formal uniforms or arms. Alongside this, and in reaction to the contemporary interest in medieval England, the sport of archery with the longbow was reintroduced.[30] George was a keen archer and was instrumental in introducing the competition rules for shooting over distances of 60, 80 or 100 yards, lengths still used at competition and known as Prince's lengths. His interest in archery remained even after his health made it unlikely he was still shooting. In 1826 a bill from Thomas Waring, the archer and archery equipment supplier, for over £60 worth of equipment, including ladies' sashes and arm guards, as well as targets, suggests he was still enjoying the sport through his friends' participation.[31]

In April 1787 the first meeting of the British Bowmen was held, and the following year they added the prefix 'Royal' in recognition of George's patronage. At Wynnstay, one of the main houses to host meetings, the dining room featured a painting of a Druid carving the words 'RBB, 1787 and HRH George Prince of Wales, Patron' onto a tree, alongside two other figures symbolising the president and the lady patroness. The prince presented a bugle to the club in 1790, which was won by one

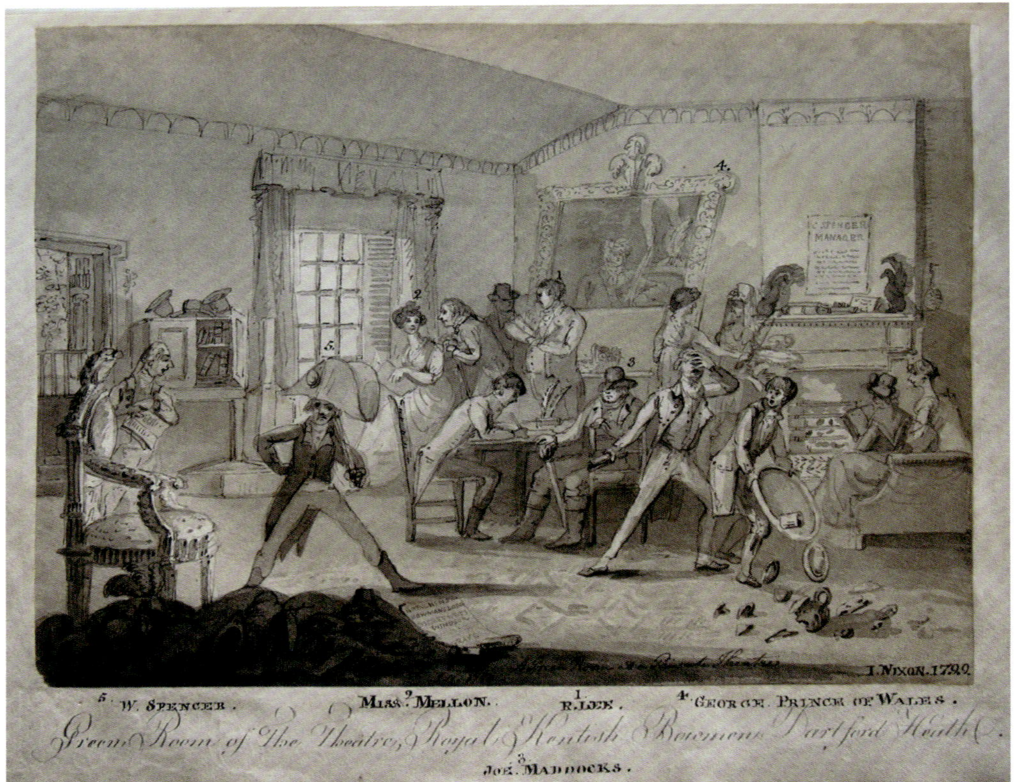

FIG. 13.12
JOHN COLLEY NIXON (*c.*1755–1818), *Green Room of the Theatre, Royal Kentish Bowmen*, 1799. Pen and ink with wash, 16.7 × 22.1 cm (The Garrick Club Collection)

Robert Hesketh shooting at 63, 96 and 128 yards. George was also a member of the Royal Kentish Bowmen, established in 1785, who met on Dartford Heath; the uniform rules and the scores for the target, established by George himself, feature in the Bowmen's rule book.[32] Members included men from the Hussey family of Scotney Castle in Kent where one of the annual prizes presented by the prince, a silver bugle won by Edward Hussey in 1794, survives. One of the other members, the Bowmen's laureate the Revd James William Dodd, won the bugle on 9 July 1792 when it was personally awarded by the prince.[33] George owned a copy of Dodd's *Ballads of Archery*, published in 1818.[34]

The prince was patron of the Royal Toxophilite Society, formed in London in 1781. One of a series of ten silver bugles presented by him to the society as an annual prize survives; its green and silver thread tassels and oak-leaf relief are very similar to those on the bugle surviving at Scotney Castle (Fig. 13.11). In 1821, the Society's minutes recorded a motion 'That the Secretary should draw up an address to His Majesty to request that he will continue his favour to the Society as King which he had before shown as Prince of Wales.'[35]

George's patronage of archery was not only marked through the commissioning of prizes. One of the most striking and attractive portraits of the prince in his youth is that which

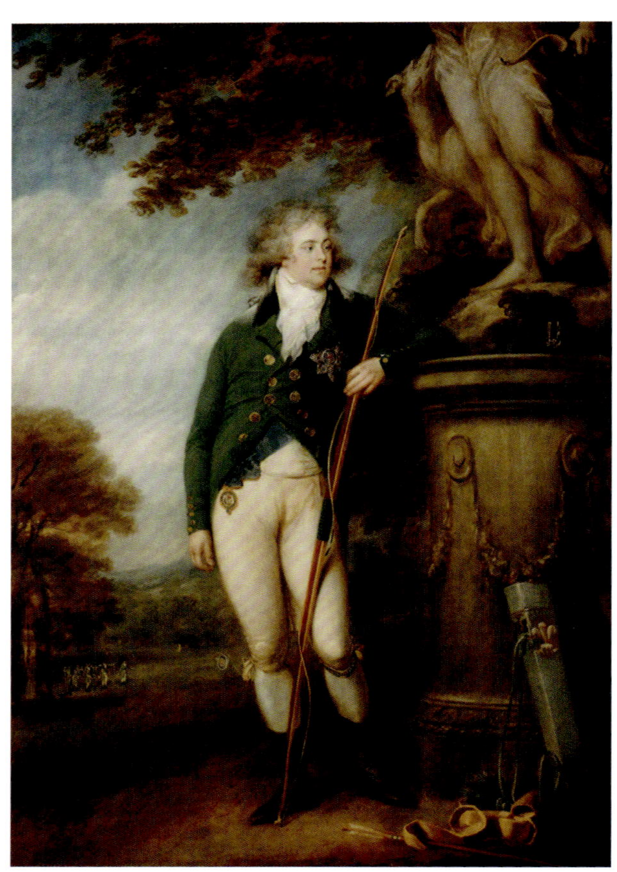

FIG. 13.13
JOHN RUSSELL (1745–1806), *George IV when Prince of Wales*, 1791. Oil on canvas, 250.2 × 180.3 cm, RCIN 405414

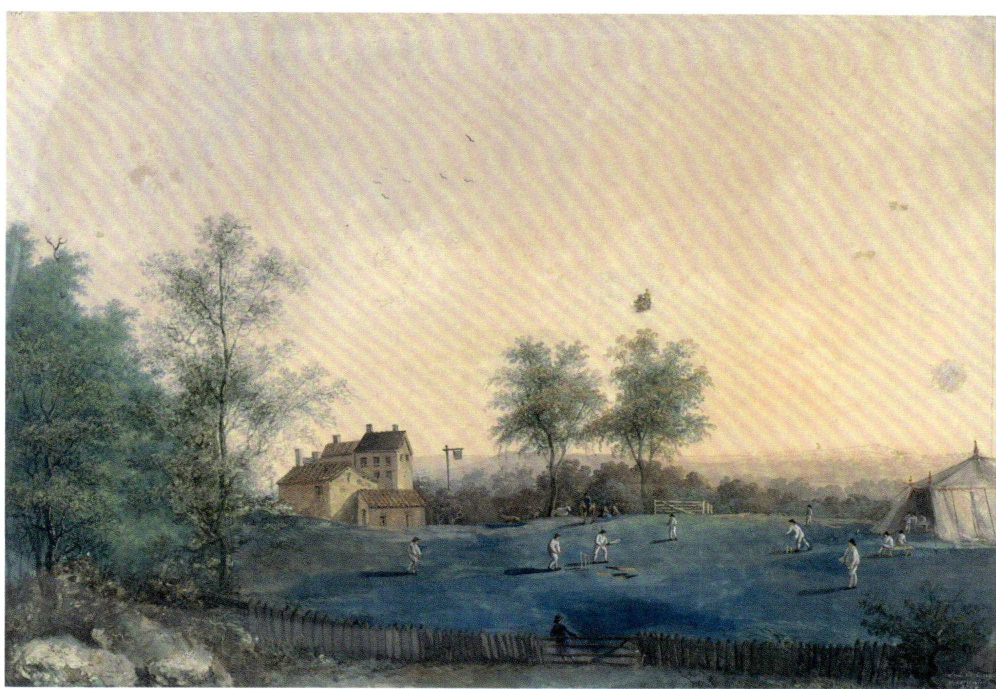

FIG. 13.14
LOUIS BÉLANGER (1736–1816), *A Cricket Match*, 1798. Bodycolour, 40.0 × 55.3 cm, RCIN 913224

he presented to hang in 'the upper room for the ladies' at the Bowmen's Lodge.[36] This was painted by John Russell in 1791 and depicts the prince in the grass-green and buff uniform of the Royal Kentish Bowmen, with a club arrow, identifiable by the colours on its shaft, lying at his feet (see Fig. 13.13). The prince's jacket bears two rows of gold buttons, as retailed by Nuttings of Covent Garden, which feature the 'RKB' initials. The yew longbow beside him shows clearly its red heartwood and white sapwood and the quiver is decorated with the Prince of Wales feathers. Russell must have had access to the uniform, although possibly not on this occasion to the prince himself, as the pose of the head is very similar to a pastel of him executed by Russell in 1790.[37] Russell's charge of £73 10s for a portrait 'as president of the Royal Kentish Bowmen in Oil whole length superior' is featured on the same bill as a pastel of Mrs Fitzherbert costing £26 5s.[38] The prince's portrait was exhibited at the Royal Academy in 1792; thereafter, the Russell portrait was hung in the first-floor room at the lodge, although a sketch of post-archery theatricals in 1799 suggests it was too tall for the room and may have been propped against the wall (Fig. 13.12). The portrait ensured the prince's presence in the club house even when he could not attend in person. It depicted him in an appropriate sporting ensemble and landscape; essentially, as a private individual, albeit one with a Garter star pinned to his jacket. An engraving after the portrait was published in 1795 with a dedication to the Bowmen.

Cricket

Although not as active a fan, or player, of the game of cricket as his brother the Duke of York, as a young man George both played in and watched matches at Brighton. The Brighton team was created as a direct result of the prince's presence there and was occasionally referred to in contemporary newspapers as 'His Royal Highness's the Prince of Wales's Brighton Club', although formal royal patronage does not appear to have been conferred. The sport in Brighton formed part of the overall entertainment available in the town, and one which women might also attend. Maria Fitzherbert was a regular spectator, and dined in Marylebone Cricket Club's marquee during one of their away games in Brighton.[39] Such a temporary structure can be seen in a watercolour by Louis Bélanger purchased by the prince on 16 April 1800, showing a match outside a public house (Fig. 13.14).[40] As King, George's interest in cricket continued. He permitted the Gentlemen of Berkshire to play the Gentlemen of Kent in the park at Windsor: 'the wickets were pitched in a fine open part of the Great Park between the Long Walk and Queen Anne's Ride and the ground, having been levelled and rolled, was in most excellent order.' A cold collation was offered for supper in marquees beside the pitch 'to which His Majesty had been graciously pleased to contribute an uncommonly fine buck'.[41]

Cricket pitches themselves had a variety of uses. In 1802 the prince was present at Lord's Cricket Ground in Marylebone

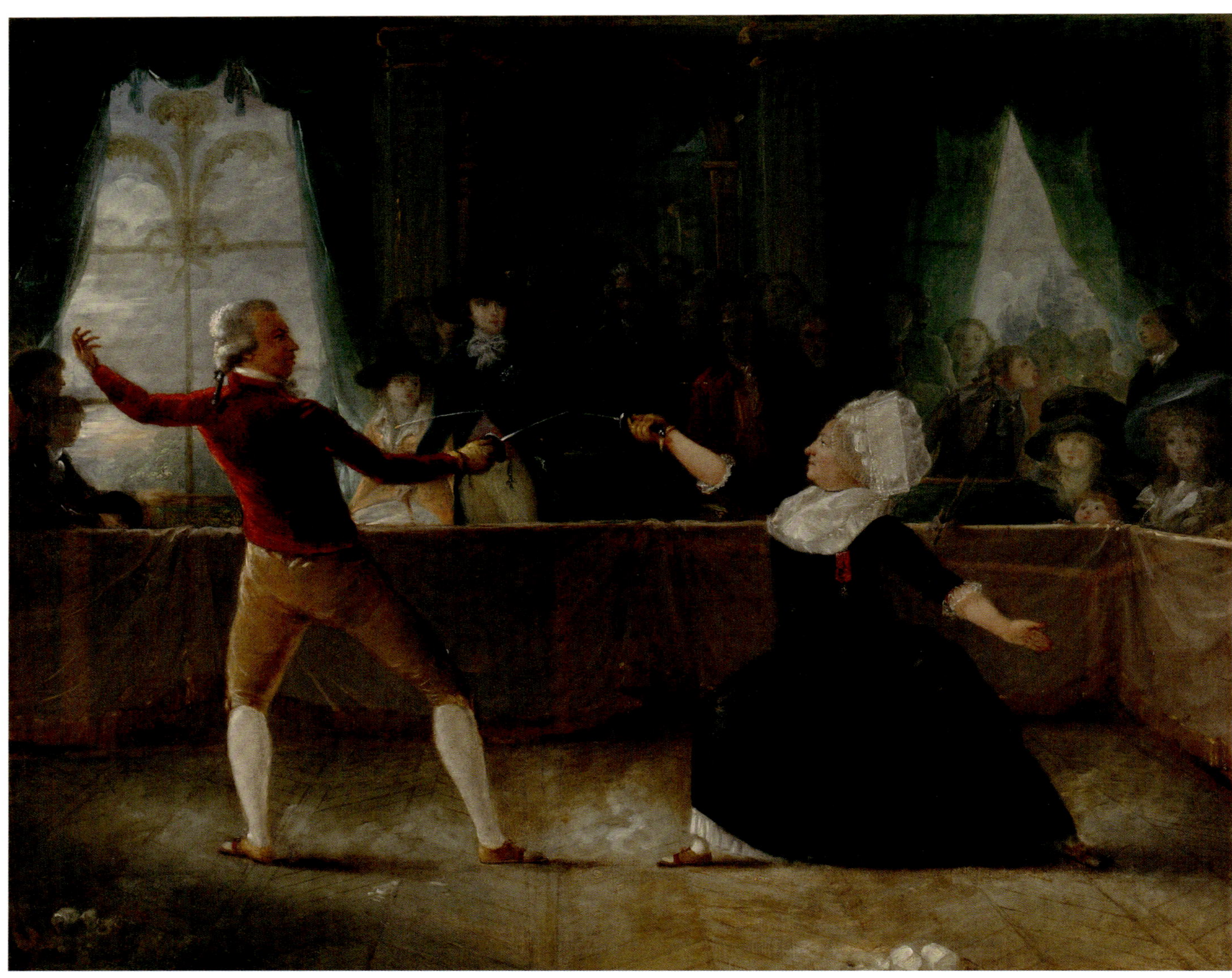

FIG. 13.15
ALEXANDRE-AUGUSTE ROBINEAU (1747–1828), *The Fencing-Match between the Chevalier de Saint-Georges (1745–99) and the Chevalier d'Eon (1728–1810)*, c.1787–9. Oil on canvas, 64.1 × 75.8 cm, RCIN 400636

to watch a balloon ascent by the French pilot André-Jacques Garnerin.[42] The Royal Kentish Bowmen's butts on Dartford Heath were also occasionally used for cricket. In 1805 Kent played Bexley there, for a prize of 500 guineas.[43] Matches had been played on Dartford Heath since before the Bowmen's existence, but the connection was undoubtedly encouraged by the fact that several of the Bowmen were also enthusiastic cricketers, including the 3rd Duke of Dorset, the 9th Earl of Winchilsea, Sir Horatio Mann and the brothers John Bligh, 4th Earl of Darnley and the Hon. Edward Bligh.[44]

Fencing

As with archery, contemporary events contributed to the reinvigoration of fencing as a gentlemanly, chivalric pursuit in the late eighteenth century. George learned the art, as did his friends Charles James Fox and Richard Brinsley Sheridan. George also enjoyed watching matches: in 1787 two fencers, the Chevalier d'Eon and the Chevalier de Saint-Georges, were invited to fence at Carlton House. Both were celebrities: the French diplomat d'Eon lived in London as a woman, remaining a competitive fencer throughout her time in the city; Saint-Georges was a mixed-race man from Guadaloupe.[45] A painting recording the bout was commissioned by George from Alexandre-Auguste Robineau (Fig. 13.15). This was later engraved by Victor-Marie Picot, perhaps on George's own initiative.[46] The prince also

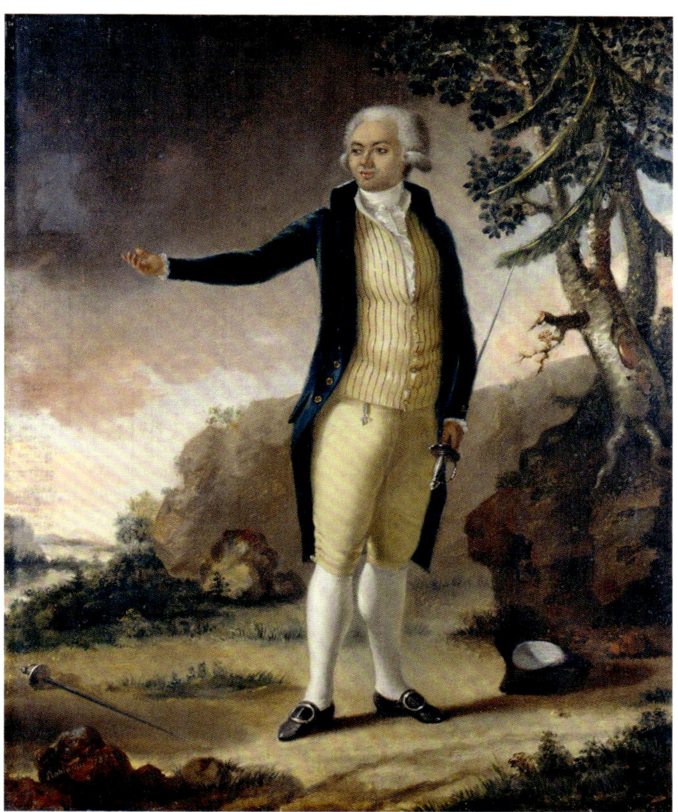

FIG. 13.16
ALEXANDRE-AUGUSTE ROBINEAU (1747–1828), *The Chevalier de Saint-Georges*, 1787. Oil on canvas, 62.0 × 51.2 cm, RCIN 404358

joined in one bout with Saint-Georges,[47] and a portrait by Robineau in the Royal Collection of the fencer ready for his next match, although rather smartly dressed, must have been commissioned at this time (Fig. 13.16).

Boxing

During George's youth he was an avid boxing spectator. As with cricket, and occasionally racing, this was a sport which he could watch on the downs north of Brighton after he acquired his home there in 1786. The rules were minimal and matches could last for hours.[48] Boxing was not officially condoned and the local militia smashed the boxing ring on the orders of the magistrate when Tom Tring, George's chairman from Carlton House, who weighed 15 stone (95 kg) and stood 6 feet 2 inches (1.9 metres) tall, was due to box Sam 'the Bath Butcher' Martin at Shepherd's Bush in 1786. The prince, along with his brother the Duke of York and the duc d'Orléans, had a more successful experience at Newmarket when they watched Richard Humphries spar with the 'Butcher' the same year. Admission was one guinea, but between thirty and forty thousand pounds was bet on the match, which the 'Butcher' won. In 1787 while at Barnet to watch racing, the prince was a spectator at a match between Daniel Mendoza and the 'Butcher'. Mendoza was presented to George, who awarded his £500 prize money, and in his memoirs Mendoza claimed to be the first Jew to meet the 25-year-old prince.[49] Thirteen years later the prince would acquire a print of Mendoza sparring against Humphries, and even later a print of Humphries after his portrait by Hoppner. Impressions of both survive in the Royal Collection although neither can be firmly connected with George's collection (Fig. 13.17).[50] The prince's brief enthusiasm for attending boxing matches ended on 6 August 1789 when he witnessed the fight between Tom 'the Tailor' Tyne and George Earl: the latter died from his injuries. The prince presented Earl's widow with a pension and never watched a match again; whether this was due to diplomatic advice or his own sensibilities is unclear.[51] However, George did not forget his generation of boxers. Concerned his estranged wife or her supporters might try to force their way in to his

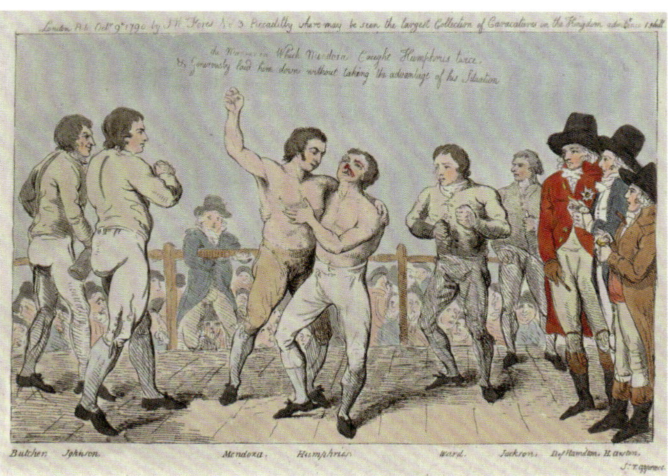

FIG. 13.17
Published by S.W. FORES (1761–1838), *The Manner in which Mendoza Caught Humphries twice*, 1790. Etching with hand colouring, 27.9 × 38.0 cm (sheet), RCIN 658760

coronation banquet, he employed John 'Gentleman' Jackson and 19 other former pugilists as pages to guard the doors.[52] Jackson, Tom Cribb and Tom Spring were employed outside the hall, and Lord Gwydyr, the Deputy Lord Great Chamberlain, presented the group with a gold coronation medal which was raffled and won by Harry Belcher.[53]

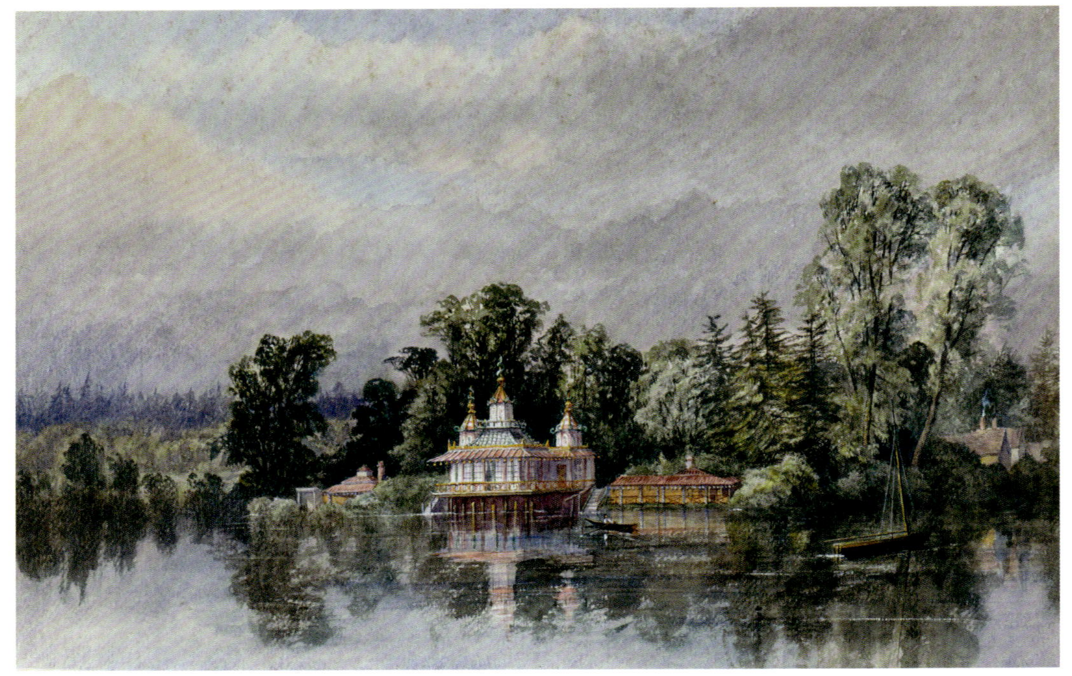

FIG. 13.18
BRITISH SCHOOL, *The Fishing Temple at Virginia Water*, before 1867. Watercolour with scraping out, 35.8 × 64.0 cm, RCIN 918355

FIG. 13.19
CHARLES WILLIAMS (1796–1830), *A King-Fisher*, 1826. Etching with hand colouring, 25.0 × 35.0 cm (sheet), RCIN 630791

FIG. 13.20
MARIA USTONSON (1784–after 1841), *George IV's fishing tackle*, 1824. Wood, brass, leather, velvet, silk, metal, bone, feathers; box: 90.0 × 22.0 × 8.0 cm, RCIN 11911

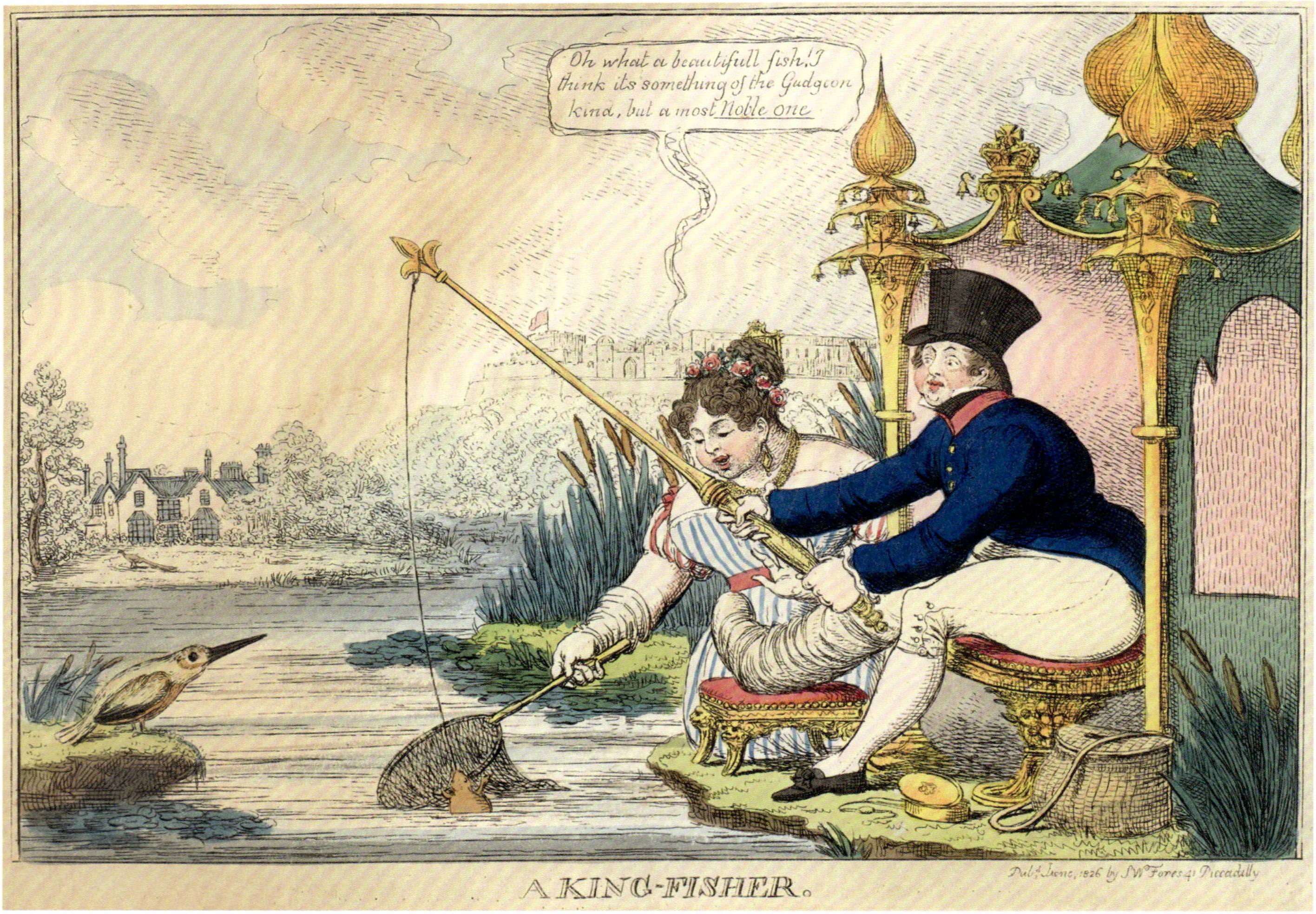

Oh what a beautifull fish! I think its something of the Gudgeon kind, but a most Noble one

A KING-FISHER.

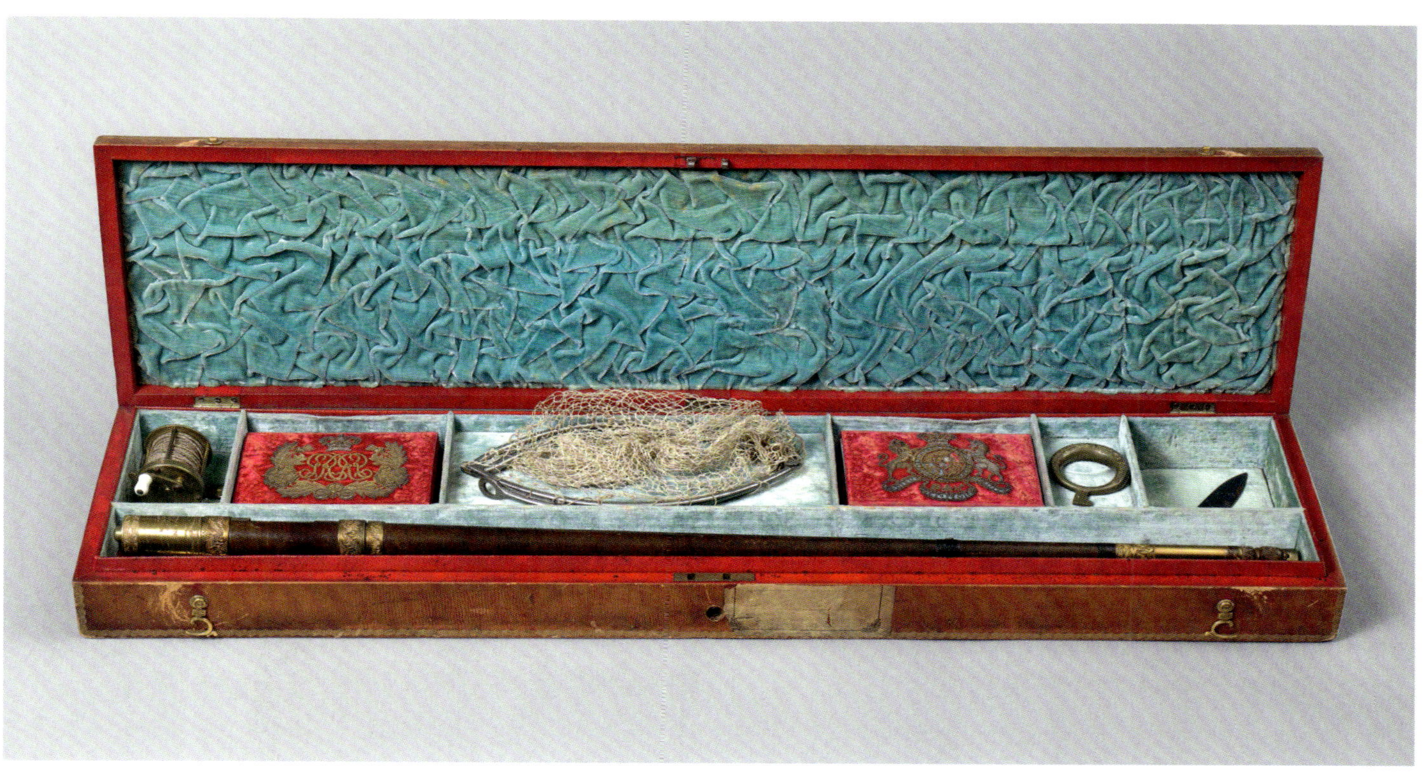

Fishing

In the final years of his life, George IV weighed over 20 stone (120 kg). Unable to ride, and only to drive out in his low pony phaeton, he began to enjoy angling, spending hours with small gatherings of friends at the chinoiserie Fishing Temple designed by his architect Jeffrey Wyatville and designer Frederick Crace on the edge of Virginia Water (Fig. 13.18). The Fishing Temple seems unlikely to have provided good casting positions, due to the overhanging architecture of the verandas. Instead, contemporary satires show George using a decorated barge for the actual pursuit of fish. The sight of the large king at Virginia Water, suffering periodically from gout, and often accompanied by Lady Conyngham, was an easy target for satirists. Some speculated that Lady Conyngham's ample proportions were the real quarry, and showed her caught on the king's hook. Others mocked the idea of a 'king-fisher', with Windsor Castle and Royal Lodge artistically moved a couple of miles to the shores of the Water to provide an obvious reference to George (Fig. 13.19).

The most remarkable sporting survivor from this late period is the king's fishing tackle (Fig. 13.20). It was retailed by Maria Ustonson at Temple Bar on the Strand. She first supplied the kit in 1824, and in 1828 it was returned to her for refurbishment. No doubt the Ustonson workshop made the reel, the rod and some of the specialist fishing equipment, but the skills involved in the working of the leather, velvet, silk and ivory, the metal-thread embroidery, fly-tying, net-making and ferrule-engraving must have involved the co-ordination of people far beyond the Ustonson business. The finished product was so extraordinary that Maria issued several hundred admission cards to her shop for viewing over a weekend in May 1828. The *Standard* described the tackle in detail, noting that 'The *tout ensemble* of the apparatus is the most beautiful specimen of the art that perhaps has been ever manufactured in this or in any other country.'[54] The king acquired a quantity of other fishing equipment for his new pastime; a bill for 1827–8 totals over £196 and includes live bait (wasps, cockchafers, grasshoppers, house flies and bluebottles), spinning minnow lures, and rods made from East India bamboo.[55]

George IV's sporting pursuits permeated every aspect of his private, and some of his public, life. They influenced his choice and promotion of staff, friends and acquaintances, and he commissioned and acquired the finest equipment, trophies and imagery to celebrate his involvement with the wide variety of sports available to a gentleman of his generation.

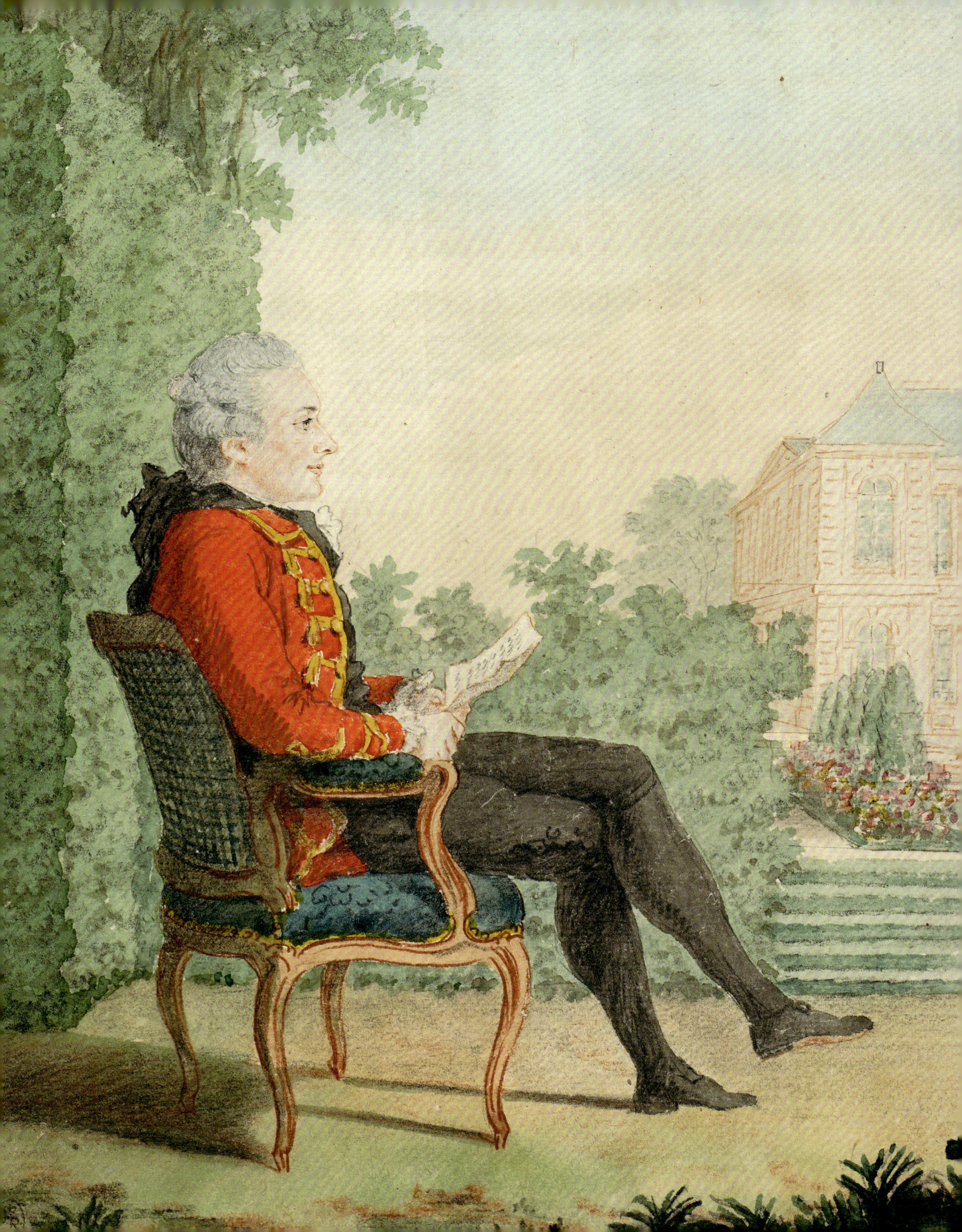

14

GEORGE IV'S INTELLECTUAL WORLD

EMMA STUART *and* KATE HEARD

IN 1789, THOMAS JEFFERSON gave a damning description of George IV's intellectual attainments, which takes the same tone as many assessments of that monarch's learning:

> As the character of the Prince of Wales is becoming interesting, I have endeavoured to learn what it truly is … My informant sat next him, and being till then unknown to the Prince, personally, … and lately from France, the Prince confined his conversation almost entirely to him. Observing to the Prince that he spoke French without the least foreign accent, the Prince told him that, when very young, his father had put only French servants about him, and that it was to that circumstance he owed his pronunciation. He led him from this to give an account of his education, the total of which was the learning a little Latin. He has not a single element of Mathematics, of natural or moral philosophy, or of any other science on earth; nor has the society he has kept been such as to supply the void of education. It has been that of the lowest, the most illiterate and profligate persons of the kingdom, without choice of rank or merit, and with whom the subjects of conversation are only horses, drinking-matches, bawdy houses, and in terms the most vulgar … In fact he never associated with a man of sense.[1]

George is often dismissed as a dissolute bore, naturally intelligent, but concerned mainly with 'horses, drinking-matches, bawdy houses' and with few intellectual instincts. Jefferson's letter is based on a first-hand account of a conversation with George, and one in which the prince seemed eager to stress his lack of learning. But George's account of his early years (probably intended more as a criticism of his upbringing than an admission of his lack of education) is belied by other evidence. In fact, George seems to have been a talented and well-read man who could discuss a wide variety of subjects with intelligence and wit, and who adapted his conversation to suit the interests of his companions: those who met him were usually extremely impressed by his learning.[2] Talking to Jefferson's Francophile contact over dinner, he played up his French credentials, but he

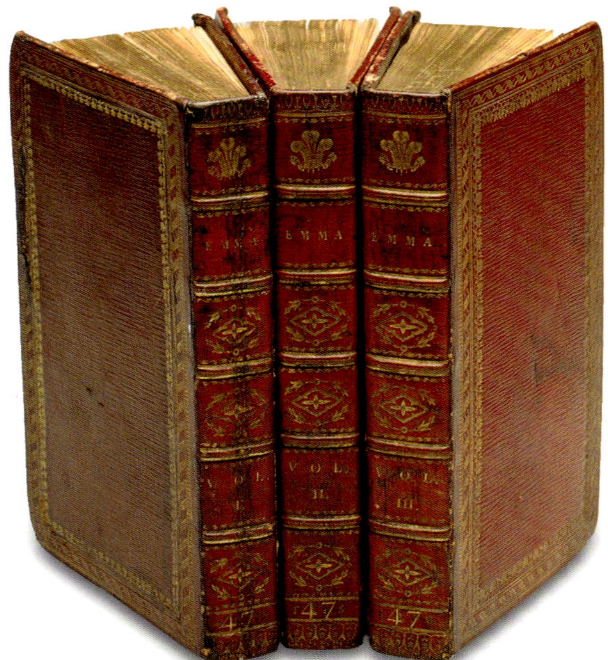

(p. 184)
Detail of Fig. 14.11, LOUIS CARROGIS DE CARMONTELLE (1717–1806), *Charles-Alexis Brûlart, comte de Genlis (1737–93)*, c.1765

FIG. 14.1
JANE AUSTEN (1775–1817), *Emma: a novel in three volumes*, 1816. Printed books, 18.3 × 11.1 cm, RCINs 1083626, 1080108, 1080109

could also turn his hand to the discussion of science and natural history, Classical and modern literature and European history. Through an assessment of his well-stocked library, the men he chose to surround him, and eyewitness accounts from those who met and conversed with him, this chapter seeks to explore the riches of George's intellectual world.

The Carlton House library

> The room is very conveniently fitted up with open book-cases, designed in the Gothic style, and partly gilt: the cornices are contrived to conceal spring rollers, which contain a fine collection of maps, that can be displayed for reference without inconvenience. The book-cases are surmounted by an ornamental parapet of embrasures, between which are introduced alternately the portcullis, the fleur de lys, and the rose. They contain a well-selected and valuable collection of books, handsomely bound, and arranged in classes under the direction of Dr. Stanier Clarke, librarian to his royal highness.
>
> The door-ways at each end of the library are concealed by imitative books and shelves, in correspondence with the cases, by which judicious contrivance the uniform effect of a library is continued without interruption.[3]

This is the most detailed existing description of the library in Carlton House, from W.H. Pyne's *Royal Residences*, but unfortunately the library was one of the few rooms that he did not illustrate.[4] Pyne was not alone in his reticence – Jane Austen famously was invited there before the publication of *Emma* (Fig. 14.1) – and its dedication to the Prince Regent – having been recognised in London by the prince's doctor, but that mistress of acute description and gentle satire did not write any detailed account of her visit.[5] Walter Scott was invited to use the library any time he was in town: 'the Prince Regent particularly wishes to see you whenever you come to London; and desires you will always, when you are there, come into his library whenever you please'.[6] While we have an account in J.G. Lockhart's *Memoirs of the Life of Sir Walter Scott* of a highly successful 'snug little dinner' in Carlton House, again, we have no description of the library.[7]

Carlton House itself no longer stands, but the ghosts of the library linger still in the Royal Collection: the remainder of George's book collection is now in the present Royal Library in Windsor Castle, where it was one of the foundation collections brought together by William IV in the 1830s. An early library furnishing scheme, distinguished by an ivory and ebony veneer (Fig. 14.2), still survives in the modern library and in St James's Palace. From these little snapshots, but more importantly, from the extensive documentation of George's purchases – bills, inventories, records of deliveries and so forth – we can begin to get a glimpse of a now-vanished apartment.

A library space appears to have been intended from the beginning of George's residence in Carlton House: an early plan from March 1784 by Henry Holland shows a library on the Lower Floor on the south side of the house, towards the west end, where it is described as unfinished.[8] Ten years later, in October 1794, a ground plan (again by Holland) shows the library situated in the bow-fronted room on the Attic Floor, next to the prince's bedroom suite.[9] Another Holland plan of the same date shows an additional or alternative library space at the north-east corner of the Principal Floor, facing Pall Mall (see Fig. 5.4).[10] Little wonder that Thomas Becket, the prince's chief bookseller at the time, complained that the library was not 'in a state of readiness' in 1787 for him to deposit books.[11] By 1806 the library had moved again, to the location described by Pyne,

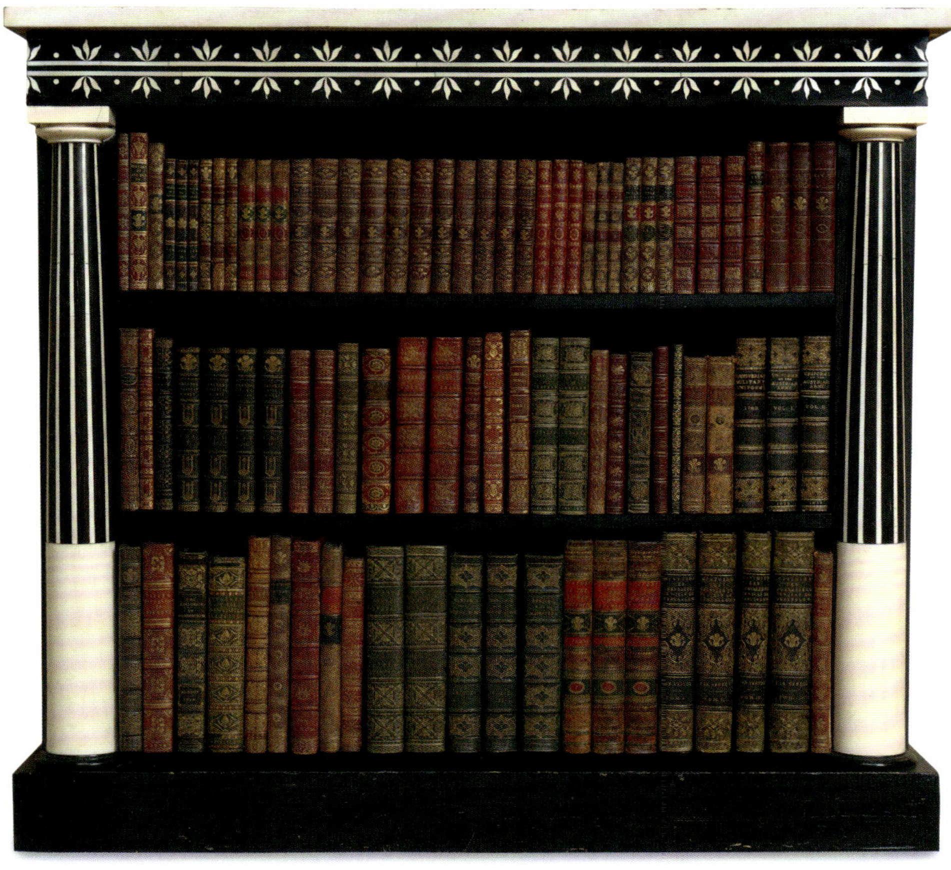

FIG. 14.2
MARSH & TATHAM, *Bookcase*, 1806 (with later alterations 1828). Ebony and ivory inlay on a pine carcase, white marble, 113.0 × 122.5 × 35.6 cm, RCIN 39475.1. The bookcase is filled with a selection of books from George IV's libraries

on the Lower Floor facing the garden, to the east of the Bow Room and Anti Room. By 1812, a year after George had been appointed Regent, the library was apparently expanding beyond the capacity of this room, since James Wyatt was asked to quote to fit up the adjacent Golden Drawing Room as an additional library room.[12] Here, a nod to Classical history was provided from 1816 by models of the triumphal arches of Constantine (Fig. 14.3), Titus and Septimius Severus (Fig. 14.4) which stood on plinths in the window embrasures. As the library's location changed, so did the decorative scheme, as David Oakey describes in chapter 5. Throughout his life, George's library spaces would be moved and adapted in accordance with his ambitious building projects at Carlton House, Buckingham Palace and Windsor Castle.

George IV's library was originally staffed by his pages. The first custodians were Cordal Powell, who had been Page in Attendance on the younger princes, and George Papendieck, brother-in-law to Queen Charlotte's Assistant Keeper of the Wardrobe.[13] Their duties included the reception of guests.[14] Acquiring books does not appear to have played a major role in their activities – instructions seem to have gone direct from the prince to his bookseller Becket, who remarked in 1787 that he had 'received H.R.H direction for these articles [books]' and that in 1784–5 'when I had an opportunity of seeing H.R.H. that I mentioned these books to him, which met his approbation, and ordered me to take care of all his Books till there was a place at Carlton House to receive them'.[15] Powell and Papendieck apparently remained in post until 1791 when they were dismissed, and in 1798 a Revd B. Clarke was listed as being Secretary for the Library.[16] By 1808 the Revd James Stanier Clarke, author of a life of Nelson (1809), and later a life of James II (1816) derived from the Stuart Papers, who had first entered the household as one of the prince's Chaplains in 1799, was signing documents as the prince's Librarian. In the same year A. Becket was named the Vice-Librarian (this post appears to have lasted only until 1812).[17] After an eventful career, which included the famous encounter with Jane Austen, Stanier Clarke was succeeded as librarian by Charles Richard Sumner, one-time tutor to the children of Lady Conyngham, George IV's mistress. After Sumner's appointment as Bishop of Llandaff in 1826 the post was taken by Dr Robert Gooch, a doctor specialising in midwifery and diseases of women, and finally by William

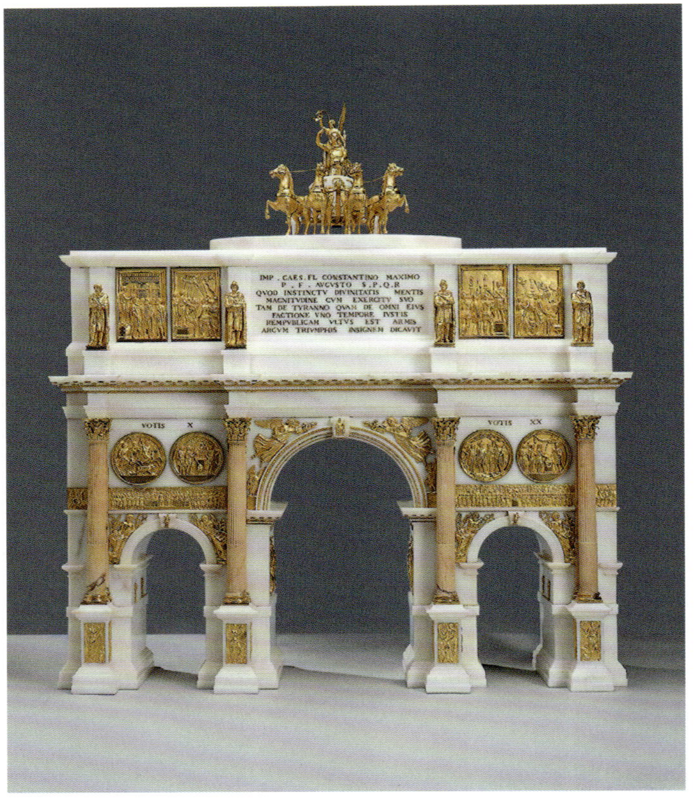

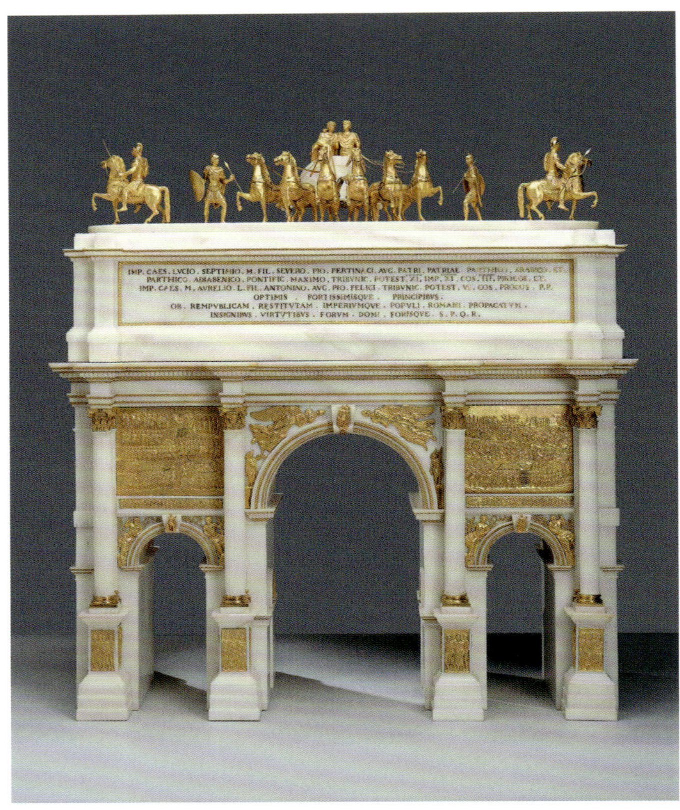

Macmichael, a surgeon and (from 1829) Physician-Extraordinary to the king, who took over at Gooch's death in February 1830. These gentlemen did not do the dirty work, though. That was left to George IV's booksellers.

The surviving bills relating to the library suggest that George IV acquired books from over 90 different booksellers, many of whom also offered other, highly specialised services. For example, William Faden, Colnaghi & Co. and Aaron Arrowsmith sold maps and charts, and maintained those in position, Thomas Daniell sold books on travels and antiquities, W. Playfair on antiquities and Rudolph Ackermann on art and travels, while Archibald Constable and John Ballantyne provided works on Scotland and Scottish history. Thomas Payne, later Payne & Foss, esteemed bookseller, to whom the renowned bibliophile Thomas Frognall Dibdin dedicated his *Library Companion* in 1824, was the chief antiquarian bookseller 1808–15, providing books for both London and Brighton. He sold the Classics (especially Greek history and literature), maps and militaria, and books on France and in French, antiquities, natural history and English literature. But these were all relatively small fry compared with the main booksellers used by George: Thomas Becket (later Becket & Porter), who supplied books until 1813, and Budd & Calkin (later Calkin & Budd), who provided books between 1813 and 1828. These booksellers also did much of the necessary library administration. Becket & Porter made the false book backs (the 'imitative books' mentioned by Pyne), they cleaned, arranged and catalogued the library, and made a fair copy of the catalogue (no copies of which survive).[18] After 1813 Budd & Calkin took over these duties, cleaning and rearranging the library, packing up and sending books to the Pavilion at Brighton, cataloguing that collection, and representing the prince at major auction sales (particularly the military sale of Lord Heathfield in 1814, where a considerable number of volumes were purchased).[19] They also organised the acquisition of binding tools and bookplates for the prince's books, payments for 'distressed literary persons' and payments to subscription libraries in Brighton (see below).[20] One of their final duties in late 1826 was to pack up the libraries in Carlton House and Warwick House (Princess Charlotte's former London residence), before the demolition of the main building.[21]

The physical maintenance of the earliest material is rarely mentioned in the surviving bills; the almanacs for the period mention Joseph Cooper as the prince's official book-binder, but no bills relating to him appear to survive.[22] Before 1808 there is little evidence for binding: we have individuals such as Charles Stuart, who in 1789 bound a copy of the Domesday Book and

(opposite left)
FIG. 14.3
GIOVACCHINO and PIETRO BELLI (1756–1822 and 1780–1828), *Arch of Constantine*, *c.*1808–15. Marble and gilt bronze, 45.0 × 55.5 × 22.5 cm, RCIN 43918

(opposite right)
FIG. 14.4
GIOVACCHINO and PIETRO BELLI (1756–1822 and 1780–1828), *Arch of Septimius Severus*, *c.*1808–15. Marble and gilt bronze, 49.5 × 57.0 × 22.5 cm, RCIN 43916

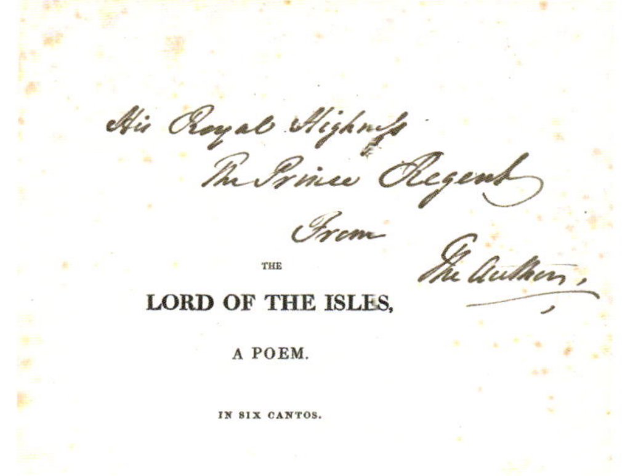

FIG. 14.5
SIR WALTER SCOTT (1771–1832), *Lord of the Isles: a poem*, 1815. Printed book, 30.6 × 24.6 cm, RCIN 1050439 (detail)

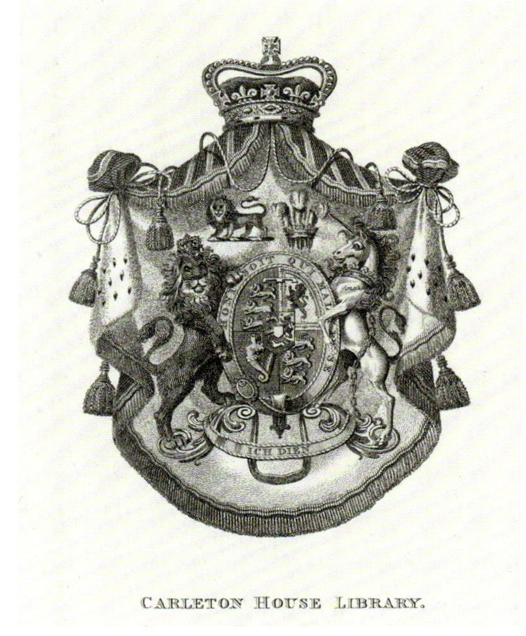

FIG. 14.6
Bookplate for George IV at Carlton House. Etching and engraving, 12.4 × 9.8 cm, within RCIN 1023588, *Clarendon's History of the Rebellion*, vol. 1, part one

187 volumes of the journals of the House of Commons and the House of Lords, or Thomas Becket, who was paid for bound sets of volumes.[23] But in 1808 (when Stanier Clarke is first mentioned as librarian) the quantity of binding took off, the large sum of nearly £340 being owed to Thomas Becket for binding in that year.[24] Thereafter there was a steady stream of binding work, usually dealt with by the principal bookseller of the time. Edward Jeffery tooled the library catalogues in 1808, and Thomas Payne, the antiquarian bookseller, bound copies of Xenophon's works and Homer's *Iliad* in 1812.[25] The Göttingen binder Charles Hering, considered to be the finest binder working in London, and his relations bound several volumes between 1813 and 1820. Some of these survive in the present Royal Library, among them a set of Shakespeare's plays (1813), an account of the visit of the Russian emperor to the Corporation of London in 1814 and Walter Scott's presentation copy of *Lord of the Isles* (Fig. 14.5).[26] Books were generally bound 'elegant', colour not often specified, and sometimes with tooling of the prince's arms. The earlier collections had plain boards but ornate gilded spines, with coloured labels and the Prince of Wales feathers badge. Later purchases were fully bound in leather, often highly decorated, in a variety of colours, red being the most popular. George used several marks of ownership both as Prince of Wales and Prince Regent; as well as his feathers badge, the prince also had an oval badge consisting of his coat of arms surrounded by the Garter, which appears on most of his surviving books acquired before 1820.[27] After George's accession, the ever-present Budd & Calkin had various armorial tools cut, and in 1822 ordered bookplates in three sizes to be printed by R. Silvester (Fig. 14.6). In total, George and his librarians used nine different bookplates.[28]

George's expenditure on books was respectable but not excessive, and by no means comparable with his outlay on (for example) furniture. We cannot compare his spending on books with that of his father, since most of George III's book bills do not survive. We do know that for the last five years of George III's life an average of £4,500 per annum was spent on his behalf on his library,[29] and that after his death George IV maintained it as a separate establishment at a cost of nearly £2,000 in 1820, and over £1,000 per annum thereafter until 1823, when responsibility passed to the British Museum. George III was, however, endeavouring to create and maintain a library for public scholarly use, whereas George IV's was purely for his own benefit and that of his friends.

The subjects accumulated by all this expenditure were predictable for one of George IV's education. Despite Jefferson's assessment, his schooling had been good, particularly equipping him with Classical languages, French, German (his German was good enough to interpret, and modify for the sake of diplomacy, General Blücher's drunken speech in Oxford during the visit there by the Emperor of Russia and the King of Prussia in 1814[30]) and even, it would appear, some Hebrew.[31] The section of his library in which he showed himself most closely aligned with

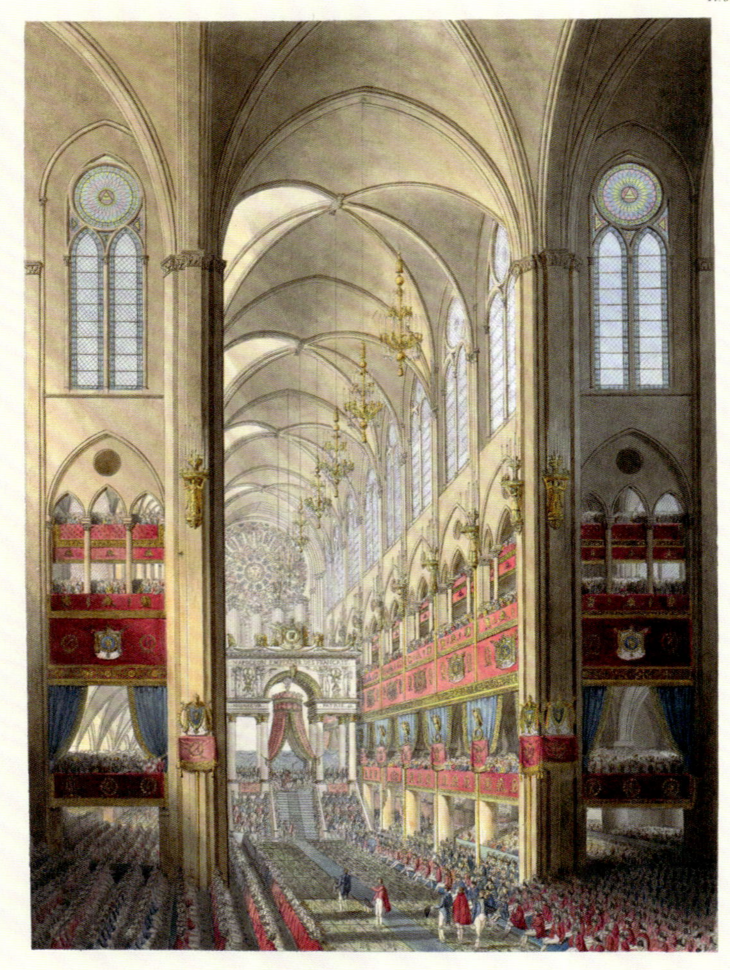

FIG. 14.7
CHARLES PERCIER (1764–1838) and PIERRE-FRANÇOIS-LÉONARD FONTAINE (1762–1853), *Description des Cérémonies et des Fêtes qui ont eu lieu pour le Couronnement de Leurs Majestés Napoléon ... et Joséphine*, 1807. Printed book, 65.8 × 50.2 cm, RCIN 1046693

popular tastes seems to have been that of English literature. Unlike his father, who bought authors only once they had become acknowledged classics, George IV seems to have been keen to buy contemporary works as they were published, reflecting the new popularity of the novel with purchases of books by such authors as Amelia Opie, Ann Radcliffe, Thomas Love Peacock, Jane Austen (Fig. 14.1), Maria Edgeworth and Walter Scott. He also acquired lesser-known works such as the English translation of E.T.A. Hoffmann's Gothic novel *The Devil's Elixirs* (1824), Lady Morgan's *Florence Macarthy* (1819) or Miss Driscoll's *Nice Distinctions* (1825).[32] His poetic purchases included Byron and Scott. He also bought the texts of several plays which had recently been performed in London, such as Frederick Reynolds's *Folly as It Flies*, played at the Theatre Royal in 1802, or *A Hint to Husbands* by Richard Cumberland, shown at the same venue in 1806.[33] The next most prevalent subject was theology, particularly later in George's life when large sums were spent (indeed over George's lifetime of acquiring books he spent the most on theological subjects, more than £2,300, compared with volumes of English literature, which were purchased in greater numbers but presumably at a lower unit cost, for a total of just over £2,000). French literature and history and militaria follow close behind; militaria was an enduring interest (see chapter 9). George's library of French literature, like its English counterpart, included modern authors such as Madame de Staël, Pigault-Lebrun, La Fontaine and Madame de Genlis, as well as the classics such as Voltaire, Racine and Molière,[34] while his interest in French history peaked during and after the Napoleonic Wars: books were purchased on the campaigns, and on Napoleon himself, including a massive £126 spent in 1816 on an account of Napoleon's coronation (Fig. 14.7).[35] Like most well-educated gentlemen of his period, he also possessed a collection of the Greek and Latin Classics, both history and literature, in the original and in translation.[36]

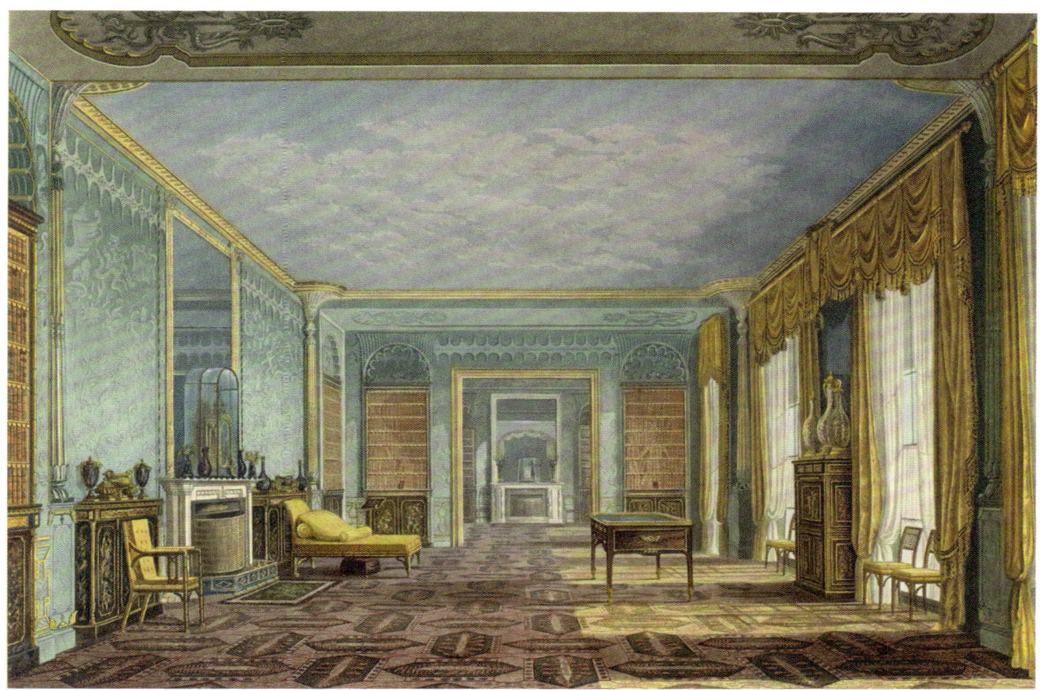

FIG. 14.8
HENRY WINKLES (active 1819–32) AFTER AUGUSTUS CHARLES PUGIN (*c.*1768–1832), *Brighton Pavilion, The Library*, 1838. Etching with aquatint and hand colouring, 20.5 × 30.0 cm (plate), RCIN 708000.au

Other libraries

When not in London, George IV had to rely on his subsidiary libraries for enlightenment and entertainment (he did not, like Napoleon, have a travelling library of small books). We have evidence for his library in the Pavilion at Brighton from 1801. This, like that at Carlton House, was serviced by his main booksellers. The library was situated in the private apartments, next door to George's bedroom, and consisted of two rooms (Fig. 14.8).[37] The contents of the library seem to have been rich in literature and history, with major purchases from 1814 when Payne & Foss acquired numerous large sets for Brighton, including the *Encyclopedia Britannica*, Shakespeare's *Works*, Chalmers's *English Poets* and *British Essayists*, Inchbald's *British Theatre* and much Walter Scott.[38] In 1822 the Pavilion library received a major injection of books when George III's library from Kew Palace, interspersed with additions by George IV (including many novels), was transported in 41 crates to Brighton.[39] In addition to his own personal collection George also subscribed to Mr Choat's library in North Street, described in a guidebook for the period as 'admirably situated in one of the most popular streets for business. It is supported by the first families and persons resorting hither ... news, literature and politics are its distinguishing characteristics'.[40] Choat's would have provided more up-to-date publications.

Closer to London, George's retreat at his 'Cottage' (Royal Lodge) in Windsor Great Park was kept well-supplied by his booksellers. The collection seems to have been in active use from 1820, when Budd & Calkin submitted bills for providing books, arranging them and 'taking down' the library, which probably implies a major spring-clean or move between rooms, since the books were arranged again not long after.[41] From 1827, however, no new additions are mentioned, and books thereafter travelled in the opposite direction – back to London. This coincided with the period when George IV was using Windsor Castle more regularly after its overhaul. In 1828 there was a concentrated purchasing effort for Windsor, in the same vein as the spending spree at Brighton, and multi-volume sets of literature, biographies and essays were bought.[42] These were presumably acquired for the Library (now the Green Drawing Room), designed by Wyatville and fitted out by Morel & Seddon as part of the suite of private apartments (see chapter 17). These complemented books selected from the Carlton House library (now in Buckingham Palace) for dispatch to Windsor.

The general character of George IV's libraries was contemporary rather than antiquarian – he was a modernist rather than a bibliophile. Yet one of his last actions with regards to the King's Library of George III was to retain over 40 items from his otherwise magnificent gift to the nation. The King's Library comprised over 65,000 volumes by 1820, and George IV,

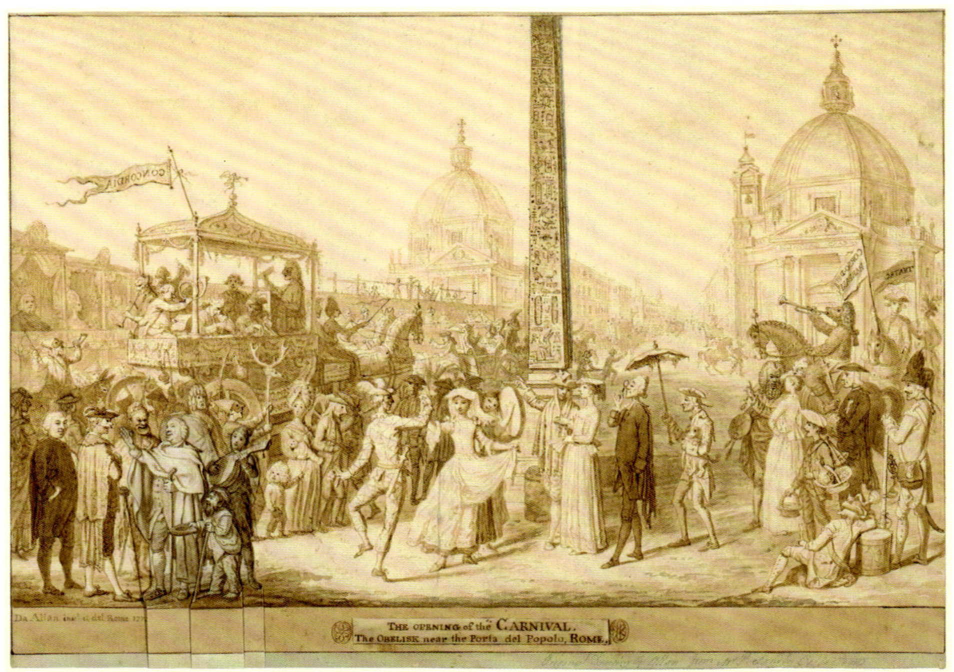

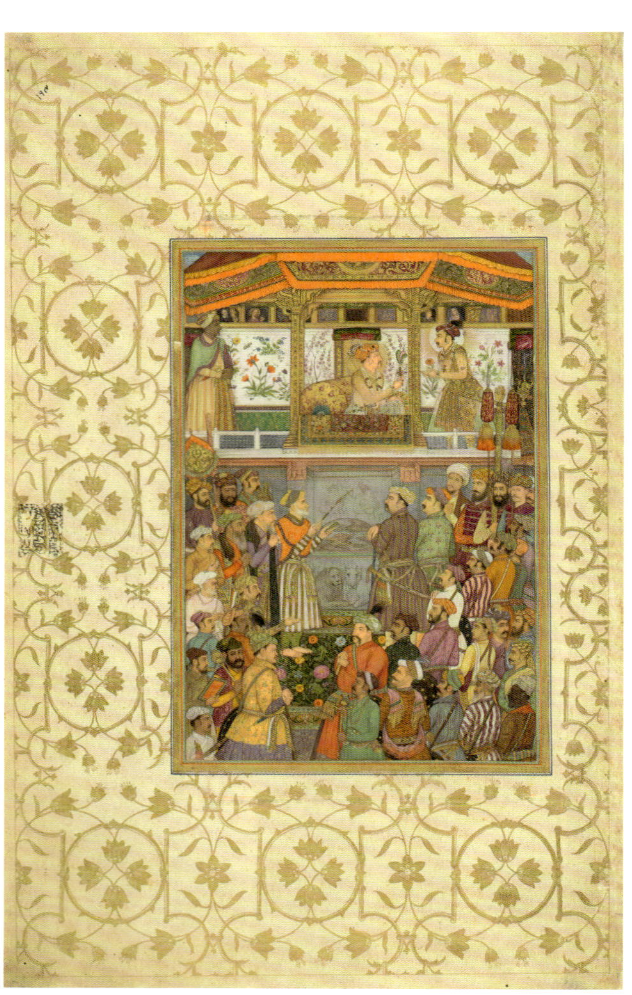

FIG. 14.9
DAVID ALLAN (1744–96), *The Opening of the Carnival: The Obelisk near the Porta del Popolo, Rome*, 1775. Pen and brown wash, some corrections in pencil, with washed mount at foot, 36.8 × 53.4 cm, RCIN 913351

FIG. 14.10
PAYAG (active 1595–1655), *Jahangir presents Prince Khurram with a turban ornament (12 October 1617)*, 1656–7. Opaque watercolour with gold paints on paper, 58.2 × 36.8 cm (sheet), RCIN 1005025.an

looking to reinvent Buckingham House as a palace, did not have room for such a large collection. Thus in 1823 he informed Lord Liverpool, the prime minister, that he intended to present the collection to the British Museum.[43] The official list of items retained included the collection of incunabula (books printed before 1501) given to George III by the antiquary Jacob Bryant in 1782, which included first and otherwise rare editions, the magnificent Mainz Psalter (1457), the second known book to be printed, Charles I's copy of the Second Folio of Shakespeare, and a small notebook in the hand of Dr Johnson.[44] He also retained six Mughal manuscripts given to George III by Lord Teignmouth at the end of his term as Governor-General of India in 1799, including the great *Padshahnama* (Fig. 14.10), a biography of the Emperor Shah Jahan, containing some of the finest Mughal miniatures ever produced.[45] It is interesting that he kept back the rarest items, not necessarily just the most splendid. George IV was no bibliophile like his father, but he was clearly aware of what was important, and what would grace a king's library.

Beyond the library

If George's books demonstrate a predominating interest in recent history and literature, military matters and current affairs, these inclinations extended to the company he kept. George's

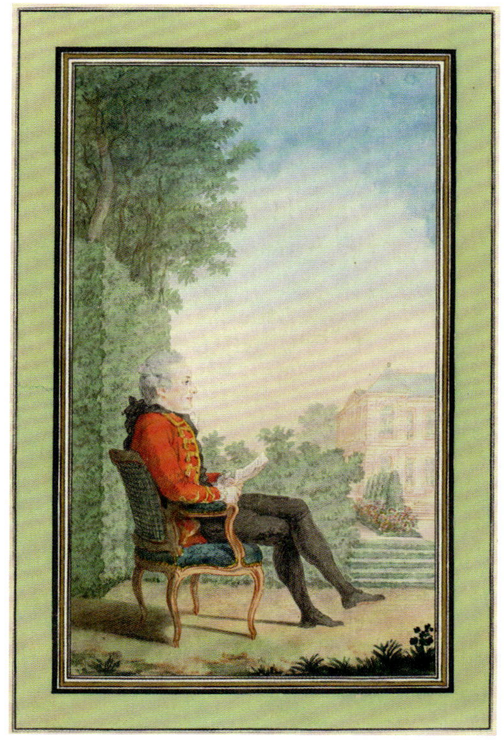

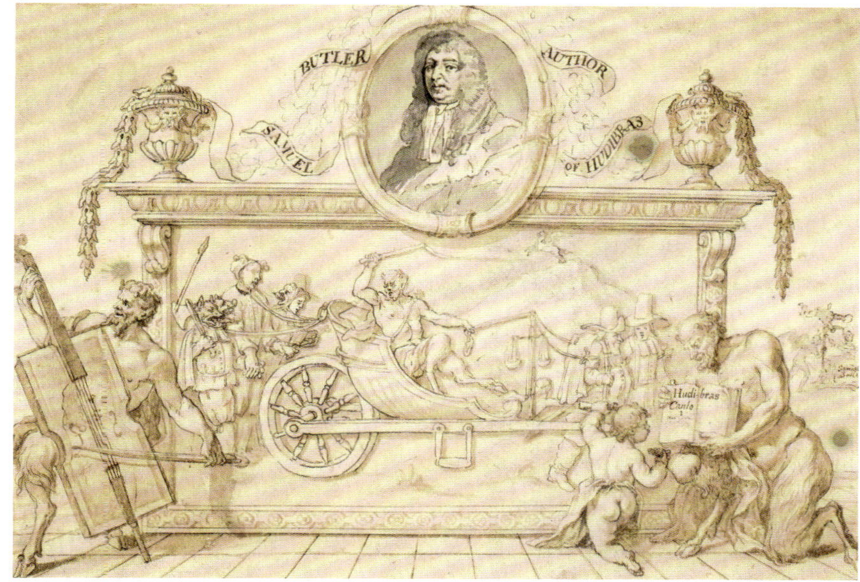

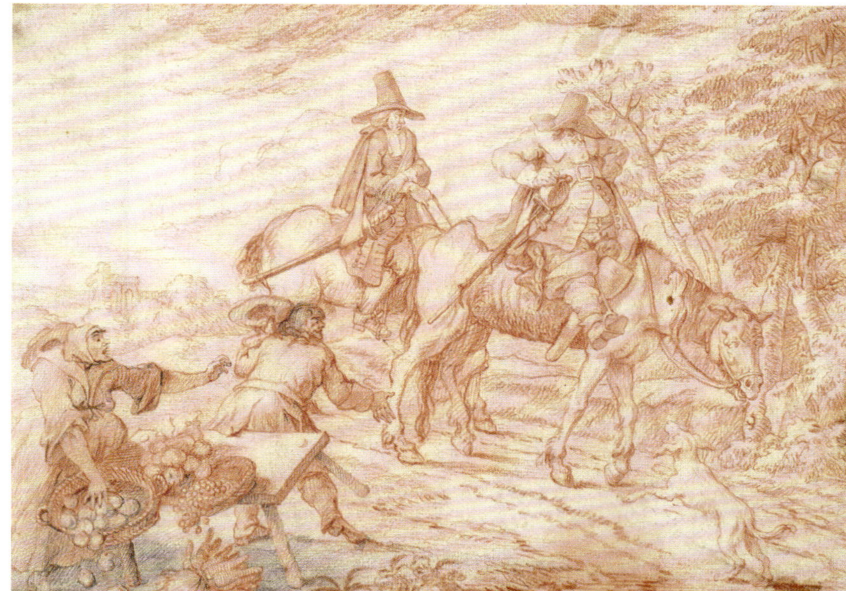

FIG. 14.11
LOUIS CARROGIS DE CARMONTELLE (1717–1806), *Charles-Alexis Brûlart, comte de Genlis (1737–93)*, *c*.1765. Watercolour with pencil and black and red chalk, 35.7 × 23.2 cm (including wash border), RCIN 913119

FIG. 14.12
WILLIAM HOGARTH (1697–1764), *Hudibras: The Frontispiece*, 1725. Pen and ink with pencil and wash, 23.8 × 33.8 cm, RCIN 913459

FIG. 14.13
WILLIAM HOGARTH (1697–1764), *Hudibras sallying forth*, 1725. Red and black chalks, 23.8 × 32.6 cm, RCIN 913460

boon companions from the 1780s to the early years of the nineteenth century were a hard-drinking set who enjoyed loud and often crude parties at Carlton House, but many of them were also cultured writers and thinkers who could provide George with stimulating conversation. Among them were Charles James Fox, leader of the Whig faction, who was a historian as well as a politician, and the playwright Richard Brinsley Sheridan. Later, Sir Thomas Lawrence and Sir Walter Scott, regular guests, would provide a link to contemporary scholars and recent literature.[46] Within George's household he benefited from the company of such men as General Sir Tomkyns Hilgrove Turner and the politician Thomas Tyrwhitt, both of whom had a deep interest in and knowledge of Classical history.

Temporary encounters, too, provided stimulating conversation. In 1783, George spoke with the poet George Crabbe at the theatre, and (to Crabbe's delight) remembered the discussion nearly 40 years later.[47] In 1784, George spent 'upwards of two hours' in conversation with the balloonist Vincenzo Lunardi.[48] In 1800, he discussed vaccination with Edward Jenner.[49] In 1812, he spoke with Lord Byron for over half an hour, impressing the 'surprised and delighted' poet with his knowledge of literature.[50] In 1813 he spent two hours discussing politics with the French writer

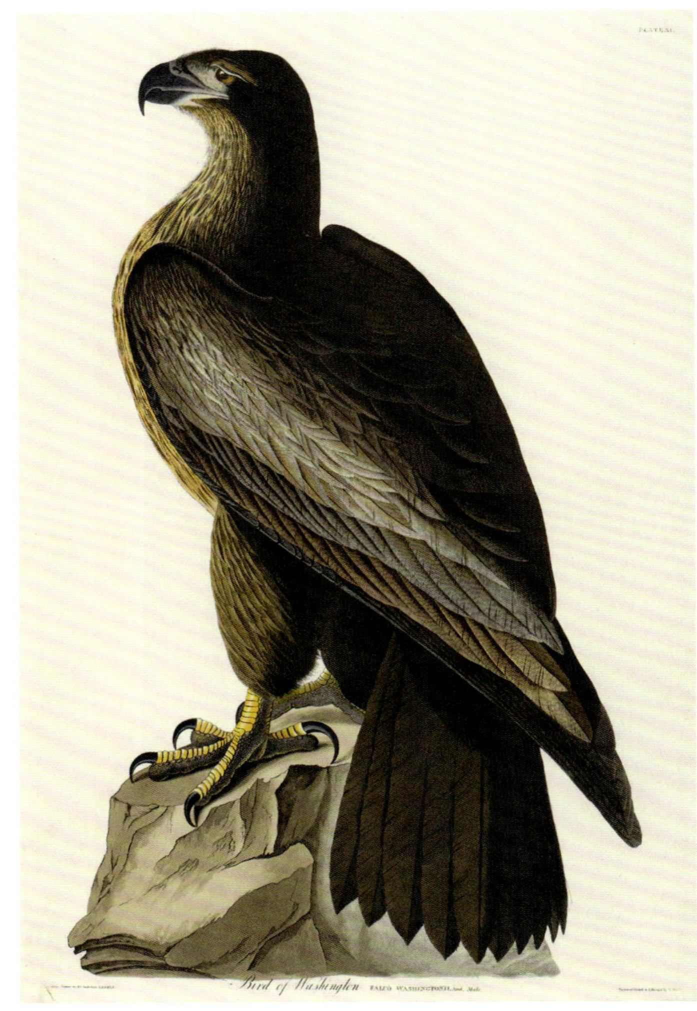

FIG. 14.14
JOHN JAMES AUDUBON (1785–1851), *Bird of Washington*, from *The Birds of America*, 1827–30. Engraving with hand colouring, 98.2 × 66.6 cm (sheet), RCIN 1122502

Madame de Staël.[51] A few months later he toured the excavations at Bignor Roman Villa with the antiquary John Hawkins, who noted 'the interest which the Prince appeared to take in the sight of the Pavements' while bemoaning the lack of practical support he had received for his project.[52] In 1814, George had lunch with the statesman Adam Czartoryski.[53] At Carlton House in 1815, he discovered a mutual love of storytelling with Sir Walter Scott, who would later co-ordinate the celebrations for his visit to Edinburgh.[54] He met the renowned scientist and explorer, Alexander von Humboldt, with whom he discussed Humboldt's planned expedition to the Himalaya Mountains in 1817.[55] In 1818 he received the naturalist Georges Cuvier, with whom he discussed natural history, and dined more than once with the ambassador Wilhelm von Humboldt, who recorded that on one occasion his fellow guests were Castlereagh and Wellington.[56] In 1822, he spent three-quarters of an hour discussing French politics with the vicomte de Chateaubriand, who reported that *il m'a fait avec une merveilleuse mémoire, l'histoire de toute société de France* ('he rehearsed the history of French society, displaying a remarkable recall').[57] Those who met him were usually impressed and George could certainly hold his own in the company of intellectuals: Wilhelm von Humboldt recorded of one evening he attended that 'during the entire dinner not a frivolous word was spoken'.[58]

George was also able to engage with the world through his vast collection of prints and drawings, which was kept separately from his library and which gave him 'great amusement' on evenings when he did not have company.[59] This assemblage of well over 50,000 sheets largely concentrated on geography, history, military matters and portraiture (Figs 14.9 and 14.11). It included a significant group of prints and drawings by Hogarth, among them the original drawings for the artist's illustrations of Samuel Butler's satirical poem *Hudibras* (Figs 14.12 and 14.13). General Turner described the collection of prints and drawings, of which he had the administration, as 'a most profitable and intelligent study, as it related to important events and distinguished characters'.[60] Such material was clearly of genuine interest to George: when his physician Sir Jonathan Wathen Waller showed him samples of the plates from John James Audubon's projected publication on American ornithology (Fig. 14.14), 'he seemed much pleased with the Prints, and ordered me to leave them with him'; as a result of the meeting George subscribed to the publication.[61] George's print collection also complemented his personal encounters: when the allied sovereigns and commanders came to London for a summit in 1814, George prepared for the visit by buying portraits of those who would attend, a practical means of familiarising himself with his guests.[62] On 1 May 1822, 12 days after meeting Chateaubriand, he paid 10s 6d for a portrait print of the vicomte, to add to the seven he already owned.[63]

George's love of theatre, too, was explored through the collection. He acquired numerous portraits of the great actor David Garrick; these ranged from small prints (Fig. 14.15) to a fine oil painting by Sir Joshua Reynolds (Fig. 14.16). Under General Turner's supervision, his staff compiled a ten-volume 'History

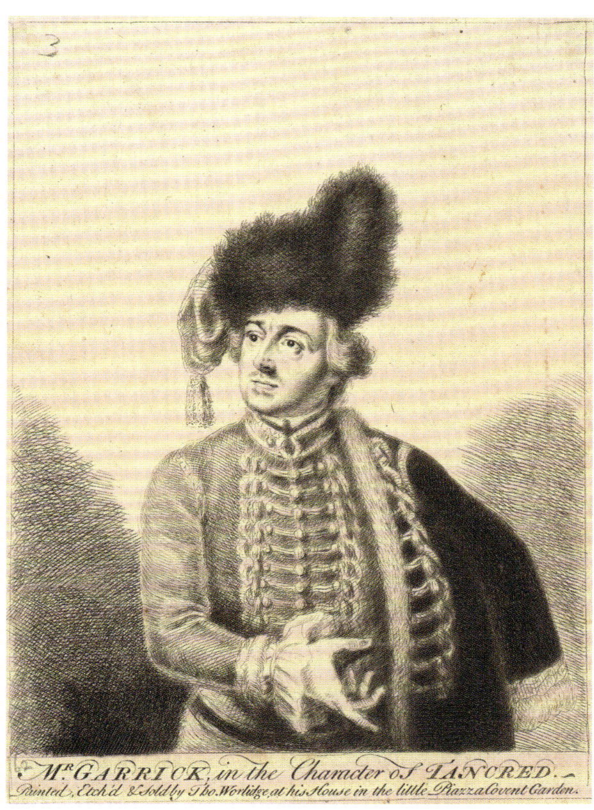

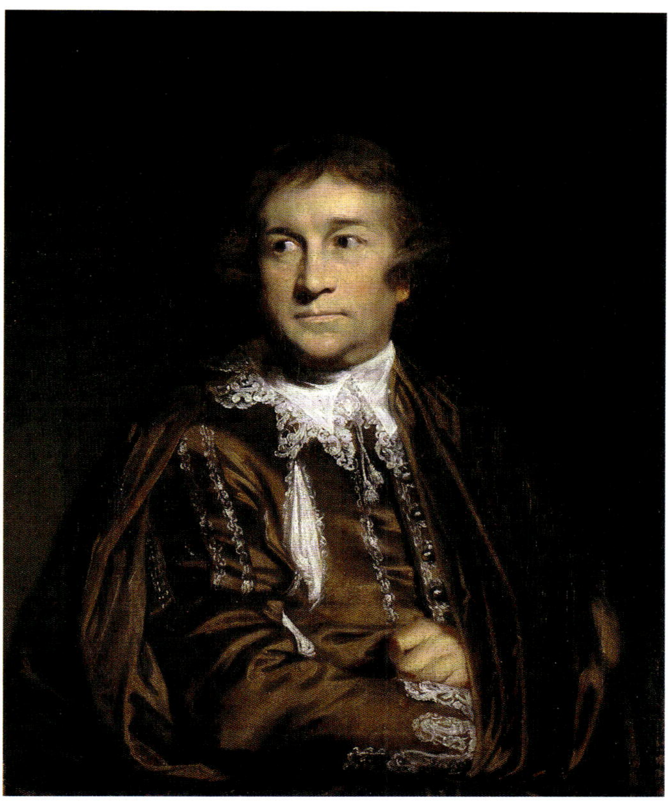

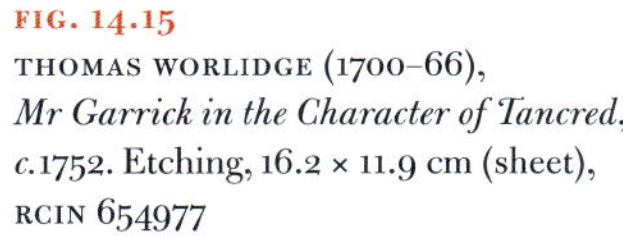
FIG. 14.15
THOMAS WORLIDGE (1700–66), *Mr Garrick in the Character of Tancred*, *c*.1752. Etching, 16.2 × 11.9 cm (sheet), RCIN 654977

FIG. 14.16
SIR JOSHUA REYNOLDS (1723–92), *David Garrick (1717–79)*, 1768. Oil on canvas, 77.0 × 64.0 cm, RCIN 406984

of the Stage' illustrated with prints and drawings, among them a portrait of the famous comic actor William Penkethman by George Vertue (Fig. 14.17) and a print by Thomas Rowlandson of Garrick's bust being crowned with a laurel wreath (Fig. 14.18).[64] These volumes were arranged chronologically from the Elizabethan period onwards, and complemented the numerous prints and drawings of contemporary theatrical performers which George collected avidly. Many of the theatrical sitters would have been known to him personally: he was a regular at the theatre, kept a box at the Theatre Royal, and was described by the comedian Joseph Grimaldi as being 'much behind the scenes of Drury Lane, delighting everybody with his affability, his gentlemanly manners and his witty remarks'.[65] If hanging around the footlights may be connected with George's playboy side, his formation of the illustrated theatrical history and purchase of plays suggests there was also a greater depth to his interest in the stage. He was sensible enough to sit on the fence when Samuel Ireland brought his son's Shakespeare forgeries to Carlton House for his examination, claiming that it was impossible to decide on the authenticity of the pieces on the basis of a short study and, according to Ireland, declaring that 'in matters of this nature so much is to be said *pro* and *con*, that the decision requires mature reflexion'.[66]

Beyond personal encounters, George acted as patron of individuals or scholarly projects.[67] His generosity funded the work of the botanist Allan Cunningham in New South Wales and he employed the music historian Edward Jones as his harpist.[68] He sponsored the Revd John Hayter's work in Naples on a group of papyri from Herculaneum, presenting Hayter's drawings to the Bodleian Library (Fig. 14.19): later he requested Sir Humphry Davy explore the difficult task of unrolling the papyri and Davy recorded in a letter to his mother that 'I had yesterday the honour of an audience from his royal highness and he commissioned me to pursue this object in the most gracious and kind manner'.[69] George was instrumental in the founding of the Royal Society of Literature.[70] He was patron of the Linnean Society, and with the Duke of Wellington established King's College, London. At Oxford, he endowed readerships in mineralogy and geology and at the Royal Society, he provided funding for Royal Medals, to be awarded for significant work in the field of science.[71] Among the societies to which he granted a

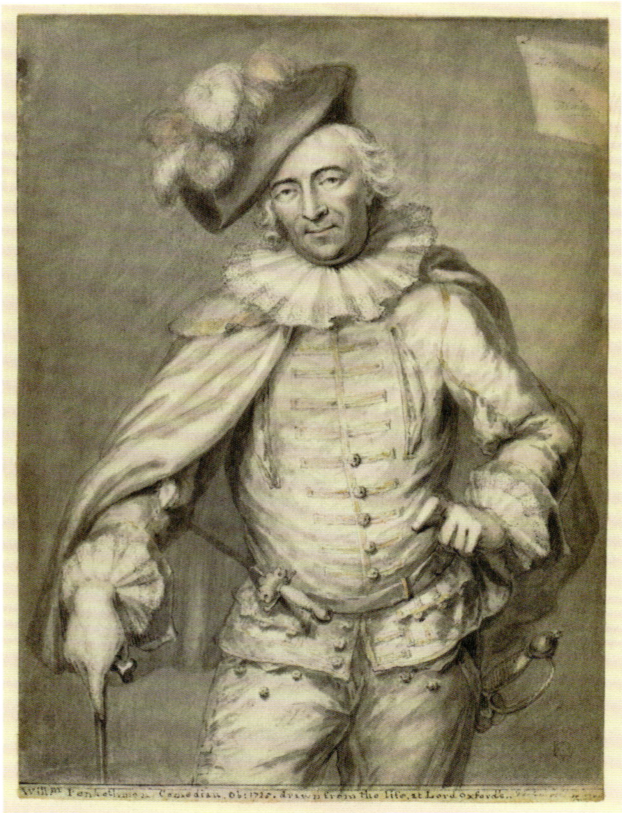

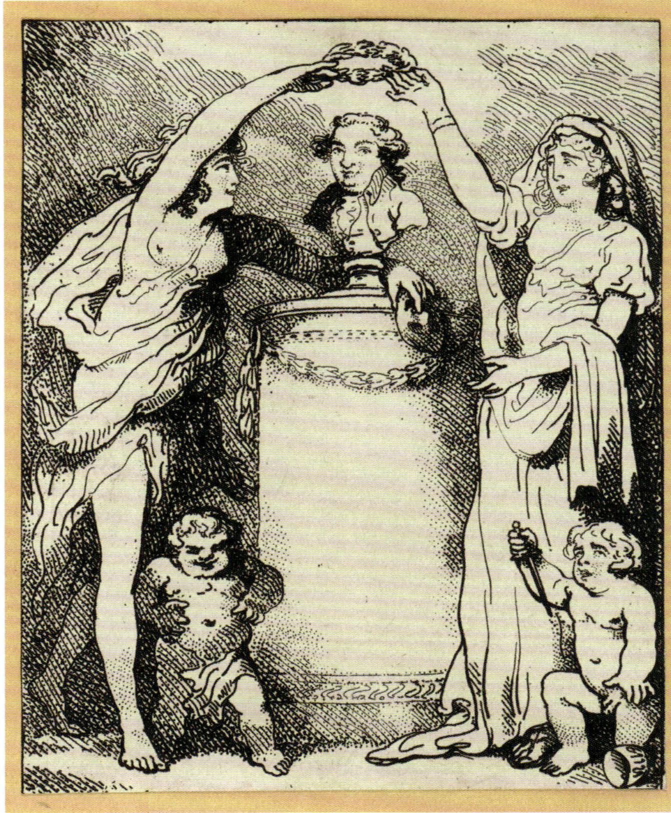

FIG. 14.17
GEORGE VERTUE (1684–1756), *William Penkethman as Don Lewis in 'Love makes a man' by Colley Cibber*, *c.*1725. Pen and grey wash with watercolour, 30.3 × 22.0 cm, RCIN 913579

FIG. 14.18
THOMAS ROWLANDSON (1757–1827), *The Bust of Garrick wreathed by Comedy and Tragedy*, *c.*1780. Etching, 12.3 × 9.9 cm (sheet), RCIN 654944

royal charter were the Royal Asiatic Society (1824), the Geological Society (1825), the Royal Society of Literature (1825), the Institution of Civil Engineers (1828), the Zoological Society (1829) and the Royal Academy of Music (1830). Imaginatively, George provided a bronze lamp to light the Great Room at the Royal Academy and gave chandeliers from the coronation to Wadham College, Oxford, to illuminate the concerts in its music room.[72]

George's patronage was not sought by individuals and learned societies primarily for financial reasons, but rather for its potential to increase the status of a project or publication. It was for this reason that numerous books (among them Austen's *Emma*) were dedicated to George; indeed, the bookseller George Nichol advised the Welsh poet Edward Williams (Iolo Morganwg) that 'as dedications to the Prince have been so common, the shorter yours is the better, as nothing new can be said on the subject' (Fig. 14.20).[73] Such dedications were usually by permission, and thus indicated an acceptance by George of the subject and premise of a text which, authors and publishers hoped, would encourage sales: his approbation must have counted for something in this area. Most dedicatory texts were gratefully respectful, but Joseph Priestley used the 1790 revised and abridged edition of his seminal *Experiments and Observation on Different Kinds of Air* to launch a startlingly strident manifesto in which he urged George to patronise the study of chemistry:

> the patronage of Princes may be eminently useful to this end, by diffusing a taste for it among those whose opulence will enable them to prosecute it to the most advantage … Hence it is that the greatest and happiest effects may be expected from the patronage of science by persons of your Royal Highness's rank and expectations, whose wishes and inclinations are often alone sufficient to give a turn to the taste and pursuits of the rich and great.

George's 'wishes and inclinations' had the potential to bring a project success.

George IV's influence on contemporary taste and culture is most clearly seen in the patronage of music, in which field

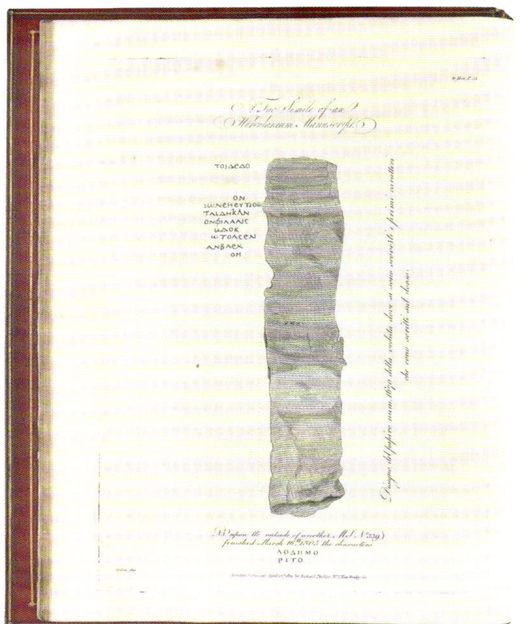

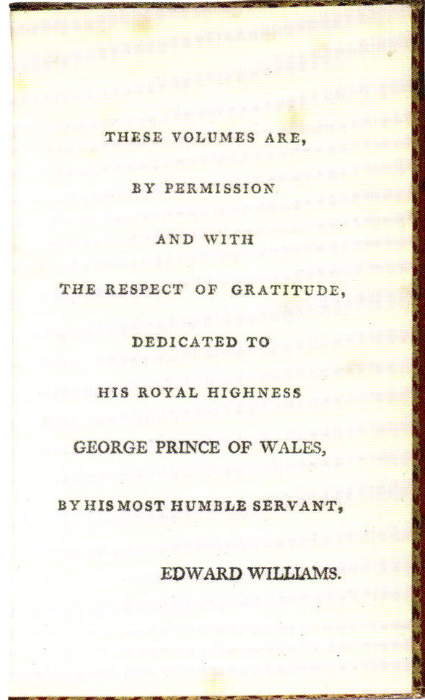

THESE VOLUMES ARE,

BY PERMISSION

AND WITH

THE RESPECT OF GRATITUDE,

DEDICATED TO

HIS ROYAL HIGHNESS

GEORGE PRINCE OF WALES,

BY HIS MOST HUMBLE SERVANT,

EDWARD WILLIAMS.

FIG. 14.19
JOHN HAYTER (1756–1818), *A Report upon the Herculaneum manuscripts, in a second letter, addressed, by permission, to His Royal Highness The Prince Regent*, 1811. Printed book, 31.3 × 25.0 cm, RCIN 1079863

FIG. 14.20
EDWARD WILLIAMS (Iolo Morganwg, 1747–1826), *Poems, lyric and pastoral, volume 1*, 1794. Printed book, 18.3 × 11.5 cm, RCIN 1087153

he has been described as 'undoubtedly the most influential arbiter' in late eighteenth-century London.[74] He maintained an important band (discussed by David Beevers in chapter 10), was a competent cellist, a regular at the opera and encouraged performance series such as the Professional Concerts and the Concerts of Antient Music (the latter also patronised by his parents).[75] Musical scores were purchased for presentation to the Royal College of Music, and to aid performances in Gloucester, Norwich, Hereford, York and Worcester in 1825.[76] He sponsored the education of Thomas Attwood, funding the promising musician's study abroad. Attwood's training included lessons with Mozart, and George has been credited with initiating the first appearance of a Mozart opera in London with the performance of *La clemenza di Tito* at a benefit for Elizabeth Billington in 1806.[77] He organised regular 'morning parties' for the performance of string quartets at Carlton House, where Haydn's 'Paris' symphonies also received their first London performance.[78] Haydn (see Fig. 1.4) was extremely impressed by George when he met him in 1787, noting that 'The Prince of Wales is the most handsome man on God's earth; he has an extraordinary love of music and a lot of feeling, but not much money. *Nota bene*, this is between ourselves. I am more pleased by his kindness than by any financial gain.'[79]

It was music that brought Charles Burney into George's circle, and the musician had an ample chance to assess George's scholarly qualities in 1805 when the two had a long conversation at an evening party. A surprised Burney wrote:

> Nobody is so prompt at polite and gratifying compliments as this gracious prince. I had no conception of his accomplishments. He quite astonished me by his learning, in conversing with my son, after my own musical *tête-à-tête* dialogue with him. He quoted Homer in Greek as readily as if quoting Dryden or Pope in English: and, in general conversation, during the dinner, he discovered a fund of wit and humour such as demonstrated him a man of reading and parts, who knew how to discriminate characters … Upon the whole, I cannot terminate my account of this prince better than by asserting it as my opinion, from the knowledge I acquired by my observations of this night, that he has as much conversational talent, and far more learning, than Charles the Second, who knew no more, even of orthography, than Molière's *Bourgeois Gentilhomme*.[80]

To those who knew him only through accusatory satires, scurrilous news stories and rumour, George would always be the irresponsible lightweight, most notable for drunken affairs and wanton excess. But to those who had the chance of personal observation, like Burney, the Humboldts, Byron and Chateaubriand, George was a man who inhabited a much richer intellectual world than most of his contemporaries were able, or willing, to acknowledge.

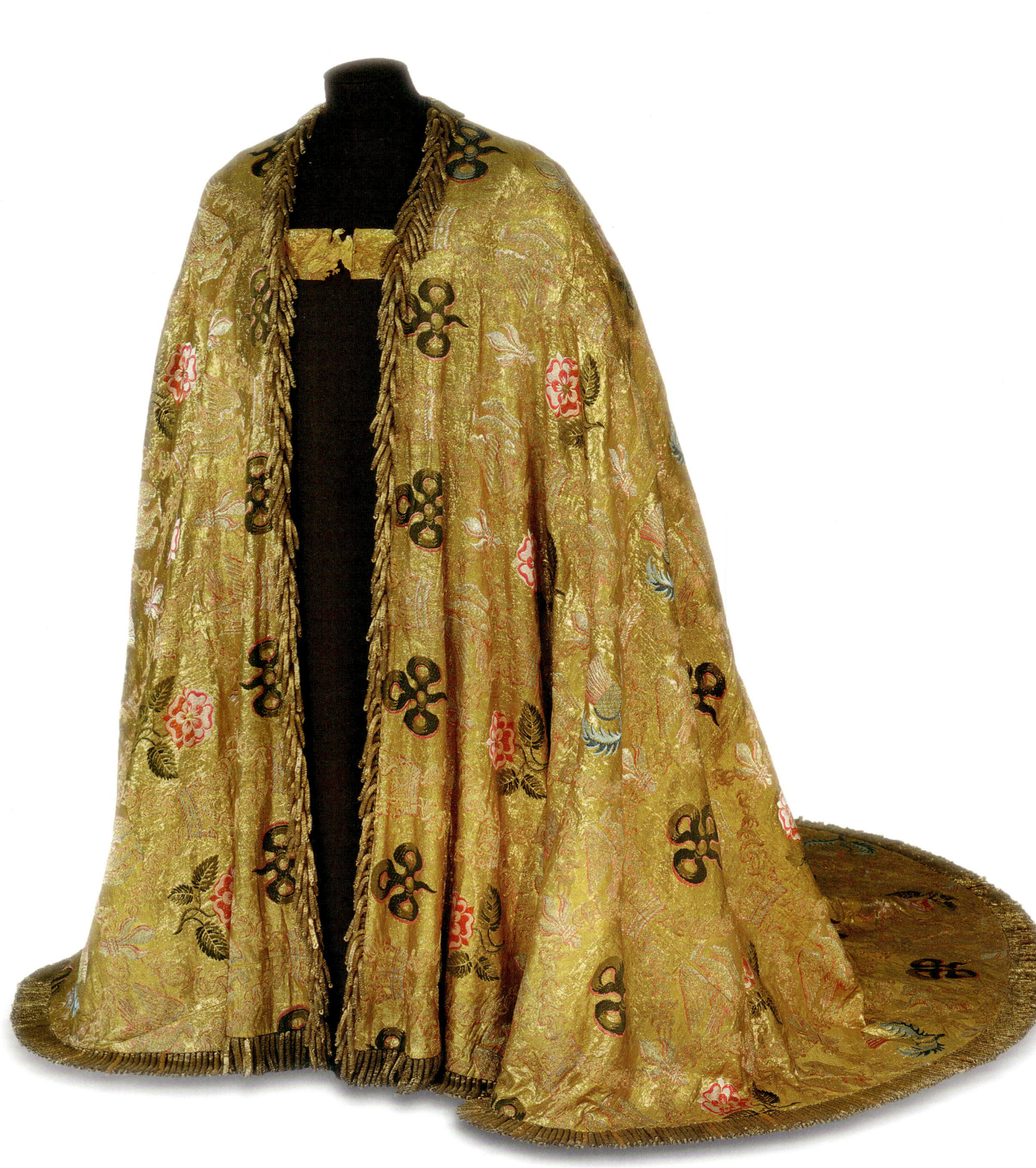

15

'NEVER SO HAPPY *as in* SHOW *and* STATE'

KATHRYN JONES

SPECTACLE PLAYED A CENTRAL ROLE IN George IV's life. If his great architectural projects are to be seen as striving to create suitably magnificent settings for the work of monarchy, then the ceremonies and celebrations of the court were the jewels to be placed in these settings. As the Dowager Lady Vernon pointed out to Mary Frampton in 1814, 'our Prince Regent is never so happy as in show and state and there he shines incomparably';[1] George was a master of such events, a natural showman, and contemporary witnesses to these occasions, although sometimes critical of the expense, could only marvel at the splendid display they made. The American ambassador Richard Rush, attending a formal Drawing Room (see below) in 1818, suggested 'foreigners agreed that the united capitals of Europe could not match the sight … the whole was harmony. Like Old English buildings and Shakespeare, it carried the feelings with it, triumphing over criticism.'[2]

In the eighteenth century there had been few opportunities for great royal spectacle, the exceptions being coronations and funerals. Traditionally these public occasions were supplemented by the opportunity to view the king dining, a tradition that had died out under George III, or by attendance at Sunday church services in the royal chapels. The latter had continued, and was kept up by George IV; at Brighton, for example, the royal pew was newly fitted up in 1822, and as many as 400 tickets were sold each week to those who wished to see the royal person during services.[3] In addition, during the late eighteenth century and into George IV's reign there were regular levées, and thrice-weekly Drawing Rooms, the former gatherings for gentlemen only, the latter for mixed company (Fig. 15.2). Conduct and dress for such occasions were carefully prescribed, although outwardly Drawing Rooms had a greater measure of informality than other opportunities to meet the royal personage. Ladies were expected to wear plumed headdresses, lace lappets or veils and hooped dresses; gentlemen to wear dress swords, orders if applicable, and what the writer Mary Berry described as 'splendid liveries and hussars of all colours'.[4] Presentation to the monarch was strictly regulated, and guests were expected to adhere to a choreographed pattern of behaviour and often follow

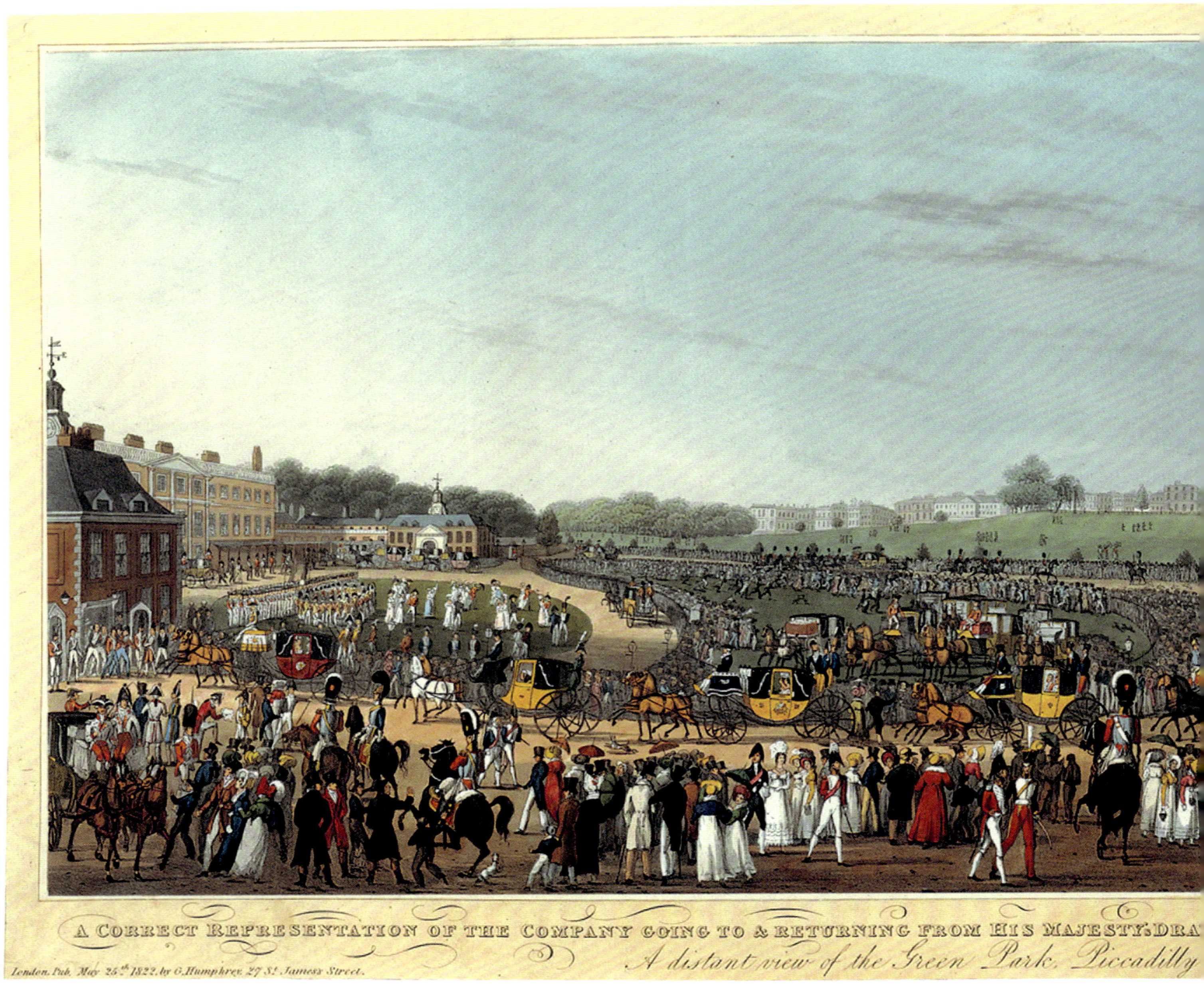

a traditional form of words. Richard Rush described his arrival at a levée at Carlton House to be presented to the Prince Regent, where he was greeted by men in an array of formal uniforms or degrees of official dress, which he noted were all very rich; he was surrounded by paintings that acted as reminders of British naval and military triumphs and commented on the weight of the political history which exuded from the walls of the house. On admittance to the Audience Room he delivered his credentials and followed the official wording required. Rush was rather taken aback when George then launched into conversation with him about John Adams, Rush's various predecessors as ambassadors and the Americans living in London.[5] Here George's talents lay – he was a genial host and seems to have been happy to discuss an entire world of subjects with his guests (see chapter 14).

Despite George's sociability there was a feeling that these events had become rather staid by the time of the Regency. Louis Simond, visiting London from France in 1810, noted that the fashions worn to court had little changed for 50 years,[6] and indeed the hooped dresses and dress swords caused something of a difficulty when as many as 1,000 guests crammed into the inadequate spaces of Carlton House or the Queen's House.

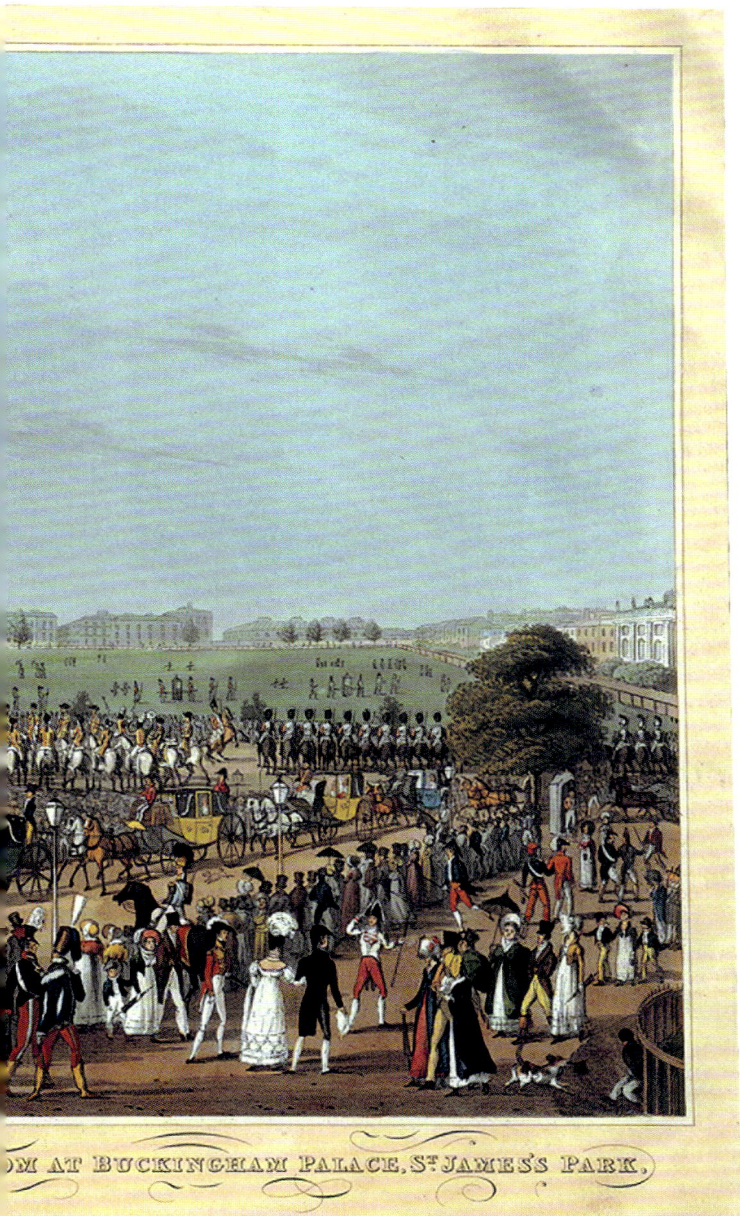

(p. 198)
FIG. 15.1
JOHN MEYER (*c.*1753–*c.*1830), *The Imperial Mantle*, 1821. Cloth of gold, silk, gold, 228.6 cm (length), RCIN 31794

FIG. 15.2
Published by GEORGE HUMPHREY (?1773–?1831), *A Correct Representation of the Company Going to & Returning from His Majesty's Drawing Room at Buckingham Palace, St James's Park*, 1822. Etching and aquatint with hand colouring, 31.4 × 56.8 cm, RCIN 750804

Nevertheless witnesses to such events were generally keen to emphasise the spectacle they created. As early as 1790, when George held his first levée, the *Microcosm of London* reported: 'His royal highness had a state levee, for the first time, at his palace at Carlton House, which was the most numerous of any thing of the kind for many years … more numerous and splendid than the generality of the drawing rooms even at St James's.'[7]

If Rush's experience illustrates that levées were used as occasions for the presentation of credentials by ambassadors, they were also the opportunity for the investiture of chivalric honours. These greatly increased in importance during and following the military campaigns of the Napoleonic Wars. In 1815 the Order of the Bath was reorganised to encompass both civil and military honours, in recognition of those who had fought at Waterloo. George also introduced new honours – in 1818 he created the Order of St Michael and St George (Fig. 15.3), for those serving in Mediterranean territories as a consequence of the Congress of Vienna. Another, the Order of Guelph, was created for the Hanoverian kingdom following its elevation to a monarchy; this was almost exclusively presented to those serving in Germany. Although both royal men and women had worn forms of more personal honours before 1820, thereafter George instituted the first official family order, the badge comprising an enamel miniature by Henry Bone, set in a diamond frame, with a crown above and royal cipher on the reverse (Fig. 15.4). These personal orders were largely reserved for female members of the family, including his sisters (see Fig. 11.1), sisters-in-law and his young niece, Victoria (see chapter 4), although the prince did also give them to political allies.

Fêtes and entertainments

There is some evidence that George wished to reduce the formality of court events. Certainly Rush recorded that George seemed determined to greet almost all the guests to a levée in person and that 'the Prince Regent was not thought to be fond of set speeches'.[8] On his accession George revised the dress code for ladies attending Drawing Rooms, no longer insisting on the cumbersome court hoops, by now long out of fashion, although ostrich-plumed headdresses were retained. As the diarist Charles Greville noted at Brighton: 'They say the King is anxious that form and ceremony should be banished, and if so it not only proves how impossible it is that form and ceremony should not always inhabit a palace.'[9] Perhaps as an attempt to reduce formality, to the more formulaic events George added ever-more spectacular fêtes and dinners, often accommodating somewhere in the region of two or three thousand guests, and there was a general move throughout the period towards music, balls and banquets.

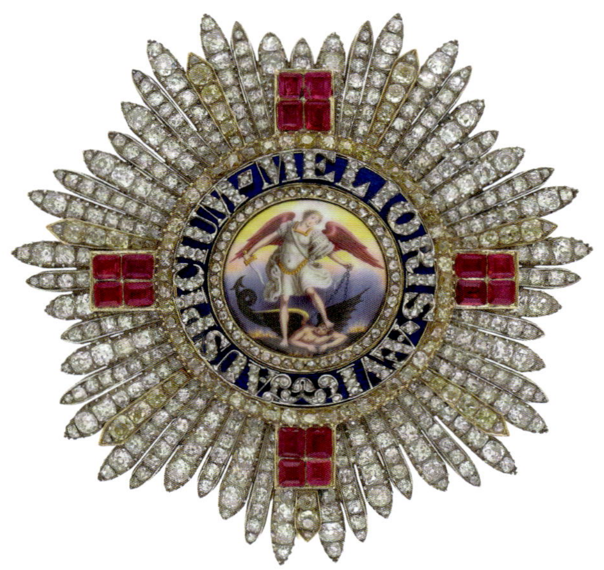

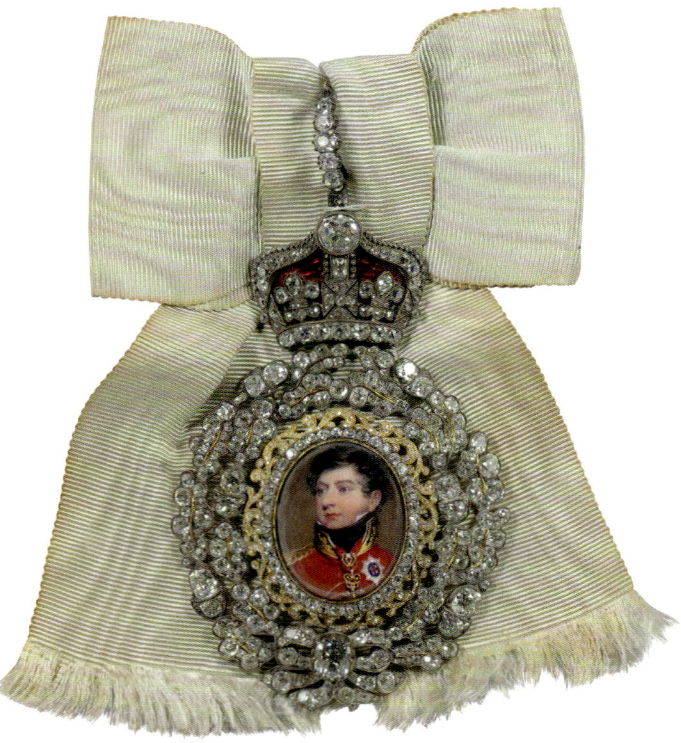

FIG. 15.3
ENGLISH, *Order of St Michael and St George: star*, *c.*1825. Diamond, yellow diamond, ruby, silver, enamel, 7.7 × 7.7 cm, RCIN 441309

FIG. 15.4
HENRY BONE (1755–1834), *Family Order of King George IV: badge*, *c.*1820–30. Enamel, gold, silver, diamond, silk, 11.5 × 6.4 cm, RCIN 441442. This badge originally belonged to Charlotte, Queen of Württemberg

Here George, clearly heavily influenced by his friend and artistic adviser Walsh Porter (see chapter 5), could give free rein to his theatrical tendencies. Carlton House was frequently re-dressed for such occasions. In 1814, for example, for a dinner held in honour of Louis XVIII on the eve of his return to France, the walls of the Throne Room were newly upholstered in silk woven with fleurs-de-lis.[10] Temporary buildings were often erected in the gardens. Something of their nature can be gleaned from a plan that details the wide range of structures built for one of the most celebrated of these parties, the 1811 fête at Carlton House, marking the start of the Regency (Fig. 15.5). At this event a whole array of temporary kitchens, marquees and seating areas was created. The Lower Floor of the house became one long space for dining, with a table some 200 feet (60 metres) in length running from the Gothic Conservatory at the western end of the building to the Gothic Dining Room at the eastern end. A buffet of silver gilt was mounted behind the Prince Regent's seat and the first delivery of the magnificent Grand Service was put into use on the table. The *Gentleman's Magazine* offers a description of the sight:

> along the centre of the table, about six inches above the surface, a canal of pure water continued flowing from a silver fountain beautifully constructed at the head of the table. Its banks were covered in green moss and aquatic flowers; gold and silver fish swam and sported through the bubbling current, which produced a pleasing murmur where it fell.[11]

Lord Colchester recorded that 'towards the Prince's end … the table widened and the water also, and fell by a succession of cascades into a circular lake surrounded with architectural decorations, and small vases, burning perfumes, which stood under the arches of the colonnade round the lake'.[12] The prince's party was served not only by his own staff but by footmen of the king and the queen in their state liveries and attended by a man in a 'complete suit of ancient armour'.[13] The celebrations apparently ran until six o'clock in the morning. By many they were considered little short of a triumph. The *Annual Register* reported 'le Vieille Cour de Versailles with all its proud presentations, could never have more attractively set forth the elegant fascinations of fashionable life and exalted rank'.[14]

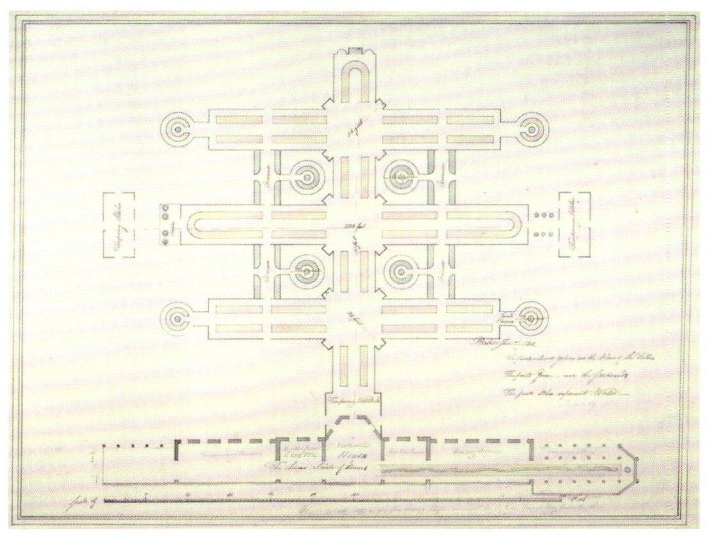

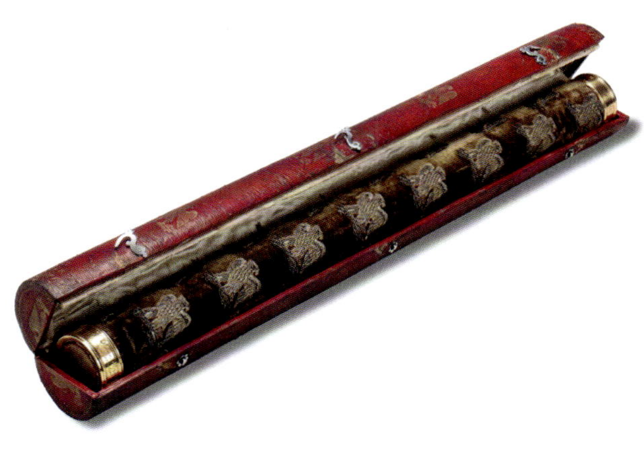

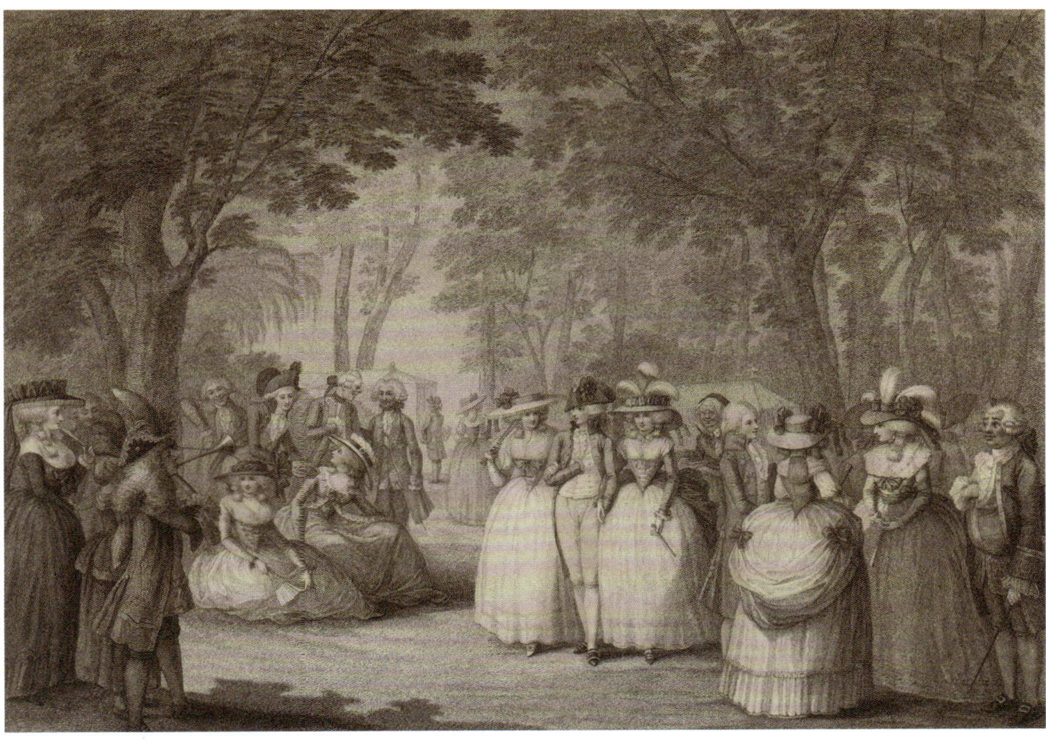

FIG. 15.5
UNKNOWN ARTIST, *Plan of the tables in the temporary rooms, Carlton House for the grand fête in 1811*, 1811. Pen and ink with wash with additions in pencil, 44.0 × 58.0 cm (British Library, London: Crace Port. 12.10)

FIG. 15.6
FRENCH, *Baton and case*, 1804. Wood, velvet, gold, gold thread, 47.7 × 4.2 cm, RCIN 61176

FIG. 15.7
WILLIAM DICKINSON (1746–1823), *The Gardens of Carleton-House with Neapolitan Ballad Singers*, 1785. Stipple with etching, printed in brown, 54.0 × 70.2 cm, RCIN 605139

On these occasions George was undoubtedly influenced by similar spectacles in Vauxhall Gardens and indeed continued to attend and support such events. In 1813, for example, at an evening celebrating the victory at the Battle of Vittoria, the Vauxhall Rotunda held 'a vast quantity of the Prince Regent's richest gold and silver plate surmounted by a bust of the Marquis of Wellington'. The great prize, Marshal Jourdan's baton (Fig. 15.6), which had been claimed by Wellington after the battle, 'was disposed among the plate, so as to be obvious to all'.[15] The scattered, temporary structures which were frequently erected in the grounds of Carlton House may have been intended to replicate such a spectacle. For example, William Dickinson's engraving recording the performance of a band of Neapolitan ballad singers illustrates a similar event (Fig. 15.7). Dickinson shows the Prince of Wales and his guests in the informal setting of the gardens at Carlton House, listening to the

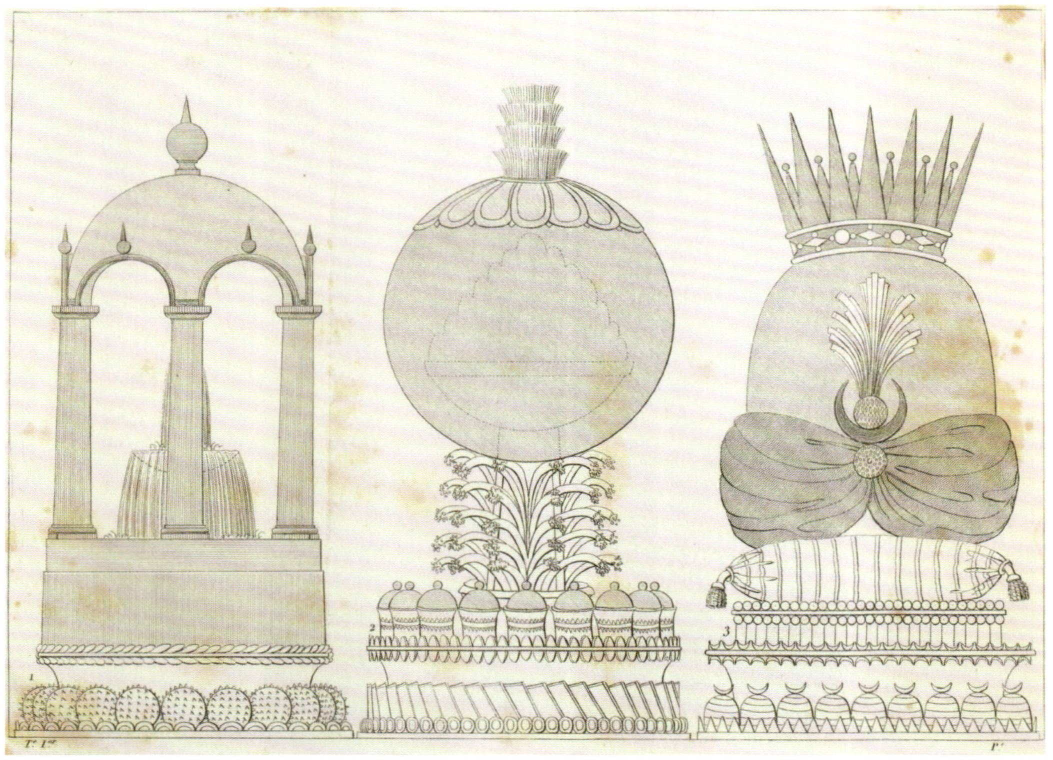

FIG. 15.8
AFTER MARIE-ANTOINE CARÊME (1784–1833), *Designs for pièces montées*, from *Le patissier royal parisien: traité élémentaire et pratique de la patisserie ancienne et moderne*, 3rd edition, Paris, 1841 (Katherine Golden Bitting Collection on Gastronomy, Library of Congress, Washington DC: TX763 .C27 1841)

singers perform; in the background two structures are visible, apparently temporary buildings erected for the entertainment. Another glimpse of such structures is offered by Mary Berry's reminiscences: 'the temporary rooms in the garden are immense, and admirably contrived, and I dare say when lighted up must have been very handsome'.[16]

The Grand Service

Such celebrations were, by their nature, ephemeral, characterised by decorations in chalk or more elaborate paintings on the floor and table, musical accompaniments, illuminations on the exterior of the buildings and fireworks, now barely remembered in the Royal Collection. The food itself was a spectacle. The celebrated French chef Marie-Antoine Carême worked for George for a brief period of eight months in 1816, providing elaborate cuisine for the prince's table. Carême later published a number of designs for the great architectural structures, or *pièces montées*, which appeared on his tables, often intended for the dessert course but only in part edible, incorporating elements in sugar, nougat and marzipan but also wax, card and wood (Fig. 15.8). George was clearly proud of the tableaux presented on such occasions and the apartments were habitually opened to public inspection on the day following a fête. Mary Berry describes such a visit: 'all the plate was still upon the table, and all the magnificent gold plate upon the sideboard, in three ranks, at the top of the room … all the knives, forks, spoons, &c, &c, yet spread upon it'.[17]

George's attitude to his plate collection perhaps reflects the fact that these objects were there to support a *mise-en-scène*. Works of silver supplied by Rundells were not infrequently returned to the goldsmiths for reworking into more elaborate forms. In 1811, for example, two centrepieces almost certainly modelled by William Theed (the Elder) were delivered to Carlton House, each formed with a central basket for flowers and three nymphs, surrounded by piping fauns and panthers. In 1816 or 1817 they were returned to Rundells to be converted into two great candelabra standing over 4 feet (1.2 metres) tall, in effect great sculptures for the table designed by John Flaxman, one showing the myth of the Apples of the Hesperides, the other Mercury delivering the infant Bacchus to the nymphs of Nysa (Fig. 15.9).[18] Similarly, a pair of candelabra formed from addorsed griffins originally began life as a single centrepiece, described in the 1811 bills as 'for the sideboard or the centre of the table, to receive a dish or basket and with a lamp in the centre'.[19] In 1818 the centrepiece was divided into the present arrangement (Fig. 15.10) and two years later new bases were added, engraved

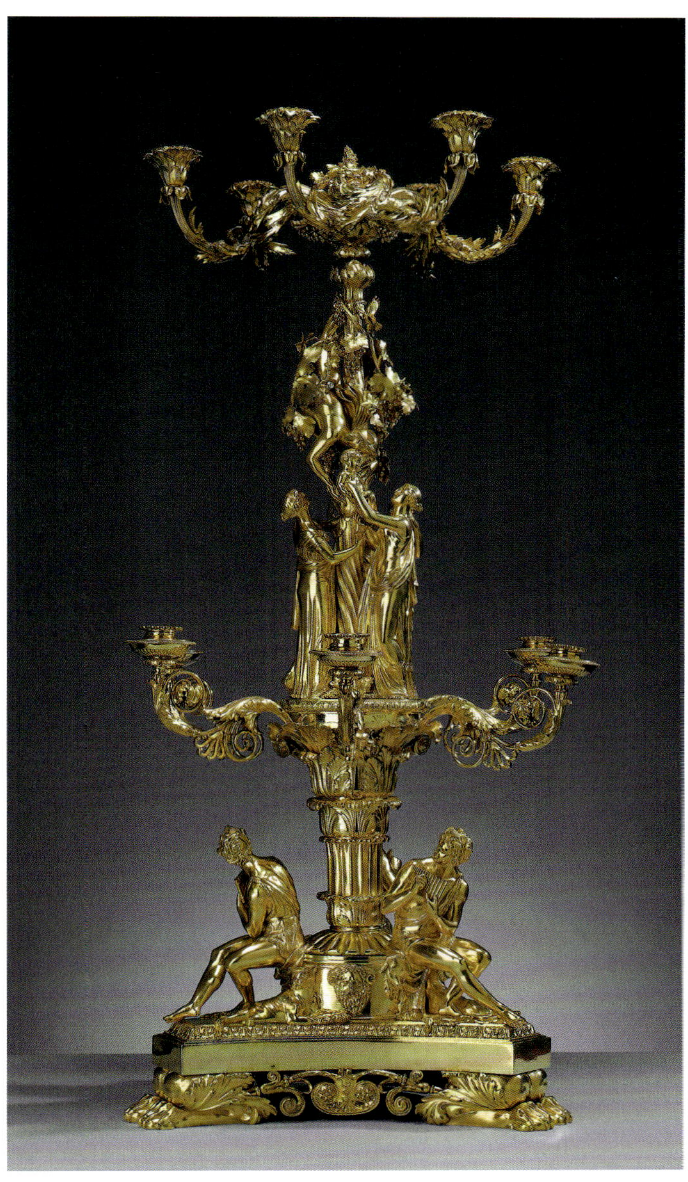

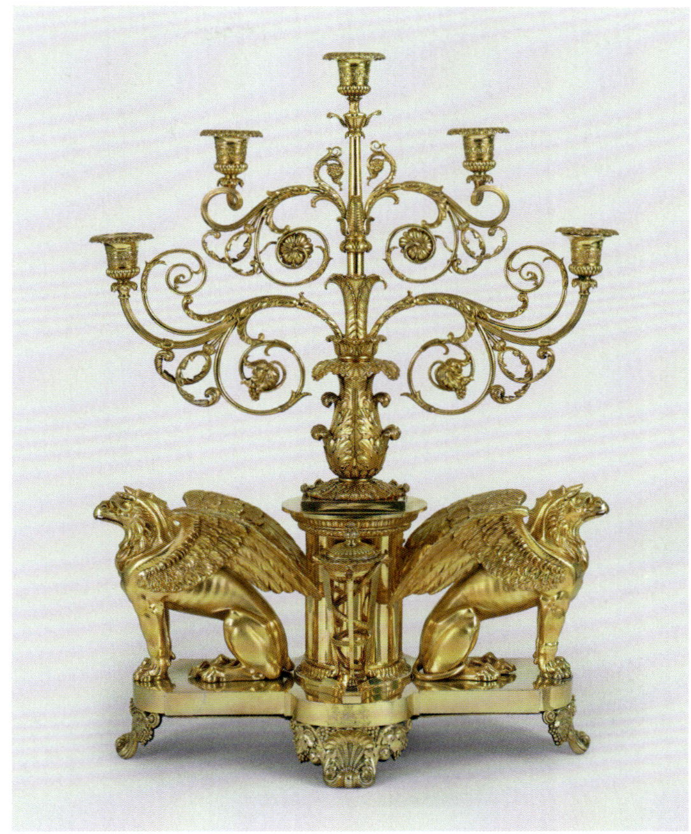

FIG. 15.9
RUNDELL, BRIDGE & RUNDELL, *Mercury and Bacchus candelabrum*, 1809–17. Silver gilt, 125.0 × 66.0 × 66.0 cm, RCIN 51977

FIG. 15.10
PAUL STORR (1771–1844), *Candelabrum*, 1811–20. Silver gilt, 82.0 × 61.0 × 28.0 cm, RCIN 51104

in reverse on the underside with the royal coat of arms, clearly intended to be placed on mirrored plateaux on the table so that the arms would read correctly in the reflections.

The entire spirit of the Grand Service, in effect an array of table-top sculptures, might be seen as the result of George's determination to increase the splendour of the entertainments at Carlton House. In the early years of his residency there he had relied on plate hired in for each occasion. Undoubtedly spurred on by Napoleon's commission of a great dining service for his coronation in 1804, known as the *Grand Vermeil*, George first ordered a prodigiously large dining service from Rundell, Bridge & Rundell around 1806. This was not a simple or homogenous service and included works which Farington noted 'will never require to be used'.[20] Instead this was a set of dining plate, and associated buffet plate, reliant on cast decoration and heavily sculptural in design, with little to link its disparate elements other than its gilded appearance and its supply by the royal goldsmiths. Over the course of the 25 years in which the individual pieces of the service were in production, Rundells were able to draw on a wide pool of artists such as Flaxman (Fig. 15.11), Theed, Thomas Stothard (Fig. 15.12), Edward Hodges Baily and A.W.N. Pugin, many of them otherwise involved in the great sculptural schemes of the day, creating national monuments. Such diversity of artistic talent led to a wide variety of design for the works of the Grand Service – the objects incorporate elements of Greek, Roman, Egyptian, baroque, rococo and Gothic styles, many also celebrating Britain's marine heritage and including patriotic symbols such as oak branches. The service might itself have been intended to act as a national monument.

It is rare to find accounts of any event held at Carlton House without some reference to this magnificent assemblage of plate.

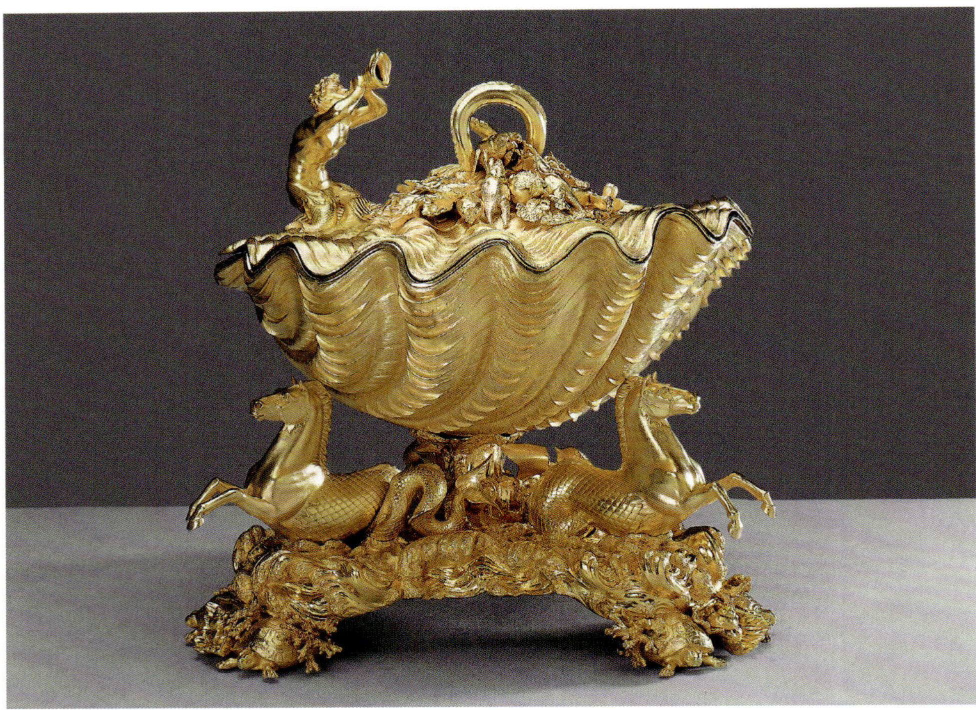

FIG. 15.11
MARK OF JOHN BRIDGE (1755–1834), for RUNDELL, BRIDGE & RUNDELL, designed by JOHN FLAXMAN (1755–1826), *Tureen*, 1826/7. Silver gilt, 42.0 × 41.0 × 38.5 cm, RCIN 50279

Lady Harriot Frampton wrote to her daughter on 22 July 1814 after attending a ball at Carlton House given in honour of the Duke of Wellington:

> the plateau down the middle of the table was covered with exquisite groups in silver gilt. The centre group was above three feet high and each one of the figures was so beautifully executed that they might have been ornaments in a drawing room, and everything else, even the salt-cellars, was in the most excellent taste.

There was some criticism of the plate left white, which by comparison looked 'poor and cold',[21] and gradually all the elements of the service were gilded. Here too the spur of Napoleon's *Grand Vermeil* may have played a role – if the French emperor was eating off gold plate in Paris, should George not be doing the same in London?

The Coronation

The most significant, the most public and the most spectacular ceremonial moment of George's life was his coronation, on 19 July 1821. The sacred nature of the service itself was of course paramount, but this was also an opportunity for George to present himself to the nation in order to revive public approbation. Rush, who witnessed the procession to dissolve Parliament on 10 June 1818, suggested such an event was 'one of the most imposing public ceremonies in England', largely, as he commented, derived from the manner in which the sovereign goes to Parliament, on public display within the glazed state coach, drawn by eight horses.[22] Greville reported that in February 1821, when George's popularity had suffered a huge downturn in the wake of Queen Caroline's controversial trial, he attended the theatre at Drury Lane for the first time since his accession. 'He was received with immense acclamations, the whole pit standing up, hurrahing and waving their hats.'[23] George never underestimated the importance of a public appearance to harness popular acclaim, and such popularity was only increased by magnificent spectacle, as his triumphant visits to Dublin, Hanover and Edinburgh were to demonstrate (see chapter 16). Nevertheless, he had no way to gauge what his reception at the time of the coronation might be, and his nervousness is clear – he ordered supplementary security, provided by pugilists at the doors to Westminster Hall (see chapter 13), and after the event he returned to Carlton House by a circuitous route to avoid any public demonstrations. Further entertainments were provided to appease the masses: the theatres of London were ordered to provide performances on the evening of the coronation, many of them opening their doors for free, and these were supplemented

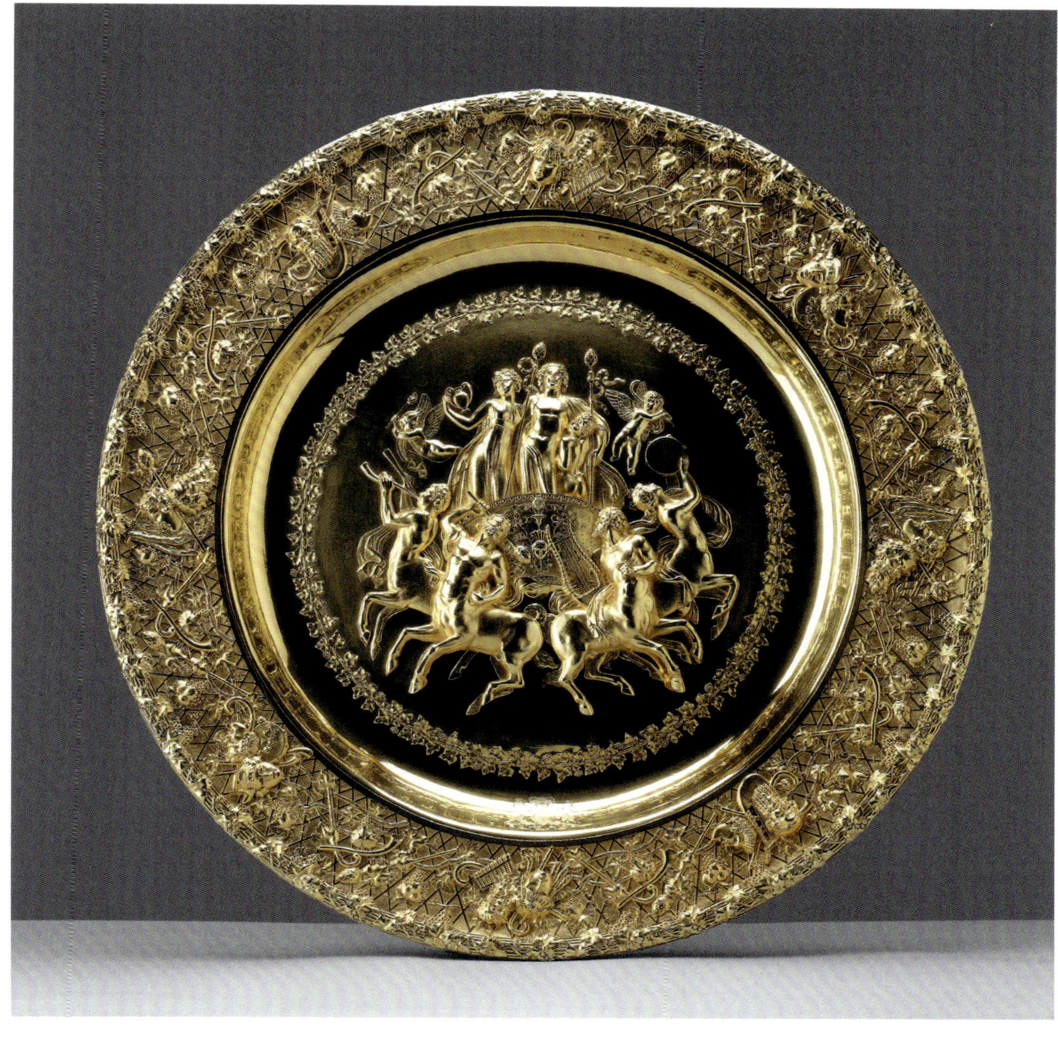

FIG. 15.12
MARK OF PAUL STORR (1771–1844), for RUNDELL, BRIDGE & RUNDELL, designed by THOMAS STOTHARD (1755–1834), *Dish (Triumph of Bacchus and Ariadne)*, 1814. Silver gilt, 7.5 × 79.0 cm (diameter), RCIN 51654

by a firework display in St James's Park choreographed by the pioneer of military rockets, William Congreve.

George had, in effect, had ten years to plan his coronation and he had studied the ceremonies of his ancestors. An eye-witness account of such study is provided by John Bridge, written on the back of a print and kept together with his ticket for admittance to the Abbey.[24] Bridge, partner in the firm of royal goldsmiths, was responsible for the refurbishment of the regalia for the coronation as well as the supply of the new diamond circlet (the Diamond Diadem; see Fig. 0.2), aigrettes, clasps and a dress sword mounted in diamonds, all commissioned by George. According to Bridge's account, on delivery of the new jewels to George's chambers in late July 1821, the king said that 'I have been reading the whole ceremony of the Coronation of King James and among other things have met with a Print of his jeweller which I have bought, indeed, I bought it for you'; he then presented Bridge with a portrait of George Heriot, Crown Jeweller to James I. George collected prints of the Stuart coronations (Fig. 15.13); he may also have owned copies of some of the variety of titles published or reissued in 1820 at his accession, relating the history of coronations, such as Edward Walker's account of Charles II's coronation. He certainly purchased similar histories by Richard Thomson and Arthur Taylor from the booksellers Budd & Calkin.[25]

For his own coronation, George chose a celebration of English history in the romanticised Hanoverian tradition. Those taking part in the ceremony were expected to wear a form of late Tudor or early Stuart costume, including doublets, ruffed collars and trunk hose. Bridge recorded that when he presented the Heriot portrait, the king spent some time examining the costume in the print and suggesting that Bridge, who would be attending the ceremony, ought to wear something similar, or at the very least a suitable cloak. George himself appears to have had a hand in the design of his own robes (Fig. 15.14), worn in

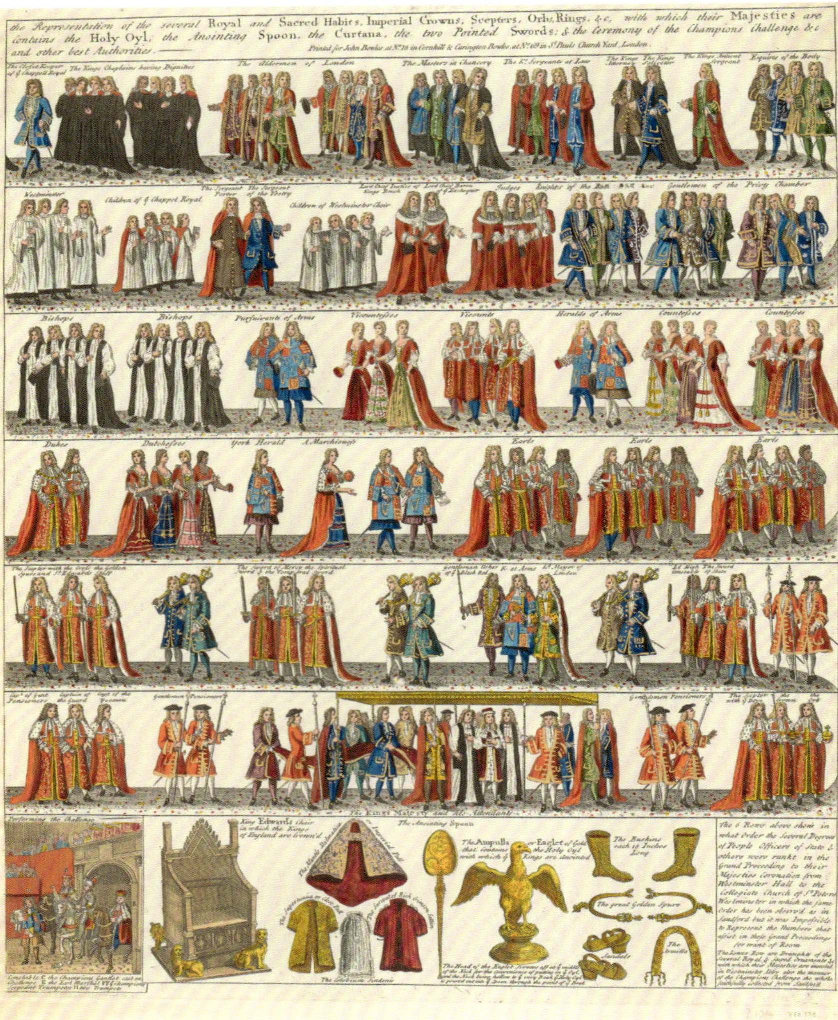

FIG. 15.13
Published by JOHN BOWLES (1701?–79) and CARRINGTON BOWLES (1724–93), *Coronation Procession of James II* (right-hand half), *c.*1790. Etching and engraving with hand colouring, 59.9 × 48.7 cm, RCIN 750178

FIG. 15.14
EDWARD SCRIVEN (1775–1841) AFTER FRANCIS PHILIP STEPHANOFF (1788–1860), *The King in his Royal Robes Wearing a Cap of Estate*, 1826. Stipple and aquatint with printed and hand colouring, 43.7 × 58.0 cm (sheet), RCIN 750784

the procession to the abbey, which included a cloth-of-silver doublet with trunk hose, trimmed in gold lace, with a ruff, an embroidered, crimson velvet surcoat (Fig. 15.15) with matching girdle or sword-belt, silver-ribbon garters with gold lace rosettes and white kid shoes with red heels with similar rosettes. There were elements here of historic dress although no direct source for any of the designs. The costume was completed by the long, crimson velvet, ermine-lined robe (the Parliament Robe) which had an additional panel in front, and a train 26 feet (8 metres) long that required more than the usual six train-bearers. On his head George wore a curled brown wig, with a broad-brimmed black velvet hat (described as a 'Spanish hat'), the brim pinned up at the front with a diamond clasp supplied by Rundells, with two or three diamond aigrettes supporting ostrich-feather plumes and the diamond circlet. These may have been intended to evoke the flavour of Stuart dress which infused the costumes worn by all other members of the procession – the curled wig in particular giving George an early seventeenth-century appearance. The king was also keen to include reference to the national flowers. His original wish was to incorporate them into the State Crown, although this was deemed inappropriate and the concept was transferred to the diamond circlet instead, where the rose, thistle and shamrock appear in the diamond sprigs which intersperse the crosses pattée. They appear again embroidered across the Parliament Robe, stole (Fig. 15.16), and in the cloth-of-gold and brocade mantle newly woven for the coronation service. The mantle also incorporates imperial eagles woven into the design and the silver-gilt clasp, again supplied by Rundells, is cast in the form of an eagle (Fig. 15.1).

This suggests that alongside his studies of historic coronations, George was keenly aware of the images of Napoleon's 1804 ceremony and incorporated a number of features into his own dress in direct response, not least the eagle motif. George appears to have collected a number of prints of Bonaparte's

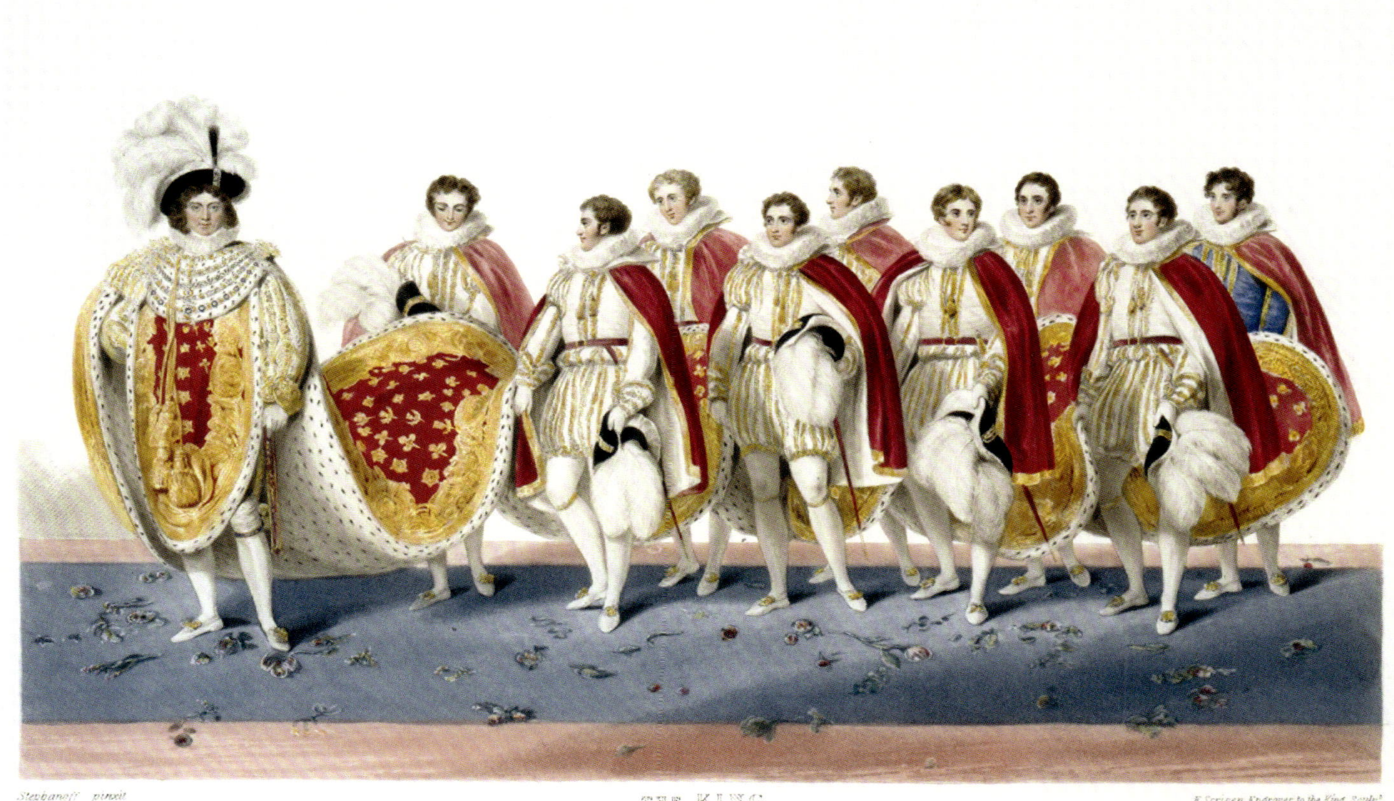

coronation (for example, Fig. 15.17). Both the emperor's *grand costume* and the *petit costume* appear to have influenced the designs for George's own. The Parliament Robe with its additional chasuble-like panel at the front is a reworking of the robe worn by Napoleon during his own ceremony, and the broad-brimmed Spanish hat with diamond-clasp worn by George was in all likelihood a response to Isabey's design for the emperor's *petit costume*, which included a hat of almost identical form.

Something of this sense of rivalry is captured in Lawrence's official state portrait (see Fig. 0.1). Lawrence, perhaps surprisingly, painted the coronation portrait over an existing image of George in Garter robes, a version of a portrait created in 1818 and presented to the Mansion House, Dublin. The 1821 image shows the king surrounded by the trappings of majesty, wearing the collars of four British and European orders and the great ermine-lined mantle, with the Imperial State Crown beside him. The crown is placed on the *Table des grands capitaines de l'antiquité* (see Fig. 1.10), a Sèvres-porcelain and gilt-bronze table originally commissioned by Napoleon, although never delivered to him, and subsequently a most prized gift to George from Louis XVIII. The coronation portrait was intended to hang in the Throne Room of St James's Palace, between two works by George Jones recording the great allied victories at Vittoria and Waterloo – there could be no doubt of the king's right to stand with those who had defeated his rival Napoleon. The Chantrey marble bust of George (see Fig. 3.1), which became his official sculptural portrait, perhaps underlines the point still further. Chantrey portrays the king as a Roman field marshal, his senatorial toga draped over a cuirass. Here is a monarch who is both an evocation of a classical emperor and a military victor.

Many of the objects created at the time of the coronation were intended to be given away – they acted as perquisites to those taking part in the ceremonies. George did, however, collect

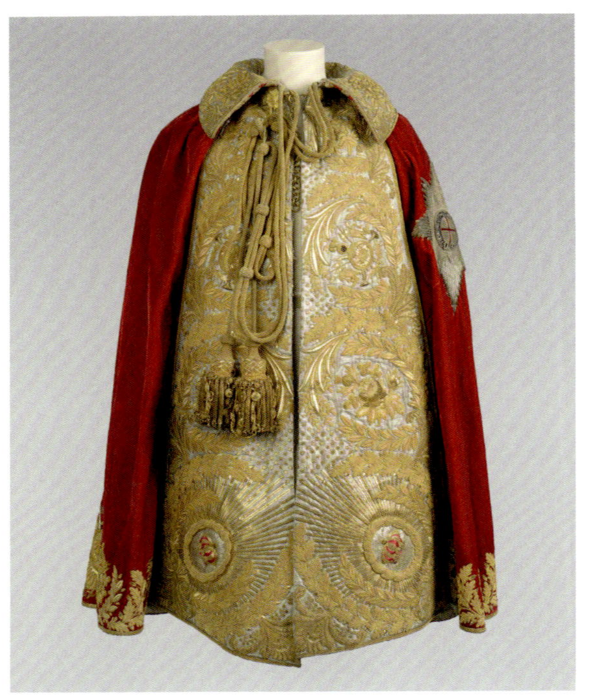

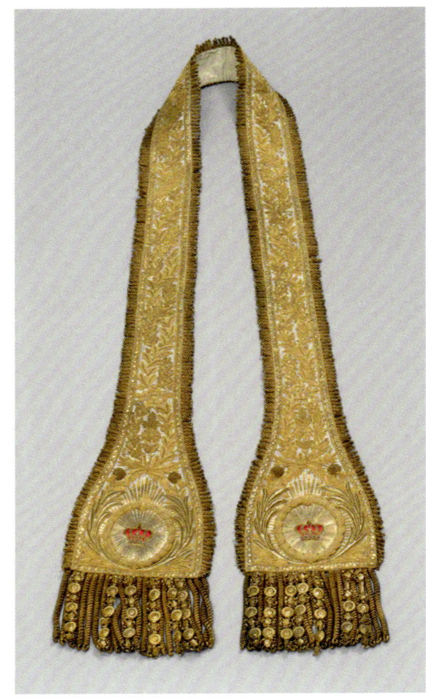

FIG. 15.15
JOHN MEYER (*c.*1753–*c.*1830), *Coronation surcoat*, 1820–1. Silk, velvet, gold and silver thread, sequins, 105.0 cm (length), RCIN 62955

FIG. 15.16
JOHN MEYER (*c.*1753–*c.*1830), *Stole*, 1821. Cloth of silver, gold thread, silk, gold, sequins, 124.5 cm (length), RCIN 62953

FIG. 15.17
BARON FRANÇOIS GÉRARD (1770–1837) AFTER BARON AUGUSTE GASPARD LOUIS DESNOYERS (1779–1857), *Napoleon le Grand*, 1808. Engraving, 70.2 × 53.2 cm (sheet), RCIN 617722

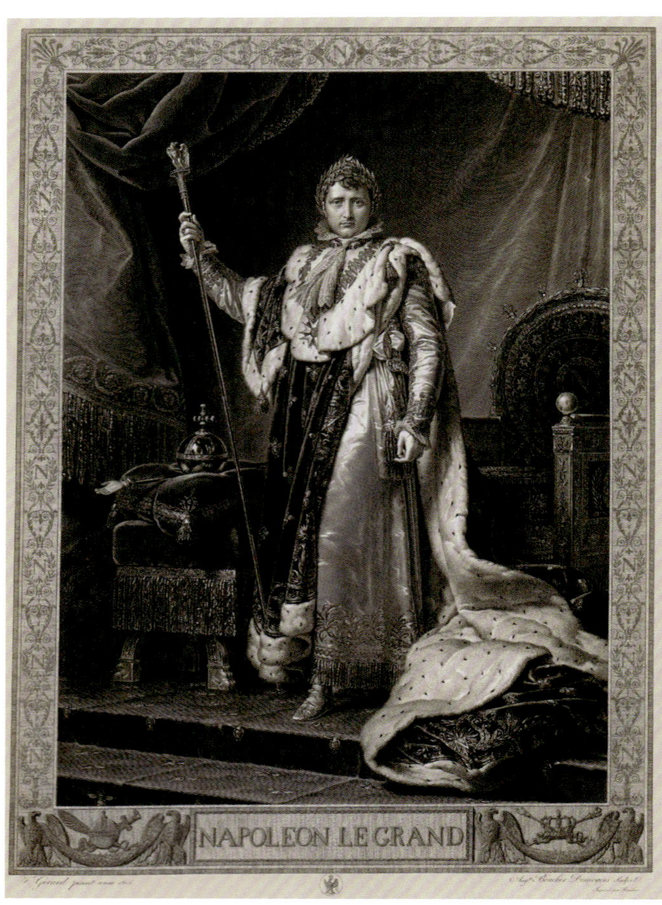

a number for himself. By tradition the Imperial State Crown was newly remade for each coronation and the stones hired in for the occasion. George wished to retain the stones after his ceremony although Parliament were not ready to support the cost of the jewels, which in George's case numbered some 12,314 individual pieces. Instead the king was obliged to commission from Rundell, Bridge & Rundell a gilt-bronze cast of the frame complete with its stones in their unbacked settings – something of a new fashion – which at least provided an idea of the crown's original appearance (Fig. 15.18).

The coronation service was followed by a banquet in Westminster Hall, the last of its kind to be held in Britain. The hall was dressed with temporary structures, including an arch through which the chief figures processed, described by Robert Huish as 'purely in the gothic style', and flanked by two sculptures representing Edward the Confessor and Richard II. The ceremonies of the banquet, like the coronation service itself, were inevitably steeped in long-standing tradition, much of it already so archaic that it meant little to those involved but was carried forward for the sake of history. The hunt for the recipe for the traditional 'dish of grout' (a form of spiced porridge) to be served to the king, for instance, is indicative of the arcane nature of some of these customs. Huish noted that 'It is not easy to give an account of this dish, which is so remarkably perpetuated by

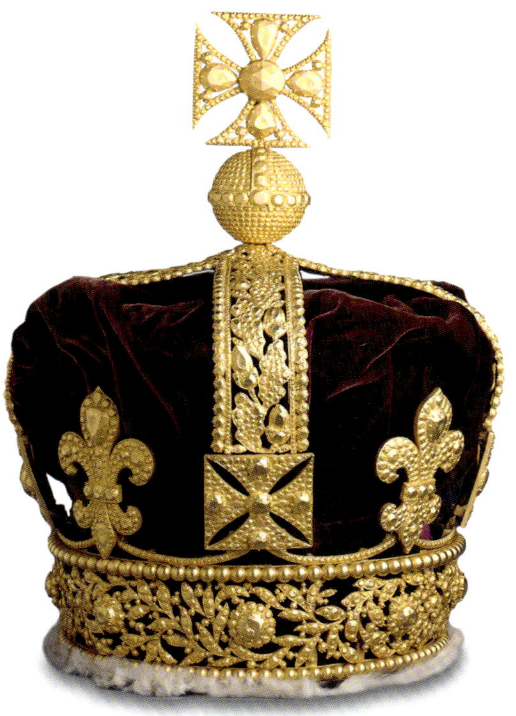

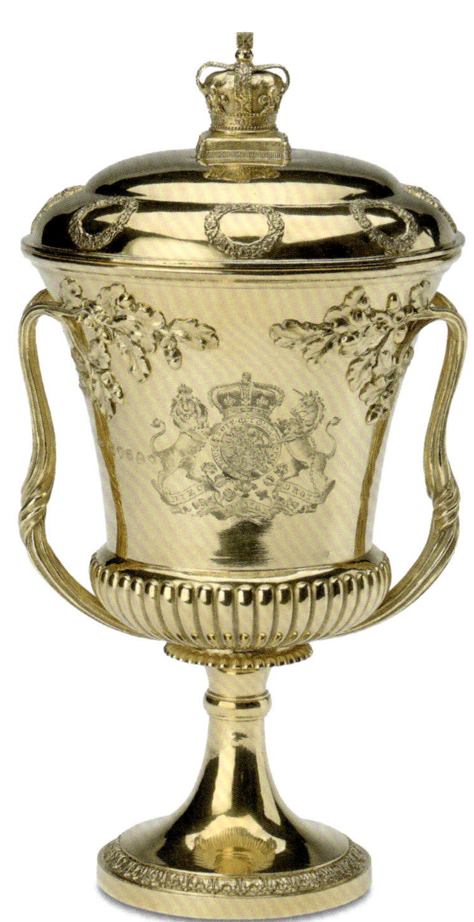

FIG. 15.18
RUNDELL, BRIDGE & RUNDELL, *Cast of George IV's Imperial State Crown*, 1823. Gilt bronze, velvet, ermine, 36.3 × 29.0 × 30.3 cm, RCIN 50435

FIG. 15.19
MARK OF PHILIP RUNDELL (1746–1827), *Cup and Cover*, 1820–1. Gold, 24.9 × 13.0 × 12.0 cm, RCIN 48383

this ancient tenure.' Similarly the King's Apothecary, Mr Walker, applied to attend the ceremonies, but to do so he would have to dress in a costume appropriate to the reign of Edward II (1307–27), which Huish recognised in his account of the coronation as 'singular' at best.[26]

Many of the objects supplied for the banquet were also perquisites – the silver and gold cups presented in sequence to the king by the Lord of the Manor of Wymondley, the King's Champion and the Lord Mayor of London, for example – but at least one remains in the Royal Collection. This is a cup based on a Greek krater vase but apparently associated with the coronation, as the domed lid is embellished with a crown finial and wreaths composed of the national flowers (Fig. 15.19). The dining plate was retained, thanks to the quick-witted actions of the Clerk Comptroller of the Kitchen, Jean-Baptiste Watier, who rescued the silver from the depredations of the assembled guests after the king had departed.

The buffet ranged behind the king at the banquet displayed silver intended to emphasise the longevity of the monarchy, including the so-called Exeter Salt and Plymouth Fountain, both associated with Charles II, as well as more contemporary works which reflected George's heroic and chivalric self-image.[27] The great silver-gilt Shield of Achilles (Fig. 15.20), marked by Philip Rundell, was also among the objects shown prominently on the buffet. This masterpiece, designed by Flaxman, was conceived as an evocation of the shield vividly described by Homer in the *Iliad*. Its overt heroic subject matter can only have helped to underline George's military credentials. This work was complemented by the large gold tray (Fig. 15.21) supplied by Rundells at the same time. No bill for this latter work exists but its iconography – the 21 European chivalric orders to which George belonged at the time of his coronation – suggests that it was almost certainly prepared for the banquet. The tray is created entirely in 18 carat gold, supported on feet cast as a lion and a unicorn, the national flowers and oak leaves incorporated into the border. Again the piece hints at imperial power – a Nemean lion's pelt motif is both a reference to Hercules and to the vanquishing of an otherwise unconquerable foe.

The most ambitious record of the coronation was the printed volume produced by John Whittaker, a large folio illustrated with coloured prints of the key protagonists in the

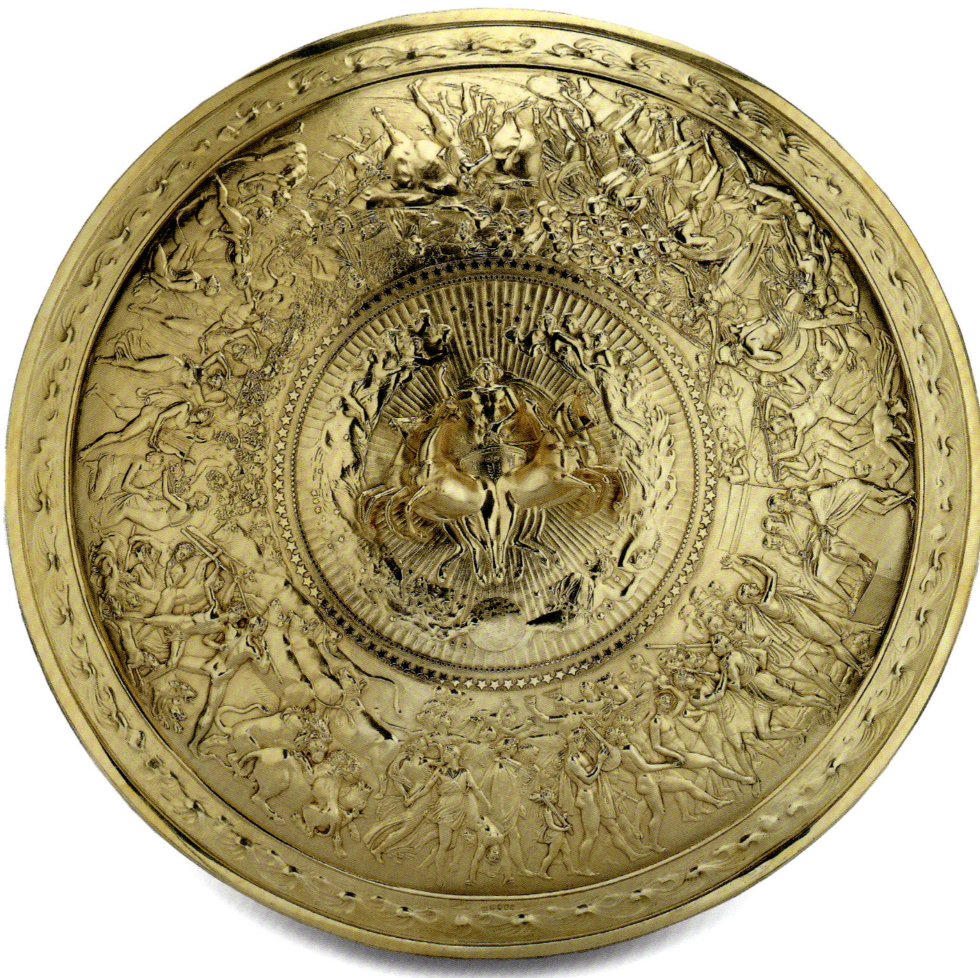

FIG. 15.20
MARK OF PHILIP RUNDELL (1746–1827), designed by JOHN FLAXMAN (1755–1826), *Shield of Achilles*, 1821. Silver gilt, 90.7 cm (diameter), RCIN 51266

procession, the letterpress printed in gold leaf using a technique invented by the publisher himself in 1816 (Fig. 15.22). Only a few copies of his *Ceremonial* are thought to have been printed, at great expense, one of which was acquired by George. Despite being awarded a grant of £5,000 towards the publication, Whittaker was bankrupted by the project.

It has been argued that George possessed an exceptional talent for presenting himself to the population of each country as one of themselves – as a decidedly Irish, Hanoverian or Scottish monarch by turns (see chapter 16). In fact, George had achieved this first at his coronation in London, presenting a quintessentially English face to the nation, underlining a form of continuity with historic monarchs as far back as Edward the Confessor, and celebrating England's traditions of chivalry and military prowess. As Walter Scott noted, 'those who witnessed it have seen a scene calculated to raise the country in their opinion and to throw into the shade all scenes of similar magnificence from the Field of the Cloth of Gold down to the present day'.[28]

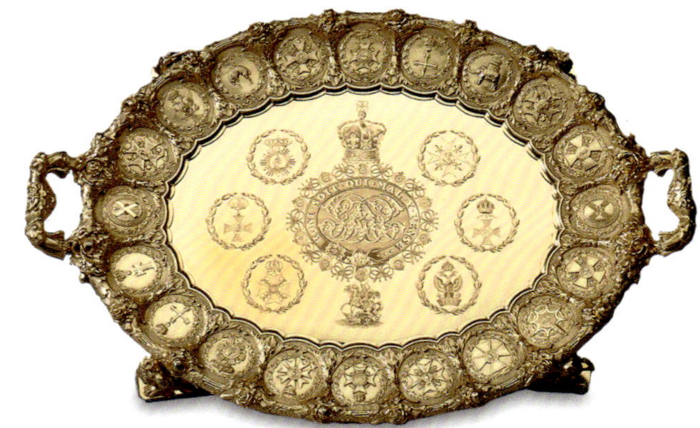

FIG. 15.21
MARK OF PHILIP RUNDELL (1746–1827), *Tray*, 1821/2. Gold, 10.0 × 67.5 × 46.0 cm, RCIN 50836

FIG. 15.22
JOHN WHITTAKER (d. 1831), *Ceremonial of the Coronation of King George IV in the Abbey of St Peter's*, 1823. Printed on japan vellum, gold letterpress, stipple engraving with etching and aquatint and hand colouring, 69.5 × 60.5 cm, RCIN 1005090

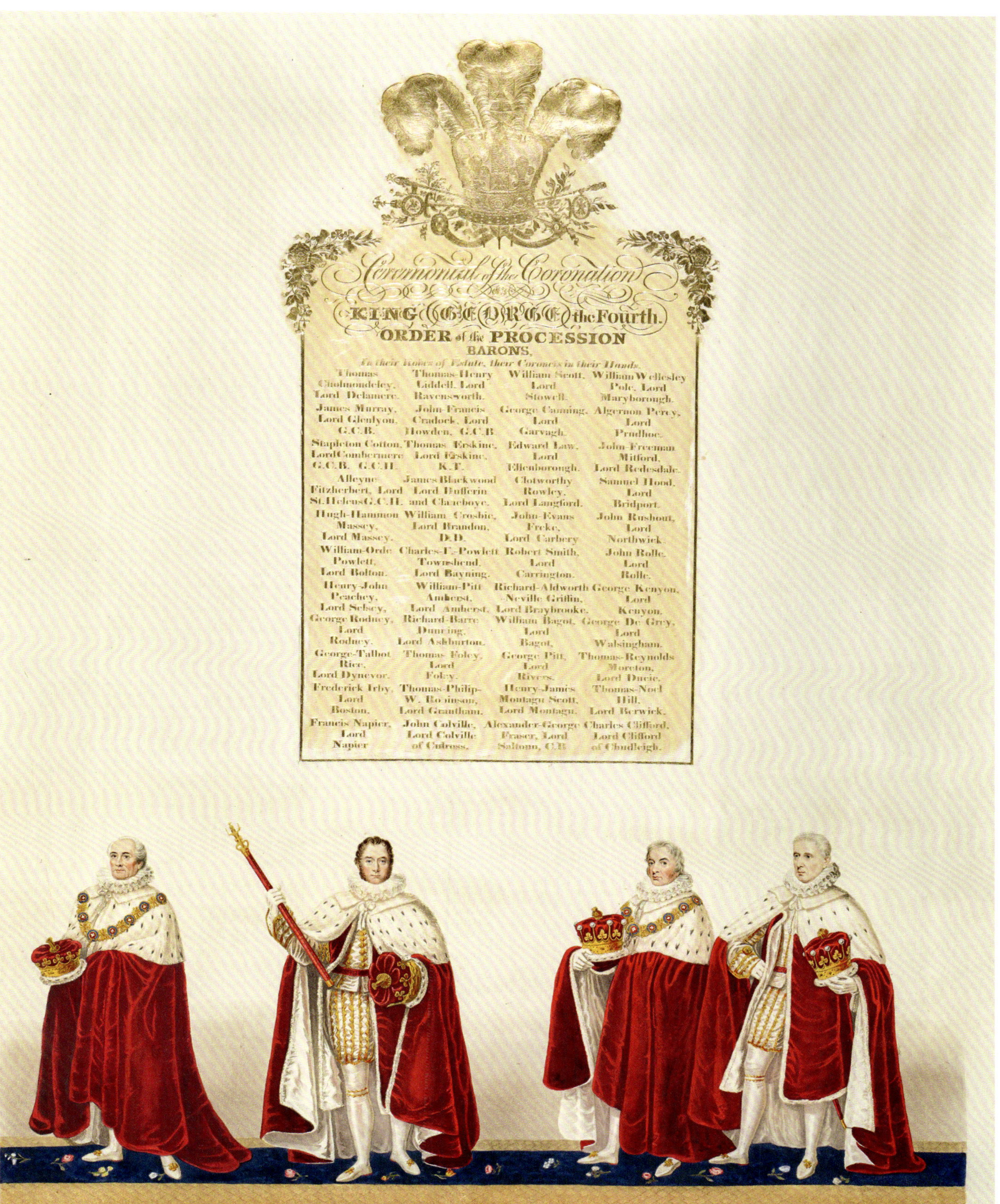

Ceremonial of the Coronation
of
KING GEORGE the Fourth.
ORDER of the PROCESSION
BARONS,
In their Robes of Estate, their Coronets in their Hands.
Thomas Cholmondeley, Lord Delamere.
Thomas-Henry Liddell, Lord Ravensworth.
William Scott, Lord Stowell.
William Wellesley Pole, Lord Maryborough.
James Murray, Lord Glenlyon, G.C.B.
John-Francis Cradock, Lord Howden, G.C.B
George Canning, Lord Garvagh.
Algernon Percy, Lord Prudhoe.
Stapleton Cotton, Lord Combermere G.C.B. G.C.H.
Thomas Erskine, Lord Erskine, K.T.
Edward Law, Lord Ellenborough.
John-Freeman Mitford, Lord Redesdale.
Alleyne Fitzherbert, Lord St. Helens G.C.H.
James Blackwood Lord Dufferin and Claneboye.
Clotworthy Rowley, Lord Langford.
Samuel Hood, Lord Bridport.
Hugh-Hammon Massey, Lord Massey.
William Crosbie, Lord Brandon, D.D.
John-Evans Freke, Lord Carbery
John Rushout, Lord Northwick.
William-Orde Powlett, Lord Bolton.
Charles-F.-Powlett Townshend, Lord Bayning.
Robert Smith, Lord Carrington.
John Rolle, Lord Rolle.
Henry-John Peachey, Lord Selsey,
William-Pitt Amherst, Lord Amherst.
Richard-Aldworth -Neville Griffin, Lord Braybrooke.
George Kenyon, Lord Kenyon.
George Rodney, Lord Rodney.
Richard-Barre Dunning, Lord Ashburton.
William Bagot, Lord Bagot,
George De Grey, Lord Walsingham.
George-Talbot Rice, Lord Dynevor.
Thomas Foley, Lord Foley.
George Pitt, Lord Rivers.
Thomas-Reynolds Moreton, Lord Ducie.
Frederick Irby, Lord Boston.
Thomas-Philip-W. Robinson, Lord Grantham.
Henry-James Montagu Scott, Lord Montagu.
Thomas-Noel Hill, Lord Berwick.
Francis Napier, Lord Napier
John Colville, Lord Colville of Culross.
Alexander-George Fraser, Lord Saltoun, C.B
Charles Clifford, Lord Clifford of Chudleigh.

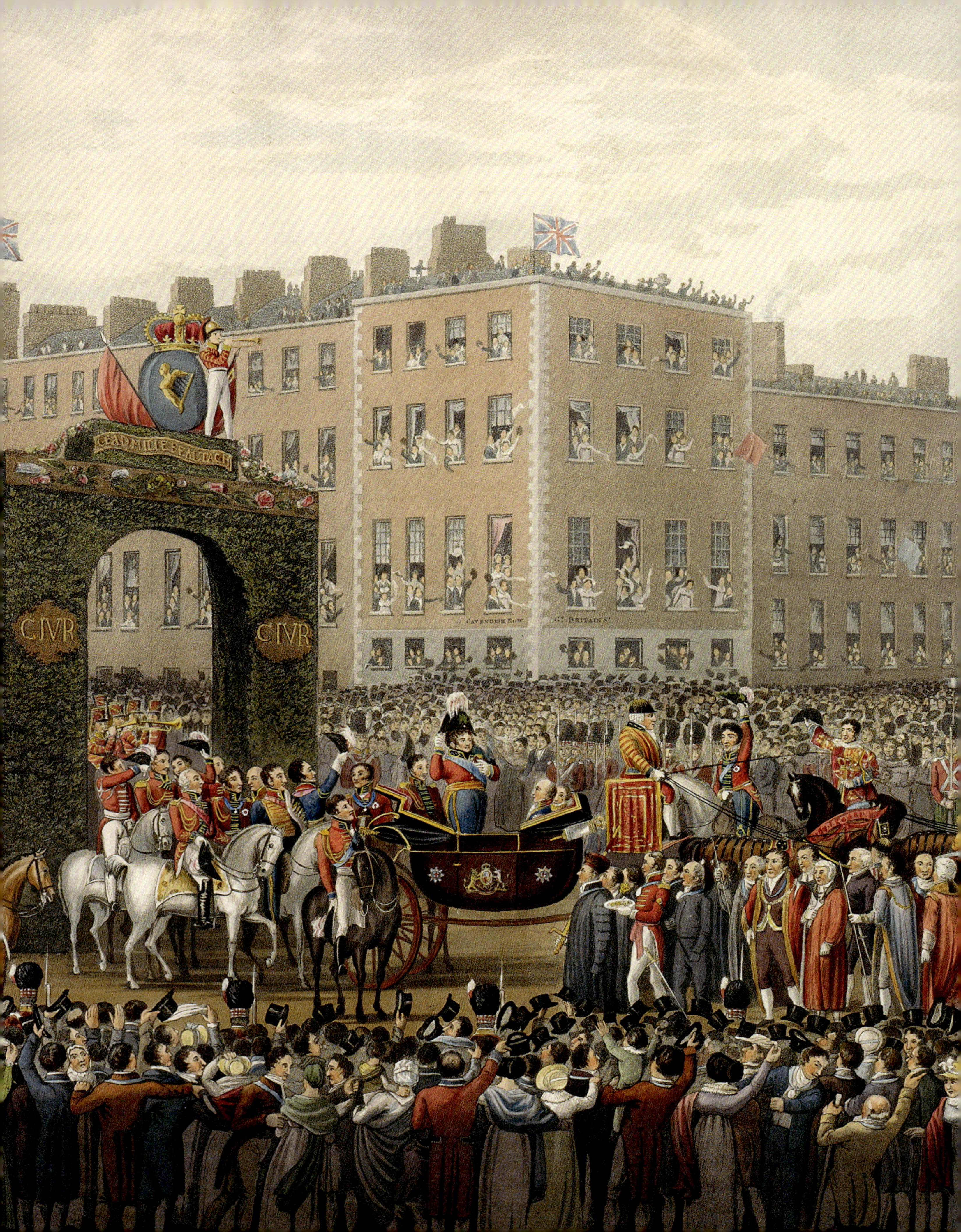
CEAD MILLE FEALTACH
CIVR
CIVR
CAVENDISH ROW
GT. BRITAIN ST.

GEORGE IV'S VISITS *to* IRELAND, HANOVER *and* SCOTLAND

DEBORAH CLARKE

After his coronation George IV embarked on a series of visits to his outlying kingdoms: to Ireland and Hanover in 1821 and Scotland in 1822. No reigning monarch had travelled to these countries for a considerable time and 'the king conceived the patriotic idea of … making himself known to the remotest of his people'.[1] During each visit, in a series of ceremonies and rituals that relied on an 'invented tradition' and a connection with the past, the king made himself visible to as large a part of the population as possible.[2] In every country, amid a whirlwind of pageantry, George showed a remarkable talent for presenting himself to the population as one of themselves, an Irish monarch, a German-speaking Hanoverian or a Highland chieftain.

Ireland

The king set sail from Portsmouth to Ireland on the *Royal George* and it was on board on 9 August 1821 at Holyhead that he received the news of Queen Caroline's death. He decided to continue his journey and on 12 August landed at Howth, a small fishing village with a harbour near Dublin, for what was to be the first peaceful visit to Ireland by a reigning British monarch.[3] Plans for the king to travel to Ireland had been discussed for some months, but it was thought expedient to wait until after the coronation.[4] Although support in Ireland for a royal visit was not wholehearted, due to religious tensions and the king's lack of support for Catholic Emancipation, George had made clear before his arrival his wish for unity among religious groups. He was motivated by the desire to build a strong relationship with the Irish, particularly the Catholics, and he was heavily involved in the preparations to ensure that all went peacefully and no offence was caused.

The royal visit was planned meticulously in Dublin and provided an opportunity to show, through certain ceremonial rituals and traditions, the loyalty of the country and its subjects to the monarch. A large temporary triumphal arch was created for Dublin, which served as the city gate for the king's official entry. Decorations and tableaux were set up throughout the city in the form of transparencies, scenes painted on paper or

(p. 214)
Detail of Fig. 16.4, ROBERT I. HAVELL (active 1808–37) AFTER JOSEPH PATRICK HAVERTY (1794–1864), *His Majesty's Public Entry into the City of Dublin on the 17th August 1821*, 1823

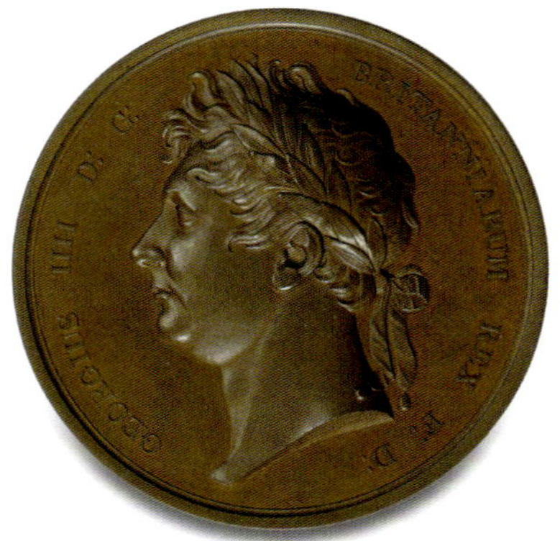

FIG. 16.1
BENJAMIN WYON (1802–58), *Medal commemorating George IV's visit to Ireland*, 1821. Bronze, 5.0 cm (diameter), RCIN 447168.a

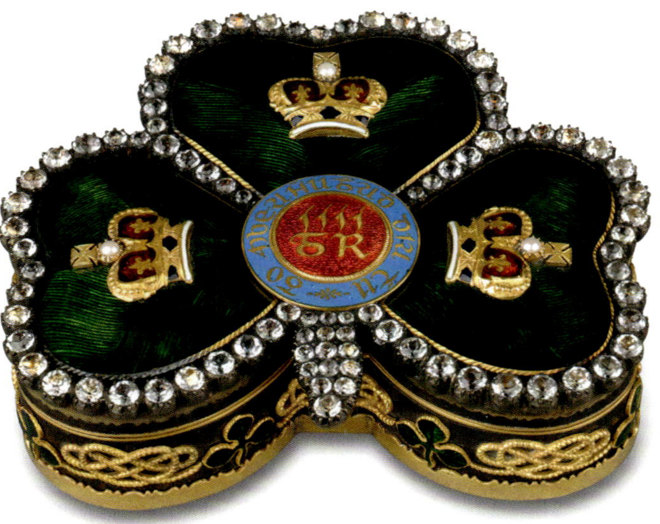

FIG. 16.2
EDWARD MURRAY (active 1812–53), *Snuffbox*, 1821. Bog oak, enamel, diamond, gold, pearl, paste (glass), 2.9 × 9.0 × 7.6 cm, RCIN 4036

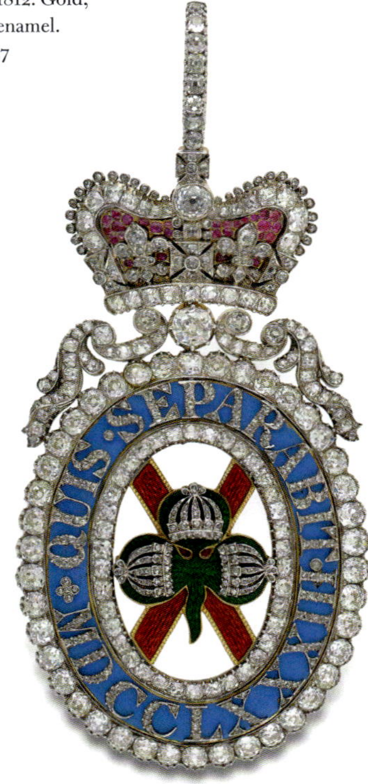

FIG. 16.3
RUNDELL, BRIDGE & RUNDELL, *Order of St Patrick: sash badge*, 1812. Gold, diamond, ruby, emerald, enamel. 10.8 × 4.8 cm, RCIN 441257

linen that were backlit to create a decorative effect, or lights and illuminations.[5] Souvenirs and commemorative objects were produced, including medals (Fig. 16.1) and prints, and gifts were made to be presented to the king (Fig. 16.2). Trade was also given a boost by George's request that all his subjects approach him in Irish-made apparel.

The royal visit proved an attraction for artists and provided the opportunity, particularly for Irish painters, to record the events for posterity. Shortly before the king's arrival, the Royal Irish Institution, founded in 1813 with the Prince Regent as patron, had announced a competition for artists. It proposed to pay £500 for the 'best picture on the subject of his Majesty's arrival and landing, which shall be painted in IRELAND by an IRISH artist'.[6] Although the name of the successful artist is not recorded, the visit did produce a number of paintings which documented particular events, such as *George IV, King of England, entering Dublin* by William Turner de Lond.[7]

Crowds grew at Howth as the ship approached and, as George disembarked, there was much waving of hats and handkerchiefs by the assembled throng. Casts were made of the royal footprints to mark the place where the king stepped on to Irish soil. Escorted by large numbers of people, George was driven to the Viceregal Lodge at Phoenix Park, the summer residence of the Viceroy, the British monarchy's representative in Ireland. The short speech he made on his arrival expressed his pleasure at the warm reception and he went on to voice his enthusiasm for the country: 'This is one of the happiest days of my life. I have long wished to visit you – my heart has always been Irish.'[8] The charming and heartfelt praise expressed by the king contributed to the enthusiastic response he received throughout the visit.

George spent the first few days of the visit in retirement, as a mark of respect for the queen's death. His formal entry into the city of Dublin took place on 17 August when, dressed in field-marshal's uniform and wearing the Order of St Patrick (Fig. 16.3), the highest order of chivalry in Ireland, he processed into the city accompanied by around 200 carriages ranked in strict order of precedence. As he passed through the triumphal

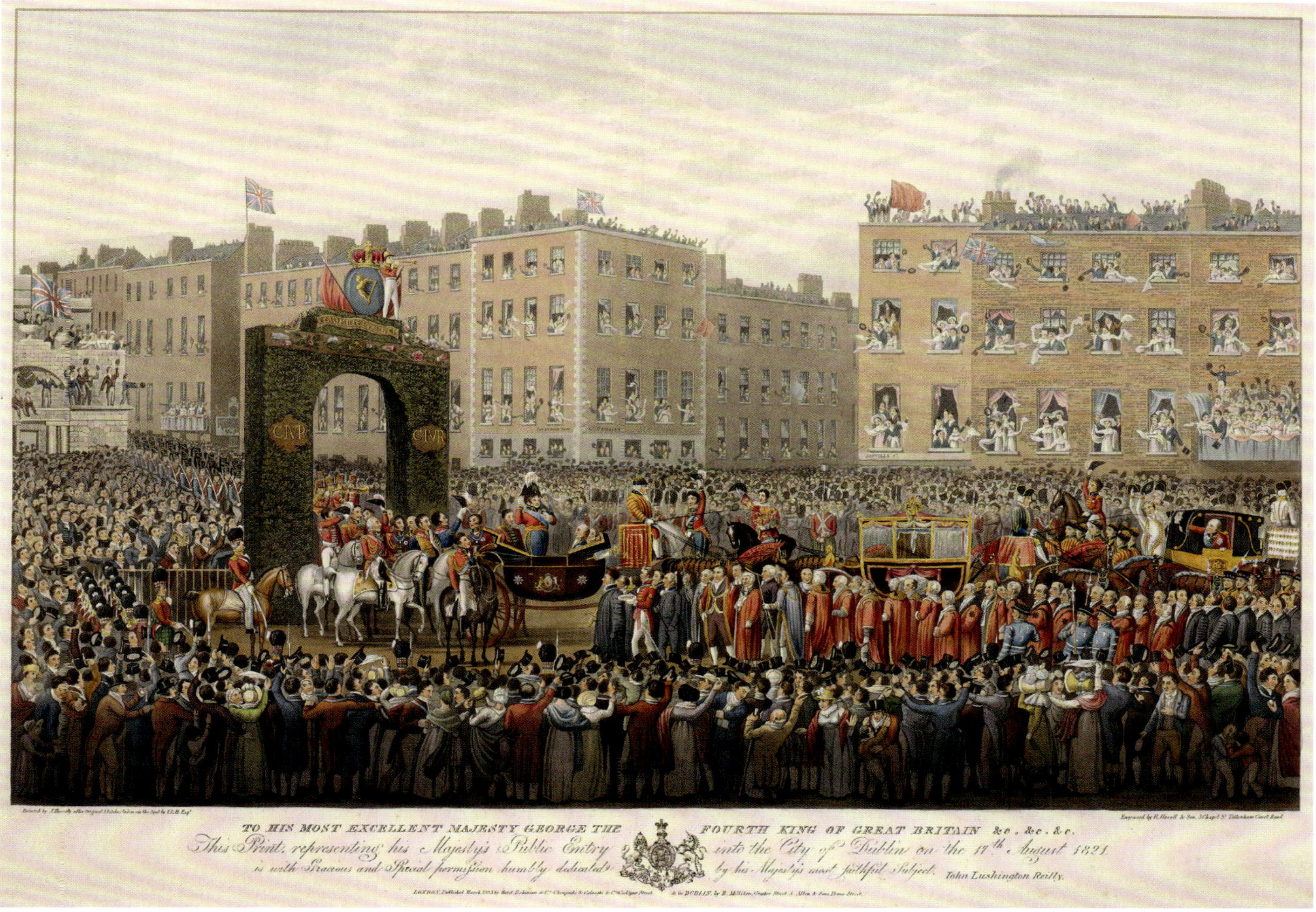

FIG. 16.4
ROBERT I. HAVELL (active 1808–37) AFTER JOSEPH PATRICK HAVERTY (1794–1864), *His Majesty's Public Entry into the City of Dublin on the 17th August 1821*, 1823. Etching and aquatint with hand colouring, 49.9 × 70.7 cm (sheet), RCIN 750802

arch, the king stood in his carriage and repeatedly pointed to the rosette composed of shamrocks which decorated his hat, 'more than twice the size of a military cockade'. Thousands of people welcomed him, flags were waved from windows and balconies were festooned with laurel as 'all eyes were fixed upon the king – his Majesty was the sole object of attention, enthusiasm, affection and love' (Fig. 16.4).[9] The royal procession moved on to Dublin Castle, the residence of the Viceroy of Ireland, Charles Chetwynd-Talbot, 2nd Earl Talbot, where the king was presented with the Irish Sword of State. Dating from the 1660s, the sword was an important part of the royal regalia and a symbol of the monarch.

The visit continued with a large number of well-attended events. These included a levée for gentlemen, a Drawing Room for ladies, visits to the theatre, the Mansion House, the Linen Hall, the Bank of Ireland, Trinity College and the Curragh (see chapter 13). The king also held an investiture for the installation of new Knights of the Order of St Patrick, when the 8th Earl of Fingall was the first Catholic to be created a member of the Order. Everywhere he was greeted with huge enthusiasm and there was a call to build a royal palace in Dublin.[10] Before leaving George paid a private visit to Slane Castle, the home of the Marquess and Marchioness of Conyngham. His adoration of the Marchioness may have provided an additional inducement for his visit to Ireland and ensured he had an extremely happy time at Slane.

The king departed from Dún Laoghaire, renamed Kingstown in his honour, on 3 September. Large crowds gathered and a number of artists were ready to record the occasion, 'busily employed with their pencils during the greater

FIG. 16.5
ATTRIBUTED TO BENEDETTO PISTRUCCI (1784–1855),
Gold ring with an intaglio of George IV, 1821.
Carnelian, gold, turquoise, seed pearl, 2.3 × 2.8 cm,
RCIN 107334

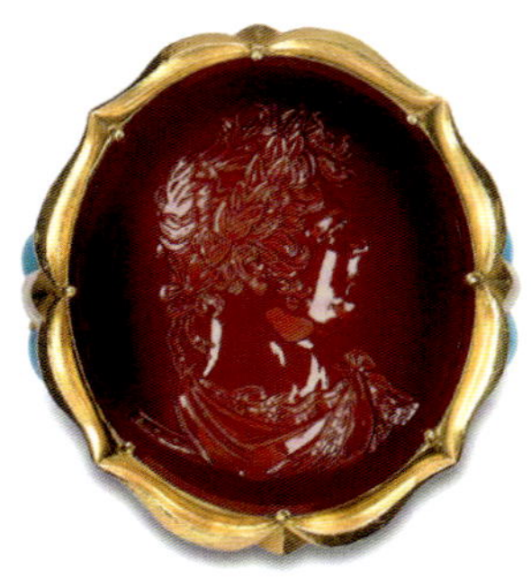

part of the day'. Daniel O'Connell, the politician and campaigner for Catholic Emancipation, presented the king with a laurel crown and the king departed, declaring, 'I never felt sensations of more delight than since I came to Ireland'.[11]

Hanover

Just over a week after his return from Ireland the king journeyed to the continent to visit Hanover. The Electorate of Hanover had been joined in a personal union with Great Britain since 1714 when the Elector, Georg Ludwig, the great-grandson of James I (and great-great-grandfather of George IV), inherited the British throne and became George I. Affirmed as a kingdom by George (as Prince Regent) on 26 October 1814 following the Congress of Vienna, and in the care of his youngest surviving brother, Adolphus, Duke of Cambridge, who had been appointed governor-general in 1816, Hanover had not received a visit from a royal ruler for 66 years.[12] The king set sail on 25 September 1821 from Ramsgate, where he enjoyed an enthusiastic reception and farewell. He travelled to Calais and journeyed on to Brussels, from where he visited Waterloo and was taken over the battlefield by the Duke of Wellington. Travelling via Dusseldorf and Osnaburgh, where he received a huge welcome, the king entered Hanover on 7 October. He went first to the royal palace of Schloss Herrenhausen, the summer residence of the rulers of Hanover, where he was to reside for the visit, before entering the city in the evening. The streets were illuminated, guns were fired, bells were rung amid great crowds, who 'all appeared animated with the most loyal and affectionate enthusiasm'.[13] Sir William Knighton, the confidential adviser who accompanied George, wrote: 'we passed through a line yesterday of ten thousand troops. It was a fine sight; and the whole population came out to greet the king.'[14]

Preparations had been under way in the city well before the king arrived and as in Ireland, commemorative items were made (Fig. 16.5). Plans were made for several days of celebrations and visits, although no Hanoverian coronation was organised.[15] Improvements were made to Herrenhausen to make it a suitable residence; Knighton described it as 'one of the most magnificent palaces you have ever beheld. It is beautifully fitted up; and the garden-walls and water-spouts make it look like enchantment ... the whole thing is in a state of grandeur that I never before witnessed.'[16] The king, wearing Hanoverian field-marshal's uniform and the insignia of the recently instituted Order of the Guelph (Fig. 16.6), made his official entry into Hanover on 10 October as thousands lined the two-mile avenue of lime trees from Herrenhausen to the city. The procession passed through a grand triumphal arch decorated by Hanover artist and court painter Johann Heinrich Ramberg with figures emblematic of the city offering gifts to the king.[17] Everywhere George was greeted enthusiastically by a delighted crowd, to whom he spoke in German and, as in Ireland, proclaimed his enthusiasm for the country: 'I have always been a Hanoverian. I will live and die a Hanoverian.'[18] Later that evening the king returned to the city to view the spectacular illuminations and the following day he held a well-attended levée for gentlemen and a Drawing Room for ladies. He also visited the theatre, recently decorated with paintings by Ramberg, watched a display of fireworks and reviewed the enormous number of troops assembled. Unfortunately an attack of gout prevented him from taking part in a large boar hunt during which 90 boars were killed,[19] but he was well enough a few days before his departure to give an audience to the Austrian Chancellor, Prince Metternich (see chapter 9).[20]

Scotland

Less than a year later, following the immense success of the visits to Ireland and Hanover, George IV travelled to Scotland. The visit was encouraged by the celebrated Scottish writer, Sir Walter Scott (Fig. 16.7), the author of *Waverley* (published in 1814). The king, an admirer of Scott's work, had invited him to dinner at Carlton House in 1815, and was 'enchanted by Scott, as Scott with him; and on all subsequent visits to London he was a frequent guest at the royal table'.[21] Scott had also attended the king's coronation in London in 1821 and had been deeply

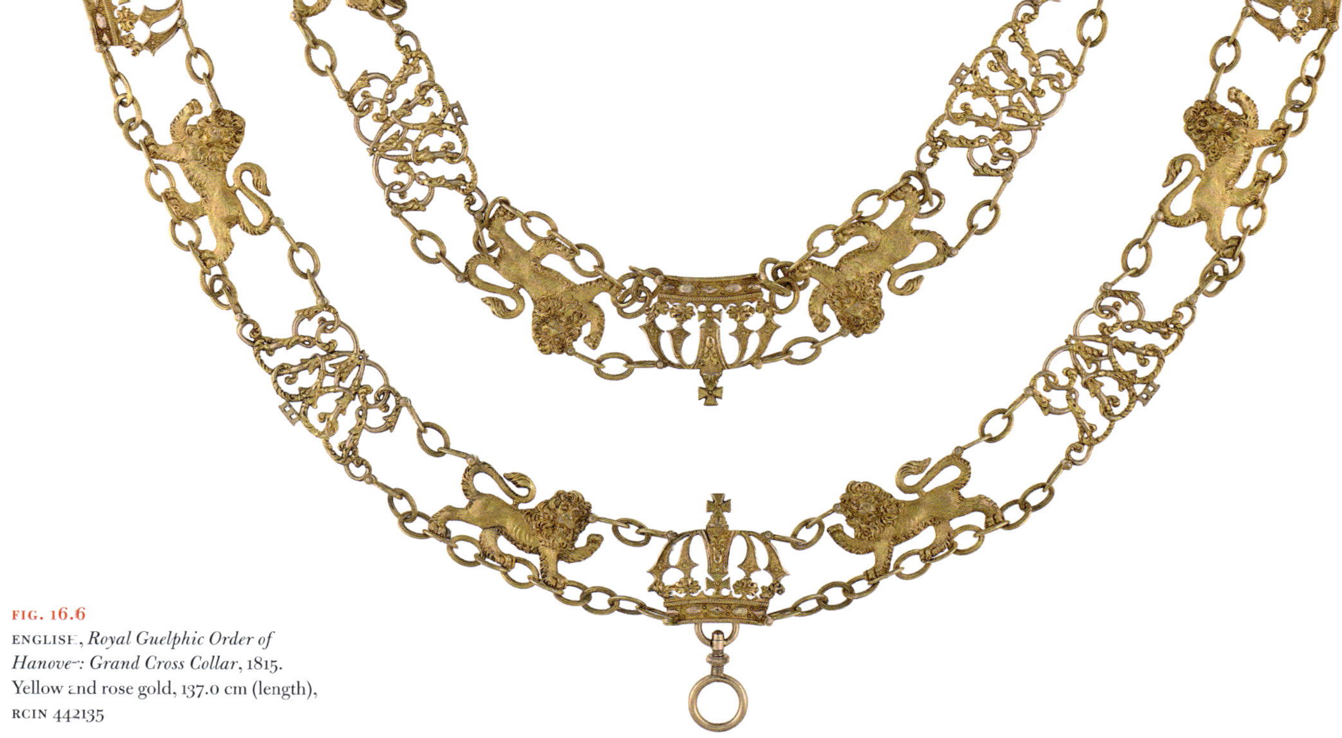

FIG. 16.6
ENGLISH, *Royal Guelphic Order of Hanover: Grand Cross Collar*, 1815.
Yellow and rose gold, 137.0 cm (length), RCIN 442135

impressed and inspired by the richness and historical nature of the ceremonial. Once the visit, to be centred on Edinburgh, had been confirmed, Scott's advice was sought and, with only three weeks' notice, he was invited by the Lord Provost of Edinburgh to organise the event.

The occasion was infused with significance and symbolism as it was to be the first visit by a monarch to Scotland since Charles II in 1650 and the first since the Act of Union in 1707. Potent memories still lingered of the Jacobite rising of 1745, when Prince Charles Edward Stuart had raised an army in Scotland and attempted to claim the British crown for his father.[22] This had divided both the Scots and the English and ended with the overwhelming defeat of the Jacobites by the Hanoverian army at Culloden in 1746. Scott, who wished to mend any lingering discord with a magnificent spectacle of loyalty to the king, seized the opportunity to present the country as a 'plaided panorama' overflowing with tartan and Highlanders.[23] He summoned Highland chiefs to the city, asking them to 'come and bring half-a-dozen or half-a-score of Clansmen, so as to look like an Island Chief as you are. Highlanders are what he [the king] will like most to see.'[24] Scott himself was an enthusiastic chairman of the Celtic Society, which promoted Highland culture and dress; wearing it had become more widespread since the lifting of the ban on tartan, proscribed following the rising of 1745. Tartan attire was encouraged during the visit and the king himself was persuaded to order a Highland dress outfit for the occasion. During the two-week-long extravaganza, Scott stage-managed a

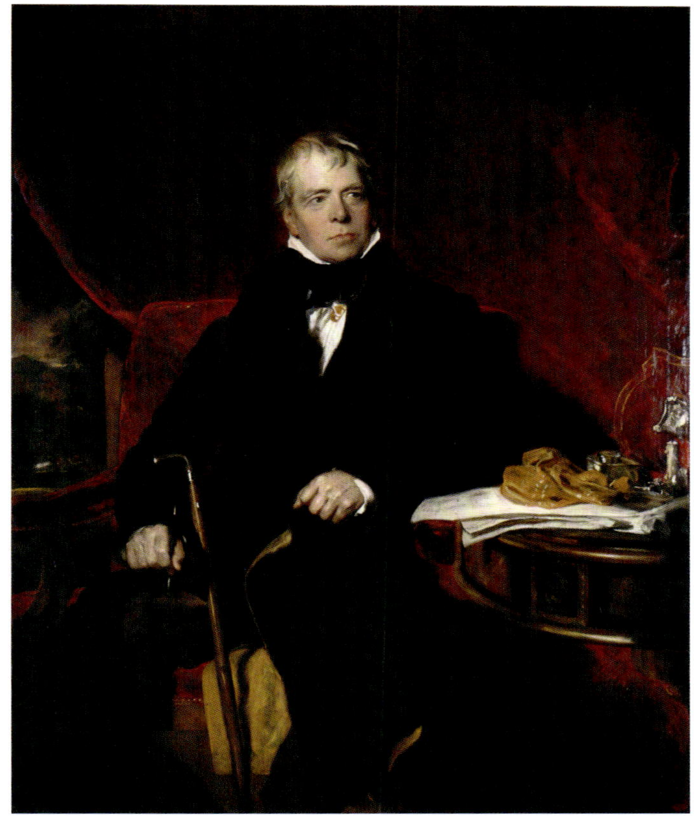

FIG. 16.7
SIR THOMAS LAWRENCE (1769–1830), *Sir Walter Scott (1771–1832)*, 1820–6.
Oil on canvas, 161.7 × 132.9 cm, RCIN 400644

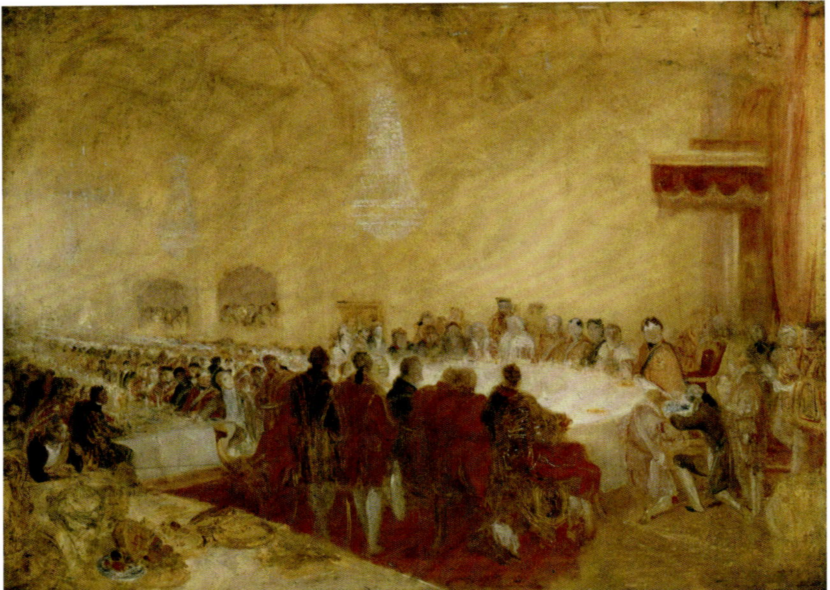

FIG. 16.8
JOSEPH MALLORD WILLIAM TURNER (1775–1851), *George IV at the Provost's Banquet in the Parliament House, Edinburgh*, c.1822. Oil on mahogany, 68.6 × 91.8 cm (The Tate Gallery, London: N02858)

FIG. 16.9
SIR DAVID WILKIE (1785–1841), *The Entrance of George IV at Holyroodhouse*, 1822–30. Oil on mahogany panel, 126.0 × 198.1 cm, RCIN 401187

FIG. 16.10
RUNDELL, BRIDGE & RUNDELL, *Order of the Thistle: sash badge*, 1812. Gold, diamond, emerald, ruby, enamel, 10.8 × 4.8 cm, RCIN 441236

series of spectacular ceremonies designed to present George IV as the legitimate king. George was introduced as the latest in a long line of Scottish monarchs, heir to both the Hanoverians and the Jacobites, and king of a country with a distinctive and unified Highland identity, as emphasised by Scott himself: 'We are THE CLAN and our king is THE CHIEF.'[25]

The visit was to prove a major fascination for many artists, who were given prime access to all events. The *émigré* Scottish artist Sir David Wilkie and the English painter J.M.W. Turner both travelled from London to record the events and festivities on this significant occasion. Turner's sketchbooks from the visit reveal that the artist planned an ambitious cycle of 19 commemorative paintings, possibly in the hope of securing the king's patronage.[26] Turner also recorded scenes in four unfinished oil paintings associated with this cycle, including *George IV at the Provost's Banquet in the Parliament House, Edinburgh* (Fig. 16.8).[27] A number of Scottish-based artists were on the spot to document proceedings, including Alexander Carse, who recorded the king's landing at Leith, and John Wilson Eubank, who depicted George's entry into the city of Edinburgh from Calton Hill.[28] In addition, other works by Scottish artists were put on display at the Palace of Holyroodhouse, to 'enable His Majesty to judge the State of the Art in this country'.[29] Artists represented included the portrait painter Henry Raeburn, whom the king knighted on the last day of the Scottish visit, together with William Allan and Alexander Nasmyth.

The king eventually arrived at Leith, the port of Edinburgh, on the *Royal George* on 14 August 1822 but, due to heavy rain, did not disembark until the following day. As he stepped ashore, wearing a thistle and sprig of heather in his hat, and a St Andrew's Cross presented by the ladies of Edinburgh, he was greeted enthusiastically by 'shouts the most hearty and prolonged that ever greeted the ears of a monarch'.[30] The king made his ceremonial entry into the city through a series of triumphal arches, by way of Leith Walk, Princes Street and Calton Hill to the royal Palace of Holyroodhouse. The various parts of the city unfolded before him, presented as a series of spectacular and staged tableaux, which culminated in the magnificent sight of the palace viewed against the dramatic backdrop of the extinct volcano, Arthur's Seat.[31] Huge crowds lined the route and the 'whole way for three miles from the shore to the palace, was one mass of hope and joy, all engrossed with one object, and responding to one pulsation'.[32]

At Holyroodhouse the king was presented with the keys of the palace by the Hereditary Keeper, the Duke of Hamilton. Wilkie, in attendance, recorded the moment in *The Entrance of George IV at Holyroodhouse* (Fig 16.9), painted for the king. George, wearing field-marshal's uniform and the green ribbon of the Order of the Thistle (Fig. 16.10), the highest order of chivalry in Scotland, is shown as he is about to enter the palace of his ancestors, 'with all the chiefs of the north on his right and left'.[33] The Honours of Scotland (the Scottish regalia) are borne on horseback as the king is acknowledged as the legitimate holder of the keys, and so the rightful King of Scotland.[34]

Although George was lodged seven miles away at the more comfortable Dalkeith Palace, the seat of the Duke of

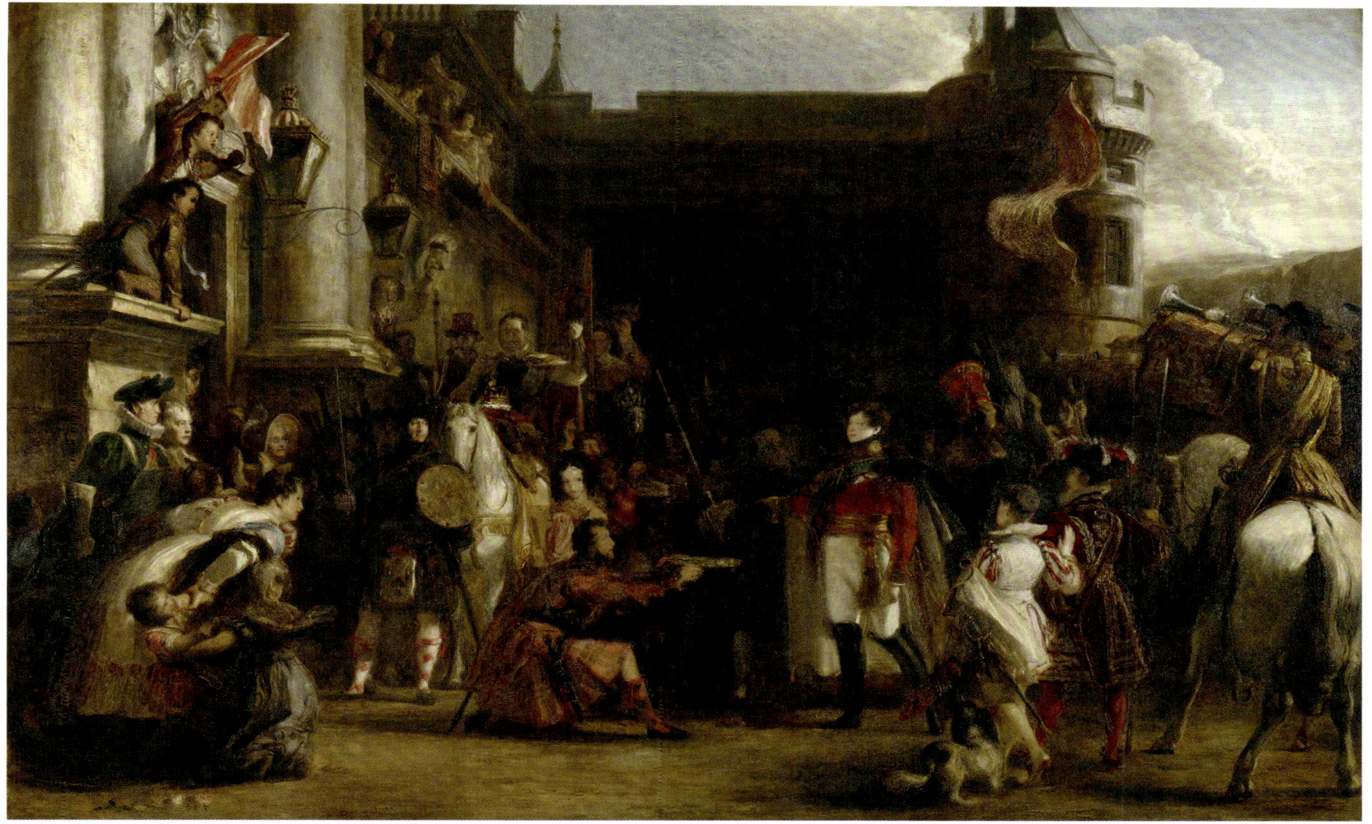

Buccleuch, repairs and redecoration were undertaken within Holyroodhouse in order to make it suitable for a number of events. The Edinburgh firm of Trotters, makers of the most fashionable furniture in the city, supplied furnishings and fitted out Charles II's old Guard Chamber as the Presence Chamber. A throne, sent up from Buckingham House, was installed complete with an elaborate canopy and hangings. A number of receptions hosted by the king took place within the palace, including a levée for 1,200 gentlemen and a Drawing Room for 500 ladies (Fig. 16.11) during which George was accompanied by the Royal Company of Archers, appointed by the king on Scott's recommendation to act as his personal bodyguard. Originally formed as an archery club in 1678, they wore the traditional uniform of tartan jacket and trews.

Wilkie obtained an invitation through Scott to the levée where gentlemen were encouraged to wear tartan. The king himself was resplendent in his Highland dress, supplied by George Hunter & Co. of Princes Street, Edinburgh, at a cost of £1,354 18s. The complete outfit included enough Royal Stewart tartan for two kilts, a goatskin sporran, a basket-hilt sword, a Highland dirk (Fig. 16.12) and a 'pair of fine gold Shoe

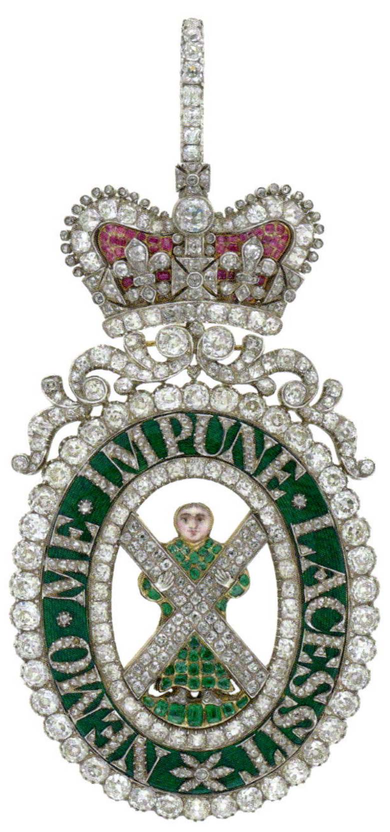

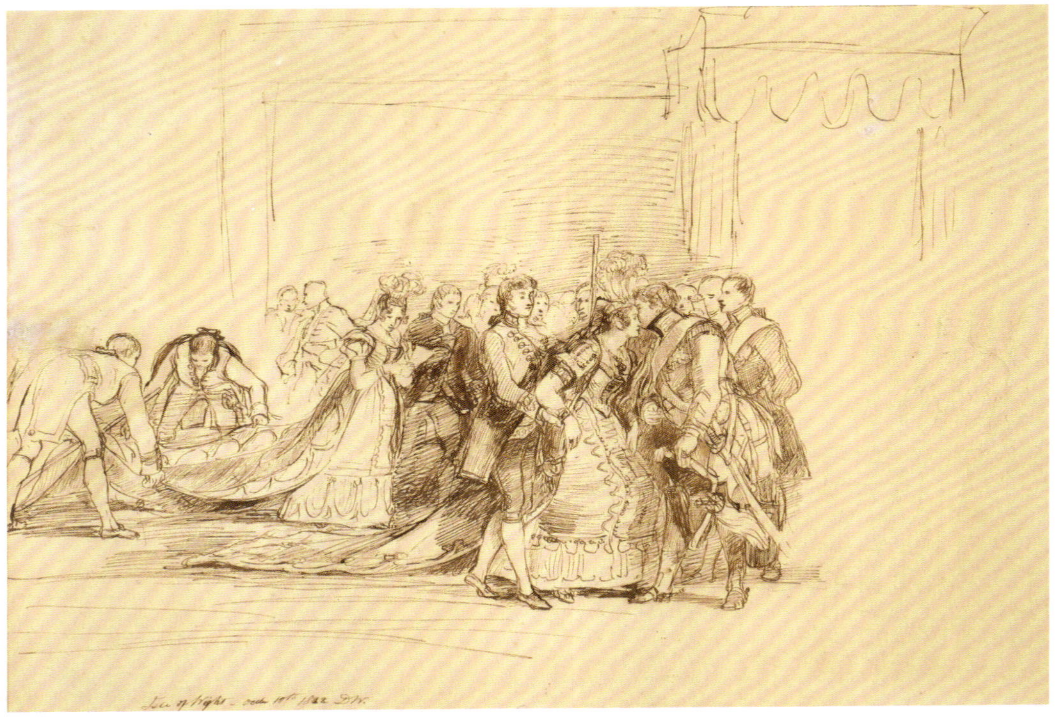

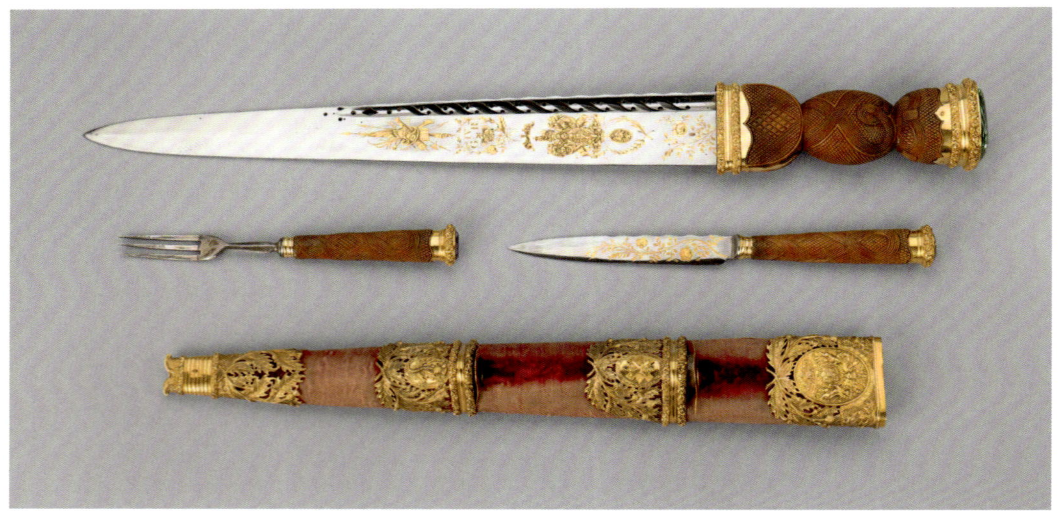

FIG. 16.11
SIR DAVID WILKIE (1785–1841), *George IV holding a Drawing Room at Holyrood*, 1822. Pencil, pen and brown ink on buff paper, 36.6 × 51.5 cm, RCIN 914768

FIG. 16.12
GEORGE HUNTER & CO., *Dirk, scabbard, knife and fork*, 1822. Boxwood, steel, gold, silver, cairngorm, aquamarine, amethyst, silk velvet; dirk: 54.4 cm (length); scabbard: 42.1 cm (length); knife: 25.5 cm (length); fork: 20.3 cm (length), RCIN 29023

Rosets with Vibrating Center'.[35] Wilkie commented, 'He looked exceedingly well in tartan. He had on the kilt and the hose, with a kind of flesh-coloured pantaloons underneath', and went on to depict the king looking like a Highland chieftain, although without the pantaloons, in a portrait completed in 1829 (Fig. 16.13).[36]

After attending a final reception at Hopetoun House on 29 August, the king boarded the *Royal George* and set sail in heavy rain for England. The visit, which was witnessed by one-seventh of the Scottish population, was proclaimed a huge success: 'Our King has seen his people, and they have seen their king.'[37] George himself had been gratified to witness 'the happiness of his subjects' and to receive 'the most convincing proofs of their faithful attachment and loyalty', and departed delighted by Scott's presentation of Scotland as an ancient and traditional clan society.[38] Sir Robert Peel wrote on the king's behalf to thank Scott for the 'deep interest you have taken in every ceremony and arrangement' for a visit designed to heal the rift between Hanoverian monarch and his northern kingdom.[39]

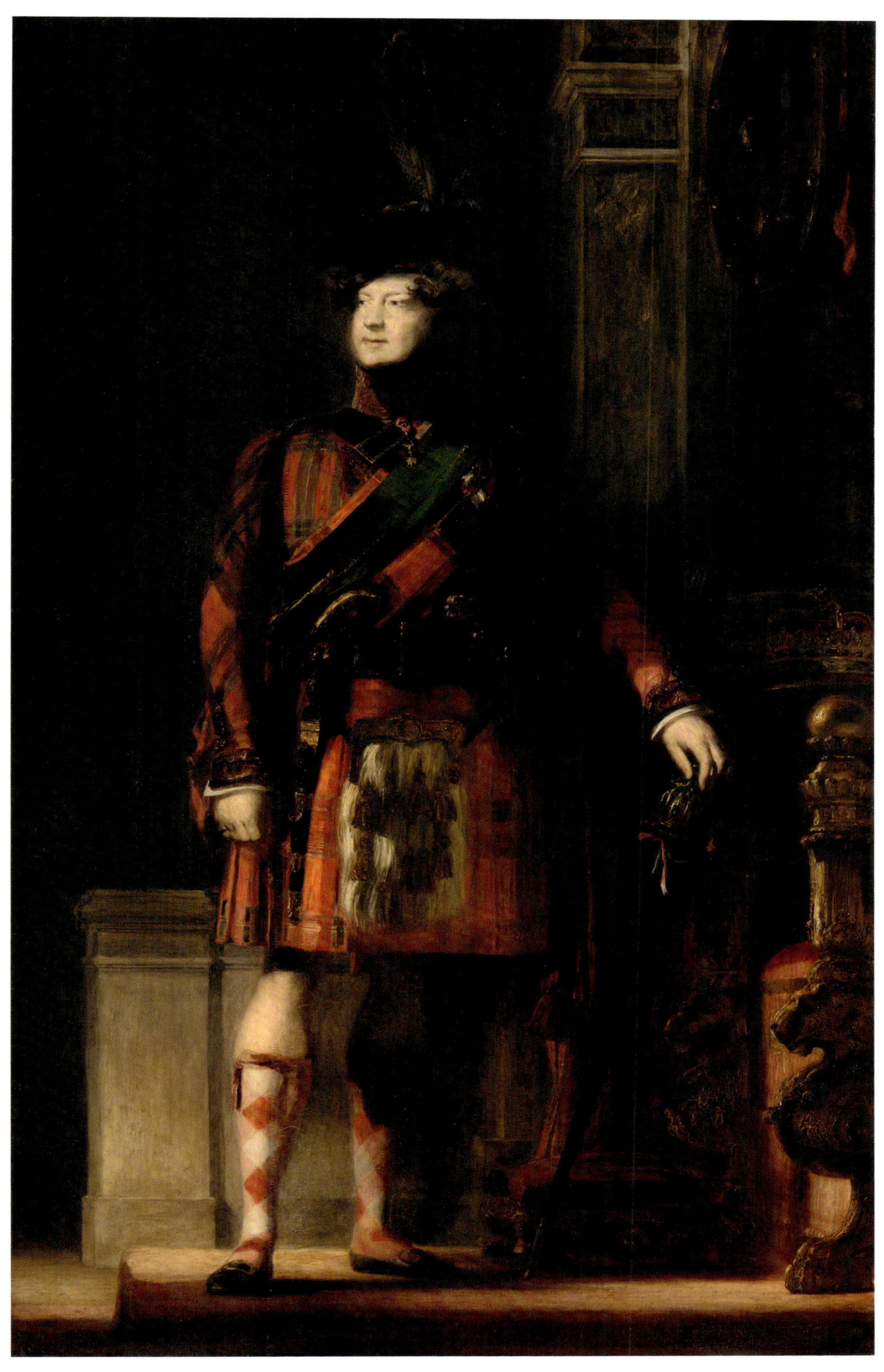

FIG. 16.13
SIR DAVID WILKIE (1785–1841), *George IV*, 1829. Oil on canvas, 279.4 × 179.1 cm, RCIN 401206

17

The HOUSES *that* GEORGE BUILT: ST JAMES'S PALACE, BUCKINGHAM PALACE *and* WINDSOR

KATHRYN JONES *and* KATE HEARD

> Poor Prinney put on a dramatic,
> royal, distant dignity to all[1]

In September 1826 the *Gentleman's Magazine* published a fictional letter purporting to be from the 'Count de Chartres to the Count de Chabrol', in which the writer commented on St James's Palace:

> You remember upon our first seeing England in 1820 our astonishment at the King of the most wealthy nation in the world dwelling in a small palace, with apparently no more state than one of his nobles, no galleries of antiquities, sculpture, or painting, no extensive library of books, or collection of works of art, nothing, in short, that announced the residence of the chief of a mighty Nation.[2]

Although this snippet was satirical in tone, it echoed the genuine sentiments of many foreign visitors to London. The motivation for all George IV's architectural schemes was to create a suitably magnificent setting for the British monarchy, reflecting properly the status of the king and allowing space for the business and ceremony of court life. It is not the intention here to relate the full architectural history of each of his residences but simply to assess some of those elements that reflected George's intentions.[3] The priority in each case was the provision of spaces for the more modern forms of early nineteenth-century entertainments, that is, music, banquets and balls; sufficient room to display the art collections and comfortable, elegant apartments for the king himself.

Until 1811, court occasions were held at St James's Palace. During the Regency much formal business had taken place in Carlton House, complemented by entertainments on occasion at Buckingham House. In practical terms, however, none of these spaces was sufficiently large to provide enough accommodation for ceremonial (Fig. 17.1). The American ambassador Richard Rush recorded his attendance at a Drawing Room at Buckingham House in 1818, where he noted that carriages delivering visitors queued for about a mile, from Tyburn to Piccadilly. Once inside,

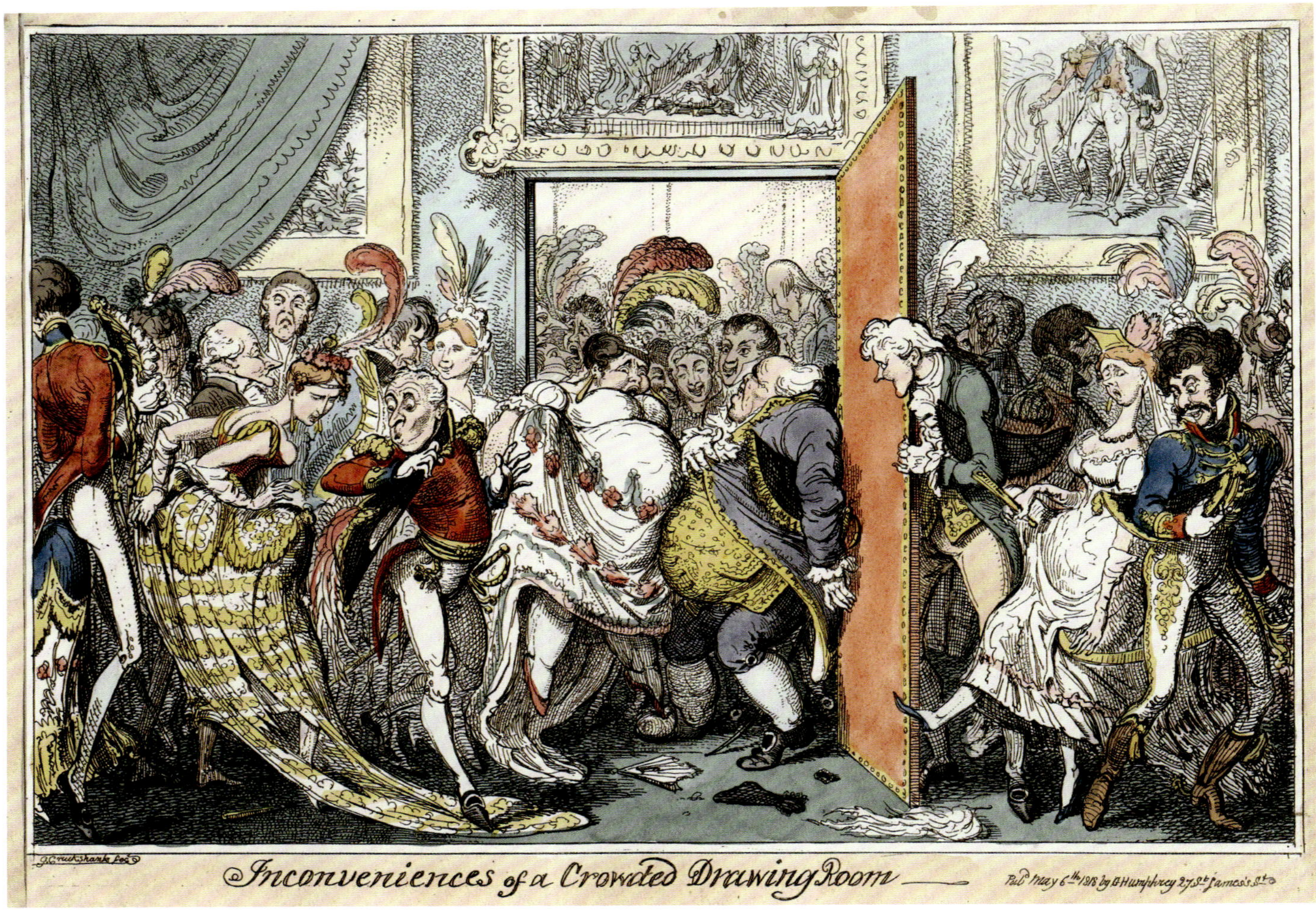

the mêlée of ladies in hooped dresses and plumed headdresses and the gentlemen with their swords caused hilarity, and the staircases were entirely inadequate: 'without pausing to describe the incidents during our progress upwards it may be sufficient to say that the party to which I was attached … reached the summit of the staircase in about three quarters of an hour'.[4] Increasingly when entertaining at Carlton House, where up to 3,000 guests were invited, George's solution was to provide temporary rooms erected in the gardens or over the porches on the upper floors, and furniture, lighting and plate were traditionally hired in.

Quite aside from the problems of entertaining, much of George's art collection was consigned to store as there was simply no wall space in his princely homes. Although he had happily acquired a number of full-length portraits and sculptures for Carlton House, these only served to underline the building's inadequacies – the intended gallery of military and political heroes of the Napoleonic campaign and subsequent peace, his Canova sculptures[5] and his great French equestrian bronze of Louis XIV[6] (Fig. 0.7) all showed that George's artistic ambitions were simply too great for the small spaces of Carlton House and the Royal Pavilion. His inheritance of St James's Palace, Buckingham House and Windsor Castle on George III's death gave George the scope to create apartments in which he could display these and other works to full advantage.

St James's Palace

The shortcomings of St James's Palace had been highlighted since the early eighteenth century. George II had put into motion plans for remodelling the rather ramshackle complex of historic buildings (Fig. 17.2), to create a satisfactory space for court ceremonial as well as sufficient accommodation for family and staff. However, the priorities at that date remained a sense of continuity with the previous dynasty, and budgetary restraint,

(p. 224)
Detail of Fig. 17.13, OFFICE OF MOREL & SEDDON, *Design for the west elevation of His Majesty's Writing Room, Windsor Castle*

FIG. 17.1
GEORGE CRUIKSHANK (1792–1878), *Inconveniences of a Crowded Drawing Room*, 1818. Etching with hand colouring, 26.0 × 37.0 cm (sheet) (Lewis Walpole Library, Yale University Library, Farmington, CT: 818.05.06.01)

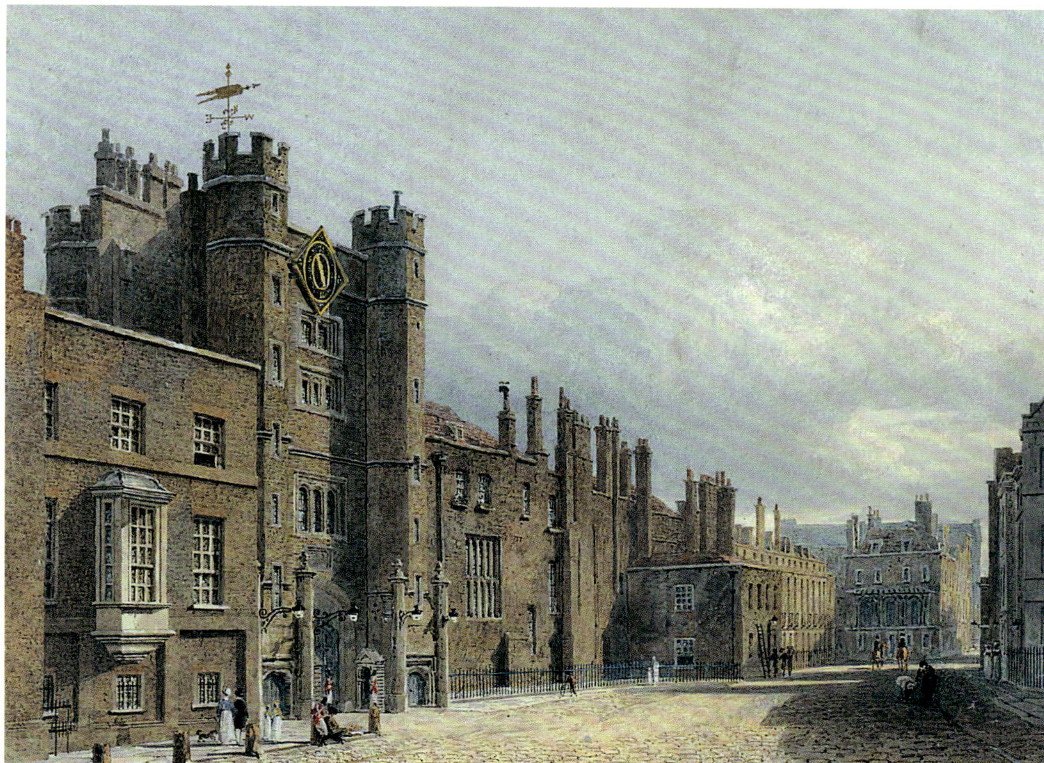

FIG. 17.2
CHARLES WILD (1781–1835), *The north front, St James's Palace, c.*1819. Watercolour and bodycolour over pencil, 19.7 × 28.8 cm, RCIN 922161

and little of the proposed schemes had come to fruition. With the acquisition of Buckingham House for Queen Charlotte and her family, the buildings of St James's had been largely neglected, although the state rooms continued to be used for formal occasions. By the 1820s, John Nash, who was asked to report on the condition of the palace, wrote to the Board of Works that 'every part of the building ... is in so ruinous a state that to repair them will be an attempt almost impracticable'.[7]

Although from the time of Queen Charlotte's death in 1818 discussions were under way to remodel Buckingham House as the seat of the monarchy, George still regarded the home of his mother as a private residence and in the early 1820s he preferred to focus on the refurbishment of St James's Palace. Despite Nash's gloomy report, the state apartments proved to be salvageable. The intention, as laid down by George, was 'the immediate execution of certain extensive arrangements ... for the necessary accommodation of the company attending ... levees and Drawing Rooms, which are in future to be held at this Palace'.[8] Nash was required to provide better access for carriages, a covered portico for those alighting from their vehicles[9] and a new grand stone staircase leading up to the state apartments. On the first floor an additional reception room, misleadingly entitled Queen Anne's Ballroom after one of the principal paintings hung within, was added to the south front of the building. Nash created an enfilade of three state rooms; in addition to the new reception room, he remodelled the Entrée Room and Throne Room, inserting grander chimneypieces (recycled from Queen Caroline's library at St James's Palace) and designing lavishly gilded ceilings; the former ballroom became a Supper or Banqueting Room. The Throne Room was the intended climax of these spaces; the national chivalric orders were picked out in the ceiling decoration and the pictures were hung to reflect British naval and military triumphs – the Lawrence state portrait of the king flanked by two works by George Jones. A small and surprisingly plain set of private apartments was created for the king on the ground floor, as *The Mirror* magazine commented: 'the decorations throughout are of a very humble description, sans glitter, sans gold, sans finery'.[10] The new apartments continued to perform the function of court spaces until the end of the reign. Even during the latter years of George's life, when he was largely living in seclusion at Windsor, he continued to hold Drawing Rooms at St James's and on 26 May 1828 he gamely hosted a state ball for 250 guests until three o'clock in the morning.[11]

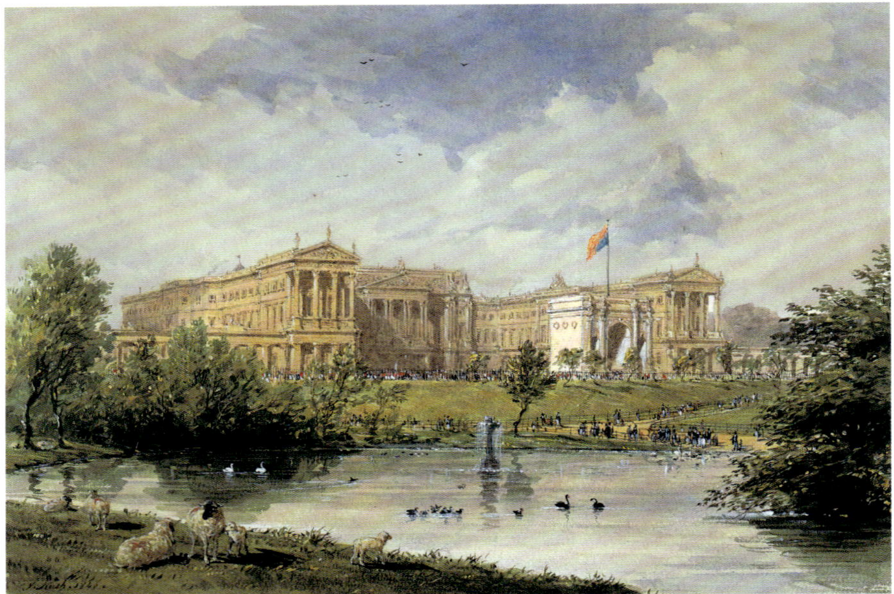

FIG. 17.3
JOSEPH NASH (1808–78), *Buckingham Palace: the East Front from St James's Park*, 1846. Watercolour and bodycolour, 27.6 × 40.3 cm, RCIN 919892

(opposite left)
FIG. 17.4
The White Drawing Room, Buckingham Palace

(opposite right)
FIG. 17.5
The Throne Room, Buckingham Palace

Buckingham Palace

In 1822 John Nash made plans for the Royal Mews to be relocated from its medieval site near Charing Cross to a new site to the south-west of Buckingham House (where it remains today), but it was not until 1825 that the first plans for converting Buckingham House into a palace were laid down.[12] Nash, who had trained in part as an architect of theatres and who had worked for George at Carlton House and the Royal Pavilion (see chapters 5 and 10), was ideally suited to create an impressive backdrop to the business of monarchy. He planned a great white marble arch as the entrance gate to the *cour d'honneur* and climax to a new processional route to the palace extending from Hyde Park Corner. This was intended as much to evoke the grand triumphal arches of Rome, and in particular that of Constantine, as to rival Napoleon's Arc de Triomphe in the centre of Paris.[13] It was originally designed to carry two friezes carved with celebrations of naval and military triumph – the battles of Trafalgar and Waterloo – and to be surmounted by a great bronze equestrian figure of George himself in the place of a Roman emperor. The arch never received this crowning glory, however, victim of later financial cuts. When Nash was removed from the project in 1830, for overspending, the arch scheme was taken over by Edward Blore and reduced in scale, and the friezes found their final place in the façades of the palace itself. Nevertheless the great three-arched gateway, clad entirely in white marble, provided a suitably awe-inspiring reminder to any visitor to the palace of the power of the monarch within (Fig. 17.3).

Nash's love of the dramatic is evident throughout the state apartments of the palace. Although frequently criticised for his rather gloomy entrance hall (in which he was constrained by a need to retain the low ceilings of the earlier building), Nash used this restrained introduction to allow for the crescendo of the Grand Staircase – a double stair top-lit by an engraved glass dome, thereby emphasising the verticality of the space, and enhanced by the dynamic scrolling design of the gilt-bronze balustrade, supplied by the metalworker Samuel Parker. Both the entrance hall and the staircase incorporated unprecedented quantities of 'snow-white' marble, from the Carrara quarries in Italy. As the *Gentleman's Magazine* reported in 1829, 'they will be the first of the kind in England, or perhaps in Europe'.[14]

Nash's original intention had been to place the king's private apartments on the ground floor, as they had been at Carlton House (and indeed as George III's had been), using one of his favourite architectural motifs – a central library with a bow window introduced on one of the long sides, flanked by two grand reception rooms. As at Carlton House, these rooms were to be garden-facing, and featured what were regarded as low ceilings, which, according to the diarist Mary Frampton's brother James, 'the King particularly insisted on, liking to inhabit low rooms himself'.[15]

The newly modelled state rooms embodied every facet of Nash's hybrid neo-classicism at its boldest and most original. Among his innovations was the reversed coving to the North (White) Drawing Room (Fig. 17.4), giving the space a tent-like appearance. Rather than traditional pilasters he introduced a purely abstract punctuation to the walls, of trellis work in

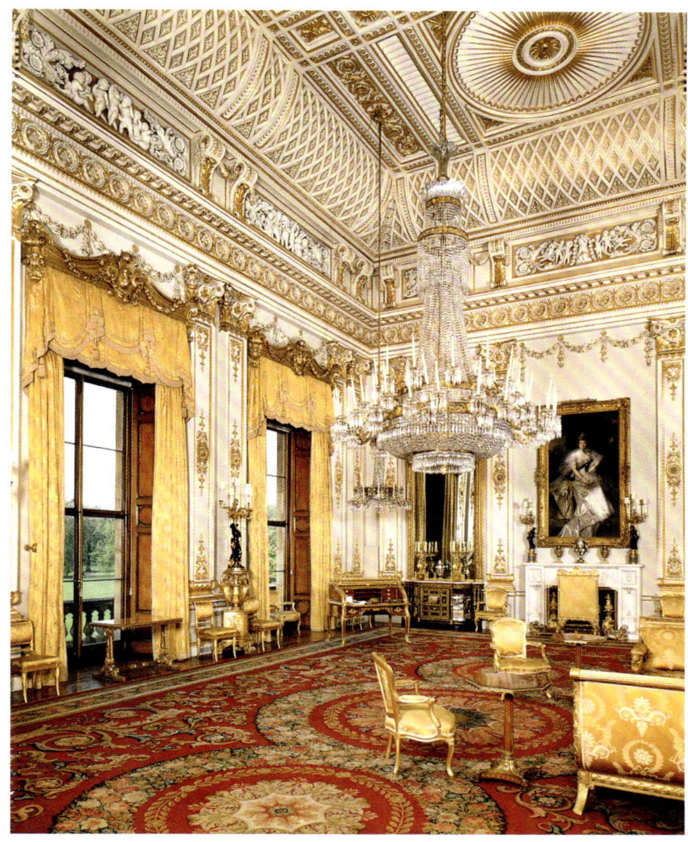

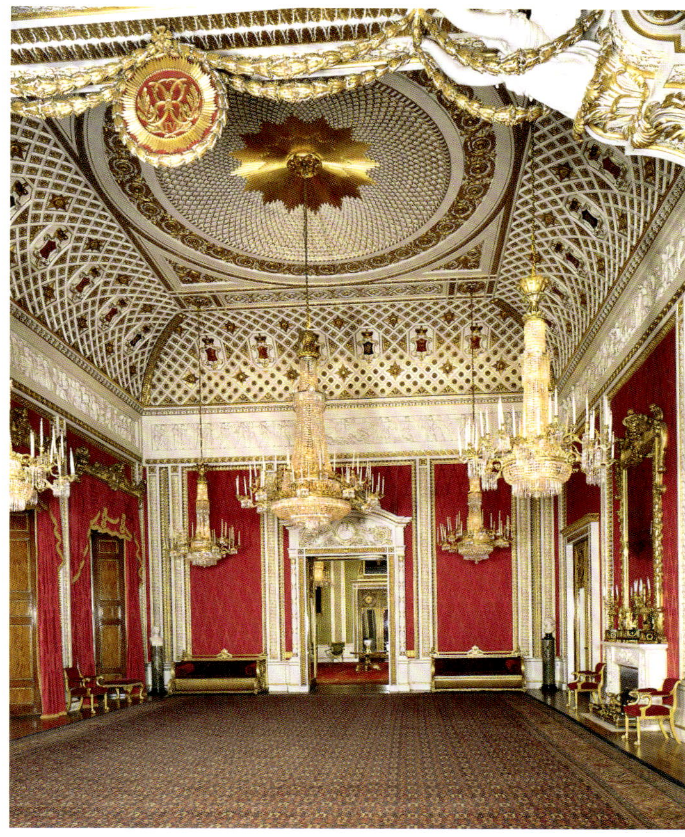

the Green Drawing Room, narrow strips of oak leaves in the Throne Room, or his own composite orders, which incorporate Garter Stars supporting friezes of triangular motifs, in the North Drawing Room. At least one visitor to the palace in its early years was unable to hide his displeasure at Nash's extension of pure classicism: 'the fantastic mixture of every style of architecture and decoration' detracted from the palace in which he noted 'fragments of Egypt, Greece, Etruria, Rome and the Middle Ages all confusedly muddled together'.[16] Such eclecticism was not unusual for George at this period. The carefully pared-down and homogenous neo-classicism of Percier and Fontaine's schemes for Napoleon, for example, was not repeated in Buckingham Palace, nor was the unifying Gothic which appeared at Windsor.

As in all George's architectural schemes, there was a strong emphasis on colour at Buckingham Palace, which was achieved through the use of rich silk damasks on the walls, and scagliola columns, some imitating real hardstones such as lapis lazuli, others purely imaginary such as the raspberry pink used in the South (Blue) Drawing Room. Parquetry floors were introduced to many of the apartments, often of extraordinarily intricate design, the most spectacular being designed by Thomas Seddon at a cost of £2,187 3s, for the Bow (Music) Room.

Francis Coghlan stated in his *A Visit to London* of 1835 that the strength of Nash's architecture was 'the impress of nationality which it exhibits'.[17] As Jonathan Marsden describes in this volume, Nash sought to celebrate British history with his impressive, partly gilded ceilings incorporating the coats of arms of the Hanoverian dynasty, the national floral emblems, most successfully in the domed ceiling of the Music Room, and the celebrated national poets – Spenser, Milton and Shakespeare – who appear in sculptural friezes in the South Drawing Room. The apogee of this celebration was the sculpted depiction of the Wars of the Roses in the Throne Room (Fig. 17.5). Elsewhere, the interior celebrated Britannia's marine heritage with overdoors by William Theed the Younger depicting figures of tritons and nautilus shells. Moreover, the *Gentleman's Magazine* of August 1829 reported that 'These apartments are to be scagliolaed by the first artists in London … The silks will be of English manufacture, as will also be the principal part of the furniture.'[18] The nationalism extended to the sculptural decoration of the building's exterior. Coade stone figures were planned for each gable to celebrate Britannia and her contributions to the arts and sciences, and bas-reliefs intended to commemorate King Alfred publishing the laws and King John accepting Magna Carta.[19]

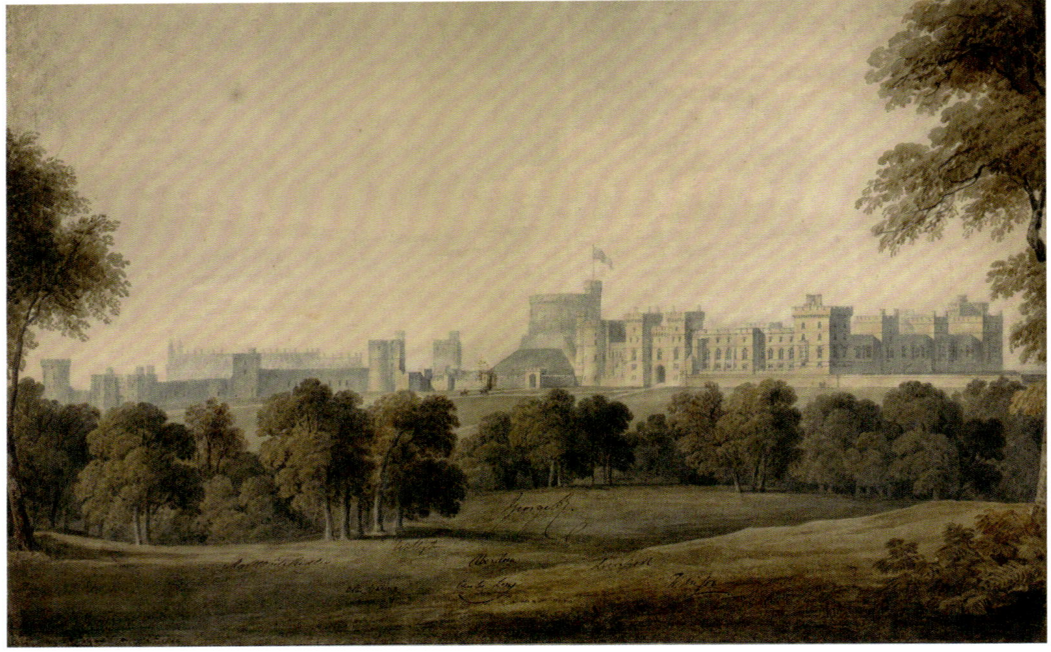

FIG. 17.6
SIR JEFFRY WYATVILLE (1766–1840), *Design for Rebuilding of Windsor Castle*, 1824. Pen and ink with watercolour and wash over pencil, 52.0 × 81.5 cm, RCIN 918420

FIG. 17.7
SIR THOMAS LAWRENCE (1769–1830), *Sir Jeffry Wyatville (1766–1840)*, 1828–30. Oil on canvas, 144.0 × 112.6 cm, RCIN 406994

Nash's new scheme allowed George to place his fine collection of paintings at the heart of the palace – the Picture Gallery formed the spine of the new state apartments, from which the reception rooms branched out, and was intended itself to act as a space for entertainment. It was top-lit by two rows of saucer domes with plaster pendentives, flanking a ceiling decorated with the chivalric orders from across Europe. Here George's collection of Dutch and Flemish Old Masters might hang for the first time as an ensemble, in a dense arrangement punctuated by marble fireplaces carved in Italy at £250 apiece, to Nash's designs, with roundels of those considered the greatest artists of the day – Dürer, Titian, Michelangelo, Rubens and Rembrandt.[20] The space was complemented on the ground floor by the sculpture gallery (or Marble Hall) – again George now had adequate space to display his full-length marble works, which had never fitted comfortably into Carlton House.

Buckingham Palace was not completed during George's lifetime and it received much criticism during the rebuilding period – what was considered reckless overspending by Nash and lavish use of materials in particular drew public disapprobation. In an attempt at economy the furnishing was largely accomplished in later reigns with pieces formerly in Carlton House or from the overflow of the great suites of seat furniture designed by Morel & Seddon for Windsor Castle. Nevertheless, on visiting the palace in 1830, James Frampton recorded that 'the reception rooms are very splendid, both as to size and in the beautiful ornaments of the ceilings, doors and inlaid floors … the private apartments are likewise very comfortable … on the whole it is much better than I at least expected'.[21]

Windsor Castle

When the French tourist Louis Simond visited Windsor in 1811, he suggested that the castle had the appearance of something out of a novel by Walter Scott 'and that is saying enough in its praise'.[22] The association of the castle with the Order of the Garter, the medieval appearance of many of the structures, and the first attempts to introduce a revived Gothic style to areas of the state apartments (most noticeably the stairs to the Queen's Guard Chamber), which had taken place under George III, all impressed on Simond the long history of the site. Although the castle was already strongly symbolic of monarchy, Windsor was, however, considered in need of remodelling in the 1820s. This project focused on making the Gothic aspects more robust, moving away from the baroque interventions that had taken place under Charles II which were felt to detract from the medieval atmosphere of the castle.

A memorandum of 1824 from Charles Long to Lord Liverpool suggested that 'The character of the Castle should be that of simplicity and grandeur and as well from its History as from the imposing style of Building belonging to the period, I should say the period of Edward the 3rd is that which should

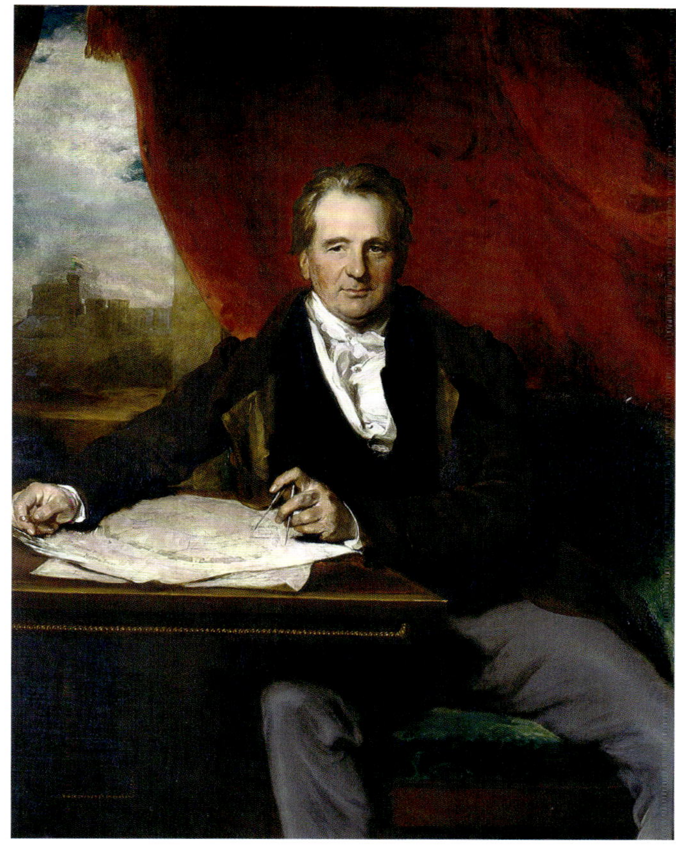

generally predominate.'[23] Long was critical of the existing early nineteenth-century attempts at reintroducing Gothic to the castle, feeling they were too fanciful in nature. The Gothic employed for George IV should be more austere, although Long did concede that 'it might be necessary to relax in some degree from the strict severity of the style'. This no doubt appealed to George's romantic view of history and stressed the importance of Edward III as founder of the Order of the Garter, but as Simond commented, the Gothic style in England was also 'considered here as national, and certainly they use it freely and as their own'.[24]

The appointed architect, Jeffry Wyatville (Fig. 17.7),[25] explained that 'though Windsor Castle is altogether an imposing and grand mass of building, it does not abound with picturesque parts',[26] and one aim of the new scheme was to address the exterior, giving it a more impressive overall appearance (Fig. 17.6). Work began on the king's birthday, 12 August 1824, George himself laying the first stone of the new gateway, which opened up the view from the State Entrance to the great avenue of trees, known as the Long Walk, planted for Charles II, and allowed access from the terrace into the inner quadrangle. At Long's suggestion Wyatville decided to turn the keep or Round Tower into the defining feature of the castle by raising its height to dominate the skyline, further towers and battlements being added to the roofline to increase the picturesque qualities of the view.

A revived Gothic style continued within, particularly in the more public spaces of the corridors, staircases and entrances, and above all in the enormous room created by the merging of the royal chapel and St George's Hall into a new, magnificent hall, measuring over 200 feet (60 metres) in length. The chivalric credentials of the king and the castle were celebrated in Wyatville's new plasterwork ceiling, which replaced baroque murals by Verrio with the coats of arms of all the Knights of the Garter since the foundation of the Order in 1348. It was noted in 1832 that 'although we miss the cupids and the Muses, and gay and gaudy paintings of the Italian artist ... still it may be supposed that the nature of the present decorations ... are more accordant with the grandeur of the hall, harmonize more with the character of the patron saint'.[27] Rather to Wyatville's distress the Gothic idiom was not universal, however. The new Ballroom or Grand Reception Room was decorated in a revived rococo style of which Wyatville would later complain that the 'old French boiseries of the age of Louis XV ... would never have appeared in the castle had the architect been guided solely by his own judgment'.[28]

At Windsor, George was able to extend many of the ideas he had begun in Carlton House – but now with the luxury of space. Among the developments planned by Long was the creation of a sculpture gallery and home for a new pantheon to the heroes – both military and political – who had come together to end the Napoleonic Wars, represented in a series of full- and half-length portraits by Sir Thomas Lawrence (see chapter 3). In essence this space, eventually created by the roofing over of a former courtyard and named the Waterloo Chamber, was an extension of the Admirals Room or the Military Tent Room at Carlton House.[29]

One of the priorities of the Windsor scheme was to create a set of private apartments for the king himself, with light, warmth and comfort being of paramount importance. Traditionally the sovereign had been housed in the apartments created for Charles II, in the northern wing of the castle, although in effect they had been little used throughout the eighteenth century. George selected for himself the south and east wings of the castle, which would allow him greater privacy. In these new apartments the style departed almost entirely from the Gothic and instead a French-influenced neo-classical dominated. On the south was a new set of reception

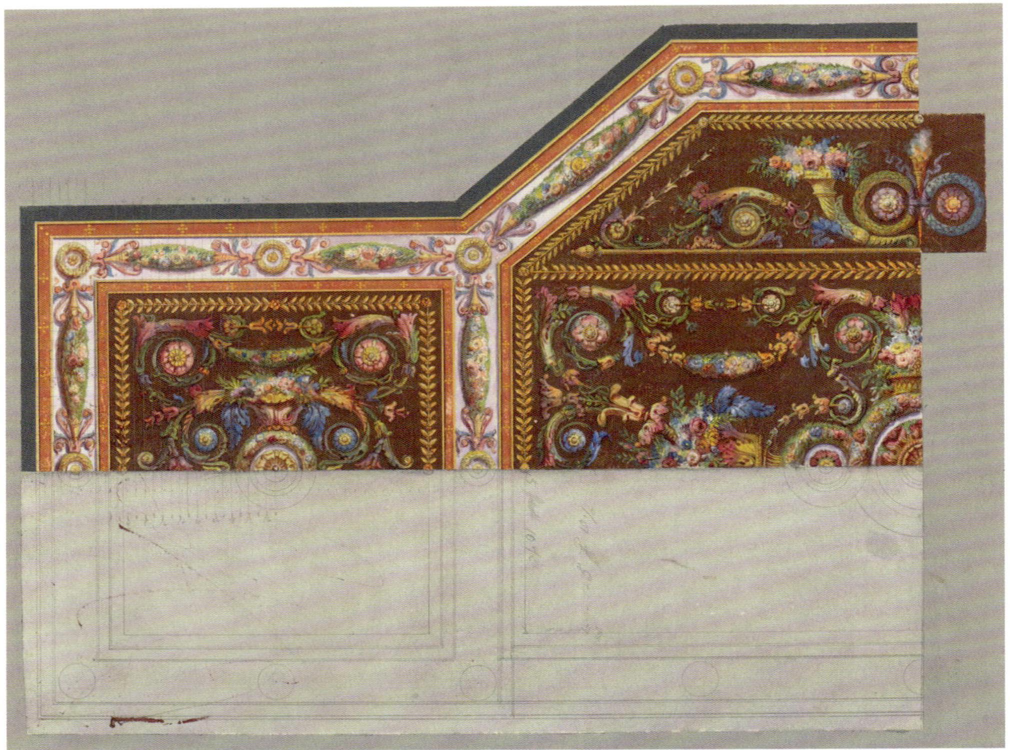

FIG. 17.8
ATTRIBUTED TO JEAN-JACQUES BOILEAU (active *c.*1787–1851), *Design for the carpet for the Large Drawing Room (The Crimson Drawing Room), Windsor Castle*, *c.*1826. Watercolour and bodycolour with pencil, 47.6 × 54.5 cm, RCIN 931283

FIG. 17.9
MOREL & SEDDON, *Open armchair*, *c.*1828 (tapestry *c.*1750). Gilded mahogany, tapestry, 103.5 × 70.0 × 71.0 cm, RCIN 33498

FIG. 17.10
ATTRIBUTED TO AUGUSTUS WELBY NORTHMORE PUGIN (1812–52), *Wine cooler*, *c.*1828. Rosewood, 41.0 × 95.5 × 61.0 cm, RCIN 29884

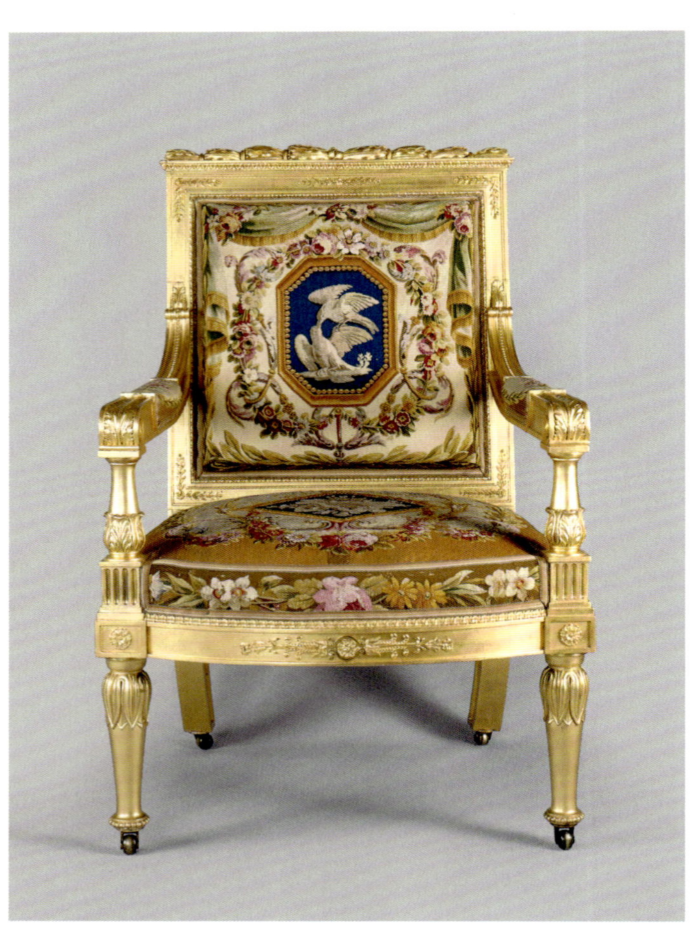

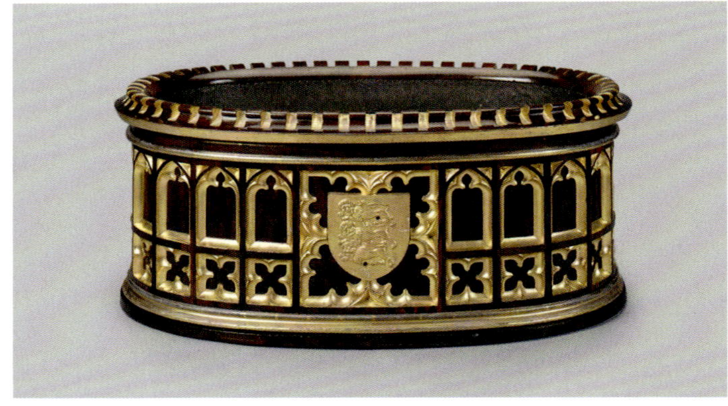

rooms for intimate guests. These rooms, a library flanked by two grand reception rooms, followed the favourite motif of a long, low-ceilinged space with a bow window on the long side. These new apartments were in essence 'an almost self-contained country house'.[30] Thomas Creevey, visiting in 1826, recorded 'all the New Living Rooms make a very good Gentleman's or Nobleman's house, nothing more', but by 1828, Harriet Arbuthnot, visiting with the Duke of Wellington, could describe the new apartments as 'quite magnificent'.[31]

Access between the two sides of the castle had historically been problematic and to overcome this inadequacy, as part of the new apartment scheme Long and Wyatville conceived a long

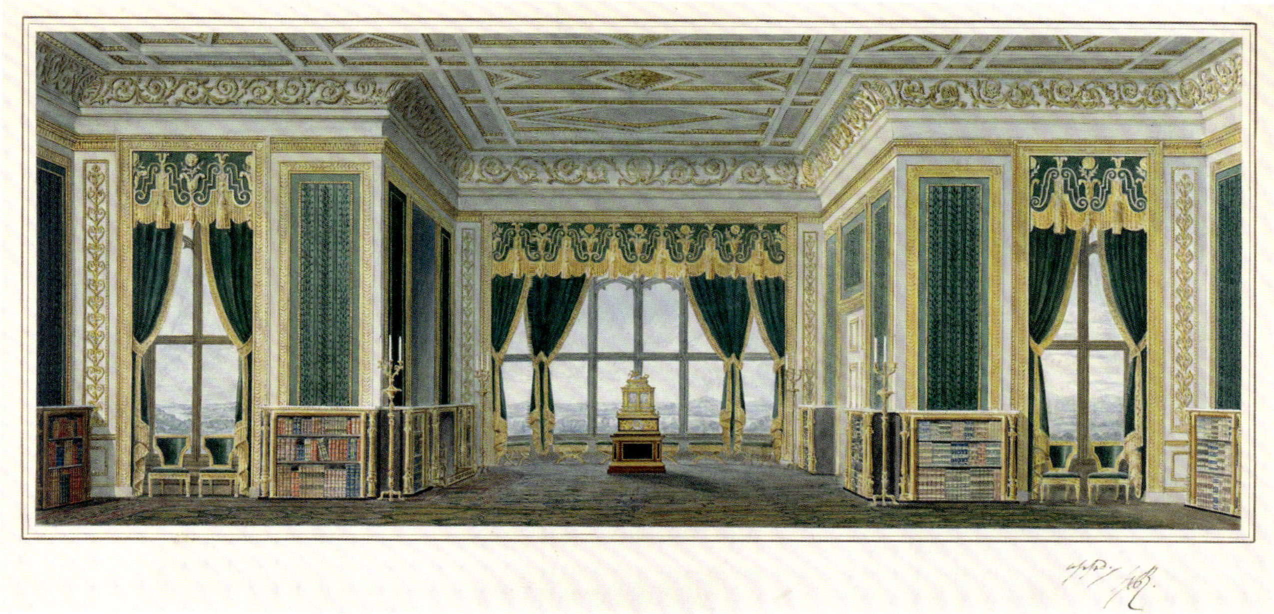

Gothic-style corridor, inserted on the quadrangle face of both east and south wings. This corridor served the twofold purpose of improving access and of acting as a long gallery, a space for a dense hang of paintings, busts and other works of art. Here George hung the entire set of paintings acquired by George III from Consul Joseph Smith, largely views of Venice by Canaletto. Among these he created a gallery of his friends, relations and political cronies, almost entirely composed of male portraits. These were punctuated by a series of marble busts, the majority by Chantrey and Nollekens, placed on scagliola pedestals supplied by Morel & Seddon; a total of 64 new pedestals were delivered in 1828.

The furniture which interspersed the busts and paintings in the corridor was largely black and gold in palette – a combination of ebony chairs thought to be Tudor in origin but in fact created on the Coromandel coast, early eighteenth-century giltwood tables and items of Boulle marquetry, both seventeenth- and nineteenth-century. These were offset by the crimson curtains, carpet and upholstery and by the scattering of colourful works of *pietra dura*, porcelain or curiosities, such as the tortoiseshell, rock crystal and *pietra dura* casket thought to have been acquired by Queen Charlotte,[32] which appeared along the length of the corridor. The gallery was liberally provided with seating – 'Gothic window stools' on one side as well as the 'Tudor' chairs on the facing wall – for those who wished to linger and enjoy the fine display of paintings, furniture and sculpture, selected by George with the sculptor Chantrey and the painter Wilkie in November 1828.[33]

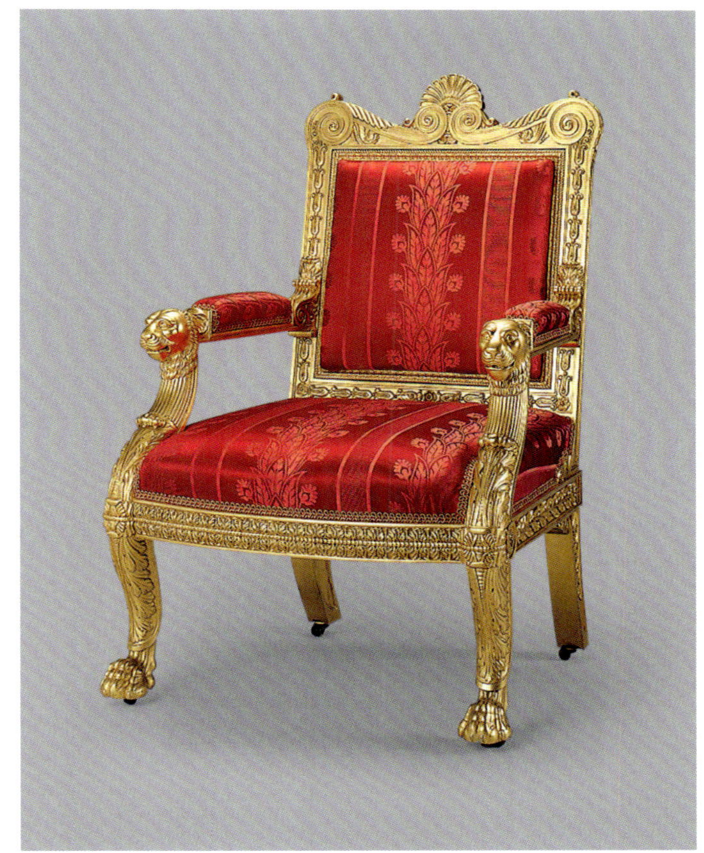

FIG. 17.11
OFFICE OF MOREL & SEDDON, *Design for the east elevation of the Library (the Green Drawing Room), Windsor Castle*, *c.*1826. Watercolour and bodycolour over pencil, 29.7 × 70.8 cm, RCIN 931282

FIG. 17.12
MOREL & SEDDON, *Open armchair*, *c.*1828. Gilded mahogany, silk damask, 109.2 × 74.9 × 71.1 cm, RCIN 2582

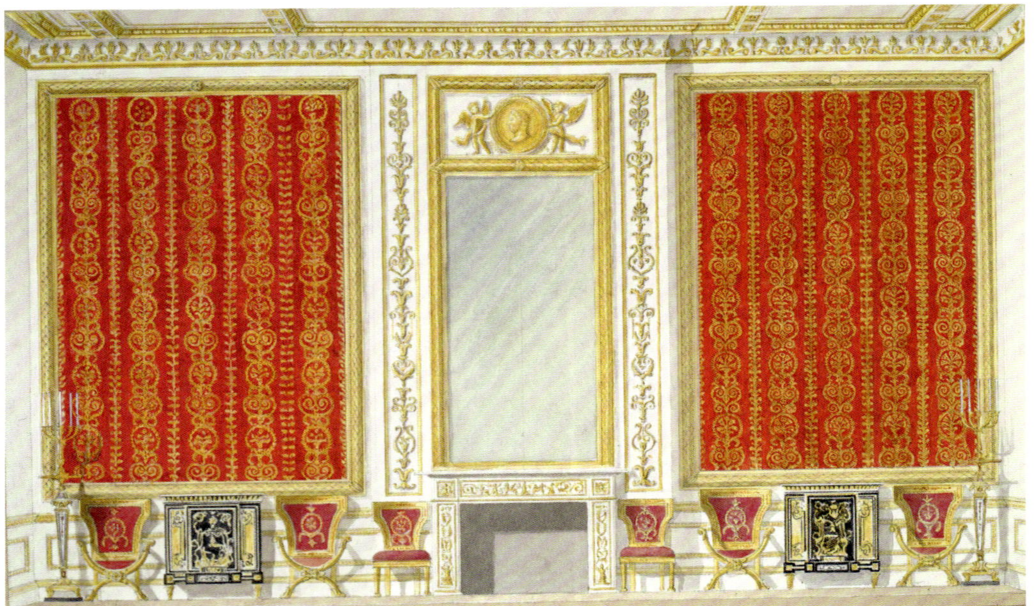

FIG. 17.13
OFFICE OF MOREL & SEDDON, *Design for the west elevation of His Majesty's Writing Room, Windsor Castle*, c.1826. Pencil and watercolour, 40.0 × 55.6 cm, RCIN 918393

FIG. 17.14
MOREL & SEDDON, *Piece of unused poppy-ground 'figured' tissue*, 1827–9. Silk damask, 54.0 cm (width) RCIN 68580

Although undertaken by a large team of architects, designers and craftsmen, the magnificence at Windsor was throughout deeply dependent on George's personal taste. The decoration of the spaces adopted many of the features that had been born in Carlton House: rich silk damask on the walls, often in panels framed in gilt, plasterwork ceilings of intricate design and lavish use of large mirrors. Elements of the fittings from Carlton House were introduced – chimneypieces by Vulliamy, carved door panels and trophies from the Throne Room reappeared at Windsor. Comfort was enhanced by the work of Morel & Seddon, a partnership formed specifically for the refitting of the castle.[34] The firm was responsible for supplying the silk damasks, curtains, carpets (Fig. 17.8) and wall panels; it provided the new mirrors and vast suites of seating and other furniture. Among this new furniture was a set of gilded mahogany open armchairs, upholstered with earlier tapestries (Fig. 17.9), and a suite of Gothic pieces designed by A.C. Pugin and A.W.N. Pugin (Fig. 17.10). Morel & Seddon are also likely to have been responsible for the painting and gilding schemes in each of the new apartments. Many of the firm's designs for these schemes survive in large watercolour images, signed by the king himself once approved (Fig. 17.11).

Morel & Seddon's designs for the interiors demonstrate George's continuing taste for French furniture and fittings; indeed Nicholas Morel had travelled to France in September 1826, shortly after receiving the commission for Windsor. Here, he may have acquired manpower as well as individual pieces of furniture: the Parisian master furniture-maker François-Honoré-Georges Jacob-Desmalter, whose influence can be seen in such French-inspired pieces as the set of mahogany armchairs designed for the Crimson and White Drawing Rooms (Fig. 17.12), subsequently travelled to England to work on the project. Architectural fittings, too, were brought from France, and in late October 'sundry large carved panels of rooms' and other carved wood arrived from Paris, to be used both as decoration and as models for further pieces.[35] The King's Writing Room (Fig. 17.13) was decorated with a crimson 'poppy-ground' silk (Fig. 17.14) woven by W.E. King and probably, like many of the textiles commissioned for Windsor, based on a French sample.[36]

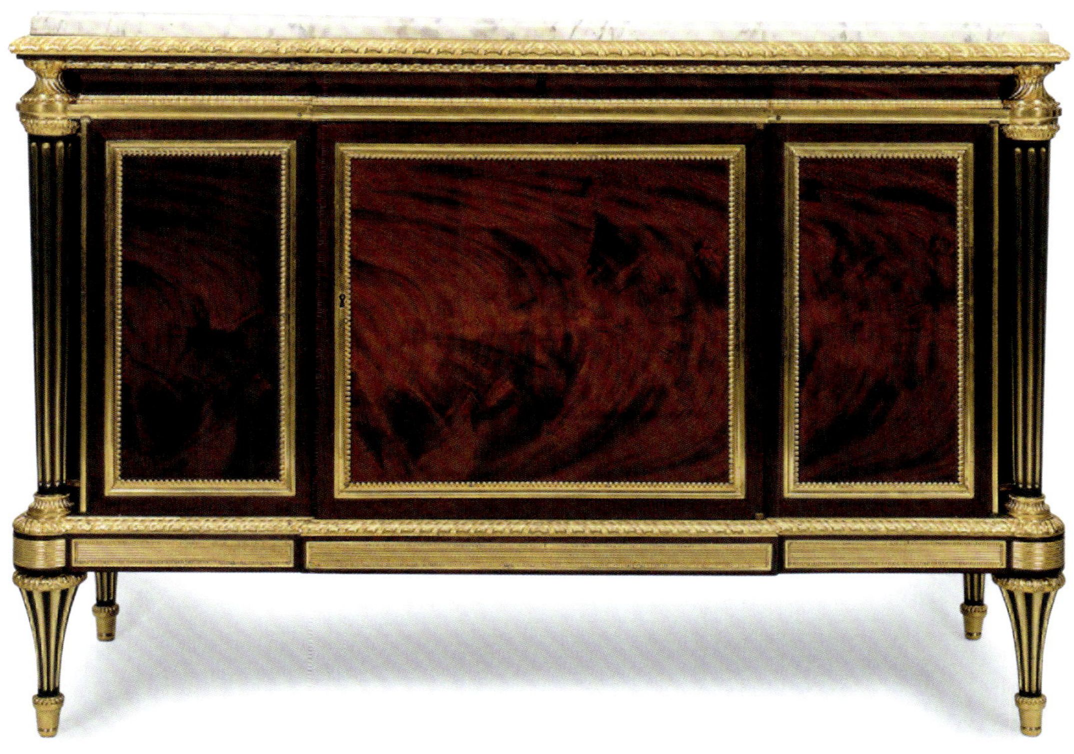

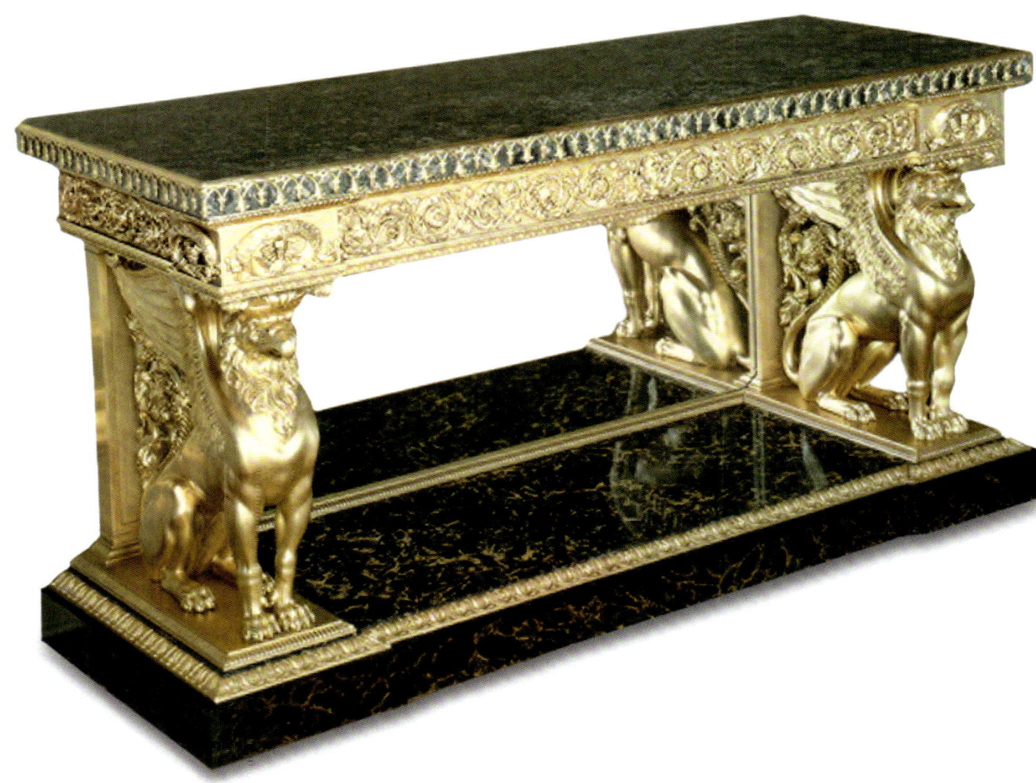

FIG. 17.15
ADAM WEISWEILER (1744–1820), *Commode*, *c.*1785. Oak, mahogany, marble, gilt bronze, 95.9 × 138.4 × 56.5 cm, RCIN 2596

FIG. 17.16
TATHAM, BAILEY & SANDERS, *Pier table*, *c.*1814–15. Gilded pine and limewood, mirror glass, scagliola, 107.2 × 205.5 × 79.0 cm, RCIN 33809

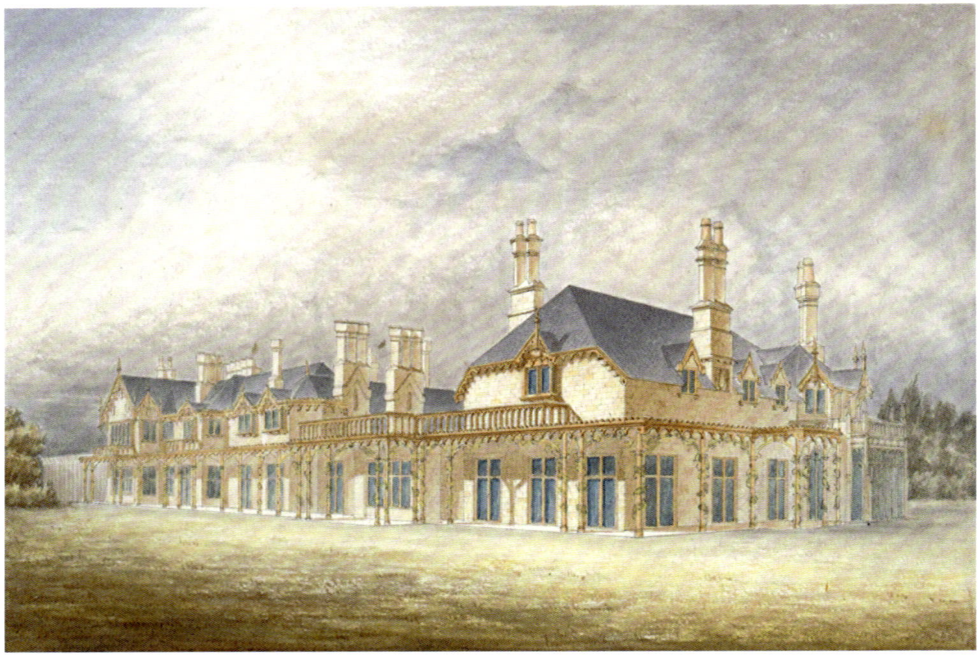

(left)
FIG. 17.17
SIR JEFFRY WYATVILLE (1766–1840), *South East View of King George the 4th cottage in Windsor Great Park*, *c.*1830. Pen and ink with watercolour, 15.5 × 35.0 cm, RCIN 932768

(opposite)
FIG. 17.18
WILLIAM HEATH (1794–1840), *Pitch in the Hole*, *c.*1827–30. Etching with hand colouring, 28.0 × 41.6 cm, RCIN 751275

In addition to the works of art already in Windsor, the furnishing of these spaces relied heavily on the contents of Carlton House, among them Weisweiler commodes (Fig. 17.15), many of them overhauled by Morel & Seddon. In 1826 in order to create a visual record for selecting these works, Long commissioned Morel to create a pictorial inventory of the smaller contents of Carlton House and the stores of Hampton Court, Brighton and Kensington Palace. This included vases, bronzes, clocks, candelabra and several of the more decorative items of furniture illustrated by A.C. Pugin and younger artists working in his office at that date and then annotated by the inventory clerk Benjamin Jutsham as various works were chosen to be transferred to Windsor. Among these were a pair of pier tables, originally made by the firm of Tatham, Bailey & Sanders for the Crimson Drawing Room at Carlton House, which were regilded and their scagliola tops repolished for the Long Gallery at Windsor in December 1828 (Fig. 17.16). Many works were transformed by the addition of plates of mirror glass, new plinth bases or gilt-bronze mounts, such as the elegant cabinet which had been in George's bedroom at Carlton House.[37] Additional works were required in the much larger spaces of Windsor, however. For the castle, George was able to acquire monumental items of furniture, such as two tall Boulle armoires that were purchased in 1825.[38] Long took responsibility for acquiring many of these works of art, often bought in France. Among them were the 37 Gobelins tapestries acquired in May 1825 in Paris, full sets of the *Story of Esther* and the *Story of Jason* designed by Jean-François de Troy, which were deployed in the seventeenth-century apartments at Windsor.

Even though the scheme was not complete before George's death, contemporaries commented on the comfort and splendour of the new accommodations. In February 1830, for example, Charles Greville recorded of Windsor that the new rooms 'are magnificent and comfortable, the corridor really delightful – furnished through its whole length of about 500 feet with the luxury of a drawing-room, and full of fine busts and bronzes and entertaining pictures, portraits and curious antiquities'.[39]

Royal Lodge, Windsor

While work was under way at Buckingham Palace and Windsor Castle, George largely retreated to a small lodge in the nearby Great Park, a residence that had previously been occupied by the park's Deputy Ranger (Fig. 17.17).[40] George had occupied the lodge since 1812, while waiting for renovations to be completed on Cumberland Lodge, which was intended to be his formal residence as Prince Regent. He immediately set about repairing and renovating the building with the help of John Nash. If he had an eye to public impression in his works at Carlton House, Brighton, Buckingham Palace and Windsor Castle – each of which he sought to make into a residence appropriate to his senior royal status – at the lodge he was able to express his private architectural ideals, in a building that was never intended to be in the public eye.

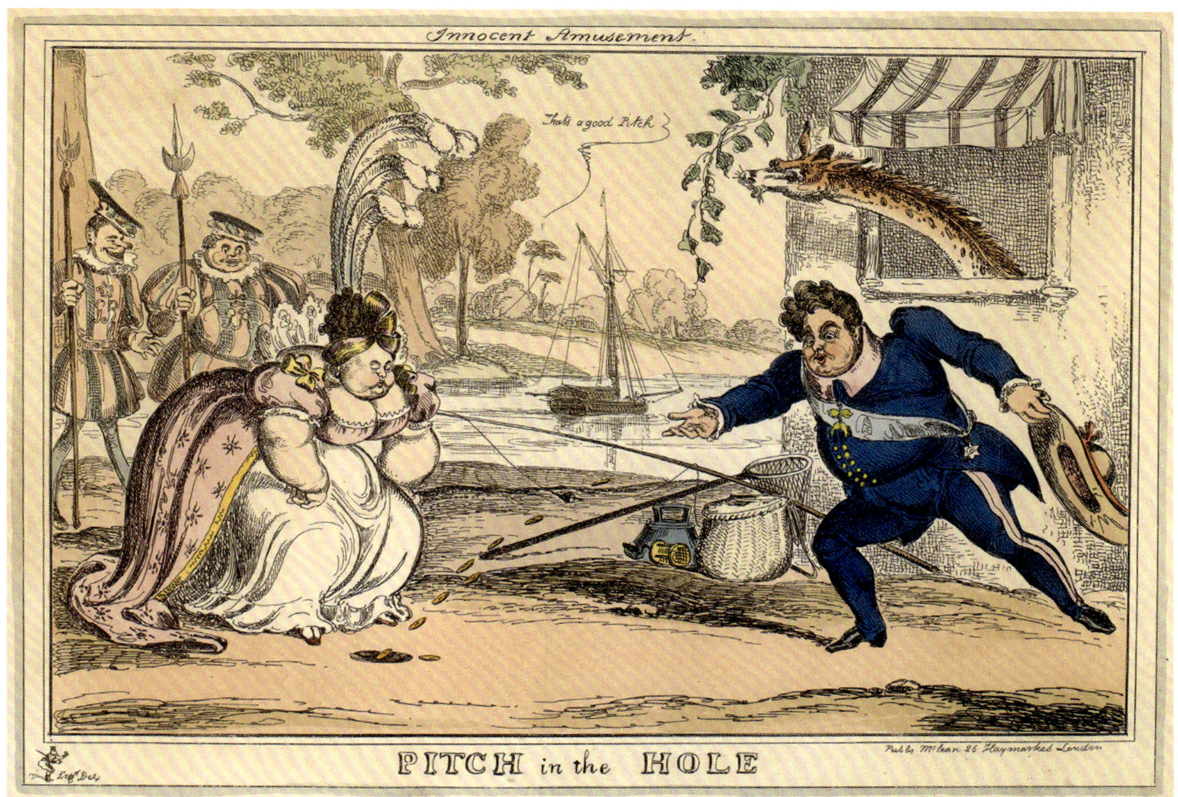

Among the surprisingly extensive works undertaken between 1812 and 1830 was the rerouting of a road which ran too close to the residence, an action intended to preserve George's privacy in the face of increasing interest in his personal life. The resulting building, largely destroyed in 1830, was something of an expensive architectural oddity: in 1824, Henry Grey Bennet, MP for Shrewsbury, could complain in the House of Commons that 'Buildings of the most strange description had already been erected in the vicinity of Windsor. One of these was a sort of Gothic cottage, with a thatched roof – a sort of thatched Henry the Seventh's chapel, the building of which cost 30,000l'.[41]

Under Nash, George's 'sort of … cottage' became a substantial residence – Royal Lodge – where the king and Lady Conyngham could entertain their closest friends. By 1823, Jeffry Wyatt (later Wyatville), who was overseeing the renovations at Windsor Castle, had succeeded Nash as architect. The building boasted a suite of reception rooms which were said to have 'a most brilliant appearance when illuminated on the occasion of any grand entertainment'. One of these rooms was an impressive conservatory which looked on to recently landscaped and planted gardens.[42] Nearby, a menagerie included a giraffe presented in 1827 by Mehmet Ali, Pasha of Egypt. The lodge had been transformed to accord with George's idea of a private idyll, where the walls were hung with paintings of his beloved horses, and his band played for his guests' entertainment. The king's rustic seclusion amused the satirists, who presented him gardening, fishing in Virginia Water (see chapter 13), and playing a suggestive game of 'pitch in the hole' with Lady Conyngham while his giraffe looks on (Fig. 17.18).

*

Few corners of the royal residences remained untouched by George IV. In each we see him celebrating the history of the monarchy, marking its links, albeit in an occasionally fanciful way, back to Edward the Confessor. This was underlined specifically at Windsor by the revival of the use of St George's Chapel for royal burials. George III was interred in the chapel in 1820 and the cenotaph to Princess Charlotte by the sculptor Matthew Wyatt, intended originally to be placed in Westminster Abbey, was inserted into a side chapel of St George's in 1824. George himself was interred in the chapel after his death in 1830. This placed him alongside that other great collector, Charles I. There is no funeral monument to George IV, but perhaps there was no need to create one – Buckingham Palace and Windsor Castle stand as his legacy.

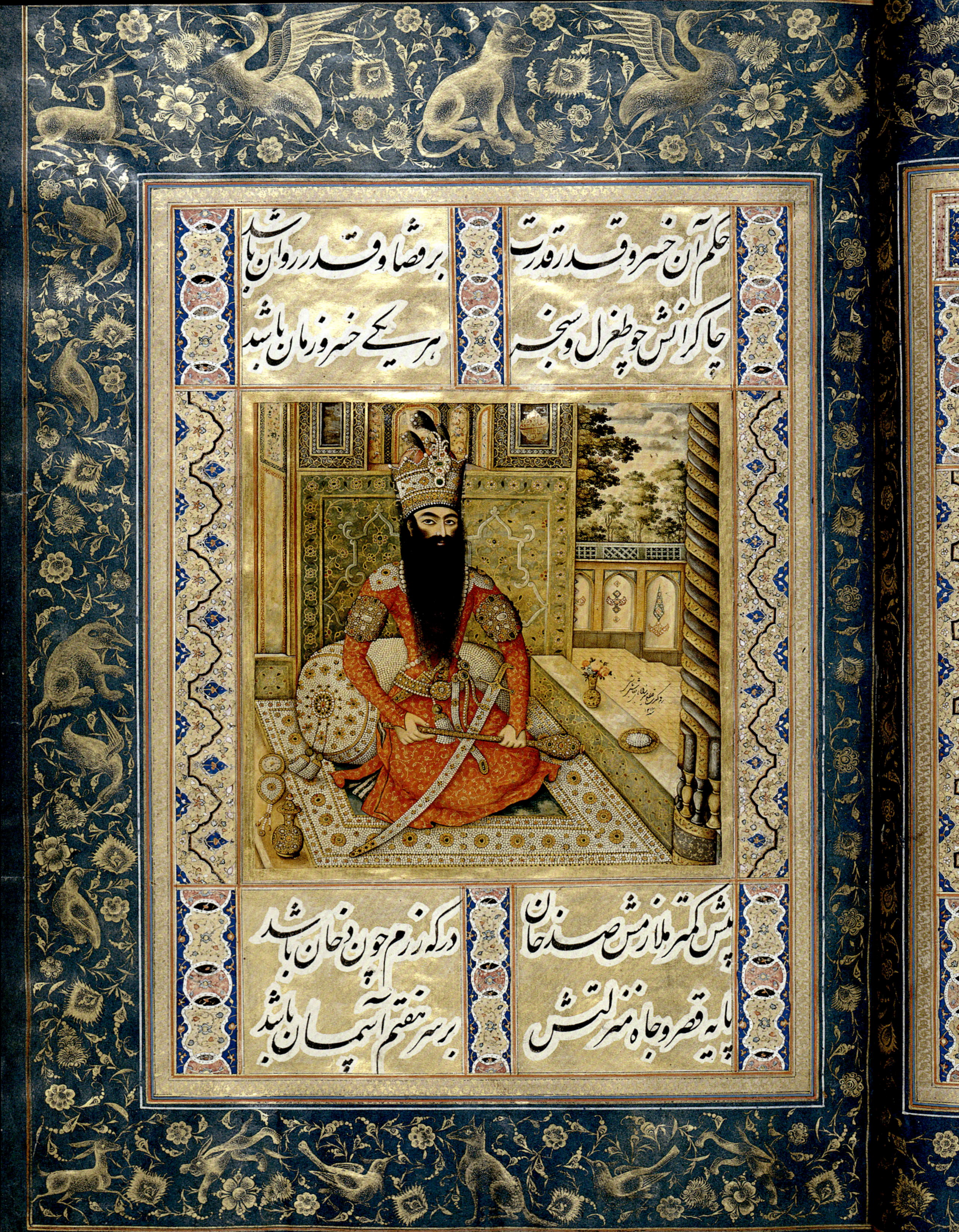
حکم آن خسرو قدر قدرت
بر قضا و قدر روان باشد
چاکرانش چو طغرل و سنجر
هر یکی خسرو زمان باشد
پیش کمتر ملازمش صد خان
درگه رزم چون دخان باشد
پایه قصر و جاه منزلتش
برسر هفتم آسمان باشد

18

GEORGE IV *and the* WIDER WORLD

RACHEL PEAT

Myriads of costly treasures …
of almost every age & country[1]

GEORGE IV LIVED IN AN ERA of exchange, empire and unprecedented global discovery. That he was a man of his time is nowhere more apparent than in his non-European collection. Yet its acquisition and appropriation evince the tastes and opportunities not of a cosmopolitan traveller or academic scholar, but of a prince. He himself never left Europe, but by virtue of his position, his passions and his purse, George amassed a collection which showed *par excellence* how the wider world might come instead to Britain.

Passions

The foremost of George's global passions was for Asian arts. In part, this reflects a contemporary fascination with the mysterious and exotic 'East', little-known and much-romanticised in Europe at this time. George's mother, Queen Charlotte, was an important early influence on his taste in this regard (see chapter 11). At Frogmore House, purchased in 1792, she assembled an array of Chinese and Japanese lacquer, as well as the 'sumptuous tents' formerly belonging to Tipu Sultan of Mysore, which George inherited after her death.[2] George also bought fans, gourd-shaped bottles, silks, furniture and specimens of 'Mandarin Dress' to the tune of £2,735 at the posthumous sale of her 'Oriental Curiosities & Porcelain' in 1819.[3] Items of this kind were integral to a series of lavish decorative schemes at Carlton House, from *c.*1788, and the Royal Pavilion, Brighton, from 1802, which are discussed in detail elsewhere in this volume (see chapters 5 and 10). There, George liberally combined wares of diverse Asian origin with European chinoiserie. In the Chinese Room at Carlton House, Eastern-style bells, lanterns and painted figures mingled with furniture by the French *ébéniste* Adam Weisweiler. Upstairs in the Bow Room or Rose Satin Drawing Room, the same pieces were from 1811 augmented by fine specimens of mounted Chinese and Japanese porcelain.

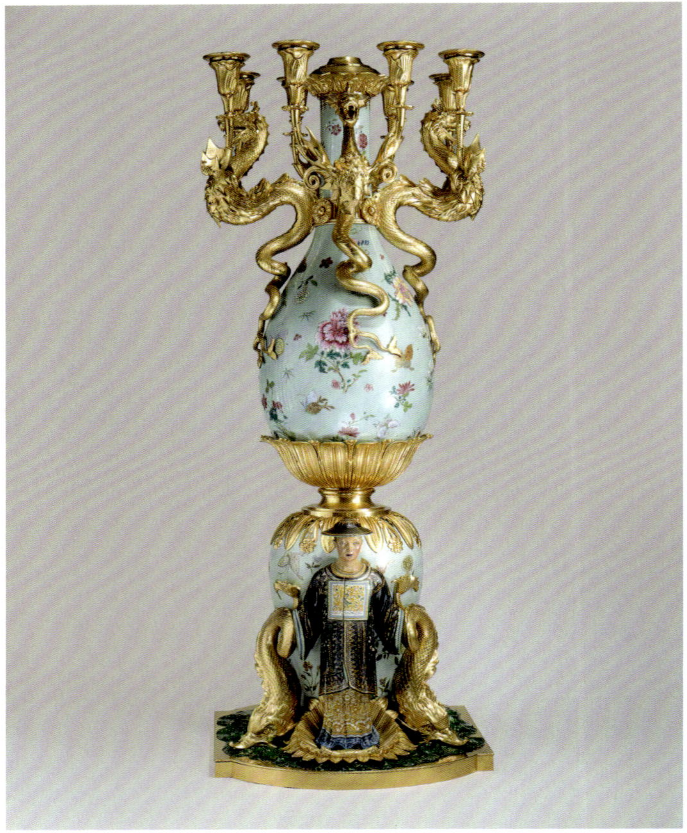

(p. 238)
FIG. 18.1
FATH 'ALI SHAH QAJAR (1772–1834), MIRZA BABA (active 1789–1810), minaturist, *Divan-i Khaqan*, 1802–3. Opaque watercolour, gold and black ink on paper, 42.5 × 28.2 cm, RCIN 1005020

FIG. 18.2
JINGDEZHEN, CHINA, *Bottle vase mounted as an eight-light candelabrum*, 1780–1810 (mounts early 19th century). Porcelain, gilt bronze, 116.0 × 47.0 × 51.0 cm, RCIN 2736

Together, such objects formed the backdrop for romantic spectacles evoking a generic and imaginary 'East'. At one entertainment, wrote Lady Elizabeth Feilding, 'a sonorous band of turbaned slaves' completed the effect of a 'Mahomet's Paradise'.[4] By 1819, most of George's 'Eastern' furnishings had been transferred to the Royal Pavilion, where ivory furniture from Vizagapatam (Vishākhapatnam) jostled with Chinese porcelain figures and imitation bamboo cabinets (see Fig. 11.11). Even the building was an architectural hybrid, 'a mixture of Moorish, Tartar, Gothic and Chinese', wrote Dorothea Lieven, wife of the Russian ambassador.[5] More playful than pedantic, George's collecting here speaks of an orientalist taste for beauty and ostentation.

George's interests nevertheless extended beyond decorative art to 'Eastern' life more broadly. His frequent and eclectic print purchases included depictions of the 'Punishments of China' in 1801, an 'Indian Idol' in 1813 and 'Persian Costumes' in 1820.[6] In 1804, he paid Dr James Garrett, surgeon aboard the East Indiaman *Warley*, £2,090 for delivering from China musical instruments, arrows, tobacco and a 'Wooden Barbers Stand', as well as porcelain and lacquer – an assortment so vast he had 'scarcely room to lie down' in his cabin.[7] Yet George had no qualms about radically adapting or 'Europeanising' such wares. Between 1800 and 1830 he assembled the largest and most important collection of European-mounted Asian porcelain in Britain. Elaborate gilt-bronze mounts were intended to harmonise with gilded interiors and in some cases completely transformed an object's function from simple jar to incense burner, candelabrum or even clock (Fig. 18.2). Several were supplied on George's orders by the Vulliamy family. For George, like other gentlemen collectors of this period, there was no fetish for the untouched 'authenticity' of overseas objects. In the fashionable interior, aesthetic appeal trumped cultural fidelity.

George's second global passion was the military. Barred from active service, he compensated by amassing at Carlton House a spectacular collection of arms and armour from almost every corner of the globe. By 1826, his Armoury (Fig. 18.4) filled five rooms and numbered some 3,300 items, including Indian mail, Malayan *kris*, Turkish saddles, Maori clubs (Fig. 18.3) and Abyssinian shields, as well as 'an immense collection of rich dresses, of all countries' (Fig. 18.5).[8] The contents were arranged 'under the immediate inspection of His Royal Highness', who had a clear predilection for the curious and the chiefly.[9] Notes in Benjamin Jutsham's five-volume inventory emphasise the romantic provenance of the pieces or their deadly capabilities: Indian arrows 'supposed to be poisoned', a Persian sword 'called … a Depriver of Life' and a Native American pouch 'worn by the King [chief] whenever he declared war'.[10] By 1808 they formed an 'unrivalled' assemblage, according to Rudolph Ackermann's *Microcosm of London*.[11] Sir Gore Ouseley, former ambassador-extraordinary to Persia, wrote in 1818 that the Prince Regent

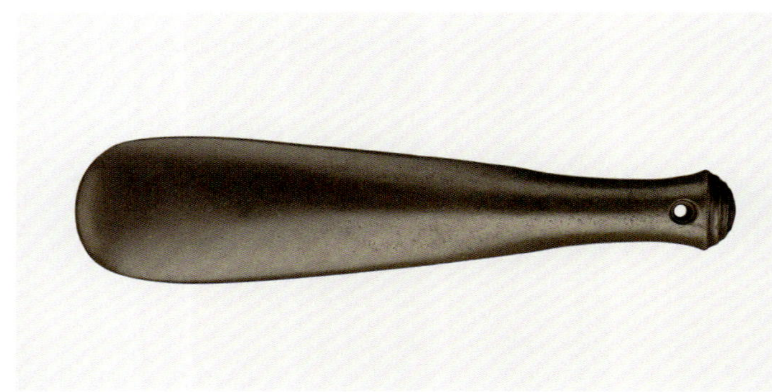

FIG. 18.3
MAORI, *Club* (*patu onewa*), 18th century. Basalt, 31.7 × 7.4 cm, RCIN 62167

FIG. 18.4
AUGUSTUS CHARLES PUGIN (*c*.1768–1832), *The Armoury, Carlton House*, 1814. Pencil, watercolour and bodycolour, 23.2 × 31.2 cm, RCIN 917092

FIG. 18.5
FIRST NATIONS, *Coat*, *c*.1800. Caribou skin, leather, 117.0 cm (length), RCIN 72705

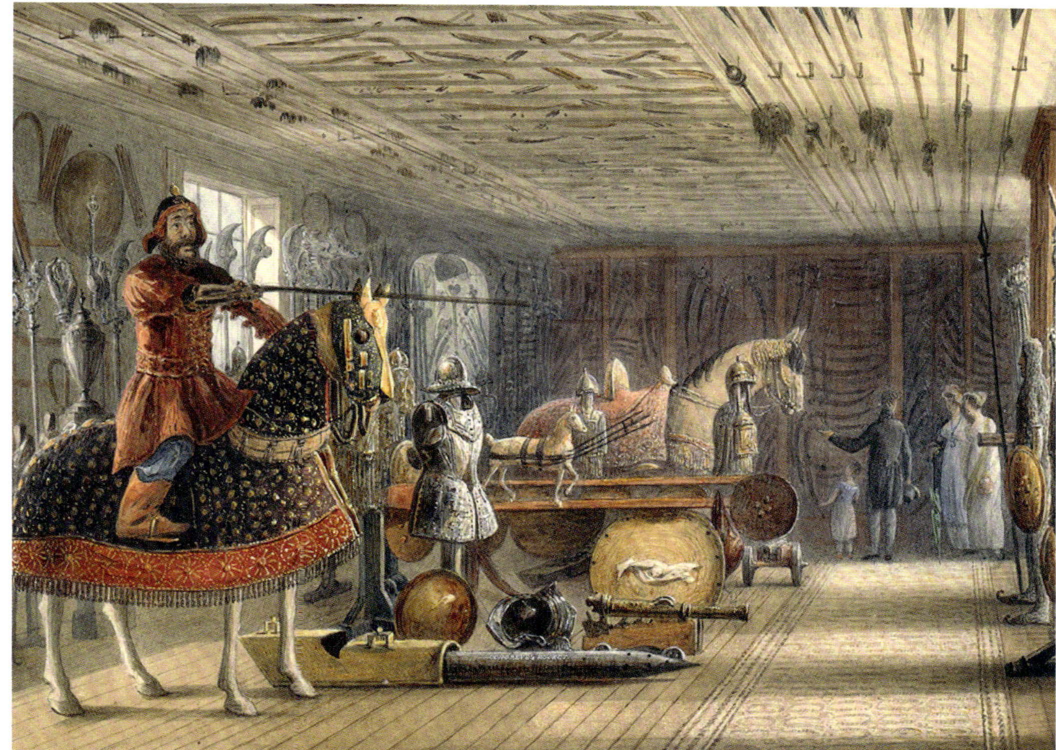

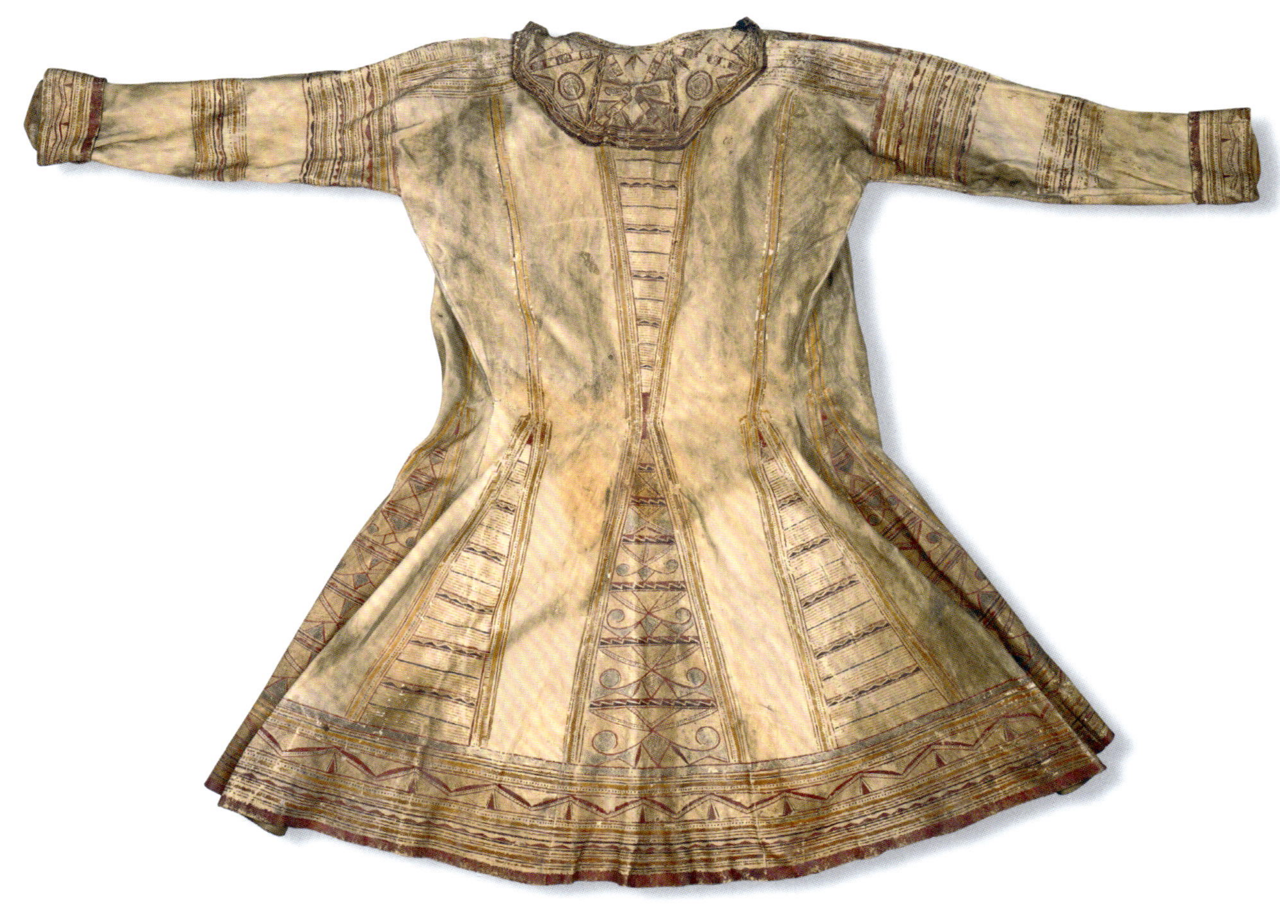

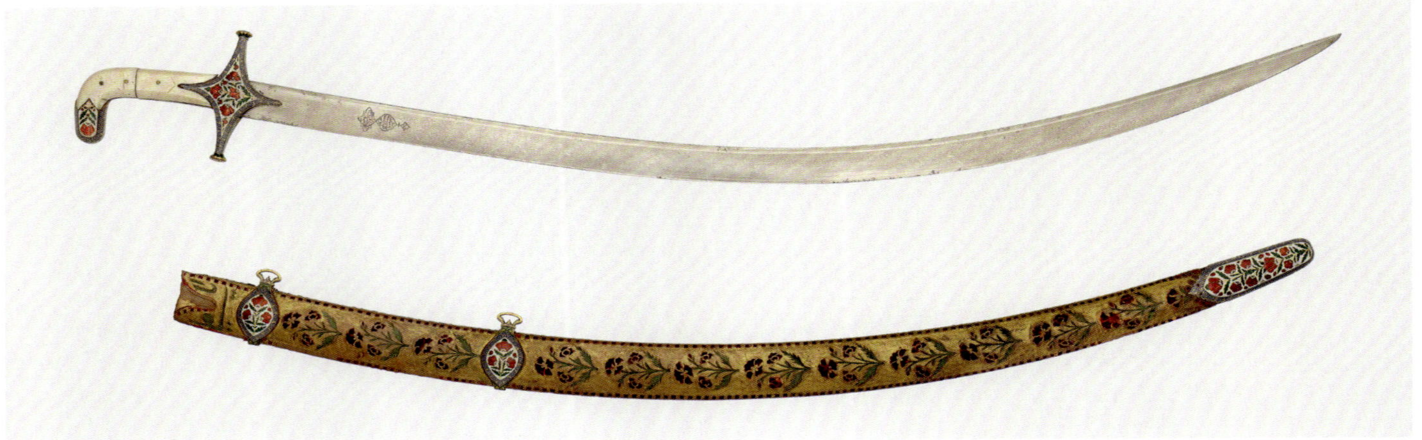

FIG. 18.6
PERSIAN, *Sword* (*shamshir*) *and scabbard*, *c.*1800. Watered crucible steel, gold, walrus ivory, wood, leather and textile, sword 91.6 cm (length), RCIN 62880

FIG. 18.7
INDIAN, *War coat*, 18th century. Brocade, silk, thread, 110.0 × 96.0 × 40.0 cm, RCIN 67229

FIG. 18.8
INDONESIAN, *Kris and sheath*, 1700–1810. Pattern-welded iron and steel, 49.3 cm (length), RCIN 67536

FIG. 18.9
ALGERIAN, *Pair of pistols*, 1800–19. Hardwood, steel, coral, silver, 49.0 cm (length), RCINS 62421 and 62422

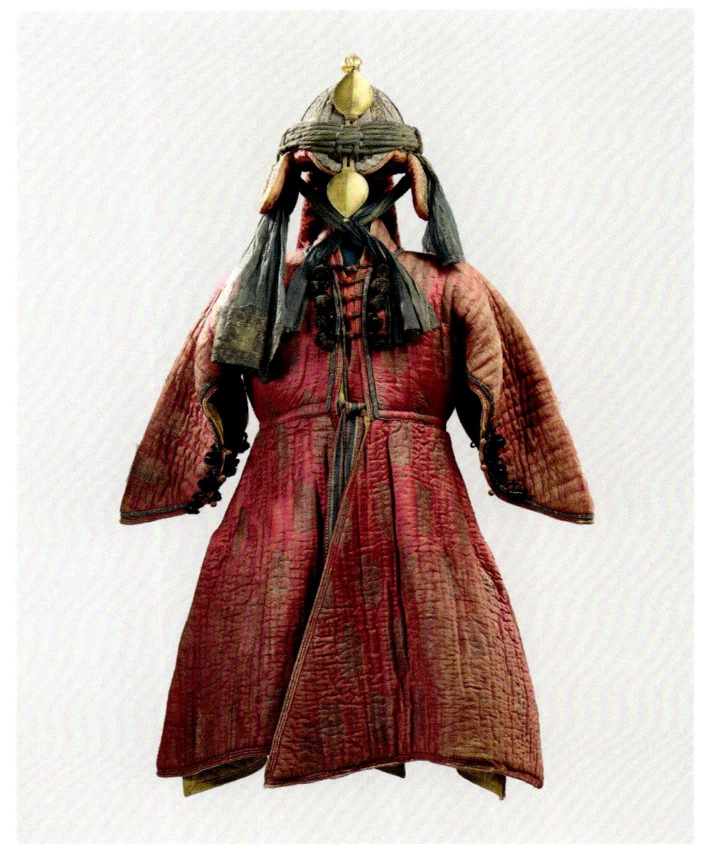

owned 'the finest Collection of Ancient Persian Swords in the World' (Fig. 18.6).[12] Costume and uniform abounded, mirrored by George's large collection of drawings 'by Foreign artists representing the military of various countries', which he showed to Benjamin West on 23 August 1810.[13]

People

Most non-European items in George's Armoury were gifts, revealing the global connections of a man who was both royal figurehead and *bon vivant*. By 1793 it was well known that the prince was 'collecting the military weapons of different countries' as well as items of 'Oriental curiosity'.[14] Friends and officials across the globe accordingly forwarded specimens as a way of currying favour and keeping George informed of their activities. In 1800, Marquess Wellesley dispatched the helmet and war coat of Tipu Sultan (Fig. 18.7), recently defeated by British forces at Seringapatam (Srirangapatna).[15] George's close friend the Earl of Moira, meanwhile, sent 'specimens of all the kinds of arrows made use of from the earliest time in Hindostan', as well as an extraordinary coat made from pangolin scales.[16] Both Wellesley and Moira held the post of Governor-General of India at the time they made these gifts. Further items were given in person by returning officials such as Stamford Raffles, who presented Indonesian spears, *kris* (Fig. 18.8) and temple sculpture following his tenure as Lieutenant-Governor of Java (1811–16). His *History of Java*, published in April 1817, was dedicated to the Prince Regent, who knighted him at Carlton House on 29 May that year.[17]

Unsurprisingly, the finest pieces in George's collection were diplomatic gifts, many received in his capacity as Regent.

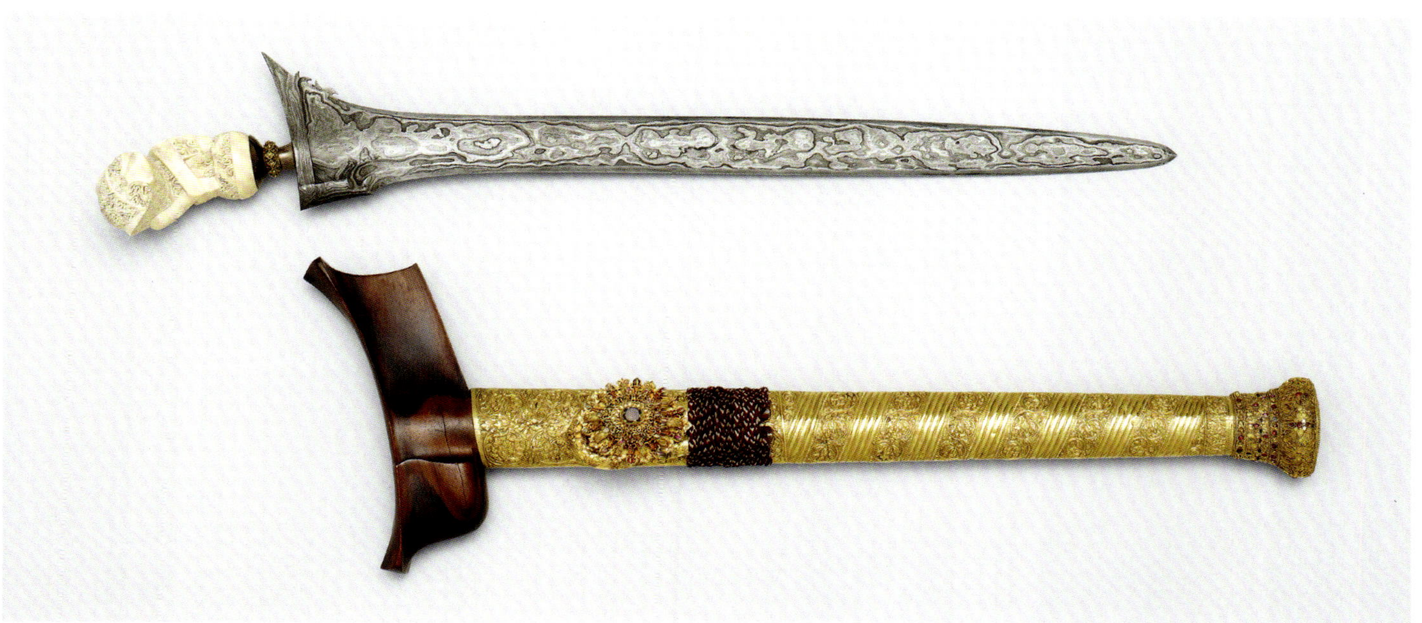

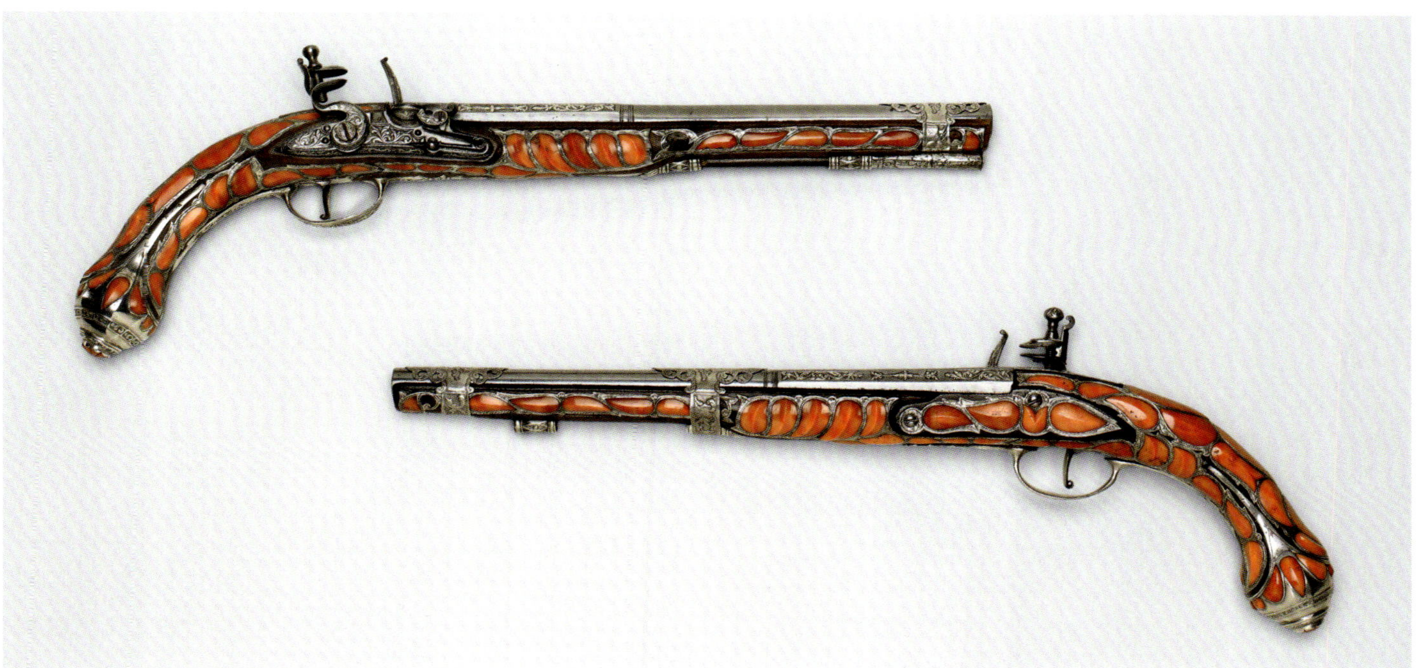

Among them were magnificent coral-encrusted guns, pistols and powder flasks sent by the Dey of Algiers in 1811 and 1819 (Fig. 18.9). Beautifully illuminated poems (*Divan-i Khaqan*), bound in lacquer, were dispatched by Fath 'Ali Shah Qajar in 1811 (Fig. 18.1). Fath 'Ali's envoy extraordinary, Mirza Abu'l Hassan Khan, later presented George with a superb *shamshir* 'celebrated in Persia for the exquisite temper of the blade'.[18] Abu'l Hassan had first come to England in 1809 and struck up a genuine friendship with George who, he wrote, 'never failed in his courtesy towards me'.[19] The two shared a long-running joke about the envoy's taste in women and George made him gifts of a clock from Carlton House and several ornate combs.[20] Not all overseas visitors received such welcome. In 1824, George delayed meeting King Kamehameha II and Queen Kamamalu of the Sandwich Islands (now Hawaii), who had made an unsolicited visit to London to request British protection for

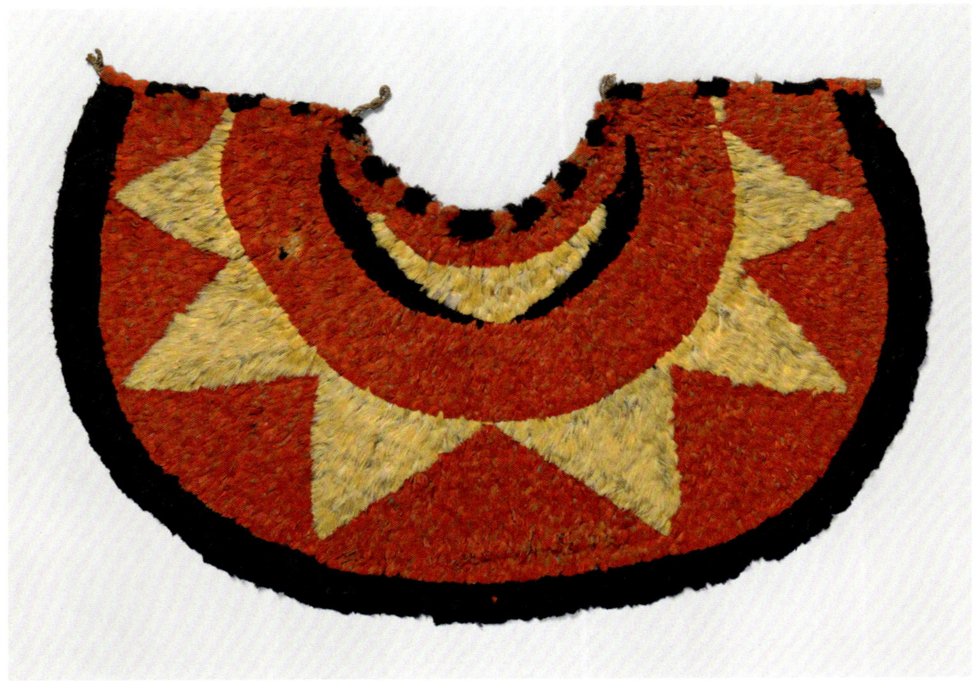

FIG. 18.10
HAWAIIAN, *Cape* (*'ahu'ula*), *c.*1824. Feather, bark cloth, 52.0 × 84.0 cm, RCIN 69994

the islands. While awaiting an audience, the royal couple died from measles, and the surviving members of their suite were left to present their costly gifts of six red and yellow feather capes (*'ahu'ula*) and a matching helmet (*mahiole*) (Fig. 18.10).[21] The garments' significance as pre-eminent symbols of chiefly status is reinforced by the melancholy record that the king and queen's own cloaks were draped over their coffins after their deaths.[22]

Places

George's collection was not geographically uniform, but mirrored the changing boundaries of British exploration and colonial activity. In keeping with a late eighteenth-century fashion for Oceanic artefacts, the prince owned several 'war instrument[s]' used 'by the natives at Botany Bay' and a club brought from Hawaii by Captain Cook's ship *Resolution*.[23] By the early nineteenth century, British explorers had turned their sights to the interior of Africa. In 1811, George accordingly received an Abyssinian shield, horn and textiles from Henry Salt, who had been dispatched by the British Government to survey what is now Ethiopia.[24] The efforts of Major Denham Dixon to trace the course of the River Niger meanwhile bore fruit in the form of spears, throwing knives and a cuirass from Bornu (now Nigeria), given to the king in 1825.[25] These objects and the men who collected them were evidently of interest to George, whose library at Carlton House contained a modest array of travel literature, including Cook's *Voyage towards the South Pole, and Round the World* (1777) and Salt's *Voyage to Abyssinia* (1814).

Spoils of war in George's collection particularly reflected the changing fortunes of British overseas power. Among them was a flintlock rifle used by American revolutionaries at the 1781 Battle of Mudlick Creek, engraved 'UNITED STATES WE ARE ONE' (Fig. 18.11).[26] By the turn of the nineteenth century, a 'swing to the East' was under way as Britain looked to India and beyond to replace the lost American colonies.[27] Central to this was the death of Tipu in 1799, whose defeat, like Napoleon's, became something of an obsession for George. In tandem with collectors such as Sir John Soane and Edward Clive, 1st Earl of Powis, George eagerly assembled items with a purported Tipu provenance, including firearms, swords and the red leather boots Tipu was said to have worn during the storming of Seringapatam (Srirangapatna).[28] Such was the prince's interest that on 29 September 1801 he bought from Colnaghi a pair of prints of Tipu, one of which showed Tipu's family grieving over his dead body, for the sizeable price of 7 guineas (Fig. 18.12).[29] Elsewhere on the Indian subcontinent, British forces deposed the Kandyan King Sri Vikrama Rajasinha in 1815, and it was the Prince Regent who received his gold-plated throne, footstool and crown.[30] By 1827 George had also been given an Ashanti war drum, replete with human jaw bones – early traces of a new era of British

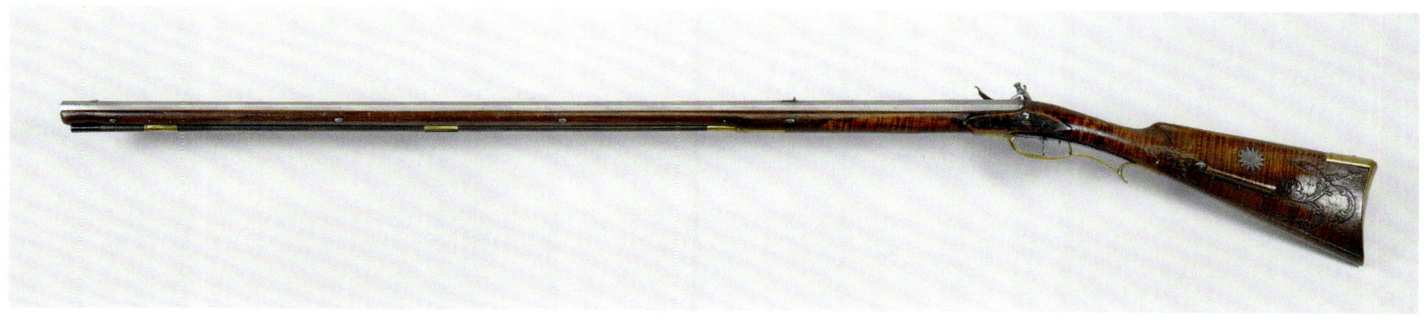

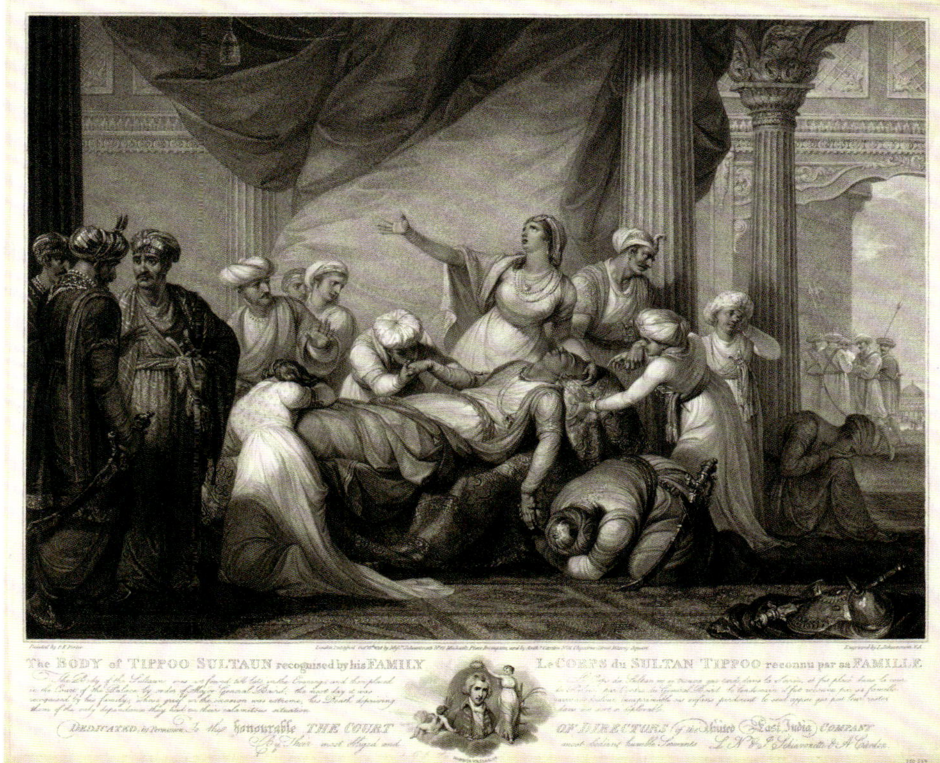

FIG. 18.11
NORTH AMERICAN, *Flintlock rifle*, 1775, with refurbishment by DURS EGG (1748–1831), *c.*1802. Maple, steel, brass, silver, 154.0 × 16.0 cm, RCIN 61069

FIG. 18.12
LUIGI SCHIAVONETTI (1765–1810) AFTER ROBERT KER PORTER (1777–1842), *Body of Tippoo Sultaun Recognised by his Family*, 1801. Stipple engraving, 57.9 × 69.0 cm (sheet), RCIN 750587

colonialism in Africa.[31] The United States ambassador, Richard Rush, saw wounded generals at a Carlton House levée and remarked, dryly, 'other nations chiefly fight on or near their own territory; the English everywhere'.[32]

By the time he became King in 1820, George's interaction with the wider world was favourite material for his satirists. He was lampooned as an obese Persian prince, 'Kouli Khan'; a bejewelled Turk, 'Sultan Sham', preying on unsuspecting ladies; and a grotesque Chinese man, 'The Great Joss', pouring coins into his Eastern-inspired building projects (see Fig. 12.6). These prints were a commentary on George's political and sexual dealings as much as his artistic ones, but they reflect a contemporary view of his engagement with the wider world as distasteful and exorbitant.

Nevertheless, some 18 years after his death, the cosmopolitan contents of George's Armoury would be transferred almost wholesale to Windsor Castle, where they were meticulously arranged by Prince Albert. Queen Victoria remarked, '[His] collection astonishes everyone, containing as it does the myriads of costly treasures inlaid with jewels & gold of every kind & of almost every age & country.'[33] George's systematic acquisition of weapons and costume from across the globe and his 30-year devotion to furnishing residences in the romantic 'Eastern' style led to the creation of one of the finest assemblages of non-European decorative art in Britain. His preservation of more serendipitous acquisitions from global friend and foe meanwhile provides a compelling outline of Britain's international standing in this period.

APPENDIX

WORKS OF ART DISPLAYED IN THE EXHIBITION *GEORGE IV: ART & SPECTACLE*

The works of art that appear in the exhibition at The Queen's Galleries in London and Edinburgh, which accompanies this volume, are listed below. The works are listed by media, and chronologically according to their acquisition where this information is available. The provenance and exhibition history of each object are given only as they concern George IV. Unless otherwise specified all works were commissioned or acquired by him; the names of his agents are given where known. Where they depart from the forms used elsewhere in this volume, room and floor names are spelled as in the documents cited. References to catalogues raisonnés are given in abbreviated form and a full list of these appears in the bibliography (pp. 285–90). Images of documents from the Royal Archives that are cited can be consulted on the Georgian Papers Project website at <www.rct.uk/collection/georgian-papers-programme>.

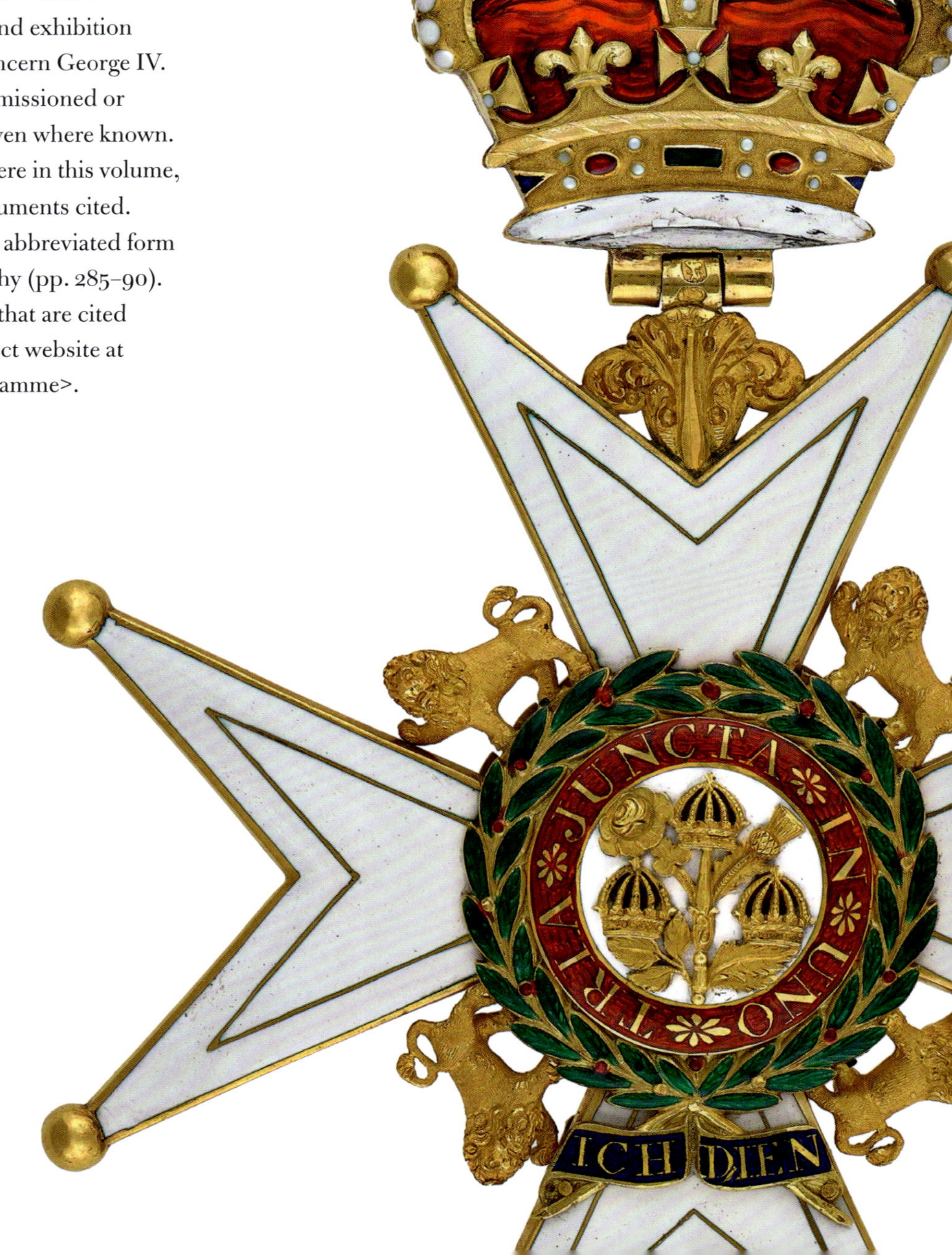

Detail of Fig. A.33
ATTRIBUTED TO RUNDELL, BRIDGE & RUNDELL, *Order of the Bath: Grand Cross sash badge*, 1814

PAINTINGS

THOMAS GAINSBOROUGH (1727–88)
The Three Eldest Princesses: Charlotte, Princess Royal (1766–1828), Augusta (1768–1840) and Elizabeth (1770–1840), 1783–4
Oil on canvas
129.7 × 179.8 cm
RCIN 400206
OM 798 FIG. 3.6

Painted to hang in the Saloon at Carlton House, at a cost of £315 (RA GEO/MAIN/26791). Recorded in store at Carlton House (CH inv. 1819, no. 352).

Exhibited at Schomberg House in 1784 and 1786.

ALEXANDRE-AUGUSTE ROBINEAU (1747–1828)
The Fencing-Match between the Chevalier de Saint-Georges (1745–99) and the Chevalier d'Eon (1728–1810), *c.*1787–9
Oil on canvas
64.1 × 75.8 cm
RCIN 400636
OMV 1050 FIG. 13.15

Painted for George IV when Prince of Wales. Recorded in store at Carlton House (CH inv. 1819, no. 257).

SIR JOSHUA REYNOLDS (1723–92)
George Brydges, 1st Lord Rodney (?1719–92), 1788–9
Oil on canvas
238.7 × 148.2 cm
RCIN 405899
OM 1026 FIG. 9.5

Said to have been painted for George IV when Prince of Wales (Graves and Cronin 1899–1901, II, pp. 840–1). Hung in the Ante-room at Carlton House in 1792; recorded in store at Carlton House in 1816 and on the Staircase in 1819 (CH inv. 1816, no. 278; CH inv. 1819, no. 523).

Exhibited at the Royal Academy in 1789 (no. 225) and at the British Institution in 1813, 1820 (no. 48) and 1827 (no. 182).

GEORGE STUBBS (1724–1806)
George IV when Prince of Wales, 1791
Oil on canvas
102.6 × 127.7 cm
RCIN 400142
OM 1109 FIG. 2.3

Painted for George IV when Prince of Wales. Recorded in store at Carlton House; sent to Royal Lodge on 31 May 1822 (CH inv. 1819, no. 262).

Probably the portrait exhibited by the artist at the Royal Academy in 1791.

JOHN HOPPNER (1758–1810)
Franz Joseph Haydn (1732–1809), 1791–2
Oil on canvas
92.1 × 71.5 cm
RCIN 406987
OM 843 FIG. 1.4

Commissioned in 1791 but not received until after Hoppner's death in 1810; the prince paid £31 10s for the 'Unfinished Portrait' (RA GEO/MAIN/26877).

Recorded in store at Carlton House (CH inv. 1819, no. 318).

THOMAS GAINSBOROUGH (1727–88)
Diana and Actaeon, *c.*1785–8
Oil on canvas
158.1 × 188.0 cm
RCIN 405077
OM 806 FIG. 0.18

Purchased by Hammond at the sale of the possessions of Gainsborough Dupont, Christie's, 10 Apr. 1797 (lot 43), for £2 3s (Spielmann 1915–16, pp. 93 and 107). Recorded in store at Carlton House (CH inv. 1819, no. 342).

JOHN HOPPNER (1758–1810)
Horatio, First Viscount Nelson (1758–1805), 1801–2
Oil on canvas
239.0 × 148.0 cm
RCIN 405901
OM 849 FIG. 3.12

Commissioned for £147 (RA GEO/MAIN/26829) but not received until after Hoppner's death in 1810. Recorded in the East Ante-Room at Carlton House (CH inv. 1819, no. 59); moved to the New Gallery (now the Grand Corridor) at Windsor Castle on 24 July 1828.

Exhibited at the British Institution in 1820 (no. 55) and 1827 (no. 157).

SIR WILLIAM BEECHEY (1753–1839)
George IV when Prince of Wales, 1803
Oil on canvas
128.4 × 101.7 cm
RCIN 400511
OM 664 FIG. 2.17

Painted for presentation to Edward, Duke of Kent at a cost of £84 (the frame an additional £10 10s) (RA GEO/MAIN/26842–3); George, Duke of Cambridge; his sale, Christie's, 11 June 1904 (73); purchased by King Edward VII.

GODFRIED SCHALCKEN (1643–1706)
The Game of 'Lady, come into the Garden', late 1660s
Oil on panel
63.5 × 49.5 cm
RCIN 405343
CW 180 FIG. 7.1

Purchased by H. Phillips at the Walsh Porter Sale, Christie's, 23 Mar. 1803 (lot 47), for £409 10s (plus £20 9s commission) (RA GEO/MAIN/26926). Hung in the Dining Room at Carlton House (CH inv. 1819, no. 70).

Exhibited at the British Institution in 1826 (no. 40) and 1827 (no. 134).

ELISABETH-LOUISE VIGÉE-LEBRUN (1755–1842)
Charles-Alexandre de Calonne (1734–1802), 1784
Oil on canvas
155.5 × 130.3 cm
RCIN 406988 FIG. 0.9

Acquired before 1806. Recorded in store at Carlton House (CH inv. 1819, no. 291).

PETER EDWARD STROEHLING (1768–*c.*1826)
George III (1738–1820), 1807
Oil on copper
60.7 × 48.2 cm
RCIN 404865
OM 1093 FIG. 11.3

Painted at a cost of 200 guineas (RA GEO/MAIN/26845–6); presented by George IV at an unrecorded date to Princess Sophia; on whose death acquired by Queen Victoria.

PETER EDWARD STROEHLING (1768–*c.*1826)
Queen Charlotte (1744–1818), 1807
Oil on copper
59.7 × 47.5 cm
RCIN 404863
OM 1094 FIG. 11.2

Princess Sophia (1777–1848), 1807
Oil on copper
60.8 × 48.3 cm
RCIN 404864
OM 1098 FIG. 3.8A

Princess Mary (1776–1857), 1807
Oil on copper
60.7 × 48.3 cm
RCIN 404866
OM 1097 FIG. 3.8B

Princess Augusta (1768–1840), 1807
Oil on copper
61.0 × 47.9 cm
RCIN 404869
OM 1095 FIG. 11.7

Princess Elizabeth (1770–1840), 1807
Oil on copper
60.8 × 48.1 cm
RCIN 404870
OM 1096 FIG. 3.8C

Princess Amelia (1783–1810), 1807
Oil on copper
61.1 × 46.1 cm
RCIN 404871
OM 1099 FIG. 3.8D

These six works were painted at a cost of 200 guineas each (RA GEO/MAIN/26845–6). Received at Carlton House in Dec. 1807 (Jutsham I, p. 31); recorded in store there and sent to Royal Lodge on 27 Sept. 1823 (CH inv. 1819, nos 484–5 and 487–90).

Returned to the artist for exhibition in 1808 (Jutsham I, p. 24).

CHARLES PARROCEL (1688–1752)
A Man on Horseback, *c*.1725–50
Oil on canvas
80.0 × 65.2 cm
RCIN 403389 FIG. A.1

Charles, Prince de Nassau (1712–75), *c*.1725–50
Oil on canvas
80.4 × 64.8 cm
RCIN 403390 FIG. 9.12

Acquired from Colnaghi on 9 May 1808 at a cost of £31 10s for the pair (RA GEO/MAIN/27462). Hung in the Armoury at Carlton House and sent to Royal Lodge on 27 Sept. 1823 (CH inv. 1819, nos 513 and 514).

ATTRIBUTED TO ADAM-FRANÇOIS VAN DER MEULEN (1632–90)
The Building of Versailles, *c*.1680
Oil on canvas
108.0 × 142.3 cm
RCIN 406554 FIG. 0.8

Purchased in or before 1809, when sent to [Edward?] 'Wyatt' for repair and regilding of the frame (Jutsham I, p. 42). Hung at Warwick House (CH inv. 1819, no. 543); sent to Royal Lodge on 21 Oct. 1823 (Jutsham III, p. 49).

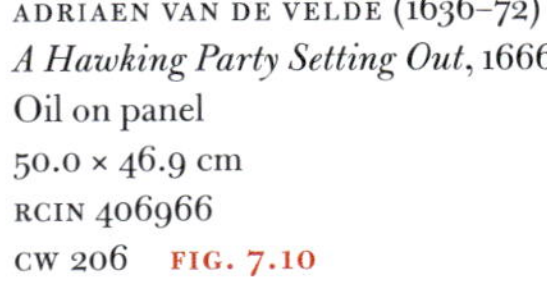

ADRIAEN VAN DE VELDE (1636–72)
A Hawking Party Setting Out, 1666
Oil on panel
50.0 × 46.9 cm
RCIN 406966
CW 206 FIG. 7.10

Purchased by Lord Yarmouth at Lord Rendlesham's sale, 28 May 1810 (Jutsham I, p. 123). Hung in the Rose Satin Room (Bow Room, Principal Floor) at Carlton House (CH inv. 1819, no. 26), where it appears in a watercolour of *c*.1817 (see Fig. 0.5).

Exhibited at the British Institution in 1826 (no. 69) and 1827 (no. 6).

EDWARD BIRD (1772–1819)
Village Choristers Rehearsing an Anthem for Sunday, 1810
Oil on panel
63.1 × 92.8 cm
RCIN 405540
OM 685 FIG. 7.3

Purchased in 1810 for 250 guineas through Benjamin West. Hung in the Upper Anti-room at Carlton House (CH inv. 1819, no. 154); sent to Royal Lodge on 27 Sept. 1823 but subsequently returned to London (Jutsham III, p. 44); sent to Royal Lodge on 17 June 1824 (Jutsham III, p. 54).

PAULUS POTTER (1625–54)
Two Sportsmen Outside an Inn, 1651
Oil on panel
53.3 × 43.7 cm
RCIN 400942
CW 156 FIG. 7.12

Purchased from William Harris, 7 Feb. 1811 (with four other pictures for a total of £2,625: RA GEO/MAIN/27087). Hung in the Rose Satin Room (Bow Room, Principal Floor) at Carlton House (CH inv. 1819, no. 28), where it appears in a watercolour of *c*.1817 (see Fig. 0.5).

Exhibited at the British Institution in 1819 (no. 5) and 1826 (no. 37).

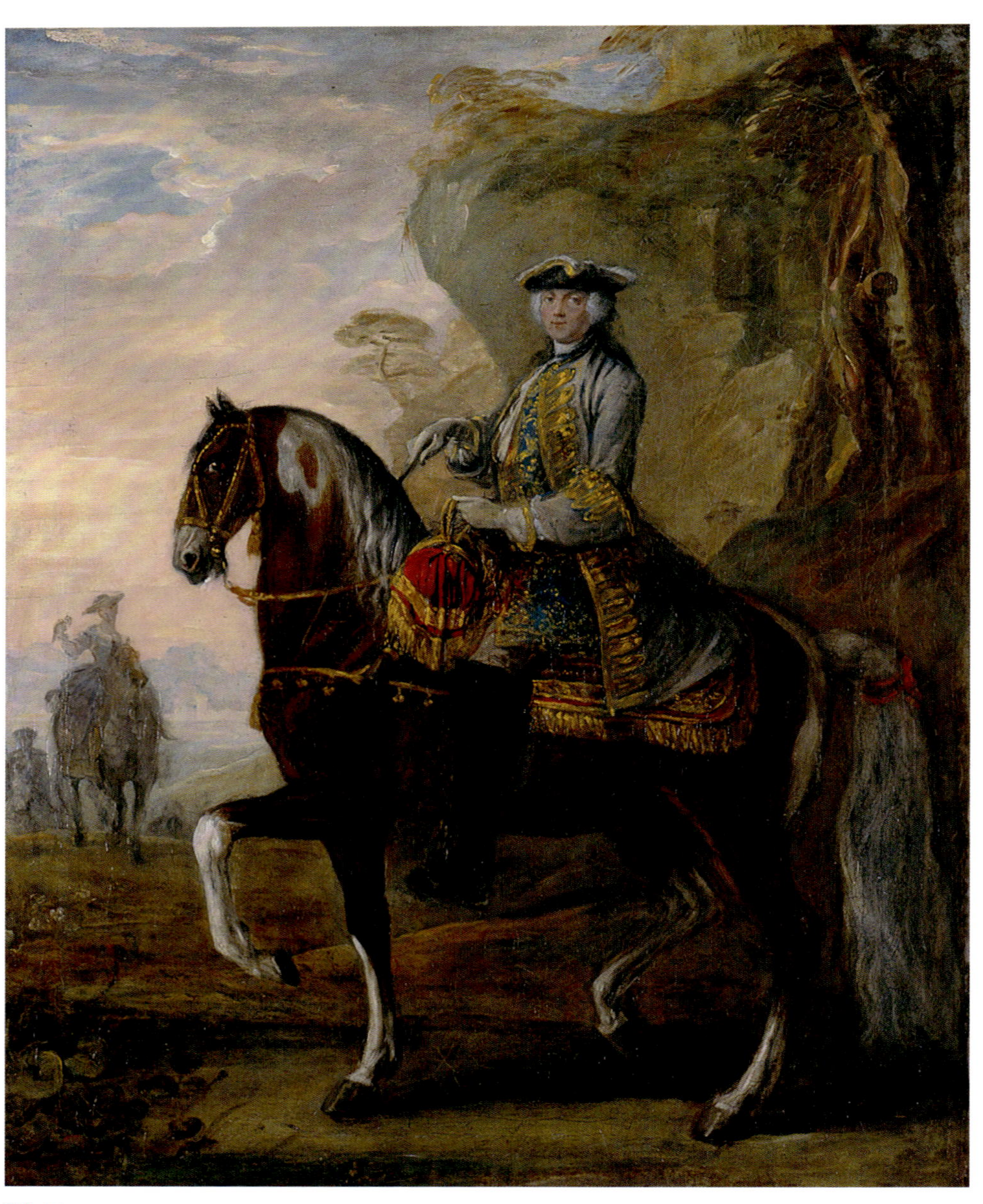

FIG. A.1

DAVID TENIERS THE YOUNGER (1610–90)
Peasants Dancing Outside a Tavern, *c.*1641
Oil on canvas
135.7 × 205.4 cm
RCIN 406363
CW 92 FIG. 7.8

Acquired at the sale of the collection of Henry Hope, 6 Apr. 1811 (lot 58; Jutsham I, p. 157). Hung in the Rose Satin Room (Bow Room, Principal Floor) at Carlton House (CH inv. 1819, no. 21), where it appears in a watercolour of *c.*1818 (RCIN 922181).

Exhibited at the British Institution in 1826 (no. 30) and 1827 (no. 57).

ADRIAEN VAN OSTADE (1610–85)
The Interior of a Peasant's Cottage, 1668
Oil on panel
49.1 × 41.2 cm
RCIN 404814
CW 132 FIG. 7.5

Purchased by Lord Yarmouth ahead of the Lafontaine sale (Christie's, 12 June 1811; Jutsham I, p. 167). Hung in the Rose Satin Room (Bow Room, Principal Floor) at Carlton House (CH inv. 1819, no. 23), where it appears in a watercolour of *c.*1817 (see Fig. 0.5).

Exhibited at the British Institution in 1826 (no. 30) and 1827 (no. 57).

JAN BOTH (*c.*1618–52)
Landscape with St Philip Baptising the Eunuch, *c.*1640–9
Oil on canvas
128.6 × 161.8 cm
RCIN 405544
CW 30 FIG. 7.6

Purchased by Lord Yarmouth ahead of the Lafontaine sale (Christie's, 12 June 1811). Hung in the Blue Velvet or Audience Room at Carlton House (CH inv. 1819, no. 49), where it appears in a watercolour of *c.*1816 (see Fig. 5.22).

Exhibited at the British Institution in 1818 (no. 10), 1826 (no. 147) and 1827 (no. 127).

REMBRANDT VAN RIJN (1606–69)
Portrait of Jan Rijcksen (1560/2–1637) and his Wife, Griet Jans ('*The Shipbuilder and his Wife*'), 1633
Oil on canvas
113.8 × 169.8 cm
RCIN 405533
CW 160 FIG. 0.10

Purchased by Lord Yarmouth at the Lafontaine sale, Christie's, 12 June 1811 (lot 63) for 5,000 guineas. Hung in the Blue Velvet or Audience Room at Carlton House (CH inv. 1819, no. 47), where it appears in a watercolour of *c.*1816 (see Fig. 5.22).

Exhibited at the British Institution in 1819 (no. 43), 1826 (no. 55) and 1827 (no. 65).

SIR JOSHUA REYNOLDS (1723–92)
David Garrick (1717–79), 1768
Oil on canvas
77.0 × 64.0 cm
RCIN 406984
OM 1021 FIG. 14.16

Presented by the artist to Edmund Burke; purchased by Lord Yarmouth at Burke's posthumous sale at Christie's, 5 June 1812 (lot 93) (Jutsham I, p. 199). Recorded in store at Carlton House (CH inv. 1819, no. 306); hung in the Grand Corridor, Windsor Castle, on 20 Aug. 1828.

Exhibited at the British Institution in 1827.

SIR PETER PAUL RUBENS (1577–1640)
Landscape with St George and the Dragon, 1630–5
Oil on canvas
152.5 × 226.9 cm
RCIN 405356
CWLF 63 FIG. 7.2

Previously in the collection of Charles I; sold during the Commonwealth; purchased from Harris in 1814 at a cost of £2,700, settled through the exchange of four paintings and £500 (Jutsham I, p. 307). Hung in the Crimson Drawing Room at Carlton House (CH inv. 1819, no. 10), where it appears in a watercolour of 1816 (see Fig. 5.20).

Exhibited at the British Institution in 1820 (no. 98), 1826 (no. 1) and 1827 (no. 26).

AELBERT CUYP (1620–91)
The Passage Boat, *c.*1650
Oil on canvas
124.0 × 144.4 cm
RCIN 405344
CW 39 FIG. 7.7

Acquired in 1814 with the Baring collection (Jutsham I, p. 305). Hung in the Blue Velvet or Audience Room at Carlton House (CH inv. 1819, no. 48), where it appears in a watercolour of *c.*1816 (see Fig. 5.22).

Exhibited at the British Institution in 1819 (no. 414), 1826 (no. 12) and 1827 (no. 61).

AELBERT CUYP (1620–91)
An Evening Landscape with Figures and Sheep, *c.*1655–9
Oil on canvas
101.6 × 153.6 cm
RCIN 405827
CW 35 FIG. 7.9

Acquired in 1814 with the Baring collection (Jutsham I, p. 301). Hung in the Bow Room, Principal Floor, at Carlton House (CH inv. 1819, no. 29).

Exhibited at the British Institution in 1826 (no. 74) and 1827 (no. 28).

GERRIT DOU (1613–75)
The Grocer's Shop, 1672
Oil on panel
41.5 × 32.0 cm
RCIN 405542
CW 46 FIG. 7.11

Purchased from Thomas Thompson Martin on 21 June 1817 for 1,000 guineas. Hung in the Bow Room, Principal Floor, at Carlton House (CH inv. 1819, no. 27).

Exhibited at the British Institution in 1826 (no. 29) and 1827 (no. 136).

SIR PETER PAUL RUBENS (1577–1640)
Portrait of a Woman, *c.*1625–30
Oil on panel
84.8 × 59.3 cm
RCIN 400118
CWLF 62 FIG. 7.14

Purchased from L.J. Nieuwenhuys via John Smith on 8 Dec. 1818 for £840 (RA GEO/MAIN/27090). Hung in the Bow Room, Lower Floor, at Carlton House (CH inv. 1819, no. 120).

Exhibited at the British Institution in 1820 (no. 99), 1826 (no. 56) and 1827 (no. 139).

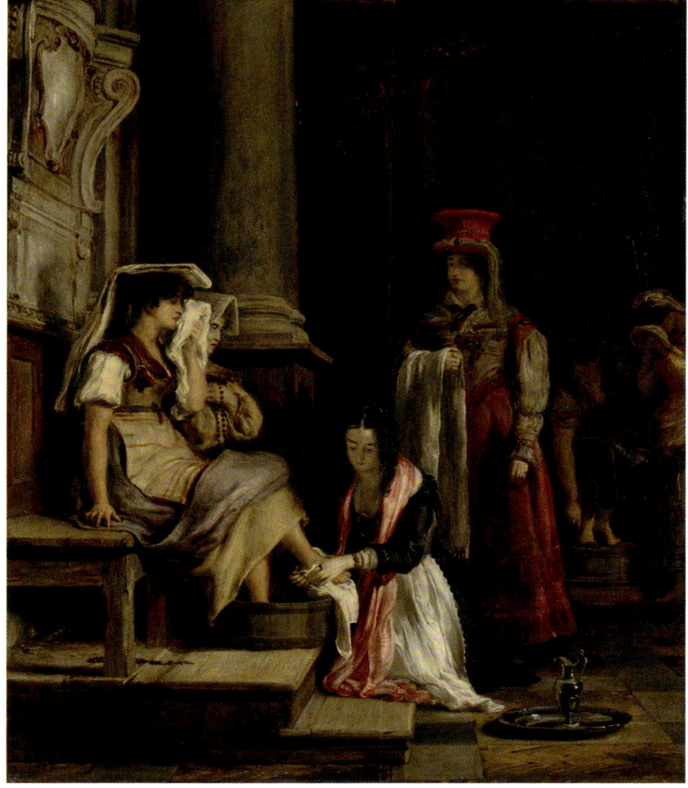

FIG. A.2

SIR THOMAS LAWRENCE (1769–1830)
Clemens Lothar Wenzel, Prince Metternich (1773–1859), c.1815
Oil on canvas
131.2 × 105.0 cm
RCIN 404948
OM 905 FIG. 9.14

Probably painted in 1815 and further worked on in Aix-la-Chapelle and Vienna in 1818 and 1819 at a cost of £315 (RA GEO/MAIN/26642). Later hung in the Waterloo Chamber at Windsor Castle.

Exhibited at the Royal Academy in 1815 (initial version, no. 15) and the British Institution in 1830 (no. 3).

SIR THOMAS LAWRENCE (1769–1830)
John, Count Capo d'Istria (1776–1831), 1818–19
Oil on canvas
128.4 × 102.8 cm
RCIN 404947
OM 888 FIG. 3.16

Painted in Vienna at a cost of £315 (RA GEO/MAIN/26642). Later hung in the Waterloo Chamber at Windsor Castle.

Exhibited at the British Institution in 1830 (no. 14).

SIR THOMAS LAWRENCE (1769–1830)
Ercole, Cardinal Consalvi (1757–1824), 1819
Oil on canvas
269.2 × 175.8 cm
RCIN 404940
OM 893 FIG. 3.15

Painted in Rome at a cost of £525 (RA GEO/MAIN/26642). Later hung in the Waterloo Chamber at Windsor Castle.

Exhibited at the British Institution in 1830 (no. 8).

SIR THOMAS LAWRENCE (1769–1830)
Charles, Archduke of Austria (1771–1847), 1819
Oil on canvas
270.1 × 179.5 cm
RCIN 405140
OM 891 FIG. 3.17

Painted in Vienna at a cost of £525 (RA GEO/MAIN/26642). Later hung in the Waterloo Chamber at Windsor Castle.

Exhibited at the British Institution in 1830 (no. 20).

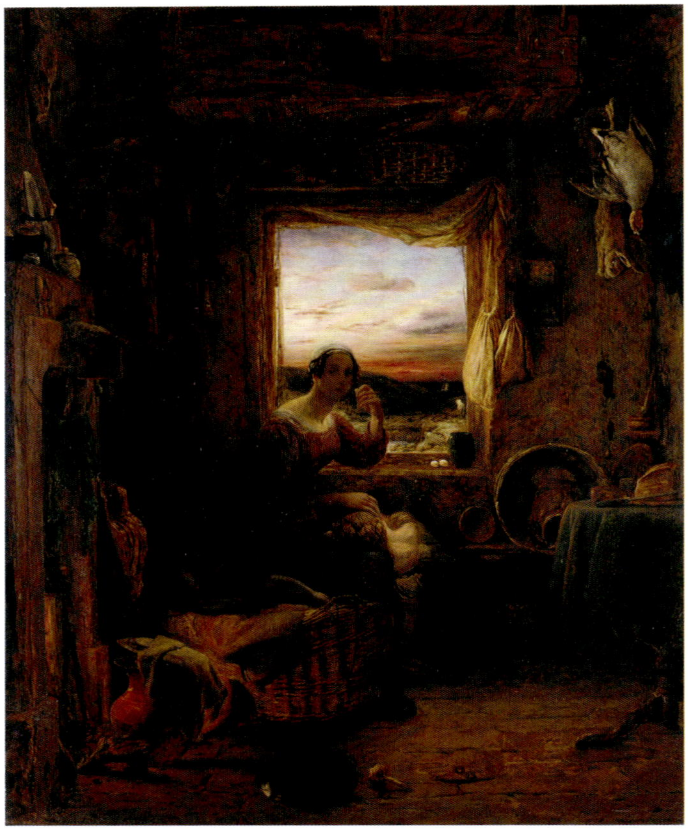

FIG. A.3

SIR THOMAS LAWRENCE (1769–1830)
Pope Pius VII (1742–1823), 1819
Oil on canvas
269.4 × 178.3 cm
RCIN 404946
OM 909 FIG. 1.1

Painted in Rome at a cost of £525 (RA GEO/MAIN/26642). Later hung in the Waterloo Chamber at Windsor Castle.

Exhibited at the British Institution in 1830 (no. 10).

REMBRANDT VAN RIJN (1606–69)
Agatha Bas (1611–58), 1641
Oil on canvas
105.4 × 83.9 cm
RCIN 405352
CW 162 FIG. 7.13

Purchased by Lord Yarmouth at an anonymous sale (Lord Charles Townshend), Robins, 4 June 1819 (lot 32), at a cost of 800 guineas. Recorded in store at Carlton House in 1821 (Jutsham III, p. 20; CH inv. 1819, no. 549).

Exhibited at the British Institution in 1821 (no. 9), 1826 (no. 29) and 1827 (no. 116).

WILLIAM MULREADY (1786–1863)
The Wolf and the Lamb, 1819–20
Oil on panel
60.0 × 51.1 cm
RCIN 405539
OM 970 FIG. 7.4

Purchased in 1820 for 200 guineas (RA GEO/MAIN/26764); sent to Royal Lodge on 17 June 1824 (Jutsham III, p. 55).

JAN STEEN (1626–79)
A Woman at Her Toilet, 1663
Oil on panel
65.8 × 53.0 cm
RCIN 404804
CW 189 FIG. 7.15

Purchased from M. Delahante in 1821 (Jutsham II, p. 147).

Exhibited at the British Institution in 1826 (no. 32) and 1827 (no. 38).

SIR THOMAS LAWRENCE (1769–1830)
Sir Walter Scott (1771–1832), 1820–26
Oil on canvas
161.7 × 132.9 cm
RCIN 400644
OM 913 FIG. 16.7

Painted at a cost of £315 (RA GEO/MAIN/26643). Sent to Windsor at the king's command in Nov. 1828 (CH inv. 1819, no. 678).

Exhibited at the Royal Academy in 1827 (no. 146).

SIR THOMAS LAWRENCE (1769–1830)
George IV, 1821
Oil on canvas
295.4 × 205.4 cm
RCIN 405918
OM 873 FIG. 0.1

Probably commissioned to hang in the Throne Room at St James's Palace, where it is mentioned on 19 May 1830 (RA GEO/MAIN/26599).

Exhibited at the British Institution in 1830 (no. 1).

JAMES WARD (1769–1859)
Monitor, 1821
Oil on canvas
81.5 × 110.6 cm
RCIN 405017
OM 1135 FIG. 13.6

Nonpareil, 1824
Oil on panel
80.2 × 111.4 cm
RCIN 405018
OM 1136 FIG. 13.7

Painted at a cost of £105 each (RA GEO/MAIN/26532).

Probably the pictures exhibited at the Royal Academy in 1825.

SIR THOMAS LAWRENCE (1769–1830)
Princess Sophia (1777–1848), *c.*1824
Oil on canvas
141.2 × 111.9 cm
RCIN 405420
OM 880 FIG. 11.1

Commissioned at a cost of £315 (RA GEO/MAIN/27042). Placed in the king's bedroom at St James's Palace in June 1826; sent to Windsor on 30 Dec. 1828; returned to St James's on 25 Apr. 1829 (Jutsham III, p. 215).

Exhibited at the Royal Academy, 1825 (no. 57).

SIR DAVID WILKIE (1785–1841)
I Pifferari, 1827
Oil on canvas
46.1 × 36.2 cm
RCIN 405861
OM 1177 FIG. 0.16

A Roman Princess Washing the Feet of Pilgrims, 1827
Oil on panel
50.2 × 42.2 cm
RCIN 405096
OM 1178 FIG. A.2

Purchased in 1828 at a cost of 400 guineas for the two (RA GEO/MAIN/26758).

WILLIAM MULREADY (1786–1863)
The Interior of an English Cottage, 1828
Oil on panel
62.1 × 50.2 cm
RCIN 405095
OM 971 FIG. A.3

Purchased through Sir Thomas Lawrence for 300 guineas in Oct. 1828 (RA GEO/MAIN/26567–8). Sent to Royal Lodge on 4 Nov. 1828.

Exhibited at the Royal Academy in 1829 (nos 298 and 224).

ALFRED EDWARD CHALON (1780–1860)
Princess Charlotte of Wales (1796–1817), Princess of Saxe-Coburg-Saalfeld, *c.*1817–19
Oil on panel
76.3 × 63.9 cm
RCIN 405449
OMV 195 FIG. 0.22

Given to Queen Victoria by the painter, June 1853.

Perhaps the portrait exhibited by Chalon at the Royal Academy in 1819.

SIR DAVID WILKIE (1785–1841)
George IV at Holyrood House: A Portrait Sketch, *c.*1822–3
Oil on panel
32.1 × 23.2 cm
RCIN 408655 FIG. A.4

Acquired 2018.

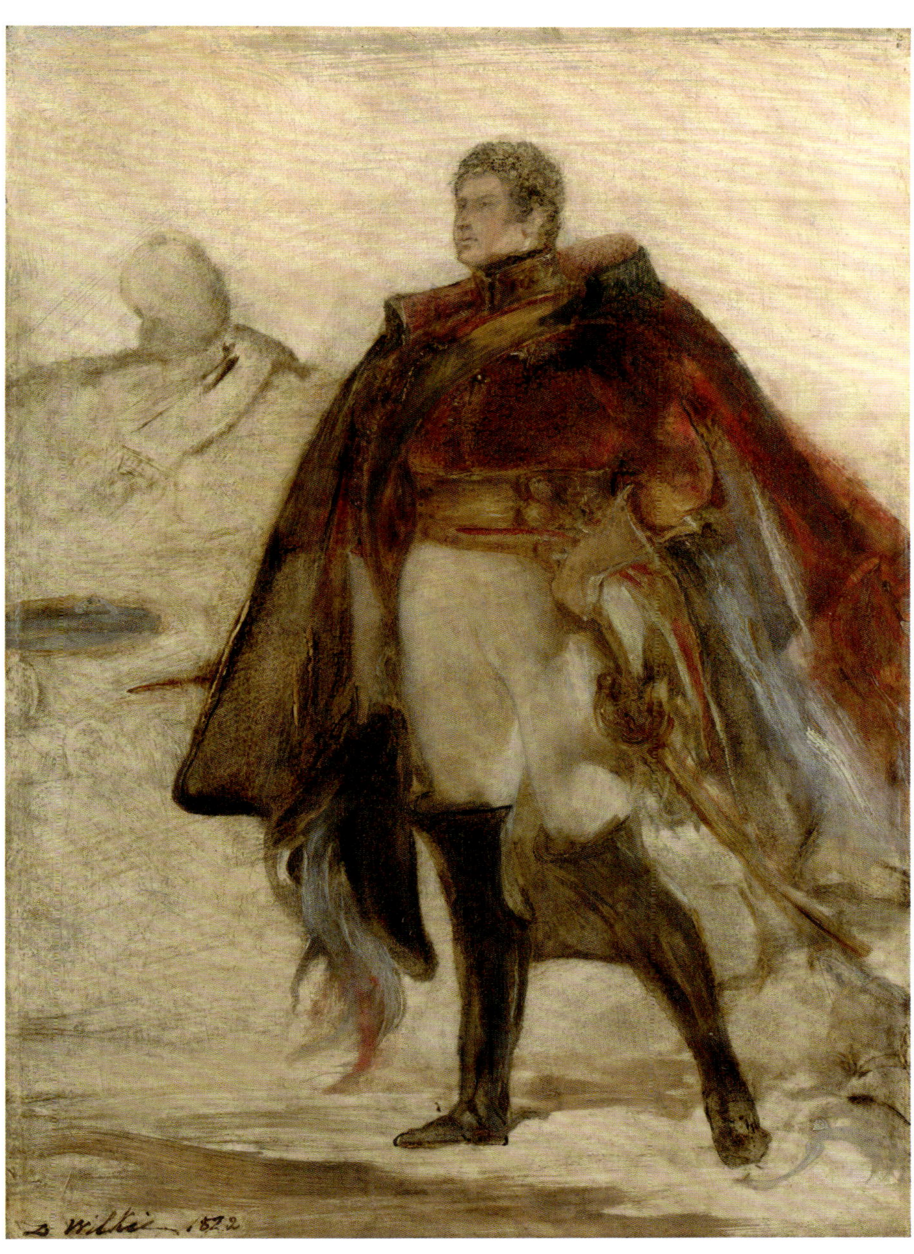

FIG. A.4

SCULPTURE

ADRIAEN DE VRIES (*c.*1556–1626)
Antiope and Theseus, *c.*1600–1
Bronze
95.0 × 36.8 × 35.6 cm
RCIN 57961 FIG. A.5

Date of acquisition not known but thought to have been purchased for Carlton House.

FRENCH SCHOOL
William III (1650–1702) Garlanded by Victory, *c.*1700–30
Bronze
90.2 cm (height)
RCIN 35463 FIG. A.6

In Kensington Palace by 1812, when dispatched to Charles Brandt for restoration (Jutsham I, p. 110). Placed in the Anti Room at Carlton House, where it appears in a watercolour of *c.*1817 (RCIN 922182); sent to Windsor Castle in Dec. 1828 (Jutsham III, p. 193).

AFTER GUILLAUME COUSTOU THE ELDER (1677–1746)
The Marly Horses, *c.*1740
Bronze
RCIN 44189.1: 63.0 × 53.0 × 23.0 cm
RCIN 44189.2: 61.5 × 45.0 × 24.0 cm
FIG. 6.8

Purchased from the dealer Pierre-Joseph-Ignace Lafontaine, Mar. 1813 (Jutsham I, p. 251), and placed in the Circular Room, Carlton House. Sent to Windsor Castle in Dec. 1828 (Jutsham III, p. 193).

GIOVACCHINO AND PIETRO BELLI (1756–1822 and 1780–1828)
Arch of Constantine, *c.*1808–15
Marble and gilt bronze
45.0 × 55.5 × 22.5 cm
RCIN 43918 FIG. 14.3

Arch of Septimius Severus, *c.*1808–15
Marble and gilt bronze
49.5 × 57.0 × 22.5 cm
RCIN 43916
FIG. 14.4

Bought at auction, together with a third model (Arch of Titus), from Pietro Santi Ammendola of Rome, Nov. 1816, for 500 guineas (Jutsham II, p. 8). One arch is shown in the library at Carlton House, through the door of the Golden Drawing Room, in a watercolour of *c.*1817 (RCIN 922188); removed to St James's Palace in Oct. 1826 (TNA LC11/53).

FRANÇOIS GIRARDON (1628–1715)
Equestrian statue of Louis XIV (1638–1715), *c.*1696
Bronze
105.5 × 92.0 × 50.0 cm
RCIN 31359

THOMIRE & CIE
Pedestal, 1826
Ebonised oak, bronze, gilt bronze
102.2 × 129.5 × 82.5 cm
RCIN 31360 FIG. 0.7

The statue purchased in 1817 by François Benois, for 360 *livres*, and placed in the Armoury at Carlton House (Jutsham II, p. 23). The pedestal commissioned by Benois in Paris at a cost of £281 3s 6d and delivered to Carlton House in 1826 (Jutsham III, p. 216).

PHILIPPE BERTRAND (1663–1724)
Psyche and Mercury, *c.*1700
Bronze
78.7 × 41.3 × 28.6 cm
RCIN 21641 FIG. 6.7

Purchased from Rundell, Bridge & Rundell on 16 Aug. 1824 for £145 (RA GEO/MAIN/26059).

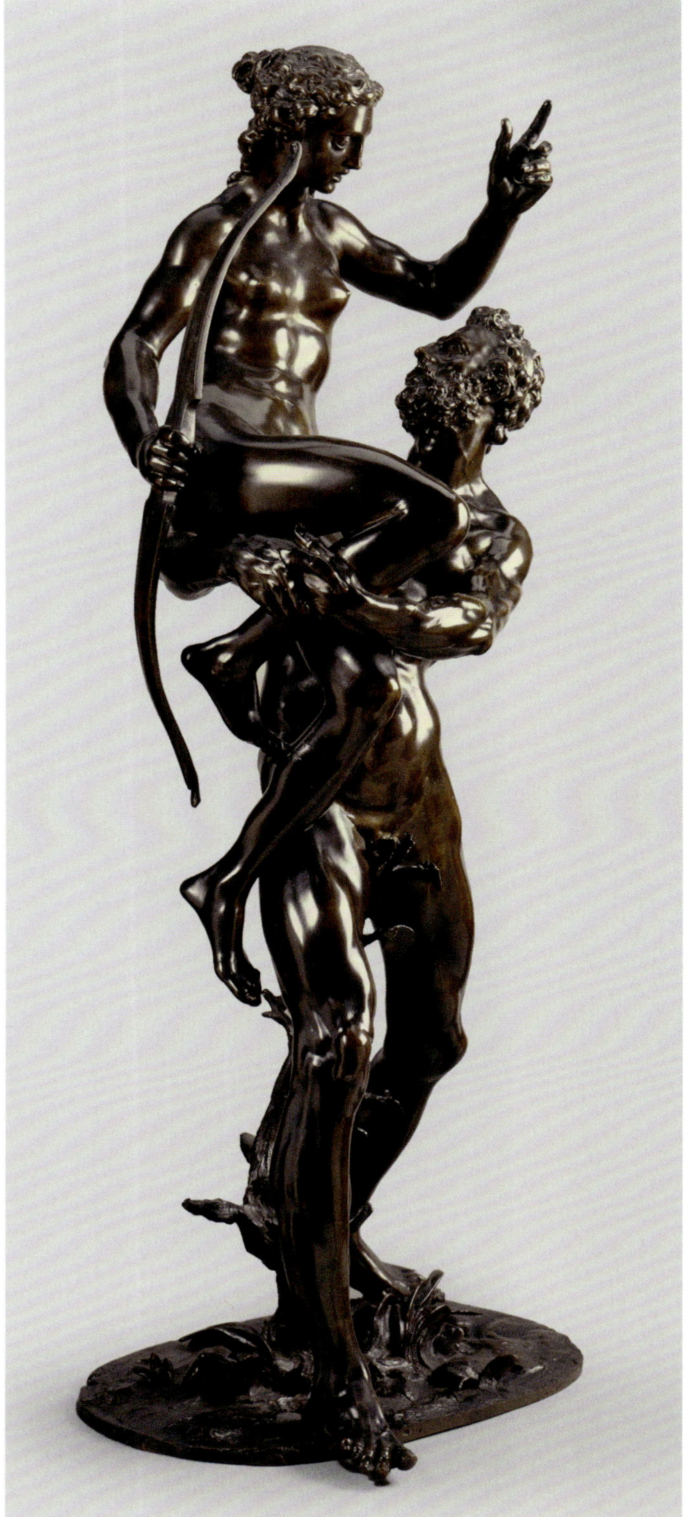

FIG. A.5

LEONE LEONI (1509–90)
Philip II (1527–98), c.1555
Bronze
88.9 × 57.5 × 30.5 cm
RCIN 35323 FIG. 6.9

Emperor Charles V (1500–58), c.1555
Bronze
95.3 × 63.0 × 34.0 cm
RCIN 35325 FIG. A.7

Purchased by Robert Fogg at the Watson-Taylor sale, held at Christie's, London, 28 May 1825 (lots 65 and 67), for £52 10s and £89 5s respectively (Jutsham II, p. 197). Placed in store at Carlton House; dispatched to Windsor, 12 Nov. 1828 (Jutsham III, p. 185).

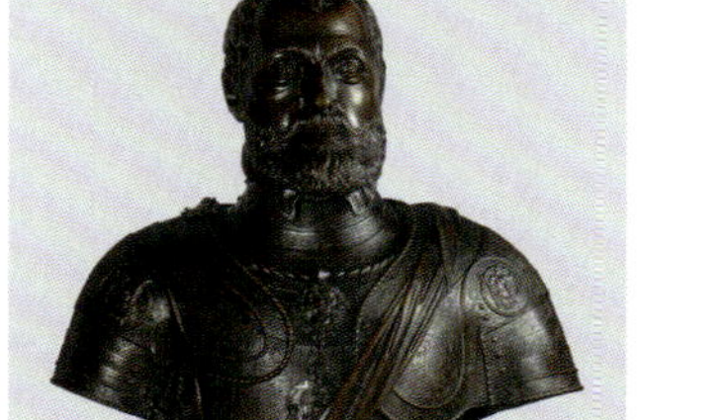
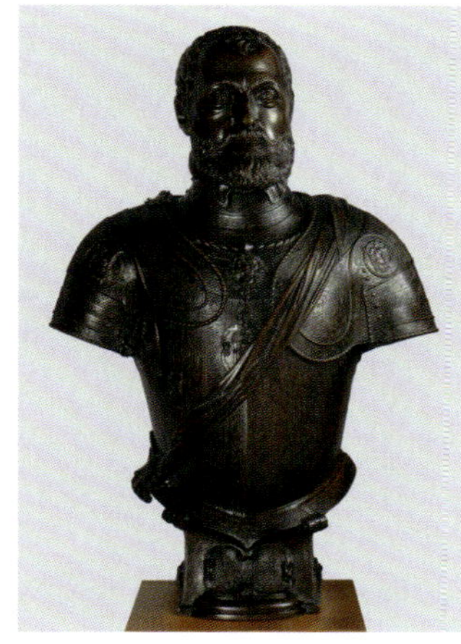

FIG. A.7

SIR FRANCIS CHANTREY (1781–1841)
George IV, 1826
Marble
80.0 × 58.0 × 27.0 cm
RCIN 2136 FIG. 3.1

Commissioned for Frederick, Duke of York in 1825 at a cost of £210, paid 1 Feb. 1825 (Chantrey 1991/2, 162a, pp. 165, 187).

SIR FRANCIS CHANTREY (1781–1841)
Arthur Wellesley, 1st Duke of Wellington (1769–1852), 1828
Marble
79.0 × 50.0 × 31.0 cm
RCIN 35422 FIG. 9.6

Commissioned for the 'gallery' (Grand Corridor), Windsor Castle, between Mar. and Nov. 1828. Delivered Mar. 1829 (Chantrey 1991/2, 211b, pp. 142, 238).

SIR FRANCIS CHANTREY (1781–1841)
Robert Stewart, Viscount Castlereagh, later 2nd Marquess of Londonderry (1769–1822), 1828
Marble
75.5 × 52.5 × 26.5 cm
RCIN 35411 FIG. A.8

Commissioned for the 'gallery' (Grand Corridor), Windsor Castle, between Mar. and Nov. 1828 (Chantrey 1991/2, 207a, p. 232).

WILLIAM THEED (1764–1817)
Thetis Returning from Hephaestus with the Arms of Achilles, 1805–12
Bronze
133.0 × 132.0 × 86.0 cm
RCIN 71833 FIG. A.9

Purchased from Rundell, Bridge & Rundell c.1829 for £787 10s (RA GEO/MAIN/26250).

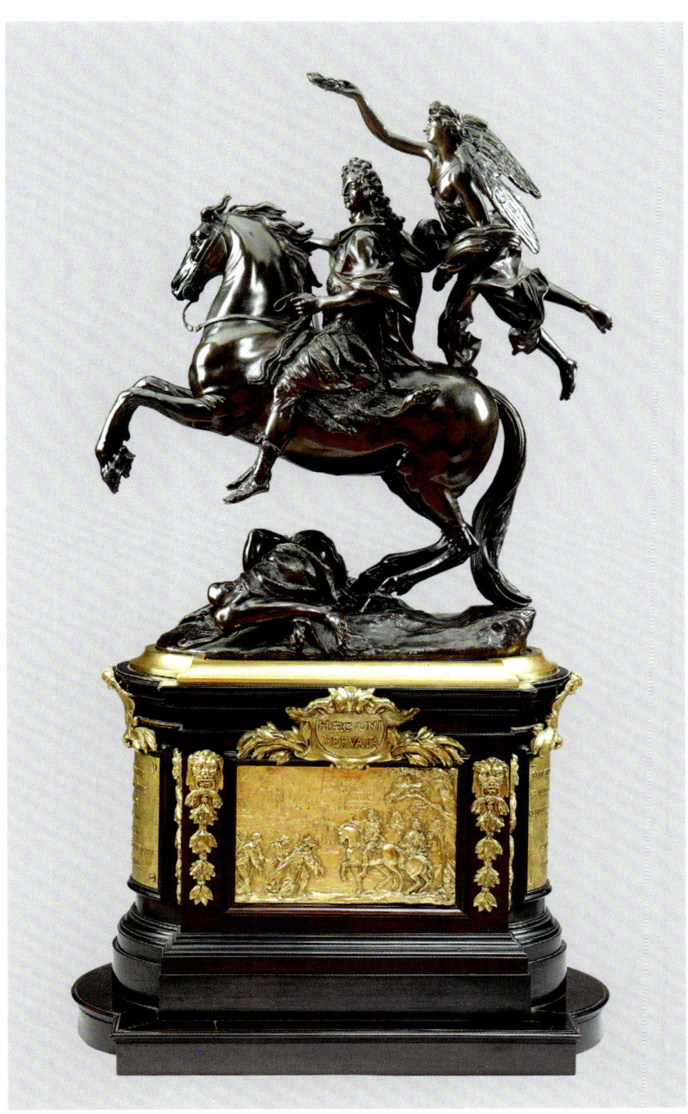

FIG. A.6

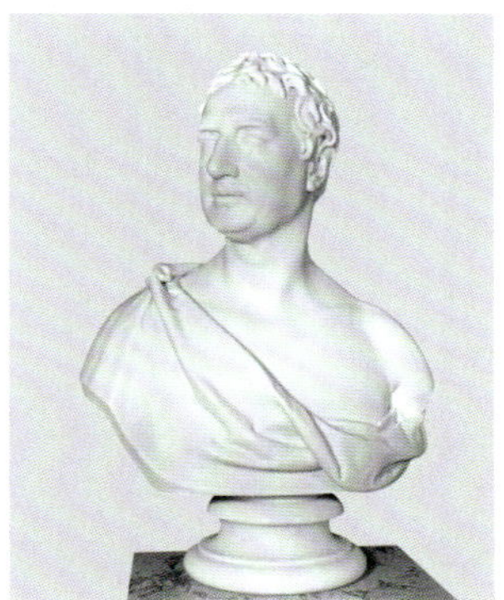

FIG. A.8

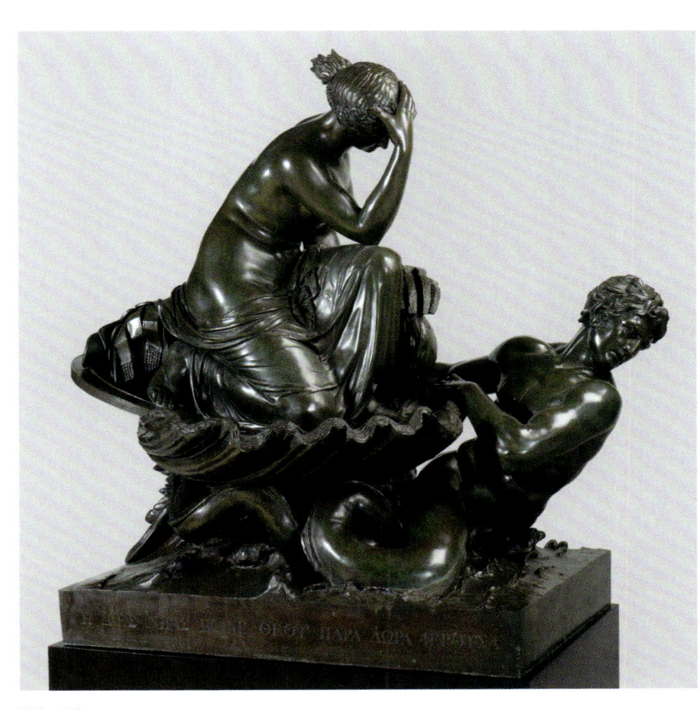

FIG. A.9

FURNITURE, CLOCKS AND GILT BRONZES

GEORGES JACOB (1739–1814)
Settee, *c.*1785
Mahogany, gilt bronze, silk damask
95.5 × 180.5 × 61.0 cm
RCIN 20590 FIG. A.10

Supplied as part of a set of seat furniture for Carlton House by Dominique Daguerre *c.*1785–90.

ATTRIBUTED TO ADAM WEISWEILER (1744–1820)
One of a pair of console tables, *c.*1787–90
Oak, ebony, gilt and painted bronze, marble
96.0 × 162.0 × 52.0 cm
RCIN 181.1 FIG. 5.16

Purchased *c.*1787–90, for the Chinese Drawing Room, Carlton House, by the *marchand-mercier* Dominique Daguerre, working to orders from Henry Holland (Coutts inv., p. 59). Transferred to Brighton Pavilion in 1819, when a pair to it was made by Tatham, Bailey & Saunders.

MARTIN CARLIN (1730–85)
Cabinet, *c.*1783
Oak veneered with tulipwood, purplewood, mahogany and boxwood, brocatello and white marble, gilt-bronze mounts, inset with soft-paste porcelain plaques
95.9 × 152.4 × 50.8 cm
RCIN 21697
Roberts 2001, no. 740 FIG. 6.3

Probably acquired direct from Dominic Daguerre, *c.*1790. Recorded in the Saloon at Carlton House, 14 Jan. 1793 (Coutts inv., p. 69), and later in the Rose Satin Drawing Room (CH inv., vol. L, pp. 130–1); delivered to Windsor Castle on 1 Oct. 1828.

ADAM WEISWEILER (1744–1820)
Commode, 1785–90
Oak, ebony, hardstones, tortoiseshell, brass, pewter, mahogany, boxwood, purplewood, gilt bronze, brocatello marble
100.3 × 149.8 × 48.3 cm
RCIN 2593
Roberts 2001, no. 491 FIG. A.11

Possibly bought at Daguerre's sale at Christie's (25 Mar. 1791, lot 59); certainly in Carlton House by 1807 when it was dispatched for repair to the mounts. In the Blue Velvet Closet, where it appears in a watercolour of *c.*1818 (see Fig. 5.23); refurbished by Morel & Seddon and delivered to the king's bedroom at Windsor Castle on 4 July 1828 (TNA LC9/366, fol. 45).

ENGLISH
Two from a set of four pedestals, *c.*1794
Gilded pine, mahogany, composition ornament and marble
122.5 × 60.9 × 40.6 cm
RCIN 2592 FIG. A.12

Originally designed as a set of eight, possibly by Dominique Daguerre; listed in Daguerre's estimate for furnishing the Great Drawing Room, Carlton House, *c.*1794 (TNA HO73/32).

ATTRIBUTED TO FRANÇOIS RÉMOND (1747–1812)
Two from a set of eight candelabra, *c.*1787
Gilt bronze, enamel
149.8 × 58.4 × 35.6 cm
RCIN 2692 FIG. 5.14

Almost certainly supplied by Dominique Daguerre with the eight pedestals above (RCIN 2592); listed in Daguerre's estimate for furnishing the Great Drawing Room, Carlton House, *c.*1794 (TNA HO73/32). First recorded in Carlton House in 1808–10 when they were regilded by Vulliamy (RA GEO/MAIN/25263, 25303 and 25315).

MARSH & TATHAM
Pair of bookcases, 1806 (with later alterations 1828)
Ebony and ivory inlay on a pine carcase, white marble
113.0 × 122.5 × 35.6 cm
RCIN 39475.1-2
Roberts 2001, nos 738–9 FIG. 14.2

Originally supplied to George III for Buckingham House. Altered and refurbished in 1806 for the library at Carlton House (RA GEO/MAIN/25205); refurbished by Morel & Seddon for the Grand Corridor at Windsor Castle in 1828.

PIERRE-PHILIPPE THOMIRE (1751–1843) with later movement by BENJAMIN LEWIS VULLIAMY (1780–1854)
Mantel clock, *c.*1810 (movement 1834)
Gilt bronze, blued steel, marble, glass
75.0 × 78.0 × 26.0 cm
RCIN 2764 FIG. 6.18

Purchased in 1810 from 'M. Boileau' (possibly Jean-Jacques Boileau) and placed in the Crimson Drawing Room, Carlton House (Jutsham I, p. 119). Sent to Royal Lodge, Windsor, in 1824 (Jutsham III, p. 66).

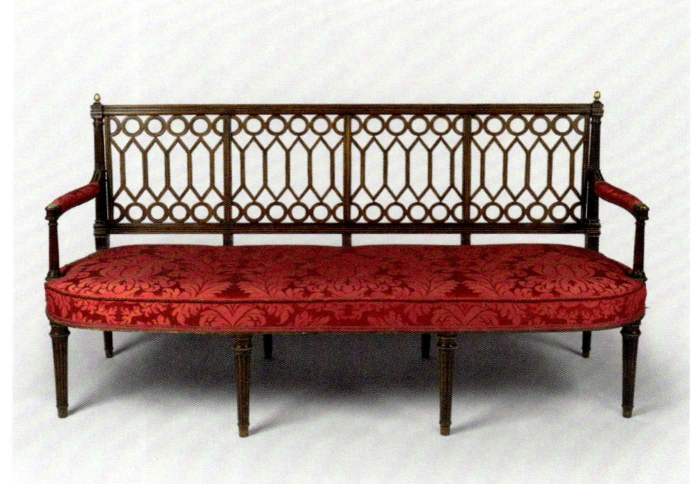

FIG. A.10

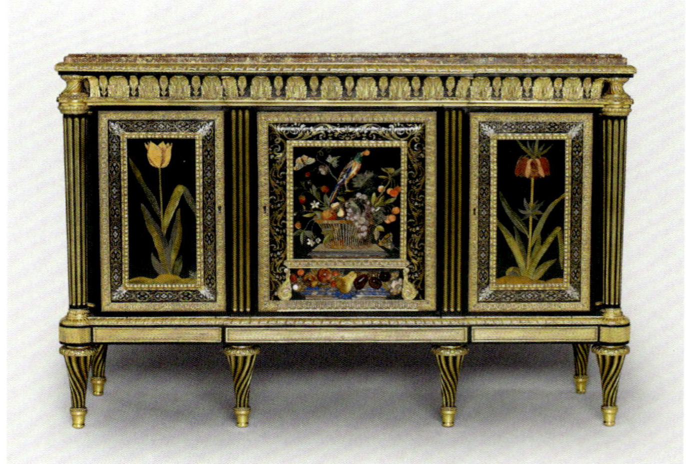

FIG. A.11

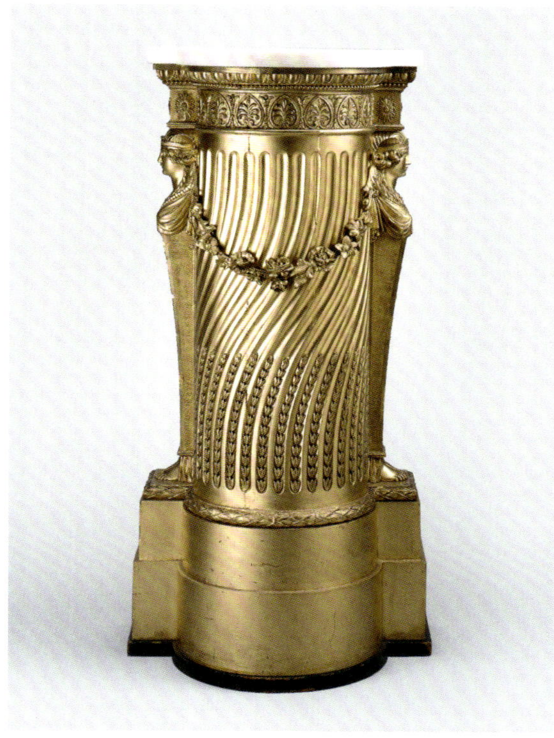

FIG. A.12

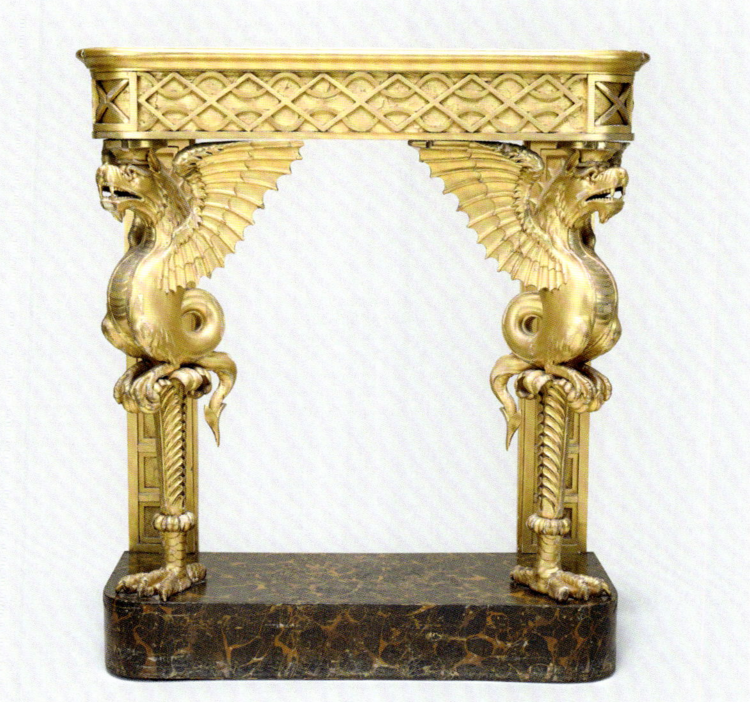

FIG. A.13

ATTRIBUTED TO TATHAM, BAILEY & SANDERS
Pair of pier tables, *c.*1811
Gilt wood, marble
91.0 × 79.5 × 40.0 cm
RCIN 769.1–2 FIG. A.13

Delivered to Carlton House, 1 Feb. 1811 (Jutsham I, p. 147), and placed in the Rose Satin Drawing Room, where they appear in a watercolour of *c.*1818 (RCIN 922181). Dispatched to Brighton in 1819 (Jutsham I, p. 324).

TATHAM, BAILEY & SANDERS
Pedestal, *c.*1811
Carved and gilt wood
99.0 × 68.0 × 68.0 cm
RCIN 3202 FIG. A.14

Seven pedestals of this design were delivered to Carlton House between 1811 and 1813 (Jutsham I, pp. 161, 233). Placed in the Crimson Drawing Room, the Blue Velvet Room and the Rose Satin Drawing Room, where they appear in watercolours of *c.*1816–18 (see Figs 5.20, 5.22 and RCIN 922181). In the last image one pedestal is shown supporting the porcelain cistern (see below, RCIN 64062).

ETIENNE LEVASSEUR (1721–98)
Secretaire, *c.*1700 (with later adaptations, *c.*1770)
Oak, ebony, tortoiseshell and brass, gilt-bronze mounts
143.5 × 135.5 × 52.0 cm
RCIN 29945 FIG. 6.16

Purchased from Robert Fogg for £367 10s (TNA LC11/16) and delivered to the South Anti Room, Carlton House, in July 1812 (Jutsham I, p. 215).

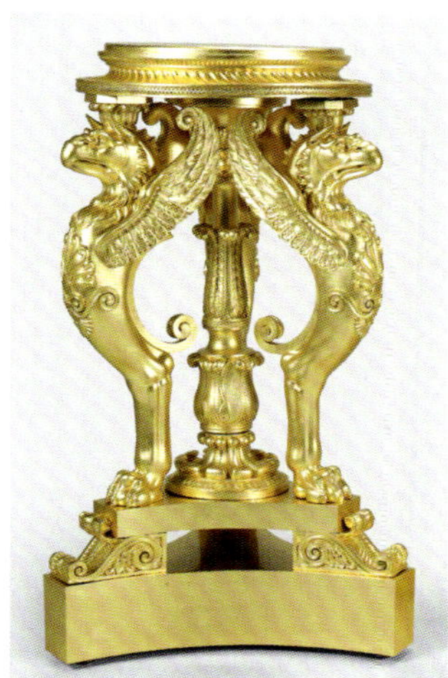

FIG. A.14

ATTRIBUTED TO ANDRÉ-CHARLES BOULLE (1642–1732)
Two medal cabinets, *c.*1740
Oak, tortoiseshell, brass
126.0 × 126.8 × 45.0 cm
RCIN 35486.1–2
Roberts 2001, no. 341 FIG. A.15

Possibly purchased from Robert Fogg, 2 Feb. 1813 (TNA LC11/14). Placed in the Blue Velvet Closet, Carlton House, where they appear in a watercolour of *c.*1818 (see Fig. 5.23); later in the library (CH inv. vol. L, p. 106); sent to His Majesty's Writing Room at Windsor Castle in July 1828 (TNA LC9/366, fols 33, 34 and 36).

THOMAS PARKER (ACTIVE 1808–30)
Pair of coffers-on-stands, 1813
Brass-inlaid tortoiseshell, gilt bronze, ebony
34.5 × 56.5 × 41.0 cm
RCIN 21624.1–2
Roberts 2001, no. 348 FIG. 6.17

Purchased from Thomas Parker in Jan. 1813 for £210 (TNA LC11/14). Placed in the Rose Satin Drawing Room and the Anti Room of Carlton House, where they appear in watercolours of *c.*1818 (RCINS 922181 and 922183); sent to His Majesty's Writing Room at Windsor Castle in Jan. 1828 (Morel Windsor Estimates, p. 97).

TATHAM, BAILEY & SANDERS
Pier table, *c.*1814–15
Gilded pine and limewood, mirror glass, scagliola
107.2 × 205.5 × 79.0 cm
RCIN 33809
Roberts 2001, no. 751 FIG. 17.16

Made for the Crimson Drawing Room, Carlton House, in 1814 (Jutsham I, p. 281). Sent to the Grand Corridor, Windsor Castle, in 1828 (Jutsham III, p. 210, and Morel Windsor Estimates, p. 102).

BREGUET ET FILS
The 'Sympathique' clock, 1814
Glazed mahogany case with chased and gilt-bronze mounts, clock with silver dial, watch with enamel dial
33.3 × 17.5 × 17.5 cm
RCIN 2861 FIG. 8.6

First recorded at Carlton House in 1826 (Jutsham III, p. 79). Although no bill survives, Clifford Smith states that it was purchased from Breguet in 1814 for 11,500 francs (Clifford Smith 1931, p. 262).

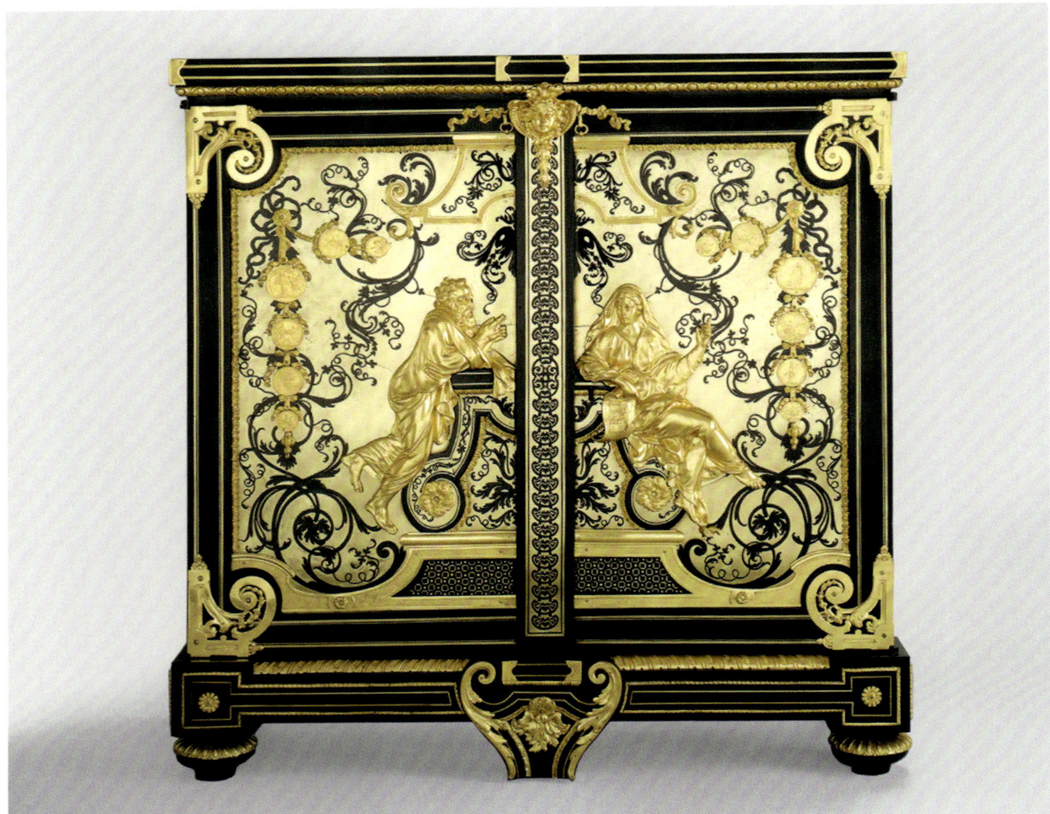

FIG. A.15

ATTRIBUTED TO DAVID ROENTGEN (1743–1807)
Mechanical cylinder bureau, *c.*1785
Oak and mahogany with gilt-bronze mounts
148.0 × 142.0 × 83.0 cm
RCIN 293 FIG. 6.14

Possibly in the collection of Louis XVI at Versailles; purchased by François Benois at a cost of £275 (RA GEO/MAIN/25366) and placed in the Attic Anti Room of the king's apartment in Carlton House, 13 May 1820 (Jutsham II, pp. 98, 112).

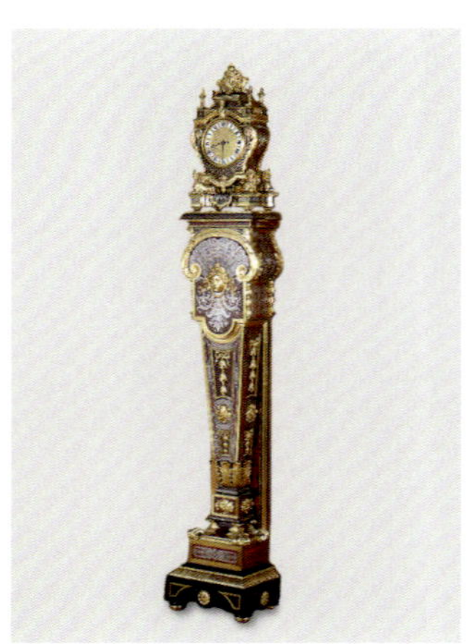

FIG. A.16

ATTRIBUTED TO ANDRÉ-CHARLES BOULLE (1642–1732)
Floor-standing clock, *c.*1685
Oak veneered in ebony, brass, pewter, tortoise shell, gilt bronze
216.5 × 38.0 × 26.5 cm
RCIN 30011 FIG. A.16

Purchased by François Benois on 13 May 1820, for 6,500 francs (RA GEO/MAIN/26438). Delivered to Carlton House in 1821 (Jutsham II, pp. 110–11), where it was placed in store.

ADAM WEISWEILER (1744–1820)
Commode, *c.*1785
Oak, mahogany, marble, gilt bronze
95.9 × 138.4 × 56.5 cm
RCIN 2596
Roberts 2001, no. 1007 FIG. 17.15

Purchased by François Benois in 1821 for 2,500 francs (RA GEO/MAIN/25375) and apparently placed in the Anti Room to the King's Bedroom at Carlton House. Sent to Windsor Castle in Jan. 1828 (Morel Windsor Estimates, p. 122).

ATTRIBUTED TO FRANÇOIS HERVÉ (ACTIVE 1781–96)
Side chair, *c.*1790
Painted and gilt wood, silk damask
95.9 × 47.0 × 47.0 cm
RCIN 31831 FIG. A.17

First recorded in Brighton Pavilion in 1823 in an engraving of the Banqueting Room Gallery by Thomas Bradley (published by John Nash, RCIN 708000.an).

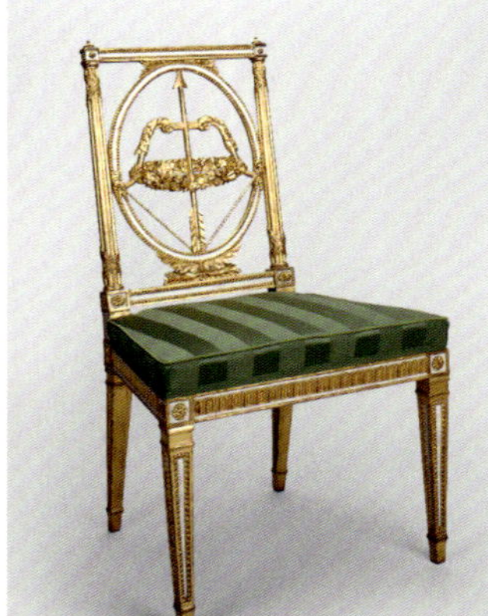

FIG. A.17

BREGUET ET FILS
Regulator clock, 1819–24
Glazed mahogany case with gilt-bronze mounts, silvered dial, zinc and steel
203.8 × 49.5 × 29.5 cm
RCIN 2767 FIG. 8.5

A coloured drawing of this clock was sent speculatively to George IV by Antoine-Louis Breguet (son of the maker) on 17 Dec. 1824 (RCIN 931506); subsequently purchased for £1,000 (RA GEO/MAIN/35792) and delivered to Carlton House on 19 Sept. 1825 (Jutsham II, p. 207).

ATTRIBUTED TO AUGUSTUS WELBY NORTHMORE PUGIN (1812–52)
Wine cooler, *c.*1828
Rosewood
41.0 × 95.5 × 61.0 cm
RCIN 29884
Roberts 2001, no. 27 FIG. 17.10

Supplied by Morel & Seddon for the Large Dining Room at Windsor Castle between 1827 and 1829 (Morel Windsor Estimates, p. 83).

MOREL & SEDDON
Two open armchairs, *c.*1828 (tapestry *c.*1750)
Gilded mahogany, tapestry
103.5 × 70.0 × 71.0 cm
RCIN 33498.1–2
Roberts 2001, nos 240–41 FIG. 17.9

Supplied by Morel & Seddon for the King's Sitting Room, Windsor Castle, between 1827 and 1829 (Morel Windsor Estimates, p. 92).

MOREL & SEDDON
Two open armchairs, *c.*1828
Gilded mahogany, silk damask
109.2 × 74.9 × 71.1 cm
RCIN 2582.1–2
Roberts 2001, no. 58 FIG. 17.12

Supplied by Morel & Seddon for the Large Drawing Room, Windsor Castle, between 1827 and 1829 (Morel Windsor Estimates, p. 85).

PORCELAIN

SÈVRES PORCELAIN FACTORY with mounts by PIERRE-PHILIPPE THOMIRE (1751–1843)
Vases à monter, *c.*1782–6
Hard-paste porcelain, gilt bronze,
41.0 × 23.0 × 13.5 cm
RCIN 35513.1–2
De Bellaigue 2009, II, no. 110 FIG. 6.25

Probably acquired through Dominique Daguerre, in the late 1780s. Recorded, after repair, in the Admirals Room, Carlton House, in 1807 (Jutsham I, p. 9).

JINGDEZHEN, CHINA, with mounts attributed to PIERRE-PHILIPPE THOMIRE (1751–1843)
Cistern with mounts, mid-18th century (mounts last quarter 18th century)
Porcelain, gilt bronze
80.7 × 57.0 × 57.0 cm
RCIN 64C62
Ayers 2016, II, no. 1364 FIG. 6.20

Purchased from Vulliamy in Mar. 1803 (TNA C1C4/58 I). In the Bow Room, Carlton House, in 1813 (Jutsham I, p. 136); dispatched to Windsor Castle in 1828 for the King's Writing Room (Jutsham III, pp. 159, 219).

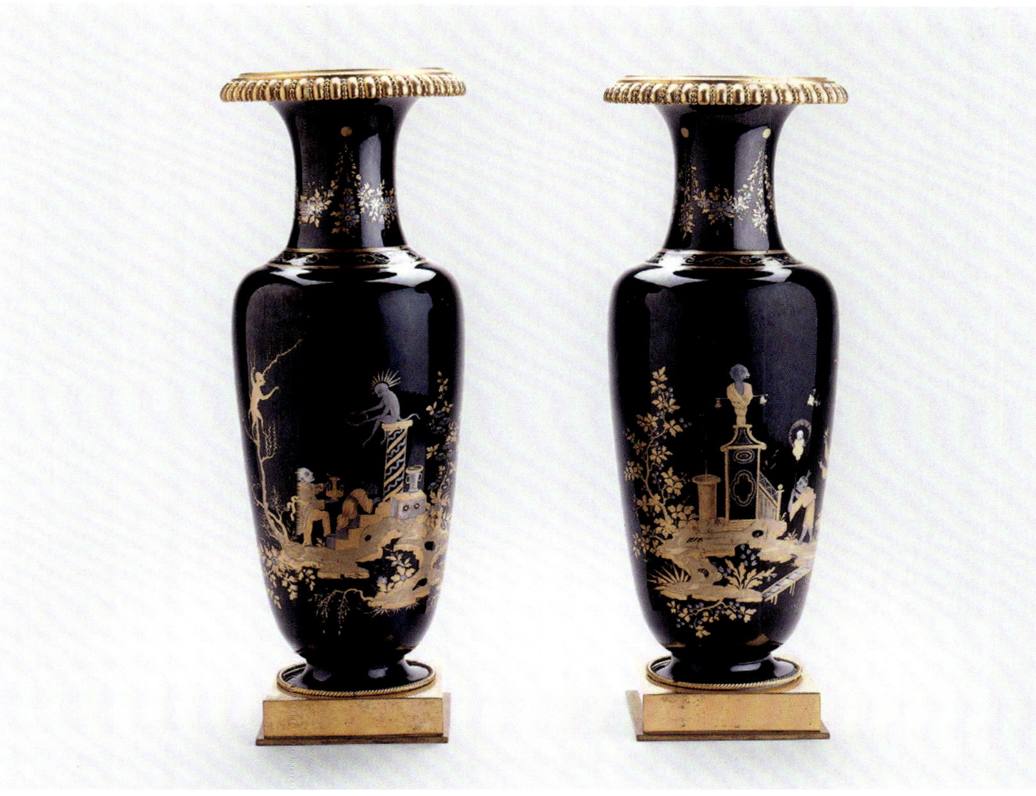

FIG. A.19

JINGDEZHEN, CHINA, with mounts by BENJAMIN VULLIAMY (1747–1811)
Vase with mounts, second half 18th century (mounts 1807)
Porcelain, gilt bronze
49.0 × 23.5 × 22.5 cm
RCIN 187
Ayers 2016, II, no. 1380 FIG. 6.19

Vase with mounts, second half 18th century (mounts 1807)
Porcelain, gilt bronze
46.5 × 26.5 × 23.0 cm
RCIN 881
Ayers 2016, II, no. 1391 FIG. A.18

Both vases, with glass shades and stands, were supplied by Vulliamy in 1807 (TNA C104/57 I and C104/58 II), and placed in the Bow Room at Carlton House (Jutsham I, p. 49), where they appear in a watercolour of *c.*1818 (RCIN 922181). Later delivered to the Music Room, Brighton Pavilion (Jutsham II, p. 310).

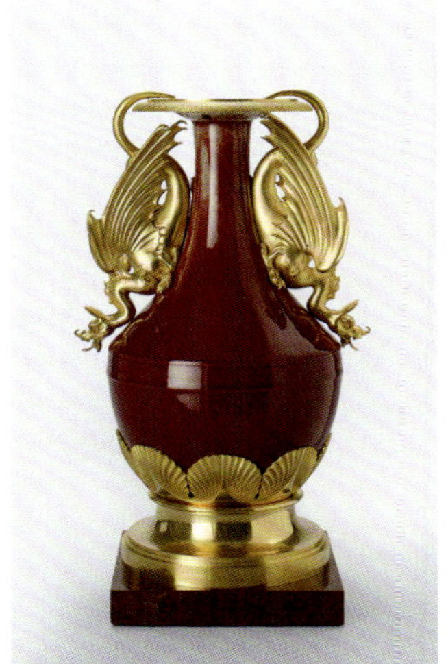

FIG. A.18

CHAMBERLAIN & CO., WORCESTER (*c.*1786–1852)
Pieces from the Harlequin Service, 1807–16
Hybrid-paste porcelain (the 'Regent body')
RCIN 5000037 FIG. 8.9

Commissioned from the factory in 1807; the 140-piece dessert service was delivered in 1811 and the dinner service five years later in Oct. 1816 (RA GEO/MAIN/26431).

SÈVRES PORCELAIN FACTORY
Pieces from the Louis XVI Service, 1783–92
Soft-paste porcelain
RCIN 5000017
De Bellaigue 1986 FIG. 6.10

Commissioned by Louis XVI in 1783; purchased through Fogg in 1811 from M. Würtz of Paris, for £1,973 4s 8d (RA GEO/MAIN/26402).

SÈVRES PORCELAIN FACTORY
Pair of mounted vases, 1789–90
Hard-paste porcelain, gilt bronze
33.5 × 11.5 × 11.5 cm
RCIN 2344.1–2
De Bellaigue 2009, II, no. 116
FIG. A.19

Probably the pair of vases purchased from Robert Fogg on 25 May 1812 (TNA LC11/13). Recorded in the Rose Satin Drawing Room of Carlton House in a watercolour of *c.*1818 (RCIN 922181).

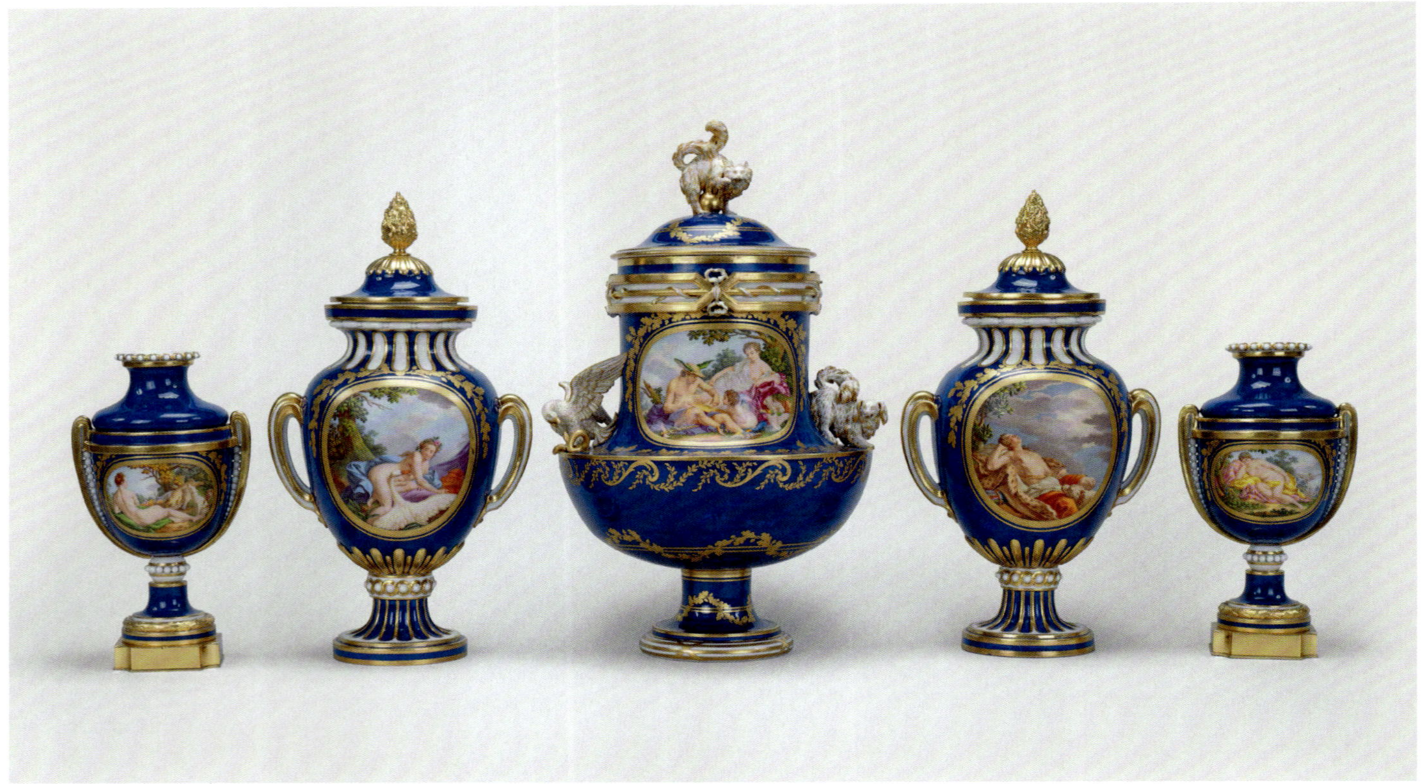

FIG. A.20

SÈVRES PORCELAIN FACTORY
Vase angora or *vase angola*, 1772
Soft-paste porcelain, gilt bronze
46.5 × 28.6 × 25.9 cm
RCIN 36101
De Bellaigue 2009, I, no. 82

Vases à batons rompus, 1772
Soft-paste porcelain, gilt bronze
39.5 × 21.5 × 16.2 cm
RCIN 36103.1–2
De Bellaigue 2009, I, no. 41

Vases chapelet, *c*.1764–72
Soft-paste porcelain
26.0 × 14.0 × 12.0 cm
RCIN 153.1–2
De Bellaigue 2009, I, no. 87
FIG. A.20

Three of the vases (36101 and 36103.1–2) were purchased from Robert Fogg in Oct. 1813 for £346 10s (TNA LC11/15) and placed in the Bow Room at Carlton House (Jutsham I, p. 269). In 1826 they were recorded in the Crimson Drawing Room with the final pair (153.1–2, date of acquisition not recorded) forming a garniture of five (CH Porcelain Inventory 1826, no. 6).

SÈVRES PORCELAIN FACTORY with mounts by PIERRE-PHILIPPE THOMIRE (1751–1843)
Vases à monter, *c*.1785
Hard-paste porcelain, gilt bronze, onyx
35.0 × 19.2 × 12.8 cm
RCIN 253.1–2
De Bellaigue 2009, II, no. 113
FIG. 6.12

Probably purchased by François Benois in 1815 from the Parisian dealer Coquille, for 500 francs (RA GEO/MAIN/26421). Placed in the Golden Drawing Room of Carlton House, where they appear in a watercolour of *c*.1817 (RCIN 922187).

SOUTH CHINA
Garniture of three vases, late 18th or early 19th century
Porcelain, craquelure glaze, slip
RCIN 11851: 45.9 cm (height)
RCIN 692.1–2: 35.4 cm (height)
Ayers 2016, I, no. 211
FIG. 11.12

Two vases are recorded as being delivered to Carlton House on 4 Sept. 1815, 'presented by the Princess Charlotte' (Jutsham I, p. 222). The third vase is not recorded.

JINGDEZHEN, CHINA, with mounts by BENJAMIN VULLIAMY (1747–1811)
Pair of pagodas, *c*.1800–15 (mounts *c*.1815–25)
Porcelain, gilt metal
192.0 × 42.5 × 36.0 cm
RCIN 812.1–2
Ayers 2016, II, nos 1178–9
FIG. A.21

Probably purchased by François Benois in Nov. 1815 (RA GEO/MAIN/26419). Additions made to the mounts in London, possibly through the agency of Robert Fogg; delivered to Brighton Pavilion on 14 Dec. 1816 (Jutsham I, p. 258).

SÈVRES PORCELAIN FACTORY
Vases japon, 1792–3
Hard-paste porcelain (with later metal additions), gilt bronze
62.7 × 37.0 × 25.3 cm
RCIN 537.1–2
De Bellaigue 2009, II, no. 120
FIG. A.22

Purchased by Jean-Baptiste Watier in Nov. 1816 (Jutsham II, p. 11). Sent to Royal Lodge in 1824 (Jutsham III, p. 65).

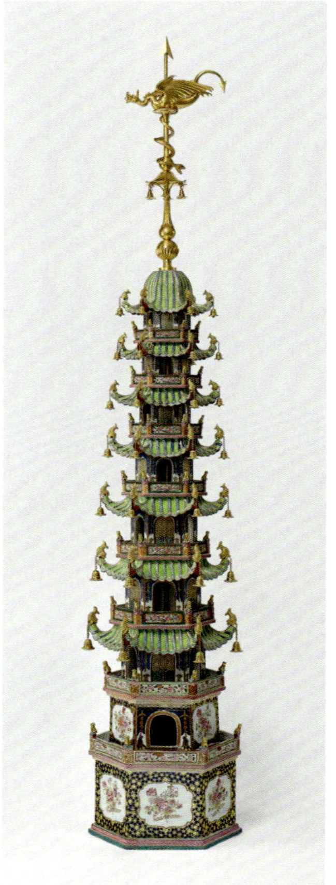

FIG. A.21

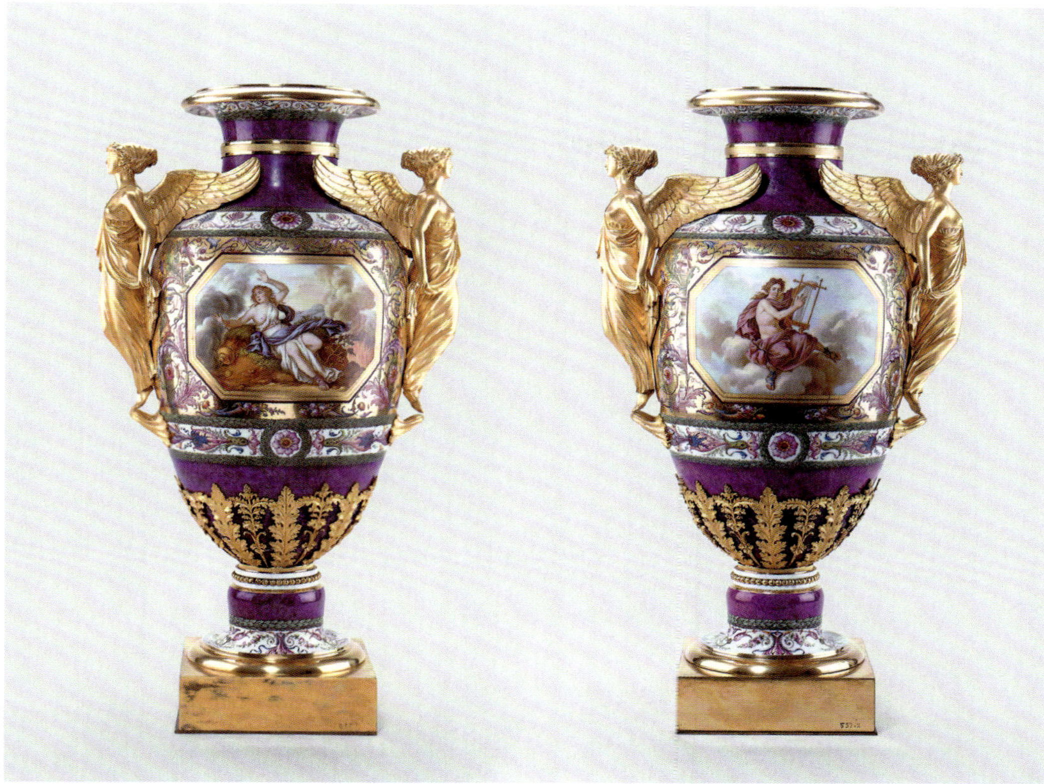

FIG. A.22

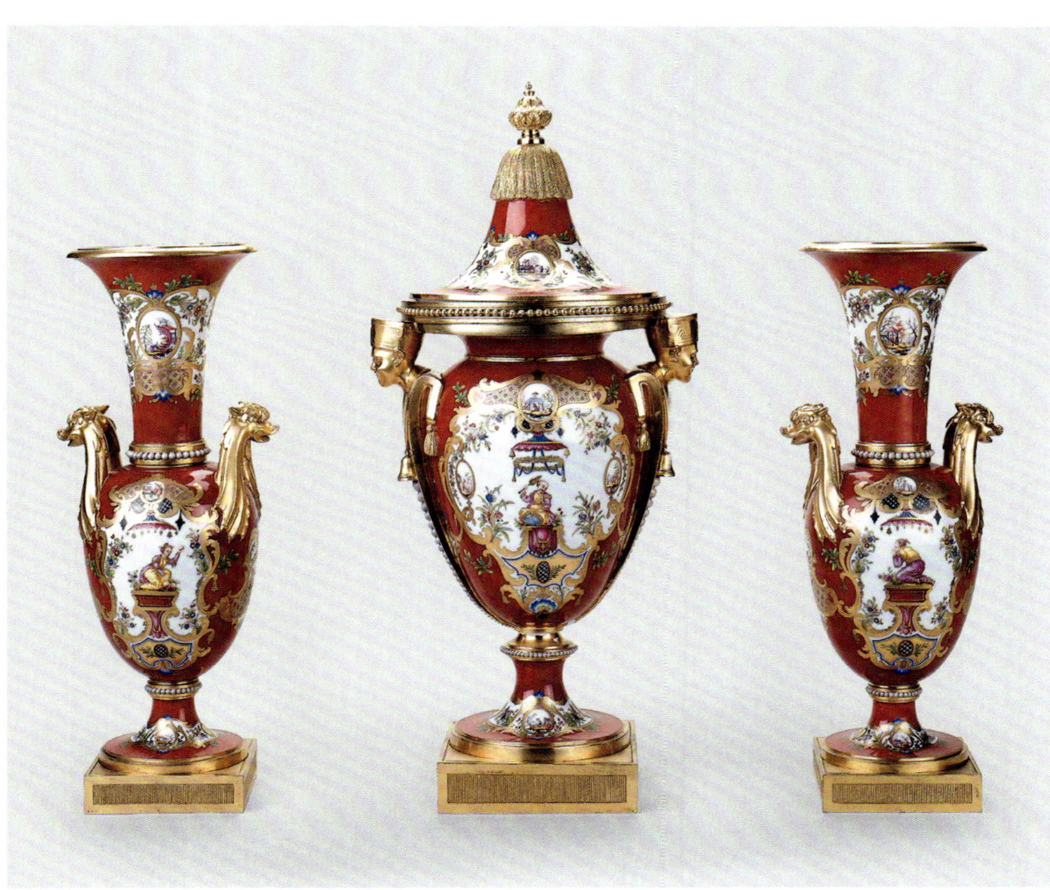

FIG. A.23

SÈVRES PORCELAIN FACTORY
Vases chinois, 1780
Hard-paste porcelain, gilt bronze
RCIN 36075: 50.0 × 22.4 × 18.5 cm
RCIN 36076.1–2: 38.5 × 15.1 × 12.8 cm
De Bellaigue 2009, II, no. 103
FIG. A.23

Sent on approval by M. Lafontaine in 1818 (RA GEO/MAIN/26432). Later sent to Brighton (Jutsham II, p. 38) and returned to Carlton House in 1826 (CH Porcelain Inventory 1826, nos 91–2).

SÈVRES PORCELAIN FACTORY
Vases ferrés, *c.*1780
Soft-paste porcelain, gilt bronze
49.5 × 19.1 × 19.1 cm
RCIN 2286.1–2
De Bellaigue 2009, I, no. 34
FIG. 6.13

Purchased by Francois Benois, Dec. 1815. Recorded in the Anti Room to the Dining Room at Carlton House in 1826 (CH Porcelain Inventory 1826, no. 93).

SÈVRES PORCELAIN FACTORY
Pot-pourri à vaisseau, 1758–9
Soft-paste porcelain, gilt bronze
55.1 × 37.8 × 19.3 cm
RCIN 2360
De Bellaigue 2009, I, no. 12
FIG. 0.11

Formerly owned by Madame de Pompadour, who acquired it in 1759 for 960 *livres*; first recorded in George IV's collection in 1826 when it was in the Bow Room of Carlton House (CH Porcelain Inventory 1826, no. 72).

MINIATURES

RICHARD COSWAY (1742–1821)
George IV when Prince of Wales, c.1783–4
Watercolour on ivory
3.3 cm (diameter)
RCIN 420005
RW 176 FIG. 4.5

Probably commissioned by George IV when Prince of Wales; bequeathed to Queen Victoria by the Duchess of Gloucester in 1857.

RICHARD COSWAY (1742–1821)
Tortoiseshell and enamel box with inset miniature of George IV when Prince of Wales, 1787–95
Watercolour on ivory, tortoiseshell, enamel, diamonds
3.7 cm (diameter)
RCIN 4412
RW 177

Perhaps commissioned by George IV when Prince of Wales; given to Queen Mary on the occasion of her coronation by Alfred Rothschild, 1911.

RICHARD COSWAY (1742–1821)
Maria Fitzherbert (1756–1837), c.1789
Watercolour on ivory laid on card
7.2 × 5.6 cm
RCIN 420928
RW 193 FIG. A.24

Probably painted for George IV when Prince of Wales.

RICHARD COSWAY (1742–1821)
Princess Amelia (1783–1810) when a Child, c.1790
Watercolour on ivory
9.1 × 7.5 cm
RCIN 420003
RW 187 FIG. A.25

Probably the miniature painted for George IV when Prince of Wales at a cost of 30 guineas (Millar 1986, p. 587); collection of Augustus, Duke of Sussex; purchased for the Royal Collection at the sale of his son-in-law, Lord Truro, Christie's, 11 May 1893 (lot 39).

RICHARD COSWAY (1742–1821)
Princess Sophia (1777–1848), c.1792
Watercolour on ivory
7.9 × 6.4 cm
RCIN 420001
RW 186 FIG. A.26

Probably the miniature painted for George IV when Prince of Wales at a cost of 30 guineas (Millar 1986, p. 587).

RICHARD COSWAY (1742–1821)
Princess Mary, Duchess of Gloucester (1776–1857), c.1795
Watercolour on ivory
7.9 × 6.4 cm
RCIN 420647
RW 185 FIG. 4.7

Probably the miniature painted for George IV when Prince of Wales at a cost of 30 guineas (Millar 1986, p. 587).

GEORGE ENGLEHEART (1752–1829)
George IV when Prince of Wales, 1801–2
Watercolour on ivory
7.1 × 5.8 cm
RCIN 420207
RW 220 FIG. 2.4

Painted for Princess Augusta; bequeathed to Queen Victoria by the Duchess of Gloucester in 1857.

JEAN PETITOT (1607–91)
Cardinal Mazarin (1602–61), c.1661
Enamel
2.5 × 2.2 cm
RCIN 421372
GR 310 FIG. A.27

Possibly the miniature purchased from Rundell, Bridge & Rundell on 20 July 1807 for £26 5s (RA GEO/MAIN/25870); if so, the tortoiseshell snuffbox into which it was set by the same firm on 7 Sept. (ibid.) has subsequently been disposed of.

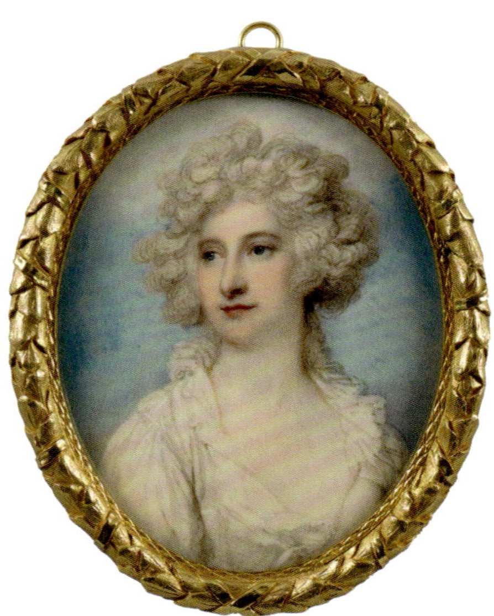

FIG. A.24

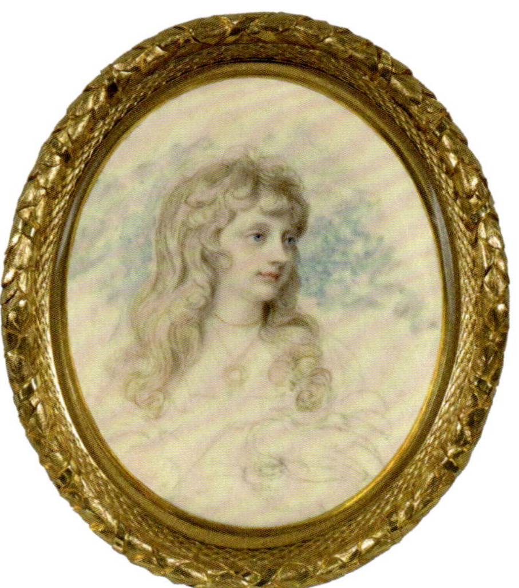

FIG. A.25

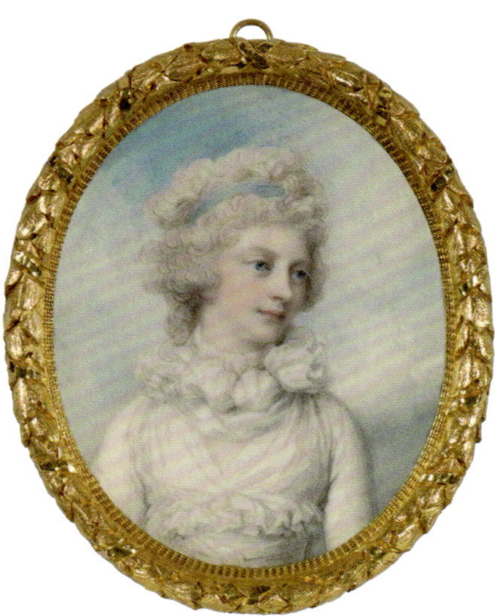

FIG. A.26

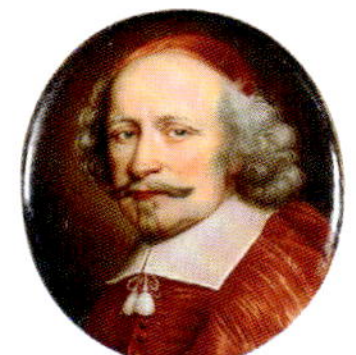

FIG. A.27

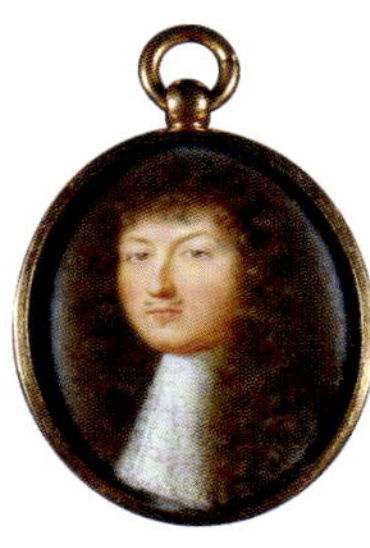

FIG. A.28

JEAN PETITOT (1607–91)
Portrait of a Lady, called Marie, Marquise de Sévigné (1626–96), c.1644–60
Enamel
2.6 × 2.3 cm
RCIN 421373
GR 329 FIG. 4.12

Probably purchased by George IV; first recorded in the Royal Collection during the reign of Queen Victoria.

RICHARD COSWAY (1742–1821)
George IV when Prince of Wales, c.1795
Watercolour on ivory
7.5 × 5.6 cm
RCIN 421469
RW 180 FIG. 4.6

In the collection of George, Duke of Cambridge; sold Christie's, 10 June 1904 (lot 322); presented to Queen Mary on her birthday by the Dowager Lady Harcourt, 26 May 1940.

JEAN PETITOT (1607–91)
Louis XIV (1638–1715), c.1660
Enamel
2.6 × 2.3 cm
RCIN 421379
GR 292 FIG. A.28

Probably acquired by George IV when Prince Regent.

ANNE MEE (1770–1851)
Isabella, Marchioness of Hertford (1760–1834), 1812–14
Watercolour on ivory
19.5 × 15.2 cm
RCIN 420869
RW 870 FIG. 4.10

Painted at a cost of £105 (RA GEO/MAIN/26978).

RICHARD COSWAY (1742–1821)
Georgiana, Duchess of Devonshire (1757–1806), c.1774–82
Watercolour on ivory
5.9 × 5.0 cm
RCIN 420124
RW 192 FIG. A.29

First recorded in the Royal Collection in 1870.

HENRY BONE (1755–1834) AFTER THOMAS PHILLIPS (1770–1845)
George IV when Prince of Wales, 1818
Enamel
18.8 × 15.0 cm
RCIN 421448
VR 111 FIG. A.30

Given to Queen Mary by Lord and Lady Mount Stephen.

HENRY BONE (1755–1834) AFTER SIR JOSHUA REYNOLDS (1723–92)
The Death of Dido, 1804
Enamel on copper
25.1 × 33.8 cm
RCIN 404284
RW 790 FIG. 4.9

Painted at a cost of 375 guineas (with an extra £50 18s 6d for a frame). Received at Carlton House on 6 Nov. 1807 and placed in the Throne Room store (Jutsham I, p. 25); hung in the Prince Regent's Bed Room by 1816 (CH inv. 1816, no. 183); recorded in the same location in 1819 (CH inv. 1819, no. 191).

Exhibited at the Royal Academy in 1805 (no. 363).

HENRY BONE (1755–1834) AFTER ANNIBALE CARRACCI (1560–1609)
Holy Family ('The Silence'), 1814
Enamel on copper
24.6 × 32.0 cm
RCIN 404281
RW 797 FIG. 4.11

Painted at a cost of 480 guineas (RA GEO/MAIN/26953). Received at Carlton House on 13 May 1814 (Jutsham I, p. 305); hung in the Prince's Bedchamber at Carlton House by 1816 (CH inv. 1816, no. 189), recorded in the same location in 1819 (CH inv. 1819, no 197).

RICHARD BULL (1721–1805)
George IV when Prince of Wales, 1793
Watercolour on ivory
7.8 × 6.2 cm
RCIN 420984
RW 146 FIG. 2.10

Acquired after 1910.

JEAN PETITOT (1607–91)
Snuffbox with inset miniature of Louis XIV, c.1680
Tortoiseshell, gold, enamel
3.9 × 7.6 × 5.4 cm
RCIN 3983
GR 297 FIG 4.13

Presented to King George V and Queen Mary in 1919.

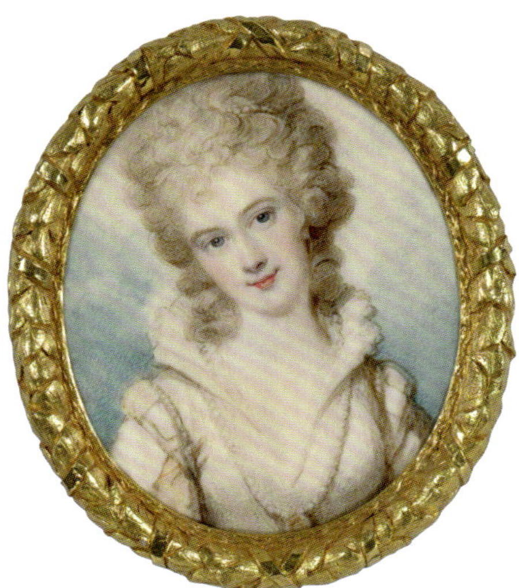

FIG. A.29

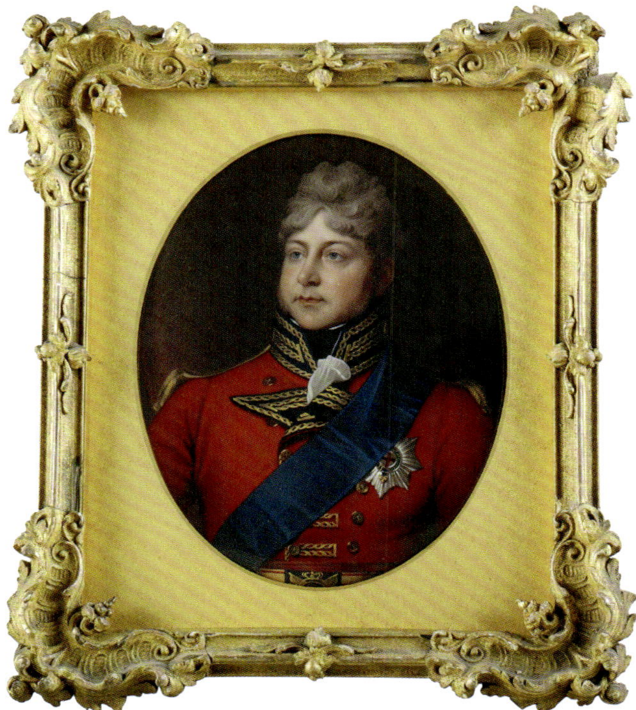

FIG. A.30

JEWELLERY, GOLD BOXES, MEDALS AND INSIGNIA

FRENCH
Henri IV (1553–1610), 1650–1700
Appliqué mother-of-pearl, cowrie shell, silver gilt
3.0 × 2.1 cm
RCIN 65197
G&J 216 FIG. 6.2

Possibly to be identified with the 'head of Henry the Fourth' purchased for £5 5s from Thomas Gray on 13 Jan. 1789 (RA GEO/MAIN/25679).

ENGLISH (?)
Locket containing hair of Charles I (1600–49), c.1620 (with later additions 1813)
Gold, enamel, Burmese ruby, diamond
8.1 × 5.0 × 1.4 cm
RCIN 43778
G&J 288 FIG. 0.14

Inscribed: *Hair of Charles the First Cut from his head April 1st 1813 Discovered on the Funeral of the Duchess of Brunswick and given to me by the Prince Regent*

In the collection of Princess Charlotte (Garrard inventory, p. 518); left to her husband, Prince Leopold, King of the Belgians; reacquired by Queen Victoria sometime before 1896.

ATTRIBUTED TO BENEDETTO PISTRUCCI (1784–1855)
Gold ring with an intaglio of George IV, 1821
Carnelian, gold, turquoise, seed pearl
2.6 × 2.1 cm (intaglio); 2.3 × 2.8 cm (ring)
Engraved: *September 1821*
RCIN 107334
G&J 272 FIG. 16.5

The inscription suggests it was a souvenir of the visit to Hanover. Purchased by Queen Elizabeth The Queen Mother before 1958.

FRENCH
Ring with a bas-relief of Louis XII of France, early 19th century
Rubelite tourmaline, gold, enamel
2.0 × 1.6 cm
RCIN 65381
G&J 213 FIG. 0.20

Purchased for £63 from Rundell, Bridge & Rundell, 24 Apr. 1827 (RA GEO/MAIN/26117).

EDWARD MURRAY (ACTIVE 1812–53), DUBLIN
Snuffbox, 1821
Bog oak, enamel, diamond, gold, pearl, paste (glass)
2.9 × 9.0 × 7.6 cm
RCIN 4036 FIG. 16.2

Presented to George IV on his visit to Ireland in 1821; sold to Rundell, Bridge & Co. after his death by William IV and, according to a label kept inside, reacquired by King Edward VII in 1902.

BENJAMIN WYON (1802–58)
Medal commemorating George IV's visit to Ireland, 1821
Bronze
5.0 cm (diameter)
RCIN 447168.a FIG. 16.1

Acquired by Queen Mary.

ENGLISH
Order of the Garter: Lesser George sash badge, 1765
Cast iron
Badge 5.7 × 3.2 cm
RCIN 441813
FIG. A.31

Reputedly worn by George IV when a young boy.

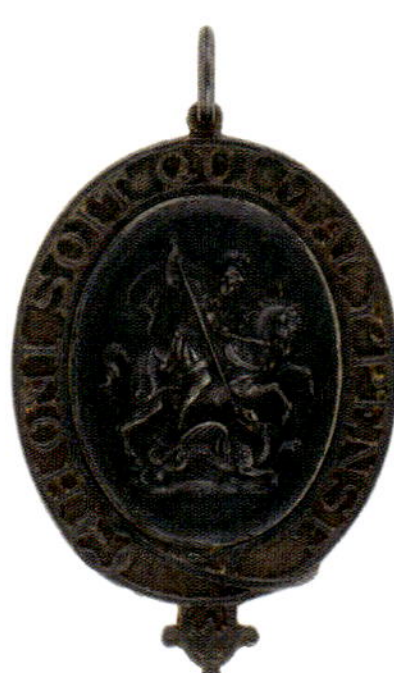

THOMAS GRAY (ACTIVE 1787–8)
Order of the Garter: Lesser George sash badge, 1787–8
Diamond, ruby, sapphire, emerald, gold
11.6 × 8.2 cm (whole object)
RCIN 441151 FIG. A.32

Supplied in 1787 for £403 15s 6d (RA GEO/MAIN/25667); the following year further diamonds were added at a cost of £420 (RA GEO/MAIN/25670).

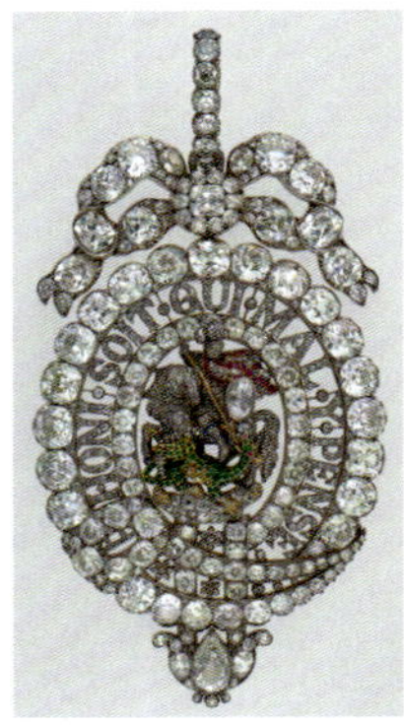

RUNDELL, BRIDGE & RUNDELL
Order of the Thistle: sash badge, 1812
Gold, diamond, emerald, ruby, enamel
10.8 × 4.8 cm
RCIN 441236 FIG. 16.10

Supplied on 10 Oct. 1812 (TNA LC9/351 fol. 8).

RUNDELL, BRIDGE & RUNDELL
Order of St Patrick: sash badge, 1812
Gold, diamond, ruby, emerald, enamel
10.8 × 4.8 cm
RCIN 441257 FIG. 16.3

Supplied on 10 Oct. 1812 (TNA LC9/351 fol. 8).

ATTRIBUTED TO RUNDELL, BRIDGE & RUNDELL
Order of the Bath: Grand Cross sash badge, 1814
11.5 × 8.7 cm
RCIN 441287 FIG. A.33

Probably one of a set of eight badges commissioned in 1814 (TNA LC9/351, fol. 9).

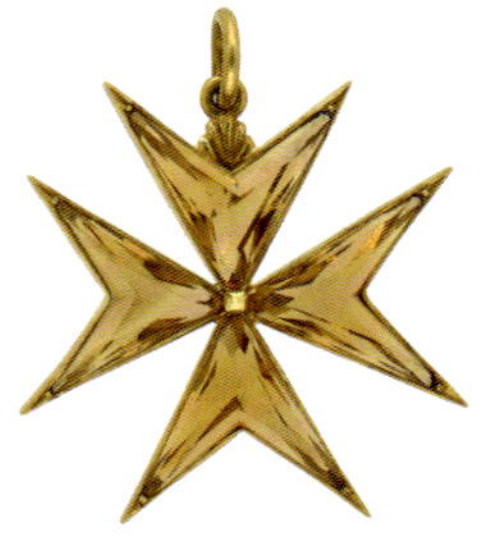

ATTRIBUTED TO RUNDELL, BRIDGE & RUNDELL
Order of St John of Jerusalem: badge, c.1815
Topaz, gold
4.5 × 4.5 cm
RCIN 52303 FIG. A.34

Possibly the 'very fine … topaz cross in gold' billed by Rundells for £31 10s on 2 May 1816 (RA GEO/MAIN/25917). Reacquired by King Edward VII when Prince of Wales in 1895.

ENGLISH
Royal Guelphic Order of Hanover: Grand Cross Collar, 1815
Yellow and rose gold
137.0 cm (length)
RCIN 442135 FIG. 16.6

Made for Adolphus, Duke of Cambridge, who was appointed a Knight Grand Cross of the Order in 1815, shortly after its foundation. Acquired 2018.

ENGLISH
Order of St Michael and St George: star, c.1825
Diamond, yellow diamond, ruby, silver, enamel
7.7 × 7.7 cm
RCIN 441309 FIG. 15.3

Made for Adolphus, Duke of Cambridge, who was appointed Grand Master of the Order by George IV in 1825.

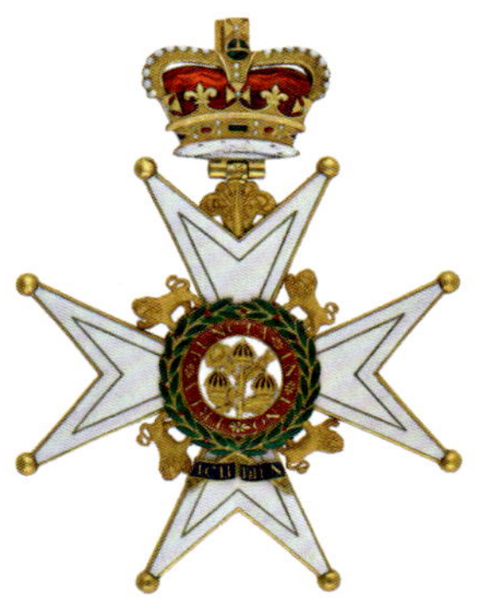

FIG. A.33

METALWORK

MARK OF PAUL STORR (1771–1844), FOR RUNDELL, BRIDGE & RUNDELL
Pair of candelabra, 1811–13
Silver gilt
64.5 × 43.0 × 43.0 cm
RCIN 50827 FIG. A.35

Two from a set of 24 candelabra, 12 of which were produced in the workshops of Benjamin Smith III between 1803 and 1810 and the remainder in the workshops of Paul Storr. Delivered to Carlton House in three groups, 1810–12 (RA GEO/MAIN/26287).

MARK OF PAUL STORR (1771–1844), FOR RUNDELL, BRIDGE & RUNDELL, DESIGNED BY THOMAS STOTHARD (1755–1834)
Tray, 1812/13
Silver gilt
11.2 × 82.8 × 60.5 cm
RCIN 50837 FIG. A.36

One of a pair of trays, one delivered to Carlton House in 1812 and the second in 1813 (£587 8s 9d and £607 19s respectively; RA GEO/MAIN/26286).

MARK OF PAUL STORR (1771–1844), FOR RUNDELL, BRIDGE & RUNDELL
Pair of wine coolers, 1812/13
Silver gilt
25.5 × 38.0 × 28.0 cm
RCIN 50810 FIG. A.37

Two from a set of four, which were supplied with four larger versions in 1813 for £3,470 5s 8d (TNA LC9/351, fol. 29).

MARK OF PAUL STORR (1771–1844), FOR RUNDELL, BRIDGE & RUNDELL
Pair of spirit lamps, 1813 (with additions 1817)
Silver gilt
24.0 × 29.5 × 30.0 cm
RCIN 50278.1–2 FIG. A.38

Originally supplied as 'stands for the sideboard' in 1813 (CH Plate inv., p. 29), with 'fluted pedestals' (TNA LC9/351, fol. 29). In Jan. 1818 new bases were supplied and at this date the phoenixes were described as lamps (TNA LC9/351, fol. 58).

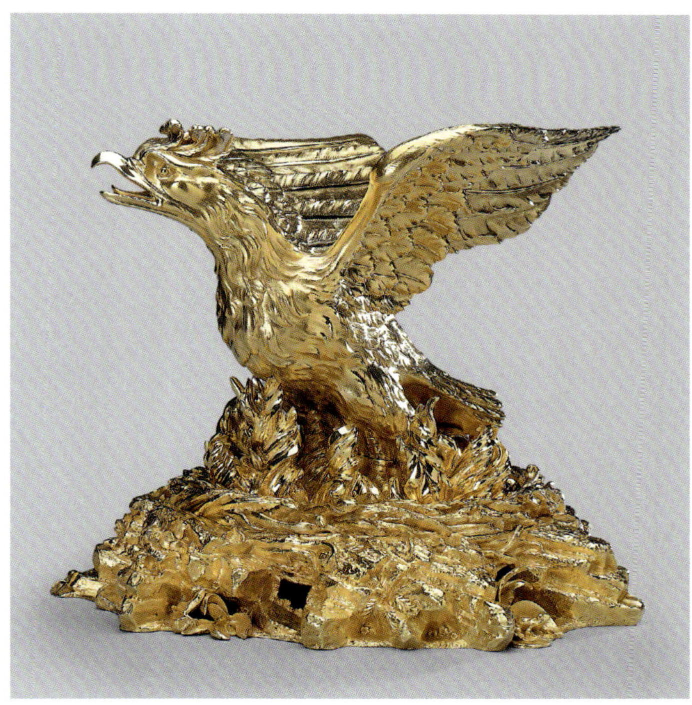
FIG. A.38

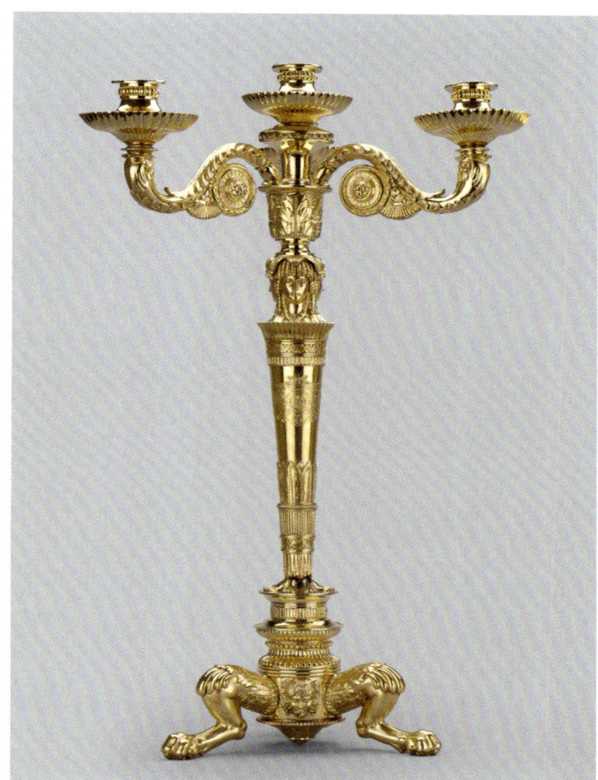
FIG. A.35

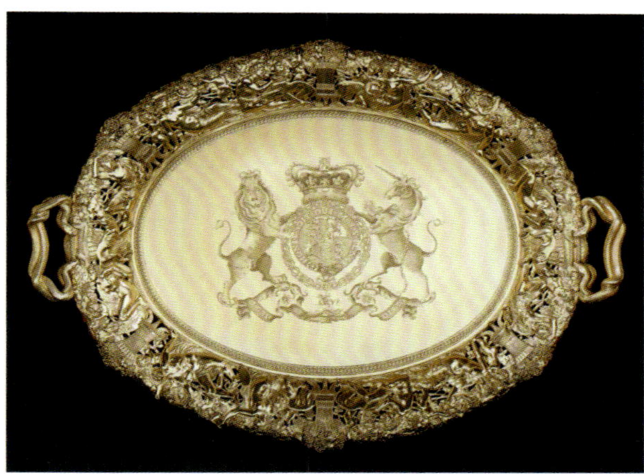
FIG. A.36

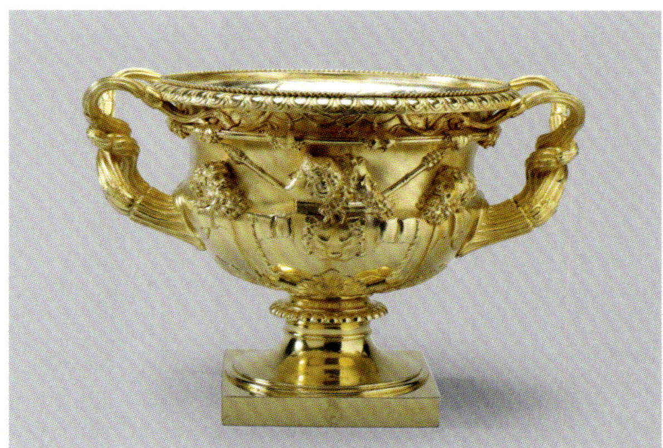
FIG. A.37

MARK OF PAUL STORR (1771–1844), FOR RUNDELL, BRIDGE & RUNDELL, DESIGNED BY THOMAS STOTHARD (1755–1834)
Dish (Triumph of Bacchus and Ariadne), 1814
Silver gilt
7.5 × 79.0 cm (diameter)
RCIN 51654 FIG. 15.12

Delivered to Carlton House on 5 Apr. 1814 (TNA LC9/351, fol. 31).

HEINRICH SADELER, HANOVER
Tankard, 1665
Silver gilt
21.8 × 19.5 × 14.8 cm
RCIN 50555
Jones 2017, no. 25 FIG. A.39

Possibly formerly in the collection of Queen Charlotte; first recorded in the collection in 1819 (CH Plate inv., p. 27).

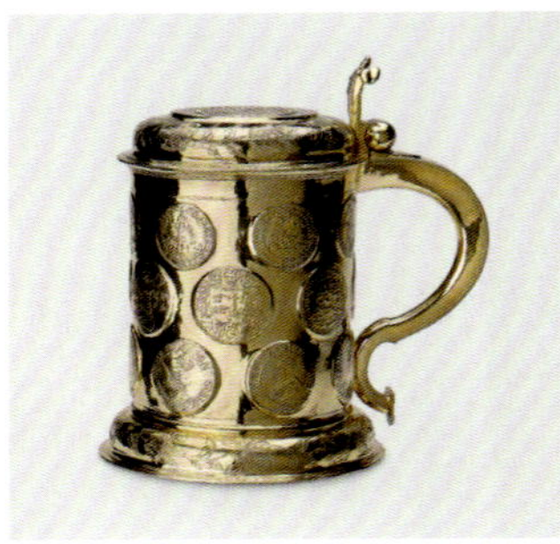

JOSEPH RODGERS & SONS, SHEFFIELD
Pocket knife, 1821
Steel, mother of pearl
31.2 cm (length)
RCIN 2451 FIG. 8.1

Engraved: *TO HIS MOST Gracious Majesty, King George the Fourth. This Specimen of the Manufacturers of SHEFFIELD, is humbly presented by his Dutiful and loyal Subjects and Servants, JOSEPH RODGERS & SONS February 1821*

According to the inscription, a gift from the firm presented in Feb. 1821.

MARK OF PHILIP RUNDELL (1746–1827) OF RUNDELL, BRIDGE & RUNDELL, DESIGNED BY JOHN FLAXMAN (1755–1826)
Shield of Achilles, 1821
Silver gilt
90.7 cm (diameter)
RCIN 51266 FIG. 15.20

Commissioned *c.*1810 from Flaxman, who received a payment for designs from Rundells in that year (letter in the Fitzwilliam Museum, Cambridge); supplied by Rundells for the coronation banquet (bill untraced).

MARK OF PHILIP RUNDELL (1746–1827) OF RUNDELL, BRIDGE & RUNDELL
Tray, 1821/2
Gold
10.0 × 67.5 × 46.0 cm
RCIN 50836
FIG. 15.21

Probably created for the coronation banquet as it is engraved with the orders of knighthood to which George IV belonged by 1821.

NIKOLAUS SCHMIDT (*c.*1550/5–1609), NUREMBERG
Nautilus cup, *c.*1600
Nautilus shell, parcel-gilt silver
52.0 × 17.0 × 24.0 cm
RCIN 50603
Jones 2017, no. 3
FIG. 6.5

Purchased from Rundell, Bridge & Rundell on 24 Apr. 1823 for 250 guineas, with a glass shade and velvet-covered stand for a further £6 18s (RA GEO/MAIN/26060).

MARK OF D.G., SOUTH GERMANY OR AUSTRIA, IVORY CARVING ATTRIBUTED TO JOHANN GOTTFRIED FRISCH (ACTIVE 1689–1716), BOGEN
Cup and cover, *c.*1700 (with later additions by Rundell, Bridge & Rundell, 1824/5)
Ivory, silver gilt, ruby, emerald, turquoise
49.8 × 16.6 × 20.2 cm
RCIN 50554
Jones 2017, no. 37 FIG. 6.1

Purchased at the Fonthill Abbey sale, 27 Sept. 1823 (lot 573), for 90 guineas. Returned to Rundells in 1824 for additions, including the jewelled mounts, for a further £148 10s (RA GEO/MAIN/26327).

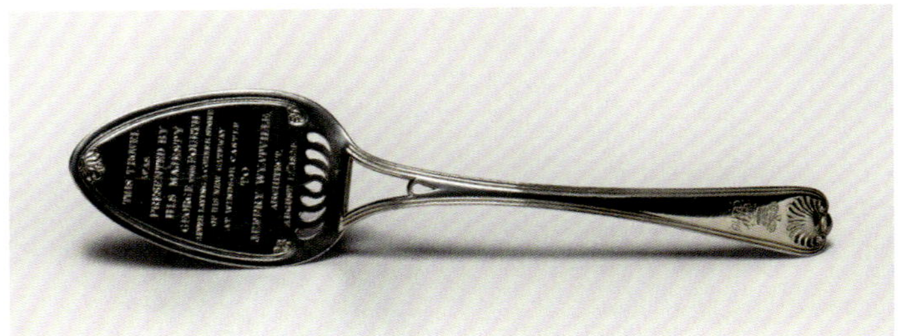

FIG. A.40

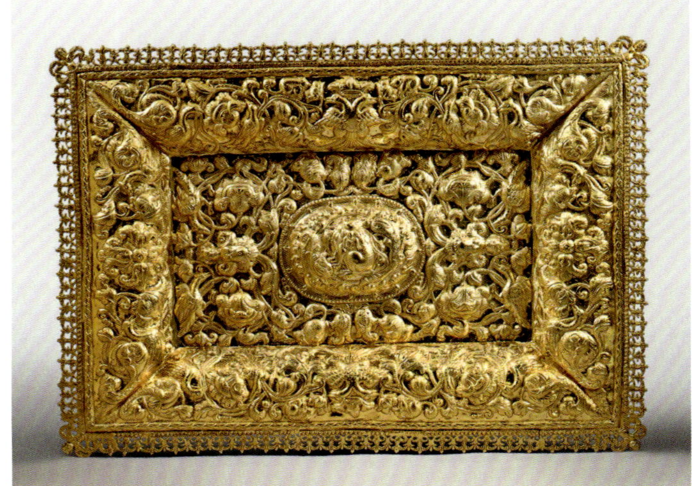

FIG. A.41

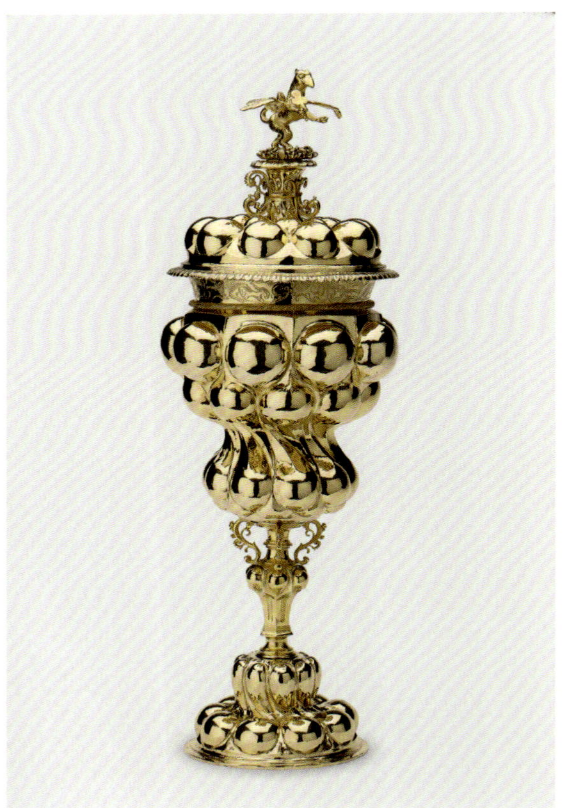

FIG. A.42

george smith iii (active 1774–86)
Trowel, *c.*1780 (hallmarks other than the maker's mark obliterated)
Silver
24.2 × 5.8 × 1.7 cm
rcin 50426 fig. a.40

Used by George IV to lay the foundation stone of the new gateway at Windsor Castle on 12 Aug. 1824; presented to Sir Jeffry Wyatville.

peruvian
Tray, early 18th century
Silver gilt
45.0 × 61.5 × 5.0 cm
rcin 50823 fig. a.41

A gift from 'one of the British Consuls' on 15 Feb. 1825 (Jutsham ii, p. 184), possibly Sir Edmund Nagle, former Groom of the Bedchamber.

georg schyrer (active 1596–1634), nuremberg
Standing cup and cover (*Bukelpokal*), 1605–9
Silver gilt
38.3 × 12.8 × 12.8 cm
rcin 51443
Jones 2017, no. 9 fig. a.42

First recorded in the collection in July 1826 (Jutsham ii, p. 217).

friedrich hillebrandt (b. 1555), nuremberg
Standing cup and cover (*Bukelpokal*), *c.*1596
Silver gilt
59.0 × 17.0 × 17.0 cm
rcin 51282
Jones 2017, no. 2 fig. 0.19

First recorded in the collection in July 1826 (Jutsham ii, p. 217).

heinrich mannlich (*c.*1625–98), augsburg
Statuette of a warrior on horseback, *c.*1675
Silver gilt
54.0 × 31.5 × 22.4 cm
rcin 51060
Jones 2017, no. 28 fig. a.43

First recorded in the collection in July 1826 (Jutsham ii, p. 217).

lorenz biller ii (1649–1726), augsburg
Nautilus cup, late 17th century (with later additions)
Nautilus shell, silver gilt, diamonds, rubies, garnets, sapphires, emeralds, turquoises
30.0 × 18.0 × 12.0 cm
rcin 50610
Jones 2017, no. 35 fig. a.44

Purchased from Rundell, Bridge & Rundell, for £94 10s in Dec. 1826 (ra geo/main/26115).

probably north germany
Tankard, *c.*1678 (with later additions)
Silver gilt, diamond, sapphire, pink sapphire, emerald, amethyst, turquoise, ruby
29.0 × 20.0 × 15.8 cm
rcin 50602
Jones 2017, no. 29 fig. a.45

Formerly in the collection of Frederick, Duke of York and sold at Christie's after his death; purchased from Rundell, Bridge & Rundell, Sept. 1827 (ra geo/main/26325).

mark of john bridge (1755–1834), for rundell, bridge & rundell, design attributed to john flaxman (1755–1826)
Pair of bottle coolers, 1827/8
Silver gilt
58.0 × 40.0 × 40.0 cm
rcin 50843.1–2 fig. a.46

Two from a set of four supplied in 1828–9 for £2,814 16s 8d (ra geo/main/26245, 26250, 26300).

mark of john bridge (1755–1834), for rundell, bridge & rundell, designed by john flaxman (1755–1826)
Pair of tureens, 1826/7
Silver gilt
42.0 × 41.0 × 38.5 cm
rcin 50279.1–2 fig. 15.11

Two from a set of four delivered (with a wainscot case) before 5 Nov. 1829 for £2,452 16s 9d (ra geo/main/26245, 26250).

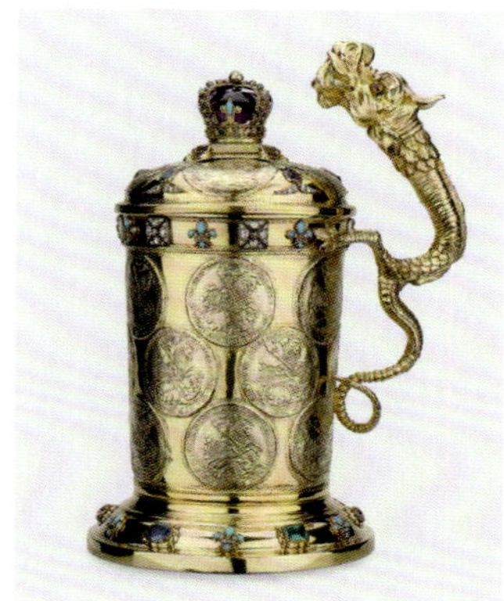
fig. a.45

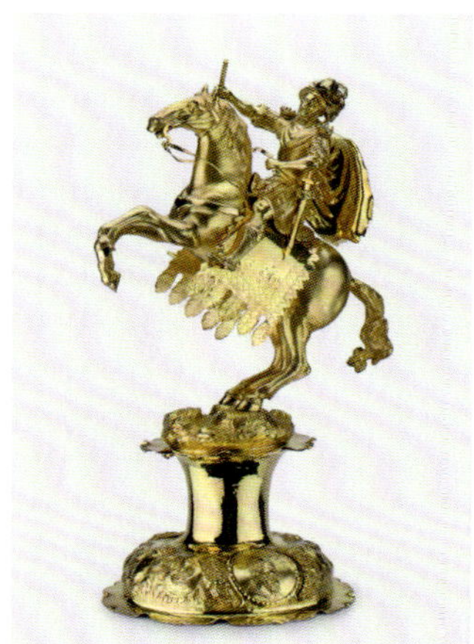
fig. a.43

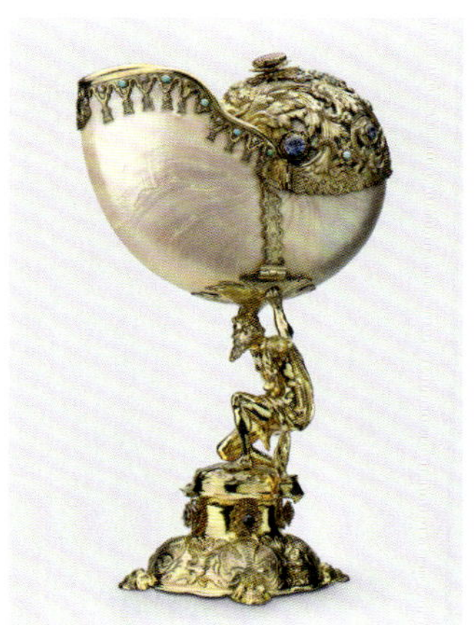
fig. a.44

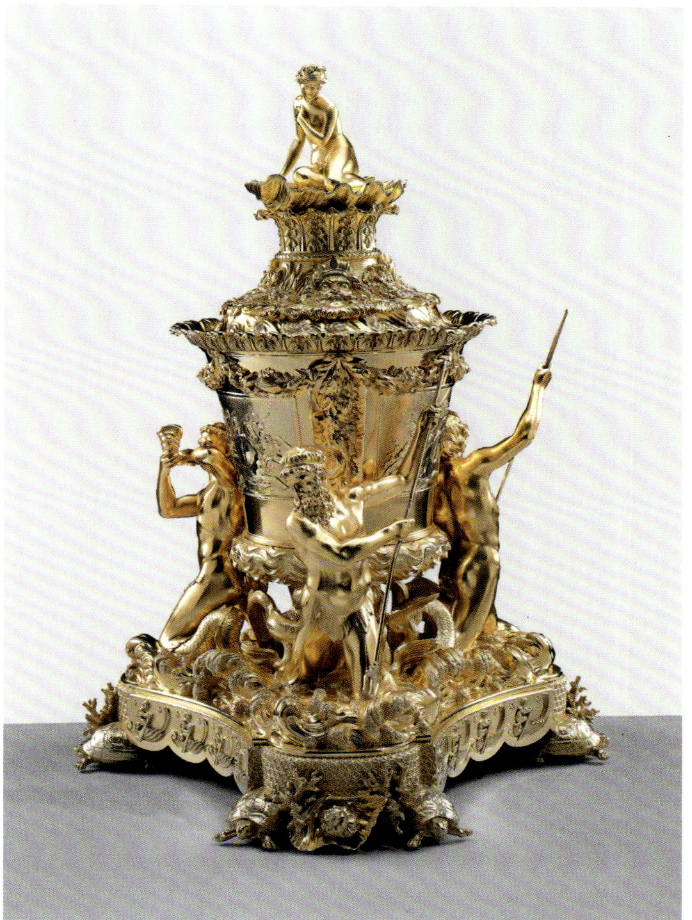
fig. a.46

PRINTS AND DRAWINGS

THOMAS ROWLANDSON (1757–1827)
The Golden Apple, or the Modern Paris, 1785
Etching
28.2 × 39.6 cm (sheet)
RCIN 810123 FIG. 12.1

Probably purchased by George IV when Prince of Wales.

THOMAS ROWLANDSON (1757–1827)
Who Kills Fi[r]st for a Crown, 1790
Etching with hand colouring
36.7 × 51.8 cm (sheet)
RCIN 810385 FIG. 12.5

Purchased from William Holland in 1790 for 3s (TNA HO73/20/1, fol. 9).

JOHANN GOTTHARD MÜLLER (1747–1830)
Louis Seize, 1792–3
Engraving
68.6 × 50.8 cm (sheet)
RCIN 617363 FIG. 0.6

Purchased from Colnaghi & Co. on 16 Dec. 1799, for £1 11s 6d (RA GEO/MAIN/27695).

FRANCESCO PANINI (1745–1812)
Veduta della Piazza di S. Pietro illuminata dalle Fiacole, c.1770
Etching with watercolour and bodycolour
55.6 × 85.6 cm (sheet)
RCIN 705163.f FIG. 6.24

Purchased from Colnaghi & Co. on 16 Dec. 1799, for £8 8s (RA GEO/MAIN/27695).

FRANCESCO PANINI (1745–1812)
Veduta della Piazza di S. Pietro illuminata dalla Luna, c.1770
Etching printed in brown with watercolour and wash
55.8 × 85.9 cm (sheet)
RCIN 705163.d FIG. A.47

Purchased from Colnaghi & Co. on 17 Dec. 1799, for £8 8s (RA GEO/MAIN/27697).

FRANCESCO PANINI (1745–1812)
Veduta dell'interno della Basilica di S. Pietro in Vaticano, c.1770
Etching with watercolour and bodycolour
53.6 × 84.2 cm (sheet)
RCIN 705163.b FIG. A.48

Purchased from Colnaghi & Co. on 17 Dec. 1799, for £8 8s (RA GEO/MAIN/27697).

FRANCESCO PANINI (1745–1812)
Prospetto Interno del' Portico della Basilica di San' Pietro nel Vaticano, c.1770
Etching with watercolour and bodycolour and gold paint
55.0 × 84.5 cm (sheet)
RCIN 705163.c FIG. 6.23

Purchased from Colnaghi & Co. on 17 Dec. 1799, for £10 10s (RA GEO/MAIN/27697).

BIAGIO REBECCA (1735–1808)
The Opera House: the auditorium, c.1787
Watercolour, bodycolour and gum arabic with pen and ink over pencil
66.5 × 54.0 cm
RCIN 917079
OE 486 FIG. A.49

Purchased from Colnaghi & Co. on 9 July 1804, for £7 7s (RA GEO/MAIN/27269).

ASSOCIATE OF SIR PETER LELY (1618–80)
Charles II (1630–85), c.1676
Red chalk (offset and worked up)
55.6 × 40.4 cm
RCIN 912839
PD 67 FIG. 0.12

Purchased from Colnaghi & Co. on 26 Mar. 1805, for £5 5s, as 'a Drawing the Port of Charles 2d by Vanderwerf' (RA GEO/MAIN/27297).

PUBLISHED BY PIERRE JEAN (1754–1829)
Plan de la Bataille d'Austerlitz, 1805
Engraving with hand colouring
48.0 × 38.5 cm (sheet)
RCIN 712608 FIG. 9.9

Purchased from Colnaghi & Co. on 9 Oct. 1806, for 5s (RA GEO/MAIN/27359).

JOHN AUGUSTUS ATKINSON (1775–1831)
Dragoons and Light Infantry, c.1805
Ink counterproof with pen and ink, pencil and watercolour
22.7 × 37.0 cm
RCIN 916415 FIG. A.50

Purchased from Colnaghi & Co. on 6 Apr. 1807, for 3 guineas (RA GEO/MAIN/27377).

JOHN AUGUSTUS ATKINSON (1775–1831)
Baggage wagon, c.1805
Ink counterproof with pen and ink, pencil and watercolour
22.4 × 37.0 cm
RCIN 916417
Haswell, Miller and Dawnay 1966, no. 370 FIG. A.51

Purchased from Colnaghi & Co. on 6 Apr. 1807, for 3 guineas (RA GEO/MAIN/27377).

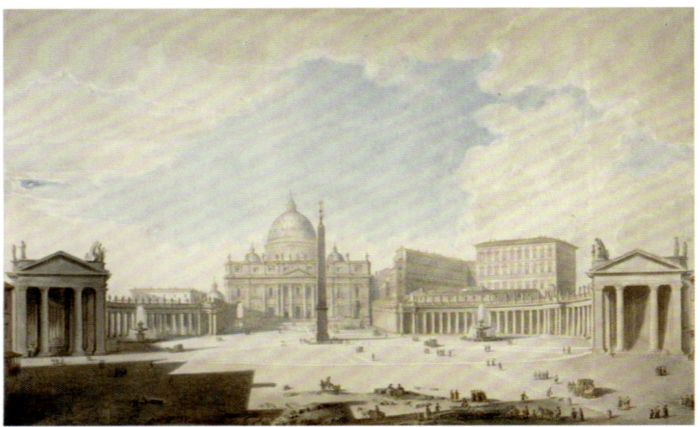
FIG. A.47

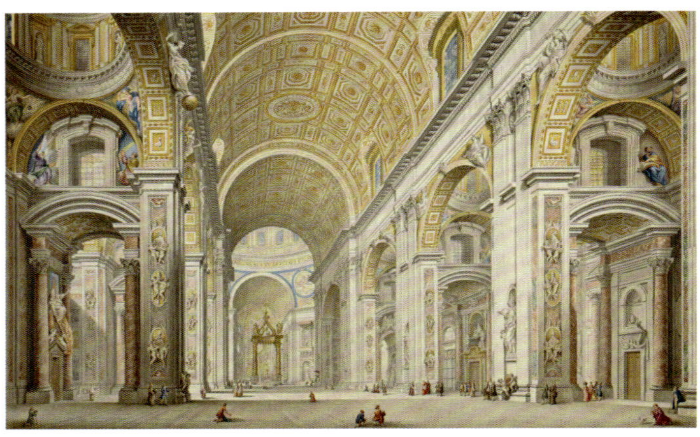
FIG. A.48

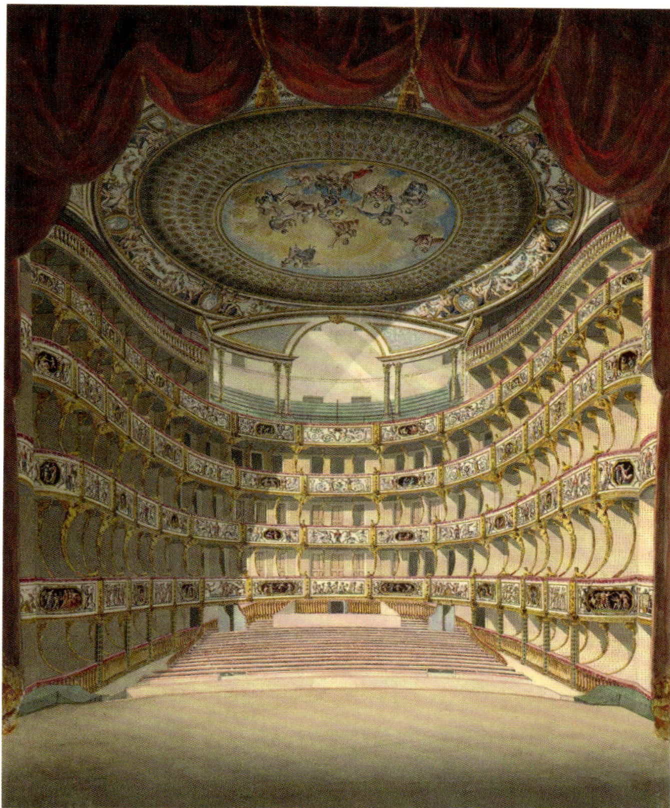

FIG. A.49

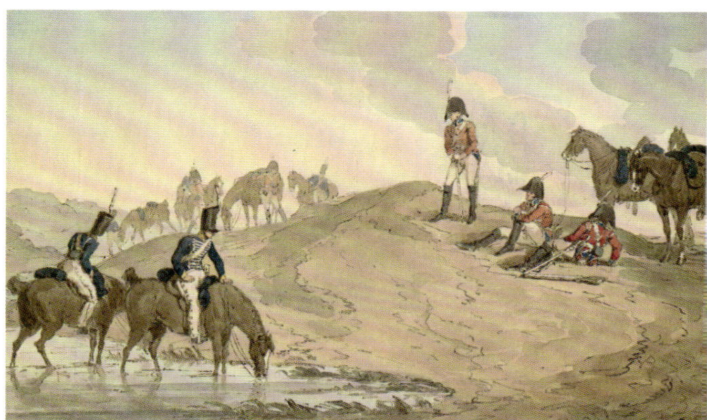

FIG. A.50

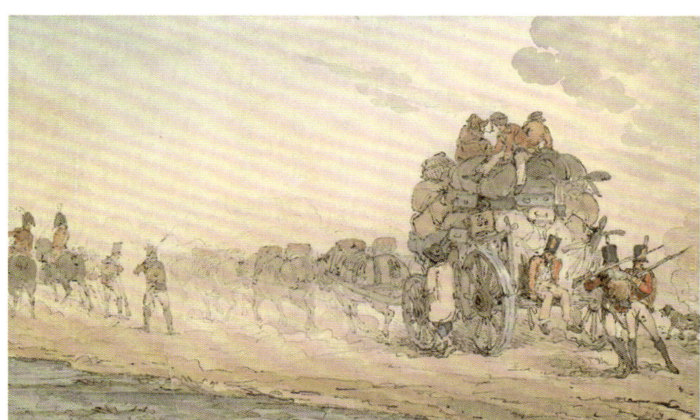

FIG. A.51

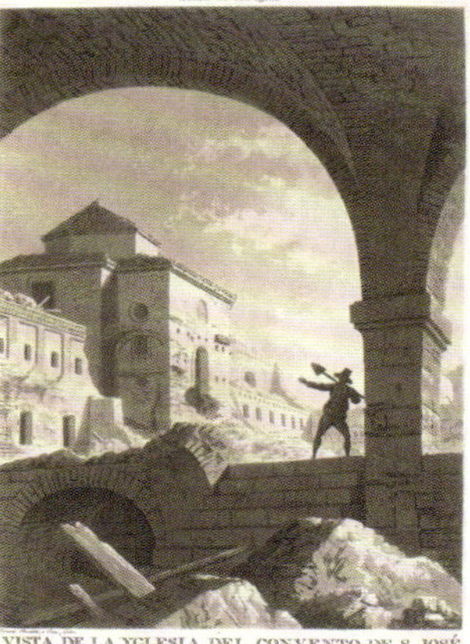

FIG. A.52

FERNANDO BRAMBILA (1763–1834)
AND JUAN GÁLVEZ (1774–1847)
Ruinas de Zaragoza: Vista de la Yglesia del Convento de S. José. Tomada desde el Patio', 1812
Etching and aquatint
38.7 × 27.4 cm (sheet)
RCIN 755999.h FIG. A.52

Presumably acquired by George IV when Prince Regent for his military collection, *c.*1812–13.

SAMUEL COOPER (1609–72)
Charles II (1630–85), 1660/62
Black and red chalks on faded brown paper
17.8 × 14.0 cm (sheet)
RCIN 914040
OE 133 FIG. 0.13

Previously in the collections of Jonathan Richardson the Elder (Lugt 2184) and Jonathan Richardson the Younger (Lugt 2170); according to a note accompanying the drawing, it was presented to George III by his son George, Prince of Wales, on 29 May (no year given) to mark the anniversary of Charles II's Restoration. First recorded in the Royal Collection *c.*1817 (Inventory A, p. 151).

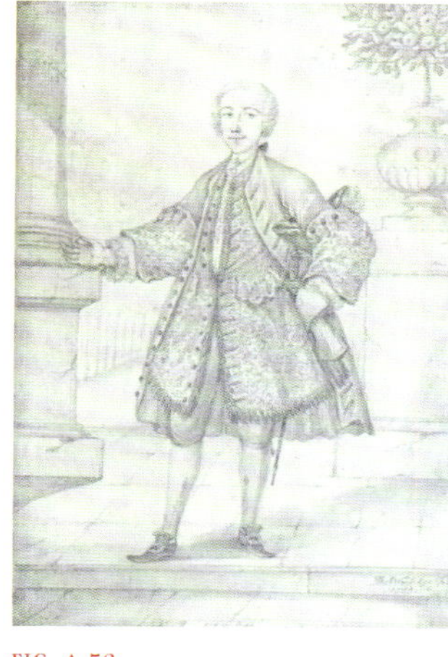

FIG. A.53

THOMAS WORLIDGE (1700–66)
Mr Theophilus Cibber (1703–58), the Comedian, 1735
Pencil on vellum
31.5 × 22.1 cm
RCIN 452429
OE 692 FIG. A.53

Purchased from Colnaghi & Co. on 21 June 1810, for £2 2s (RA GEO/MAIN/27534).

BARON FRANÇOIS GÉRARD (1770–1837)
AFTER BARON AUGUSTE GASPARD LOUIS DESNOYERS (1779–1857)
Napoleon le Grand (1769–1821), 1808
Engraving
70.2 × 53.2 cm (sheet)
RCIN 617722 FIG. 15.17

Purchased from Colnaghi & Co. on 1 Feb. 1811, for £63 (RA GEO/MAIN/27596).

JACQUES-FABIEN GAUTIER D'AGOTY (1716–85)
Henri IV (1553–1610), King of France, *c.*1741–60
Mezzotint with engraving printed in four colours
51.7 × 48.8 cm (sheet)
RCIN 616654 FIG. A.54

Probably one of the three coloured prints of Henri IV purchased by George IV, perhaps that acquired from Colnaghi & Co. on 1 Feb. 1811, for £1 1s (RA GEO/MAIN/27596).

DAVID ALLAN (1744–96)
The Opening of the Carnival: The Obelisk near the Porta del Popolo, Rome, 1775
Pen and brown wash, some corrections in pencil, with washed mount at foot
36.8 × 53.4 cm (sheet)
RCIN 913351
OE 21 FIG. 14.9

Previously in the possession of Paul Sandby; acquired from Colnaghi & Co. on 23 Mar. 1812, for £3 3s, along with another nine from the series at £3 3s each (RA GEO/MAIN/27835).

WILLIAM WALKER (1729–93) AFTER JAMES ROBERTS (1753–*c*.1810)
Mr Garrick and Mrs Yates in the Characters of Lusignan and Zara, 1776
Etching
14.7 × 16.9 cm (sheet)
RCIN 655005 FIG. A.55

Purchased from Colnaghi & Co. on 21 Oct. 1812, for 1s 6d (RA GEO/MAIN/27893).

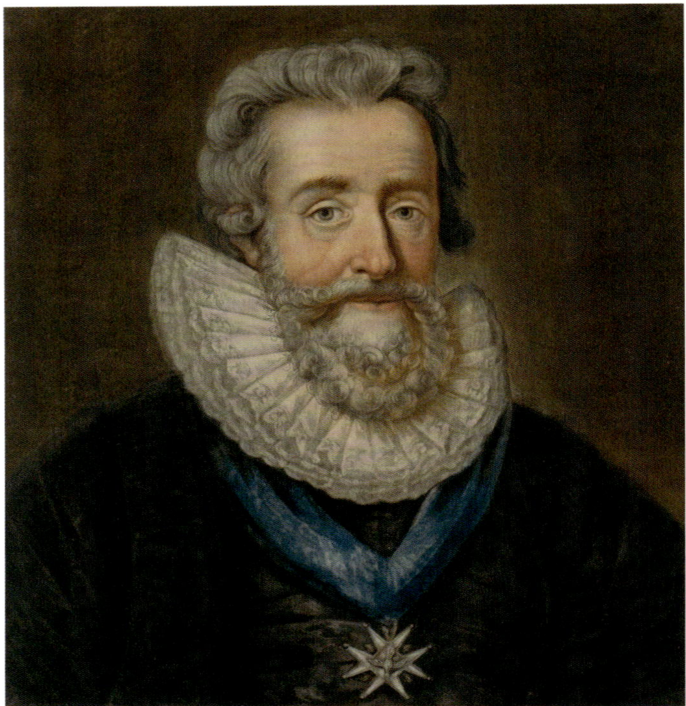

FIG. A.54

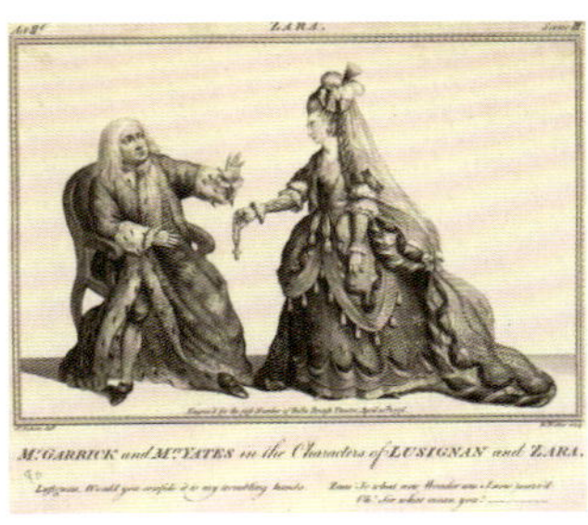

FIG. A.55

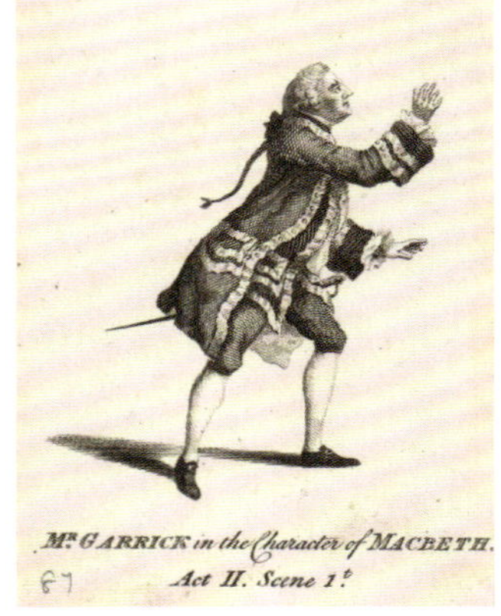

FIG. A.56

THOMAS ROWLANDSON (1757–1827)
The Bust of Garrick wreathed by Comedy and Tragedy, *c*.1780
Etching
12.3 × 9.9 cm (sheet)
RCIN 654944 FIG. 14.18

Probably acquired as part of a job lot of theatrical prints for George IV's extra-illustrated 'History of the Stage', and retaining the orange mount associated with this project.

PUBLISHED BY THOMAS BOWEN (ACTIVE 1769–86)
Mr Garrick in the Character of Macbeth, 1769
Etching
9.0 × 6.1 cm (sheet)
RCIN 655002 FIG. A.56

Probably acquired as part of a job lot of theatrical prints.

CHARLES GRIGNION (1721–1810) AFTER JOHANN LUDWIG FÄSCH (1739–78)
Mr Garrick in the Character of Macbeth, 1769
Etching
9.6 × 7.8 cm
RCIN 655001 FIG. A.57

Probably acquired as part of a job lot of theatrical prints.

JOHN HALL (1739–97) AFTER EDWARD EDWARDS (1738–1806)
Mr Garrick in the Character of Don John, 1777
Etching
15.0 × 8.9 cm (sheet)
RCIN 654982 FIG. A.58

Probably acquired as part of a job lot of theatrical prints.

JOSEPH COLLYER (1748–1827) AFTER ISAAC TAYLOR (1730–1807)
Mr Garrick in the Character of Tancred, 1776
Etching
16.8 × 9.3 cm (sheet)
RCIN 654980 FIG. A.59

Probably acquired as part of a job lot of theatrical prints.

CHARLES GRIGNION (1721–1810) AFTER JOHAN JOSEPH ZOFFANY (1733–1810)
Mr Garrick in the Character of Sr John Brute in the Provok'd Wife, 1769
Etching
8.7 × 6.9 cm (sheet)
RCIN 654992 FIG. A.60

Probably acquired as part of a job lot of theatrical prints.

THOMAS WORLIDGE (1700–66)
Mr Garrick in the Character of Tancred, *c*.1752
Etching
16.2 × 11.9 cm (sheet)
RCIN 654977 FIG. 14.15

Probably acquired as part of a job lot of theatrical prints.

CHARLES GRIGNION (1721–1810) AFTER JOHANN LUDWIG FÄSCH (1739–78)
Mrs Barry and Mr Garrick in the Characters of Donna Violante and Don Felix in the Wonder, 1769
Etching
9.7 × 8.0 cm (sheet)
RCIN 654975 FIG. A.61

Probably acquired as part of a job lot of theatrical prints.

JOHN RAPHAEL SMITH (1751–1812) AFTER SIR JOSHUA REYNOLDS (1723–92)
His Most Serene Highness Louis Philippe Joseph, Duke of Orleans, 1786
Mezzotint
67.3 × 47.7 cm (sheet)
RCIN 640933 FIG. 2.1

Purchased from Colnaghi & Co. on 10 May 1813, for 1 guinea (RA GEO/MAIN/27844).

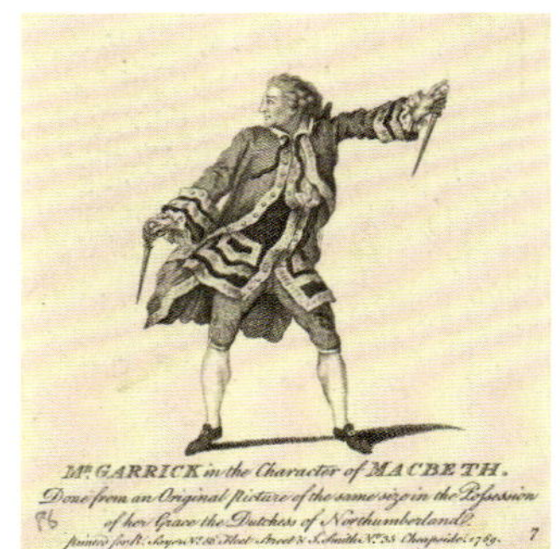

FIG. A.57

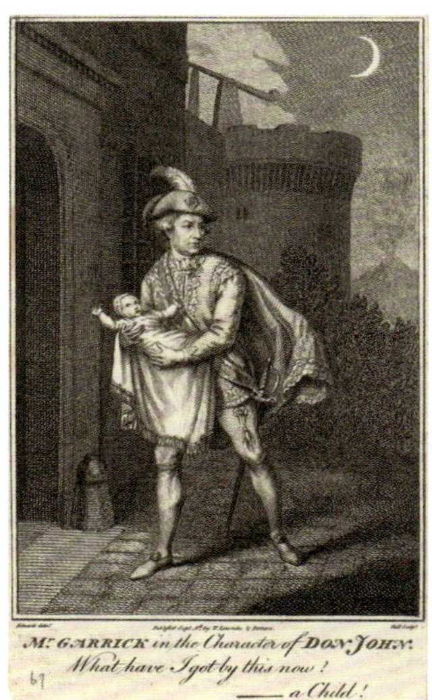

FIG. A.58

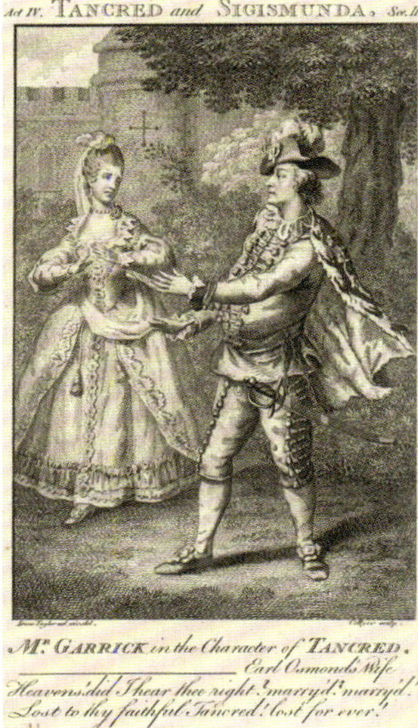

FIG. A.59

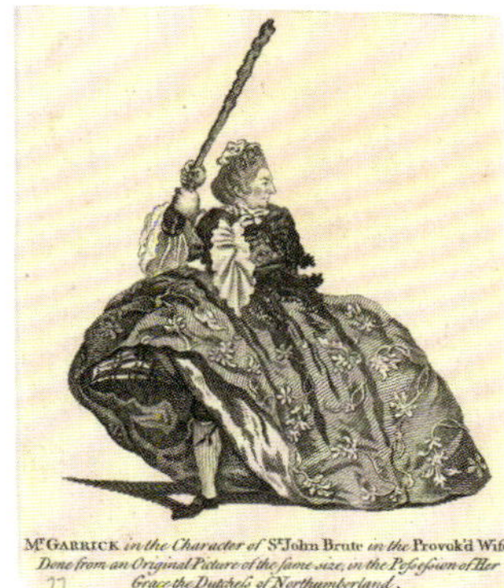

FIG. A.60

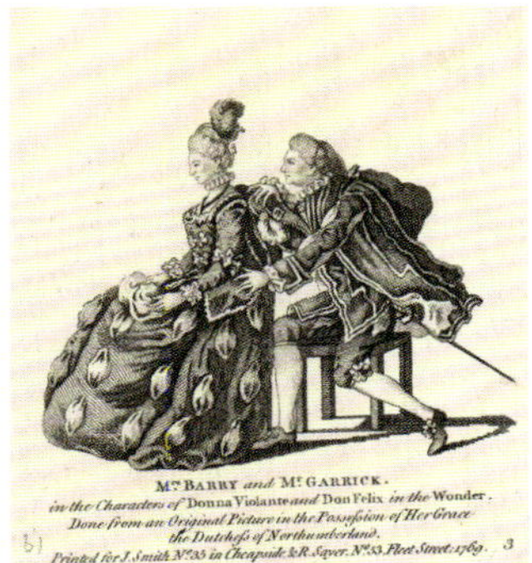

FIG. A.61

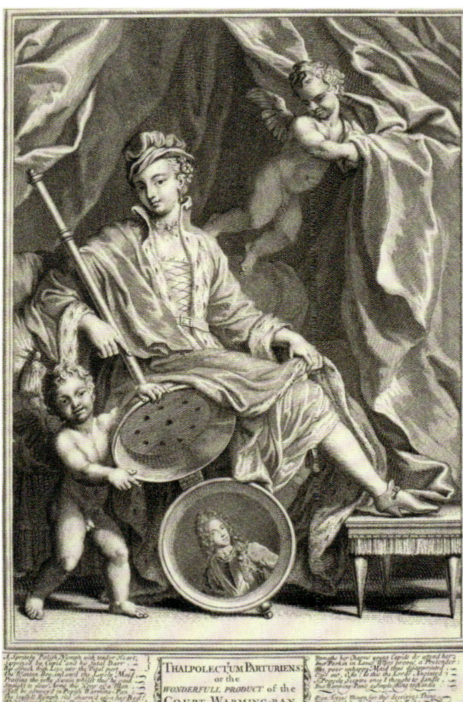
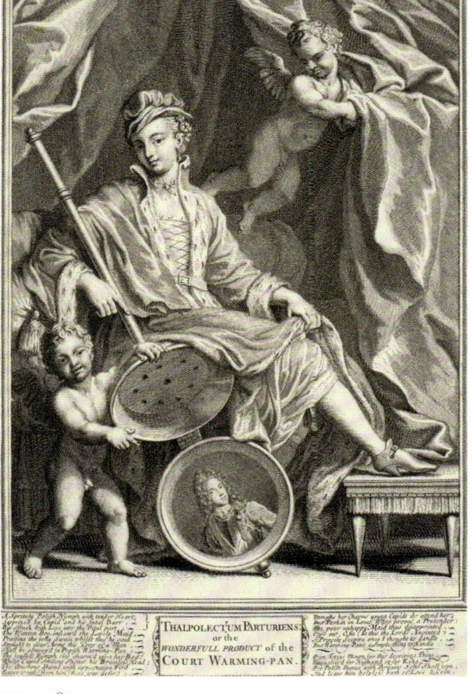

FIG. A.62

FIG. A.63

WILLIAM HOGARTH (1697–1764)
Hudibras: The Frontispiece, 1725
Pen and ink with pencil and wash
23.8 × 33.8 cm
RCIN 913459
OE 332 FIG. 14.12

Purchased with the collection of George Barker, via Colnaghi, on 5 June 1813 (RA GEO/MAIN/28547).

WILLIAM HOGARTH (1697–1764)
Hudibras sallying forth, 1725
Red and black chalks
23.8 × 32.6 cm
RCIN 913460
OE 333 FIG. 14.13

Purchased with the collection of George Barker, via Colnaghi, on 5 June 1813 (RA GEO/MAIN/28547).

ANONYMOUS
Thalpolectrum Parturiens: or the Wonderful Product of the Court Warming-Pan, c.1719–66
Engraving
37.7 × 24.4 cm (sheet)
RCIN 603552 FIG. A.62

Purchased from Colnaghi & Co. on 22 Nov. 1813, for 10s 6d (RA GEO/MAIN/27960).

DENIS DIGHTON (1792–1827)
Russian Army: Officer of the Imperial Guard, 1814
Watercolour over pencil with gum arabic
50.9 × 37.2 cm
RCIN 915144
Haswell, Miller and Dawnay 1966, no. 605 FIG. 9.15

Purchased from the artist on 10 June 1814, for £12 12s (RA GEO/MAIN/26945).

AFTER LIEUTENANT PYM (ACTIVE c.1811)
French Imperial Eagle of the 8th regiment taken at Barrosa, 1811
Etching with hand colouring
35.9 × 25.6 cm (sheet)
RCIN 750667 FIG. A.63

Purchased from Colnaghi & Co. on 31 Oct. 1815, for 5s (RA GEO/MAIN/28080).

GERARD EDELINCK (1640–1707)
Jacques III. Roy d'Angleterre &c, c.1704–7
Engraving
48.5 × 37.6 cm (sheet)
RCIN 603505 FIG. O.15

Purchased from Colnaghi & Co. on 15 Apr. 1816, for 15s (RA GEO/MAIN/28093).

JAMES WATSON (c.1739–90) AFTER CATHERINE READ (1723–78)
His Royal Highness George Prince of Wales & Prince Frederick, c.1766
Mezzotint
52.2 × 40.0 cm (sheet)
RCIN 605074 FIG. A.64

Purchased from Colnaghi & Co. on 29 Apr. 1800, for 12s (RA GEO/MAIN/27147).

JEAN-BAPTISTE ISABEY (1767–1855)
The Congress of Vienna, 1815
Pen and ink with wash
61.0 × 83.0 cm (sight)
RCIN 451893.a
B(MF) 10 FIG. 1.5

Commissioned by Charles Maurice de Talleyrand, but remained in the artist's possession; exhibited by Isabey in London in 1820, where purchased for £600 (with another drawing by the same artist). Arrived at Carlton House on 31 July 1820 (Jutsham II, p. 105).

GEORGE VERTUE (1684–1756)
William Penkethman as Don Lewis in 'Love makes a man' by Colley Cibber, c.1725
Pen and grey wash with watercolour
30.3 × 22.0 cm
RCIN 913579
OE 624 FIG. 14.17

Purchased from Colnaghi & Co. on 16 May 1821, for £14 14s, for George IV's extra-illustrated 'History of the Stage' (RA GEO/MAIN/28323).

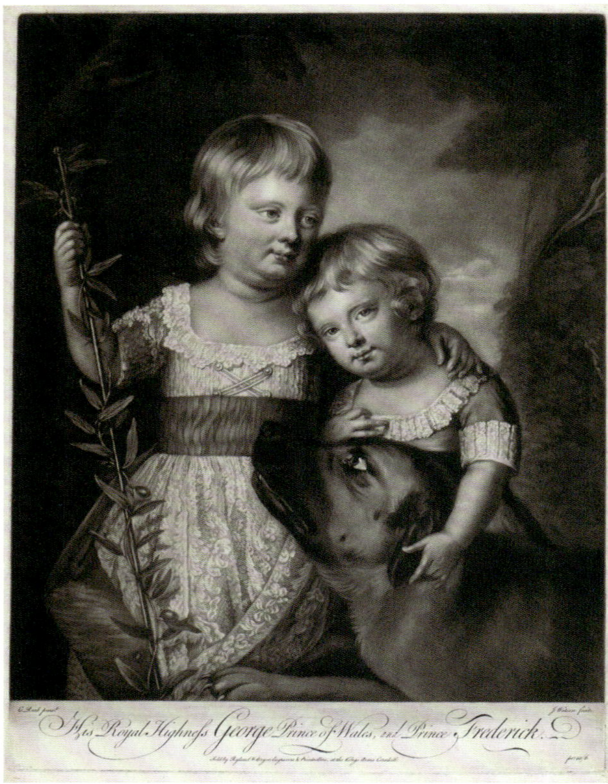

FIG. A.64

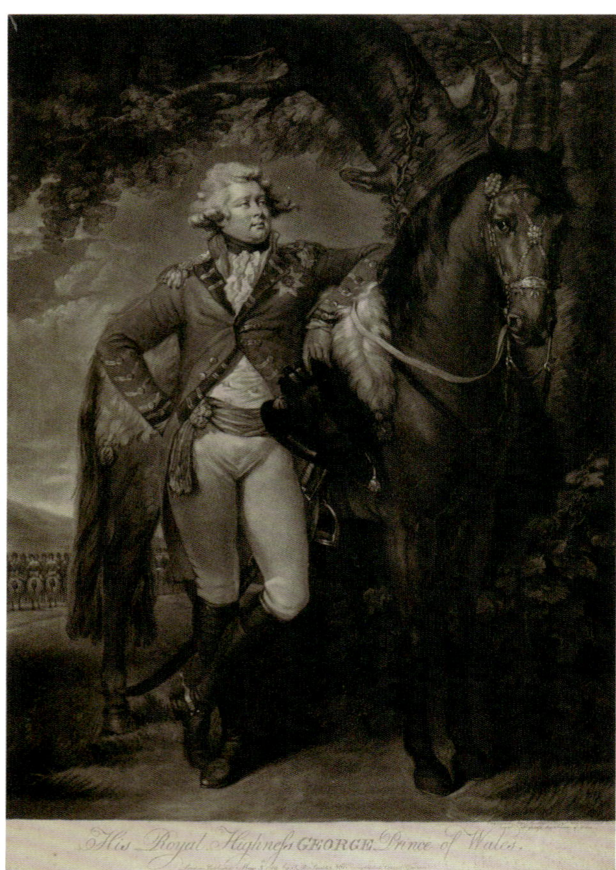

FIG. A.65

PUBLISHED BY JOHN BOWLES (1701?–79) AND CARRINGTON BOWLES (1724–93)
Coronation Procession of James II (right-hand half), *c.*1790
Etching and engraving with hand colouring
59.9 × 48.7 cm
RCIN 750178 FIG. 15.13

Probably the impression purchased on 18 June 1821 (RA GEO/MAIN/28331).

LOUIS CARROGIS DE CARMONTELLE (1717–1806)
Charles-Alexis Brûlart, comte de Genlis (1737–93), *c.*1765
Watercolour with pencil and black and red chalk
35.7 × 23.2 cm (including wash border)
RCIN 913119
B(F) 315 FIG. 14.11

Purchased from Colnaghi & Co. on 20 Sept. 1828 for £1 11s 6d (RA GEO/MAIN/28376).

THOMAS ROWLANDSON (1757–1827)
Filial Piety!, 1788
Etching with hand colouring
25.6 × 37.5 cm (sheet)
RCIN 810287 FIG. 12.9

Probably one of the prints acquired by Queen Victoria from the descendants of Samuel Fores in 1854.

RICHARD COSWAY (1742–1821)
Caroline, Princess of Wales (1768–1821), and Princess Charlotte (1796–1817), *c.*1797
Pencil and watercolour
29.0 × 20.6 cm (sight)
RCIN 452410
OE 151 FIG. 0.21

Probably commissioned by the sitter or by George IV when Prince of Wales in 1797, but not paid for by 1820 (Lloyd 2004, p. 197). According to a note in the Lord Chamberlain's inventory, presented by Caroline, Princess of Wales to Lady Willoughby d'Eresby; in the Royal Collection by 1883–7.

JOHN RAPHAEL SMITH (1751–1812)
George IV when Prince of Wales, *c.*1783
Mezzotint with pencil
61.4 × 45.5 cm (sheet)
RCIN 605110 FIG. 0.23

In the Royal Collection by *c.*1900?

JOHN RAPHAEL SMITH (1751–1812)
AFTER THOMAS GAINSBOROUGH (1727–88)
His Royal Highness George Prince of Wales, 1789
Mezzotint
65.9 × 45.6 cm (sheet)
RCIN 605116 FIG. A.65

Previously in the collection of Thomas Kirk (d. 1797); in the Royal Collection by *c.*1900?

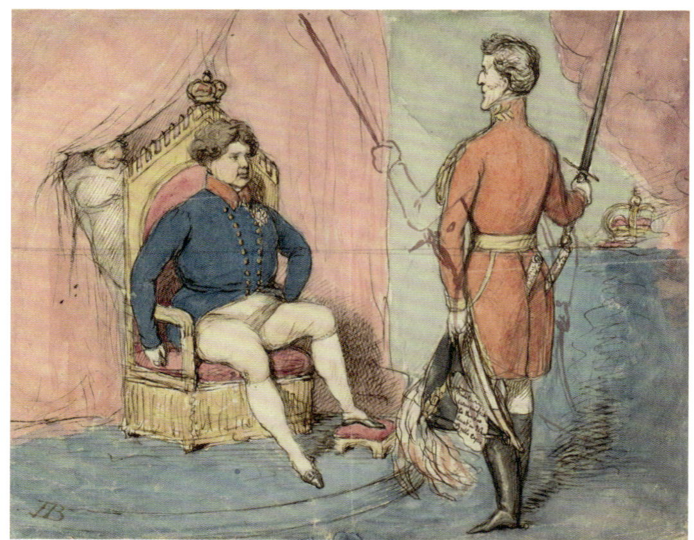

FIG. A.66

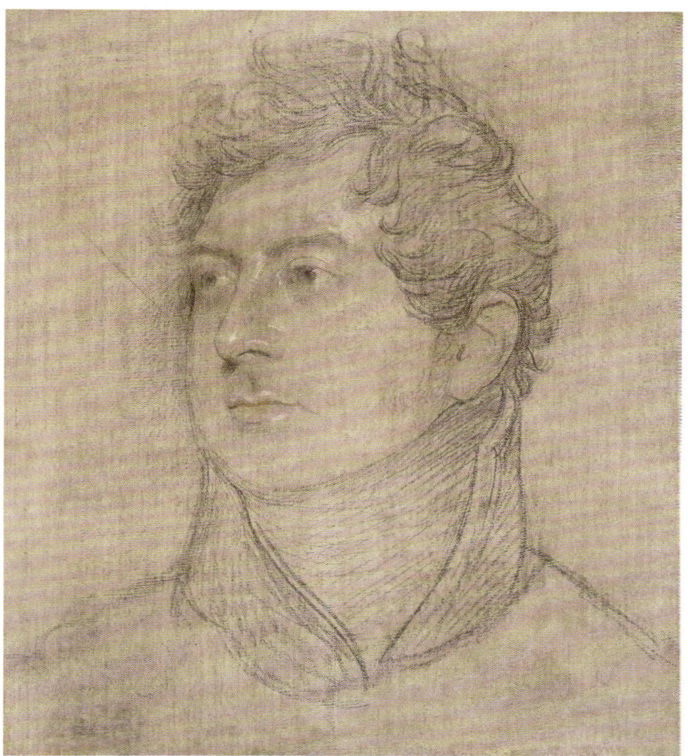

FIG. A.67

JOHN DOYLE (1797–1868)
The Throne in Danger, 1828
Pen and ink over pencil, coloured with watercolour, some changes made to the design in brush
22.8 × 28.5 cm (sheet)
RCIN 917823 FIG. A.66

Purchased 1957.

CHARLES WILLIAMS (1796–1830)
A King-Fisher, 1826
Etching with hand colouring
25.0 × 35.0 cm (sheet)
RCIN 630791 FIG. 13.19

Purchased 2003.

SIR THOMAS LAWRENCE (1769–1830)
Head of George IV, *c.*1820
Black and coloured chalks
40.0 × 36.5 cm (sight)
RCIN 933873 FIG. A.67

Purchased 2004.

ROBERT SEYMOUR (1798–1836)
The Great Joss and his Playthings, *c.*1829
Etching with hand colouring
25.2 × 35.3 cm
RCIN 751279 FIG. 12.6

Presented 2017.

PUBLISHED BY JOHN MARSHALL JUNIOR (ACTIVE 1820)
The Kettle calling the Pot ugly names, 1820
Etching with hand colouring
27.9 × 38.4 cm (sheet)
RCIN 751290 FIG. 0.3

Purchased 2018.

RICHARD COSWAY (1742–1821)
Maria Fitzherbert, *c.*1789
Pencil and watercolour
30.1 × 22.0 cm
RCIN 935221 FIG. 0.17

Purchased 2019.

ARCHITECTURAL PLANS AND VIEWS; INTERIOR DESIGN

CARLTON HOUSE

HENRY HOLLAND (1745–1806)
Carlton House in March 1784, 1784
Pen and ink with wash, annotated in pencil
34.9 × 46.5 cm
RCIN 918937 FIG. A.68

Prepared for George IV when Prince of Wales.

LOUIS BÉLANGER (1736–1816)
The Rebuilding of Carlton House
Pen and ink and watercolour over pencil
31.8 × 44.3 cm
RCIN 913030
OE 61 FIG. 5.2

In the Royal Collection by *c.*1900.

JIROUARD LE GIRARDY (ACTIVE *c.*1789–1800)
Design for the decoration of an interior, perhaps Carlton House, *c.*1795
Pen and ink with watercolour and bodycolour
18.7 × 43.4 cm
RCIN 927995 FIG. A.69

Purchased 1988.

JIROUARD LE GIRARDY (ACTIVE *c.*1789–1800)
Design for the decoration of an interior, perhaps Carlton House, *c.*1795
Pen and ink with watercolour and bodycolour
18.8 × 35.0 cm
RCIN 927996 FIG. A.70

Purchased 1988.

HENRY HOLLAND (1745–1806)
Carleton House, October 1794. Plan of the Principal Floor, 1794
Pen and ink with watercolour and wash
34.0 × 48.6 cm
RCIN 918943 FIG. 5.4

Prepared for George IV when Prince of Wales.

HUMPHRY REPTON (1752–1818)
Conservatory, Carlton House, *c.*1808
Pen and ink with watercolour over pencil
26.5 × 55.4 cm (maximum)
RCIN 917090
OE 489 FIG. A.71

Prepared for George IV when Prince of Wales.

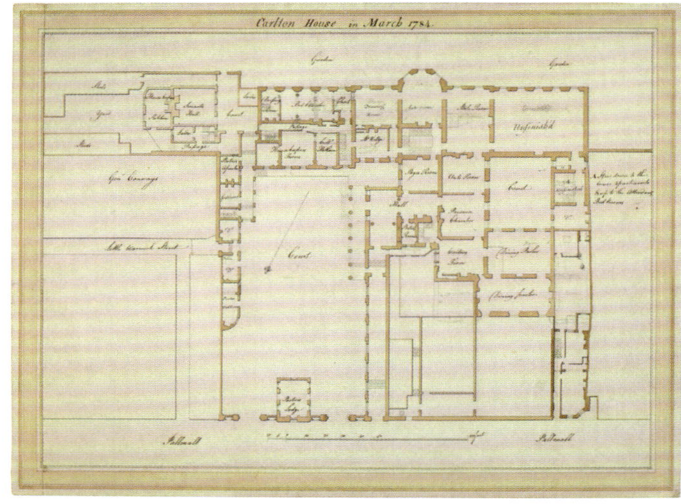

FIG. A.68

HUMPHRY REPTON (1752–1818)
View from the Principal Floor of Carlton House, 1808
Pen and ink with watercolour over pencil
36.5 × 49.0 cm (maximum)
RCIN 917091.a and .b
OE 488 FIGS A.72–73

Prepared for George IV when Prince of Wales.

CHARLES WILD (1781–1835)
The Rose Satin Drawing Room, Carlton House, c.1817
Watercolour and bodycolour with gum arabic over pencil
20.6 × 27.0 cm
RCIN 922180 FIG. 0.5

CHARLES WILD (1781–1835)
The Blue Velvet Room, Carlton House, c.1816
Watercolour and bodycolour with gum arabic over pencil
20.1 × 25.2 cm
RCIN 922184 FIG. 5.22

CHARLES WILD (1781–1835)
The Vestibule, Carlton House, c.1819
Watercolour and bodycolour with gum arabic over pencil
21.1 × 25.4 cm
RCIN 922172 FIG. A.74

CHARLES WILD (1781–1835)
The Gothic Dining Room, Carlton House, 1817
Watercolour and bodycolour with gum arabic over etched outlines
19.5 × 26.3 cm
RCIN 922189 FIG. 5.25

WILLIAM WESTALL (1781–1850)
The South Front, Carlton House, c.1819
Watercolour and bodycolour over pencil
21.2 × 26.9 cm
RCIN 922169 FIG. 0.4

CHARLES WILD (1781–1835)
The Blue Velvet Closet, Carlton House, c.1818
Watercolour and bodycolour with gum arabic over pencil
20.2 × 25.0 cm
RCIN 922185 FIG. 5.23

Presumably acquired for the library at Carlton House, c.1819.

OFFICE OF MOREL & SEDDON
Inventory of Clocks Etc [The Pictorial Inventory], vol. A
Album of watercolours
40.2 × 30.0 cm
RCIN 935559 FIG. 6.15

Prepared by the firm of Morel & Seddon, at a cost of £224 14s (RA LC/ACC/BILLS/1456).

BRIGHTON

HENRY HOLLAND (1745–1806)
Marine Pavilion, Brighton, 1801
Pen and ink with watercolour over pencil
17.2 × 21.4 cm (sight)
RCIN 918957.d FIG. 10.4

Prepared for George IV when Prince of Wales.

HUMPHRY REPTON (1752–1818)
Designs for the Pavilion at Brighton humbly inscribed to His Royal Highness The Prince of Wales, 1806
Manuscript on paper, watercolour illustrations
54.5 × 38.2 cm
RCIN 970493 FIG. A.75

Presented by the artist, 1806.

FIG. A.69

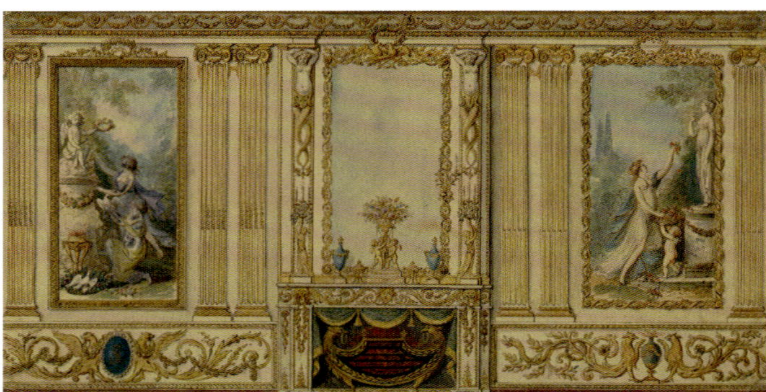

FIG. A.70

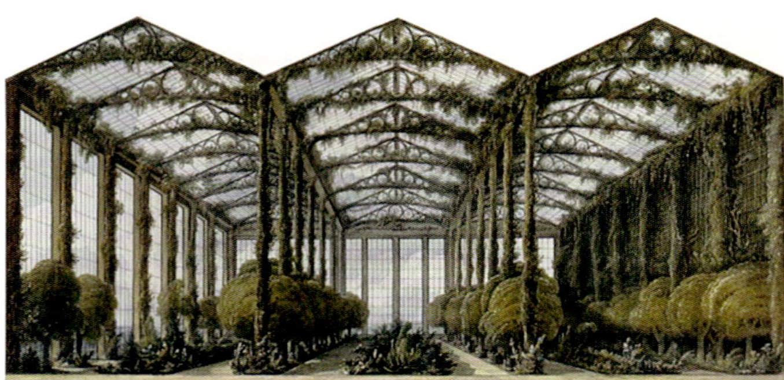

FIG. A.71

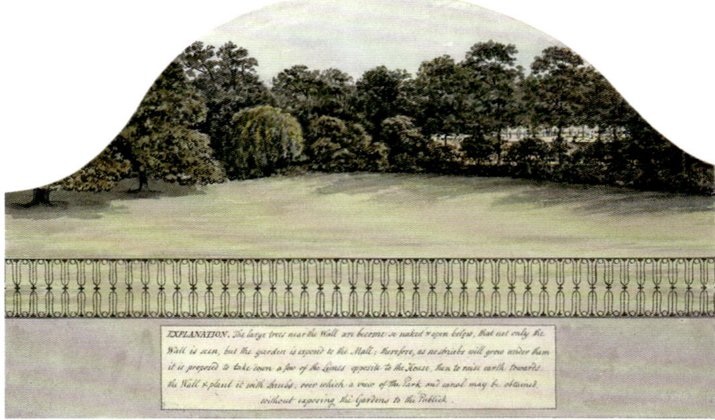

FIG. A.72

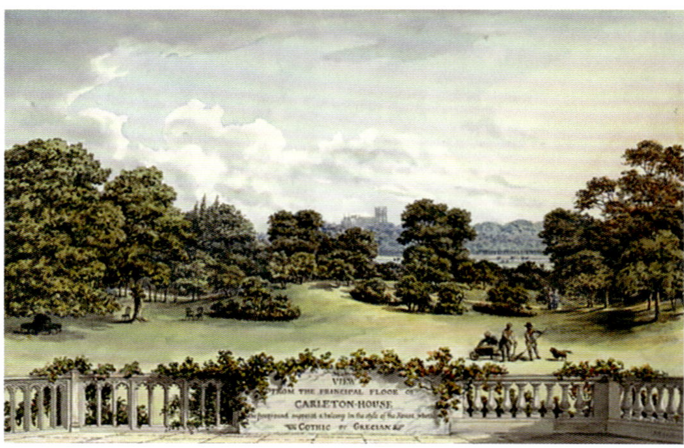

FIG. A.73

WINDSOR CASTLE

OFFICE OF MOREL & SEDDON (ATTRIBUTED TO AUGUSTUS CHARLES PUGIN (*c.*1768–1832))
Design for the south elevation of the Dining Room, Windsor Castle, *c.*1827
Pen and ink with watercolour over pencil
48.7 × 80.9 cm
RCIN 918386 FIG. A.76

Prepared for George IV; purchased 1970.

OFFICE OF MOREL & SEDDON
Design for the west elevation of His Majesty's Writing Room, Windsor Castle, *c.*1826
Pencil and watercolour
40.0 × 55.6 cm
RCIN 918393 FIG. 17.13

Prepared for George IV; purchased 1970.

OFFICE OF MOREL & SEDDON
Design for the east elevation of the Library (the Green Drawing Room), Windsor Castle, *c.*1826
Watercolour and bodycolour over pencil
29.7 × 70.8 cm
RCIN 931282 FIG. 17.11

Prepared for George IV; purchased 1990.

ATTRIBUTED TO JEAN-JACQUES BOILEAU (ACTIVE *c.*1787–1851)
Design for the carpet for the Large Drawing Room (The Crimson Drawing Room), Windsor Castle, *c.*1826
Watercolour and bodycolour with pencil
64.7 × 47.6 cm
RCIN 931283 FIG. 17.8

Prepared for George IV; purchased 1990.

ROYAL LODGE

SIR JEFFRY WYATVILLE (1766–1840)
South East View of King George the 4th cottage in Windsor Great Park, *c.*1830
Pen and ink with watercolour
15.5 × 35.0 cm
RCIN 932768 FIG. 17.17

Purchased 1994.

BOOKS AND MANUSCRIPTS

Statutes of the Most Noble Order of the Garter, 1770–71
Manuscript on paper, watercolour illustrations. 58 pages
26.9 × 21.7 cm
RCIN 1104858 FIG. A.77

Prepared for George IV's installation as a Knight of the Garter, 25 July 1771 (when Prince of Wales).

Acquired 2018.

SIR DAVID DUNDAS (1735–1820)
Cavalry formations, 1775
Manuscript on paper; watercolour illustrations. 86 pages
32.0 × 20.5 cm
RCIN 1047113 FIG. 9.7

Acquired for the library at Carlton House.

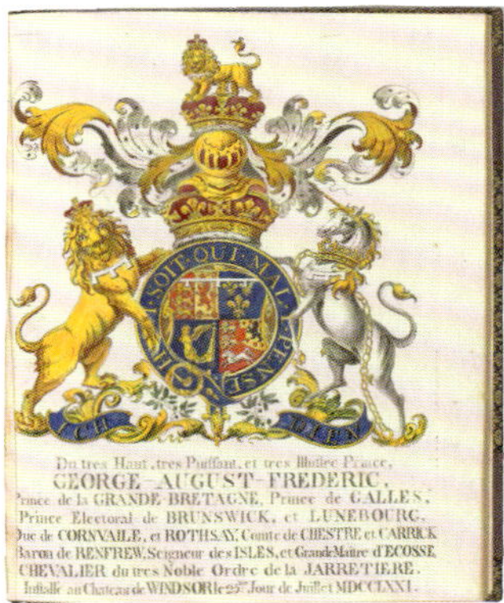

FIG. A.77

PUBLISHED BY MAGIMEL, PARIS
Réglement sur l'uniforme des Généraux, des Officiers des Etats-majors des armées et des places, 1803
Printed book
20.6 × 12.7 cm
RCIN 1082268 FIG. 9.8

Acquired for the library at Carlton House before 1815.

FREDERICK, BARON EBEN (1771–1832)
Observations on the utility of good riflemen both in the infantry & cavalry … to which is added a short manual exercise for mounted chasseurs, *c.*1804–6
Manuscript on paper; watercolour illustrations. 102 pages, 21 illustrated plates
25.0 × 20.7 cm
RCIN 1047356 FIG. 9.3

Dedicated to George IV when Prince of Wales, *c.*1806.

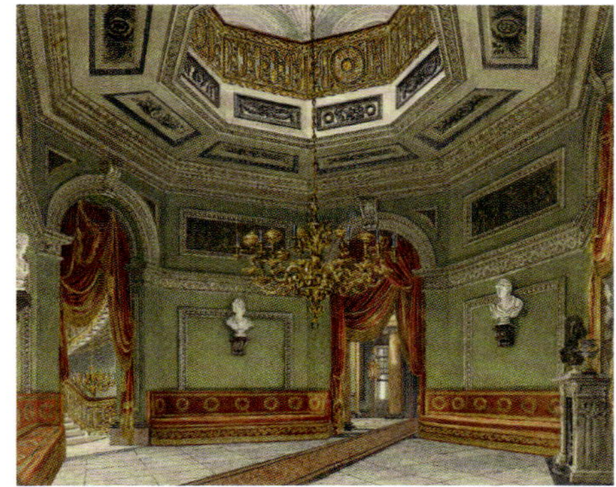

FIG. A.74

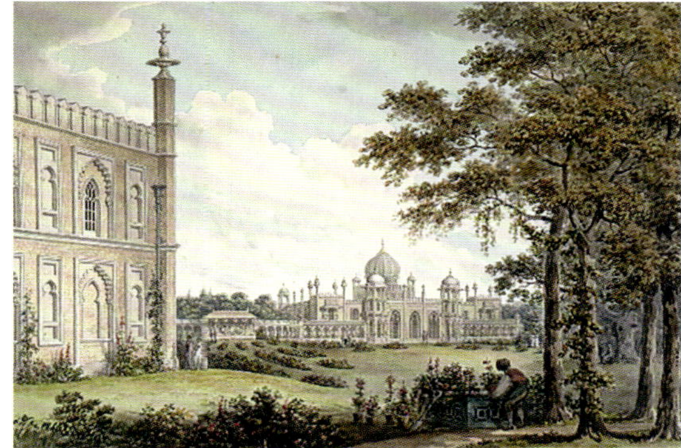

FIG. A.75

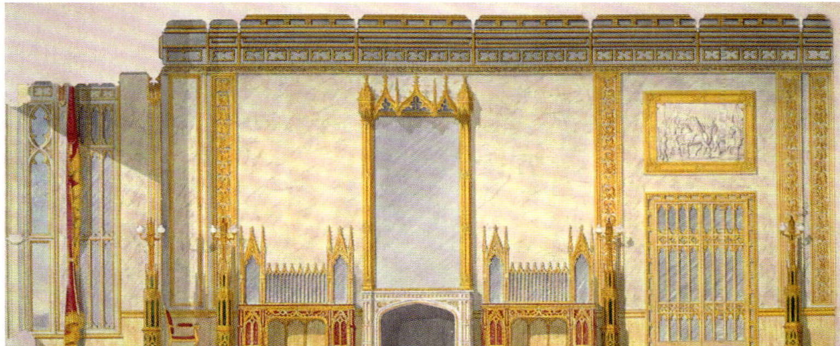

FIG. A.76

BEDFORD MASTER (ACTIVE *c.* EARLY 15TH CENTURY)
The Sobieski Hours, *c.*1430–40
Manuscript on vellum; decorated initials and borders in bodycolour and gold leaf. 234 folios
28.6 × 19.7 cm
RCIN 1142248 FIG. A.78

Bequeathed to George IV when Prince of Wales by Henry Benedict Stuart, Cardinal York in 1807.

CHARLES PERCIER (1764–1838) AND PIERRE-FRANÇOIS-LÉONARD FONTAINE (1762–1853)
Description des Cérémonies et des Fêtes qui ont eu lieu pour le Couronnement de Leurs Majestés Napoléon … et Joséphine, 1807
Printed book
65.8 × 50.2 cm
RCIN 1046693 FIG. 14.7

Acquired for the library at Carlton House, after 1807.

JOHN HAYTER (1756–1818)
A Report upon the Herculaneum manuscripts, in a second letter, addressed, by permission, to His Royal Highness The Prince Regent, 1811
Printed book
31.3 × 25.0 cm
RCIN 1079863 FIG. 14.19

Probably a presentation copy to George IV when Prince Regent from the author, 1811.

JANE AUSTEN (1775–1817)
Emma: a novel in three volumes, 1816
Printed books
18.3 × 11.1 cm
RCINs 1083626, 1080108, 1080109
FIG. 14.1

The presentation copy sent by the publishers John Murray on behalf of the author, Dec. 1815 (John Murray Archive, MS 42001, letter from Austen to Murray, 11 Dec. 1815).

PUBLISHED BY MARTINET, PARIS
Galerie des Enfans de Mars, ou collection des divers uniformes de tous les Corps composant la ci-devant Garde, *c.*1817
28.6 × 20.7 cm
RCIN 1082307 FIG. A.79

Presented by Louis Philippe, duc d'Orléans in 1817.

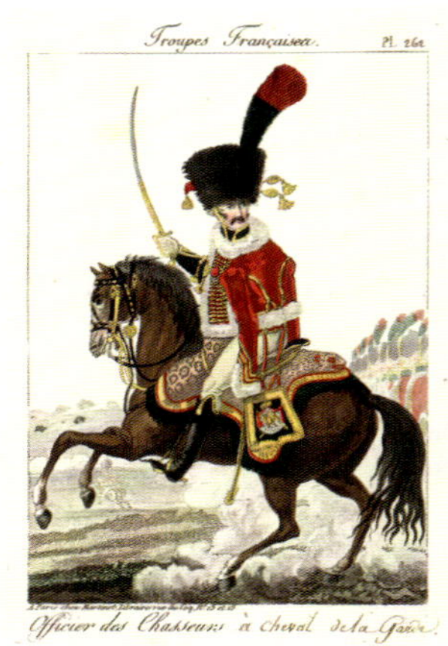

FIG. A.79

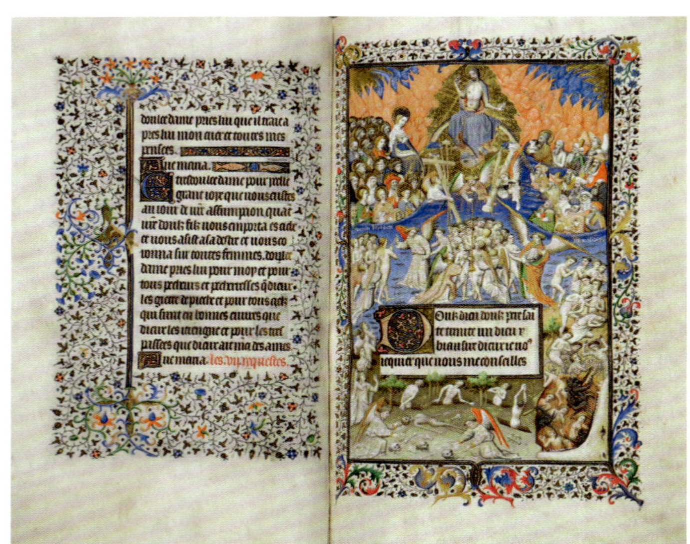

FIG. A.78

ITEMS FROM THE ARMOURY

DURS EGG (1748–1831)
Pair of pistols, 1787
Walnut, steel, gold, silver
38 cm (length)
RCIN 61166.1–2 FIG. 6.22

Purchased from Durs Egg in 1787 (CH Arms Cat., no. 704).

GERMAN (?) WITH LATER ADDITIONS BY RUNDELL, BRIDGE & RUNDELL
Dress sword, mid-17th century
Ivory, steel
96.5 cm (length), blade 80.5 cm (length)
RCIN 67142 FIG. A.80

The hilt purchased from Rundells, 6 July 1802, for £21 (RA GEO/MAIN/26264); blade added subsequently (bill untraced).

PERSIAN
Sabre and scabbard, *c.*1802
Steel, iron, gold, leather
92.3 cm (length)
RCIN 62882 FIG. A.81

Presented by George Pitt, Baron Rivers on 16 Jan. 1802 (CH Arms Cat., no. 1354).

MAORI
Club (*patu onewa*), 18th century
Basalt
31.7 × 7.4 cm
RCIN 62167 FIG. 18.3

First recorded in the Armoury at Carlton House before 1804 (CH Arms Cat., no. 1045).

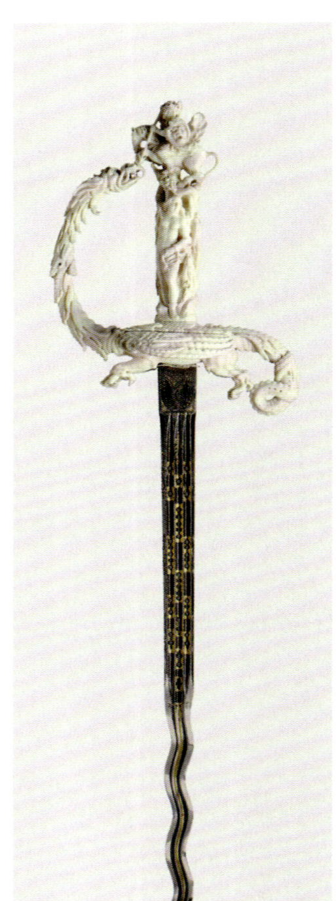

FIG. A.80

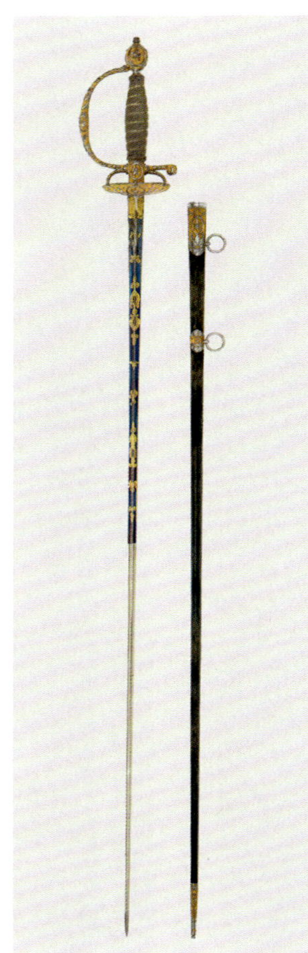

FIG. A.82

FRENCH/GERMAN AND ENGLISH
Small sword and scabbard, 1780
Steel, wood, silver-gilt wire
101.0 cm (length)
RCIN 61292 FIG. A.82

Purchased from Bland of St James's, London, before 1804 (CH Arms Cat., no. 146).

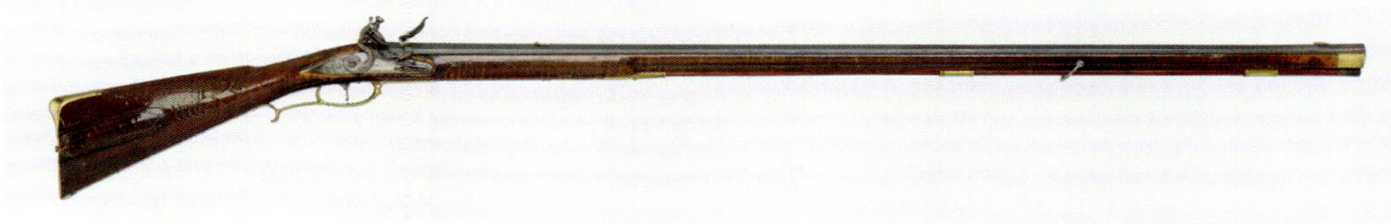

FIG. A.83

NORTH AMERICAN, *Flintlock rifle*, 1775 WITH REFURBISHMENT BY DURS EGG (1748–1831), *c.*1802
Maple, steel, brass, silver
154.0 × 16.0 cm
RCIN 61069 FIG. 18.11

Presented by Colonel George Hanger, before 1804 (CH Arms Cat., no. 794).

JOHN CHRISTIAN OERTER (ACTIVE 1747–77)
Flintlock long gun, 1775
Maple, steel, brass, silver
154.0 × 20.0 × 5.0 cm
RCIN 61071 FIG. A.83

Presented by Colonel George Hanger, before 1804 (CH Arms Cat., no. 796).

ENGLISH OR FRENCH WITH BLADE FROM SOLINGEN, GERMANY
Arming sword, 1600–25
Steel, iron, wood
102.3 cm (length), blade 85.9 cm (length)
RCIN 62964 FIG. 9.16

Presented by Major-General Sir Francis Thomas Hammond, before 1804 (CH Arms Cat., no. 222).

INDIAN (?)
Dagger and sheath, *c.*1800
Jade, gold, silver, steel, enamel (dagger); wood, rubies, emeralds, textile (sheath)
37.8 cm (length)
RCIN 11509 FIG. A.84

Acquired *c.*1802–4 (CH Arms Cat., no. 1249).

ENGLISH (BIRMINGHAM)
Parade breastplate, 1806
Steel, velvet, silk
49.6 × 38.8 cm
RCIN 67162
Norman and Eaves 2016, no. 46
FIG. 9.13

Made for George IV when Prince of Wales, 1806. Possibly presented by Baron Charles Hompetsch to act as a pattern for the uniform of the 10th Light Dragoons (CH Arms Cat., no. 1808).

JOHANN GOTTFRIED HÄNISCH (1696–1778), DRESDEN
Crossbow, *c.*1750–75
Steel, mahogany, ebony, horn
65.3 × 55.0 cm
RCIN 61425 FIG. 6.21

Purchased from Colonel Benningson in 1807 (CH Arms Cat., no. 1873).

FIRST NATIONS
Coat, *c.*1800
Caribou skin, leather
117.0 cm (length)
RCIN 72705 FIG. 18.5

Presented by Benjamin Bloomfield in 1807 (CH Arms Cat., no. 1874).

INDIAN (?)
Dagger and sheath, 1807
Jade, gold, silver, steel, enamel (dagger); wood, rubies, emeralds, textile (sheath)
27.7 × 4.5 × 1.4 cm
RCIN 11508 FIG. A.85

Presented by Francis Seymour, 3rd Marquess of Hertford on 21 July 1807 (CH Arms Cat., no. 1848).

NORTHERN EUROPEAN WITH BLADE FROM SOLINGEN, GERMANY
Rapier, *c.*1640
Iron, gold
107.6 cm (length)
RCIN 62994 FIG. 9.17

Presented by Walsh Porter on 12 Aug. 1807 (CH Arms Cat, no. 1868).

PERSIAN
Sword (shamshir) and scabbard, *c.*1800
Watered crucible steel, gold, walrus ivory, wood, leather and textile
91.6 cm (length)
RCIN 62880 FIG. 18.6

Purchased from Mr Jackson, 15 Oct. 1809 (CH Arms Cat., no. 1993).

JAPANESE
Samurai sword and scabbard, 1813
Steel, *shakudo*, gold, lacquer, wood
79.2 cm (length)
RCIN 72783 FIG. A.86

Presented by James Duff, 4th Earl of Fife on 23 Apr. 1813 (CH Arms Cat., no. 2345).

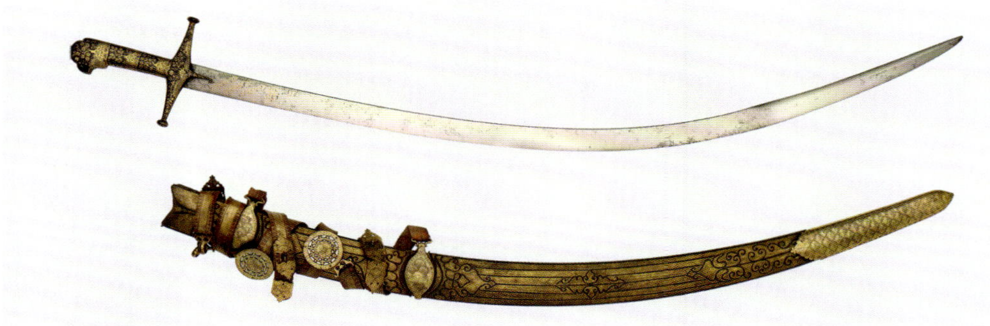

FIG. A.81

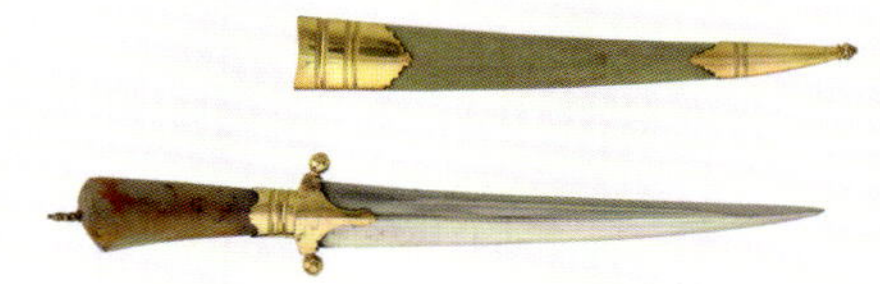

FIG. A.84

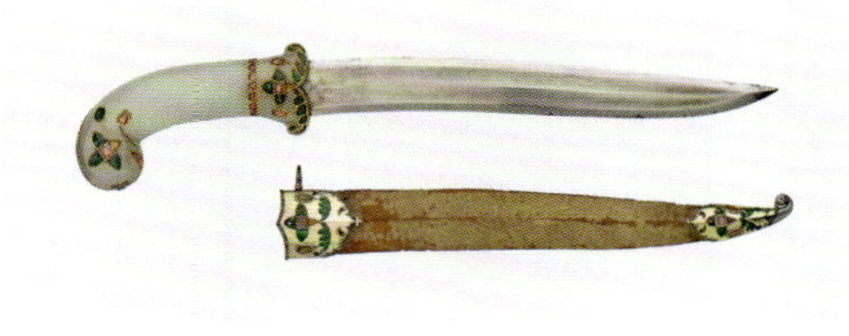

FIG. A.85

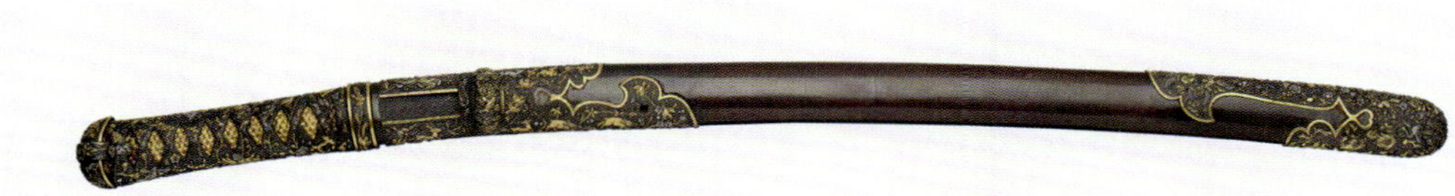

FIG. A.86

INDONESIAN (?)
Kris and scabbard, 1813
Steel, ivory, wood, gold, diamonds
47.4 cm (length)
RCIN 62064 FIG. A.87

Presented by Sir Robert Townsend Farquhar, Governor of Mauritius, on 23 June 1813 (CH Arms Cat., no. 2355).

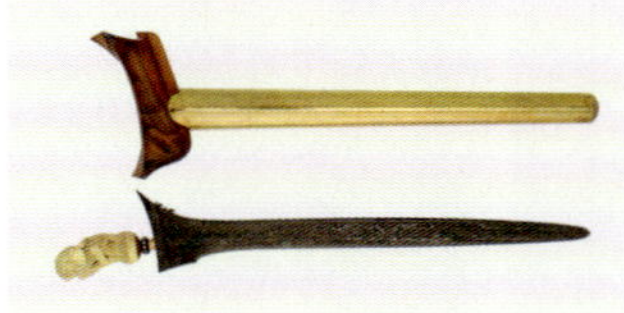

FRENCH
Baton and case, 1804
Wood, velvet, gold, gold thread
47.7 × 4.2 cm
RCIN 61176 FIG. 15.6

Created for Marshal Jean-Baptiste Jourdan and taken by Arthur Wellesley (later Duke of Wellington) as a prize at the Battle of Vittoria; presented by him on 5 July 1813 (CH Arms Cat., no. 2358).

INDONESIAN
Kris and scabbard, 1817
Steel, wood, diamonds, gold
47.5 cm (length)
RCIN 62066 FIG. A.88

Presented by Stamford Raffles on 10 May 1817 (CH Arms Cat., no. 2716).

INDONESIAN (?)
Kris and scabbard, 1819
Steel, ivory, wood, gold, diamonds
47.4 cm (length)
RCIN 62063 FIG. A.89

Presented by Sir Evan Nepean, 26 Oct. 1819 (CH Arms Cat., no. 2391).

ALGERIAN
Pair of pistols, 1800–19
Hardwood, steel, coral, silver
49.0 cm (length)
RCINS 62421 and 62422 FIG. 18.9

Part of a gift from the Dey of Algiers, presented in 1811 and 1819.

TURKISH (?)
Pistol, late 18th century
Steel, silver gilt
49.0 cm (length)
RCIN 62922 FIG. A.90

Purchased from Mr Davis, Jan. 1819 (CH Arms Cat., no. 2875).

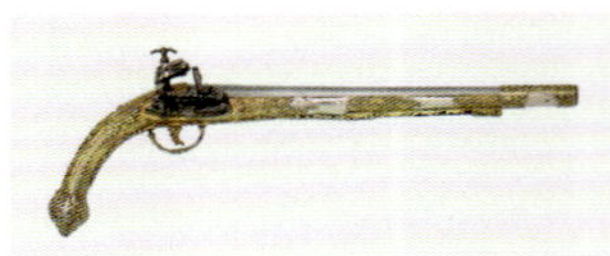

GEORGE HUNTER & CO., EDINBURGH
Dirk, scabbard, knife and fork, 1822
Boxwood, steel, gold, silver, cairngorm, aquamarine, amethyst, silk velvet
Dirk: 54.4 cm (length); scabbard: 42.1 cm (length); knife: 25.5 cm (length); fork: 20.3 cm (length)
RCIN 29023 FIG. 16.12

Supplied for George IV's visit to Edinburgh in Aug. 1822 (RA GEO/MAIN/29600).

HAWAIIAN
Cape ('ahu'ula), *c.*1824
Feather, bark cloth
52.0 × 84.0 cm
RCIN 69994 FIG. 18.10

A gift from King Kamehameha II and Queen Kamamalu of the Sandwich Islands in 1824 (CH Arms Cat., no. 3216).

ITEMS ASSOCIATED WITH THE CORONATION

RUNDELL, BRIDGE & RUNDELL
The Diamond Diadem, 1820–1
Diamond, pearl, silver, gold
19.0 × 19.0 × 7.5 cm
RCIN 31702 FIG. 0.2

Purchased for £8,216, adjusted to £7,126 (RA GEO/MAIN/25994).

JOHN MEYER (*c.*1753–*c.*1830)
Surcoat, 1820–1
Silk, velvet, gold and silver thread, sequins
105.0 cm (length)
RCIN 62955 FIG. 15.15

For the coronation (bill untraced).

JOHN MEYER (*c.*1753–*c.*1830)
Stole, 1821
Cloth of silver, gold thread, silk, gold, sequins
124.5 cm (length)
RCIN 62953 FIG. 15.16

Supplied for the coronation, for £134 (LC2/50 p.18).

PROBABLY GERMAN, WITH ADDITIONS BY RUNDELL, BRIDGE & RUNDELL
Sword and scabbard, *c.*1750–1820
Steel, gold, diamond, ruby; wood, fishskin, diamond, gold (scabbard)
96.6 cm (length); 78.0 cm (blade length)
RCIN 67134 FIG. 6.6

A bill for alterations and the mounting of additional diamonds to an existing sword hilt was submitted by Rundells on 7 Aug. 1820 (RA GEO/MAIN/25995).

BENEDETTO PISTRUCCI (1784–1855)
Medal commemorating the coronation of George IV, 1821
Silver
3.5 cm (diameter)
RCIN 443328 FIG. 3.2

Acquired during the present reign.

RUNDELL, BRIDGE & RUNDELL
Cast of the Imperial State Crown, 1823
Gilt bronze, velvet, ermine
36.3 × 29.0 × 30.0 cm
RCIN 50435 FIG. 15.18

Bought, together with a stand and glass shade, in May 1823, for £38 (RA GEO/MAIN/26304).

JOHN WHITTAKER (d. 1831)
Ceremonial of the Coronation of King George IV in the Abbey of St Peter's, 1823
Printed on japan vellum; gold letterpress, stipple engraving with etching and aquatint, and hand colouring
69.5 × 60.5 cm
RCIN 1005090 FIG. 15.22

Probably belonged to George IV.

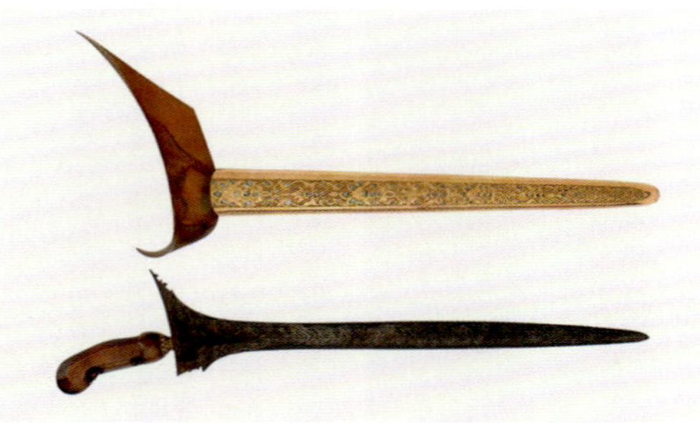

FIG. A.88

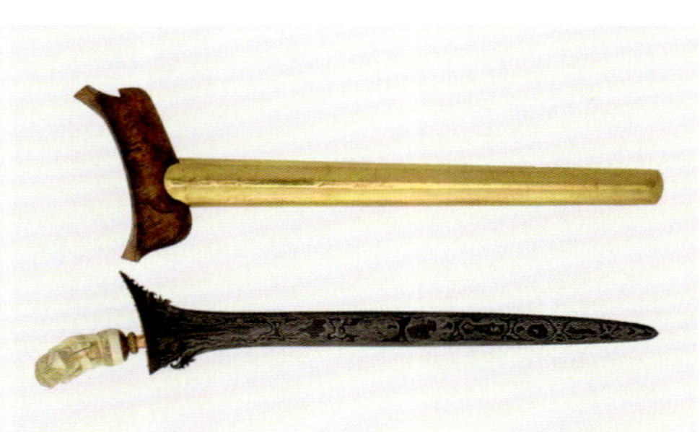

FIG. A.89

NOTES

INTRODUCTION

GEORGE IV: ART AND SPECTACLE

1. Gallatin 1914, p. 72, entry for 5 May 1815.
2. Ibid., p. 269, entry for 15 Apr. 1827.
3. Jerningham 1896, II, p. 155.
4. *The Times*, 16 July 1830, editorial.
5. Pyne 1819; Watkin 1984.
6. H. Roberts 2001, p. 26, quoting Wyatville's pupil, Henry Ashton, who attributed this taste entirely to George IV.
7. Ibid., pp. 27–8.
8. CW, p. 39.
9. There is no existing bill for this purchase but the piece is recorded in the Bow Room of Carlton House in 1826 (CH Porcelain Inventory 1826, no. 73).
10. RCIN 2431; now believed to have been in the collection of Marie Adélaïde, daughter of Louis XV.
11. RCINs 31207 and 2544 respectively.
12. RCIN 61171.
13. Wilkie was knighted in 1836.
14. General Sir Tomkyns Hilgrove Turner, quoted in Loveday 1964, p. 101.
15. See Jones 2017, pp. 24–6.
16. Smith 1999, p. 26.
17. Ibid., p. 30.
18. RA GEO/MAIN/16476–7 and 41822–3; Aspinall 1963–71, I, no. 128, p. 164, Col. G. Hotham to the Prince of Wales, 27 Oct. 1784.
19. See, for example, the instances cited in J. Goodison 2017.
20. Gash 1979; Hilton 2006.
21. Quoted in Hilton 2006, p. 270.
22. The prices in the following text, where possible, are given in the same form as they appear in the original invoices and so both guineas and pounds, shillings and pence are used.
23. London 1991 (which built on the extensive research of Sir Geoffrey de Bellaigue); H. Roberts 2001.
24. CW, Millar 1986, Norman and Eaves 2016, Ayers 2016 and De Bellaigue 2009 respectively.
25. Parissien 2001 and Lloyd 1995 respectively.

CHAPTER 1

'FIRST GENTLEMAN OF EUROPE'

1. Melville 1906, p. 1.
2. As he was called – perhaps through gritted teeth – by the Duke of Wellington in Parliament shortly after his death; *The Times*, 30 June 1830, p. 4, quoting the duke's speech in the House of Lords on 29 June.
3. Robbins Landon 1959, pp. 122–3, J. Haydn to Maria Anna von Genzinger, 20 Dec. 1791, following a two-day visit to Oatlands, Surrey (home of the Duke and Duchess of York) at the invitation of the Prince of Wales.
4. De Bellaigue 2009, I, pp. 7–9.
5. George's use of agents is discussed by Rufus Bird in ch. 6.
6. Granville 1916, II, p. 120, Lady Bessborough to Granville Leveson Gower, 9 Oct. 1805.
7. Reeve 1899, I, p. 246, entry for 29 Nov. 1829.
8. Williams 1831, I, pp. 338–9, T. Lawrence to Miss Croft, May 1814.
9. Taylor 1926, I, pp. 169, 197.
10. The remark is only recorded at second-hand, as reported in a letter from the poet Thomas Moore to James Corry: Russell 1853–6, VIII, p. 97.
11. Summerson 1980, chs 5 and 6.
12. *The Times*, 21 Apr. 1814.
13. For the visit of the Russian emperor and the King of Prussia, see Nicolson 1945, ch. VII.
14. Maxwell 1903, I, p. 196; T. Creevey to his wife, 14 June 1814.
15. Summerson 1980, pp. 97–9.
16. *Quarterly Review*, 56 (1836), p. 309.
17. Quoted in Londonderry 1830, p. 335.
18. *Dublin University Magazine*, 25, Mar. 1845, p. 343.
19. For the gift of casts to the Royal Academy see Postle 2018, pp. 482–6.
20. For Canova's mission see Eustace 1997.
21. RCIN 2038. Quoted from a letter from Canova to Count Leopoldo Cicognara, Jan. 1816; Honour and Mariuz 2002, p. 39, no. 26.
22. Marsden 2013, p. 164.
23. Ibid., p. 163, with sources.
24. Williams 1831, I, p. 352.
25. RCIN 2039.
26. Leoni 2013, p. 135.
27. RA GEO/MAIN/27064–5; Aspinall 1938, III, no. 1210, p. 123, W.R. Hamilton to Sir C. Long, 12 August 1825.
28. Vigée-Lebrun 1984, II, p. 130.
29. MS HCB Br 208, Hans Conrad Bodmer collection, Beethoven-Haus, Bonn.
30. Kelly 2003, pp. 121–54.
31. H. Roberts 2001, pp. 78, 82 and 93 (fig. 85). The present-day location of this object is unknown.
32. RCIN 918414.
33. See also Rebecca Lyons' discussion of the Waterloo Chamber paintings in ch. 3.
34. The author ('W.H.') of a description of the vase published in *The Naval and Military Magazine* (2, 1827, pp. 368–73) pointed out the parallel with a story told by Pausanias of the fate of some blocks of marble taken by the Persian army to Greece in readiness to carve a monument to their forthcoming victory. After they were in fact defeated, Phidias was instructed to use the blocks for a statue of Nemesis. See also Busco 1994, pp. 53–7.
35. The reliefs were never fitted to the arch. Later they were applied to the East Front of the palace itself. The bronze statue was subsequently erected in Trafalgar Square. See Saint 1997.
36. Coghlan 1833, p. 8.
37. Two early drawings on this theme, which their format would suggest were for the Throne Room, are in the Yale Center for British Art, New Haven, CT, B1975.2.44–5.
38. See Marsden 2001.
39. See especially the contributions of E. van Wezel and A. von Buttlar in Bergvelt *et al.* 2009.
40. Londonderry 1853, II, p. 429.
41. Ibid., p. 453.
42. For a description of London as a commercial capital as distinct from a court city, see Fox 1992.
43. These are terms that recur in the accounts of Morel & Seddon for the furnishing of Windsor Castle. See H. Roberts 2001.

CHAPTER 2

MAN OF FASHION: GEORGE, PRINCE OF WALES AND HIS IMAGE

1. Thackeray 1879, p. 92. Thackeray's American lectures were first published in 1860.
2. Ellenborough 1881, II, p. 100. Awkward though the picture's composition was, Wilkie's portrait still tactfully omitted George's flesh-coloured leggings.
3. Bessborough 1955, p. 289.
4. RA GEO/MAIN/43404–7; Aspinall 1963–71, I, pp. 55–6, Prince George to Prince Frederick, 30 Mar. 1781.
5. Steuart 1910, II, pp. 404–5.
6. On 30 Mar. 1782 Grace Dalrymple Elliott gave birth to a daughter, Georgina, allegedly fathered by the prince. She was subsequently passed on as mistress to the duc d'Orléans, and in 1786 moved to Paris to be nearer to him. Imprisoned in 1793, she survived the Terror and died in Paris in 1823.
7. Aspinall 1963–71, II, p. 96.
8. Lloyd 1995, p. 8.
9. Barnett 1995, p. 170.
10. Mansel 2005 (p. 57) provides an example of George III dressing splendidly.
11. See, for example, Williams's cruel print of Aug. 1816, *A View of the R-G-T's Bomb* (BM SATIRES 12803).
12. Brummell had enlisted in the 10th as a cornet in 1794.
13. Jesse 1844, I, pp. 30–1.
14. Ribeiro 1995, p. 100.
15. Wilson 1825, I, p. 101.
16. Ribeiro 1995, pp. 100–1.
17. Jesse 1844, I, p. 62.
18. Kelly 2005, p. 172.
19. Brummell's use of buff-and-blue combinations derived not, as the Whig doctrine had it, from George Washington's troops, but from the uniform he had worn at Eton as a 'poleman' at the school's annual Montem initiation ceremony on Salt Hill in Slough.
20. Ribeiro 1995, p. 99.
21. Ibid., p. 100.
22. RA GEO/MAIN/29583.
23. Jesse 1844, II, p. 7.
24. RA GEO/MAIN/29210, 29230, 29231.

25. Farington 1978–84, V, p. 1932, entry for 10 Nov. 1802.
26. Millar 1967, pp. 530–2.
27. RA GEO/MAIN/48576; Aspinall 1963–71, IV, p. 298, Duke of Cambridge to George, 24 July 1802.
28. RA GEO/MAIN/44916–7; Aspinall 1963–71, IV, p. 423, Duke of Clarence to Prince of Wales, ?autumn 1803.
29. RA GEO/MAIN/39041–3; Aspinall 1963–71, III, p. 34, Prince of Wales to Henry Dundas, 1 Mar. 1795.
30. RA GEO/MAIN/39065–8; Aspinall 1962–70, II, p. 313, Prince of Wales to George III, 9 Mar. 1795.
31. Amherst's age – he had been born in 1717 – had already prompted his supercession by George's brother, the Duke of York, in Feb. 1795.
32. RA GEO/MAIN/39076–7; Aspinall 1962–70, II, p. 329, George III to the Prince of Wales, 8 Apr. 1795.
33. Nigel Arch in London 1991, p. 144.
34. See for example Isaac Cruikshank's *The Dandy Taylor* of May 1819.
35. RA GEO/MAIN/39480–1; Aspinall 1963–71, III, pp. 427–8, Prince of Wales to George III, 25 Apr. 1798.
36. RA GEO/MAIN/39900–1; Aspinall 1963–71, IV, p. 386 (Prince of Wales to H. Addington, 18 July 1803); RA GEO/MAIN/39968–9; Aspinall 1963–71, IV, p. 425 (Prince of Wales to Duke of York, 2 Oct. 1803); RA GEO/MAIN/42365–8; Aspinall 1963–71, IV, p. 395 (Prince of Wales to George III, 6 Aug. 1803); RA GEO/MAIN/39922; Aspinall 1963–71, IV, p. 396 (George III to Prince of Wales, 7 Aug. 1803).
37. RA GEO/MAIN/42950; OM, I, p. 5.
38. Excerpt from a poem first published in *The Examiner*, 15 Mar. 1812.
39. Quoted in Mollo 1997, pp. 99, 104.

CHAPTER 3

PRINCELY SPLENDOUR AND POSTERITY: GEORGE IV'S PATRONAGE AND DISPLAY OF PORTRAITURE

The author would like to thank the Paul Mellon Centre and Wolfson College, Cambridge, for supporting her research.

1. For this threat see Solkin 2018.
2. For a discussion of portraits of George IV at the Royal Academy see Hallett 2004.
3. For more information see L. Brown 1980, I, 84, pp. 172–3.
4. RA GEO/MAIN/43482–3; Aspinall 1963–71, I, no. 53, p. 79, Prince of Wales to Prince Frederick, 24 Dec. 1781.
5. RA GEO/MAIN/43508–9; Aspinall 1963–71, I, no. 60, p. 85, Prince Frederick to the Prince of Wales, 29 Mar. 1782.
6. RA GEO/MAIN/43498–9; Aspinall 1963–71, I, no. 57, p. 83, Prince of Wales to Prince Frederick, 1 Mar. 1782. 'Gerrard' refers to Viscount Lake, at the time First Equerry to the Prince of Wales, and the picture is referenced in the bill illustrated as Fig. 3.3.
7. RA GEO/MAIN/43537–9; Aspinall 1963–71, I, no. 66, pp. 93–4, Prince of Wales to Prince Frederick, 15 Oct. 1782.
8. RA GEO/ADD/10/4; Aspinall 1963–71, II, no. 762, p. 367, Princess Augusta to the Prince of Wales, 25 June 1793.
9. RA GEO/MAIN/26791 or version in TNA HO73/19.
10. RA GEO/MAIN/26793.
11. Reynolds Ledgers Vols I and II, Fitzwilliam Museum, Cambridge, transcribed in Cormack 1968–70, pp. 105–69.
12. The original work is recorded in a mezzotint; it was cut down in the reign of Queen Victoria and the strips that were removed were destroyed. The cropped painting survives as RCIN 400206.
13. RA GEO/MAIN/26806.
14. The original was given to the equally Francophile Mrs Fitzherbert and has remained outside the Royal Collection. It is represented in the Collection by a large enamel copy by Henry Bone (RCIN 405173). George also acquired Vigée-Lebrun's portrait of Charles-Alexandre de Calonne (RCIN 406988), the epitome of *ancien régime* style and nobility.
15. The contemporary portraits purchased and commissioned by George are among those catalogued in OM.
16. Farington 1978–84, XI, p. 3919, entry for 27 Apr. 1811.
17. See, for example, Hallett 2018.
18. Farington 1978–84, II, p. 621, entry for Weds. 27 July 1796.
19. *Morning Herald*, Tues. 11 Apr. 1786.
20. *General Evening Post*, 25–27 Apr. 1786.
21. RA GEO/MAIN/43646–7; Aspinall 1963–71, I, pp. 145–6, Prince of Wales to Prince Frederick, 16 May 1784.
22. Coutts inv. document no. 15145 of 1793 also records busts of these two brothers displayed in Carlton House.
23. *Morning Post and Daily Advertiser*, Fri. 12 Mar. 1784.
24. Coutts inv. document no. 15145.
25. A more comprehensive discussion of these pictures at Carlton House can be found in Shawe-Taylor 2013.
26. TNA HO73/23.
27. CH inv. 1816, no. 45, and CH inv. 1819, no. 48.
28. CH inv. 1819 nos 60, 62 and 63. *Francis Russell, 5th Duke of Bedford* (RCIN 405408; OM 841); *Francis Rawdon-Hastings, 2nd Earl of Moira and 1st Marquess of Hastings* (RCIN 405410; OM 842); and *John Jervis, Baron Jervis and Earl St Vincent*, RCIN 405902 (OM 851).
29. Both works, along with others, were victims of a fire at Carlton House in 1824.
30. These were commissioned by the 1st Marquess Townshend and were presented to George in 1810 by Townshend's widow.
31. For a more detailed account of the genesis of the Waterloo Chamber, see again Shawe-Taylor 2013.
32. This work is now in the National Gallery, London (NG 4257). It was shown at the Royal Academy in 1790 but not favourably received by the king and queen, and remained with the artist.
33. OSB, MS File 19614: Sir Thomas Lawrence to Anne Bloxam, 1814.
34. OM (pp. xxxii–vi) and Levey 2005 (pp. 184–5) note the original idea from Lady Anne Barnard for two group portraits; some of the beginnings of the correspondence with Lady Anne can be found in the Royal Academy archives at LAW/2/77.
35. Levey 2005 (pp. 176 and 191) gives a good overview of the reception and the behaviour of these two sitters in London.
36. Williams 1831, II, p. 6.

CHAPTER 4

GEORGE IV AS A COLLECTOR OF PORTRAIT MINIATURES

1. Benson and Esher 1907, I, p. 16.
2. For example, Henry Bone's accounts for 18 June to 4 Aug. 1806 list two enamels of the Prince of Wales set in lockets and two in rings, for which the prince paid £105: RA GEO/MAIN/27343.
3. Toynbee 1928, p. 79.
4. Lloyd 1995, p. 6.
5. *Princess Sophia* (RCIN 420001); miniature of Princess Charlotte in a ring, untraced.
6. Lloyd 2004, p. 196.
7. RA GEO/MAIN/50258; Aspinall 1963–71, I, no. 148, p. 201, Prince of Wales to Mrs Fitzherbert, 3 Nov. 1785.
8. Sold Christie's, London, 6 July 2017 (lot 14).
9. *The Lady's Monthly Museum*, 1814, 16, p. 2.
10. RA GEO/MAIN/25872.

CHAPTER 5

THE CONSTRUCTION, DECORATION AND DEMOLITION OF GEORGE IV'S CARLTON HOUSE

1. The history of the house before the prince's involvement is outlined in 'Carlton House' in Gater and Hiorns 1940, pp. 69–76, and Colvin 1976, pp. 138–9.
2. The site is today occupied by Waterloo Place.
3. Colvin 1973, p. 308.
4. In the early 1780s he was still the duc de Chartres, succeeding as duc d'Orléans in 1785.
5. Such as Benham Park (1774–5) for the 6th Baron Craven and Berrington Hall (1778–81) for Thomas Harley, former Lord Mayor of London.
6. Stroud 1966, p. 73.
7. See Pearce and Salmon 2005.
8. See Colvin 1973.
9. Clerisseau and Holland had both worked for the prince's friend Lord Shelburne in the 1770s; it is likely they were in touch.
10. Séguier 1759.
11. Similar ideas are evidenced in Parisian houses such as Claude-Nicolas Ledoux's Hôtel de Thelusson (1778), which featured a passage for carriages that passed under the house.
12. Neufforge 1757–68, I. I am grateful to the late Professor David Watkin for this information.
13. Holland also used doubled Ionic columns at his own home, Sloane Place, and another of his projects, Southill Park.
14. Bill from Robert Campbell, upholsterer and furniture maker: TNA HO73/18.
15. Braham 1980, p. 87.
16. RA GEO/MAIN/35014.
17. See V&A, D:1486–1898.
18. RA GEO/MAIN/35043.
19. They cost £67: TNA HO73/19.
20. H.S. Robinson 1942, p. 345.
21. It cost £800: TNA HO73/22.
22. The total cost of these glass half-domes was £1,064: TNA HO73/22. Some pieces were reused at Windsor Castle.
23. TNA HO73/19.
24. W.S. Lewis 1937–83, 33, 17 Sept. 1785, p. 499.
25. Blondel argued that corridors dissected a plan; Etlin 1978, p. 144.
26. The caryatids were featured in detail in Stuart and Revett's *Antiquities* (1762), and in the earlier French publication by Julian-David Le Roy, *Les Ruines des plus beaux monuments de la Grèce* (1758).
27. TNA HO73/19 and RIBA SKB122/3, fol. 13r.
28. TNA HO73/19.

29. Robert Campbell's bill mentions Mr Schwertzel, the prince's gamekeeper, having apartments over the stables: TNA HO73/19.
30. RA GEO/MAIN/35014.
31. McCormick 1990, p. 152.
32. W.S. Lewis 1937–83, XXXIII, p. 498–9, H. Walpole to the Countess of Upper Ossory, 17 Sept. 1785.
33. The prince's first levée was held there in 1790. Ackermann 1808, I, p. 113.
34. Quoted in Hellman 1999, p. 418.
35. Bélanger was in England in 1766 and visited Bowood; he returned again in 1778 when he worked at Lansdowne House.
36. For a detailed examination of Dominique Daguerre's relationship with Britain and the British, see De Bellaigue 1995, pp. 157–79.
37. TNA HO73/19.
38. De Bellaigue 1995, pp. 173–4.
39. Stroud 1966, p. 74.
40. See Baulez 2007.
41. Cornforth 1991, p. 75.
42. Ibid.
43. TNA HO73/21.
44. TNA HO73/19.
45. Stroud 1966, p. 80.
46. See De Bellaigue 1967.
47. Green *cipollino* columns were also installed in the dining room on the Lower Floor: TNA HO73/17.
48. Holland's final contributions were alterations to the house to provide accommodation for the prince's new wife, Caroline of Brunswick, in 1794. He eventually left the prince's service in 1803.
49. Although the prince did manage to continue to acquire French furniture and ceramics: see Rufus Bird's essay in ch. 6.
50. A medieval manuscript in the collection of the New York Public Library (Spencer Collection MS 193) has the inscription 'Given me by Walsh Porter descended from Endymion Porter'.
51. Dominique Vivant, Baron Denon, joined Bonaparte's expedition to Egypt in 1798 and published his hugely influential compendium of Egyptian architecture and design, *Voyage dans la basse et la haute Egypte*, in 1802.
52. Thorne 1876, I, p. 233.
53. Croker 1860, p. 213.
54. RA GEO/MAIN/40668–9, letter from Walsh Porter to George, Prince of Wales, 23 Aug. 1806.
55. Ibid.
56. TNA LC1/40.
57. Colvin 1973, p. 312.
58. RA GEO/MAIN/25197.
59. RA GEO/MAIN/25239.
60. Jutsham I, p. 4.
61. For more on this redecoration, see De Bellaigue 1990.
62. Jutsham I, p. 54.
63. RA GEO/MAIN/25260; TNA C104/58, C104/57.
64. RA GEO/MAIN/25234.
65. RA GEO/MAIN/25273–4.
66. V&A, W.21:1 to 3-1987; and see H. Roberts 1990.
67. RA GEO/MAIN/25300–1; Jutsham I, p. 63. One chair may survive from this scheme (RCIN 33747) and is discussed in H. Roberts 2007, pp. 49–52.
68. 'A Gothic Oak Book Case with Brass wire Doors … did belong to the piers in Gothic Library, lent to Lady De Clifford' on Dec. 8 1809 (Jutsham I, p. 42) – and another on 3 Jan. 1810 (Jutsham I, p. 46).
69. RA GEO/MAIN/35180–82.
70. RA GEO/MAIN/25214.
71. Jutsham I, p. 187.
72. RA GEO/MAIN/25251.
73. RA GEO/MAIN/35194.
74. I am grateful to Patrick Baty for this information. See <http://patrickbaty.co.uk/2011/04/20/tor-royal-dartmoor> (accessed 15 July 2019).
75. Jutsham I, p. 86.
76. It was described as such by John Nash in 1822: TNA WORK 9/11. James Parker had patented his 'Roman Cement' in 1796.
77. Repton also produced his own design for a conservatory at Carlton House (RCIN 917090); Fig. A.71.
78. RA GEO/MAIN/35195.
79. 'By order of Walsh Porter Esq.': RA GEO/MAIN/25309.
80. They cost £95 4s: RA GEO MAIN/25281.
81. Jutsham I, p. 167.
82. Ibid., p. 131.
83. Jackson 1873, I, p. 270.
84. Farington 1978–84, VII, p. 2745, entry for 3 May 1806.
85. RA GEO/MAIN/40458–9.
86. Colvin 1973, p. 315.
87. The trophies cost an impressive £584: RA GEO/MAIN/25340.
88. John Nash, *A Gothic Design for Carlton House*, *c.*1814, RCIN 405844 and *A Classical Design for Carlton House*, *c.* 1814, RCIN 406951.
89. Anderson 2001.
90. TNA LC1/6 F346.
91. Farington 1978–84, XI, p. 3952.
92. Canova's commissions for the prince had to be placed in incongruous locations; the *Fountain Nymph* was installed in the Gothic Conservatory in 1819 and *Mars and Venus* in the centre of the Circular Room in 1824.
93. Colvin 1973, pp. 320–1.
94. TNA WORK 9/11.
95. Colvin 1973, p. 322.
96. The Corinthian columns from the portico were redeployed on the flanking entrances on the façade of the National Gallery, and the Ionic columns from the screen were used on the pavilions at Buckingham Palace.
97. *The European Magazine*, Mar. 1784, p. 234.
98. Britton and Pugin 1825–8, p. 201.
99. W.S. Lewis 1937–83, XXXIII, p. 499, Horace Walpole to the Countess of Upper Ossory, 17 Sept. 1785.

CHAPTER 6

GEORGE IV AND THE ART MARKET

1. RA GEO/MAIN/25141, M.-E. Lignereux to George, Prince of Wales, 20 June 1803. Lignereux had been in partnership with Daguerre 1789–96.
2. T. Lewis 1865, II, p. 146, entry for 22 Mar. 1802 (Paris).
3. Spieth 2018, pp. 397–400.
4. Buchanan 1824, I, pp. xii–xiii.
5. RA GEO/MAIN/25051. See RA GEO/MAIN/25075 for a list of craftsmen and artists employed to work at Carlton House under the guidance of Gaubert, at a total cost (to 29 May 1786) of £38,023 11s 4d.
6. CW, p. 40.
7. RA GEO/MAIN/40668–9; Aspinall 1963–71, V, no. 2207, pp. 417–18, Walsh Porter to the Prince of Wales, 23 Aug. 1806.
8. Jutsham I, p. 255, and Jutsham II, p. 25.
9. RCIN 405352; CW 2015, no. 162, p. 315.
10. Farington 1978–84, XV, p. 5361, entry for 6 May 1819.
11. RCIN 50603; Jones 2017, no. 3. Sale of William Pole-Tylney-Long-Wellesley, Wanstead House, Essex, 18 June 1822, lot 331 (£120).
12. RCIN 100032.
13. RCIN 67134.
14. RCIN 31702.
15. RA GEO/MAIN/25994; London 2002, no. 154, pp. 231–2.
16. RA GEO/MAIN/25780. The bill totalled £1,563 8s 0d and included the purchases of 36 objects from 5 Feb. to 7 Sept. 1807. The portrait of Henry VIII is probably similar to RCIN 404438, which was recorded in Kensington Palace in 1790 (Kensington inv. 1790, King's Gallery, no. 5).
17. RA GEO/MAIN/26059; RCIN 33464 (*Prometheus*); RCIN 20797 (*Henri IV*); RCIN 21929 (*Hercules and Antaeus*); RCIN 33466 (*Turenne*); RCIN 44189 (*Marly horses*); RCIN 35451 (*Nile river god*). The three most expensive bronze groups were *Psyche and Mercury* (RCIN 21641), the *Reposing Hercules* (RCIN 31361), and a *Centaur*, each costing £145.
18. RCIN 35858.
19. RCIN 72636 (*Prometheus*); RCIN 2138 (*Vespasian*); RCIN 2139 (*Augustus*).
20. The larger version (RCIN 44191) stands at 3 ft 2 in. (97 cm); the smaller version (RCIN 2172) is 1 ft 9 in. (53 cm) high.
21. H. Roberts 2000, pp. 117–19.
22. RCIN 1, the first pair acquired in 1804 and the second in 1817.
23. RA GEO/MAIN/25158.
24. RA GEO/MAIN/26411, and see De Bellaigue 2009, I, p. 17.
25. De Bellaigue 2004, pp. 388–9.
26. Ibid., p. 392. I am also grateful to Diana Davis for allowing me to see volume 2 of her unpublished PhD thesis, 'British dealers and the making of the Anglo-Gallic interior, 1785–1853', University of Buckingham, 2016.
27. Rowell and Burchard 2016, pp. 181–2.
28. RA GEO/MAIN/26405.
29. RCIN 5000021; see De Bellaigue 2009, II, no. 169, esp. pp. 673–4.
30. RA GEO/MAIN/25354.
31. RA GEO/MAIN/25355. The table was the first of a group of four commissioned by Napoleon from the manufactory. In the event only two were completed and only one, the *Table des maréchaux*, was delivered to the emperor in 1810. The second of the group, the *Table des grands capitaines de l'antiquité*, was eventually presented as a gift to George by Louis XVIII in 1817. De Bellaigue 1999, p. 112.
32. RA GEO/MAIN/25354–9.
33. RCIN 293.
34. The Pictorial Inventory consists of three volumes (RCINs 933559–61) containing a total of 230 drawings. It was originally created in the late 1820s as a pictorial record of the clocks, vases, candelabra and other miscellaneous items from Carlton House, as well as selected items from the stores at Buckingham House, Brighton Pavilion, Hampton Court and Kensington Palace to be considered for use in the refurbishment of Windsor Castle.
35. RA GEO/MAIN/26430.
36. RA GEO/MAIN/25358.
37. De Bellaigue 2004, p. 393, n. 37.
38. RCIN 64049.
39. RCIN 20593.
40. De Bellaigue 1975a; De Bellaigue 1975b.
41. RCIN 1382.
42. RCIN 35289.
43. Van Duin 1989.
44. Murdoch 1992, p. 121.
45. RCIN 39208.
46. RA GEO/MAIN/32767.
47. London 2014, no. 122, p. 221.
48. RCIN 64062; Ayers 2016, II, no. 1364, p. 567.
49. Norman and Eaves 2016, p. 22.
50. RA GEO/MAIN/29165. Brandt is recorded in Frith Street in 1817 and in 1821 at 62 Jermyn Street. He was declared bankrupt in 1823:

London Gazette, 13 May 1823. I am grateful to Angus Patterson for this information.

51. The quotation is from RA GEO/MAIN/43498–9. The pistols are RCIN 61166. See London 1991, p. 149, no. 120; Norman and Eaves 2016, p. 23.
52. Kate Heard's contribution on George's print-collecting activities is here gratefully acknowledged. See Heard (forthcoming) for a detailed discussion. There are a number of similarities between George's purchases of works on paper and books, which are discussed by Emma Stuart in the present volume.
53. RA GEO/MAIN/27839 and following Colnaghi invoices.
54. RA GEO/MAIN/27129.

CHAPTER 7

GEORGE IV AND THE LOW COUNTRY MASTERS

1. OM 1200 (RCIN 404709).
2. The paintings hanging in this room were described 20 years later in an inventory of 1785 (BP 1785, p. 44) and illustrated some 30 years after that in a watercolour by James Stephanoff of 1818 (RCIN 922143).
3. Reynolds 1997, pp. 42–4, *Discourse III*, 14 Dec. 1770.
4. For a fuller account of the Georgian collecting and display of Old Master painting, see London 2014, pp. 223–9.
5. BP 1785, pp. 43–4; BP 1819, nos 659–99; see also watercolours by Stephanoff and Wild (RCINs 922142–4).
6. The displays at Carlton House appear in inventories of 1816 and 1819 and in Pyne 1819.
7. The inventory of 1819 (CH inv. 1819) carried current valuations of the works; for an analysis of the collection as an 'asset portfolio' of holdings of the various artists, see Shawe-Taylor 2018, pp. 216–19.
8. Reynolds provides a sample of such views in his *Discourse VI* of 10 Dec. 1774: Reynolds 1997, pp. 108–10. For attitudes towards Dutch art at this time in England, see London 2015, pp. 20–9.
9. See Buchanan 1824, pp. 21–2, for the taste for Dutch and Flemish Masters and its French origins.
10. CWLF, pp. 21–5, for Flemish acquisitions by Frederick, Prince of Wales and George III, and CW, pp. 33–6, for their Dutch acquisitions.
11. CWLF 93 (RCIN 407274) and CWLF 107 (RCIN 405342); impressions of both engravings are in the Royal Collection (RCINs 820068 and 820188).
12. See BP 1785, p. 46.
13. George IV could afford copies in enamel from Henry Bone of Old Masters, such as Correggio, Parmigianino, Annibale Carracci, Domenichino, Cantarini and Reynolds: CH inv. 1819, nos 187–98.
14. Walsh Porter advised at Carlton House from 1805 to 1809: see London 1991, p. 12.
15. RA GEO/MAIN/40668–9; Aspinall 1963–71, V, no. 2207, p. 417, Walsh Porter to the Prince of Wales, 23 Aug. 1806.
16. I am very grateful to Isobel Muir for her invaluable help in reconstructing Walsh Porter's collection, using Christie's sales (see W. Roberts 2017) and the Getty Trust Sales Catalogue Archive.
17. Teniers, *Drummer*, CWLF 97 (RCIN 406577); Le Nain, *Young Card Players* (RCIN 405944); De Keyser, *Couple Riding*, CW 281 (RCIN 405202); Walsh Porter sale, 22 Mar. 1803 (lot 28); 23 Mar. 1803 (lots 45, 47 and 48).
18. CW 180 (RCIN 405343).
19. Walsh Porter sale, 23 Mar. 1803 (lot 47); CH inv. 1819, no. 70.
20. Walsh Porter's sale of 14 Apr. 1810 included Rubens's *Madonna and Saints* (lot 45; Christie's, 30 Apr. 2015, lot 424); Claude's *Enchanted Castle* (lot 44; National Gallery, London, NG 6471); Titian's *Magi* (lot 38; untraced); and Murillo's *Magdalen* (lot 35; Wallraf-Richartz Museum), not to mention Correggio's *Danae* (lot 52; Borghese Gallery).
21. CW 263 (RCIN 400940) and CW 172 (RCIN 405538); Walsh Porter sale, 14 Apr. 1810 (lots 8 and 18). Rubens's *Pan and Syrinx*, CWLF (RCIN 404637), lot 45, and Teniers' *Fishermen*, CWLF 91 (RCIN 405348), lot 26, were both acquired by George IV two years later, on 18 Jan. and 11 Apr. 1812; Jutsham I, pp. 183 and 191.
22. CW 179 (RCIN 405337). It arrived on 24 Nov. 1810 (Jutsham I, p. 135) and was hung in the Dining Room, Lower Floor, making a pair with the earlier Schalcken acquisition (CW 180, RCIN 405343), CH inv. 1819, nos 66 and 70.
23. CH inv. 1819, no. 174 (RCIN 400672).
24. OM 685 (RCIN 405540); CH inv. 1819, no 154; Jutsham I, p. 135.
25. Lamb 1811, p. 64.
26. Ibid., p. 76.
27. OM 617 (RCIN 405954); CH inv. 1819, no. 57; see London 2014, p. 378, no. 251.
28. OM 970 (RCIN 405539). Whitley 1928, pp. 316–17; George IV ordered 'three choice proofs' of the print made after the painting: letter from F. Scotney to Sir William Knighton, 12 Dec. 1828, RA GEO/MAIN/26572.
29. It was acquired for 175 guineas; see receipt of 3 May 1830, RA GEO/MAIN/26782; CH inv. 1819, no 686. The painting is no longer in the Royal Collection but its composition is recorded in a print of 1854, published by Charles Henry Jeens (BM 1872,1012.2417).
30. For the appreciation of Ter Borch's work at this date, see Nieuwenhuys 1834, pp. 245–6.
31. For the 3rd Marquess of Hertford, see Stephen Duffy in Duffy *et al.* 2005, pp. 7–8.
32. There had been a sale in Amsterdam of the same collection on 1 and 2 Aug. 1810: see Nieuwenhuys 1834, p. 154.
33. CW 242 (RCIN 406736); CW 249 (RCIN 405334); CW 208 (RCIN 404137); and CW 132 (RCIN 404814). Three hung together in the Bow Room, Principal Floor, CH inv. 1819, nos 22–4; Wouwerman's *Hawking Party* (RCIN 406736) hung in the Anti-Room to the Dining Room, Lower Floor; CH inv. 1819, no 100; see also Jutsham I, p. 169; Nieuwenhuys 1834, pp. 174–5.
34. OM 164 (RCIN 405325) and CW 160 (RCIN 405533).
35. Jutsham I, p. 169. The Van Dyck was valued at 1,000 guineas: CH inv. 1819, no. 50; the Rembrandt at 2,500 guineas: CH inv. 1819, no. 47.
36. At the start of George IV's reign there were four other Rembrandts in the collection: *Young Man* (CW 159, RCIN 404522) in the King's Gallery at Kensington Palace, KP 1818, no. 331; *Old Man* (CW 167, RCIN 405519) in the Coffee Room at Buckingham Palace, BP 1819, no. 769; *Female Portrait* (CW 165, RCIN 400045) in Queen Mary's Work Closet at Hampton Court, Pyne 1819, II, p. 61; and *Rembrandt's Mother* (CW 158, RCIN 405000) in the King's Dressing Room at Windsor, Pyne 1819, I, pp. 150–1.
37. Jutsham I, pp. 299–305, dated 8 May 1814.
38. Farington 1978–84, XV, p. 5312, entry for 13 Jan. 1819, quoting Mr Watson (Frederick Beilby Watson), Assistant Private Secretary to George.
39. Jutsham I, pp. 152–68.
40. Among the sold appear familiar names: Teniers, Wouwerman, Dou, Schalcken, Mieris, Cuyp and Berchem; Jutsham I, pp. 164–8, nos 9, 68, 83–4, 89. Flower paintings by Rachel Ruysch and Jan van Huysum were also sold: Jutsham I, pp. 164–8, nos 1, 31, 49–50.
41. Jutsham I, pp. 152–64, nos 90, 135, 139, 142, 156, 229, 240, 243, 357, 365–7, 372 and 374–5.
42. CWLF 63 (RCIN 405356). Jutsham I, pp. 153, 301, 303, 305 and 307.
43. George IV had Rubens's *Self-portrait* (CWLF 61, RCIN 400156), painted for Charles while Prince of Wales, brought from Kensington Palace to Carlton House on 18 Apr. 1812: CH inv. 1819, no. 119. Walsh Porter secured for him Van Dyck's famous triple portrait of the king (OM 146, RCIN 404420) for 1,000 guineas from Mr Wells, though delay over payment meant that it arrived at Carlton House in 1819: CH inv. 1819, no. 548; Buchanan 1824, pp. 183–4.
44. CW 27 (RCIN 406574); CH inv. 1819, nos 10 and 12. The 'Rembrandt' is now thought to be a Ferdinand Bol of an unknown sitter; it was acquired at the Hope sale of 1 July 1816.
45. The illustrations commissioned by Pyne were published between 1816 and 1819.
46. CW 30 (RCIN 405544) and CW 39 (RCIN 405344). CH inv. 1819, nos 48–9; Jutsham I, p. 305, no. 91.
47. CH inv. 1819, nos 19–36, 51–8 and 65–176.
48. CWLF 109 (RCIN 405207) and CWLF 110 (RCIN 405206); CH inv. 1819, nos 145–6.
49. *Sporting Magazine* 1795, 6, p. 102; see Shawe-Taylor 2018, p. 226.
50. We may assume that the remaining rooms, described but not illustrated, were hung in one of these two patterns, or some variant thereof.
51. CW 101 (RCIN 405534) and CW 100 (RCIN 405535); CH inv. 1819, no. 51 and 58. As so often this is a pairing of a Baring picture (Metsu) with a work already in the collection (Maes), bought at Christie's through Lord Yarmouth on 26 Jan. 1811: RA GEO/MAIN/26881.
52. CW 46 (RCIN 405542); CW 206 (RCIN 406966); and CW 156 (RCIN 400942). This is the arrangement in the Bow Room, Principal Floor, described in the 1819 inventory, CH inv. 1819, nos 26–8, though not quite that shown in Charles Wild's watercolour of *c.*1817 (RCIN 922180).
53. The Van de Velde was acquired in 1810, the Potter in 1811 (Jutsham I, pp. 123 and 153) and the Dou in 1817 (see below, note 55).
54. Buchanan 1824, p. 371.
55. CW 46 (RCIN 405542). CH inv. 1819, no. 27 states that this is 'From the Duke de Praslin's Collection', presumably meaning Choiseul-Praslin: RA GEO/MAIN/26994–5; Buchanan 1824, p. 358.
56. CW 181 (RCIN 404624) and CW 162 (RCIN 405352); Jutsham I, pp. 80–1; CH inv. 1819, nos 549–50. The title of the Schalcken is provided by Nieuwenhuys 1834, pp. 305–7.
57. CWLF 62 (RCIN 400118). For the acquisition of Rubens's *Portrait of a Woman* (no longer thought to be the artist's wife), see Nieuwenhuys 1834, pp. 208–10; CH inv. 1819, no. 120; Jutsham I, p. 43. Smith's

receipt is dated 8 Dec. 1818: RA GEO/MAIN/27090.
58. CW 240 (RCIN 404589) and CW 184 (RCIN 404812). The exchange occurred on 10 July 1819; Jutsham I, pp. 318–20; CH inv. 1819, nos 55, 85, 99, 150, 161, 170, 222 and CH 1816, no. 32.
59. CW 161 (RCIN 404816). The exchange occurred on 9 Nov. 1819; Jutsham I, p. 86; CH inv. 1819, nos 65, 69, 175 and 313.
60. CW 164 (RCIN 405350) and CWLF 57 (RCIN 405335); Jutsham I, pp. 1 and 301, no. 34; CH inv. 1819, nos 116 and 124.
61. CWLF 100 (RCIN 405952), CW 189 (RCIN 404804) and CWLF 58 (RCIN 405333). Jutsham I, pp. 146–7; CH inv. 1819, nos 578–80, where the Rubens and Teniers were each valued at 1,500 guineas and the Steen at 500 guineas; see also Buchanan 1824, pp. 371–3.
62. CW 120 (RCIN 404795). CH inv. 1819, no. 626; RA GEO/MAIN/26778. For the rising reputation of the painter at this time, see Nieuwenhuys 1834, pp. 165–7.
63. RCIN 405357; RA GEO/MAIN/26779; CH inv. 1819, no. 628.
64. CW 85 (RCIN 405951); RA GEO/MAIN/26766; CH inv. 1819, no. 599.
65. CW 84 (RCIN 405331; RA GEO/MAIN/26778; CH inv. 1819, no. 627.
66. Nieuwenhuys 1834, pp. 154–6.

CHAPTER 8

GEORGE IV AND MODERN MANUFACTURING

1. *The Times*, 30 June 1830, p. 4, quoting the duke's speech of 29 June.
2. London 1991, p. 37.
3. N. Goodison 2002, p. 356.
4. RCIN 21532.
5. Stroud 1966, p. 80.
6. Jutsham I, pp. 331, 365, RA GEO/MAIN/31757 and Jutsham II, p. 117.
7. Several versions of the Galvanic Goblet exist, in the City Museum and Art Gallery, Birmingham, Museum of Fine Arts, Boston, Dallas Museum of Art and Toronto Museum. The latter forms part of a tea service commissioned by George and supplied to Lady Conyngham in 1818.
8. RCIN 2747.
9. RCIN 2831.
10. TNA LC1/5.
11. Louw 1991, p. 61.
12. By late 1806 Jutsham notes numerous Argand lamps in use at Carlton House: Jutsham I, p.1.
13. Mundy 1886, pp. 158–9, Lady E. Fielding to M. Frampton, 10 Feb. 1813.
14. This metallic composition was noted in *The Times*, 23 Jan. 1826 as 'patronized by Mr Nash' but without further information (the term is usually applied to a bronze powder based on tin rather than an apparently solid material for manufacturing railings as here).
15. See London 1991, p. 46.
16. RA GEO/MAIN/26398.
17. Binns 1877, pp. 238–43.
18. Rush 1833, p. 249.

CHAPTER 9

A NAIVE AND SENTIMENTAL SOLDIER? GEORGE IV AND THE ART OF WAR

1. Maxwell 1903, II, p. 233.
2. R.R. Brown 2010, p. 50 (brass guns); Blackmore 1960, p. 230; CH Arms Cat., nos 138–9.
3. Clarke 1978, p. 74; Hots 2004.
4. Home 1970, III, p. 430, journal entry for Saturday, 27 July 1771.
5. As recounted in Anon. 1798.
6. RCINs 98892 and 98894.
7. Huish 1830, I, p. 137.
8. Augustus, Duke of Sussex was unable to pursue a military career through ill health.
9. RA GEO/MAIN/38968–9; Aspinall 1963–71, II, no. 885, p. 481, Ernest, Duke of Cumberland to George from Arnhem, 6 Nov. 1794.
10. *Star*, 29 Oct. 1791. Frederick's 'campaign of *love*' was his marriage, in Berlin, to Frederica Charlotte of Prussia.
11. RA GEO/MAIN/39352–4; Aspinall 1963–71, III, no. 1250, p. 328, H. Dundas to Lord Keith, 18 Mar. 1797.
12. RA GEO/MAIN/39900–1; Aspinall 1963–71, no. 1720, pp. 386–7, Prince of Wales to H. Addington, 18 July 1803.
13. Monod 2009, p. 282.
14. For Darby see Mollo 1997, pp. 38 and 82. For Howard and Ponsonby see Aspinall 1963–71, no. 559, Queen Charlotte to George after the Battle of Waterloo, 22 June 1815.
15. Murray 1922, p.182, Byron to Lady Melbourne, 21 Sept. 1813.
16. Mollo 1997, p. 13.
17. George's involvement with the 10th is discussed in detail in Mollo 1997.
18. Mollo 1997, p. 13; Smith 1999, pp. 68–9.
19. Mollo 1997, p. 25; Parissien 2001, p. 110.
20. Heard (forthcoming).
21. 'Abstract of Foreign Occurrences Spain and Portugal', *Gentleman's Magazine*, June 1817, p. 553.
22. Millar 1969, no. 711. RCIN 409290 is a reduced copy; the prime version is now in the Museum of Fine Arts in Boston, inv. no. 25.98.
23. London 1991, p. 24. The 'Admirals Room' would a few years later become the Large Blue Velvet Room (see the table on p. viii).
24. London 1991, p. 26.
25. Thomas Gainsborough, *Charles, 2nd Earl and 1st Marquess Cornwallis*, after Jan. 1782 (RCIN 4007487), and Thomas Phillips, *John Hely-Hutchinson, 1st Baron Hutchinson and 2nd Earl of Donoughmore*, 1811 (RCIN 402776).
26. Jordan and Rogers 1989 assess the public reputation of naval heroes in the 18th century.
27. RA GEO/MAIN/28555 and 28558–61 (Heathfield), 28623 (James), 28637 (Dowdeswell). I am grateful to Emma Stuart for these references.
28. RA GEO/MAIN/28410, invoice from Egerton, Feb. and Mar. 1799; RA GEO/MAIN/28417, invoice from Thomas Becket, July to Oct. 1800. For the Dighton drawings see Haswell Miller and Dawnay 1966, nos 435–507. It is often impossible to determine the date of purchase of the Dighton drawings, since the artist did not always specify individual works in his invoices.
29. RA GEO/MAIN/27447.
30. Maxwell 1903, I, p. 49.
31. Ramsey 2011, *passim*. Ramsey notes (p. 41) that such memoirs were 'directed towards that class of reader who identified with the gentleman military officer, not his common counterpart'.
32. Ramsey 2011, p. 163. The copy presented to George has not been identified.
33. Sherer 1824, p. 4. Sherer's account is considered at length in Ramsey 2011.
34. CH Arms Cat., no. 2115; RA GEO/MAIN/26116.
35. RA GEO/MAIN/26968, memorandum from Robert Gray to Colonel McMahon, 14 Sept. 1815.
36. Howard Blackmore in Norman and Eaves 2016, pp. 22–9.
37. Anon. 1818, p. 82.
38. London 1991, pp. 14 and 47.
39. Ackermann 1808, I, p. 109.
40. 'So to commence: - Our R-g-nt Prince, / A wond'rous passion doth evince, / To guard in armoury, with care, / Types of *old saddles militaire*': Ireland 1814, p. 169.
41. For the history of collecting arms and armour see Cripps-Day 1925, and Wainwright 1989, pp. 60–9.
42. Stanley 1821, lot 108; Wainwright 1989, p. 64.
43. RA GEO/MAIN/28397, invoice from Thomas Becket for books delivered Jan. to Mar. 1787.
44. Cripps-Day 1925, p. xl.
45. CH inv. 1826, p. 71
46. RA GEO/MAIN/27376, bill from Colnaghi & Co., 23 May 1807.
47. CH Arms Cat.
48. For example, CH Arms Cat., nos 2068–70, 2192, 2289, 2319.
49. CH Arms Cat., no. 1645 (Chabraque); RCIN 67162, CH Arms Cat., 1808 (breastplate). Norman and Eaves 2016, no. 46. Geoffrey de Bellaigue has observed that a number of pieces of uniform in the Armoury were 'probably used by the Prince and his circle almost as a form of fancy dress, in which they could imagine themselves in the roles of romantic, savage, warrior kings and princes' (London 1991, p. 144).
50. 'Le Roi était étendu sur une chaise longue, enveloppé dans une capote de hussard autrichien, d'une coupe passablement fantaisiste'; Metternich 1881, III, p. 518.
51. Farington 1978–84, X, p. 3715.
52. Wilkie was lent a Highland target (RCIN 67310) for use in his portrait of George in Highland costume (Norman and Eaves 2016, no. 53) and Lawrence was sent a sabre, sword belt and sword knot 'to paint from' in Mar. 1815 (CH Arms Cat., nos 2412, 2469 and 2470).
53. Ackermann 1808, I, p. 112.
54. Blackmore (1960, p. 233) notes that particular guns appealed to George due to their provenances.
55. CH Arms Cat., nos 230, 233 and 222.
56. Ireland 1805, p. 10.
57. CH Arms Cat., nos 2358 and 2412.
58. Ibid., nos 138 and 1661. The sword was presented to Henry Fitzclarence, George's illegitimate nephew, in 1808.

CHAPTER 10

THE ROYAL PAVILION AT BRIGHTON

1. Croly 1841, I, p. 111.
2. RA GEO/MAIN/33498.
3. Morley 1984, p. 86. The designs are attributed to Boileau in Croft-Murray 1970, II, p. 305.
4. RA GEO/MAIN/33498.
5. Highfill *et al.* 1973, p. 454.
6. *London Chronicle*, 17 Aug. 1802.
7. *Morning Advertiser*, 17 Aug. 1802.
8. The Craces' work at the Pavilion is itemised in a typescript copy of the Crace accounts from 1802 to 1822 held at the Royal Pavilion.
9. Granville 1916, II, p. 120, Lady Bessborough to Granville Leveson Gower, 9 Oct. 1805.
10. Walker 1809, p. 23.
11. Summerson 1980, p. 104.
12. Gore and Carter 2005, p. 151.
13. Quoted in Musgrave 1959, p. 65.
14. *Sussex Weekly Advertiser*, 27 Nov. 1820.
15. Ibid., 4 Dec. 1820.
16. Ibid., 22 Jan. 1821.

17. Jennings 1885, I, p. 127.
18. Aldrich 1990, p. 24.
19. RA GEO/MAIN/34223; H.D. Roberts 1939, p. 134.
20. The compass was said to run from CCC with a double diapason throughout: Sickelmore 1824, p. 26.
21. RA GEO/MAIN/34223; H.D. Roberts 1939, p. 134.
22. Brighton inv. 1828, p. 42.
23. TNA LC11/31, Bailey & Sanders account 5 Apr. 1821. 'India work' was a term frequently used to describe Chinese or Japanese lacquer.
24. *Sussex Weekly Advertiser*, 16 Nov. 1818.
25. Wright 1818, p. 44.
26. RA GEO/MAIN/29064, List of His Majesty's Private Band 27 Feb. 1826.
27. For the band see Carse 1946, Frisby 1996 and Frisby 1997.
28. 'Royal Patronage of Music', *Quarterly Musical Magazine & Review*, I, no. 2, 1818, p. 162.
29. *Morning Herald*, 1 Jan. 1824.
30. *Morning Post*, 1 Jan. 1824, quoted in *The Musical Times and Singing Class Circular*, 41, no. 683, 1 Jan. 1900, p. 19.
31. Conner 2008, p. 65.

CHAPTER 11

THE FEMALE INFLUENCE ON GEORGE IV'S TASTE AND COLLECTING HABITS

1. New Haven and London 2017 *passim* and p. 335 (essay by Lee Prosser).
2. Beevers 2008, p. 21.
3. W. Chambers 1763, p. 5.
4. Brighton inv. 1828, p. 7.
5. For Queen Mary's collection of Chinese and Japanese porcelain, see Ayers 2016, I, pp. 104–12.
6. New Haven and London 2017, p. 125.
7. London 2004, p. 120.
8. Pyne 1819, II, p. 21.
9. London 2004, p. 120.
10. For the artistic work of Charlotte and her daughters, see J. Roberts 1987, pp. 74–80, and New Haven and London 2017, pp. 375–83 (essay by Jane Roberts).
11. New Haven and London 2017, p. 359 (essay by Samantha Howard).
12. Pyne 1819, I, p. 18.
13. Ibid., p. 19.
14. London 2004, pp. 147–8.
15. Pyne 1819, I, p. 21.
16. London 2004, p. 150.
17. Pyne 1819, I, pp. 20–1.
18. Ibid., p. 148. See also Ayers 2016, I, p. 8.
19. Alexander 1805.
20. RA GEO/ADD/2/87–8.
21. For George IV's purchases at Queen Charlotte's sale, see Matthew Winterbottom in London 2004, pp. 385–9 and no. 477 (Indian chairs).
22. Among the Chalons in Princess Charlotte's collection was RCIN 409134, of one of her favourite horses with a groom; the Bristows included RCIN 409133, a portrait of a pony belonging to Prince Leopold.
23. Williams 1831, II, p. 79.
24. J.M. Robinson 1979, p. 180. The monument to the princess was funded by public subscription.

CHAPTER 12

THE GREAT JOSS AND HIS PLAYTHINGS: GEORGE IV AND SATIRICAL PRINTS

1. See, for example, K. Baker 2005; J. Baker 2014.
2. For further information on George IV's relationship with the British satirical print market, and his attempts to censor criticism, see Heard (forthcoming), on which this essay is based.
3. This number is unlikely to have included the 582 satirical prints acquired by George III, since the father and son's collections appear to have remained separate until the Victorian period (see Heard 2018).
4. MS VIII.C, fol. 5, Sir John Soane's Museum, London. For Wigstead, see Payne and Payne 2003.
5. For the evidence that George used his print collection, and that prints added to the collection required his approval, see Heard (forthcoming).
6. TNA HO73/20, part one. I am grateful to David Oakey for drawing this to my attention and to the conservators at the National Archives for making the document available for study.
7. For an analysis of the Holland invoices, see Heard (forthcoming).
8. For William Humphrey's invoice see RA GEO/MAIN/27681, which includes a mixture of satirical and fine art prints. George's first invoice from Hannah Humphrey is RA GEO/MAIN/27722.
9. *Fraser's Magazine for Town and Country*, June 1841, p. 685, includes an apparently well-informed account of Turner visiting Humphrey's shop to select satires for George.
10. RA GEO/MAIN/27722, dated 1803 (*Flannel Armour*); RA GEO/MAIN/27725, dated 1804 (*Rogues*).
11. For an in-depth discussion of the antagonism between George and Fores, see Heard (forthcoming).

CHAPTER 13

GEORGE IV AND SPORTING ART

1. Dixon 1912, p. 88.
2. It was later revised by Freeman Strickland; a presentation copy of this revised version survives in the original binding from the Carlton House Library (RCIN 1074847).
3. The prince was 16 when this was painted so is unlikely to have been the original patron. The Hanoverian Cream was a breed of horse, now extinct, with luxuriant cream mane and tail, and cream coat, blue eyes and pink Roman nose.
4. J. Roberts 1997, pp. 62 and 182.
5. J. Harris 2007, p. 182. A chimneypiece by John Deare, ordered by the Duke of Gloucester in Rome in 1795 on behalf of his brother and intended for Kempshott, was de-accessioned from the St Louis Art Museum, Missouri, in the mid-20th century.
6. RA GEO/ADD/3/81.
7. *Hampshire Chronicle*, 1 Feb. 1790.
8. J. Roberts 1997, p. 53.
9. Fitzgerald 1990, p. 38.
10. Melville 1906, p. 256.
11. Chifney's version is now in the United States. A copy after Stubbs by John Nost Sartorius also survives in the Royal Collection (RCIN 406005).
12. Ross 1982, p. 50.
13. Fitzgerald 1990, p. 69.
14. RCIN 50269.
15. RA GEO/MAIN/25756.
16. *Finn's Leinster Journal*, 5 Sept. 1821.
17. D'Arcy 1991, p. 96. Unfortunately, none of these calendars survive in the Royal Collection.
18. Creevey quoted in Gore 1937, p. 212.
19. RCIN 914676.
20. RA GEO/MAIN/26532. Nygren 2013, letter 93. The horses face different directions, but the paintings are similar sizes and would hang well as a group; it is not clear whether they ever did.
21. Nygren 2013, letter 93 (*Monitor* and *Soothsayer*) and letter 94 (*Nonpareil*).
22. Shawe-Taylor 2016, pp. 7–10.
23. Gardner Williams 1987, p. cxxiv.
24. RA GEO/MAIN/41985; Aspinall 1963–71, II, no. 665, p. 247, the Prince of Wales to Sir J. Lade, 15 Apr. 1792.
25. Raikes 1856, I, entry for 8 June 1836 (referring to earlier undated incident).
26. Norman and Eaves 2016, p. 26.
27. Guns by these makers remain in the Royal Collection but it is not clear whether any were from this transaction.
28. RA GEO/MAIN/28424 (advertisement for subscription); RCINS 1074769–71 (volumes).
29. RA GEO/MAIN/27301, 27353, 27354, 27407, 27375, 27446, 27837, 27907, 27929, 27968.
30. Credland 1996, p. 20.
31. RA GEO/MAIN/29188.
32. An example is in the collection of the National Trust, Scotney Castle, Kent.
33. Dodd 1818, p. 140.
34. RCIN 1088024.
35. Anon., *Minutes of the Royal Toxophilite Society*, entry for 25 May 1821; private collection.
36. *World*, 12 Nov. 1789.
37. Now at Antony House, Cornwall, and a similar example in Harvard Art Museums, Cambridge, MA, 1943.754.
38. TNA HO73/23.
39. *South West Advertiser*, 12 Sept. 1791.
40. Purchase recorded in RA GEO/MAIN/27145.
41. *Kentish Gazette*, 26 Aug. 1826.
42. Harris and Ashley-Cooper 1920, p. 50.
43. Harris and Ashley-Cooper 1929, p. 94.
44. Credland 1996, p. 43.
45. Hopton 2007, pp. 179–80.
46. Heard (forthcoming).
47. *Morning Herald*, 9 Apr. 1787.
48. David 1998, p. 287.
49. Sawyer 1989, p. 117.
50. Purchases recorded in RA GEO/MAIN/27133 and 28011.
51. David 1998, p. 288.
52. D.M. Stuart 1953, p. 202.
53. The medal was believed to be in his ownership when he died. Its present location is unknown.
54. *Standard*, 1 May 1828.
55. RA GEO/MAIN/29194–4a.

CHAPTER 14

GEORGE IV'S INTELLECTUAL WORLD

1. Boyd 1958, pp. 429–31, Thomas Jefferson to John Jay, 11 Jan. 1789.
2. For an assessment of differing views of George's education see Gardner Williams 1987, pp. xxi–xxv.
3. Pyne 1819, III [Carlton House section], pp. 56–7.
4. For a detailed study of the library at Carlton House, see E. Stuart 2001.
5. Austen-Leigh 1870, p. 147.
6. Lockhart 1837, III, p. 340.
7. Ibid., p. 341. For more of George's intellectual connections, see Gardner Williams 1987, pp. liii ff. For an extended discussion of George IV and Walter Scott, see Gardner Williams 1987, pp. lxviii–ci.
8. RCIN 918936.
9. RCIN 918944.
10. RCIN 918943; Fig. 5.4.

11. RA GEO/MAIN/28399.
12. TNA WORK 6/26, p. 29.
13. *Royal Kalendar*, 1785, p. 277; Kassler 2015, p. 83.
14. Kassler 2015, p. 96.
15. RA GEO/MAIN/28399.
16. *Court and City Register*, 1798, p. 296; Kassler 2015, pp. 108, 352 n. 542.
17. *Royal Kalendar*, 1808, p. 138.
18. RA GEO/MAIN/28499–500 (false book backs, sorting and arranging library), 28508 (cleaning and arranging), 28525 (cleaning and arranging), 28473 (from Edward Jeffrey, for lettering the binding of the catalogue), 28549 (making a fair copy of the catalogue).
19. RA GEO/MAIN/28553–4 (dusting and cleaning), 28566 (sorting, packing and transporting), 28585 (transporting), 28616 (cataloguing at Brighton), 28555 (Heathfield sale). Both Budd & Calkin and Payne & Foss made purchases for George at this sale.
20. RA GEO/MAIN/28598 (bookplates), 28603 (tools), 28679 ('distressed literary persons'), 28581 (subscription to Choat's library).
21. RA GEO/MAIN/28875.
22. E.g. *Royal Kalendar*, 1788, p. 277.
23. RA GEO/MAIN/28401 (Stuart), 28427, 28432, 28436 (Becket).
24. RA GEO/MAIN/28474–7, 28479.
25. RA GEO/MAIN/28473 (Jeffrey) and 28521 (Payne). Payne had already undertaken binding work in 1811 (RA GEO/MAIN/28513).
26. RA GEO/MAIN/28582; RCINs 1050439 (Scott, *Lord of the Isles*), 1059025–45 (Shakespeare), 1081287 (1814 visit).
27. RA GEO/MAIN/28603 (cutting binding tools, 1817); the mark appears on 1,256 books in the present Royal Library; RA GEO/MAIN/28544 (cutting new binding tools to reflect Regency); new arms and feathers were cut after he became Prince Regent.
28. B.N. Lee 1992, nos 78–83 (pre-1820) and nos 84–6 (1820 and later). Five of these (nos 78, 80, 81, 82 and 83) are recorded in the present Royal Library.
29. Brooke 1977, p. 39; P.R. Harris 1998, p. 32.
30. Richardson 1966, p. 139.
31. Rush 1833, p. 124.
32. RA GEO/MAIN/28585 (Opie), 28442 (Radcliffe), 28776 (Peacock), 28539 (Scott), 28553 (Edgeworth), 28827 (Austen), 28616 (Morgan), 28647 (Driscoll).
33. RA GEO/MAIN/28518 (Byron), 28449 (Scott poetry), 28427 (*Folly*), 28453 (*Hint*). For George's interest in the works of Sir Walter Scott, see ch. 16 below.
34. RA GEO/MAIN/28551 (de Stäel), 28549 (Le Brun and de Genlis), 28554 (Pigault-Lebrun and Fontaine), 28584 (de Genlis), 28400 (Voltaire, Racine, Molière).
35. RA GEO/MAIN/28589.
36. RA GEO/MAIN/28512 (Thucydides, Tacitus, Cicero), 28568 (*Life of Cicero*, Classical dictionary), 28821 (numerous works of Classical literature, including Livy, Juvenal, Ovid, Martial, Cicero, Catullus).
37. For a detailed description, see Brayley 1838, pp. 13–14.
38. RA GEO/MAIN/28568.
39. Jutsham II, p. 154.
40. Sickelmore 1815, p. 60.
41. RA GEO/MAIN/28832 (providing books for Royal Lodge), 28835 (arranging), 28863 (removing), 28864 (arranging).
42. RA GEO/MAIN/28911–2.
43. Goldfinch 2009, pp. 282–4.
44. Royal Library 1826 (retained items); Bryant 1782; RCINs 1071478 (Mainz Psalter), 1080415 (Second Folio), 1047020 (Johnson); Goldfinch 2009.
45. RCIN 1005025.
46. Bruce Redford demonstrates Lawrence's connections to the members of the Society of Dilettanti (Redford 2008). For more of George's intellectual connections, see Gardner Williams 1987.
47. Powell 2004, pp. 100 and 330.
48. Lunardi 1784, p. 14.
49. Fisk 1959, p. 172.
50. MacCarthy 2002, p. 161, quoting a letter from John Murray to Sir Walter Scott.
51. Goodden 2008, p. 230.
52. Steer 1966, pp. 12–13, Hawkins to Samuel Lysons, 2 Nov. 1813. We are very grateful to the Revd Professor Martin Henig for this reference.
53. Zawadzki 1993, p. 228.
54. Lockhart 1837, III, p. 341; and see ch. 16 below.
55. Théodoridès 1966, p. 43.
56. For Cuvier, see S. Lee 1833, p. 37; Taquet 2006, p. 10. For Humboldt, see Sweet 1980, p. 299.
57. Riberette 1986, no. 1571, Chateaubriand to Montmorency, 19 Apr. 1822.
58. Sweet 1980, p. 299. The translation is Sweet's from a letter from Humboldt to his wife, 7 Aug. 1818.
59. Loveday 1964, p. 101. The description is General Turner's.
60. Loveday 1964, p. 101.
61. Ford 1988, p. 445 n., Waller to Sir Thomas Lawrence, 26 Aug. 1827; RA GEO/MAIN/28895, 28922, 28926, 28931, 28936 (all purchases of Audubon plates).
62. Heard (forthcoming).
63. RA GEO/MAIN/28346 (invoice from Colnaghi & Co.).
64. See Heard (forthcoming).
65. For George's box at the Theatre Royal, Haymarket, see RA GEO/MAIN/30007. Grimaldi quoted in Dickens 1968, p. 130.
66. The episode is recounted in Ireland 1805, p. 216, and discussed in Gardner Williams 1987, pp. xliv–xlv, and Richardson 1966, p. 74. Richardson's use of the encounter as an indication of George's learning may be overconfident: Ireland's awed description of George's learning is undoubtedly exaggerated.
67. A fuller list is given in Gardner Williams 1987, see particularly p. cxxxix.
68. N. Chambers 2014, VII no. 154, letter from Sir Joseph Banks to Allan Cunningham, 13 Feb. 1817, describing 'the Prince ... from whose Royal bounty & purse your establishment issues.'; Morgan 2004.
69. Quoted in Knight 1992, p. 118.
70. Gardner Williams 1987.
71. Brock 1997, p. 17.
72. N. Goodison 1997.
73. Jenkins, Jones and Jones 2007, p. 488, Mary Nichol to Iolo Morganwg, reporting the advice of George Nichol, 2 May 1792. The presentation copy is RCIN 1087153–4. David Gardner Williams compiled a list of over 200 literary dedications to George (Gardner Williams 1987, pp. cxxix and 607–70).
74. McVeigh 1993, p. 20.
75. For opera see Hall-Witt 2007, pp. 91–4, 115.
76. RA GEO/MAIN/28849, 28850.
77. Senici 1995, p. 4.
78. McFarlane and McVeigh 2004, p. 195 (quoting the *Public Advertiser* of 1787); McVeigh 1993, p. 20.
79. Robbins Landon 1959, pp. 122–3, J. Haydn to Maria Anna von Geuzinger, 20 Dec. 1791.
80. Burney 1833, pp. 340–41.

CHAPTER 15

'NEVER SO HAPPY AS IN SHOW AND STATE'

1. Mundy 1886, p. 225, Dowager Lady Vernon to M. Frampton, 1814.
2. Rush 1833, p. 105.
3. Sickelmore 1824, p. 33; Carder 1990, p. 114.
4. T. Lewis 1865, II, p. 458, entry for 26 Feb. 1811.
5. Rush 1833, p. 84.
6. Simond 1815, I, p. 56.
7. Ackermann 1808, I, p. 113, entry for 8 Feb. 1790.
8. Rush 1833, p. 81.
9. Reeve 1899, I, p. 50.
10. Jutsham I, pp. 329, 331.
11. *Gentleman's Magazine*, June 1811, p. 587.
12. Abbot 1861, II, p. 336.
13. Buckingham 1859, I, p. 99.
14. *The New Annual Register, for the year 1811*, 1812, p. 70. It is worth noting perhaps that there were dissenters from this view, among them Percy Bysshe Shelley, who published the poem 'On a Fête at Carlton House' to highlight his disgust at such excess.
15. *Morning Chronicle*, 21 July 1813; and see Doderer-Winkler 2013, p. 94.
16. T. Lewis 1865, II, pp. 480–81, entry for 24 June 1811.
17. Ibid.
18. RA GEO/MAIN/26920; TNA LC11/23, 5 July 1817.
19. RA GEO/MAIN/26284.
20. Farington 1978–84, VII, p. 2745, entry for 3 May 1806.
21. Mundy 1886, p. 236, Lady H. Frampton to M. Frampton, 22 July 1814.
22. Rush 1833, p. 239.
23. Reeve 1899, I, p. 44.
24. RCIN 1104542.
25. Richard Thomson, *An Account of the Processions and Ceremonies Observed in the Coronation of the Kings and Queens of England*, London, 1820, purchased 'by special order', 10 Apr. 1820 (RA GEO/MAIN/28646); Arthur Taylor, *The Glory of Regality*, London, 1820, purchased 24 Mar. 1820 (RA GEO/MAIN/28639).
26. Huish 1821, pp. 95, 42, 41.
27. RCIN 31772 (Exeter Salt); RCIN 31742 (Plymouth Fountain).
28. Walter Scott in Huish 1821, p. 278.

CHAPTER 16

GEORGE IV'S VISITS TO IRELAND, HANOVER AND SCOTLAND

1. Simpson 1822, p. 6.
2. Cannadine 2003, p. 106; Milligan 2017, p. 202.
3. William III had led an army to Ireland in 1690 and fought the Battle of the Boyne against his predecessor, James II.
4. RA GEO/MAIN/22565–6, Aspinall 1938, no. 905, Lord Liverpool to Sir Benjamin Bloomfield, 14 Mar. 1821.
5. Milligan 2017, pp. 216–17, 234.
6. Ibid., pp. 205, 232.
7. National Gallery of Ireland, NGI 1148.
8. *Freeman's Journal*, 12 Aug. 1821.
9. Ibid., 18 Aug. 1821.
10. Ibid., 20 Aug. 1821.
11. Ibid., 4 Sept. 1821.
12. The last royal visit had been from George II, who departed on 16 Sept. 1755.
13. *The Times*, 15 Oct.1821.
14. Knighton 1838, p. 85.
15. The king's activities are reported in *The Times*, 20–30 Oct. 1821; and Dittmer 1822.

16. Knighton 1838, p. 84.
17. *Morning Post*, 22 Oct. 1821.
18. Quoted in Harding 2007, p. 265.
19. *The Times*, 30 Oct. 1821.
20. Metternich 1881, III, p. 518.
21. Lockhart 1837, III, p. 340.
22. Prince James Francis Edward Stuart, the Catholic son of James II.
23. Lockhart 1837, V, p. 193.
24. Quoted in Prebble 1988, p.105.
25. Scott 1822, p. 3.
26. London and Edinburgh 1981, pp. 15, 32, 45.
27. Ibid., p. 38.
28. Both paintings in the collection of the City of Edinburgh Council. For further details about artists' responses to the visit see Coltman (forthcoming).
29. NRS RH4/446.4; [Scott] 1822, p. 8, William Adam to Thomas Mash, 19 Aug. 1822.
30. Mudie 1822, p. 99.
31. Dorrian 2006, p. 32.
32. Simpson 1822, p. 47.
33. Cunningham 1843, II, p. 89.
34. The Honours of Scotland (the Crown, Sword of State and Sceptre) were Scotland's ancient symbol of royal authority. They had been missing since 1707 and were rediscovered by Scott in Edinburgh Castle in 1817.
35. RA GEO/MAIN/29600. For further details see Norman 1996–7, who records (p. 10) that the king ordered enough tartan for two kilts, but in fact only wore one.
36. Cunningham 1843, II, p. 86.
37. Simpson 1822, p. 11.
38. Edinburgh 1961, p. 35.
39. Lockhart 1837, III, p. 215.

CHAPTER 17

THE HOUSES THAT GEORGE BUILT: ST JAMES'S PALACE, BUCKINGHAM PALACE AND WINDSOR

1. Maxwell 1903, II, p. 211.
2. *Gentleman's Magazine*, Sept. 1826, p. 223.
3. Windsor Castle has been the subject of new publications in recent years: see especially H. Roberts 2001 and Brindle 2018. St James's Palace is covered in Thurley (forthcoming). The following discussion is indebted to these studies.
4. Rush 1833, p. 102.
5. The *Fountain Nymph* had been placed in the Gothic Conservatory and *Mars and Venus* in the Circular Room of Carlton House.
6. RCIN 31359.
7. TNA WORK 19/19, p. 56.
8. TNA WORK 4/25, pp. 225 and 247.
9. See ch. 5 for the introduction of a *porte cochère* at Carlton House.
10. *The Mirror of Literature, Amusement and Instruction*, 3 Feb. 1827, p. 92.
11. *The Times*, 28 May 1828, p. 2.
12. TNA WORK 1/10, p. 142 and 1/11, p. 105.
13. Saint 1997. Nash himself in a letter to Wellington called it 'a plagiarism of the Arch of Constantine'; Wellington 1877, p. 3, letter of 2 July 1829.
14. *Gentleman's Magazine*, Aug. 1829, p. 163.
15. Mundy 1886, letter from J. Frampton to M. Frampton, 25–26 May 1830, pp. 346–7.
16. Von Raumer 1835, p. 252.
17. Coghlan 1833, p. 8.
18. *Gentleman's Magazine*, Aug. 1829, p. 163.
19. Colvin 1973, p. 298.
20. Colvin 1973, p. 299; and see London 2016, p. 37. The identification of these artists has been revised several times since their installation; this represents the current roll call.
21. Mundy 1886, letter from J. Frampton to M. Frampton, 25–26 May 1830, pp. 346–7.
22. Simond 1815, II, p. 115.
23. BL Add. MS 38371, fol. 1.
24. Simond 1815, II, p. 239.
25. The architect was originally named Jeffry Wyatt but on the day that the first stone was laid, George granted him the chance to change his name to Wyatville, which was thought to be more medieval in character.
26. Wyatville's introductory text to his designs for Windsor Castle (RCIN 918409).
27. J.B. Brown 1832, p. 36.
28. Ashton 1841, I, preface.
29. Shawe-Taylor 2013, p. 248.
30. Brindle 2018, p. 6.
31. Gore 1937, p. 226; Bamford 1950, II, p. 193, entry for 9 June 1828.
32. RCIN 35474.
33. H. Roberts 2001, pp. 236, 237 and 239.
34. For a history of this successful partnership and their work at Windsor see H. Roberts 2001.
35. H. Roberts 2001, p. 33.
36. Ibid., p. 165.
37. RCIN 35510.
38. RCINs 21630 and 21642, each 8 ft 7in (262 cm) in height.
39. Reeve 1899, I, p. 285, entry for 25 Feb. 1830.
40. For Royal Lodge see Morshead 1965; and J. Roberts 1997, pp. 311–21, which are the sources for the following discussion.
41. Hansard, HC Deb., 11, cols 147–71, 5 Apr. 1824 <https://api.parliament.uk/historic-hansard/commons/1824/apr/05/repairs-of-windsor-castle> (accessed 3 Mar. 2019).
42. *Visitants* 1828, p. 66. For the gardens, see J. Roberts 1997, pp. 323–30.

CHAPTER 18

GEORGE IV AND THE WIDER WORLD

1. RA VIC/MAIN/QVJ (W) 2 Nov. 1848 (Princess Beatrice's copies).
2. Pyne 1819, I, [Frogmore], p. 2; RA GEO/MAIN/36823.
3. RA GEO/ADD/2/88. The sale, held by Christie's, took place 7–10 May 1819.
4. Mundy 1886, pp. 158–9.
5. Quenell 1937, p. 76.
6. RA GEO/MAIN/27156, 27911, 28297.
7. RA GEO/MAIN/25158.
8. Ackermann 1808, I, p. 112.
9. Ibid., p. 109.
10. CH Arms Cat., nos 1177, 1003, 1502.
11. Ackermann 1808, I, p. 112.
12. CH Arms Cat., no. 2818.
13. Farington 1978–84, X, p. 3715.
14. RA GEO/MAIN/38808–15; Aspinall 1963–71, II, pp. 359–61, Robert Percival Pott to the Prince of Wales, 30 May 1793.
15. RA GEO/MAIN/39670–71.
16. RA GEO/MAIN/21215–6; Aspinall 1938, I, p. 338, the Earl of Moira to the Prince Regent, 6 Dec. 1813. CH Arms Cat., no. 2981.
17. *London Gazette*, 7 June 1817, p. 1295.
18. *The Times*, 24 May 1819, p. 3.
19. Abu'l Hassan 1988, p. 265.
20. Ibid., pp. 131, 113, 181, 240.
21. CH Arms Cat., no. 3216; RCINS 69990–95. The helmet no longer survives.
22. *The Times*, 13 July 1824, p. 3, and 17 July 1824, p. 118.
23. CH Arms Cat., nos 1048, 948, 1522.
24. Ibid., nos 2143–51.
25. Ibid., nos 3258–75.
26. Ibid., no. 794.
27. Harlow 1952, I, p. 10.
28. CH Arms Cat., no. 1215.
29. RA GEO/MAIN/27162.
30. CH Arms Cat., nos 2510, 2511, 3040. These items were returned to Ceylon (now Sri Lanka) by the Duke of Gloucester in 1934.
31. CH Arms Cat., no. 3320; RCIN 69929.
32. Rush 1833, p. 86.
33. RA VIC/MAIN/QVJ (W) 2 Nov. 1848 (Princess Beatrice's copies).

BIBLIOGRAPHY

ABBREVIATIONS

B(F)
A.F. Blunt, *The French Drawings in the Collection of His Majesty The King at Windsor Castle*, London, 1945

BL
British Library, London

B(MF)
E. Schilling and A.F. Blunt, *The German Drawings and Supplements to the Catalogues of Italian and French Drawings in the Collection of Her Majesty The Queen at Windsor Castle*, London, 1971

BM
British Museum, London

BM SATIRES
F.G. Stephens and M.D. George, *Catalogue of Political and Personal Satires in the Department of Prints and Drawings in the British Museum*, 11 vols, London, 1870–1954

CW
C. White, *Dutch Pictures in the Collection of Her Majesty The Queen*, London, 2015

CWLF
C. White, *The Later Flemish Pictures in the Collection of Her Majesty The Queen*, London, 2007

G&J
K. Aschengreen Piacenti and J. Boardman, *Ancient and Modern Gems and Jewels in the Collection of Her Majesty The Queen*, London, 2008

GR
G. Reynolds, *The Sixteenth and Seventeenth-Century Miniatures in the Collection of Her Majesty The Queen*, London, 1999

LUGT
F. Lugt, *Les Marques de Collections de Dessins & d'Estampes*, Fondation Custodia, Paris, online edn <http://www.marquesdecollections.fr/> (accessed 7 June 2019)

NRS
National Records of Scotland

ODNB
Oxford Dictionary of National Biography

OE
A.P. Oppé, *English Drawings (Stuart and Georgian Periods) in the Collection of His Majesty The King at Windsor Castle*, London, 1950

OM
O. Millar, *The Later Georgian Pictures in the Collection of Her Majesty The Queen*, 2 vols, London, 1969

OMV
O. Millar, *The Victorian Pictures in the Collection of Her Majesty The Queen*, 2 vols, Cambridge, 1992

OSB
Osborn Collection, Beinecke Rare Books and Manuscript Library, Yale University

PD
L. van Puyvelde, *The Dutch Drawings in the Collection of His Majesty The King at Windsor Castle*, London, 1944

RA
Royal Archives, Windsor

RA GEO/ADD
Georgian Papers, Royal Archives

RA GEO/MAIN
Georgian Papers, Royal Archives

RA LC/ACC/BILLS
Lord Chamberlain's Accounts, Royal Archives

RA VIC/MAIN
Victorian Papers, Royal Archives

RCIN
Royal Collection Inventory Number

RW
R. Walker, *The Eighteenth and Early Nineteenth Century Miniatures in the Collection of Her Majesty The Queen*, Cambridge, 1992

TNA C
The National Archives, Court of Chancery Papers

TNA HO
The National Archives, Home Office Papers

TNA LC
The National Archives, Lord Chamberlain's Papers

TNA WORK
The National Archives, Office of Works' Papers

V&A
Victoria and Albert Museum, London

VR
V. Remington, *Victorian Miniatures in the Collection of Her Majesty The Queen*, 2 vols, London 2010

MANUSCRIPT SOURCES

BP 1785
Inventory of Buckingham House, 1785, MS, part of RCIN 1112546

BP 1819
Catalogue of Pictures at the Late Queen's House St James's Park and St James's Palace, 1819, MS, RCIN 1112572 (Queen's House, nos 662–1010; St James's, nos 1011–1088)

BRIGHTON INV. 1828
The 1828 Pavilion Inventory, MS, The Royal Pavilion and Brighton Museums, acc. no. 23006

BRYANT 1782
Mr [Jacob] Bryant's list of books given to the King Oct 1 1782, RCIN 1145267

CH ARMS CAT.
A catalogue of Arms: the property of HRH The Prince of Wales at Carlton House, 1781–1828, MS, 6 vols, RCIN 1113368–1113372, 1113374

CH INV. 1816
M. Bryan, *A Catalogue of pictures forming the collection of His Royal Highness The Prince Regent in Carlton House, December 1816*, MS, RCIN 1112585

CH INV. 1819
W. Seguier (ascribed to), *Catalogue of His Majesty's Pictures in Carlton House*, 1819, MS, RCIN 1112591

CH INV. 1826
A list of furniture &c. at Carlton House supplied by the Lord Chamberlain's Department, 1826, MS, RCIN 1114764

CH INV. VOL. L
A list of various articles delivered from Carlton Palace at various times to be used for Windsor Castle, 1828 MS, RCIN 1114773

CH PLATE INV.
An Inventory of Plate belonging to His Majesty George the Fourth at Carlton House and Brighton, *c.*1829, MS, RA GEO/ADD/19/8

CH PORCELAIN INVENTORY 1826
A Descriptive list of his Majesty's ornamental Seve porcelain at Carlton House, 1826, MS, RCIN 1114752

COUTTS INV.
Inventory of the contents of Carlton House … drawn up as security for a loan, 14 Jan. 1793, MS, Coutts & Co. Archives, London

GARRARD INVENTORY
Garrard & Co., *Inventory of Jewels &c., the property of Her Majesty The Queen*, 1896, MS, RCIN 1114856

INVENTORY A
A Catalogue of the drawings & prints as they are arranged in the book cases [at Buckingham House], *c.*1800–20, MS, RCIN 1155585

JUTSHAM I
An account of Furniture &c. Received and Deliver'd by Benjamin Jutsham … at Carlton House, 31 December 1806–21 June 1816 (Receipts); 7 January 1807 – October 1820 (Deliveries), MS, RCIN 1112484

JUTSHAM II
Ledger of Furniture &c. received by Benjamin Jutsham, 23 June 1816–7 December 1829, MS, RCIN 1112775

JUTSHAM III
Ledger of Furniture &c. received by Benjamin Jutsham, 23 October 1820–4 February 1830, MS, RCIN 1112485

KENSINGTON INV. 1790
A Catalogue of His Majesty's Pictures at Kensington Palace, 1790, MS, RCIN 1112542

KP 1818
B. West (ascribed to), *Catalogue of Pictures at Kensington Palace*, 1818, MS, RCIN 1115431

MOREL WINDSOR ESTIMATES
Morel & Seddon, *Windsor Estimates*, *c.*1828–9, MS, RCIN 1115774

ROYAL LIBRARY 1826
List of books commanded by His Majesty George IV to be selected from the Royal Library previously to its removal from Kensington Palace to the British Museum [*no.1*], *c.*1826, MS, RCIN 1146159.b

PUBLISHED SOURCES

ABBOT 1861
C. Abbot, *The Diary and Correspondence of Charles Abbot, Lord Colchester, Speaker of the House of Commons, 1802–1817*, 3 vols, London

ABU'L HASSAN 1988
M. Abu'l Hassan Khan, *A Persian at the Court of King George, 1809–1810* (trans. M.M. Cloake), London

ACKERMANN 1808
R. Ackermann, *The Microcosm of London*, 3 vols, London

ALDRICH 1990
M. Aldrich (ed.), *The Craces: Royal Decorators 1768–1899*, Brighton

ALEXANDER 1805
W. Alexander, *The Costume of China: Illustrated in Forty-eight Coloured Engravings*, London

ANDERSON 2001
J. Anderson, 'John White Senior and James Wyatt: an early scheme for Marylebone Park and the new street to Carlton House', *Architectural History*, 44, pp. 106–14

ANON. 1798
The Conquest of France; with the Life and Glorious Actions of Edward the Black Prince, Glasgow

ANON. 1818
A Visit to Uncle William in Town; or, a description of the most remarkable Buildings and Curiosities in the British Metropolis, London

ASHTON 1841
H. Ashton (ed.), *Illustrations of Windsor Castle, by the late Sir Jeffry Wyatville*, 2 vols, London

ASPINALL 1938
A. Aspinall (ed.), *The Letters of King George IV, 1812–1830*, 3 vols, London

ASPINALL 1962–70
A. Aspinall (ed.) *The Later Correspondence of George III*, 5 vols, Cambridge

ASPINALL 1963–71
A. Aspinall (ed.), *The Correspondence of George, Prince of Wales, 1770–1812*, 8 vols, London

AUSTEN-LEIGH 1870
J.E. Austen-Leigh, *A Memoir of Jane Austen*, London

AYERS 2016
J. Ayers, *Chinese and Japanese Works of Art in the Collection of Her Majesty The Queen*, 3 vols, London

J. BAKER 2014
J. Baker, 'The royal brat: making fun of George Augustus Frederick', in A. Kremers and E. Reich (eds), *Loyal Subversion? Caricatures from the Personal Union between England and Hanover (1714–1837)*, Göttingen and Bristol, pp. 69–91

K. BAKER 2005
K. Baker, *George IV: A Life in Caricature*, London

BAMFORD 1950
F. Bamford (ed.), *The Journal of Mrs. Arbuthnot, 1820–32*, 2 vols, London

BARNETT 1995
G. Barnett, *Richard and Maria Cosway*, Tiverton, Devon

BAULEZ 2007
C. Baulez, 'François Rémond and chimneypieces for Carlton House, 1787–1790', *Furniture History*, 43, pp. 9–19

BEEVERS 2008
D. Beevers (ed.), *Chinese Whispers: Chinoiserie in Britain 1650–1930*, Brighton

BENSON AND ESHER 1907
A.C. Benson and Viscount Esher (eds), *The Letters of Queen Victoria*, 3 vols, London

BERGVELT *ET AL.* 2009
E. Bergvelt, D.J. Meijers, L. Tibbe and E. van Wezel (eds), *Napoleon's Legacy: The Rise of National Museums in Europe 1794–1830*, Berlin

BESSBOROUGH 1955
Lord Bessborough, *Georgiana: Extracts from the Correspondence of Georgiana, Duchess of Devonshire*, London

BINNS 1877
R.W. Binns, *A century of potting in the city of Worcester*, 2nd edn, London

BLACKMORE 1960
H.L. Blackmore, 'The Prince Regent as a gun collector', *The Connoisseur*, Dec., pp. 230–6

BOYD 1958
J.B. Boyd (ed.), *The Papers of Thomas Jefferson. Vol. 14: 8 October 1788 to 26 March 1789*, Princeton, NJ

BRAHAM 1980
A. Braham, *The Architecture of the French Enlightenment*, London

BRAYLEY 1838
E.W. Brayley, *Illustrations of Her Majesty's Palace at Brighton*, London

BRINDLE 2018
S. Brindle (ed.), *Windsor Castle: A Thousand Years of a Royal Palace*, London

BRITTON AND PUGIN 1825–8
J. Britton and A.C. Pugin, *Illustrations of Public Buildings of London, with historical and descriptive accounts of each edifice*, 2 vols, London

BROCK 1997
M.G. Brock, 'The Oxford of Peel and Gladstone, 1800–1833' in M.G. Brock and M.C. Curthoys, *The History of the University of Oxford*, VI: *Nineteenth-Century Oxford*, Part 1, Oxford, pp. 7–71

BROOKE 1977
J. Brooke, 'The library of King George III', *Yale University Library Gazette*, 52, no. 1, pp. 33–45

J.B. BROWN 1832
J.B. Brown, *The Royal Windsor Guide*, Windsor

L. BROWN 1980
L. Brown, *British Historical Medals Vol. 1: The Accession of George III to the Death of William IV*, London

R.R. BROWN 2010
R. Rhynas Brown, '"For the instruction and amusement": guns for George, Prince of Wales', *International Committee of Museums and Collections of Arms and Military History Magazine*, no. 4, Apr., pp. 50–3

BUCHANAN 1824
W. Buchanan, *Memoirs of Painting: with a chronological history of the importation of pictures by the great masters into England since the French Revolution*, 2 vols, London

BUCKINGHAM 1859
R.P. Temple-Nugent-Brydges-Chandos-Grenville, Duke of Buckingham and Chandos, *Memoirs of the Court of George IV 1820–1830*, 2 vols, London

BURNEY 1833
F. Burney, *Memoirs of Doctor Burney*, London

BUSCO 1994
M. Busco, *Sir Richard Westmacott, Sculptor*, Cambridge

CANNADINE 2003
D. Cannadine, 'The context, performance and meaning of ritual: the British monarchy and the "invention of tradition", *c.*1820–1977', in E. Hobsbawm and T. Ranger (eds), *The Invention of Tradition*, 10th edn, Cambridge, pp. 101–64

CARDER 1990
T. Carder, *The Encyclopedia of Brighton*, Brighton

CARSE 1946
A. Carse, 'The Prince Regent's band', *Music and Letters*, XXVII, pp. 149–51

N. CHAMBERS 2014
N. Chambers (ed.), *The Indian and Pacific Correspondence of Sir Joseph Banks. Vol. VIII: Letters 1810–1821*, London

W. CHAMBERS 1763
W. Chambers, *Plans, Elevations, Sections, and Perspective Views of the Gardens and Buildings at Kew in Surr*[*e*]*y, the Seat of Her Royal Highness the Princess Dowager of Wales*, London

CHANTREY 1991/2
I. Lieberman, A. Potts and A. Yarrington (eds), 'Sir Francis Chantrey's ledgers of accounts, 1809–1841', *Walpole Society*, 56

CLARKE 1978
M.L. Clarke, 'The education of royalty in the eighteenth century: George IV and William IV', *British Journal of Educational Studies*, 26, no. 1, Feb., pp. 73–87

CLIFFORD SMITH 1931
H. Clifford Smith, *Buckingham Palace, Its Furniture, Decoration and History*, London

COGHLAN 1833
F. Coghlan, *A Visit to London, or Stranger's Guide to every object worthy of attention in the Metropolis*, London

COLTMAN (FORTHCOMING)
V. Coltman, *Art & Identity: A Cultural History of Scots and Scotland, 1745–1832*

COLVIN 1973
H. Colvin (ed.), *History of the King's Works. Vol. VI: 1782–1851*, London

COLVIN 1976
H. Colvin (ed.), *History of the King's Works. Vol. V: 1660–1782*, London

CONNER 2008
P. Conner, 'Chinese style in 19th-century Britain', in Beevers 2008, pp. 55–64

CORMACK 1968–70
M. Cormack, 'The ledgers of Sir Joshua Reynolds', *Walpole Society*, 42, pp. 105–69

CORNFORTH 1991
J. Cornforth, 'The roots of Regency taste', *Country Life*, 185, 25 Apr., pp. 74–7

CREDLAND 1996
A.G. Credland, 'Archery and its art in Britain', *The British Sporting Art Trust*, 26, essay no. 29

CRIPPS-DAY 1925
F.H. Cripps-Day, *A Record of Armour Sales 1881–1924*, London

CROFT-MURRAY 1970
E. Croft-Murray, *Decorative Painting in England 1537–1837*, 2 vols, London

CROKER 1860
T. Crofton Croker, *A Walk from London to Fulham*, London

CROLY 1841
G. Croly, *The Personal History of His late Majesty George the Fourth*, 2nd edn, London

CUNNINGHAM 1843
A. Cunningham, *The Life of Sir David Wilkie*, 3 vols, London

D'ARCY 1991
F. D'Arcy, *Horses, Lords and Racing Men: The Turf Club 1790–1990*, County Kildare

DAVID 1998
S. David, *Prince of Pleasure: The Prince of Wales and the Making of the Regency*, New York

DE BELLAIGUE 1967
G. de Bellaigue, 'The furnishings of the Chinese Drawing Room, Carlton House', *Burlington Magazine*, 109, no. 774, Sept., pp. 518–28

DE BELLAIGUE 1975A
G. de Bellaigue, 'Edward Holmes Baldock – part I', *Connoisseur*, 189, no. 762, Aug., pp. 290–9

DE BELLAIGUE 1975B
G. de Bellaigue, 'Edward Holmes Baldock – part II', *Connoisseur*, 190, no. 763, Sept., pp. 18–25

DE BELLAIGUE 1986
G. de Bellaigue, *The Louis XVI Service*, London

DE BELLAIGUE 1990
G. de Bellaigue, 'The Crimson Drawing Room, Carlton House', *Furniture History*, 26, pp. 10–19

DE BELLAIGUE 1995
G. de Bellaigue, 'Dominique Daguerre in England', in U. Leben (ed.), *Bernard Molitor 1755–1833*, Luxembourg, pp. 157–79

DE BELLAIGUE 1999
G. de Bellaigue, 'A royal keepsake: the Table of the Grand Commanders', *Furniture History*, 35, pp. 112–41

DE BELLAIGUE 2004
G. de Bellaigue, 'Philippe-Claude Maëlrondt, supplier to George IV', *Burlington Magazine*, 146, no. 1215, June, pp. 386–95

DE BELLAIGUE 2009
G. de Bellaigue, *French Porcelain in the Collection of Her Majesty The Queen*, 3 vols, London

DIBDIN 1824
T.F. Dibdin, *The Library Companion; or, the young man's guide, and the old man's comfort, in the choice of a library*, 2 vols, London

DICKENS 1968
C. Dickens, *Memoirs of Joseph Grimaldi*, London

DITTMER 1822
H. Dittmer (ed.), *Authentische und vollständige Beschreibung aller Feierlichkeiten, welche in dem Hannoverschen Lande, bey ... Georgs des Vierten*, Hanover

DIXON 1912
[H.H. Dixon], 'The Druid', *The Post and the Paddock*, London

DODD 1818
J.W. Dodd, *Ballads of Archery*, London

DODERER-WINKLER 2013
M. Doderer-Winkler, *Magnificent Entertainments: Temporary Architecture for Georgian Festivals*, New Haven, CT, and London

DORRIAN 2006
M. Dorrian, 'The king and the city: on the iconology of George IV in Edinburgh', *Edinburgh Architecture Research*, 30, pp. 32–6

DUFFY *ET AL.* 2005
S. Duffy, R. Fox, E. West and others, *The Wallace Collection*, London

EDINBURGH 1961
Visit of George IV to Edinburgh 1822 (exh. cat.), Scottish National Portrait Gallery, Edinburgh

ELLENBOROUGH 1881
E. Law, Lord Ellenborough, *A Political Diary 1828–30*, 2 vols, London

ETLIN 1978
R. Etlin, '"Les Dedans": Jacques François Blondel and the system of the home', *Gazette des Beaux Arts*, VI, no. 91, Apr., pp. 137–47

EUSTACE 1997
K. Eustace, '"Questa Scabrosa Missione": Canova in Paris and London in 1815', in *Canova: Ideal Heads* (exh. cat.), Oxford, pp. 9–38

FARINGTON 1978–84
K. Garlick, A. Macintyre and K. Cave (eds), *The Diary of Joseph Farington*, 16 vols, New Haven and London

FISK 1959
D. Fisk, *Dr Jenner of Berkley*, London

FITZGERALD 1990
A. Fitzgerald, *Royal Thoroughbreds: A History of the Royal Studs*, London

FORD 1988
A. Ford, *John James Audubon: A Biography*, New York

FOX 1992
C. Fox, 'A visitor's guide to London – world city 1800–40', in C. Fox (ed.), *London: World City, 1800–1840* (exh. cat.), Essen and London, pp. 11–20

FRISBY 1996
J. Frisby, '"The Finest in Europe": George IV's private band of wind musicians', *Royal Pavilion & Museums Review*, July, pp. 3–6

FRISBY 1997
J. Frisby, '"Long Among us in the Character of Settled Inhabitants": the members of George IV's private band in Brighton', *Royal Pavilion and Museums Review*, Apr., pp. 2–5

GALLATIN 1914
J. Gallatin, *A Great Peace Maker: The Diary of James Gallatin, Secretary to Albert Gallatin, 1813–1827*, London

GARDNER WILLIAMS 1987
D. Gardner Williams, *The Royal Society of Literature and the Patronage of George IV*, New York

GASH 1979
N. Gash, *Aristocracy and People: Britain, 1815–65*, Cambridge MA

GATER AND HIORNS 1940
G.H. Gater and F.R. Hiorns (eds), *Survey of London*, Vol: 20, *St Martin-in-The-Fields. Pt III: Trafalgar Square and Neighbourhood*, London

GOLDFINCH 2009
J. Goldfinch, 'Moving the King's Library: argument and sentiment 1823–1998', in G. Mandelbrote and B. Taylor (eds), *Libraries within the Library: The Origins of the British Library's Printed Collections*, London, pp. 280–95

GOODDEN 2008
A. Goodden, *Madame de Staël: The Dangerous Exile*, Oxford

J. GOODISON 2017
J. Goodison, *The Life and Work of Thomas Chippendale Junior*, London

N. GOODISON 1997
N. Goodison, 'Let There Be Light, said the Prince Regent: Vulliamy's "Great Lamp" for the Royal Academy', *Furniture History*, 33, pp. 217–24

N.GOODISON 2002
N. Goodison, *Matthew Boulton: Ormolu*, London

GORE 1937
J. Gore (ed.), *Creevey's Life and Times: A Further Selection from the Correspondence of Thomas Creevey*, London

GORE AND CARTER 2005
A. Gore and G. Carter (eds), *Humphrey Repton's Memoirs*, London

GRANVILLE 1916
C. Granville (ed.), *Lord Granville Leveson Gower (First Earl Granville): Private Correspondence 1781–1821*, 2 vols, London

GRAVES AND CRONIN 1899–1901
A. Graves and W.V. Cronin, *A History of the Works of Sir Joshua Reynolds, P.R.A.*, 4 vols, London

HALLETT 2004
M. Hallett, 'Reading the walls: pictorial dialogue at the British Royal Academy', *Eighteenth-Century Studies*, 37, no. 4, pp. 581–604

HALLETT 2018
M. Hallet, '1792: a guided tour', at 'The Royal Academy Summer Exhibition: A Chronicle, 1769–2018' <https://chronicle250.com/1792> (accessed 26 Apr. 2019)

HALL-WITT 2007
J. Hall-Witt, *Fashionable Acts: Opera and Elite Culture in London, 1780–1880*, Durham, NH

HARDING 2007
N. Harding, *Hanover and the British Empire 1700–1831*, Woodbridge, Suffolk

HARLOW 1952
V. Harlow, *The Founding of the Second British Empire*, 2 vols, New York

J. HARRIS 2007
J. Harris, *Moving Rooms: The Trade in Architectural Salvages*, New Haven, CT, and London

P.R. HARRIS 1998
P.R. Harris, *History of the British Museum Library*, London

HARRIS AND ASHLEY-COOPER 1920
G.R.C.H. Harris and F.S. Ashley-Cooper, *Lord's and the Marylebone Cricket Club*, London

HARRIS AND ASHLEY-COOPER 1929
G.R.C.H. Harris and F.S. Ashley-Cooper, *Kent Cricket Matches, 1719–1880*, Canterbury

HASWELL MILLER AND DAWNAY 1966
A.E. Haswell Miller and N.P. Dawnay, *Military Drawings and Paintings in the Collection of Her Majesty The Queen*, London

HEARD 2018
K. Heard, 'The British royal family and satirical prints, 1760–1901', in A. Gáldy and S. Heudecker (eds), *Collecting Prints and Drawings*, Newcastle upon Tyne

HEARD (FORTHCOMING)
K. Heard, *Ridicule and Spectacle: George IV and the Market for Prints*, London

HELLMAN 1999
M. Hellman, 'Furniture, sociability and the work of leisure in eighteenth-century France', *Eighteenth Century Studies*, 32, pp. 415–45

HIGHFILL *ET AL.* 1973
P.K. Highfill, Jr, K.A. Burnim, and E.A. Langhans, *A Biographical Dictionary of Actors, Actresses, Musicians, Dancers and Other Stage Personnel in London, 1660–1800. Vol. 2: Belfort to Byzand*, Carbondale and Edwardsville, IL

HILTON 2006
B. Hilton, *A Mad, Bad, and Dangerous People?: England, 1783–1846*, Oxford and New York

HOME 1970
J.A. Home (ed.), *The Letters and Journals of Lady Mary Coke*, 4 vols, Bath

HONOUR AND MARIUZ 2002
H. Honour and P. Mariuz (eds), *A. Canova Epistolario, 1816–17*, Edizione nazionale delle opere di Antonio Canova, XVIII, Rome

HOPTON 2007
R. Hopton, *Pistols at Dawn: A History of Duelling*, London

HOTS 2004
S. Hots, 'Leonard Smelt (*bap.* 1725, *d.*1800)', *ODNB*, online edn <https://doi.org/10.1093/ref:odnb/25754> (accessed 22 Oct. 2018)

HUISH 1821
R. Huish, *An Authentic History of the Coronation of King George the Fourth*, London

HUISH 1830
R. Huish, *Memoirs of George IV*, 2 vols, London

IRELAND 1805
W.H. Ireland, *The Confessions of William Henry Ireland*, London

IRELAND 1814
[W.H. Ireland], 'Satiricus Sculptor', *Chalcographimania; or, the Portrait-Collector and Printseller's Chronicle, with Infatuations of every Description*, London

JACKSON 1873
Lady Jackson (ed.), *The Bath Archives: A Further Selection from the Diaries and Letters of Sir G. Jackson, from 1809 to 1816*, 2 vols, London

JENKINS, JONES AND JONES 2007
G.H. Jenkins, F.M. Jones and D.C. Jones, *The Correspondence of Iolo Morganwg. Vol. 1: 1770–1796*, Cardiff

JENNINGS 1885
L.J. Jennings (ed.), *The Correspondence and Diaries of the late Rt. Hon. John Wilson Croker*, 2nd edn, 3 vols, London

JERNINGHAM 1896
F.D. Jerningham, *The Jerningham Letters (1780–1843): being excerpts from the correspondence and diaries of the Honourable Lady Jerningham and of her daughter Lady Bedingfield*, 2 vols, London

JESSE 1844
W. Jesse, *The Life of Beau Brummell, Esq*, 2 vols, London

JONES 2017
K. Jones, *European Silver in the Collection of Her Majesty The Queen*, London

JORDAN AND ROGERS 1989
G. Jordan and N. Rogers, 'Admirals as heroes: patriotism and liberty in Hanoverian England', *Journal of British Studies*, 28, no. 3, July, pp. 201–24

KASSLER 2015
M. Kassler (ed.), *Memoirs of the Court of George III. Vol. 1: The Memoirs of Charlotte Papendieck (1765–1840)*, London

KELLY 2003
I. Kelly, *Cooking for Kings: The Life of Antonin Carême, the First Celebrity Chef*, London

KELLY 2005
I. Kelly, *Beau Brummell*, London

KNIGHT 1992
D. Knight, *Humphry Davy: Science and Power*, Oxford

KNIGHTON 1838
[D. Knighton] Lady Knighton, *Memoirs of Sir William Knighton*, London

LAMB 1811
C. Lamb, 'On the genius and character of Hogarth', *The Reflector*, II, no. 3, pp. 61–77

B.N. LEE 1992
B.N. Lee, *British Royal Bookplates and Ex-libris of Related Families*, Aldershot

S. LEE 1833
[S. Lee], *Memoirs of Baron Cuvier*, London

LEONI 2013
F. Leoni, 'John Campbell Committente di Canova', *Studi Neoclassici*, I, pp. 127–46

LEVEY 2005
M. Levey, *Sir Thomas Lawrence*, New Haven, CT

T. LEWIS 1865
T. Lewis (ed.), *Extracts of the Journals and Correspondence of Miss Berry from the Year 1783 to 1852*, 3 vols, London

W.S. LEWIS 1937–83
W.S. Lewis, *The Yale Edition of Horace Walpole's Correspondence*, 48 vols, New Haven

LLOYD 1995
S. Lloyd, 'Fashioning the image of the prince: Richard Cosway and George IV', in D. Arnold (ed.), *'Squanderous and Lavish Profusion': George IV, His Image and Patronage of the Arts*, London, pp. 5–14

LLOYD 2004
S. Lloyd, 'The Cosway inventory of 1820: listing unpaid commissions and the contents of 20 Stratford Place, Oxford, London', *Walpole Society*, 66, pp. 163–218

LOCKHART 1837
J.G. Lockhart, *Memoirs of the Life of Sir Walter Scott, Bart.*, 7 vols, Edinburgh and London

LONDON 1991
Carlton House: The Past Glories of George IV's Palace (exh. cat.), The Queen's Gallery, London

LONDON 2002
J. Roberts (ed.), *Royal Treasures: A Golden Jubilee Celebration* (exh. cat.), The Queen's Gallery, London

LONDON 2004
J. Roberts (ed.), *George III and Queen Charlotte: Patronage, Collecting and Court Taste* (exh. cat.), The Queen's Gallery, London

LONDON 2014
D. Shawe-Taylor (ed.), *The First Georgians: Art & Monarchy 1714–1760* (exh. cat.), The Queen's Gallery, London

LONDON 2015
D. Shawe-Taylor and Q. Buvelot, *Masters of the Everyday: Dutch Artists in the Age of Vermeer* (exh. cat.), The Queen's Gallery, London

LONDON 2016
A. Reynolds, L. Peter and M. Clayton (eds), *Portrait of the Artist* (exh. cat.), The Queen's Gallery, London

LONDON AND EDINBURGH 1981
G. Finley, *Turner and George the Fourth in Edinburgh 1822* (exh. cat.), London and Edinburgh

LONDONDERRY 1830
C.W. Vane, Marquess of Londonderry, *Narrative of the War in Germany and France in 1813 and 1814*, London

LONDONDERRY 1853
C.W. Vane, Marquess of Londonderry (ed.), *Correspondence, Despatches and Other Papers of Viscount Castlereagh, Second Marquess of Londonderry*, 3rd ser., 4 vols, London

LOUW 1991
H. Louw, 'Window-glass making in Britain, *c.*1660–*c.*1860 and its architectural impact', *Construction History*, 7, pp. 47–68

LOVEDAY 1964
A.F. Loveday, *Sir Hilgrove Turner, 1764–1843: Soldier and Courtier under the Georges*, Dover

LUNARDI 1784
Lunardi's Grand Aerostatic Voyage through the Air, containing a complete and circumstantial account of the grand aerial flight made by that enterprising foreigner, in his air balloon, on September 15, 1784, London

MACCARTHY 2002
F. MacCarthy, *Byron: Life and Legend*, London

MCCORMICK 1990
T.J. McCormick, *Charles-Louis Clérisseau and the Genesis of Neo-Classicism*, New York

MCFARLANE AND MCVEIGH 2004
M. McFarlane and S. McVeigh, 'The string quartet in London concert life, 1769–1799', in S. Wollenberg and S. McVeigh (eds), *Concert Life in Eighteenth-Century Britain*, Aldershot, pp. 161–90

MCVEIGH 1993
S. McVeigh, *Concert Life in London from Mozart to Haydn*, Cambridge

MANSEL 2005
P. Mansel, *Dressed to Rule: Royal and Court Costume from Louis XIV to Elizabeth II*, New Haven, CT, and London

MARSDEN 2001
J. Marsden '"England's Raphael" and his lost Parnassus', *Georgian Group Journal*, 11, pp. 29–46

MARSDEN 2013
J. Marsden, 'Canova and George IV, Prince Regent and King', *Studi Neoclassici*, 1, pp. 157–70

MAXWELL 1903
H. Maxwell (ed.), *The Creevey Papers: A Selection from the Correspondence and Diaries of the Late Thomas Creevey, M.P.*, 2 vols, London

MELVILLE 1906
L. Melville, *The First Gentleman of Europe*, London

METTERNICH 1881
Prince Richard de Metternich (ed.), *Mémoires, documents et écrits divers laissés par le prince de Metternich*, 8 vols, Paris

MILLAR 1967
O. Millar, 'Gainsborough and George IV: a lost portrait', *Burlington Magazine*, 109, no. 774, Sept., pp. 530–2

MILLAR 1969
O. Millar, *The Later Georgian Pictures in the Collection of Her Majesty The Queen*, 2 vols, London

MILLAR 1986
O. Millar, 'George IV when Prince of Wales: his debts to artists and craftsmen', *Burlington Magazine*, 128, no. 1001, Aug., pp. 586–92

MILLIGAN 2017
K. Milligan, 'Royal visits to Dublin, 1821–1911: pier, procession, presence chamber', in M. Campbell and W. Derham (eds), *Making Majesty: The Throne Room at Dublin Castle. A Cultural History*, Newbridge, pp. 200–35

MOLLO 1997
J. Mollo, *The Prince's Dolls*, Barnsley, Yorkshire

MONOD 2009
P. Kléber Monod, *Imperial Island: A History of Britain and Its Empire 1660–1837*, Oxford

MORGAN 2004
P. Morgan, 'Williams, Edward [*pseud.* Iolo Morganwg] (1747–1826)', *ODNB*, online edn <https://doi.org/10.1093/ref:odnb/29498> (accessed 26 Apr. 2019)

MORLEY 1984
J. Morley, *The Making of the Royal Pavilion Brighton*, London

MORSHEAD 1965
O. Morshead, *George IV and Royal Lodge*, Brighton

MUDIE 1822
R. Mudie, *A Historical Account of His Majesty's Visit to Scotland*, Edinburgh

MUNDY 1886
H.G. Mundy (ed.), *The Journal of Mary Frampton from the Year 1779, until the Year 1846*, 3rd edn, London

MURDOCH 1992
T. Murdoch (ed.), *Boughton House: The English Versailles*, London

MURRAY 1922
John Murray, (ed.) *Lord Byron's Correspondence*, 1, London

MUSGRAVE 1959
C. Musgrave, *Royal Pavilion: An Episode in the Romantic*, London

NEUFFORGE 1757–68
J.-F. de Neufforge, *Recueil élémentaire d'architecture*, 8 vols, Paris

NEW HAVEN AND LONDON 2017
J. Marschner, D. Bindman and L.L. Ford (eds), *Enlightened Princesses: Caroline, Augusta, Charlotte, and the Shaping of the Modern World* (exh. cat.), New Haven, CT, and London

NICOLSON 1945
H. Nicolson (ed.), *Der Wiener Kongress oder über die Einigkeit unter Verbündeten 1812–1822*, Zurich

NIEUWENHUYS 1834
C.J. Nieuwenhuys, *A Review of the Lives and Works of Some of the Most Eminent Painters*, London

NORMAN 1996–7
A.V.B. Norman, 'George IV and Highland dress', *Review of Scottish Culture*, x, pp. 5–15

NORMAN AND EAVES 2016
A.V.B. Norman and I. Eaves, *Arms & Armour in the Collection of Her Majesty The Queen: European Armour*, London

NYGREN 2013
E. Nygren, 'James Ward (1769–1859), papers and patrons', *Walpole Society*, 75, pp. 1–438

PARISSIEN 2001
S. Parissien, *George IV: The Grand Entertainment*, London

PAYNE AND PAYNE 2003
M. Payne and J. Payne, 'Henry Wigstead, Rowlandson's fellow-traveller', *British Art Journal*, IV, no. 3, pp. 27–38

PEARCE AND SALMON 2005
S. Pearce and F. Salmon, 'Charles Heathcote Tatham in Italy, 1794–96: letters, drawings and part of an autobiography', *Walpole Society*, 67, pp. 1–91

POSTLE 2018
M. Postle, 'The cast collection', in R. Simon (ed.), *The Royal Academy of Arts: History and Collections*, New Haven, CT, and London, pp. 462–89

POWELL 2004
N. Powell, *George Crabbe: An English Life, 1754–1832*, London

PREBBLE 1988
J. Prebble, *The King's Jaunt*, London

PYNE 1819
W.H. Pyne, *The History of the Royal Residences*, 3 vols, London

QUENELL 1937
P. Quenell (ed.) and D. Powell (trans.), D. Lieven, *The Private Letters of Princess Lieven to Prince Metternich, 1820–1826*, London

RAIKES 1856
T. Raikes, *A Portion of the Journal Kept by Thos. Raikes, Esq. 1831–47*, 2 vols, London

RAMSEY 2011
N. Ramsey, *The Military Memoir and Romantic Literary Culture, 1780–1835*, Farnham, Surrey

REDFORD 2008
B. Redford, *Dilettanti: The Antic and the Antique in 18th-Century England*, Los Angeles

REEVE 1899
H. Reeve (ed.), *The Greville Memoirs: A Journal of the Reigns of King George IV, King William IV and Queen Victoria*, 8 vols, London

REYNOLDS 1997
J. Reynolds, *Discourses on Art* (ed. R.R. Wark), New Haven, CT, and London

RIBEIRO 1995
A. Ribeiro, *The Art of Dress*, New Haven, CT

RIBERETTE 1986
P. Riberette (ed.), *Chateaubriand, correspondence générale. Vol. 5: 1er avril 1822–31 décembre 1822*, Paris

RICHARDSON 1966
J. Richardson, *George IV: A Portrait*, London

ROBBINS LANDON 1959
H.C. Robbins Landon (ed.), *The Collected Correspondence and London Notebooks of Joseph Haydn*, London

H. ROBERTS 1990
H. Roberts, 'Metamorphoses in wood: Royal Library furniture in the eighteenth and nineteenth centuries', *Apollo*, June, pp. 382–90

H. ROBERTS 2000
H. Roberts, '"Quite appropriate for Windsor Castle": George IV and George Watson Taylor', *Furniture History*, 36, pp. 115–37

H. ROBERTS 2001
H. Roberts, *For the King's Pleasure: The Furnishing and Decoration of George IV's Apartments at Windsor Castle*, London

H. ROBERTS 2007
H. Roberts, 'Thrones revisited', *Furniture History*, 43, pp. 46–52

H.D. ROBERTS 1939
H.D. Roberts, *A History of the Royal Pavilion, Brighton*, London

J. ROBERTS 1987
J. Roberts, *Royal Artists: From Mary Queen of Scots to the Present Day*, London

J. ROBERTS 1997
J. Roberts, *Royal Landscape: The Gardens and Parks of Windsor*, New Haven, CT, and London

W. ROBERTS 2017
W. Roberts, *Memorials of Christie's: A Record of Art Sales from 1766–1896*, Ancarano, Abruzzo

H.S. ROBINSON 1942
H.S. Robinson, 'The Tower of the Winds and the Roman market-place', *American Journal of Archaeology*, 47, no. 3, pp. 291–305

J.M. ROBINSON 1979
J.M. Robinson, *The Wyatts: An Architectural Dynasty*, Oxford

ROSS 1982
A. Ross, *The Turf*, Oxford

ROWELL AND BURCHARD 2016
C. Rowell and W. Burchard, 'Francis Benois, Martin-Eloi Lignereux and Lord Whitworth: leasing, furnishing and dismantling the British embassy in Paris during the Peace of Amiens 1802–3', *Furniture History*, LII, pp. 181–213

RUSH 1833
R. Rush, *A Residence at the Court of London*, London

RUSSELL 1853–6
J. Russell (ed.), *Memoirs, Journals and Correspondence of Thomas Moore*, 8 vols, London

SAINT 1997
A. Saint, 'The Marble Arch', *Georgian Group Journal*, VII, pp. 75–93

SAWYER 1989
T. Sawyer, *Noble Art: An Artistic and Literary Celebration of the Old English Prize-ring*, London

SCOTT 1822
W. Scott, *Hints Addressed to the Inhabitants of Edinburgh, and others, in Prospect of His Majesty's visit. By an Old Citizen*, Edinburgh

SÉGUIER 1759
J.-F. Séguier, *Dissertation sur l'ancienne inscription de la Maison carrée de Nismes*, Paris

SENICI 1995
E. Senici, '"Adapted to the Modern Stage": *La clemenza di Tito* in London', *Cambridge Opera Journal*, 7, no. 1, Mar., pp. 1–22

SHAWE-TAYLOR 2013
D. Shawe-Taylor, 'The Waterloo Chamber before the Battle of Waterloo', in G. Perry, K. Retford and J. Vibert (eds), *Placing Faces: The Portrait and the English Country House in the Long Eighteenth Century*, Manchester, 2013, pp. 244–63

SHAWE-TAYLOR 2016
D. Shawe-Taylor, 'Sporting art in the Royal Collection', *The British Sporting Art Trust*, essay no. 69, Autumn

SHAWE-TAYLOR 2018
D. Shawe-Taylor, 'The pictures at Carlton House', in K. Retford and S. Avery-Quash (eds), *The Georgian Town House: Building, Collecting and Display*, London and New York, pp. 211–30

SHERER 1824
M. Sherer, *Recollections of the Peninsula*, London 1824

SICKELMORE 1815
R. Sicklemore, *An Epitome of Brighton …, involving its history from the earliest to the present period*, Brighton

SICKELMORE 1824
R. Sickelmore, *Sickelmore's History of Brighton*, third edn, Brighton

SIMOND 1815
L. Simond, *Journal of a Tour and Residence during the years 1810 and 1811*, 2 vols, Edinburgh

SIMPSON 1822
J. Simpson, *Letters to Sir Walter Scott, BART., on the Moral and Political Character and Effects of the Visit to Scotland in August 1822, of his Majesty King George IV*, Edinburgh

SMITH 1999
E.A. Smith, *George IV*, New Haven, CT

SOLKIN 2018
D.H. Solkin, '1786: Endangered royalty on display' at 'The Royal Academy Summer Exhibition: A Chronicle, 1769–2018' <https://chronicle250.com/1786> (accessed 26 Apr. 2019)

SPIELMANN 1915–16
M.H. Spielmann, 'A note on Thomas Gainsborough and Gainsborough Dupont', *Walpole Society*, 5, pp. 91–108

SPIETH 2018
D.A. Spieth, *Revolutionary Paris and the Market for Netherlandish Art*, Leiden and Boston

STANLEY 1821
A catalogue of the very curious and valuable Assemblage of Miscellaneous Articles of Taste and Virtu, the Property of that distinguished Artist and Virtuoso, Richard Cosway, Esq. R.A … which will be Sold by Auction by Mr Stanley … on Tuesday May 22, 1821, London

STEER 1966
F.W. Steer (ed.), *The Letters of John Hawkins and Samuel and Daniel Lysons, 1812–1830*, Chichester

STEUART 1910
A.F. Steuart (ed.), *The Last Journals of Horace Walpole*, 2 vols, London

STROUD 1966
D. Stroud, *Henry Holland: His Life and Architecture*, London

D.M. STUART 1953
D.M. Stuart, *Portrait of the Prince Regent*, London

E. STUART 2001
E. Stuart, 'A prince's library: an examination of George IV's library at Carlton House', unpublished MA thesis, University of London

SUMMERSON 1980
J. Summerson, *The Life and Work of John Nash, Architect*, London

SWEET 1980
P.R. Sweet, *Wilhelm von Humboldt: A Biography*, Columbus, OH

TAQUET 2006
P. Taquet, *Georges Cuvier: Naissance d'un genie*, Paris

TAYLOR 1926
T. Taylor (ed.), *The Autobiography and Memoirs of Benjamin Robert Haydon*, 2 vols, London

THACKERAY 1879
W.M. Thackeray, *The Four Georges*, London

THÉODORIDÈS 1966
J. Théodoridès, 'Humboldt and England', *British Journal for the History of Science*, 3, no. 1, June, pp. 39–55

THORNE 1876
J. Thorne, *Handbook to the Environs of London, alphabetically arranged*, 2 vols, London

THURLEY (FORTHCOMING)
S. Thurley (ed.), *St James's Palace: A History*, London

TOYNBEE 1928
P. Toynbee (ed.), 'Horace Walpole's journals of visits to country seats &c.', *Walpole Society*, 16, pp. 9–80

VAN DUIN 1989
P. van Duin, 'Two pairs of Boulle caskets on stands by Thomas Parker', *Furniture History*, 25, pp. 214–20

VIGÉE-LE BRUN 1984
E.-L. Vigée-Le Brun, *Souvenirs*, 2 vols, Paris

VISITANTS 1828
The Visitants Guide to Windsor Castle, 2nd edn, Windsor

VON RAUMER 1835
F. von Raumer, *England in 1835: being a series of letters written to friends in Germany, during a residence in London and excursions into the provinces*, Philadelphia, PA

WAINWRIGHT 1989
C. Wainwright, *The Romantic Interior: The British Collector at Home, 1750–1850*, London

WALKER 1809
C. Walker, *Brighton and Its Environs*, London

WATKIN 1984
D. Watkin, *Royal Interiors of Regency England from Watercolours First Published by W.H. Pyne in 1817–20*, London

WELLINGTON 1877
Despatches, Correspondence and Memoranda of Field Marshal Arthur, Duke of Wellington. Vol. VI: July 1829 to April 1830, London

WHITLEY 1928
W.T. Whitley, *Art in England 1800–20*, Cambridge

WILLIAMS 1831
D.E. Williams, *The Life and Correspondence of Sir Thomas Lawrence Kt.*, 2 vols, London

WILSON 1825
H. Wilson, *The Memoirs of Harriette Wilson*, 4 vols, London

WRIGHT 1818
C. Wright, *The Brighton Ambulator*, London

ZAWADZKI 1993
W.H. Zawadzki, *A Man of Honour: Adam Czartoryski as a Statesman of Russia and Poland, 1795–1831*, Oxford

INDEX

CONTRIBUTORS

DAVID BEEVERS is Keeper of the Royal Pavilion, Brighton

RUFUS BIRD is Surveyor of The Queen's Works of Art, Royal Collection Trust

DEBORAH CLARKE is Senior Curator, Palace of Holyroodhouse, Royal Collection Trust

SALLY GOODSIR is Curator of Decorative Arts, Royal Collection Trust

KATE HEARD is Senior Curator of Prints and Drawings, Royal Collection Trust

KATHRYN JONES is Senior Curator of Decorative Arts, Royal Collection Trust

ALEXANDRA LOSKE is Curator, Royal Pavilion, Brighton

REBECCA LYONS is Director of Learning and Collections at the Royal Academy of Arts and Director of Royal Collection Studies

JONATHAN MARSDEN was formerly Director of the Royal Collection and Surveyor of The Queen's Works of Art

DAVID OAKEY is an independent researcher and curator of a private collection

STEVEN PARISSIEN is Chief Executive, The National Horseracing Museum

RACHEL PEAT is Assistant Curator, Non-European Works of Art, Royal Collection Trust

VANESSA REMINGTON is Senior Curator of Paintings, Royal Collection Trust

DESMOND SHAWE-TAYLOR is Surveyor of The Queen's Pictures, Royal Collection Trust

EMMA STUART is Senior Curator of Books and Manuscripts, Royal Collection Trust

ACKNOWLEDGEMENTS

The authors would like to thank the following for their help in the preparation of this volume:

Her Majesty The Queen for permission to quote from the Royal Archives.

Megan Aldrich, Stella Beddoe, Rupert Burgess, Jane and Ted Burnham, Meaghan Clarke, Nicola Coleby, Alexander Collins, Viccy Coltman, Sara Duke and her colleagues in the Prints and Photographs Division at the Library of Congress, Washington DC, Tracey Earl, Alison Effeny, Henrietta Graham, Gordon Grant, Chris Hassall, Martin Henig, Maurice Howard, Adrian Hunt, Stephen Lloyd, Peter Mandler, Charles May, Colin Parrish, Deborah Phipps, Mark Pomeroy, Frances Pressner, Hugh Roberts, Jane Roberts, Marie Selwood, Guy Wilson, Natalie Zimmer and Beverly Zimmern.

We would also like to thank our colleagues within Royal Collection Trust: Polly Atkinson, Tjeerd Bakker, Lynnette Beech, Hannah Bowen, Andrew Brown, Irene Campden, Wilhelmina Castelijns van Beek, Stephen Chapman, Nicola Christie, Martin Clayton, Carly Collier, Paul Cradock, Steven Davidson, Allison Derrett, Ann Geary, Megan Gent, Roxanna Gilhooley, Martin Gray, Gary Gronnestad, Alison Guppy, Emily Hannam, Sam Harris, Laura Hobbs, Nick Kingswell, Tim Knox, Sarah Laing, Karen Lawson, Isabella Manning, Simon Metcalf, Theresa-Mary Morton, Fiona Norbury, Kate Owen, Daniel Partridge, Shruti Patel, Clara de la Peña McTigue, Camille Polkownik, Rosie Razzall, Georgina Seage, Puneeta Sharma, Susan Shaw, Steve Sheasby, Jane Simpkiss, Rachael Smith, Laura Staccoli, Chris Stevens, Bill Stockting, Kate Stone, Tung Tsin Lam, Emma Turner, Shaun Turner, Oliver Walton, David Wheeler, Sophy Wills and Eva Zielinska-Millar.

PHOTOGRAPHIC ACKNOWLEDGEMENTS

Unless otherwise stated below, all works reproduced are Royal Collection Trust / © Her Majesty Queen Elizabeth II 2019

All items in the Royal Archives: Royal Archives / © Her Majesty Queen Elizabeth II 2019: Figs 3.3, 11.10, endpapers
Royal Collection Trust / All Rights Reserved: Figs 2.19, 9.1, 16.5, A.75, A.77
Royal Collection Trust / © Her Majesty Queen Elizabeth II 2019. Photographer: John Freeman: Figs 17.4, 17.5
Royal Collection Trust / © Her Majesty Queen Elizabeth II 2019. Photographer: Relic Imaging: Fig. 3.18
Royal Collection Trust / Photograph © Christie's Images: Fig. 0.17

Royal Collection Trust is grateful for permission to reproduce the items listed below:

British Library, London, © British Library Board 2019. All Rights Reserved / Bridgeman Images: Figs 5.3, 15.5
British Museum, London, © The Trustees of the British Museum: Fig. 12.8
Cooper Hewitt, Smithsonian Design Museum. Image copyright Cooper Hewitt, Smithsonian Design Museum 2019 / Art Resource / Scala, Florence; museum purchase through gift of Mrs John Innes Kane: Figs 10.5, 10.6
The Garrick Club, London: Fig. 13.12
Lewis Walpole Library, Yale University, Farmington, CT: Figs 9.2, 17.1
Library of Congress, Washington DC: Fig. 12.4
Library of Congress, Washington DC, Katherine Golden Bitting Collection on Gastronomy: Fig. 15.8
The Light Dragoons: Fig. 13.10
Metropolitan Museum of Art, New York, gift of Adele S. Gollin, 1976: Fig. 2.7; Harris Brisbane Dick Fund, 1917: Fig. 2.21
Musée Condé, Chantilly, France / Bridgeman Images: Fig. 3.13
National Portrait Gallery, London, © National Portrait Gallery: Figs 2.5, 3.5 (on loan to the National Portrait Gallery, by consent of the owners)
National Trust, © National Trust / Andrew Fetherston: Fig. 1.6
National Trust, The Rothschild Collection, Waddesdon, Aylesbury, © National Trust: Fig. 3.10
Private collection / Photograph © Christie's Images / Bridgeman Images: Fig. 4.8
Private collections: Figs 2.8, 2.16, 13.11
RIBA Collections: Fig. 5.9
Royal Hospital Chelsea, London / Bridgeman Images: Fig. 1.2
The Royal Pavilion and Museums, Brighton and Hove: Figs 10.11, 12.7
Sir John Soane's Museum, London: Fig. 5.11
The Tate Gallery, London; accepted by the nation as part of the Turner Bequest, 1856: Fig. 16.8
Victoria and Albert Museum, London, © V&A Images: Figs 1.12, 5.24
Yale Center for British Art, New Haven, CT: Figs 2.15, 5.7

Every effort has been made to contact copyright holders; any omissions are inadvertent, and will be corrected in future editions if notification of the amended credit is sent to the publisher in writing.

June For the Bo

309¾ Yds green Gro. d

186½ Yds richest broad

302¼ Yds Middle Br

108 Yds Narrow

1791 For the My

Jan 7. 416¼ Yds white Gro. d

Eagle

365½ Yds rich.d Brocad

£

Nov.r 17. 30 Yds rich white